THE ROMAN REPUBLIC OF LETTERS

The Roman Republic of Letters

SCHOLARSHIP, PHILOSOPHY, AND POLITICS IN THE AGE OF CICERO AND CAESAR

KATHARINA VOLK

PRINCETON UNIVERSITY PRESS

PRINCETON & OXFORD

Published by Princeton University Press
41 William Street, Princeton, New Jersey 08540
6 Oxford Street, Woodstock, Oxfordshire OX20 1TR

press.princeton.edu

All Rights Reserved

Library of Congress Cataloging-in-Publication Data

Names: Volk, Katharina, 1969– author.
Title: The Roman republic of letters : scholarship, philosophy, and politics in the age
    of Cicero and Caesar / Katharina Volk.
Description: Princeton ; Oxford : Princeton University Press, [2021] |
    Includes bibliographical references and index.
Identifiers: LCCN 2021029270 (print) | LCCN 2021029271 (ebook) |
    ISBN 9780691193878 (hardback) | ISBN 9780691224343 (ebook)
Subjects: LCSH: Rome—History—Republic, 265–30 B.C. | Rome—Politics
    and government—265–30 B.C. | Learning and scholarship—Rome—History. |
    Politics and culture—Rome—History. | Politics and literature—Rome—History. |
    Republicanism—Rome—History. | Rome—Intellectual life. | Rome—Social life
    and customs. | BISAC: PHILOSOPHY / Political | HISTORY / Ancient / Rome
Classification: LCC DG254.2 .V65 2021 (print) | LCC DG254.2 (ebook) |
    DDC 937/.03—dc23
LC record available at https://lccn.loc.gov/2021029270
LC ebook record available at https://lccn.loc.gov/2021029271

British Library Cataloging-in-Publication Data is available

Editorial: Rob Tempio & Matt Rohal
Production Editorial: Ali Parrington
Jacket Design: Karl Spurzem
Production: Erin Suydam
Publicity: Alyssa Sanford & Amy Stewart

Jacket Credit: From *Portrait of Two Friends*, by Jacopo Carucci
(Jacopo da Pontormo), ca. 1552. Art Heritage / Alamy Stock Photo

This book has been composed in Arno

Printed on acid-free paper. ∞

Printed in the United States of America

10 9 8 7 6 5 4 3 2 1

To Jim

socio studiorum, socio uitae

CONTENTS

PREFACE

THE LEARNED Roman senators who are the subject of this book were not in the habit of prefacing their works with lists of acknowledgments. Then as now, however, intellectual activities—researching, writing, and publishing—were intensely social and sociable pursuits, in which individual scholars drew on extensive networks of learned friends, Greek professionals, and skilled freedmen and slaves. As I hope to show in these pages, the likes of Cicero valued the communal effort that went into their studies and liked to present themselves and their peers as engaged in an enjoyable process of συμφιλολογεῖν (*Fam.* 16.21.8).

I, too, have in the course of writing this book greatly profited from the assistance of many individuals and institutions. My work has been supported by a Columbia University/Michael I. Sovern Affiliated Fellowship to the American Academy in Rome (2016), a Fellowship at the Wissenschaftskolleg zu Berlin (2016–17), a Heyman Center Fellowship at Columbia University (2018–19), and a Fellowship by the National Endowment for the Humanities (2019–20; I am bound to point out that any views, findings, conclusions, or recommendations expressed in this publication do not necessarily reflect those of the National Endowment for the Humanities). My profound thanks go to the grant-giving bodies, as well as to the many people affiliated with them who have furthered my research in diverse and significant ways.

I have over the years had the pleasure of presenting aspects of my work at Humboldt Universität Berlin, Canterbury, Cologne, Columbia, Cornell, Dublin, Durham, Edinburgh, Harvard, the University of Illinois, Johns Hopkins, Munich, Penn, Penn State, Sydney, and the University of Virginia. I am most grateful to the audiences at these venues for their hospitality and for their many helpful comments.

My special thanks go to the following colleagues who have answered queries on particular points and/or have been so kind as to share unpublished material: Yelena Baraz, David Blank, Nathan Gilbert, Margaret Graver, Phillip Horky, John Izzo, Evan Jewell, Bob Kaster, Joshua Katz, Duncan MacRae, Tobias Reinhardt, James Rives, Chris van den Berg, Iakovos Vasiliou, and Gareth Williams. They have shown themselves true fellow citizens of the Republic of

Letters. In addition, Nathan Gilbert, Bob Kaster, and Chris van den Berg read drafts of my manuscript either in part or in its entirety, encouraging me in the project and offering numerous valuable comments and suggestions for improvement. I am greatly in their debt.

A particular thank-you is owed to Rob Tempio at Princeton University Press for believing in this project and shepherding it so expertly to publication. Ali Parrington deftly steered the book through production, while Kim Hastings did an outstanding job as copyeditor. I am grateful also to the Press's anonymous readers for their perceptive comments, suggestions, and corrections.

One paratextual convention that was observed already by this book's protagonists is the dedication: Cicero, Caesar, Varro, Brutus, and their contemporaries never published anything without highlighting a special individual to whom they felt themselves bound and who they hoped would take a personal interest in the work. This book is dedicated to the person who has lived with it and with me for a happy near-decade: Jim Zetzel, beloved husband and symphilologist extraordinaire.

KV
New York
December 2020

THE FOLLOWING abbreviations for works of scholarship are used in the text and notes:

FGRH   Jacoby, F. et al. (ed.)(1923–). *Fragmente der griechischen Historiker.* Berlin: Weidmann/Leiden: Brill.

FRHIST Cornell, T. J. (ed.) (2013). *The Fragments of the Roman Historians.* 3 vols. Oxford: Oxford University Press.

OLD   Glare, P. G. W. (ed.) (1983). *Oxford Latin Dictionary.* Oxford: Oxford University Press.

RRC   Crawford, M. H. (1974). *Roman Republican Coinage.* 2 vols. Cambridge: Cambridge University Press.

Abbreviations for ancient authors and texts, unless otherwise indicated, follow those of S. Hornblower and A. Spawforth (eds.) (2012). *The Oxford Classical Dictionary.* 4th ed. Oxford: Oxford University Press.

Abbreviations used in the bibliography follow those of the *American Journal of Archaeology* 95 (1991), 1–16, supplemented from *L'Année philologique.*

THE ROMAN REPUBLIC OF LETTERS

1

Introduction

The past is an immense area of stony ground that many people would like to
drive across as if it were a road, while others move patiently from stone to
stone, lifting each one because they need to know what lies beneath.

—JOSÉ SARAMAGO, *THE ELEPHANT'S JOURNEY*

1. Senator Scholars

In 54 BCE, Julius Caesar dedicated to Cicero his *De analogia*, a treatise in two
books on the proper use of Latin. The work was to some extent a response to
Cicero's *De oratore*, written only the year before: when laying out the qualities
of the good orator, Cicero had given short shrift to the issue of linguistic correctness; Caesar, by contrast, considered this an important enough topic in its
own right, proposing morphological regularity or analogy as a significant criterion in the assessment of idiomatic and elegant speech. When in 46 BCE,
Cicero composed his history of Roman oratory, the *Brutus*, he took the occasion to come back to the debate, expressing his appreciation of the earlier
dedication but also assessing Caesar's own style—in a manner that, while
superficially complimentary, made it clear that the two men remained far from
agreement on what constituted an effective and aesthetic use of language.

The *Brutus* was named for M. Iunius Brutus, a younger friend of both Cicero
and Caesar. Cicero dedicated the work to him at least in part as a thank-you
for a philosophical treatise, *De uirtute*, that Brutus had just dedicated to him
and that Cicero had read with great enjoyment. The two men shared a vivid
interest in philosophy and especially in the question at issue in *De uirtute*,
namely, whether virtue should be deemed a sufficient condition for happiness.
When Cicero in the following months proceeded to write a whole series of
philosophical works of his own, he addressed four of them (*Paradoxa Stoicorum,
De finibus, Tusculans,* and *De natura deorum*) once more to Brutus.

Another person to receive a Ciceronian philosophical text during this period was M. Terentius Varro. Varro had hinted to Cicero that he was working
on a major piece of scholarship that he intended to dedicate to his friend, and
had expressed an interest in receiving a token of appreciation in turn. To oblige

Varro, Cicero made him both an interlocutor in his dialogue *Academica* and its dedicatee (45 BCE). Varro in turn did not fail Cicero and two years later dedicated to him his monumental *De lingua Latina*. In this monograph on the Latin language, Varro, among other topics, picked up the question of analogy previously treated by Caesar, devoting six of twenty-five books to its discussion. Caesar himself had been the dedicatee of another Varronian work in 46 BCE, the sixteen books of the *Antiquitates rerum diuinarum*, on Roman religion.

What I have just outlined are a few moments in the intellectual history of the late Republic. In the mid-first century BCE, Rome went through a period of cultural flourishing. Some of the most influential pieces of Latin scholarship and philosophy were penned by a close-knit group of intellectuals, men who knew each other, read and reacted to each other's texts, and received the dedications of their colleagues' books. Caesar, Cicero, Brutus, and Varro, among others, created a body of works on topics ranging from ethics to linguistics, from politics to religion to agriculture and beyond, that would shape the ways the Romans thought of themselves and of their world for centuries to come.

What is wrong with this picture? The story I have been telling is, of course, ludicrously one-sided. The mid-first century BCE has gone down in history primarily as a time of violent political conflict and civil war, and when people think of Julius Caesar, what usually comes to mind is not his achievements as a linguist but his exploits as a politician and general. Even *De analogia* was, we are told, written while its author was crossing the Alps on one of his many campaigns to Gaul, and when Caesar's actions a few years later led to the Civil War, he found himself fighting against not only Pompey, but also his erstwhile dedicatee Cicero and many other learned senators, including Brutus and Varro. The rest is history: Caesar emerged victorious, and most of Brutus's, Cicero's, and Varro's philosophical and scholarly works mentioned above were written in the uneasy time of his dictatorship, after the three men had received the victor's pardon. In the end, of course, it was none other than Brutus who led the conspirators who—to the applause of Cicero—assassinated Caesar on the Ides of March 44 BCE. Less than three years later, Brutus and Cicero were both dead, victims of the turbulent developments in the aftermath of Caesar's death, events in which they themselves had played crucial parts. Varro too barely survived, having seen his life and property twice threatened by proscription and having lost part of his library, including valuable copies of his own works.

My purpose in this book is to combine the two narratives just sketched and to treat them as one and the same story. As we have just seen, some of the most important intellectuals of the late Republic were also leading politicians—or, to look at the other side of what I think of as the same coin, some of the most important political actors in this time of turmoil also engaged in significant scholarly activity. This fascinating historical phenomenon raises a number of questions: Why are the same men political players and intellectual luminaries? What are the social, political, and larger cultural circumstances that enable this convergence of roles? How do these men's political and intellectual activities relate to one another? And what is the relationship (if any) between the late Republic's cultural flourishing and its concomitant political collapse?

In the following chapters, I hope to arrive at some answers to these questions by studying the intellectual and political activities of Roman senators, and the mutual relationships of and connections among these diverse actions and behaviors. To put it slightly differently, what I aim to offer in this book is a work of intellectual history on the knowledge-producing practices of the late Republican political elite in their historical and cultural contexts. Before I lay out my methodological approach and the structure of my discussion, two preliminary qualifications are in order. I have no ambition to write a general history of scholarship or intellectual life in the late Roman Republic, projects that have been admirably undertaken by other scholars in the past (see 1.3 below), but have chosen a topic much more closely confined both in time and in subject matter. As for time, I will concentrate on the twenty years from 63 to 43 BCE, that is, from Cicero's consulship to his death, with a special focus on the mid-50s to mid-40s. This is when most of the important late Republican works of scholarship and philosophy were written; it is also the time during which the Republican system finally collapsed in chaos and civil war, never to recover.

The second restriction is even more significant. As already hinted, my story's cast of characters will consist nearly exclusively of members of the Roman senate (with the occasional walk-on from a nonsenator, Cicero's friend Atticus being the most prominent). Needless to say, not all writers, scholars, and philosophers in late Republican Rome were senators—far from it. Numerous members of the equestrian order as well as many resident Greeks played crucial roles in the intellectual developments of the period and interacted in multiform ways with the "senator scholars" who are my topic. Since, however, my specific interest is in the roles intellectual activity played in the lives and careers of politically active men, I will touch on the practices and achievements of nonsenators only where they impinge on my narrative.

Conversely, of course, many important Roman politicians and other members of the senate did not apparently spend any time penning or discussing works on virtue or the Latin language (though note that in most cases, we simply do not know: absence of evidence is not evidence of absence). Such men too will therefore appear in these pages only as supporting characters of the central cast—Caesar, Cicero, Brutus, Varro, Cato, Cassius Longinus, Nigidius Figulus, and numerous less well-known senators with an intellectual bent. We will get to know these protagonists in detail in the following chapters; the remainder of this introduction is devoted to considerations of methodology—how the intellectual history of the late Republic has been, and might be, written.

2. A Social History of Late Republican Knowledge

The term "intellectual history" has meant many different things to many different people, and the field's definition and relationship to such sister, or rival, disciplines as, among others, the history of ideas, cultural history, *Geistesgeschichte*, or *histoire de mentalités* is anything but clear.[1] Despite this theoretical and methodological diversity, for many decades one basic tenet has been central to much work on the history of scholarship, literature, philosophy, religion, and science, namely, that ideas and the linguistic structures in which they are expressed arise not in a vacuum but in a historical, political, social, and cultural context. In contrast to a history of thought that views ideas as interacting with and responding to other ideas in a purely intellectual realm, such contextualizing approaches work on the assumption that all processes and products of thought are deeply enmeshed in the culture of their time and place and cannot be properly understood without taking account of the circumstances in which they arise.

As a corollary to this stress on context, intellectual historians have increasingly been directing their focus away from intellectual products (e.g., books or other publications) and toward intellectual practices (e.g., researching, writing, teaching, conducting scientific experiments, attending conferences, etc.). While published works can to some extent be understood as participating in a timeless world of thought—at the very least, they have the potential to transcend the immediate concerns and circumstances of their production and become meaningful to readers in different times and places[2]—the activities of thinkers are always taking place in a particular historical situation. Furthermore, such practices are very often inherently social, involving not just the individual intellectual but entire communities dedicated to similar pursuits,

1. For helpful introductions, see Brett 2002, Bavaj 2010, Whatmore 2016, and the essays in Whatmore and Young (eds.) 2016, as well as (from the wider perspective of cultural history) Burke 2008 and Arcangeli 2012. The description of the intellectual historian in Rorty, Schneewind, and Skinner 1984 (though meant to be a "sympathetic caricature," 9) is one that I would very much endorse.

2. Note, though, that any expression of thought, whether in oral or written form, can itself be viewed as a—historically contextualized—action or activity. Compare Quentin Skinner's famous application of speech-act theory to the history of ideas (Skinner 2002 [1969]; cf. Gotter 2003: 174): by *saying* something, intellectuals are *doing* something, i.e., intervening in an ongoing intellectual argument.

be they teachers and students at an educational institution, scholars in the same academic field, authors and their publishers and readers, or any other group engaged in some form of intellectual exchange.

As we have seen at the beginning of this chapter, the intellectual efforts of senators in the late Republic were likewise strongly interactive:[3] Caesar, Cicero, Brutus, and Varro wrote for one another as well as for other men with similar interests, participated in scholarly debates, and created networks of exchange through the mutual dedication of books. Their activities thus lend themselves to the kinds of social analysis that have fruitfully been brought to bear on other periods of intellectual history. However, as will become clear, there are certain aspects of my protagonists and their pursuits that make them somewhat peculiar exhibits in the greater history of knowledge.

The social aspects of knowledge production have been much studied and theorized in multiple ways, often under such headings as "sociology of knowledge" or "social history of knowledge."[4] Such approaches examine the ways in which social structures inform intellectual activity as well as the social forms of such activity itself. Needless to say, the relationships and behaviors that constitute intellectual life differ greatly from period to period and place to place (Italian humanists, say, operate differently from twenty-first-century American academics); nevertheless, there are certain key elements that appear to underlie knowledge production through the ages and on which intellectual historians have therefore often concentrated.

First, intellectual history frequently takes the form of a history of intellectuals.[5] In other words, its focus is on (groups of) individuals who are the "main discoverers, producers and disseminators of knowledge" (Burke 2000: 18). Depending on the context, such people may be fittingly described as, for

---

3. A note on terminology: in this book, I use "senators/senatorial class," "nobles/nobility," and "aristocrats" interchangeably to refer to politically active Roman males, as defined through membership in the senate, with its requisite property requirements and election at least to the quaestorship (unlike some scholars, I do not reserve "nobility" for a specific subcategory, however defined, within this group); by contrast, "elite" and "upperclass" include both senators and *equites*.

4. "Sociology of knowledge" is the translation of German *Wissenssoziologie*, an approach most famously associated with Karl Mannheim; see Mannheim 1936 and compare Ringer 1990 and McCarthy 1996. For "(social) history of knowledge," see Burke 2000, 2012, 2016. Since I am not here concerned with writing the history of these scholarly approaches themselves, I will be using these two terms interchangeably and without the wish to express adherence to any particular theory or school.

5. See Ringer 1990: 281: "The social group that most interests the historian of knowledge, of course, is the group or category of the intellectuals."

example, scholars, academics, philosophers, or scientists or, collectively, as the "intelligentsia" or "clerisy."[6] Men and women of these descriptions are usually first and foremost dedicated to whatever their intellectual activities may be,[7] and may well define themselves, or be defined by their contemporaries, by an appropriate label ("Posidonius is a philosopher," "Volk is a professor"). In many, if not all, cases, such intellectuals can even be designated professional "brain workers," that is, people who (attempt to) make a living through researching, teaching, writing, and similar pursuits.

Second, intellectual history is often the history of institutions.[8] Scholars are so called because they attend or teach at *scholae* "schools," ranging from the philosophical schools of ancient Greece to medieval classrooms to modern research universities. Scientists conduct experiments in laboratories; men and women of letters congregate at academies and learned societies; intellectuals are employed by courts, by the church, by publishing houses, by museums, libraries, and cultural institutions of all descriptions. By studying the workings of such establishments and of the communities they foster, historians are able to reconstruct the intellectual life and developments of a given period and (sub)culture.

If we now turn back to the men of letters of the late Republic, we encounter a problem: Cicero, Caesar, Brutus, Varro, and their friends emphatically do not fit the mold of the traditional sociology of knowledge as sketched above. These men were not members of an intellectual class; they did not define themselves first and foremost via their erudite activities; and they certainly did not practice scholarship or philosophy as a profession.[9] On the contrary: they were at pains to distinguish themselves from full-time scholars (usually Greeks) and disdained such labels as *philosophus*,[10] showing no sign of

6. See Burke 2000: 18–31. For the manifold meanings of the term "intellectual," see Collini 2006: 13–65.

7. Compare the definition of the "Person des Gebildeten" by Keck, Wiersing, and Wittstadt 1996: 8 as someone "dessen Berufs- oder bevorzugte Hauptbeschäftigung während einer längerfristigen biographischen Konstellation das Denken und das 'Mitteilen' von Gedachtem ist."

8. On the importance of institutions in the intellectual history of the (early) modern period, see Burke 2000: 32–52, 2012: 239–44 and passim.

9. This distinguishes them from, among others, the learned individuals who are the subject of Kendra Eshleman's recent study of intellectuals in the Roman Empire (2012): the "sophists, philosophers, and Christians" of her subtitle did very much think of themselves as belonging to groups of like-minded thinkers or practitioners (cf. also the following n.).

10. For such efforts at demarcation, see the detailed discussion in 2.1 below. On the rejection of the designation *philosophus* by Latin philosophical writers of the Republic, see Hine 2016; as Trapp 2017 shows, this attitude changed in the Empire.

considering themselves anything but members of the senatorial class.[11] In studying the intellectual life of these men, then, we are considering the social behaviors not of a separate group of literati, but of noblemen whose erudite pursuits were part and parcel of their identity as politically active Romans.[12]

Since the second chapter of this book is dedicated to a detailed examination of the kinds of intellectual activity my protagonists engaged in and the ways in which they represented and defined their scholarly pursuits, I here just add some further methodological considerations. Throughout my explorations of the late Republican history of knowledge, I will focus precisely on the ways in which the studies and writings of Cicero, Caesar, Varro, Brutus, and others are inextricably linked to their public life and political actions. In doing so, however, I hope to go beyond an approach that views political and social circumstances as the mere context in which intellectual developments unfold and on which they are ultimately dependent.

What events or circumstances are "contexts" for which others—rather than the other way around—is largely a matter of perspective. Thus, we might say that Caesar's dictatorship provided the context for Cicero's philosophical work of the early 40s; at the same time, it would also make sense to state that the author's philosophical considerations and beliefs informed his experience and actions at this time. While men like Cicero did distinguish between their intellectual and political activities, and often reflected on the relationship between the two, it is also the case that there is no way in which such pursuits can be neatly compartmentalized and kept apart: if the same person wrote scholarship and attended the senate, both activities need to be viewed as part of the totality of that man's actions and personality.

Furthermore, as this book aims to show, there is a deep connection between my senators' scholarship and politics: not only were their writings influenced by their political views, but they frequently constituted political interventions in their own right. At the same time, these men's public actions themselves were colored or even motivated by their intellectual views. Finally, we might even go so far as to question any neat distinction between intellectual discourse and social and political structures on general theoretical grounds. In the wake of the so-called linguistic turn, often associated with such

11. Compare Gotter 2003: 175: "Intellektuelle gab es nicht . . . dem Angehörigen der regimentsfähigen Gruppe stand die *persona* des Intellektuellen nicht zu Gebot."

12. I will therefore henceforth no longer refer to the subjects of my study as "intellectuals" or "scholars," modern terms that tend to refer to distinct social or professional groups and are thus misleading in the late Republican context (cf. Fantham 2009: 141–43). I will, however, continue to use "intellectual," "scholarly," and "scholarship," which appear to me to be sufficiently vague. For ancient terminology for intellectual activity, see 2.2 below.

theorists as Michel Foucault and Pierre Bourdieu, cultural historians have increasingly shifted from examining the ways in which historical reality informs thought to exploring how this reality is itself discursively constructed.[13] On this view, the realm of the social and political is not a world given a priori and external to discourse; it is part of discourse itself.

While I am not interested in larger theories of discourse formation, and while the focus of this book, qua intellectual history, will be on scholarship and learning rather than political events, I do consider the intellectual and political lives of my protagonists single entities and in my interpretations will not privilege one over the other. In particular, I wish to avoid a currently widespread way of thinking about intellectual life in ancient Rome, that is, the view that cultural pursuits were engaged in not for their own sake, but merely to fulfill ulterior social or political functions. While perhaps no scholar would state this "functionalist argument" so baldly, it is in fact pervasive in discussions of the learned pursuits of the Roman elite. Thus, we are told, for example, that senators practiced religious scholarship for the sake of "elite self-assertion," that philological or philosophical discussions acted as "social glue" among upperclass individuals, or that private readings of literature "served to cement friendships, make new social contacts, and perpetuate . . . the habits of the cultured élite."[14] While such analyses are not wrong—there was, of course, fierce competition among aristocrats, and as we will see again and again, intellectual activity did play an enormous social role—there has been a tendency in scholarly discussion for sociological abstractions to become reified and to be considered the unquestioned motivators of a vast array of practices and behaviors. By contrast, I in what follows concentrate on the practices and behaviors themselves, not on any functions they might fulfill in any posited social mechanism.

As will have become clear, my focus in this book is—somewhat unfashionably—on individuals and their intentions. This approach distinguishes my project not only from the functionalist perspective just sketched, but also from discourse analysis in the vein of Foucault and others, which radically downplays the role of individuals;[15] instead, it puts me closer to the brand of intellectual history practiced by Quentin Skinner and other members of the

---

13. This paradigm shift is neatly described by McCarthy 1996: 1–10; its implications for the practice of intellectual history are discussed by Brett 2002: 119–26.

14. "Elite self-assertion": MacRae 2016: 59 (cf. his entire discussion on pp. 55–59); "social glue": Damon 2008: 175; "served to cement . . .": Cavallo 1999: 75.

15. For historical discourse analysis, see Landwehr 2008.

so-called Cambridge School.[16] I certainly do not consider my focus on a few "great men" the only way to analyze the intellectual life of this or any other period; however, I believe that it makes sense in the context of what I hope to achieve, for the following reasons.

First, our sources are skewed toward (these) individuals. Not only is the greater part of all written evidence from Greco-Roman antiquity concerned with the elite, but historiographical sources for my period have understandably focused on such important political actors as Caesar, Cicero, Brutus, and Cato. In addition, there is what we might call the Cicero problem, which is that Cicero's voluminous writings—whether speeches, rhetorical and philosophical treatises, or letters—are our single most important source for the political and intellectual life of the period and that these works, for obvious reasons, concentrate on both Cicero's own doings and those of his fellow senators.[17]

Second, it can be argued that my "great men" were, in fact, great men.[18] Setting aside the larger historical significance of such individuals as Caesar, Cicero, Cato, and Brutus, there is no question that Cicero, Varro, and Nigidius Figulus played central roles in the intellectual history of ancient Rome and beyond. Cicero's towering influence on Latin style and on the development of European philosophy and political theory cannot be overstated, and while Varro and especially Nigidius have fared less well in terms of the transmission of their texts, they were throughout antiquity regarded as the two "most learned" Romans, with Varro's work in particular acting as a standard reference point in many disciplines.[19] While not all my protagonists were equally important as either scholarly or political players, these learned senators were at the forefront of the intellectual deveopments of their times, and it thus makes sense for the intellectual historian to concentrate on them.

16. See esp. Skinner 2002 [1969]. For brief introductions to the Cambridge School, see Landwehr 2008: 40–43, Bavaj 2010: 6–8, and Whatmore 2016: 39–44 and passim; many of the essays in Whatmore and Young (eds.) 2016 touch on methodologies and individuals associated with the School.

17. See Levene 2005. On the pitfalls and pay-offs of using Cicero's writings as historical sources, see Lintott 2008.

18. Needless to say, they were also all men: while some upperclass Roman women were well educated and engaged in intellectual exchange with their male contemporaries, they were of course barred from political careers. On women in Roman intellectual life, see Rawson 1985: 46–48; on one attested late Republican woman with learned interests, Cicero's correspondent Caerellia, see McCutcheon 2016.

19. On the trope of Varro as *doctissimus*, see Volk 2019: 184 with further references. For the pairing of Varro and Nigidius, see 6.2 below.

Third and finally, I believe that my focus on individuals is appropriate for a social and political system that was predicated on individual agency. In the absence of parties or larger administrative institutions, the aristocracy that was the Roman Republic functioned as the sum of its parts: events took place as more or less powerful individuals acted and interacted, aligning and realigning their loyalties according to political, personal, financial, familial, and other concerns. Both in theory and in practice, it was the men who held, or had held, magistracies and made up the senate who by their individual decisions made Roman history. Even if this system was failing at the very period I study in this book, my model of intellectual history as the history of the intellectual activities of individuals is, I suggest, germane to the spirit of the age.[20]

As hinted above, the analysis of these individuals' activities—including, crucially, their writings—should ideally lead to an uncovering of their thoughts and intentions. I ultimately consider the main question of intellectual history to be, "What were they thinking?," in the sense of not just "What was the intellectual content of their thought?" but also "What were they trying to do?" To quote Skinner, "Any statement is inescapably the embodiment of a particular intention on a particular occasion, addressed to the solution of a particular problem, and is thus specific to its context in a way that it can only be naive to try to transcend" (2002 [1969]: 88). The determination of such intentions is always bound to remain speculative. Nevertheless, such speculation is an intrinsic part of the intellectual historian's task and will play a major role in this book.

3. What This Book Is Not

Given its narrow focus on the doings of a particular group of men over a period of twenty years, my book is by no means intended as a study of the intellectual scene of late Republican Rome in general. Versions of such a history have already been written, by two great scholars in two great, if very different, books: Elizabeth Rawson's *Intellectual Life in the Late Roman Republic* (1985) and Claudia Moatti's *La Raison de Rome* (1997; English translation 2015). I very much admire both works, whose influence will be felt throughout these pages even where I do not explicitly refer to them. Rawson's painstakingly detailed reconstruction of the erudite personnel and processes of the period has been indispensable for my own study; at the same time, I have been inspired by Moatti's analysis of the spirit of the age and especially her insistence on the specificity and originality of Roman intellectual activity (even if I do not always agree with her larger narrative; see below).

---

20. Individualist models of agency are found also in some of the period's theoretical writings; see now Woolf 2015, esp. 170–200 on the individualism of Cicero's ethics.

Among the individual subfields of intellectual activity, it is the religious scholarship of the late Republic that has been studied the most systematically. As part of the renaissance of Roman religious studies in the past few decades, the Romans' own attempts at describing and interpreting their practices and beliefs have likewise been subjected to scrutiny, including—to mention just three prominent examples—in Beard, North, and Price's standard text *Religions of Rome*, the work of Jörg Rüpke, and Duncan MacRae's 2016 monograph on civil theology in the first century. There has not been an equally sustained effort to write the history of Roman philosophy,[21] though over the years a number of edited volumes have helped put this neglected area of philosophical history back on the map.[22] Of course, there are, and have always been, innumerable studies of the works and life of Cicero, while the intellectual contributions of Varro and even Julius Caesar are slowly beginning to receive more scholarly attention as well.[23]

What this means for my book is that while my perspective is more restricted than that of the *opera magna* of Rawson and Moatti, it is more encompassing and synthetic than that of much other work on the period, which has tended to concentrate on individual fields, figures, and works. Despite this wider scope, however, my focus is mostly synchronic. I am concerned with painting the picture of the thoughts and actions of a particular social set at a particular time, and while certain lines of development and possible chains of cause and effect will emerge in the course of my discussion, it is not my purpose to plot my observations onto a preconceived historic narrative. This approach sets me apart from many other discussions of the culture of the late Republic, which are predicated on the idea that the political change from Republic to Empire went hand in hand with what has memorably been called a "cultural revolution."[24] While individual scholars differ on the exact details of such a change, a much

21. Morford 2002, Maurach 2006, and Maso 2012 are very basic introductions, focusing on individual thinkers; Garbarino 1973 covers only the 2nd c. BCE.

22. See esp. Griffin and Barnes (eds.) 1989, Barnes and Griffin (eds.) 1997, Williams and Volk (eds.) 2016, Vesperini (ed.) 2017, and Müller and Mariani Zini (eds.) 2018.

23. The works of Varro have long been the subject of specialist studies, but few attempts have been made to interpret his oeuvre as a whole (the only recent monograph is the helpful general introduction of Cardauns 2001; compare also Volk 2019); however, recent conference volumes (Butterfield [ed.] 2015 and Arena and Mac Góráin [eds.] 2017) attest to renewed interest. Caesar's scholarship is given its due by Garcea 2012 and chapters in two recent *Companions* (Fantham 2009 and Pezzini 2018).

24. The phrase "Roman cultural revolution," pointedly calqued on Syme's famous title, was put on the map by Habinek and Schiesaro (eds.) 1997 (compare their introduction to the volume); the concept has been explored and theorized most thoroughly by Wallace-Hadrill 1997, 2008.

simplified version of a narrative widespread in current historiography might run something like the following:[25]

In earlier periods of the Roman Republic, the Roman nobility was a well-functioning body whose members were inspired by a system of shared values, known as the *mos maiorum*; the Republican political system, as well as the nobles' commitment to the common good, prevented the concentration of power in the hands of individuals. Certain forms of knowledge—for example, religious or legal—were a de facto monopoly of the senatorial class, which passed on this expertise from generation to generation without resorting to written systematization or codification. When with the extension of Rome's empire, the Republican form of government and senatorial esprit de corps came under increased pressure and ultimately collapsed, the structures of knowledge, too, underwent a change. What had been unwritten know-how became the subject of rational analysis and written record, as the control over knowledge was wrested from the nobility and passed into the hands of specialists.

While this is, in many ways, a plausible story, there are a number of serious problems with it. First, in positing a pristine early Republican period in which the *mos maiorum* ruled supreme, scholars seem to be overly trusting in the Romans' own narratives of decline.[26] The idea that the *res publica* had fatally deteriorated from a former state of glory to the present ruin was a common refrain of late Republican literature, and the *mos maiorum* was the idealizing retrojection of whatever values a particular speaker or writer wished to promote. While there obviously were political and social developments in the course of Republican history, it is highly unlikely that there ever was a period of blithe aristocratic consensus, when values, policies, or knowledge were uncontested.[27] The *maiores* never existed; they are the symbolic guarantors of invented tradition.[28]

A second, related difficulty is the nature and chronology of the supposed cultural revolution. Claudia Moatti and Jörg Rüpke both posit an increasing

---

25. Versions of this narrative are found or implied in, among others, Minyard 1985; Hölkeskamp 1996; Moatti 1988, 1997, 2003a; Wallace-Hadrill 1997, 2008; Rüpke 2009b, 2012; and Leonardis 2019.

26. Compare Beard, North, and Price 1998: 1.117–18: "One of the reasons that *decline* has entered the analysis is precisely because several ancient writers themselves chose to characterize the religion of the period in this way" (emphasis theirs).

27. See Mouritsen 2017: 111: "We should therefore accept the possibility that our picture of the 'middle' republic as a period of broad elite consensus and stable senatorial control—over the *res publica* as well as its own members—may be a myth born out of hindsight."

28. On the invention of tradition, see Hobsbawm 1983. For late Republican constructions of their past, see ch. 5.

dominance of reason or rationality, though the former bases her model on the European enlightenment (*raison*) while the latter uses the terminology of Max Weber (*Rationalisierung*).[29] In both cases, there is a danger of anachronism, but we might nevertheless agree that it makes sense to describe Roman writings on civil law, augural methods, or pretty much any other field as attempts to impose some rational order on the material at hand. The real problem is that this form of rationalization is inherent in each and every form of scholarly or technical writing, from any period: ordering, explaining, analyzing, and the very act of putting into language are rationalizing practices. Thus, as soon as the Romans began writing on history, philosophy, grammar, science, and other subjects—that is, as far as our evidence goes, in the early second century BCE, but possibly earlier—they were already rationalizing. What this means is that the posited intellectual sea change begins in the middle Republic and is a long and drawn-out process[30]—and indeed, both Moatti and Rüpke study material from at least the second century BCE to the beginning of the Augustan period. Since the start of this "enlightenment," then, coincides more or less with the beginning of Latin literature, it becomes methodologically questionable to contrast it with a supposedly different earlier period, given that we do not have any contemporary sources for what was going on then. As far as we can tell, the Romans were always rationalizers, and they always engaged in intellectual activity.[31]

The less abstract claim that there was a change in the sociology of knowledge production—intellectual mastery passed from senatorial amateurs to nonsenatorial specialists—likewise has some truth to it. We certainly find in the late Republic an increasing "differentiation" of knowledge:[32] forms of expertise that had previously been part and parcel of any elite male's know-how now became distinct subjects of theoretical discussion and publication. Thus, for example, while every magistrate knew how to take the auspices and

---

29. Note the title of Moatti 1997; the epigraph of her book is Kant's famous definition of *Aufklärung* (p. 11). Rüpke's Weberian approach is laid out in, among other places, Rüpke 2012: 2–4.

30. I do not mean to deny that there are changes and developments within this period, or that there appears to be an increase in volume and sophistication of attempts at ordering knowledge in the late Republic (indeed, the very existence of my book is predicated on the latter observation). At the same time, owing to the scarcity of our sources, there is a real danger of underestimating the intellectual achievement of the second century, which remains a seriously understudied period.

31. For a somewhat different argument against the "rationalization" narrative, specifically in the field of Roman religion, see MacRae 2013: 513, 2016: 53–75.

32. See Beard, North, and Price 1998: 1.149–56; generally on "structural differentiation" as a model of sociohistorical change in the course of the Republic, see Hopkins 1978: 74–96.

engaged with many other officially sanctioned predictive practices, the many treatises on augury that appeared in the mid-first century, not to mention Cicero's philosophical discussion in *De diuinatione*, suddenly put "divination" on the map as a scholarly subject.[33]

It is also undoubtedly the case that sociological specialization and/or professionalization occurred.[34] New fields of knowledge, especially those with a Greek pedigree, including grammar and philosophy, came with their own teachers; skills previously passed on informally from generation to generation, such as oratory, gradually became subjects of institutionalized instruction; and increased specialization in elite knowledge, most prominently in law, ultimately led to the emergence of classes of experts, who no longer pursued political careers themselves. Especially once we move into the Augustan period, we find nonsenatorial specialists gaining prominence in a variety of fields and making their voices heard in publications, including both freeborn professionals (e.g., the architect Vitruvius) and imperial freedmen (e.g., the librarian Hyginus).

Nevertheless, it is striking how at least in the period with which I am concerned, the increasing differentiation of knowledge very often did *not* go hand in hand with professionalization. It is exactly senators—such as Cicero, Varro, and Nigidius—who were the most prominent practitioners and innovators in many intellectual fields, without therefore making up some new scholarly class or calling into question the Republican status quo.[35] As a matter of fact, this type of "dilettante" persisted into the changed political situation of the Empire, where such eminent scholarly and philosophical writers as Seneca and Pliny the Elder also held public office and had busy political careers.

In addition to the individual problems just discussed, the narrative of the Roman cultural revolution that explicitly or implicitly underlies much scholarship on late Republican intellectual history is questionable, in my opinion, for

33. Compare Volk 2017: 329–34 and 6.1 below.

34. See Wallace-Hadrill 1997, 2008: 213–58.

35. See MacRae 2016: 55–59, who shows that the religious scholarship of the late Republic was largely carried out by members of the senatorial class. Wallace-Hadrill 2008: 213–58 has to contend with the awkward fact that his posited dismantling of the traditional knowledge of the nobility was driven largely by two men, Cicero and Varro, who were not only senators but fairly conservative in their outlook. He concludes, "Cicero and Varro were key figures in articulating this sense of disintegration; but though they implied that the nobility *ought* to be successfully preserving the ways of their *maiores*, they were actively engaged in dismantling their authority" (258; emphasis his). In a similar vein, Binder 2018 attempts to play a "professional" Varro against an aristocratic Cicero.

the very reason that it posits a grand historical arc in the first place. At least since Hegel, Roman Republican history has been haunted by the specter of teleology: since we know that the Republic fell, all events must be inexorably moving toward this end point, and it is the task of the historian to explain the mechanisms through which this development came to pass.[36] On the same model, intellectual and cultural events are seen as leading up to the "golden age" of the Augustan period and must likewise be understood as chapters in a story of progress.

In recent decades, the teleological view of Republican political history has at least occasionally been challenged and replaced with a more complex picture of individual and group motivation and action that led to certain results (such as the end of Republic) not because they "had to happen," but because they "just so happened," owing to a highly complex and ever-changing set of individual factors and events.[37] I view my work on the intellectual history of the period inspired by a similar methodology. To quote from the passage of José Saramago used as an epigraph for this chapter, rather than "drive across" the past as if it were a road that leads to a particular end point, I hope to lift up numerous individual stones in order to find out "what lies beneath" (Saramago 2010: 21). Throughout the book, I wish to draw attention to the intricate synchronic details of learned pursuits from the mid-60s to the mid-40s BCE, always attuned to the multiformity, individuality, and serendipity of intellectual (and, indeed, political) behavior. As mentioned above, my interest is in what my protagonists "were thinking" at the time. If in the end a somewhat larger diachronic tale does emerge, I believe it will be less abstract and messier and more diverse than other stories that have been told before.

One of the corollaries of this approach is that I will attempt, as far as this is possible and makes sense, to employ "actors' categories," that is, my protagonists' own words and concepts, in analyzing their statements and behaviors.[38] My goal is to get, if not inside these men's heads, at least inside their language, that is, the ways in which *they* represented the world to themselves at the time, as opposed to how *we* might designate their thoughts and actions with

---

36. Schneider 1998: 1–55 provides a helpful overview of modern historiography on the period; see also Walter 2009. Prominent proponents of some version of the idea that the Republic found itself in a "crisis without alternative" ("Krise ohne Alternative," C. Meier 1997: 201–5) and was doomed to fall include Theodor Mommsen, Mathias Gelzer, Ronald Syme, and Christian Meier, among many others.

37. See Strasburger 1968 and esp. Gruen 1974.

38. To use another set of terms to describe the same approach, my account will strive to be "emic" rather than "etic."

hindsight. My approach is thus comparable to that of Craig Williams in his recent study of Roman friendship (2012: 28; emphasis his):

> Instead of trying to get behind the rhetoric, I stay *with* it and examine its workings: always alert to the non-textual, non-linguistic environments in which these texts arose, circulated, and had their meaning, but keeping my focus firmly on language.

While it is of course impossible to think or speak about the past (or anything else) without applying one's own mental and linguistic structures, there is still an enormous methodological difference between scholarly approaches that describe historical societies and events in deliberately anachronistic terms (e.g., ones drawn from particular modern theories) and others that aim to reconstruct the ways of thinking and speaking of a particular period or set of individuals themselves.[39] While I would thus not agree with Quentin Skinner's strong claim that "no agent can be said to have meant or achieved something which they could never be brought to accept as a correct description of what they meant or achieved"[40]—it might make perfect sense, in certain historiographical contexts, to describe an agent's doings with designations alien to his or her own conceptual language—my own approach will be to understand and represent my protagonists' practices as far as possible in their own terms.

4. Overview of Chapters

In this spirit, the following chapter 2 explores the social world of late Republican intellectual activities and the ways in which my protagonists thought, spoke, and wrote about it. I first attempt to debunk the widespread view that learned pursuits carried a stigma among the practically minded Romans and that upperclass men therefore felt the continuous need to justify their intellectual activities. Instead, such studies were a regular part of the educated elite's lifestyle, though Roman aristocrats were at pains to demarcate their own forays into philosophy and other scholarly fields from the activities of Greek professionals, whose practices were felt to belong to a different social and intellectual sphere.

Drawing mostly on the corpus of Cicero's letters, I identify a vocabulary of learned pursuits, which were most often generically referred to as *studia* or *litterae* and felt to consist of reading and writing. Such activities were intensely social, involving the studying aristocrat in multiform interchanges with Greek intellectuals, skilled slaves and freedmen, and his own *amici* with similar

---

39. Compare Williams 2012: 26–27.

40. Skinner 2002 [1969]: 77; cf. Rorty, Schneewind, and Skinner 1984: 1.

interests. From the acquisition of books to the composition and circulation of written works, the learned senator drew on the labor, support, and feedback of a wide variety of individuals and represented such collaboration (especially when it involved members of his own social class) as intrinsically valuable and conducive to forging a closer interpersonal bond.

The letters to and from Cicero are testimony to the value accorded to such instances of *societas studiorum* ("companionship of study"), whose repeated invocation by the letter writers is itself part and parcel of the creation of such intellectual networks. I conclude the chapter with a look at Cicero's *Brutus*, an amicable dialogue between the author and his friends Atticus and Brutus, which both depicts an idealized instance of "studying together" and—through its publication and dedication to Brutus—aspires to furthering in the real world the close-knit intellectual companionship that is projected by the text. *Studia* and *societas studiorum* clearly mattered to the learned senators at the center of my study; how the practice and content of their studies affected their private and public lives is the question at issue in the remainder of the book.

Chapters 3 through 6 are divided by intellectual field, with chapters 3 and 4 treating philosophy, chapter 5 considering reconstructions of Roman histori-cal and linguistic identity, and chapter 6 focusing on science and theology. Chapter 3 opens with a question. We know that late Republican Romans were enthusiastic about the study of philosophy, and that philosophy billed itself as an "art of life" designed to assist its practitioners with the conduct of their lives—but did mid-first-century senators ever apply their philosophical teach-ings and beliefs to their own political activities and decisions? In the course of the chapter, I consider three test cases for potentially "engaged philosophy" in the period leading up to and including the Civil War.

I first focus on the younger Cato, the optimate diehard who after his suicide at Utica was turned into both a Republican martyr and a Stoic paragon. While his Stoicism did not shape the content of his conservative politics, I suggest that Cato's single-minded pursuit of his political goals was crucially informed by Stoic ethical theory, in particular its privileging of (virtuous) intention over (uncontrollable) outcome. In stubbornly pursuing his agenda, including by spectacular methods at odds with customary Roman practice, Cato self-consciously fashioned for himself a recognizable public persona, setting in motion the creation of the Cato legend even during his own lifetime.

By contrast, the period's most famous Roman student of philosophy, M. Tullius Cicero, subscribed to the Skepticism of the New Academy, submitting epistemological and ethical issues to careful scrutiny and adopting any posi-tion only provisionally. His dedication to philosophical studies was compli-cated by the fact that according to his own understanding of human nature, the ideal lifestyle was the active, not the contemplative life, and in particular the life dedicated to the welfare of the commonwealth. Following this "political imperative," Cicero aimed to bring his philosophical insights to bear on late Republican politics, in terms both of his theoretical work on government, *De re publica*, and of his own public actions, in which—as we can follow in detail in his letters—he attempted to conform to his ethical convictions.

The chapter concludes with a discussion of the philosophical school most popular in mid-first-century Rome: Epicureanism. Given that Epicurus counseled withdrawal from public life in order to achieve the desired psychological freedom from disturbance, the fact that a fair number of Roman senators displayed allegiance to a doctrine at odds with their political commitments calls for an explanation. Focusing on three prominent Epicureans (C. Cassius Longinus, L. Calpurnius Piso Caesoninus, and T. Pomponius Atticus), I explore the diverse ways in which upperclass Roman Epicureans were successfully able to reconcile their philosophical beliefs and their political (dis)engagement.

Chapter 4 considers the interlinking of politics and philosophy in the period after the Battle of Pharsalus. I first focus on what I call "Pompeian group therapy," the recourse to sociable philosophizing on the part of defeated Republicans. As Cicero's letter collection *Ad familiares* shows, both Cicero and his *amici* (many still in exile after the Civil War) turned to philosophy for consolation and the reassurance that they had done, and were continuing to do, the morally right thing.

I then turn to the question of freedom of speech (and the absence thereof) under Caesar's dictatorship, showing how Cicero and others attempted to cope with the changed political situation. Cicero's *Brutus* addresses the altered conditions that make a continuation of Republican oratory near-impossible, while the author's own speech *Pro Marcello* explores new means of expressing one's political opinions even when speaking to Caesar himself. As the lively publicity war over the legacy of Cato attests (with the most prominent pamphleteers being none other than Cicero and Caesar), a fair amount of *libertas dicendi* still obtained, with aristocratic politeness assuring that personal offense was largely avoided.

The main philosophical product of the period was Cicero's encyclopedic corpus. The project's purpose and possible political import have been much discussed, and I examine once more Cicero's own statements as found especially in the works' prefaces. By writing his philosophical works, the author clearly meant to comfort himself over the loss of both his daughter and the Republic, while also doing a service to his countrymen that was at the same time cultural, ethical, and political. While there is little overt anti-Caesarianism in the texts themselves, I argue that both their cast of interlocutors and the networks in which they circulated were meant to create a "Caesar-free" zone that signaled clearly who was excluded from the *uita beata* achieved through virtuous conduct.

The chapter concludes by considering the uses of philosophy in the assassination of Caesar and its aftermath. The most prominent conspirators, Brutus and Cassius, were known for their philosophical interests and, I argue, at least partly motivated by theoretical convictions about the evils of tyranny. After the Ides of March, Cicero became a major apologist of the "liberators," arguing in speeches, letters, and philosophical works for the primacy of the morally good (*honestum*) over all other considerations, including personal loyalty. Caesar's friends and supporters, by contrast, maintained that Brutus et al. were traitors for having broken the sacred bonds of friendship, a narrative that won out when Octavian declared himself the avenger of his wronged father.

Chapter 5 turns from the "imported" subject of philosophy to more intrinsically Roman concerns, discussing mid-first-century explorations of Roman identity. I first provide a general survey of the period's proliferating antiquarian studies, while also considering modern explanations for why late Republican authors were so fascinated by their own past. While disillusionment with the present political crisis may have played a role, Roman antiquarianism on closer examination turns out to be far less nostalgic and conservative than often depicted; furthermore, efforts to codify traditional knowledge were often guided not so much by abstract ideals of reason (*ratio*)—as some of the current narratives of late Republican intellectual history would have it—as by the recognition and embrace of the shared habits and usages (*consuetudo*) that had shaped Roman practices over the centuries.

Thus, Cicero in book 2 of his *De re publica* describes the establishment of the Roman mixed constitution as a long and not always straightforward process, which involved a multitude of individual actors. Similarly, in his *Antiquitates rerum diuinarum* Varro depicts Roman religion as a work in progress, in which cults and particular manners of worship are established, and occasionally again fall into disuse, at different points in time. Concerned specifically with the civic religion of his own community, Varro admits that current cult practices are not necessarily in agreement with philosophically informed ideas about the divine, but considers it his own task to trace the messy reality of the grown customs of his "old people" rather than impose a more rational system.

Similar attitudes are found in late Republican discussions of the Latin language. While *Latinitas* (the use of correct Latin) is considered an ideal and much debated in works of the period, authors like Cicero and Varro not only admit that linguistic *consuetudo* condones many verbal forms that are not strictly speaking correct, but even openly accept such usages, whether for aesthetic reasons or simply because individual speakers, however learned, are bound by the common speech of the *populus*. Even more rationally inclined linguistic thinkers, such as Julius Caesar, go only so far in promoting the use of morphologically analogical forms; even though the Latin language becomes more standardized during our period, there was never an attempt to systematize it from the top down.

Chapter 6 finally moves from *urbs* to *orbis*, considering late Republican attempts at "coopting the cosmos," that is, situating Rome or individual Romans within the universe as a whole and connecting them to the sphere of the divine. Roman civic religion was predicated on the assumption that the gods favored the *res publica* and its endeavors, and its ritual practices were designed to maintain that favor. By the mid-first century, however, this religious system had become subject to various strains and innovations, as political strife led to increasingly partisan and obstructive uses of its rituals, and powerful individuals furthermore began to seek and claim divine support outside the parameters of the state religion. At the same time, the spread of scientific and philosophical ideas led to new ways of understanding the workings of the universe, affecting the ways in which learned Romans viewed the role of the gods, the question of fate and its predictability, and the status of human beings, both in life and after death.

After an introductory section, the chapter discusses the words and deeds of three prominent Roman senators with particular interests and expertise in these topics. I first turn to Nigidius Figulus, a firm anti-Caesarian, whose learned endeavors go considerably beyond the genteel studies of a Cicero and Varro. Labeled a "Pythagorean and sorcerer" by Jerome, Nigidius wrote about grammar, but also about natural history, astronomy and astrology, and numerous forms of divination. Strikingly, he is credited with having been active as a diviner himself, using child mediums in one of our sources and casting horoscopes in others. His astrological interventions as well as his publication of an Etruscan calendar of thunder omens point to a strongly political aspect of Nigidius's prediction making: apparently, the senator used his esoteric knowledge to warn against the rise of a sole ruler, prophecies that, as it happens, turned out to be only too correct.

I next consider the man whose ascent to power Nigidius tried to prevent both on the battlefield and in his divinatory practice. Arguably, Julius Caesar's greatest achievement is his reform of the Roman calendar, which for the first time brought the civic year into lasting agreement with the changes of the seasons and the risings and settings of the constellations. A powerful symbol of both Rome's embeddedness in the cosmos and Caesar's own control over time, the new calendar presents the only good example of the "rationalization" narrative of late Republican intellectual history; unsurprisingly, it was resented by those of a more Republican persuasion as an imposition of despotic power.

Caesar's most spectacular cooption of the cosmos was, of course, his own apotheosis. In the years of his dictatorship, consecutive decrees of the senate increasingly approximated Caesar to a god, with actual introduction into the state cult apparently voted in shortly before the Ides of March 44. After his death, Caesar was associated with the comet that appeared at his funeral games and—at the initiative of Octavian/Augustus—finally received a proper temple and lasting place in the Roman pantheon. Whether Caesar himself had been actively planning on becoming a god can no longer be determined; his immediate contemporaries, at any rate, appear to have been less alarmed at the dictator's alleged divinity than at his increasingly monarchic demeanor.

It is fitting for a book so dependent on Ciceronian evidence to conclude with yet another discussion of Cicero himself. The master orator was highly adept at claiming divine support for himself, most notably concerning his actions during the Catilinarian conspiracy, when—as Cicero discusses at length in the third *Catilinarian* and in his poem about his consulship—numerous dire portents warned of danger, and his own countermeasures were obviously approved by the gods. In his philosophical work, however, the Skeptic Cicero calls into question the existence of communication from gods to humans, going so far as to debunk in hilarious fashion the very portents of his consulship when discussing divination in *De diuinatione*. Generally, it seems as if Cicero would like to believe in an ordered cosmos where gods care for humans, the soul is immortal, and virtuous statesmen receive a celestial afterlife—but, owing to his Skepticism, cannot quite assent to such propositions. The one thing that he remains certain about, however, is the primacy of virtue: in the absence of clear divine favor, human beings still are able, and required, to do the morally right thing, following what Cicero terms the "auspices of virtue."

The book ends with a brief conclusion, which summarizes its results and stresses once more the interconnectedness of knowledge production and political activity among the late Republican Roman senatorial class. While the period's turbulent political events certainly acted as a catalyst for developments in the intellectual sphere—and occasionally vice versa—the perhaps most striking aspect of mid-first-century senatorial *studia* is their "Republican" nature. The Republican political process was driven by individual actors with their own agendas, who cooperated with or opposed one another in ever-shifting alliances, all the while keeping up their base assumption of mutual *amicitia* and weathering disagreements with the help of aristocratic politeness. Similarly, the scholarly efforts of these same men present a diverse nexus of intensely sociable practices, characterized by both intellectual independence and competitive engagement with one's peers. When the political system collapsed and was replaced by a monarchy, the cultural landscape likewise underwent a momentous shift, as the senators' loss of political power went hand in hand with the emperors' increasingly top-down shaping of the intellectual sphere. The unique Roman Republic of Letters did not survive the fall of the actual Republic.

2

Res publica of Letters

THE TITLES both of this chapter and of the book as a whole nod to the early modern term "Republic of Letters" or *res publica litterarum*. In the Renaissance, scholars across Europe viewed themselves as equal citizens of an intellectual commonwealth that transcended political and institutional frontiers and was imagined as functioning according to its own laws and customs.[1] I wish to suggest that in the late Roman Republic, educated senators likewise conducted their intellectual activities in a community of equals—except that in their case, the group of their learned peers significantly overlapped with that of their fellow politicians. In other words, the mid-first-century Republic of Letters was wholly embedded within the actual *res publica*, the Republican political system run by the same men who also engaged in scholarship.[2] It is the very convergence of these two spheres that is the topic of this book.[3]

1. On the concept of the Republic of Letters, see Bots and Waquet 1997 and Fumaroli 2015; Grafton 2009: 9–34 discusses some of the interactive practices of the Republic's "citizens."

2. Fascinatingly, Renaissance authors themselves frequently likened their putative Republic of Letters to the most famous republic, that of ancient Rome; see Bots and Waquet 1997: 22–23.

3. My conceit (which I intend to be playful more than anything else) of a *res publica* of letters, with its focus on the social aspects of late Republican intellectual activity, is thus different from such superficially similar metaphors found in recent scholarship on the period as "written republic" (Baraz 2012), "literary republic" (Gurd 2012: 49–76), or "paper forum" (Stroup 2010: 161–67), terms meant to evoke the use of writing as an alternative or additional arena for political expression and action (cf. also Moatti 1997: 159–61), esp. in reference to Cicero's publications under Caesar's dictatorship (see also "republic in letters," used by Gildenhard 2018 for Cicero's community-building through letter-writing in the same period). This phenomenon will play an important role in my book as well but is not the focus of this chapter. I also note "Letters of the Republic," the title of ch. 3 in MacRae 2016, with reference to learned literary production in the late Republic; "Republic of Letters," the title of ch. 3 in Elder and Mullen 2019, on code-switching in Cicero's letters; and *Empire of Letters*, the title of Frampton 2018, on the theme of writing in Roman literature.

In what follows, I first discuss general views of intellectual activity in the late Republic, including not only the attitudes of the Romans themselves but also the judgments of modern scholars (2.1). I then move on to an examination of the basic Latin terminology for learned pursuits, relying mostly on Cicero's letters; this exploration of actors' categories provides us with a rough map of the intellectual practices in which the period's elite men engaged (2.2). To conclude, I turn to some more sophisticated ways in which Roman writers represented and constructed the manifold interactions in the intellectual community that was their own *res publica* of Letters (2.3).[4]

1. These So Learned Times

In a letter to Atticus of 11 March 45, Cicero dwells again on a topic that has been central to the friends' correspondence for the last few days: Cicero's grief over the recent death of his daughter Tullia and his plan to construct a shrine to her memory. He envisages memorializing his daughter with "all kinds of monuments taken from the genius of all Greeks and Latins," an ambitious vision that he qualifies with the proviso, "as far as this can be realized in these so learned times (*his temporibus tam eruditis*)."[5] While it is not entirely clear what Cicero has in mind—a series of inscriptions on the physical structure of the *fanum*?[6]—it is clear that he believes that any such selection cannot possibly be representative of "all" appropriate sentiments that "genius" can come up with: the age he lives in is simply too erudite and sophisticated.

My concern in this section is not with what Cicero was thinking when writing these lines, but with his characterization of his time as "this age of culture" (thus the translation of Shackleton Bailey 1999). As we will see in the course of this book, the period of the late Republic was indeed a time of cultural flourishing unprecedented in Roman history. Men of the upper classes, typically functionally bilingual, received literary and rhetorical education in both Latin and Greek; increasingly studied in Greek centers of learning; and habitually consorted with Greek intellectuals at home and abroad. They were often well versed in philosophy, making and appreciating philosophical allusions

---

4. On late Republican intellectual life as discussed in this chapter, compare generally Boyancé 1936; Rawson 1985, esp. chs. 1–7; Griffin 1994; Fantham 1996, ch. 1; Arweiler 2003: 225–35; Heil 2003; Sánchez Vendramini 2010, ch. 3; Stroup 2010; and MacRae 2016: 28–75. On the intellectual life of the Roman nonelite, see Toner 2017.

5. *Att.* 12.18.1: *quantum his temporibus tam eruditis fieri potuerit ... omni genere monimentorum ab omnium ingeniis sumptorum et Graecorum et Latinorum.* All translations from Greek and Latin are my own.

6. Compare Shackleton Bailey 1965–70 ad loc.

and jokes in speeches, letters, and conversation; many went further and declared their own allegiance to particular philosophical schools, including Stoicism, Epicureanism, and the various shades of Academic philosophy. Senators and equestrians imported Greek artwork; built town houses, country villas, and gardens with sophisticated designs and decoration; and amassed and displayed Greek and Latin libraries. They patronized poets of both languages and often wrote poetry themselves. Finally, they produced an unprecented volume of prose works (typically in Latin but sometimes in Greek) on such topics as philosophy, rhetoric, grammar, history, religion, and science, among others.

It is beyond the scope of this book to trace the developments that led to this proliferation of learning and learned practices. The history of Roman cultural development is to a great part the history of Hellenization, a process that had been ongoing since the beginnings of the city but had intensified with the conquest of the eastern Mediterranean and the subsequent movement of people, material, and knowledge. The emergence of a Latin literature on the model of the Greek—viewed by the Romans as a conscious choice datable to a particular moment in time, the year 240 BCE—was perhaps the single most important aspect of this development, leading to the existence of a literate culture that not only translated, adapted, and transformed Greek thoughts and writings, but created a discourse of its own, specific in both Latin form and Roman content. In keeping with my synchronic approach, I am here taking these developments for granted, focusing on my particular period—the very times that were, by the assessment of one of their most prominent thinkers and writers, "so learned."

Or is the tag phrase I have taken out of context and chosen as this section's heading in need of revision or at least further probing? Have I been painting too simplistic a picture of elite intellectual activity in the late Republic? How learned were these times really? After all, scholars have often taken a dim view of Roman intellectual achievement, dismissing the efforts of the period's authors as unoriginal or otherwise of less than stellar quality. And even if we reject such verdicts as based on stereotype and prejudice, we still have to contend with a second, more sophisticated objection that is often made, namely, that the Romans themselves regarded learned activities with suspicion or at least ambivalence, considering them potentially un-Roman or unfitting for an upperclass male. If it is indeed the case that the men of the late Republic viewed intellectual practices as inherently problematic, how does this affect my project of studying such activities?

As for the first point, the stereotype of Roman cultural inferiority—based in large part on Romantic ideas about originality and the idealization of Greek culture especially in eighteenth- and nineteenth-century Germany—is still alive and well, for all scholarly efforts to the contrary. Leaving aside anecdotal evidence (such as the Hellenist colleague who keeps informing me cheerfully that my class on "Roman philosophy" cannot possibly have any content), it is the apologetic tone of many studies of Roman philosophy and scholarship themselves that signals to the reader that the intellectual bona fides of their subject matter is somehow in doubt. We are often left with the impression that the efforts of, say, a Cicero or Varro were pretty good—for a Roman. What may be meant as a historicizing effort to stress cultural specificity (e.g., the observation that the Romans were particularly interested in practical and political philosophy) can come across as a disparagement (viz. they apparently had no sense for the finer points of theory). Even openly revisionist works that set out to prove the independent quality of their subject matter—such as Raphael Woolf's recent vindication of Cicero's philosophy (2015) or Daryn Lehoux's championing of Roman science (2012)—raise the question of why such a gallant defense is necessary in the first place.[7]

If the specter of secondariness will thus unfortunately most likely continue to haunt Roman studies, the question of intellectual quality is luckily beside the point of this book. However much I may personally be convinced of the superior intelligence of many of my protagonists and of the excellence of their written works (and I am), my aim here is not to critique the intellectual products of the late Republic but to describe and analyze the period's intellectual practices. The question, for example, of whether Cicero's philosophical works do or do not compare well with those of either Greek or modern philosophers (whatever this could possibly mean) is of little concern to me; what this book is about is the fact that Cicero wrote these works, and that is undisputed.

Prejudices against Roman culture are typically based on an implicit or explicit comparison with other cultures, in particular that of ancient Greece or otherwise our own (e.g., Roman philosophy stacks up poorly against Greek; Roman science seems ludicrous from a modern perspective). They are thus anachronistic and ultimately irrelevant to a more historicist inquiry, as mine in this book. The same, however, is not true for the second possible objection to my "most learned times" scenario, namely, that the Romans themselves viewed intellectual activity with ambivalence or even hostility. While my focus is, again, primarily on Roman activities rather than Roman attitudes, the question of what my protagonists and their contemporaries thought about the manifold learned practices of their society is obviously of importance to my project.

Needless to say, while many historical actions and activities are well documented (e.g., Cicero was consul in 63 BCE; Varro wrote a book on the Latin

---

7. One major work that is unusually and pleasantly free of any apologetic tone is Moatti 1997.

language), it is next to impossible to determine what historical agents, let alone groups of agents, actually believed. First, just as there exists no single opinion on any subject among any group of people at any moment today, it makes no sense to posit that "the Romans" had one specific view of intellectual pursuits or of anything else.[8] Second, our sources are both scarce and extremely skewed; as with so many other issues, evidence for late Republican attitudes to learned activities comes nearly exclusively from the works of Cicero, a person who was anything but an uninvolved observer.

Despite these caveats, though, it is certainly true that we find in Roman sources a number of interrelated tropes and arguments that point to potentially negative attitudes to intellectual pursuits in general, or Roman intellectual activities in particular. These include (i) the expression of feelings of cultural inferiority vis-à-vis the Greeks; (ii) anti-intellectual and xenophobic sentiments; (iii) apologetic defenses of learned pursuits; and (iv) reflections on what types of activities are or are not appropriate for a Roman upperclass male. I will discuss these four sets of topoi and attitudes in turn.

First, what might be called the Roman inferiority complex vis-à-vis the Greeks is a motif widespread in Latin writing, and has no doubt partly inspired the modern prejudices mentioned above. To choose just two famous examples from Augustan poetry, Horace in his Letter to Augustus describes Rome's adoption of Greek culture as a form of reverse conquest: "captured Greece took captive its savage conqueror and brought the arts to boorish Latium."[9] Though victorious in battle, the Romans are rustic savages and are forced to submit to capture by their erstwhile captives. Despite this mental colonization, however, the suspicion remains that they will never reach the point where they will be able to meet the Greeks on their own ground. Thus, Anchises in his prophetic speech at the end of the sixth book of Vergil's *Aeneid* states in no uncertain terms that "others" (*alii*, 6.847)—clearly the Greeks—will remain superior to the Romans in such diverse fields as sculpture, oratory, and astronomy (847–50).

Such acknowledgments of Greek achievement, however, not infrequently go hand in hand with the assertion that the Romans are by no means out of the running. These competitive challenges typically take one of two forms. In one scenario, the Romans are said to surpass the Greeks in turn in some other skill that is more congenial to their national character and/or more valuable

---

8. This point is banal in the extreme but seems necessary to make in the face of the proliferation of blanket statements found even in serious scholarship about supposed Roman attitudes and values.

9. Hor. *Epist.* 2.1.156–57: *Graecia capta ferum uictorem cepit et artis / intulit agresti Latio.*

or important. Thus the rousing conclusion of Anchises's speech: the Romans are called upon to "rule peoples by their command" (*regere imperio populos*, 851) and to excel in empire building and lawgiving. Alternatively, the Romans turn out to beat the Greeks at their cultural game after all: as, for example, Quintilian aims to demonstrate in his surveys of Greek and Latin literature in book 10 of his *Institutio oratoria*, the Romans in time mastered all literary genres, with the result that they eventually challenged and even surpassed their Greek models.[10] This competitive urge is a fundamental motif in much Roman writing, with authors more or less explicitly setting out to become the Roman Homer (Ennius, Vergil), Plato (Cicero), Demosthenes (Cicero), Hesiod (Vergil), Callimachus (Propertius), and so forth.

Avowals of cultural inferiority can thus not be taken as straightforward evidence for actual Roman beliefs but need to be read within their larger rhetorical contexts, where they not infrequently serve to set up subsequent claims of Roman equality or even superiority.[11] Of course, the very fact that many Roman writers apparently felt the need to prove their people's, and their own, worth in the face of the dazzling cultural achievements of the Greeks points to some kind of underlying anxiety. What it does not point to, on the whole, is a widespread Roman sense of resignation in the face of Greek superiority: the Greeks are good, but the Romans may yet turn out to be better. After all, even Anchises's steering his descendants away from the arts and sciences and toward a set of particularly Roman *artes* occurs in an ambitious piece of Latin literature specifically designed to vie with the most celebrated poet of the Greeks.[12]

10. A combination of the two lines of attack is found in Cicero's preface to *Tusculans* 1, which nicely exemplifies Roman hedging and ambivalence in light of Greek cultural achievements. After stating his proud belief that the Romans "either came up with everything on their own more wisely than the Greeks or improved what they had taken over from them" (*omnia nostros aut inuenisse per se sapientius quam Graecos aut accepta ab illis fecisse meliora, Tusc. 1.1*), Cicero first claims that the Romans clearly surpass the Greeks in terms of their social and political customs and institutions, as well as their military achievements (1.2), before admitting that the Greeks are superior in *doctrina* and *litterae* (1.3). This concession, however, is immediately tempered by the observation that Greek victory in these fields was easy because the Romans originally did not compete, given that their civilization arose at a later date (1.3). While it is still the case that the Greeks excel in some arts and sciences (1.4–5), Romans are increasingly and successfully challenging them in other fields, including oratory (1.5)—and now, with Cicero, philosophy as well (1.5–6).

11. The same is true of the related topos of the "poverty" of Latin language, according to which Latin is inferior to Greek, especially in terms of (often philosophical) vocabulary: this claim typically appears in contexts where Latin writers wish to draw attention to their own verbal skills and ingeniosity. On the motif, see Fögen 2000.

12. On the metapoetics of Anchises's injunction to the Romans, see Volk 2009a.

The second motif to be discussed is the open embrace of anti-intellectual attitudes or invective, often tinged with specifically anti-Greek bias. There are plenty of places in our sources where we find Romans disparaging intellectual activity and ridiculing its practitioners, especially Greeks. Philosophers in particular are the butt of numerous jokes: their endless discussions are removed from everyday concerns and contain the most absurd propositions; as Varro puts it in his *Menippean Satires*, "no sick man dreams up something so unspeakable that some philosopher wouldn't say it."[13] No wonder that a practical Roman could get fed up with such pointless theorizing. Thus the proconsul L. Gellius in 93 BCE summoned all Athenian philosophers and urged them "finally to put an end to their controversies. If they agreed that they didn't want to spend their lives in quarrels, some arrangement could be found, and he himself promised them his help to find an agreement among them."[14] Alternatively, a Roman could simply refuse to engage with such drivel and, like Trimalchio, decide to "never listen to a philosopher."[15]

Even such a highly educated man as Cicero on more than one occasion engages in this kind of discourse. Thus, for example, in the *Verrines*, he professes ignorance of Greek sculpture; in *Pro Murena*, he pokes fun at Cato's Stoic beliefs and practices; and in a letter to C. Memmius of 51 BCE, he speaks in the most condescending terms of the Athenian Epicureans, who are being a nuisance to his addressee on account of his building plans on the site of Epicurus's former house.[16] Connoisseurship is a waste of time, philosophy is for nerds, and those Greeks can be so annoying about their cultural heritage.

As these examples show, though, such anti-intellectual, anti-Greek utterances are little more than rhetorical ploys, means of playing on stereotypes to raise a laugh or win over an audience. Such strategies are by no means particularly Roman: the unworldly intellectual was a running joke throughout the ancient world,[17] and disdain for high culture continues to play well in populist speechifying the world over. In all the Ciceronian examples cited, it is quite

---

13. *Sat. Men.* fr. 122 Astbury: *nemo aegrotus quicquam somniat / tam infandum, quod non aliquis dicat philosophus*; cf. Cic. *Div.* 2.119.

14. Cic. *Leg.* 1.53: *eisque [sc. philosophis Atheniensibus] magnopere auctorem fuisse [sc. Gellium] ut aliquando controuersiarum aliquem facerent modum. quodsi essent eo animo ut nollent aetatem in litibus conterere, posse rem conuenire, et simul operam suam illis esse pollicitum, si posset inter eos aliquid conuenire.* On this episode, see Gotter 2003: 165–66.

15. Petron. *Sat.* 71.12: *nec umquam philosophum audiuit*.

16. Cic. 2 *Verr.* 4.4–5, 13; *Mur.* 3–6, 58–66, 74–77; *Fam.* 13.1.

17. Compare, e.g., Aristophanes's spoofing of Socrates in the *Clouds* or the preponderance of *scholastikos* ("egghead") jokes in the late antique joke book *Philogelos* (see Beard 2014, index s.v. "*scholastikos* jokes").

clear that the author is putting it on. Cicero's pretend ignorance of Praxiteles and Polyclitus may well be a joke;[18] his mockery of Cato is part of the rhetorical strategy of *Pro Murena*, which also involves making fun of the field of civil law as represented by Cato's fellow prosecutor, Cicero's friend Ser. Sulpicius Rufus;[19] and the letter to Memmius not only contains a discussion of Cicero's own philosophical allegiance but is addressed to a man who was the patron of Catullus and Lucretius, and presumably chose Athens as his place of exile (after being convicted of *ambitus*) exactly because of the city's cultural attractions.[20]

That an anti-intellectual attitude could be adopted for rhetorical purposes without any commitment on the part of the speaker or writer is demonstrated by a passage from the *Paradoxa Stoicorum*, where Cicero declares that, in the context of a discussion of Stoic philosophy among educated men, he does not need to pretend ignorance of such matters:[21]

> praeclare enim est hoc usurpatum a doctissimis—quorum ego auctoritate non uterer si mihi apud aliquos agrestes haec habenda esset oratio; cum uero apud prudentissimos loquar quibus haec inaudita non sunt, cur ego simulem me si quid in his studiis operae posuerim perdidisse?—dictum est igitur . . .

> For it has been very well said by most learned men—and I wouldn't refer to their authority if I had to give this speech to some rustics; but since I am speaking to very intelligent people to whom these matters are not unknown, why should I pretend that I have wasted the time that I have dedicated to such studies?—so, it has been said . . .

18. See Zetzel 2003: 123, who suggests that the modern equivalent would be, "What's the name of that Dutch painter? Rembrandt? Thank you very much; I never pay attention to that sort of thing."

19. On the rhetorical purpose of Cicero's ridicule of Cato in *Pro Murena*, see Craig 1986. Cicero himself acknowledges at *Fin.* 4.74 that he was joking on that occasion (*iocabar*) and playing to an uneducated audience (*apud imperitos tum illa dicta sunt, aliquid etiam coronae datum*). Cicero's attitude to Cato's Stoicizing will be discussed further in 3.1.

20. See Morgan and Taylor 2017 (whose further contentions—that Memmius was a committed Epicurean and in fact planned to erect a statue of Epicurus on the contested site—are sadly unsupported by any positive evidence), as well as Koch Piettre 2017.

21. *Parad. Stoic.* 33. Slyly, Cicero uses a version of the same argument to introduce his digs against Cato's Stoicism in *Pro Murena*: it is exactly because he is not speaking "in an uncivilized crowd or some gathering of peasants" (*aut in imperita multitudine aut in aliquo conuentu agrestium*, 61), the speaker claims, that he feels emboldened to talk "about intellectual matters" (*de studiis humanitatis*, 61). Cicero manages simultaneously to flatter his audience for their high culture and to denigrate Cato for his.

Cicero can play the anti-intellectual card at will, and he and his contemporaries can laugh at eggheaded Greeks and their silly Roman followers—or, alternatively, at stolid Romans who are too dumb to get what, say, philosophy is all about (thus, the Cicero character in *De legibus* declares the story about L. Gellius's attempt at ending philosophical controversy simply "hilarious," *ioculare*, 1.53[22]). None of this proves that the Romans of the late Republic were less inclined or more hostile to intellectual activity than any other group of people in human history.

Still, it is often maintained that men who seriously engaged in learned pursuits had to contend with criticism. We have thus come to the third trope on our list, the apology for intellectual activity, and are now in exclusively Ciceronian territory. In the prefaces to his rhetorical and philosophical works, Cicero reflects at length on his studies; his motivations and goals in writing his works; and the place of philosophy and other forms of theorizing in his own life and in Roman society in general. These rich texts provide important insights into Cicero's cultural context, his intellectual attitudes and development, and his literary ambitions and techniques, and have accordingly been much studied.[23] On a number of occasions, Cicero mentions and responds to criticism of his intellectual pursuits, and it is these passages that have been taken as evidence for the existence of a strongly negative view of such activities in Roman culture, a view against which Cicero felt he had to push back.

The prime exhibit in this context is the preface to the first book of *De finibus*, a work that is part of Cicero's great philosophical corpus of the mid-40s. In it, the author anticipates that his project of presenting Greek philosophy in Latin will raise a number of objections (1.1), to which he undertakes to respond in turn. Some people, even educated ones, do not like philosophy altogether; others consider it a leisure-time activity to which not too much effort should be dedicated; still others believe it is fine but only in Greek; and a fourth group (Cicero suspects) will think that this field is inappropriate specifically for Cicero's *persona* and *dignitas*. Cicero accordingly launches into an extended defense of philosophy in general; the dedicated and detailed study of philosophy; the writing of philosophy in Latin; and the appropriateness of his own undertaking this task.

---

22. Or was Gellius already being playful, offering his arbitration to the philosophers bogged in controversy as a joke (thus, Görler 1974: 202, Rawson 1985: 7 n. 17, and Griffin 1989: 14–15)? If so, who is laughing at whom?

23. See Schmidt 1978–79, Habinek 1994, Kurczyk 2006: 335–46, Gildenhard 2007, and Baraz 2012, as well the discussion in 4.3 below.

In light of this and similar Ciceronian passages,[24] scholars have concluded that "literary pursuits by a Roman senator were thought to be in need of justification" and that there were "real social and cultural pressures" on a man who chose, for example, to write philosophy: in the eyes of the Romans, "philosophy is ultimately incompatible with public life and, if practiced too seriously, will cause the practitioner to abandon his duties as an (elite) Roman."[25] Now it is possible that such an attitude existed and was widespread, but can the preface to *De finibus* in fact count as evidence? We have only Cicero's word for the criticism of his philosophical writing—and even this criticism is anticipated only for the future. Within the preface, the four supposed objections to Cicero's project provide the framework for the development of the author's own program, ultimately serving to elevate his work and abilities: the message is that philosophy should indeed be practiced by Romans and written in Latin, and that Cicero is the man to do it. Response to purported criticism is a time-honored rhetorical strategy in contexts of self-legitimation and -glorification: in Callimachus's famous *Aetia* prologue, for example, the poet cites and refutes objections to his poetry by the mysterious Telchines, and in the prologues to his comedies, Terence vehemently combats criticism of his plays that he claims has been voiced before even they reached the stage.[26] In these and similar cases, one suspects that the criticism has been invented or at least greatly exaggerated. The same may very well be true for Cicero, too.

The fact of the matter is that we simply do not know. Perhaps Cicero, and his intellectually inclined friends, did indeed get a lot of flak for dedicating themselves to scholarship and philosophy, but the only evidence is that of Cicero's own highly rhetorical and self-serving prefaces.[27] Other authors apparently did not see the need to justify their learned endeavors,[28] and from

---

24. Compare esp. the prefaces to *De or.* 2; *Tusc.* 1, 2, 3; *Nat. D.* 1; *Off.* 2.

25. The quotations are from Gildenhard 2007: 45 and Baraz 2012: 14, 15–16. See also Christes 1996: 115–16 and Bishop 2019: 16–26.

26. Callim. *Aet.* frr. 1–1e Harder; Ter. *An.* 1–27; *Haut.* 1–52; *Eun.* 1–45; *Phorm.* 1–34; *Ad.* 1–25.

27. Ironically, there is much better evidence for pressure on Cicero to devote himself *more* to his studies and to abandon public life; see, e.g., *De or.* 3.13 for Quintus's attempts to discourage Cicero from political strife in the 50s, and *Att.* 14.20.5 for Atticus's Epicurean advice to stay out of politics after the death of Caesar.

28. Baraz 2012: 22–43 adduces as parallels the prefaces to Sallust's *Catiline* and *Jugurtha* as well as that to the *Rhetorica ad Herennium*. However, unlike Cicero, these authors do not refer to any societal pressure or criticism. Sallust reflects on the relationship between doing and writing history (*Cat.* 3) and the *Auctor ad Herennium* on that between *otium* and *negotium* (1.1); neither expresses anxiety that his literary activities might be considered inappropriate or problematic.

Cicero's letters as well as from historiographic sources we get the impression that learned men of the upper classes engaged in intellectual activity without incurring criticism or experiencing anxiety. Admittedly, our sources are both scarce and skewed: unfortunately, we have little prefatory material from any of the non-Ciceronian scholarly works written at the time, and, as ever, the Ciceronian corpus provides a large portion of our evidence for the intellectual life of the period. Still, while absence of evidence is not evidence of absence, it is certainly not evidence of presence, and I conclude that we have no positive reason to believe that elite intellectual activity in the late Republic was subject to widespread censure and criticism—or even much hand-wringing or anxiety.

But is—and this finally brings me to my fourth point—the very fact that Cicero reflects so extensively on, and often positively agonizes over, the appropriateness of scholarly pursuits for a Roman statesman like himself not a sign that such activities were viewed with ambivalence? Yes: by Cicero himself. Throughout his oeuvre—not just the theoretical works, but also the speeches, poetry, and letters—Cicero shows an abiding concern with the status of intellectual activity in Roman culture. To what extent and under what circumstances should a member of the Roman elite dedicate himself to learned pursuits? How do Roman cultural achievements relate to Greek ones? Is there, or should there be, a specifically Roman way of doing, say, philosophy? What is the significance of the Latin language? And finally, and perhaps most importantly, what role does Cicero himself have to play, given his political career, cultural interests, and verbal mastery?

These questions are central to the intellectual landscape of Cicero, a man who—as his works, especially his letters, show—was unusually given to probing reflection, if not tortured agonizing, over what ways of behavior and courses of action might be appropriate for him. While his contemporaries obviously shared the same cultural background, and may have had some of the same concerns, we cannot simply extrapolate from Cicero's sophisticated cultural criticism to general attitudes that "the Romans" might have held at the time.[29] In the course of this book, I will return on occasion to Cicero's project of intellectual self-positioning;[30] however, my focus is not on the expressed thoughts of one extraordinary individual, but on the practices of an entire social group.

29. Compare Romano 2006: 16, who warns (in the context of a discussion of the preface of *Tusc.* 1) of interpreting "una rappresentazione ideologicamente orientata . . . come se fosse una ricostruzione storiografica attendibile, una testimonianza anziché un'interpretazione"—a frequent mistake in modern scholarship, in Romano's opinion.

30. See esp. 3.2, 4.3, and 6.4.

As this survey of four sets of supposed evidence has demonstrated, there is indeed some support for occasional ambivalent, hostile, or anxious attitudes to intellectual activity on the part of some Romans. What the sources do not support is the belief there was a prevalent anti-intellectual bias in Roman society, one that rendered learned activities on the part of senators automatically suspect and in need of justification. I am thus in this book working with a base assumption of a "normal," that is, societally largely unquestioned, state in which upperclass Roman males as a matter of course were well educated and engaged in study and occasional writing: those are the "most learned times" of my heading. The rest of this chapter lays out the parameters of this normality, and while the following chapters will certainly touch on unusual activities in unusual circumstances, these too need to be interpreted before the background of established and customary practices.

Before moving on to an exploration of these practices, one main clarification is in order. In the context of positing a hostile environment for elite intellectual activity in the late Republic, scholars often state that it would have been impossible for a member of the senatorial class to dedicate himself to full-time scholarship.[31] While this is perhaps not entirely true—some men who could have entered a political career decided instead to dedicate themselves to their studies and/or other pursuits (e.g., Cicero's father and Atticus, though this course would have been more difficult for men born into senatorial families); others retired from politics for age, health, or other reasons[32]—the basic point is valid and highly significant. The men who are the subject of my study engaged in serious intellectual activity, but did so as part of an accepted way of senatorial life, not as a separate career. Cicero, Caesar, Varro, Nigidius, Brutus, and Cato were not scholars or intellectuals in the modern sense, and it would not have crossed their minds to define themselves as such. Their intellectual pursuits were part and parcel of their elite Roman way of life, not a profession.

This "amateur" status of my protagonists is intimately linked to an issue raised above, that of the relationship of Roman intellectual acitivity to Greek.[33] Most of the fields in which these men were active—philosophy, grammar, rhetoric, science, and various literary genres—were ones that had been pioneered by Greeks and were represented in Rome and in the eastern Mediterranean

31. E.g., Fantham 2009: 141: "For the Roman elite, being an intellectual was not a career option."

32. Cicero's father: Cic. *Leg.* 2.3; Atticus: Cic. *Att.* 1.17.5; Nep. *Att.* 6 (on Atticus's choice, see further 3.3 below). One gets the impression that after the Civil War, Varro (in his late sixties at this point) simply retired to his studies, while Sallust turned to writing history after his political disgrace. Compare Griffin 1994: 725 with n. 189.

33. For the following, compare and contrast the discussion in Christes 1975: 211–17.

by Greek professionals. What I mean by "professionals" is men who dedicated their lives to whatever fields they practiced and were either attached to institutions of learning (such as philosophical or rhetorical schools) or employed by private individuals.[34] While they may not all have been "paid" for their services (in the sense of cash transactions), they were often dependent on patronage and the "gifts" or other benefits they received from their students or other "employers."

Members of the Roman elite who dedicated their own studies, or even writing, to such fields thus found themselves confronted with a group of traditional practitioners who were ethnically different, potentially culturally superior but socially inferior, and accustomed to doing, say, philosophy in ways and social settings significantly different from those of the Roman dilettantes. Being intellectuals in the modern sense, the Greek professionals operated in contexts that we might term (again, in the modern sense) academic, that is, both educational and scholarly. Roman men of letters, by contrast, were not out to make a living or establish themselves in a particular academic community, and often viewed Greek professional practices, including their formalism and high level of theorizing, as remote from their own interest and concerns. Cultural stereotypes about garrulous, quarrelsome, and impractical Greeks no doubt added to a sense that the intellectual activity of Roman elite men had to be different from that of their Greek teachers.

We thus find in Cicero's works not only the author but a number of his dialogues' interlocutors expressing ridicule for the Greek *schola*, meaning both "school" and the formal lecture that takes place in such an institution. *Scholae* are suspect for using a mind-numbing format of instruction that is inferior to the free and genial conversation among elite Romans, and for peddling the kind of arid knowledge that has no application in real life and can even be detrimental to proper Roman morale.[35] In his invective against L. Calpurnius Piso, Cicero presents his Epicurean fellow senator as *politus ex schola* ("polished right out of the lecture room," 59), which accounts for his suspicious disdain for glory, and satirically imagines Piso as delivering a *schola* himself (60), lecturing his son-in-law Caesar on why triumphs are no good.[36]

As Ingo Gildenhard has observed, the *schola* "functions as the 'Greek other'" (2007: 14), an intellectual institution and/or practice that is typically

---

34. Compare my discussion in 1.2 above.

35. Gildenhard 2007: 12–14 surveys Cicero's use of *schola*, in the context of attempting to explain the fact that in the *Tusculans*, Cicero unusually terms his own teachings *scholae* (*Tusc.* 1.7–8). Generally on the meanings of Greek/Latin *schola* and *scholastikos* and their shift over time, see Manuwald 1923.

36. See further 3.3 below.

mentioned only to be rejected. In Varro's *De re rustica*, the interlocutor Stolo thus disparages Theophrastus's botanical works as "books of use not so much to those who want to cultivate the soil as to those who [want to frequent] the schools of philosophers,"[37] and the character Cicero at the beginning of the second book of *De finibus* introduces his own speech as follows (2.1):

> "primum," inquam, "deprecor, ne me tamquam philosophum putetis scholam uobis aliquam explicaturum, quod ne in ipsis quidem philosophis magnopere umquam probaui."

> "First," I said, "please don't think that like a philosopher, I will give you some lecture—a practice I have never much approved of even among philosophers themselves."

Scholae are for the professional practitioners of philosophy (though, in Cicero's opinion, not a great medium even for them). A member of the Roman elite goes about treating philosophy in a different way.

As this last example shows, Cicero, even in the process of writing a philosophical treatise, pointedly distances himself from *philosophi*. In his recent survey of Roman uses of the term *philosophus* (2016), Harry Hine shows that not only in the Republic but still in the early Empire, members of the Roman elite were happy to avow their dedication to *philosophia* and *philosophari*, but carefully avoided referring to themselves or their peers as *philosophi* (in the few cases where Cicero does use *philosophus* of himself or another member of the upper classes, he is typically making some kind of joke; see Hine 2016: 14–19). As Hine points out, the reason Romans do not call themselves *philosophi* "is because for them a *philosophus* is a professional, typically someone who offers teaching in philosophy to young men or offers public lectures on philosophy, and usually someone of lower social status, generally Greek."[38]

The complexity and occasional anxieties of intellectual life in the late Roman Republic are thus not so much a matter of Roman inferiority complexes, anti-intellectualism, or xenophobia as an expression of the period's sociology of knowledge, which involved individuals from different social strata with different levels of professionalism and different practices and purposes.[39] After a survey of "intellectuals in Rome" in chapters 5 and 6 of her magisterial work on the period, Elizabeth Rawson thus concludes that "there were various

---

37. Varro, *Rust.* 1.5.2: *libri non tam idonei iis qui agrum colere uolunt, quam qui scholas philosophorum.*

38. Hine 2016: 13; cf. also Gildenhard 2013: 260–63.

39. Compare Zetzel 2003, esp. 134–35 on the "sociology of culture" (134) that Cicero develops in holding Roman cultural activity against Greek.

classes, not one class, of intellectuals" (1985: 98). While certain disciplines were dominated by members of one group (e.g., doctors were Greek, lawyers Roman), others, such as philosophy, attracted both professionals and amateurs. The Roman elite men who engaged in *philosophia* interacted in numerous important ways with Greek *philosophi*—as students, patrons, readers, and correspondents. At the same time, they also, more or less self-consciously, developed their own intellectual practices. The rest of this chapter explores the ways in which they went about their learned activities.

2. *Studia*

While many ancient texts touch on the intellectual life of the social group that is my focus, there is one source that is especially rich and informative and that will therefore play a central role in the following discussion. We have over nine hundred letters written by, and occasionally to, Cicero, a corpus that abounds in references to the learned activities of a large number of correspondents and provides a more immediate access to elite intellectual practices than our other main contemporary sources, including Cicero's own, highly rhetorical speeches and treatises.[40] Although it would be naive to view the letters as unembellished reflections of "real" life—recent scholarship has demonstrated both the painstaking verbal craft of Ciceronian epistolography and the careful social strategies employed in the correspondence[41]—they nevertheless provide a wealth of information about upperclass activities. The fact that intellectual pursuits are often mentioned in passing and as matters of fact, rather than being made the center of an argument, renders the letters a less biased source than, for example, the Ciceronian prefaces discussed above, while the large number of correspondents and wide range of situations make the corpus more representative than any other contemporary set of texts. Of course, the agenda of the letter writer, whether Cicero or one of his friends, must always be taken into account. By definition, each letter is a speech act, designed to accomplish something, and as we will see, Cicero's correspondence does not just reflect upperclass intellectual practice but is itself an important part of it.

How, then, did members of the late Republican elite talk about their learned pursuits? Cicero's letters contain a wealth of different terms for intellectual activities.[42] Most of these expressions are generic, denoting dedication to study

40. In using the letters, I am generally following the dating of Shackleton Bailey 1965–70, 1977, 1980. For other Ciceronian dates, I rely mostly on Marinone and Malaspina 2004.

41. See especially Hutchinson 1998, J. Hall 2009a, P. White 2010, Wilcox 2012, Bernard 2013, De Giorgio 2015, and Bishop 2019: 219–57.

42. The following word studies are largely restricted to the letters, for the reasons just mentioned, with only occasional reference to other sources. However, the terms discussed are

and writing without specifying a subject matter: with the occasional exception of philosophy, the learned senator does not present himself as working in a particular field but as employed in scholarly pursuits in general. Thus, the two words most commonly used in this context are *studia* and *litterae*, which on account of their very vagueness are able to function as convenient umbrella terms for the nonspecific, nonprofessional activities in which members of the upper classes engaged.

Studia is an idiomatic expression for "intellectual activity" or "studies," a specialized use of the common noun *studium*, meaning "eagerness" or "pursuit."[43] The base meaning of the word makes it possible for *studia* in the specialized sense to appear as situated at one end of a spectrum of a number of activities and interests a person might pursue: a man like Cicero would give his *studium* to many matters, including, but not restricted to, his *studia*.

The second term, *litterae*, is likewise helpfully indeterminate. It is idiomatically used to denote "literary works, writings," "literary activities or pursuits," "what is learnt from books, scholarship," or "erudition or culture" and can be employed to encompass any activity that includes "letters," that is, both reading (whether for its own sake or as research for the reader's own works) and writing.[44] In fact, *legere* and *scribere* are two other words that in Cicero's letters appear in combination to refer to the activities a person would engage in as part of his studies.[45] Given this use, it is tempting to interpret the following well-known fragment from Varro's *Menippean Satires* as an exhortation to the kind of intellectual activity so often mentioned in his friend's correspondence: *legendo autem et scribendo uitam procudito.*[46]

---

employed widely in many additional texts, most notably Cicero's other works, and there would certainly be scope for a more wide-ranging study.

43. Cf. *OLD* s.v. *studium* 7a, though note that the dictionary fails to point out the idiomatic use of the plural; see also Gunderson 2016. *Studia* in Cicero's letters: *Att.* 1.20.7; 2.16.3; 4.18.2; 8.11.1; *Fam.* 1.9.23; 2.13.2; 3.10.7, 3.13.2; 4.4.4, 5, 4.13.4; 5.13.5, 5.15.2; 6.6.1, 6.9.1, 6.10.4; 7.23.2, 7.30.2, 7.33.2; 9.2.5, 9.6.5 (2x), 9.8.1, 2; 12.16.1, 2, 12.17.3, 12.24a; 13.12.2, 13.16.1, 4, 13.22.1, 13.28.2, 13.29.1 (2x), 5, 13.30.1; 15.4.13, 16; 16.4.3; *QFr.* 1.1.22, 28; 3.9.2.

44. Cf. *OLD* s.v. *littera* 8a, c, 9a, b. *Litterae* in Cicero's letters: *Att.* 4.10.1, 4.11.2, 4.18.2; 9.10.2; 12.13.1, 12.14.3, 12.15, 12.16, 12.20.1, 12.28.2, 12.38a.1, 12.46.1; 14.7.2, 14.13.3; *Fam.* 1.7.10, 1.8.3, 1.9.2; 5.15.3–4, 5.19.2, 5.21.3; 6.4.3, 6.6.12, 6.12.5, 6.18.5; 7.33.2 (2x); 9.2.5, 9.20.3, 9.26.1 (2x); 11.27.6; 13.16.4, 13.30.1; 16.4.3, 16.14.1, 2, 16.16.2; *QFr.* 3.5.4 (2x), 3.7.2. The diminutive *litterulae* occurs in *Att.* 7.2.8; *Fam.* 5.21.2; 16.10.2.

45. Cf. Cic. *Fam.* 9.20.3, 9.26.3; 16.22.1.

46. Fr. 551 Astbury: "fashion your life through reading and writing"; cf. Cèbe's commentary ad loc. (1972–99: 2052). Unfortunately, this quotation—chosen by the Italian postal service for a commemorative stamp at the bimillenary of Varro's death in 1974—has come down to us (transmitted, like most fragments of the *Menippeans*, by the late antique lexicographer Nonius) without any indication of context.

That a learned Roman's *studia* typically centered around written material is apparent also from the collocation *studia litterarum*,[47] as well as from the fact that Cicero can use *libri* or *libelli* "books" metonymically for intellectual activity in general.[48] The writer also on occasion employs *philologia*, being the first Roman to use this Greek loanword, which appears to refer indistinctly to "literary study, the pursuit of learning," without any reference to a particular variety of textual scholarship (by contrast to modern uses of "philology").[49] Cicero even once coins a mock-Homeric phrase, ἔργα λόγοιο "the works of the word," to refer to his intellectual activities. Pondering his political options in a letter to Atticus from 26 April 44 (14.13)—whether to join either Brutus or Sextus Pompeius and get ready for the bloodshed of civil war, or otherwise retreat into private life—Cicero quotes the words with which Zeus in *Iliad* 5.427–28 sends Aphrodite from the battlefield, replacing γάμοιο "of marriage" with λόγοιο (2):

τέκνον ἐμόν, οὔ τοι δέδοται πολεμήια ἔργα,
ἀλλὰ σύ δ' ἱμερόεντα μετέρχεο ἔργα λόγοιο.

My child, the works of war are not given to you; instead, concern yourself with the delightful works of the word.

Thanks to the intertext and the adjective ἱμερόεντα, Cicero's "philological" pursuits come across as highly eroticized and accordingly desirable.

Additional Ciceronian terms for intellectual activity, which do not highlight its logocentricity but share the indeterminacy of the expressions already discussed, include *artes* and *doctrina(e)*, as well as, more poetically, *Musae*.[50] As mentioned above, the one exception to the general looseness of Cicero's references to his and his peers' studies is those cases where the pursuit in question is explicitly labeled "philosophy."[51] As we will see in chapter 3, philosophy was an intellectual subject especially enthusiastically pursued by Roman upperclass men of the period, and it is likely that a fair percentage of the *studia* of Cicero and others were in fact philosophical in nature.

47. Cf. Cic. *Fam.* 1.8.3; 13.30.1.

48. Cf. Cic. *Att.* 2.6.1; 9.10.2; 10.14.2; 12.3.1; 13.40.2; *Fam.* 9.1.2, 9.2.5.

49. Cf. *OLD* s.v. and Cic. *Att.* 2.17.1; cf. *Att.* 13.52.2; 15.15.2. The only attested earlier borrowing into Latin of Greek φιλόλογ- is Ennius's use of a feminine *philologa* in an unclear context (fr. I 42 Vahlen = *Opera incerta* fr. 20 Goldberg and Manuwald = Festus 278.8–12 Lindsay).

50. *Artes*: *Fam.* 3.13.2; 4.3.3, 4.13.4; 7.3.4; 9.3.2; 13.29.1; 15.4.16; *QFr.* 1.1.28; *Ad Brut.* 1.17.5; *doctrina(e)*: *Att.* 9.10.2; 10.14.2; *Fam.* 3.10.7; 4.3.3, 4.4.4; 9.6.4; 13.1.5, 13.30.1; *Musae*: *Att.* 2.4.2, 2.5.2; *Fam.* 1.9.23; 16.10.2.

51. *Att.* 1.16.13; 2.5.2, 2.13.2; 15.13a.2; *Fam.* 4.3.4, 4.4.4; 7.30.2; 9.17.2; 15.4.16.

Typically, the "reading and writing" of a Roman senator takes place during his *otium*, the time when he is not engaged in political, legal, or other business, and often outside Rome, at one of his villas in the Italian countryside.[52] Exceptions are attested, but get typically mentioned for the very purpose of highlighting the unusualness of such behavior. Thus, the younger Cato reportedly read in the senate while his fellow senators were assembling, doing so "quietly" (ἡσυχῇ) and under the cover of his toga, which he had stretched in front of his book.[53] Caesar, we are told, composed his *De analogia* while crossing the Alps en route to Gaul or even while engaged in combat in his province.[54] The claim that he wrote about linguistics matters *inter tela uolantia* ("amid flying missiles") is clearly intended to stress Caesar's remarkable abilities, which transcend the traditional division of the spheres of *otium* and *negotium*.[55]

What were Cicero and his peers "reading and writing"? The content of their studies will be the subject of the remaining chapters of this book, while I will here dwell some more on the "how," the ways and circumstances in which they went about their "works of the word." From the evidence discussed so far, we might get the impression that the intellectual activities of the Roman elite were solitary pursuits, with men retiring to their villas to study on their own; even Cato, though in the middle of the senate, isolates himself while in the process of reading. However, in his letters Cicero again and again depicts *studia* as communal enterprises. Thus, to mention just a few examples, he describes Atticus as his "comrade in studies" and wishes that he and Varro might "live together in our studies."[56] Similarly, Cicero's son Marcus, writing to his father's freedman Tiro from Athens and describing his studies there, ends his letter with a wish for future *una* συμφιλολογεῖν ("joint studying together," *Fam.* 16.21.8).

---

52. On the Roman concept of *otium* and its association with intellectual activity, see André 1966 and Wiegandt 2016. On villa culture in the late Republic, see D'Arms 1970: 39–72 and (specifically on Cicero) O'Sullivan 2011: 77–96, Narducci 2003, and Hutchinson 2016. For both topics, compare Rawson 1985, ch. 2.

53. Plut. *Cat. Min.* 19.1; see also Cic. *Fin.* 3.7; Val. Max. 8.7.2. It is unclear whether Cato's "cover-up" is meant to increase privacy or to hide his unusual activity: as Cicero reports, Cato's reading attracted *reprensionem . . . uulgi inanem* ("the empty criticism of the crowd"), which the senator, however, paid no heed. On Cato as a reader, see further 3.1 below.

54. Suet. *Iul.* 56.5; Fronto, *Parth.* 9, 224.12–17 van den Hout = Caes. *De an.* T1, 2 Garcea. Citation from Suetonius here and throughout this book follows the numbering of the *OCT* (Kaster 2016).

55. Fronto, *Parth.* 9, 224.15 van den Hout. Dugan 2005: 188 attractively suggests that these accounts go back to Caesar's own presentation in *De analogia* of the work's genesis.

56. *Fam.* 7.30.2: *socium studiorum meorum*; *Fam.* 9.2.5: *una uiuere in studiis nostris*.

Such συμφιλολογεῖν could take many forms: preceding, following, accompanying, and supplementing a man's private study, numerous practices combined to make intellectual activity an often intensely social behavior. First, despite the stress on the written word in some of the above-mentioned terms for an elite man's *studia*, oral communication played an enormous role in the intellectual life of the period. Education proceeded largely orally, ranging from one-to-one instruction by private tutors to the attending of lectures by Greek philosophers and rhetors, especially during sojourns in Greek centers of learning.[57] In the first century BCE, study abroad became a common practice among the Roman upper classes:[58] just as Marcus Cicero junior went to Athens in 45 to study with the Peripatetic Cratippus and others, his father had engaged in philosophical and rhetorical training in Athens and Rhodes in 79–77. Many other Roman students—including Caesar, Brutus, and Cassius—put in the ancient equivalent of their junior year abroad, or otherwise embarked on a kind of grand tour, covering both historical and intellectual highlights. Such activities were not just for the young: educated Romans traveling in the eastern Mediterranean on political or military business frequently took the opportunity to stop off at, or prolong their sojourns in, certain Greek cities in order to meet intellectuals and hear their lectures.

However, by the first century, it was no longer necessary to travel abroad to find Greek teachers. While Greeks, including philosophers and other intellectuals, had been coming to Rome in various capacities for a long time, the Mithridatic Wars and especially Sulla's sack of Athens in 86 led to an increased influx of both prisoners of war and free Greek professionals who were fleeing the turmoil in the east and hoping to make a livelihood in the new cultural center that was Rome.[59] Romans were thus able to interact with Greek scholars on their own turf, and often developed close patronage relationships or friendships with particular individuals. Thus, to mention two prominent examples, the distinguished grammarian Tyrannio the Elder, first brought to Rome by Lucullus, was friendly with Caesar, Atticus, and Cicero; served as a tutor to Cicero's son and nephew; and generally appears to have been his intellectual go-to person in all kinds of situations.[60] Philodemus of Gadara,

57. On Roman encounters with Greek intellectuals both at Rome and throughout the Mediterranean, see Hutchinson 2013: 43–132.

58. On Roman study abroad, see Daly 1950, Rawson 1985: 9–13, Ferrary 2007: 38–41, and Howley 2014.

59. Rawson 1985, ch. 1 thus considers the Mithridatic Wars a watershed in Roman intellectual history. On Greek intellectuals in Rome, see further Ferrary 2007: 41–46 and Hutchinson 2013: 52–64; Balsdon 1979: 54–58 provides a handy list of Greek scholars attached to prominent Romans, from the late third century to Augustus.

60. On Tyrannio, see Rawson 1985, index s.v. and Johnson 2012.

Epicurean philosopher and epigrammatist, enjoyed the patronage of L. Piso, and it may be his library whose charred remnants have been found in the Villa dei Papiri (possibly Piso's villa) in Herculaneum.[61]

Relationships between Roman nobles and their Greek protégés could become quite close and even affect living arrangements. A number of Greeks stayed as guests in the houses of their Roman patrons or accompanied them on their journeys. Cicero, for example, for many years hosted the blind Stoic philosopher Diodotus, who died in his house in about 60. According to Plutarch, Cato on his ill-fated African campaign had among his entourage at least two philosophers, "Apollonides the Stoic" and "Demetrius the Peripatetic,"[62] with whom he discussed philosophical problems right before committing suicide.

Even in less dramatic circumstances, it is clear that well-to-do, educated Romans could draw on a wealth of scholarly expertise from within their own households. In addition to "live-in" philosophers, highly trained freedmen and slaves would be on hand to assist their masters' *studia*.[63] Cicero, for one, was very attached to (if occasionally enraged by) Atticus's freedman Dionysius, who tutored the young Marcus and Quintus and helped Cicero himself in a number of matters. His beloved secretary Tiro—first a slave, then manumitted—was clearly indispensable to Cicero's intellectual as well as private life.

In addition, informal conversations among friends must have played an important role in the development of Roman philosophy and scholarship. Such interactions are stylized in Cicero's rhetorical and philosophical dialogues, which present upperclass men talking among themselves in a variety of settings.[64] While a number of these works take place in the past, the majority feature contemporaries and not infrequently Cicero himself as a participant. It is obvious that these conversations are fictional and never took place as such,[65] but it is also clear that Cicero went to great lengths to achieve

---

61. The secondary literature on Philodemus is extensive and cannot be surveyed here. For a recent discussion of the library at the Villa dei Papiri, see Houston 2014: 87–129. See further 3.3 below, with n. 119.

62. Plut. *Cat. Min.* 65.5; see further 3.1 below, with n. 26. Citation from Plutarch here and throughout this book follows the numbering of the *Loeb* (Perrin 1914–26).

63. See Treggiari 1977, with special attention to Cicero.

64. See Linderski 1989, who surveys the participants of all Ciceronian dialogues (108–12), pointing out that they are mostly senators, often very high-ranking; as he shows (118), the same is true for Varro's *Logistorici* (on the assumption that these were dialogues), while the humbler topic of agriculture makes for a more socially varied cast of characters in *De re rustica* (116–18).

65. Cicero himself points this out, tongue in cheek, in the letter in which he dedicates the *Academica posteriora* to Varro: *puto fore ut, cum legeris, mirere nos id locutos esse inter nos quod*

verisimilitude in the set-up of his dialogues; we may thus read these texts as highly stylized versions of the kinds of exchanges among peers that an educated Roman man might engage in—or at least imagine or fantasize about.[66]

Cicero carefully outlines the settings of his dialogues, presenting his upperclass interlocutors in a variety of probable scenarios, which tell us much about the conduct of intellectual life in this social group. Most of the conversations take place in the villa of one of the interlocutors, that accepted locus of *otium* and learned pursuits.[67] In a variation on this theme, books 3 and 4 of *De finibus* are set specifically in the library of the Tusculan villa of the younger Lucullus: Cicero has gone there to consult this famous collection of books (on which see further below) and unexpectedly encounters Cato, who has come for the same purpose and is sitting surrounded by Stoic works—which naturally leads to a discussion of the Stoic view of the highest good. The conversation in book 5 of the same treatise takes place in Athens during Cicero's sojourn in 79. A group of Roman expatriates, including Cicero, his brother Quintus, his cousin Lucius, Atticus, and M. Pupius Piso, decide to take a walk to Plato's Academy and there, after a discussion of their fascination with Greek cultural sites, embark on a debate of the views of the Academic philosopher Antiochus.

When people were unable to communicate in person, they wrote to each other, and we are fortunate to possess the more than nine hundred letters of the Ciceronian corpus. The significant social functions served by these letters have been much studied: Roman men and women corresponded not only to exchange information, but to construct and maintain their manifold and ever-changing relationships and social networks, employing a vast variety of linguistic strategies while adhering to a basic code of politeness. As we have already observed, and will see again and again, much of the evidence for the sociology of knowledge of late Republican Rome comes from this source; however, the letters do not simply reflect intellectual practice, but in creating communities of like-minded individuals, they are themselves an important part of such practice.

Turning now to the specifics of *studia*, we may observe that even a man's actual reading and writing were always bound up in a variety of interactions

---

numquam locuti sumus; sed nosti morem dialogorum ("I bet that when you read you will be surprised that we talked with each other about things that we never talked about—but you know the convention of dialogues," *Fam.* 9.8.1).

66. See Steel 2013: 230 on this aspirational aspect of the dialogues.

67. Compare the synopsis of *dialogorum loca* in Linderski 1989: 107–8.

with other people. First, the act of private reading itself frequently involved listening to a *lector*, just as much writing consisted in dictation.[68] The recitation of literary works could also take the form of a more social occasion, as hosts had trained readers entertain their guests at dinner parties.[69]

A major concern for late Republican Romans engaged in intellectual pursuits was the availability of books. In the absence of public libraries,[70] readers had to rely on their own book collections or those of their friends, and there is evidence that owners of significant private libraries made their holdings available to those with a legitimate interest.[71] The library of Lucullus that provides the setting for Cicero's conversation with Cato in *De finibus* 3 and 4 is a prime example:[72] L. Licinius Lucullus apparently amassed his book collection in the Mithridatic Wars, housed it in his villa in Tusculum, and opened it up for the use especially of Greek intellectuals. In 52 BCE, the dramatic date of Cicero's dialogue, Lucullus was dead and the library had passed to his son, but men like Cicero and Cato were still able to use it, both to read books there (as Cato does) and to borrow (as is Cicero's declared intention).[73] Of course, book borrowing could take place without an actual visit to someone's library: in the letters to Atticus, we find Cicero again and again asking his friend to bring or send him a particular book.[74]

68. The evidence for *lectores* is assembled in Starr 1990–91. The question of whether the Greeks and Romans read silently or aloud, or were mostly read to, is a long-standing controversy; see Johnson 2010: 4–9 for a *historia quaestionis*. H. N. Parker 2009 makes a forceful case that Roman literary reading was predominantly silent and private.

69. See Rawson 1985: 51–52. Atticus's entertainment of his dinner guests through trained *lectores* is especially well attested; see Nep. *Att.* 13.3, 14.1; Cic. *Att.* 16.2.6.

70. In the 40s, Caesar was planning the first public library in Rome, putting Varro in charge of organizing it (Suet. *Iul.* 44.2). The Ides of March put an end to this project, and the first public library was established only in the late 30s/early 20s by Asinius Pollio (Plin. *HN* 7.115; 35.10).

71. On book collections and use in the late Republic, see Rawson 1985, chs. 3 and 4; Dix 2000, 2013; Tutrone 2013; Houston 2014; and Frampton 2016.

72. On this collection, see Dix 2000, with a survey of the evidence, and Tutrone 2013: 157–60. On the scene at the beginning of *Fin.* 3, see Frampton 2016. Another library scene is invoked at the beginning of Cicero's *Topica*, where Trebatius's discovery of Aristotle's *Topics* in Cicero's library sparks his interest in the subject matter (*Top.* 1–2).

73. *Nam in Tusculano cum essem uellemque e bibliotheca pueri Luculli quibusdam libris uti, ueni in eius uillam ut eos ipse, ut solebam, depromerem* ("for when I stayed on my Tusculan estate and wished to use some books from the library of the young Lucullus, I went to his villa to take them, as was my custom," *Fin.* 3.7). Dix 2000: 457 wonders "whether Cicero would have taken books from the library so nonchalantly while Lucullus was alive as he seems to have done when the library came into the possession of Lucullus' son."

74. Cic. *Att.* 2.3.4, 2.4.1, 2.20.6; 8.11.7, 8.12.6; 13.8, 13.31.2, 13.32.2, 13.33.2, 13.39.2, 13.44.3, 13.48.2.

In *De finibus*, Cato is made to wonder aloud why Cicero is consulting Lucullus's library, given that he owns so many books himself (3.10). Indeed, as we can see over the course of his lifelong correspondence, Cicero was an avid book collector and enlisted the help of numerous individuals both to acquire books and to arrange them in actual library spaces.[75] Most significant are two sequences of letters to Atticus. First, in 67–66 we find Cicero corresponding with his friend, then resident in Greece, about a collection of Greek books that Atticus apparently has got his hands on and that Cicero is eager to purchase (and, we assume, ultimately did).[76] Ten years later, three letters reveal a project to rearrange (parts of) Cicero's library at his villa in Antium, an effort apparently made necessary by partial loss and destruction during the owner's exile in 58–57.[77] For this, Cicero drew on the services not only of the learned Tyrannio, who took care of arranging the books, but also of skilled slaves provided by Atticus, who glued on labels and constructed and painted the shelves.

Moving on from reading to writing, we find that intellectual production, too, involved not only the writer, but other people consulted for information or asked for feedback. Cicero's correspondence provides fascinating insight into the genesis of his rhetorical, philosophical, and other works and reveals the extent to which the author drew on the input of others.[78] Thus, we find Cicero not only querying Atticus on points of historical fact,[79] but also discussing with his friend the suggestions he has received from others[80] and his own thinking about the structuring and restructuring of his dialogues. Unfortunately, of course, the Atticus side of the correspondence is lost, but it is clear that the two men habitually bandied about ideas about content, setting, and interlocutors.[81] Cicero appears to have been quite receptive to criticism and

75. On Cicero's library, see Dix 2013 and Houston 2014: 18–19, 217–20.

76. The letters are (in chronological order) *Att.* 1.7, 1.10.4, 1.11.3, 1.4.3.

77. Cicero refers to the "remains" (*reliquiae, Att.* 4.4a.1) of his books; Dix 2013: 222–24 suggests that after the destruction of various Ciceronian properties by Clodius's gangs, the surviving parts of his book collection were brought together in the library at Antium. The letters in question are (in chronological order) *Att.* 4.4a.1, 4.8.2, 4.5.3.

78. On the practice of literary revision in ancient Rome, see Gurd 2012, whose third chapter discusses Ciceronian practice.

79. Cic. *Att.* 6.1.8, 18, 6.2.3; 12.5b, 12.20.2, 12.22.2, 12.23.2, 12.24.2; 13.4.1, 13.5.1, 13.6.4, 13.30.2, 13.32.3, 13.33.3; 16.13a(b).2.

80. See esp. Cic. *Att.* 12.40.1, 12.51.2, 12.52.2; 13.1.3, 13.26.2, 13.27.1, 13.28.2–3, 13.31.3, 13.44.1 on Cicero's advisory letter to Caesar, a project shelved after criticism from Oppius and Balbus; on this work, see McConnell 2014: 195–219 and 4.2 below.

81. Especially well known is the revision history of the *Academica*, where Cicero, in consultation with Atticus, changed the entire set-up of the dialogue from a conversation of Lucullus,

ready to revise his works in reaction to the input of others; Sean Gurd, in his recent study of the sociability of literary revision in Rome, ascribes to him a "committed vision of literature as a form of sociality cemented through the exchange of corrections."[82]

One of the recurring topics Cicero discusses with Atticus is the important question of whom to dedicate a work to. Book dedications among the educated Roman elite were a means to honor individuals and to recognize and cement relationships.[83] Since writers frequently engaged in mutual dedications, we may view the granting and receiving of such honors as a specialized part of the general exchange of *beneficia* that formed the basis of Roman *amicitia*; participating in this process meant being a member of a community that was both socially and intellectually elevated.

I cannot here provide a survey of all late Republican dedications,[84] but wish to draw attention to the close-knit nature of the network of writers who dedicated books to one another. Thus Cicero received the dedication of Brutus's *De uirtute* and dedicated to its author the *Brutus, Paradoxa Stoicorum, Orator, De finibus, Tusculans,* and *De natura deorum. De senectute* and *De amicitia* were inscribed to Atticus, who had dedicated his *Liber annalis* to his friend. In exchange for the dedication of the *Academica,* Varro dedicated to Cicero his *De lingua Latina;* his *De uita populi Romani* and *Atticus de numeris* went to Atticus, and his *Antiquitates rerum diuinarum* to Caesar. Caesar himself dedicated his *De analogia* to Cicero.

The practice of dedication raises the larger issue of the publication and circulation of books. Most scholars agree that in the Ciceronian period, there was not much of a professional book trade and that "publication" consisted in the presentation of copies to individuals of one's acquaintance.[85] These copies

---

Hortensius, and Catulus to one of Varro, Atticus, and himself. See Griffin 1997b, Gurd 2012: 71–74, and Cappello 2019: 11–81.

82. Gurd 2012: 74. Gurd finds a political meaning in the giving and receiving of feedback concerning Cicero's works, especially of the 40s: the author's openness to revision and the collective nature of the process exhibit a commitment to Republicanism in opposition to Caesar's autocratic rule; "revision, in Cicero's view, *was* politics" (51; emphasis his). Compare also Cappello 2019: 11–81.

83. On the practice of book dedication in the late Republic, see Ambaglio 1983: 22–28, Stroup 2010, and (specifically on Cicero) Baraz 2012: 111–12, 150–86, 204–12.

84. Ambaglio 1983 surveys the dedication of Greek and Latin works up to the Flavian period and provides indices of dedicators and dedicatees on pp. 49–52.

85. Compare the appropriately minimalist definition in Dortmund 2001: 113 of ancient "publication" (Lat. *edere*) as "heraus-geben," that is, the author's simple "giving" his work to any "outside" or public, without any of the associations of modern publishing (cf. van Groningen

might be further circulated or copied at the recipients' wish or the request of other interested parties. Through this process of private copying and recopying, as well as lending and borrowing, works were able to reach a small readership of individuals who were most likely known to each other and for whom the writing and reading of their friends' books were just one element of their manifold social interactions.

Publication, then, was an intensely social matter, with individuals furnishing copies not necessarily only of their own books, but also of those of others. Atticus apparently took some role in disseminating Cicero's works by having copies made—no doubt by trained slaves—and distributing them according to the author's wish.[86] The old belief that the wealthy *eques* ran a kind of professional publishing business has long been discredited as anachronistic: Atticus simply took an especially active part in the exchange of written works customary among members of the Roman elite.

To conclude this survey, we have found Roman senators habitually engaged in intellectual activity vaguely referred to as *studia*, which were conceptualized as consisting in reading and (though clearly not in all cases) writing. Such studies involved the man in question in a variety of social interactions, with Greek intellectuals, skilled slaves and freedmen, and—crucially, from the perspective of this book—other members of his own class. Learned conversation, research and library assistance, the circulation of texts pre- and postpublication, and the practices of revision and dedication were part and parcel of the social life of the educated Roman elite and took place among men who— rather than being brought together as a group of "intellectuals" specifically by these activities—were interacting with each other on many levels by virtue of many shared concerns, including first and foremost their political activity and membership in the senate. While the described intellectual sociability was obviously not restricted to senators (we have already seen the important role of the equestrian Atticus), there is clearly a significant overlap between, say, the network of men with whom Cicero interacted in the political arena and that of those with whom he shared literary and philosophical interests. In fact, trying to distinguish between these two groups may be impossible and ultimately pointless: for a Cicero, political and intellectual activity were certainly two different things, but they were engaged in by the same man, often at the same time, and in close interaction with some of the same groups of people.

1963). On the circulation of books in late Republican Rome, see further Starr 1987, Murphy 1998, and McCutcheon 2016: 25–27.

86. See first and foremost Sommer 1926, as well as J. J. Phillips 1986, Dortmund 2001, and Iddeng 2006: 64–68.

3. Societas studiorum

As we have seen, *studia* were one set of practices among the wide range of activities in which elite men of the late Republic engaged. At the same time, owing to the social nature of many learned pursuits, *studia* were also one significant subsection of the manifold interactions among such men, interactions that constituted the vast informal social network that held together the elite and enabled the functioning of the Republican political system. The Latin term for such affiliative relationships among presumed equals is *amicitia* "friendship," and joined *studia* were—and were perceived to be—an important manifestation of the friendships of Roman upperclass men.

The meaning of Roman *amicitia* has been hotly debated in scholarship (Does the term refer narrowly to quid-pro-quo political alliances? What is its relationship to ancient philosophical or modern popular views of friendship?). I am here adopting Craig Williams's inclusive approach, which follows Latin linguistic usage and regards as *amicitia* any relationship the Romans termed thus.[87] In particular (owing to the focus of this book) I consider *amicitia* all minimally positive and cooperative connections among Roman senators and/ or equestrians—which under most circumstances would have encompassed the vast majority of relationships in this group.[88] This does not mean, of course, that *amicitia* was never contested in Roman society and that people never asked themselves, "What is a (or: who is my) true *amicus*?" My point is simply that my protagonists would have considered most positively valenced interactions with their peers as aspects of *amicitia*, and I will thus be using the same Latin terms, as well as English "friend(ship)," without wishing to commit to any more specific definition.

To return to *studia*, it is apparent from Cicero's letters that common interest in intellectual pursuits could be viewed as a strong bond between individuals and invoked in a variety of contexts.[89] We have already seen examples of expressed wishes to "study together" (see 2.2), a scenario that is presented as mutually enjoyable and beneficial. Depending on the circumstances, such an invitation to joint intellectual pursuits can take on a heightened significance.

---

87. Williams 2012: 54 states his approach as follows: "If writers of Latin texts refer to a relationship as *amicitia* or describe a person as someone's *amicus*, then, in the absence of any explicit indication that the words are being used in a transferred, metaphorical, or nonliteral sense, it is *amicitia* and they are *amici*, regardless of what else they might be." See also already Brunt 1965, a classic article that goes a long way toward discrediting narrowly political interpretations of *amicitia*.

88. Compare Brunt 1965: 11–13 on the rarity of declared *inimicitiae*.

89. Compare Damon 2008.

Thus when Cicero enjoins Varro to *una uiuere in studiis nostris* ("live together in our studies," *Fam.* 9.2.5), this exhortation is part of an effort to rekindle the two men's *amicitia* in the traumatic situation post-Pharsalus and to cast their envisaged joint intellectual pursuits not only as a consolation for the loss of, but also as a substitute for, political activity (ibid.):

> si nemo utetur opera, tamen [sc. nobis stet illud] et scribere et legere πολιτείας et, si minus in curia atque in foro, at in litteris et libris, ut doctissimi ueteres fecerunt, gnauare rem publicam et de moribus ac legibus quaerere.

> If no one calls on our help, let us nevertheless both read and write "Republics" and—if not in the senate house and the forum, then in writing and books—serve the Republic as did the learned men of old, and inquire about customs and laws.

For Cicero and Varro, then, communal *studia* are one category of appropriate social activity on a spectrum that crucially also includes politics. The wish for joint intellectual pursuits remains a leitmotif throughout Cicero's letters to his friend, with whom the author feels connected through their *coniunctio studiorum amorisque nostri*.[90]

As Cicero's correpondence shows, a shared interest in intellectual matters was perceived as creating a connection between individuals and could be invoked as a token of *amicitia* in a variety of contexts. Thus in a letter of April 50 to Appius Claudius Pulcher, the author mentions "similarity of *studia*" as one of the many bonds that bind him to Appius: "the similarity of our pursuits, the delight of our interactions, the enjoyment of our lifestyle, the exchange of our conversation, and our more recondite studies."[91] More blatantly, if also somewhat playfully, Cicero in a famous letter to Cato attempts to capitalize on the *societas studiorum atque artium* that he has going with his forbidding fellow senator (*Fam.* 15.4.16), even enlisting their common friend Philosophy to plead with his correspondent to support in the senate Cicero's bid for a *supplicatio*.

The repeated references in Cicero's letters to a communality of *studia* confirms both the social character of elite intellectual pursuits and the significance

---

90. *Fam.* 9.8.1: "bond of our studies and our affection." On the—not always easy—friendship of Cicero and Varro, see Kumaniecki 1962, Rösch-Binde 1998, and Cappello 2019: 45–60. On their correspondence, see further 4.1.

91. *Fam.* 3.10.9: *studiorum similitudo, suauitas consuetudinis, delectatio uitae atque uictus, sermonis societas, litterae interiores*; cf. also *Fam.* 3.13.2.

of such joint activities within the larger practice of *amicitia*.[92] While the letter writer may remind a *socius studiorum* directly of the bond that links them (either to create fellow feeling through fond reminiscences or, more pointedly, to persuade the correspondent to a certain course of action), the avowed sharing of *studia* can also serve to recommend a third party. Thus, in a set of letters from late 46/early 45, Cicero first invokes the *studiorum parium coniunctio* that connects him to Aulus Caecina when writing to his friend himself, but subsequently refers to these *studia communia* when commending Caecina (a *homo omnibus mecum studiis officiisque coniunctissimus*) to Furfanus Postumus and P. Servilius Isauricus, respectively.[93] Similarly, Cicero's assurance that he is very close (*amicissimus*) to T. Pinarius "not only because of all his virtues but because of our shared *studia*"[94] is meant as a point in favor of Pinarius, whom Cicero in this particular letter is recommending to Cornificius.

Shared intellectual interests might even create a bond between men who were as yet unaware of any *studiorum similitudo*. When asking Ser. Sulpicius Rufus in 46 to further the business interests of L. Mescinius Rufus, Cicero predicts that Sulpicius will enjoy dealing with his recommendee. The reason is that Mescinius commands not only *uirtus, probitas, officium*, and *obseruantia*, but also "those studies of ours, which were previously our enjoyment and are now our life."[95] Whose *studia* are these? Clearly Cicero's (the reference to the vital, all-encompassing importance of intellectual pursuits is a leitmotif of his writings under Caesar's rule), but the use of the first-person plural draws Sulpicius into the nexus of lovers of *studia* that are truly "ours" (*nostra*). In these difficult times, Cicero and Sulpicius find emotional support in their intellectual pursuits, a fact that does (or, in the case of Sulpicius, should) make them especially well disposed toward Mescinius, who shares their interests.[96]

If Cicero's letters demonstrate the interpersonal importance that at least some members of the late Republican elite ascribed to the sharing of intellectual interests, it is in his dialogues that we find idealized depictions of how a *societas studiorum* could play out in practice. I will focus here on the *Brutus*, a work whose set-up is not only fairly elaborate but also appears to aim at particular realism and immediacy: the dialogue is presented as having taken place

92. For the use of a similar argument in a speech, see *Lig.* 21, where Cicero appeals to his opponent L. Aelius Tubero by invoking their "great bond on account of always having engaged in the same studies" (*magnum . . . uinculum quod isdem studiis semper usi sumus*).

93. See *Fam.* 6.6.1, 6.9.1; 13.66.1.

94. *Fam.* 12.24a: *cum propter omnis uirtutes tum etiam propter communia studia.*

95. *Fam.* 13.28.2: *studia illa nostra quibus antea delectabamur, nunc etiam uiuimus.*

96. For further discussion of Cicero's correspondence with Sulpicius during this period, see 4.1 below.

not in the past but immediately before its composition (early 46 BCE), and the interlocutors are Cicero himself as well as Atticus and Brutus, the first one of his oldest friends, the second an increasingly important connection. While the narrated conversation obviously never took place as such, the interactions described can be taken as a stylized version of what joint *studia* among the Roman elite may have looked like.

Cicero begins with a eulogy of the recently deceased orator Hortensius (*Brut.* 1–9), who, he says, has come up as a topic in a recent conversation—that is, the very conversation the dialogue purportedly records. Cicero stresses the informal nature of the colloquy: it is in the course of "some talk" (*ex sermone quodam*, 9) that he and his interlocutors "chance upon" (*incidissemus*, ibid.) the recollection of Hortensius, and the conversation itself arises from an everyday situation, a visit of Atticus and Brutus to Cicero's house in Rome, when their host happens to be at leisure (*otiosus*, 10) and taking a walk in his garden. The friendship among the three men is stressed: not only are Atticus and Brutus "accustomed" (*consueuerat*, ibid.) to drop in on Cicero but they are "men both close to each other and dear and delightful to me."[97]

Given the social status of the three friends (two senators and recently pardoned ex-Pompeians, one equestrian with ample political connections and interests) and the historical situation (news from Caesar's campaign in Africa is anxiously expected), it is unsurprising that the conversation turns first to the *res publica* (10); however, Atticus immediately asserts that he and Brutus have come to take their (and Cicero's) minds off this sore topic and are hoping to hear their friend discourse on a different subject (11). We are thus approaching the alternative realm of *studia*, and indeed Cicero avows not only that he has recently returned to his former intellectual pursuits but that he has done so inspired by his two friends' written communications.[98]

This statement introduces a major topic of the preface, the exchange of scholarly works and the reciprocity that is at the heart of these men's *societas studiorum*.[99] It turns out that the *litterae* Cicero has received were not simple letters but two learned treatises his friends have dedicated to him: Atticus's *Liber annalis*, on chronology, and Brutus's *De uirtute*, on ethics.[100] Cicero

---

97. *Brut.* 10: *homines cum inter se coniuncti tum mihi ita cari itaque iucundi.*

98. *Brut.* 11: *uestris primum litteris recreatus me ad pristina studia reuocaui.*

99. On this motif, see Marchese 2011: 22–31.

100. That Atticus's work is the *Liber annalis* is clear from Cicero's subsequent references in *Brut.* 14, 15, 19, 42–44, 72 (for further discussion of the work, see 5.1 below, with n. 18); there is no hint in the text as to what Brutus's *litterae* are, but the identification with *De uirtute*, first proposed by Hendrickson 1939, makes sense and has been generally accepted (for a dissenting voice, see Dettenhofer 1992: 199–201 and compare Garbarino 2003: 92). On Cicero's use of and

expresses his thanks and declares that his friends' gifts have put him under obligation to reciprocate, a theme that the three men keep playfully riffing on for the next five paragraphs (15–19). First, Cicero employs a version of the modesty topos, claiming that he is unable to pay back Atticus. Leading off with a quotation from Hesiod's *Works and Days* (15), he launches into an extended agricultural metaphor, maintaining that his intellectual fields are currently lying fallow (16).

While Atticus graciously acquiesces, extending his "loan" for an unspecified period, Brutus appoints himself Atticus's agent (*procurator*, 17) and declares that he will take it upon himself to hound Cicero to repay his debt. With the adoption of legal language, scholarly reciprocity has turned into a financial transaction that can be pursued in court, and the three men—well-acquainted with the lingo—delight in ringing changes on this theme (18–19).[101] In the end, Atticus, in order to reward Brutus for taking up his case, decides in turn to support Brutus in his demands against Cicero, with the result that the author now sees himself confronted with two "creditors" clamoring for repayment (19).

The kind of repayment Brutus and Atticus have in mind is, of course, a written work by Cicero himself: *ut scribas ... aliquid* ("that you write something," 19). For the moment, however, they have a different demand, one that Cicero is happy to accede to immediately: he and Atticus have recently had a conversation out in Tusculum about the history of oratory; Atticus has told Brutus about it; and the two want Cicero to continue his account then and there (20). After some preliminaries, the friends sit down next to a statue of Plato (24), and the dialogue begins.

The introduction to the *Brutus*, then, presents three members of the Roman elite in the process of συμφιλολογεῖν. The three are close friends, and the described conversation is but one part of their ongoing interactions. In addition to concerning themselves with the *res publica*, Cicero, Brutus, and Atticus engage in joint intellectual pursuits, conducted both via correspondence and in face-to-face conversation; the latter takes place during *otium* and more often than not in a country villa (while the dialogue itself is set at Rome, the earlier conversation with Brutus occurred *in Tusculano* [20], and future exchanges are anticipated as happening *in Cumano aut in Tusculano aliquando* [300]). All

---

response to *De uirtute*, see Dugan 2005: 236–48. The relationship of Cicero and Brutus in the 40s is considered in greater detail in ch. 4; further discussion of the *Brutus* can be found in 4.2 and 5.3.

101. Perlwitz 1992: 60–61, Narducci 1997: 106, and Dugan 2005: 210 n. 114 further suggest that Cicero here uses legal and economical language to allude playfully to Brutus's and Atticus's money-lending practices.

three interlocutors write scholarly works, which they dedicate to one another, and there is a strong expectation that such gifts will be reciprocated.[102] At the same time, Cicero is at pains to establish that these dedications and counterdedications are not just mechanical steps in the aristocratic exchange of *beneficia*, but provide genuine intellectual stimuli: the character Cicero presents his friends' books as intellectual and emotional lifesavers (11–15), and Atticus avows that it was Cicero's own *De re publica* that inspired his work on chronology (19). In turn, Cicero on a number of occasions in the *Brutus* draws on Atticus's historical reconstructions, whether playfully to disagree with them (42–44) or otherwise to adopt them (72–74). It was Atticus's work, he says, that "inflamed me with the eagerness to trace the lives and times of famous men."[103] At this point in the dialogue, it becomes clear that Brutus, too, has read the *Liber annalis* and enjoyed it (*delector*, 74); he agrees with Cicero on its importance for the author's project at hand.

Similarly to the passing references to *societas studiorum* in the letters, Cicero's elaborate depiction of his learned interactions with Atticus and Brutus in the *Brutus* is not only a (highly idealized) representation of intellectual comradeship, but a speech act that itself contributes to constituting this relationship. It is by declaring and describing the bond that joint interest in *studia* creates that this bond is strengthened or, in some cases perhaps, created from scratch. Both the letters and the *Brutus* and other dialogues are thus not simply sources (however skewed) for the social aspects of intellectual practices of the late Republic; they are a crucial part of these practices themselves.[104]

This is especially obvious in the *Brutus*, which not only presents a picture of learned activity as a mutual exchange among peers, but is itself, qua written work, an important element in this exchange. For, of course, the *Brutus* itself is the very repayment for the *Liber annalis* and *De uirtute* that the authors of these works demand with such spirit at the beginning of the dialogue.[105]

---

102. As Dugan 2005: 176–77 points out, there is a fourth, absent participant in this network of intellectual and textual exchange: Julius Caesar, whose *De analogia* was likewise dedicated to Cicero and, together with its author, receives some very cautious discussion in *Brut.* 252–62 (see Dugan 2005: 177–89). On the rhetorical and linguistic controversies between Cicero and Caesar, see van den Berg forthcoming and the discussion in 5.3 below.

103. *Brut.* 74: *me inflammauit studio illustrium hominum aetates et tempora persequendi.*

104. Compare G. M. Müller 2015 on the dialogues as Cicero's "inszenierte Diskursgemeinschaft" (293) and Gildenhard 2018 on community-building in the letters.

105. That the *Brutus*—named after all for the man who is not just an interlocutor but (apparently) the work's dedicatee—is meant to be a repayment for *De uirtute* seems fairly obvious; that it is at the same time meant as a response to Atticus's gift is suggested not only by the preface but by the many references to the *Liber annalis* in the course of the dialogue. Compare the brief

Cicero is having some fun with the different levels of reality and fictionality inside and outside his work. Brutus and Atticus are real people and have really dedicated treatises to their friend, for which Cicero reciprocates by writing a real book, that is, the *Brutus*. At the same time, the three men are characters in a fictional dialogue, whose conversation—both about the hoped-for dedication exchange and about the history of Roman oratory—is, as it were, the plot of the work. Whereas within the dialogue, Cicero's writing of the "repayment" for Brutus and Atticus is postponed while an actual conversation among the friends is taking place (20), in reality this conversation is already part of the published text.

Cicero self-referentially draws attention to the paradoxical double nature of his dialogue with Brutus and Atticus when raising the question of why his history of Roman oratory steers clear of evaluating contemporary speakers (231). The character Cicero claims that he is refraining from discussing the rhetorical merits of men still alive because he suspects that Brutus and Atticus have too prurient an interest in Cicero's (possibly quite negative) opinions about their contemporaries. As Brutus immediately objects, this reasoning is obviously phony: Cicero simply does not wish to offend anybody. Of course, within the fictional world of the dialogue, such offense could take place only if details of the private conversation leaked out, and Brutus believes that Cicero is afraid that he and Atticus will spill the beans. Cicero pretends to be shocked:

> "quid? uos," inquam, "tacere non poteritis?"
> "nos quidem," inquit, "facillime; sed tamen te arbitror malle ipsum tacere quam taciturnitatem nostram experiri."

> "What," I said, "can't you keep silent?"
> "We easily can," said he. "But I think you prefer to keep silent yourself rather than put our discretion to the test."

Coming perilously close to breaking the fourth wall, Cicero's character calls out Cicero the author on the fictionality of the dialogue in which they both appear.[106]

The *Brutus* is a bravura performance, and Cicero, Brutus, and Atticus (both inside and outside the dialogue) are presumably unusual in their dedication

---

and reasonable discussion by Douglas 1966 ad *Brut.* 16.1, who concludes that "the work is a gift to both."

106. See Dugan 2005: 208–9 and compare his general discussion of the *Brutus* as an "ironic text" (pp. 204–12). Another slippage occurs at *Brut.* 181, where Cicero states that it is difficult to "write" (*scribi*) anything about past orators whose speeches do not survive.

to *studia*, even in "these so learned times." While my focus in the rest of the book will be on the politics of knowledge as practiced by these and similar outstanding individuals, I hope to have established that despite the unavoidable Ciceronian bias of our sources, there is evidence for widespread intellectual practices among the late Republican elite, and that "studies," of whatever kind and intensity, were a type of often very social leisure-time activity that Roman upperclass men engaged in as a matter of course. How a number of particularly well-documented senators (and some *equites*) went about their *studia*, what exactly they studied, and how they integrated their knowledge-producing practices into their private and public lives will be the topic of the following chapters.

3

Engaged Philosophy

WHEN IN 63 BCE Cicero defended L. Murena against a bribery charge, he scored points by making fun of the Stoic beliefs of one of the prosecutors, the tribune-elect M. Porcius Cato. When, at a trial in 56, he berated P. Vatinius, a witness against Cicero's client Sestius, the orator cast aspersions on this former tribune's conduct by hinting that he belonged to a group of Pythagoreans. And when a year later Cicero in the senate embarked on a savage attack against the consular L. Calpurnius Piso, whom he held partly responsible for his exile three years earlier, Cicero attempted to denigrate his opponent by dwelling on his adherence to Epicureanism.[1]

These incidents can tell us much about Ciceronian rhetorical strategy, the wide scope in Roman oratory for ad hominem attacks, and—provided we take the orator's words with a grain of salt—Cicero's views of philosophical doctrines that he did not share. What they also tell us, however, is that in the mid-first century BCE, Roman senators were sufficiently versed in philosophy to declare allegiance to individual schools, and that discussion—and mockery—of philosophical doctrine and behavior could be used to good effect in public speeches that were designed to sway and entertain not only senate and jury but also a larger audience.

The cases of Cato, Vatinius, and Piso are part of a wider phenomenon. Late Republican Rome was saturated in philosophy. David Sedley speaks of the "feverish interest shown by leading Romans of Cicero's day in acquiring a philosophical education and allegiance," a development that represents a culmination point of "the great Roman love-affair with philosophy" that had begun in the previous century.[2] As so often, Cicero's letters provide an

---

1. Cic. *Mur.* 3–6, 58–66, 74–77; *Vat.* 14; *Pis.* passim.

2. Sedley 2010: 702 (cf. 2009: 29). The history of this great love-affair remains to be written. For short general introductions to Roman philosophy, see Morford 2002, Maurach 2006, Maso 2012, and Volk forthcoming b; Griffin and Barnes (eds.) 1989, Barnes and Griffin (eds.) 1997, Williams and Volk (eds.) 2016, Vesperini (ed.) 2017, and Müller and Mariani Zini (eds.) 2018

excellent gauge of the zeitgeist. As Pierre Boyancé and Miriam Griffin have shown, the correspondence abounds in philosophical references, many of them joking and allusive;[3] the very fact that the letter writers and recipients appear to be able to pick up on passing remarks, and to make and understand in-jokes, attests to the widespread currency of philosophical language and ideas.

First-century Romans acquired their philosophical expertise by studying with Greek philosophers, both at home and abroad, and by maintaining formal and informal ties with such intellectuals, including on a number of occasions the hosting of a philosopher in a Roman noble's household or entourage. In addition, Romans were able to study Greek texts, including whole libraries that had reached the city as booty from the conquest of the Greek east.[4] By the late Republic, however, Romans were also writing philosophical works in their own language. These included poems, such as Lucretius's and Egnatius's *De rerum natura* and the *Empedoclea* of Sallustius; prose works, such as the Epicurean treatises of Amafinius, Rabirius, and Catius Insuber, Brutus's *De uirtute*, Varro's *De philosophia*, and Cicero's extensive philosophical corpus; and, in a mix of poetry and prose, the Cynically inspired *Menippean Satires* of Varro.[5]

Among the cultural practices adopted and adapted from the Greeks, philosophy was but one option from many types of *studia* an educated member of the Roman elite might embrace. At the same time, philosophy held a special status. It not only presented an intellectually stimulating exercise that offered cultural capital, but advertised real solutions to ethical and emotional problems, ultimately holding out the promise of "happiness" or the "good life" (Gk. *eudaimonia*, Lat. *bene* or *beate uiuere*). Philosophy was considered an "art of life" (*ars uitae*), providing models of judgment and action meant to be successfully applied to situations in which its practitioners might find themselves. In a society where theoretical explanation and practical guidance were not

---

are collections of essays. Garbarino 1973 documents the beginnings of Roman philosophy in the 2nd c. BCE. On philosophy in the late Republic, see Jocelyn 1977; Rawson 1985, ch. 19; Griffin 1989; Bringmann 2003; Gotter 2003; and Vesperini 2012.

3. See Boyancé 1936: 302–4 and Griffin 1995, 1997a, as well as now McConnell 2014 and Gilbert 2015, who show that philosophy in Cicero's letters is not restricted to badinage, but also encompasses serious and often profound discussion. I return to some philosophical aspects of the correspondence in 3.2 (further scholarly literature is cited in n. 96) and 4.1.

4. On Roman interactions with Greek intellectuals and the availability of books and libraries, see 2.2 above.

5. On Republican didactic poetry, including the lost works of Egnatius and Sallustius, see Kruschwitz and Schumacher 2005. Epicurean prose works are discussed by Gilbert 2015: 35–62, with earlier literature. On Varro's *Menippean Satires* as evidence for a late Republican philosophical scene apart from the (Ciceronian) mainstream, see Zetzel 2016. Fragments of Latin philosophical writings prior to Seneca are collected by Garbarino 2003.

supplied by religion—as they were to be in medieval and early modern western societies—philosophy had the potential of answering a real intellectual and emotional need and to play an accordingly significant role. The question, as far as the late Roman Republic is concerned, is: Did it actually do so?

While scholars acknowledge the Roman elite's acquaintance with and enthusiasm for philosophy, they are often reluctant to believe that philosophical ideas made a real impact on their Roman students or informed their actions. Cases have been made by both ancient and modern historians for the philosophical inspiration of a number of individual figures and events, but many of these remain controversial, owing to the difficulty of fathoming the psychological motivation of poorly documented historical actors of more than two thousand years ago. It is hard to find a "smoking gun," and Miriam Griffin in her seminal article "Philosophy, Politics, and Politicians at Rome" thus comes to the conclusion that "attempts to establish connections between philosophical doctrines and particular policies and decisions fail," and that the contribution of philosophy to the political world of the late Republic consisted more generally in providing a "moral vocabulary for weighing alternatives and justifying decisions."[6]

Griffin arrives at her negative assessment after setting down two "minimal requirements" (22) that need to be fulfilled before we can assert that a person's actions were influenced by a certain philosophical creed (22–23):

(1) to show that the man adhered to the sect in general or that there is reason to think he was under its influence at the time.

(2) to show that the policy or decision would be the one clearly indicated by the creed of that sect for these circumstances.

While there are a number of good candidates for (1), Griffin is certainly correct that (2) is barely ever fulfilled.[7] As she points out, "the ethical doctrines of the dogmatic schools themselves were usually too general to give unambiguous directives in particular situations" (32). Matters are further complicated by the fact that "[f]or a Roman in public life, it can be even harder to show that he has chosen a course of action because it was prescribed by his philosophy, for he may have been following Roman tradtion [sic]" (23).

---

6. Griffin 1989: 32, 36; the author reiterates her view in Griffin 1994: 725–28. To my knowledge, no one else has tackled the issue in a systematic way since then. In the introduction to a 2003 volume on the relationship of philosophy and "real life" in antiquity, Karen Piepenbrink still refers to Griffin when stating that in the case of the late Republic, it is difficult "tatsächliche oder zumindest denkbare Transfers philosophischer Überlegungen auf die politische Praxis nachzuweisen" (Piepenbrink 2003: 13; compare, however, the different approach of Gotter 2003 in the same volume).

7. She provides a number of case studies at 1989: 22–32.

On Griffin's criteria, then, it is nearly impossible to ascribe a philosophical motivation to any political choice made by a particular Roman. Stoicism, Epicureanism, and other philosophical schools indeed offered little concrete guidance on how to vote in the senate, what legislation to champion, or how to behave in the case of a civil war. The very fact that throughout Roman history, adherents of the same philosophical school are found on opposite ends of the political spectrum shows that specific philosophical systems—nothwithstanding their teachings on ethics in general and political theory in particular—did not provide blueprints for political action.[8] But does this mean that individual political actions could not, among other things, have been informed by philosophy? Even if, say, a man's Stoicism did not "clearly indicate" a particular decision so as to satisfy Griffin's requirements, who is to say that he was not (also) motivated by his Stoicism in taking it?

The same objection applies to the observation—unobjectionable in itself—that "Roman tradition" must have been a major factor in many political decisions. Scholarly resistance to considering philosophy a motivating force in late Republican political decision-making is often predicated on a misguided application of Occam's razor: as long as there is one plausible motivation (e.g., political calculation, aristocratic competition, family connections), this is deemed enough to explain any individual decision, and philosophy (or any other possible motivating factor) need not be adduced.[9] Nothing, however, prevents a person from being motivated by a number of factors at the same time, and I for one consider it more likely that late Republican Romans, like us, were complex characters capable of maintaining numerous ideas at the same time.[10] Furthermore, "Roman tradition" itself miserably fails Griffin's

8. See, e.g., Sedley 2009: 43–44 on Epicureanism in the Republic and Brunt 1975 and Trapp 2007: 226–30 on Stoicism during the Empire.

9. Compare, e.g., Maurach 2006: 52 on Cato ("Cato war vor allem von optimatischen Grundsätzen bestimmt und von gentilizischen Interessen beherrscht. Sein Charakter war nicht erst durch die Stoa geformt, diese war nur Bestärkung"; see also Drogula 2019, passim), Perlwitz 1992: 97 on Atticus ("Die Zurückhaltung des Atticus gegenüber den angestammten Formen politischer Betätigung wird dabei zu großen Teilen aus den politischen Verhältnissen dieser Zeit selbst zu erklären sein und den Rückgriff auf geistesgeschichtliche Erklärungsmuster überflüssig machen"), and Gotter 1996b: 225 on the assassination of Caesar ("Hierfür waren die Kategorien des römischen Nobilis im übrigen völlig ausreichend, einer irgendwie idealisierten Tyrannophobie griechischer Provenienz bedurfte es nicht. Wenn griechische Motive anklangen, hat man darin nur die Stilisierung in den geistig verbindlichen Formen zu sehen, in denen sich ein gebildeter Römer bewegte"). Cf. also Syme 1939: 57.

10. Cf. Gilbert 2015: 96 n. 55: "we should view the actions of committed Roman Epicureans (or adherents of any other sect) as the result of hybridized motivations."

second requirement: in no case was a historical policy or decision ever "clearly indicated" by that most slippery concept; in fact, most Roman political actors at most times probably thought of, or presented, themselves as upholding their traditional aristocratic values, even if in their attitudes and actions they violently clashed with one another.

While I thus fully agree with Griffin that rather than prescribing specific policies, philosophy provided interested Romans with a theoretical framework for thinking and speaking about ethical choices, I am working on the assumption that such modes of thought cannot be neatly separated from the rest of a person's existence. A Roman noble did not check his *studia* at the door when entering the senate,[11] and I believe it is well worth asking to what extent political figures known to have had a strong interest in philosophy may have applied their mental habits to their actions and used the purported art of life to master their own lives, which were by definition political. This and the following chapter discuss a number of cases where I believe philosophy and politics intersected in the late Republic, including both the application of philosophical teaching to political action and the employment of philosophy itself—the (speech) act of discussing and writing philosophy—*as* political action. This chapter largely focuses on the period leading up to the Civil War of the early 40s and considers two very different men known for both their philosophical interests and their political engagement: the Stoic M. Porcius Cato (3.1) and the Academic Skeptic M. Tullius Cicero (3.2). I conclude by considering the apparent conundrum that what appears to have been the period's most popular philosophical school, Epicureanism, advocated a withdrawal from politics that seems to sit ill with Roman upperclass values and ideology (3.3). In the following chapter, I move on to the post-Pharsalus years and consider what philosophy may have offered its Roman practitioners in the tense years under Caesar's rule.

1. The Importance of Being Cato

M. Porcius Cato (95–46 BCE) is perhaps the best candidate for a late Republican "philosopher in politics."[12] His professed adherence to Stoicism must have been well known already in 63 for Cicero's persiflage in *Pro Murena* to be

---

11. This observation is not as self-evident as it sounds: many scholars have argued for a strict mental division between Roman *otium* and *negotium*. Thus, Zanker 1987: 40 writes that, conversely, "[m]it der *toga* legte man in der Freizeit gleichsam sein Römertum ab" (quoted approvingly by Haltenhoff 2003: 238 n. 64 as the *communis opinio*).

12. This phrase is adapted from Miriam Griffin's 1976 designation of the younger Seneca. If Cato followed the practice of his contemporary Cicero and, indeed, Seneca himself, he

effective. Elsewhere, Cicero refers to him as a "(most) perfect Stoic,"[13] and in *De finibus* 3 and 4, written not long after Cato's death, he casts his late fellow senator as a spokesman for Stoic ethics. Cato reportedly employed philosophical arguments even in his public speeches,[14] and generally often behaved in ways that were socially unexpected but could be interpreted as informed by his philosophy. Later authors took Cato's Stoicism for granted, transforming him into an *exemplum* of virtuous action or even a Roman manifestation of that ultimate Stoic ideal, the wise man.[15]

At the same time, Cato's exact views and motivations are hard to establish. Unlike most of the major protagonists of this book, he did not publish anything. According to Plutarch, the speech he delivered in the senate on 5 December 63 to argue for the execution of the Catilinarians was his only oration to circulate—not by his own decision, but because the consul Cicero had made sure that the debate was taken down in shorthand.[16] The one product of Cato's stylus to have come down to us verbatim is a single short letter to Cicero of April 50 BCE (*Fam.* 15.5).

In addition, our understanding of Cato is made difficult by the bias of many of our sources. The hagiography—as well as, conversely, vilification—of the Republican diehard set in immediately after his death, with the publication of warring pamphlets by Cicero, Caesar, Brutus, and others,[17] and continued for centuries and indeed millennia. It is difficult to find the real man behind the idealizations of, say, a Lucan or Addison; more than any of his contemporaries, Cato has turned into a symbol designed to elicit emotional responses rather than historical analysis.

In an attempt to get as close as possible to the historical Cato, I will thus, where feasible, rely on contemporary sources, which here as elsewhere means

---

presumably did not label himself a philosopher (cf. Hine 2016); significantly, however, Plutarch designates him thus (unusually for a Roman: see Swain 1990: 197) at *Cat. Mai.* 27.5, *Brut.* 2.1, and *Pomp.* 40.1—though, interestingly, not in his own *Life*.

13. Cic. *Parad. Stoic.* 2: *perfectus mea sententia Stoicus*; *Brut.* 118: [Brutus speaking:] *in quo perfectissimo Stoico*.

14. Cic. *Parad. Stoic.* 3: *Stoice...solet dicere*; Plut. *Cat. Min.* 54.5–6 (speech to the soldiers at Dyrrhachium). Cicero stresses that unlike most Stoics, Cato was an accomplished orator (see also *Brut.* 118–19 and Stem 2005–6). On the effectiveness of Cato's speeches to the Roman people, see van der Blom 2012.

15. On Cato's literary and philosophical afterlife, see Pecchiura 1965, Goar 1987, Beßlich 2008, and Gäth 2011.

16. Plut. *Cat. Min.* 23.3. This is, of course, the speech recreated by Sallust in *Cat.* 52. As Cato's only written work, Plut. *Cat. Min.* 7.2 mentions juvenile iambic poetry against Metellus Scipio, who had stolen his bride (see Cowan 2015).

17. These "Cato Wars" of the mid-40s will be discussed in 4.2.

primarily the writings of Cicero. Cicero was well acquainted with Cato, if never close to him; while they stood on the same side in many political conflicts as well as in the Civil War, the pragmatic consular found the inflexibility of his younger contemporary hard to take and not infrequently counterproductive. Though many of his references to Cato do show a (grudging) admiration, Cicero can certainly not be accused of a blind pro-Catonian bias.

The same is true for Plutarch's biography, our main source for Cato's life. Plutarch himself had well-informed sources, most importantly a life of Cato by Thrasea Paetus (1st c. CE), which in turn followed an account by Cato's own friend Munatius Rufus.[18] Munatius's life was presumably part of the flurry of publications shortly after Cato's death, when friends and enemies competed in shaping Cato's legacy; even if he was an ardent apologist, however, Munatius nevertheless was in a position to provide valuable inside information on his subject not otherwise available. As for Thrasea Paetus, this Stoic "martyr" of the Neronian era may well have adapted Munatius's text to serve as a blueprint for his own resistance to Imperial power, which culminated in his Catonian suicide of 66 CE. By contrast, Plutarch paints a more balanced picture of Cato, depicting him generally positively but also deploring his unwillingness to compromise and general rigor of attitude. As a professed Platonist, Plutarch had no time for hardline Stoicism and may have devised especially his account of Cato's death as the cautionary tale of a man whose actions did not live up to his philosophy.[19]

In using Cicero, Plutarch, and other sources, I will attempt to steer clear of their explicit and implicit value judgments while working on the cautious assumption that their accounts of what Cato himself did and said are reasonably reliable. The man's beliefs and thought processes will have to be reconstructed from his actions (and, to some extent, the reactions of his contemporaries), a process that is of necessity speculative. At the same time, our knowledge of the intellectual and political context, the res publica of letters of which Cato too was a member, should assist us in gaining a better understanding of why this unusual character acted the way he did.

The younger Cato was the great-grandson of the famous Censor, a man whom he appears to have regarded as a role model.[20] With excellent political

---

18. On Plutarch's sources, see Geiger 1979, Pelling 1979, and Scardigli 1979: 136–40. Plutarch himself signals his reliance on Munatius/Paetus at 25.1 and 37.1–2. See FRHist 37 and 81 for the surviving fragments of Munatius and Paetus, as well as further discussion.

19. On Plutarch's depiction and judgment of Cato, see Pelling 1989: 228–32, Swain 1990: 197–201, Duff 1999: 131–60, Trapp 1999, Zodorojnyi 2007, and Beck 2014: 470–75.

20. See Cass. Dio 37.22.1 and compare Cic. Mur. 32. On Cato's life and political career, see Afzelius 1941, Miltner 1953, Gelzer 1963 [1934], Fehrle 1983, Stein-Hölkeskamp 2000, and now

and family connections,[21] Cato entered the *cursus honorum* with the quaestor-ship in 64, followed by the tribunate in 62. From 58 to 56, he was in Cyprus on a special commission, arranging the annexation of the island from Ptolemaic rule; his appointment to this ad hoc position had been engineered by the tribune P. Clodius Pulcher—no doubt with the support of the members of the First Triumvirate[22]—who was keen on removing a political enemy from Rome. On his return, Cato failed to be elected praetor for 55 but attained the office the following year; his bid for the consulship of 51 was unsuccessful.

Throughout his political career, Cato evinced a meticulous adherence to the letter of the law. This is apparent in his scrupulous financial administration as quaestor and propraetor, as well as in his persistent and often original attempts to curb bribery and election fraud. Most famous, of course, is his unwavering support for the unwritten constitution of the Republic: Cato vigorously opposed extraordinary commands, which repeatedly brought him into conflict with Pompey, Caesar, and their supporters.[23] From his tribunate onward, he acted as the leader of a shifting hyperconservative faction, working to uphold the traditional power of the senate and oppose triumviral and other *popularis* initiatives. In the Civil War, he joined Pompey without apparent enthusiasm, and together with such other intellectually inclined Pompeians as Cicero and Varro was garrisoned at Dyrrhachium during the party's defeat at Pharsalus in August 48. Unlike his more moderate colleagues, however, he decided to carry on the war, leading an army into northern Africa, where he joined forces with Metellus Scipio. When the latter was decisively defeated by Caesar at Thapsus in April 46, Cato was holding the town of Utica. Realizing that further resistance was pointless, but unwilling to surrender to Caesar and be granted his much-vaunted *clementia*, Cato committed suicide, turning himself into a martyr for the Republican cause.

It is clear from our sources that Cato's contemporaries considered his personality and behavior unusual and remarkable. While his conservative stance may have been shared by many, his single-minded and often unorthodox pursuit of his beliefs must have raised many an eyebrow. Cicero famously

---

Drogula 2019. Sources for individual events can be found in these treatments; I will provide references only for incidents central to my own discussion.

21. Most interesting, from this book's sociology-of-knowledge perspective, is Cato's half-sister Servilia, the erstwhile mistress of Caesar and mother of Brutus; Cato posthumously became his nephew's father-in-law when Brutus married Cato's daughter Porcia in 45.

22. As is well known, the so-called First Triumvirate of Caesar, Pompey, and Crassus was not an official "board of three men" (unlike the Second Triumvirate of Antony, Octavian, and Lepidus). I will nevertheless use this traditional denomination, while also following historiographical convention in referring to the men in question as "dynasts."

23. For constitutional debates in the late Republic, see Straumann 2016.

lamented that Cato behaved as though he lived "in the *Republic* of Plato rather than among the dregs of Romulus";[24] however, this idealistic stance did not translate into unworldly remoteness but instead into an aggressive political style that involved not only Cato's infamous harangues and filibusters,[25] but also fairly courageous physical confrontations in the kinds of melees that became a more and more common feature of Roman politics in the 50s. In addition, Cato drew attention to himself with his unconventional attire—he was wont to walk about without shoes and tunic—and invited gossip by divorcing his wife Marcia to allow her to marry Hortensius and subsequently remarrying her after Hortensius's death. Even among the colorful cast of characters that is the last generation of the Roman Republic, Cato stands out for what may well be termed sheer eccentricity.

He also was remarkable for his *studia*. We know little about his early training (unlike other Romans of his generation, he does not seem to have studied abroad in Greece), but we find the adult Cato surrounding himself with Greek philosophers and participating in philosophical drinking and debating parties.[26] He was apparently an avid reader, taking books with him into the senate and spending the last hours before his suicide reading through Plato's *Phaedo*, not once but twice.[27] In *De finibus*, Cicero paints a lively scene of encountering Cato in the library of Lucullus (3.7):

> quo cum uenissem, M. Catonem, quem ibi esse nescieram, uidi in bibliotheca sedentem multis circumfusum Stoicorum libris. erat enim, ut scis, in eo auiditas legendi, nec satiari poterat, quippe qui ne reprensionem quidem uulgi inanem reformidans in ipsa curia soleret legere saepe dum senatus cogeretur, nihil operae rei publicae detrahens. quo magis tum in summo otio maximaque copia quasi helluari libris, si hoc uerbo in tam clara re utendum est, uidebatur.

> When I got there, I saw M. Cato—who I had not known would be there—sitting in the library surrounded by many Stoic books. For he had,

---

24. Cic. *Att.* 2.1.8: *tamquam in Platonis* πολιτείᾳ, *non tamquam in Romuli faece,* quoted by Plut. *Phoc.* 3.1.

25. On Cato's filibusters, see Groebe 1905.

26. The following Greek philosophers are associated with Cato: Antipater of Tyre (Stoic; Plut. *Cat. Min.* 4.1), Athenodorus Cordylion (Stoic; Plut. *Cat. Min.* 10, 16.1), Apollonides (Stoic; Plut. *Cat. Min.* 45.5, 66.4, 69.1, 70.1), and Demetrius (Peripatetic; Plut. *Cat. Min.* 45.5, 67.2, 69.1, 70.1). For *symposia*, see Plut. *Cat. Min.* 6.2, who makes the suggestion, echoed in modern scholarship, that it was Cato's taste for alcohol-fueled philosophical debates that gave rise to his reputation as a drunkard, a theme exploited by Caesar in his *Anticato* (frr. 4, 5 Tschiedel).

27. Reading in the senate: Cic. *Fin.* 3.7; Val. Max. 8.7.2; Plut. *Cat. Min.* 19.1; cf. 2.2 above; reading the *Phaedo*: Plut. *Cat. Min.* 68.2–3, 70.1; cf. Sen. *Ep.* 24.6, 71.11.

as you know, such a greed for reading, and could not get enough, that without fearing the empty criticism of the crowd he often used to read even in the curia, while the senate was assembling, in no way neglecting public business. At this time, when he was wholly at leisure and had the best conditions, he seemed even more so, as it were, to be glutting himself with books, if I may use this expression for such a noble pursuit.

Cato's binge-reading is, as so many of his other behaviors, single-minded and extreme: he is as fervently committed to his *studia* as to his politics, eschewing convention in pursuing both.[28]

Both ancient sources and modern historians have often assumed that Cato's politics were influenced by his philosophical beliefs, but little consensus has emerged as to which aspects of his policies and behavior were particularly "Stoic."[29] In approaching this question, it is important to realize that Stoicism was not an especially popular choice among late Republican Romans looking for a philosophical creed to embrace. No doubt misled by the widespread adoption of Stoic beliefs and attitudes under the Empire, when Stoicism became a kind of default weltanschauung of the Roman elite, scholars sometimes assume that mid-first-century BCE Romans were as enthusiastic about the school as their Imperial descendants.[30] As a matter of fact, while we are aware of numerous late Republican Epicureans, a handful of prominent Academics, and at least two potential Pythagoreans,[31] Cato is the single unambiguously attested professed Stoic of the mid-first century.[32] Rather than assuming, as

28. Compare the description of Valerius Maximus: *doctrinae cupiditate flagrauit* ("he was burning with the desire for knowledge," 8.7.2). On Cicero's depiction of Cato's reading orgy at the beginning of *Fin.* 3, see Frampton 2016.

29. Among modern historians, Afzelius 1941, Gelzer 1963 [1934], and Morrell 2017 are especially inclined to consider Cato's politics influenced by his Stoicism; by contrast, Drogula 2019 maintains that Stoicism played next to no role in his attitudes and actions. On Cato in the history of Roman philosophy, see the fairly cursory discussions of Morford 2002: 46–48 and Maurach 2006: 50–53.

30. E.g., Stein-Hölkeskamp 2000: 296: Stoic ethical teachings "fanden in Rom zu seiner [sc. Cato's] Zeit zumal bei der *jeunesse dorée* zahlreiche Anhänger"; Drogula 2019: 28: "Stoicism was popular among Roman elites."

31. Epicureans: see 3.3 below; Academics: Cicero (Skeptic), Varro, Brutus (both Antiochean); Pythagoreans: Vatinius, Nigidius Figulus. What adherence to Pythagoreanism in the late Republic would have entailed is quite unclear; compare Volk 2016b: 43–49 and 6.2 below with nn. 81–82.

32. Cato's friend and admirer M. Favonius is sometimes considered a Stoic, on next to no evidence (see Geiger 1974: 167–70). Prominent earlier Roman Stoics include P. Rutilius Rufus and Q. Aelius Tubero (late 2nd/early 1st c. BCE; note also Sp. Mummius and C. Fannius [Cic.

people often do, some vague affinity between Stoicism and traditional Roman values, we should work on the assumption that Cato's creed was one shared by few people and removed from mainstream ideas. As Cicero puts it in his *Paradoxa Stoicorum*, "Cato believes that of which one can hardly persuade the multitude," and Stoic tenets (especially the infamous paradoxes) "run counter to everybody's opinion."[33] In later ages, Cato became everybody's favorite role model; in his own time, his views and behavior were decidedly unusual.[34]

As far as Cato's politics are concerned, it is unlikely that his conservatism and his committed defense of senatorial power were as such inspired by Stoicism. While it is sometimes assumed that the Roman Republican system with its "mixed constitution" would have particularly appealed to Stoics as being in keeping with their political ideals, there is little evidence that this was in fact the case, and none at all that Cato himself thought or acted along those lines.[35] If Cato took his philosophy seriously, he would of course have attempted to determine rationally what choice of lifestyle and individual actions would be morally right for him (indeed, Plutarch reports that "he chose politics as being the task of a good man"[36]), and subsequently to make every effort to pursue

Brut. 94, 118]). Less significant are Sex. Pompeius, Q. Lucilius Balbus (the spokesman for Stoicism in Cic. *Nat. D.* 2), L. Lucilius Balbus, and M. Vigellius, all credited with Stoic sympathies in Cic. *De or.* 3.78 (dramatic date 91 BCE). Who the "rustic Stoics" (*rusticos Stoicos*, Cic. *Fam.* 15.19.1) are whom Cassius jokingly threatens to unleash against Cicero in a letter of January 45 is anyone's guess (cf. Zetzel 2016: 52).

33. Cic. *Parad. Stoic.* 2: *Cato ... ea sentit quae non sane probantur in uulgus*; 4: *contra ... opinionem omnium.* The mockery of Cato's Stoic principles in *Mur.* 58–66 is likewise predicated on the assumption that such ideas contradict common sense and popular sentiment.

34. This does not mean that late Republican Romans were unfamiliar with the tenets of Stoicism. Beginning with Diogenes of Babylon at the famous embassy of 155 BCE, numerous Stoic philosophers sojourned in Rome (including Panaetius and Posidonius) or interacted with members of the Roman elite abroad.

35. For the idea that Cato viewed the traditional Roman Republican system as a kind of Stoic ideal state, see Afzelius 1941: 114–15 and Gelzer 1963 [1934]: 267. Cf. Brunt 1975: 17–18, who states that "Cato could probably have cited Stoic texts to justify his struggle to preserve the Republic" (18), while also pointing out that there is little positive evidence for general Stoic championing of the Roman mixed constitution. For an argument that Cato's theory and practice of provincial adminstration were strongly influenced by Stoic cosmopolitanism, see Morrell 2017; see also n. 55 below.

36. Plut. *Cat. Min.* 19.2: ὡς ἴδιον ἔργον ἀνδρὸς ἀγαθοῦ τὴν πολιτείαν ἑλόμενος. Plutarch stresses that Cato went into politics neither for the sake of his reputation nor out of greed, nor indeed by rote or chance, but because of this belief, adding that Cato "held that he ought to be more dedicated to the public good than the bee to its honeycomb" (μᾶλλον ᾤετο δεῖν προσέχειν τοῖς κοινοῖς ἢ τῷ κηρίῳ τὴν μέλιτταν).

the chosen goals. The exact thought processes by which Cato decided on the correctness of his general attitude and particular decisions are lost, but there is nothing remarkable about his conservative and pro-senate stance as such. In many ways, it would have been a default attitude for any politically active Roman, and indeed many others, with different or no philosophical convictions, espoused the same cause. One might go even further and maintain that in a political climate where conflict was barely ever ideologically motivated, probably every political player would have maintained and indeed believed that he was acting for the public good and maintaining the *res publica*. No one, not even Julius Caesar or others of Cato's most *popularis* opponents, was out to destroy the Republican system or held theoretical beliefs about its unsuitability.[37]

If there was thus nothing particularly Stoic about the *contents* of Cato's politics, I posit that the *form* of his public conduct was strongly inspired by philosophy, and that it is indeed his Stoicism that explains much of his more unusual behavior. Stoicism famously holds that virtue—that is, moral stance and action, based on the knowledge of what is right—is the only good and as such sufficient for happiness. All apparent goods and evils are instead "indifferents" of no consequence for a person's living a good and blessed life. Nevertheless, some of these indifferents are "preferred" (e.g., health, wealth), others "dispreferred" (e.g., illness, poverty). The wise man's virtue consists in knowing which preferred indifferents he ought to pursue and how, and in dedicating himself to this pursuit. Doing so will ensure his happiness regardless of the outcome: attaining the envisaged preferred indifferent will make him no happier than failing to do so.[38] Indeed, within the larger framework of Stoic cosmology, the outcome is fated and happens according to divine providence, and the individual can take solace in the fact that the universe is perfect at all times and that apparent individual setbacks are in fact part of the greater cosmic good.

This kind of dogged pursuit of the perceived good regardless of public opinion or chance of success is the very modus operandi associated with Cato, the "Don Quixote of the aristocracy," as Mommsen sneeringly put it.[39] In sticking to his guns, the senator defied not only his contemporaries but what in hindsight could be judged the "course of history" or otherwise Fortune or even the

37. Compare C. Meier 1997 on the absence of an alternative model to the system of senatorial rule, as well as Mouritsen 2017: 105–72 for the nonideological nature of most Republican politics.

38. In *Fin.* 3.22, Cicero has Cato himself explain this doctrine with the image of the archer, whose task consists in shooting straight; whether he actually hits the target (something that is subject to circumstances beyond his control) is of no relevance to his excellence in archery.

39. Mommsen 1868–69: 3.157: "Don Quixote der Aristokratie."

gods. Thus Seneca stated that Cato "demonstrated that a brave man can live against the will of Fortune and die against the will of Fortune," a sentiment that Lucan pithily brought to the point with his famous line about the Civil War, that "the victorious cause was pleasing to the gods, but the defeated one to Cato."[40]

Viewing Cato as motivated by Stoic principles—principles that would have been considered extreme by his contemporaries—goes a long way toward explaining not only his inflexibility and disinclination to compromise but also his undeniable courage in the pursuit of his goals. Rather than examining the totality of Cato's career under this aspect, I here mention just three rather different incidents that show the senator as a "just man sticking to his purpose."[41] First, Cato's participation in the prosecution of the obviously guilty L. Murena for *ambitus* in late 63 demonstrates his unwavering commitment to the integrity of the electoral process—even at a time when (as the opposing counsel Cicero did not tire of pointing out) invalidating a consular election, especially that of an experienced military man and reliable conservative like Murena, might have contributed to the dangerous political destabilization owing to the Catilinarian conspiracy. Murena was acquitted, but Cato had made his point.

Second, as an example of Cato's physical courage, we may point to his behavior during the elections for 55, when, following the Conference of Luca, Pompey and Crassus were both running for the consulship against the optimate, and Cato's brother-in-law, L. Domitius Ahenobarbus. Being opposed by the two dynasts was not a comfortable or even safe position to be in, and according to Plutarch, it was Cato who persuaded Domitius not to abandon his stand, declaring that this was a matter "not of office but of the liberty of the Romans."[42] When on election day the two men and their supporters were viciously attacked on the Campus Martius by Pompey's supporters (with at least one casualty, that of their torchbearer), Cato, though wounded in the arm, physically held back his brother-in-law and exhorted him to stand his ground. Less inclined to heroism, Domitius fled to his house, and Pompey and Crassus were duly elected.

Finally, Cato's own bid for the consulship four years later ended in resounding defeat, no doubt at least in part because of his refusal to run a vigorous campaign or attempt to ingratiate himself with the electorate. When his friends

---

40. Sen. *Ep.* 104.29: *ostendit . . . uirum fortem posse inuita fortuna uiuere, inuita mori*; Luc. 1.128: *uictrix causa deis placuit sed uicta Catoni.*

41. Thus Hor. *Carm.* 3.3.1: *iustum et tenacem propositi uirum.* Horace's generic description has often been believed to be alluding to Cato (see esp. L. P. E. Parker 2002); *iustum* may be a matter of opinion, but *tenacem propositi* is undoubtedly correct.

42. Plut. *Cat. Min.* 41.2: οὐ περὶ ἀρχῆς . . . ἀλλὰ περὶ τῆς Ῥωμαίων ἐλευθερίας.

and relatives were dejected at Cato's *repulsa*, he himself "bore what had happened so easily that he anointed himself and played ball on the Campus Martius."[43] While he realized that his own manner had cost him the election, he declared that changing his ways for the sake of others was not something a man of any sense would do.[44] The Stoic will not be upset when not achieving the preferred indifferent he has been pursuing, nor will he submit to change in reponse to external pressures. Even when he failed as a politician, Cato's moral integrity—thus the anecdote would have us believe—was unaffected.

Viewing Cato's political behavior as partly philosophically inspired by no means obliges us to find Stoic explanations for everything he said and did, or to assume an inherent consistency in his actions. Despite his later reputation, Cato was obviously not a sage, and ancient and modern writers have pointed out his many self-contradictions and failures. For all his famed inflexibility, Cato was enough of a politician occasionally to compromise and espouse the expedient over the ideal (one case in point is his support of Pompey's wholly unconstitutional consulship *sine collega* in 52); in the best Roman tradition, he let family connections override considerations of right and wrong (thus, when prosecuting Murena in 63, he pointedly did not go after his own equally guilty brother-in-law Silanus; he abetted the outrageous electoral bribery of his son-in-law Bibulus in 60; and after refusing to support Cicero's bid for a *supplicatio* in 50, he voted for a lavish thanksgiving for Bibulus); and as a notoriously excitable man, he was far from achieving the Stoic ideal of freedom from passion. Even his philosophical suicide was marred by his angry outburst against the slaves who had hidden his sword, in the course of which Cato hit one of them so hard that he hurt his own hand.[45] My purpose is not to show that Cato was a perfect or even a good Stoic, but simply to demonstrate that on many occasions, if by no means always, he acted, or attempted to act, in a Stoic fashion. I would further maintain that Cato was well aware of what he was doing, and in fact self-consciously fashioned his own Stoic behavior for his political purposes.

As we have seen, Cato turned into a legend upon his death: his displayed *uirtus* turned him into the proverbial just man[46] and a poster child for

43. Plut. *Cat. Min.* 50.1: οὕτως ἤνεγκε ῥᾳθύμως τὸ συμβεβηκὸς ὥστε ἀλειψάμενος . . . ἐν τῷ πεδίῳ σφαιρίσαι.

44. Plut. *Cat. Min.* 50.3: ὃν [sc. τρόπον] οὔτε μεταθέσθαι πρὸς ἑτέρων χάριν . . . νοῦν ἔχοντος ἀνδρός ἐστι.

45. Plut. *Cat. Min.* 68.3, 70.5. Even though this episode appears only in Plutarch, its very bizarreness suggests to me that it is authentic, rather than having been invented by Plutarch to render his account more novelistic (Tandoi 1966: 25) or cast doubt on Cato's Stoic *apatheia* (Zodorojnyi 2007, esp. 218–19).

46. On the afterlife of Cato in Latin proverbial expressions, see Otto 1890 s.v. "Cato."

Stoicism, while his resistance to Caesar and ultimate suicide solidified his image as a martyr for the lost Republic. However, this Cato legend was started by none other than Cato himself.[47] I suggest that Cato was fully aware that his Stoically inspired actions not infrequently defied cultural norms and expectations and that he deliberately fashioned for himself a persona that was immediately recognizable: the "Cato brand," as it were. Scholars have often remarked that the senator was a spirited public performer and relished displaying the odd but admirable behavior that had come to be expected from him.[48] In other words, Cato was highly accomplished at playing Cato.

One aspect of this role was Cato's defying of the Roman dress code by going about without a tunic underneath his toga or even without shoes.[49] This eccentricity has been variously explained—Was Cato imitating the attire of the Romans of yore? Was there a heat wave during his praetorship in 54?[50]—but it seems most likely that he was on the one hand imitating the famously unshod and uncloaked Socrates and on the other demonstrating a Stoically or even Cynically inflected "life according to nature." According to Plutarch, Cato was training himself "to be ashamed only of shameful things,"[51] that is, not to regard indifferents (such as unconventional clothing) as "bad," but to reserve this label for the morally wrong. This seems to be a fair assessment; however, I rather doubt that, as Plutarch also maintains, "Cato was not pursuing notoriety through this unusual behavior."[52] I suspect that this is exactly what he was doing.

The famous anecdote about Cato at the Floralia of 55 (Val. Max. 2.10.8) illustrates both the extent to which the Catonian persona had become part of the popular perception (pop culture, as it were) and Cato's skill at playing his role, especially in the inherently spectacular context of the games. When the audience hesitated to call for the traditional striptease in the presence of stern

47. Compare L. P. E. Parker 2002: 103.

48. See, e.g., Fehrle 1983: 174 ("'Sonderlichkeit', die Cato bewußt kultiviert hatte"), Stein-Hölkeskamp 2000: 303 ("bewußte[] Stilisierung seiner Besonderheit"), and van der Blom 2012: 49 ("his flair for theatricality in public performances"). For a detailed examination of Cato's deliberate self-fashioning, see now Drogula 2019.

49. See Hor. *Epist.* 1.19.12–14; Val. Max. 3.6.7; Plut. *Cat. Min.* 6.3, 44.1, 50.1; Asc. *Scaur.* 29.7–11 Clark.

50. The idea that Cato was modeling his attire on statues of Romulus, Tatius, and Camillus is found in Asc. *Scaur.* 29.8–11 Clark and accepted by Drogula 2019: 29–31. The heat wave of 54 is well attested (Cic. *QFr.* 2.16.1; 3.1.1), but Cato is reported to have dressed down on other occasions as well.

51. Plut. *Cat. Min.* 6.3: ἐπὶ τοῖς αἰσχροῖς αἰσχύνεσθαι μόνοις.

52. Plut. *Cat. Min.* 6.3: οὐ δόξαν ἐκ ταύτης τῆς καινότητος θηρώμενος.

Cato, the latter diffused the embarrassing situation by making a grand exit from the theater—a performance that both solidified his virtuous image and demonstrated his gracious disposition toward the people. On that day, the audience was treated to not one but two great shows: "Cato" *and* the disrobing mime actresses.[53]

Of course, most of Cato's performances took place in the political arena, where his stubborn resistance to Pompey, Caesar, and their followers took spectacular forms that must soon have become predictable or even expected. Senators of the 50s knew that Cato, once he had put down the book that he insisted on bringing into the senate, was always good for a filibuster or for letting himself be dragged off to the *carcer*,[54] for proposing an outlandish anticorruption scheme or for bringing some outrageous motion, such as handing Caesar over to the Germans.[55] The predictability of Cato's political behavior—or, to put it Stoically, the constancy of the wise man—is nicely encapsulated in his famous speech against the convicted Catilinarians, as reported by Sallust (*Cat.* 52.7):

> saepenumero, patres conscripti, multa uerba in hoc ordine feci, saepe de luxuria atque auaritia nostrorum ciuium questus sum, multosque mortalis ea causa aduorsos habeo.

> Often, conscript fathers, have I spoken at length in the senate, often have I lamented the licentiousness and greed of our citizens, and for that reason I have many enemies among men.

---

53. Critics from Martial (*Pref.* 1) onward have pointed out that Cato must have known full well what was on the Floralia program. Perhaps he did not expect the people to consider his presence problematic (in the version of the story told by Valerius Maximus, his friend Favonius needs to point the popular reaction out to an unsuspecting Cato)—or did he in fact come to the theater specifically to put on his show of leaving again (thus Martial: *cur in theatrum, Cato seuere, uenisti? / an ideo tantum ueneras, ut exires?*)?

54. There are two separate incidents when his opponents reportedly had Cato marched off to prison but were forced to release him under popular pressure: a senatorial debate in 59, when Cato spoke against Caesar's agrarian law, and a *contio* in 55, when he opposed a law assigning the provinces Syria and Spain to the consuls Crassus and Pompey.

55. After Caesar had defeated the Usipetes and Tencteri in 55, the senate debated the granting of a *supplicatio* to the victorious general. Cato, however, considering this "victory" an unprovoked massacre that violated the Roman principle of just war, instead proposed handing Caesar over to the Germans and taking religious precautions against bringing the wrath of the gods against the Roman people as a whole (see Gelzer 1961 and Morrell 2015). It has been suggested that Cato was at least partly inspired by Stoic ideas of cosmopolitanism and natural law; see Gelzer 1963 [1934]: 265; Strasburger 1968: 25, 75; and Fehrle 1983: 178–79.

Though Sallust was presumably working from Cato's actual speech (on whose circulation, see above), it seems unlikely that the tribune elect would have uttered these words in 63, having at that point not had many opportunities to harangue the senate. The historian, who himself must have heard many of Cato's later performances, presumably added this sentence because it fit so well with his and his contemporaries' experience of the stubborn senator, who throughout his speeches would ring changes on the same theme of corruption and danger to the *res publica*, whether this made him popular or not.

Cato's most famous mise-en-scène was, of course, his suicide, an act that for us remains entangled in an endless cycle of art imitating life imitating art.[56] It seems clear that Cato took pains to style his death on that of Socrates, spending his last hours debating philosophical questions with friends and attempting (not always successfully) to evince a Socratic calm and steadfastness of purpose. In doing so, he himself followed a literary model, that of Plato's *Phaedo*, the work that Cato reportedly perused in his dying hours as though studying a script. As soon as the martyr of Utica had breathed his last, his own death became the object of competing literary and even visual representations,[57] and itself turned into a paradigm of philosophical suicide to be followed by such later Stoic dissidents as Seneca and Thrasea Paetus—and by the historians who described their deaths. Cato's reported annoyance with those trying to prevent his killing himself—it bears keeping in mind that, unlike, say, Socrates or later Seneca, he was under no duress and could presumably have obtained Caesar's pardon—can be read as resistance to any attempt to divert him from his chosen path, his decision to play his role to the end. When he finally obtained the sword with which to stab himself, he reportedly uttered the highly Stoic sentiment "Now I am my own."[58]

I have been arguing that both during his life and at his death, Cato was committed to "being Cato." To some extent, this was a typically Roman endeavor. Upperclass Roman men were highly aware of what they owed their personal *dignitas*, an ill-defined sense of worth and identity based on family traditions and connections, military and political positions and achievements, and individual character traits and beliefs. Thus, for example, we find Cicero, with his oversensitive self-awareness, worrying at length at various stages of

---

56. On the ancient versions of Cato's death, see Tandoi 1965, 1966. On the suicide's reception and crucial role in shaping Roman ideas of political and philosophical death, see Griffin 1986; Hill 2004: 6–7, 65–71, 186–87; Edwards 2007: 1–5, 113–160; and S. H. Rauh 2018.

57. According to App. *B Civ.* 2.101.420, at his quadruple triumph of 46 Caesar displayed a graphic image of Cato's suicide, a propagandistic strategy that backfired when the crowd expressed distress at this and other depictions of Caesar's defeated Roman enemies.

58. Plut. *Cat. Min.* 70.1: νῦν ἐμός εἰμι.

his life over what would be worthy of his own "Cicero-ness," as it were. When in 45, he is grieving over the death of his daughter Tullia in ways that his friends consider excessive, it is his friend Sulpicius Rufus who tries to jolt him out of this unbecoming behavior by exhorting him, "Do not forget that you are Cicero!"[59]

At the same time, in sticking so consistently to his chosen life script, Cato may well have been influenced specifically by Stoic persona theory.[60] Championed, among others, by Panaetius (2nd c. BCE), whose treatise *On Duties* was adapted by Cicero in his *De officiis* of 44, and later playing a central role in the work of Epictetus (1st/2nd c. CE), this ethical doctrine held that in determining right action, we need to keep in mind that we are, as it were, playing two roles (Gk. *prosōpa*, Lat. *personae*): that of human being and that of our own individual self.[61] We need to know—and to some extent decide—what our own persona is and then act in accordance with it. What is right for one individual is therefore not necessarily right for another, as Cicero explains, with reference to none other than Cato:[62]

> atque haec differentia naturarum tantam habet uim ut nonnumquam mortem sibi ipse consciscere alius debeat, alius in eadem causa non debeat. num enim alia in causa M. Cato fuit, alia ceteri qui se in Africa Caesari tradiderunt? atqui ceteris forsitan uitio datum esset si se interemissent, propterea quod lenior eorum uita et mores fuerant faciliores; Catoni cum incredibilem tribuisset natura grauitatem, eamque ipse perpetua constantia roborauisset semperque in proposito susceptoque consilio permansisset, moriendum potius quam tyranni uultus aspiciendus fuit.

> And this diversity of human nature is so important that sometimes one person ought to kill himself but another one in the same situation ought not. For was M. Cato in a different situation from all those who in Africa surrendered to Caesar? But the others would perhaps have been blamed had they killed themselves, for the reason that their lifestyles had been softer and their characters more easy-going. But since nature had endowed

59. Cic. *Fam.* 4.5.5: *noli te obliuisci Ciceronem esse.*

60. Compare Brunt 1975: 15, Rawson 1985: 95, Griffin 1986: 201 n. 14, Dyck 1996: 282 n. 160, and Edwards 2007: 148, 152.

61. Generally on Stoic *personae*, see Brunt 1975: 13–16 and Sorabji 2007: 141–46. The differences between the Panaetian/Ciceronian theory, which ultimately reckons with four *personae* (see De Lacy 1977, Gill 1988, and Lévy 2006), and that of Epictetus are of no concern here.

62. Cic. *Off.* 1.112. On this passage, see Gill 1988: 186–88, Dyck 1996 ad loc., Hill 2004: 66–71, Edwards 2007: 148, and S. H. Rauh 2018: 79. As Griffin and Atkins 1991: 44 n. 2 and Dyck 1996 ad loc. point out, it is likely that in providing this example, Cicero is uneasily reflecting on his own decision not to kill himself after his party's defeat. For Cicero's "survivor's guilt" post-Pharsalus, compare *Fam.* 4.13.2; 9.18.2.

Cato with incredible gravitas, which he himself had strengthened through perpetual consistency, and since he had always persisted in his purpose and the course he had once decided on, therefore it was right for him to die rather than look upon the face of the tyrant.

It is exactly because Cato is Cato that he is acting—in fact, according to his creed, must act—the way he is. There is no expectation, even on his part, that others will or should follow what he has determined to be the right course of action for himself. Thus, for example, when after the defeat of Pharsalus, Cicero and others decided not to join Cato in carrying on the war, Cato not only accepted their decision but calmed down Pompey's son, who was so enraged by this perceived act of treason that he wanted to kill one prominent defector, Cicero (Plut. *Cat. Min.* 55.3). Right before his death, Cato admonished his own son not to engage in politics "since the circumstances no longer allowed him to do so in a manner worthy of a Cato."[63] After Cato himself had played his role to the end, there would not be a repeat performance.

Epictetus compares the individual who has chosen a *persona* that stands out positively from those of his or her contemporaries with a purple thread that distinguishes itself from the monochrome uniformity of the rest of the fabric into which it is woven (*Discourses* 1.2.17–18). Whether Cato already knew this particular image or not, I suggest that this is exactly what he endeavored to be: an extraordinary person held to extraordinary standards, wholeheartedly committed to living up to his ideal of being Cato. I believe that his Stoicism was sincere and goes a long way toward explaining his sometimes bizarre political *modus operandi*. Of course, Cato's politics turned out to be singularly unsuccessful, though whether his inflexibility itself hastened the fall of the Republic and a different approach on his or other political actors' parts might have led to a different outcome is a moot question. What is clear is that it was exactly Cato's drawn-out defeat—from his quixotic fight against the likes of Caesar to his suicide—that turned him into a legendary character and handy *exemplum* for future generations.

Like his model Socrates, Cato never put pen to paper to explain his philosophical views, preferring to discuss them with his friends around the banquet table. Also not unlike Socrates, this first prominent Roman Stoic became a reference point and model for later adherents of the same philosophical creed. It is striking that the rise of Stoicism's popularity at Rome coincides with the establishment of an autocratic regime: the idea of the wise person's autonomy,

---

63. Plut. *Cat. Min.* 66.3: τὸ μὲν γὰρ ἀξίως Κάτωνος οὐκέτι τὰ πράγματα δέξασθαι (cf. Cass. Dio 43.10.5). Compare also the argument Cato allegedly made to Cicero in Pompey's camp in Greece, claiming that while it was appropriate for him to have joined forces with Pompey, this was not the case for Cicero, who should have remained neutral and in Italy (Plut. *Cic.* 38.1).

which is not subject to any external power, must have resonated in a political system where upperclass political freedom of action and expression was increasingly curtailed. Of course, only a small number of Imperial Stoics were members of an active opposition, but even to those who were not, their doctrine held out the promise of perfect control over their own rational lives, no matter what outer limits or pressures they were experiencing. And for those who—like Seneca and Thrasea Paetus—did lose their lives as a result of real or perceived resistance to the regime, Cato's Stoic death provided inspiration and legitimation. Once the Republic had irrevocably come to an end, elite Romans no longer strove to assert their political autonomy or restore a system of government that had become unviable. What they needed was an assurance not that the Caesars could be stopped—they couldn't—but that they themselves would be able to live and die morally even, as Seneca put it, "against the will of Fortune."[64] It was Cato who provided that assurance.[65] While to some extent our idealized image of Cato was shaped by his Imperial admirers, the behavior and decisions of this "perfect Stoic" themselves crucially shaped the direction Roman Stoicism was to take. Already during his lifetime, Cato was busily writing the Cato legend, and with it an important chapter in the history of philosophy at Rome.

2. Cicero and the Political Imperative

In late 51/early 50, Cicero wrote to Cato to persuade him to join a senatorial vote in favor of awarding Cicero a *supplicatio* for his military exploits in Cilicia, appealing to his fellow senator by invoking their *societas studiorum* and especially their shared commitment to philosophy.[66] He and Cato, so Cicero maintained, had more or less single-handedly injected philosophy into Roman politics (*Fam.* 15.4.16):

> soli prope modum nos philosophiam ueram illam et antiquam, quae quibusdam oti esse ac desidiae uidetur, in forum atque in rem publicam atque in ipsam aciem paene deduximus.

> The two of us practically on our own have brought that true and ancient philosophy, which to some people seems to be a pursuit for leisure and idleness, into the forum and the *res publica* and even nearly onto the battlefield itself.

64. Cf. once again Sen. *Ep.* 104.29.
65. Cf. Griffin 1989: 10–11.
66. Cic. *Fam.* 15.4. Cicero's appeal to personified *Philosophia* and *societas studiorum atque artium nostrarum* occurs at 15.4.16; compare 2.3 above.

Cato, unfortunately, was unimpressed: he did not support the motion, and in his brief reply (*Fam.* 15.5) enumerated his own arguments why a public thanksgiving was not warranted, without responding to Cicero's flowery appeal to their supposed joint intellectual project.

As we have seen in the previous section, it is hard to know what Cato thought he was doing (and whether he believed it bore any resemblance to Cicero's endeavors); any intentions on his part need to be reconstructed from his actions and his contemporaries' reactions. By contrast, this snatch from a personal letter is only one of dozens of statements, made over a lifetime in a wide variety of genres and contexts, in which Cicero offers an interpretation of his own application of philosophy to politics. While his views and their expressions shifted in keeping with political and private circumstances, the gist of Cicero's proud statement to Cato is probably something he would have subscribed to at all times of his life: bringing philosophy into the *res publica* was at the heart of the self-conception and self-fashioning of this most-documented man of our period.

As a politician, Cicero was both singularly successful and woefully on "the wrong side of history." Despite being a *homo nouus*, he breezed through the *cursus honorum*, which culminated in his consulship of 63 and the successful suppression of the Catilinarian conspiracy. This proudest moment, however, led to his exile in 58–57, and the First Triumvirate and changed political scene of the 50s meant that he never recovered the influence that he felt was his due. After reluctantly following Pompey in the Civil War and subsequently receiving Caesar's pardon, Cicero spent the years of the dictatorship largely dedicated to his studies and the writing of his philosophical corpus. Reentering the political fray after the Ides of March, he attempted to curb the rising power of Antony but badly miscalculated in supporting Caesar's young heir Octavian. When in 43 Octavian joined Antony and Lepidus in the Second Triumvirate, Cicero was immediately proscribed and assassinated. Infamously, his severed head and hand were publicly exhibited on the rostra in the Roman forum.

Of course, the significance of Cicero is not to be measured by his political career alone. Already during his lifetime, he was considered Rome's leading orator and famous for his verbal mastery. Cicero was a prolific writer, producing a vast corpus of speeches, poetry, philosophy, rhetorical works, and personal letters, moving at the forefront of his period's intellectual developments and crucially shaping the course of western literature and thought. Still, despite ancient and modern attempts to do so, Cicero the eloquent writer and "intellectual" cannot be separated from Cicero the doomed politician. Political engagement and the belief in the traditional Republican form of senate-directed government were central to Cicero's life and work from beginning to end. He was a profoundly political animal, who not only made a career in the political arena but also continually reflected on politics and his own role as a political actor. In doing so, Cicero was deeply influenced by his second and related great interest: philosophy.[67]

In the preface to *De natura deorum* (45 BCE), Cicero affirms his lifelong commitment to philosophy (1.6–7):

> nos autem nec subito coepimus philosophari nec mediocrem a primo tem-
> pore aetatis in eo studio operam curamque consumpsimus et, cum minime
> uidebamur, tum maxime philosophabamur; quod et orationes declarant
> refertae philosophorum sententiis et doctissimorum hominum familiari-
> tates, quibus semper domus nostra floruit, et principes illi Diodotus Philo
> Antiochus Posidonius, a quibus instituti sumus. et si omnia philosophiae
> praecepta referuntur ad uitam, arbitramur nos et publicis et priuatis in
> rebus ea praestitisse quae ratio et doctrina praescripserit.

> But I didn't just suddenly begin to philosophize nor did I spend only a little
> bit of time and effort on this pursuit of mine from the very beginning of my
> life: when I seemed to do so the least, then I was philosophizing the most.
> My speeches confirm this, stuffed as they are with the opinions of philoso-
> phers, and my friendship with most learned men, who always graced my
> home, and especially Diodotus, Philo, Antiochus, and Posidonius, who
> were my teachers. And if indeed all philosophical precepts apply to life,
> then I think that in both public and private affairs I have lived up to what
> reason and teaching prescribed.

Philosophy, for Cicero, has been a serious pursuit that has lasted a lifetime; it has colored his doings, including his oratory, throughout, even if this has not always been readily apparent; it has involved serious study and personal friendships with leading Greek philosophers; and it has informed and guaranteed the ethics of Cicero's behavior as a person and a politician. This is a strong statement but one that Cicero keeps repeating in various shapes and forms throughout his oeuvre. As he states in *De legibus*, philosophy "made me who I am."[68]

As Cicero mentions in the passage from *De natura deorum* just quoted, he studied with a number of Greek thinkers from a variety of philosophical schools.[69] Most influential among these was his first teacher, the Academic

---

67. The interconnections and mutual reinforcement of Cicero's philosophical thought and political engagement are increasingly being recognized and explored in scholarship; see esp. the recent discussions of Gildenhard 2007, 2011; Baraz 2012; McConnell 2014; and Zarecki 2014.

68. *Leg.* 1.63: *quaeque* [sc. *philosophia*] *me eum quicumque sum effecit.*

69. On Cicero's teachers and studies, see Treggiari 2015: 241–45.

Skeptic Philo of Larissa, who came to Rome in 88 BCE, fleeing the Mithridatic Wars. After Philo's death in 84/83, Cicero continued his studies with the Stoic Diodotus, who subsequently became his house guest and stayed with Cicero until his death in about 60. When in 79–77 Cicero traveled to Greece to restore his failing health and work on a way of delivering his speeches that would not ruin his voice, he attended lectures in Athens by the "Old" Academic Antiochus of Ascalon as well as by the Epicureans Phaedrus and Zeno; on Rhodes, he met with the Stoic Posidonius.

Cicero thus received personal instruction from representatives of all leading schools except for the Peripatos, and in addition read widely across the philosophical board (a process we can partly follow through his letters with Atticus, on whom Cicero often calls for copies of individual books). His own declared allegiance was to the Skeptic "New" Academy in the probabilist variant of his teacher Philo:[70] the Skeptic will consider all approaches to a philosophical question, typically by marshaling the arguments for all in the procedure known as *disputare in utramque partem* ("arguing in each direction"), but will suspend judgment as to the veracity of any position, believing truth to be unattainable; nevertheless, he may still espouse any position as his own on the ground that it is "probable" (Gk. *pithanon*, Lat. *probabile*) or "similar to the truth" (Lat. *uerisimile*). Cicero himself discusses the Skeptic approach in his *Academica* (unfortunately surviving only in parts) and employs variations of it in many of his philosophical dialogues, where different characters argue different positions and critique those of their interlocutors.[71]

Academic Skepticism appealed to Cicero for a number of reasons: its Platonic pedigree (the New Academics saw themselves as upholding Plato's true

70. On Philo, see Brittain 2001. Philo's exact epistemology and its development over time are controversial; the matter cannot be discussed here. Doubts have been raised as to whether Cicero remained committed to Academic Skepticism throughout his life or instead went through a dogmatic, Antiochean phase in the 50s; see esp. Glucker 1988 and cf. Steinmetz 1989, 1995 (see also Long 1995a for the idea that Cicero was, as it were, "both a Philonian and an Antiochean Academic at the same time," 41). This view now seems to have largely been laid to rest, thanks esp. to the rebuttal of Görler 1995. For different views of Cicero's Skepticism, see Lévy 1992, 2017; Gawlik and Görler 1994: 1084–1125; Görler 1997; Leonhardt 1999; Brittain 2006; Thorsrud 2009: 84–101; Woolf 2015; Nicgorski 2016; Cappello 2019; and Wynne 2018, 2019. This list makes no claim to completeness. See further 6.4 below.

71. Cf. Süß 1952, Leonhardt 1999: 13–88, and Schofield 2008. Among the fully extant dialogues, *Lucullus*, *De finibus*, *De natura deorum*, and *De diuinatione* follow this principle. Note also the competing speeches of Philus and Laelius on justice in *De re publica* 3, staged explicitly as a reenactment of the most (in)famous instance of Academic *disputare in utramque partem*, Carneades's speeches pro and contra justice in 155 BCE.

method as seen in the early, Socratic dialogues); its affinity to and employment of rhetoric, especially in debates *in utramque partem*; and, more than anything, the intellectual independence that came with the Skeptic refusal of any un-examined dogma, coupled with the freedom to choose any position found plausible, without regard to school affiliation.[72] Throughout his life, we see Cicero probing, doubting, arguing with himself and others, and changing his mind on more than one occasion. In his letters, his speeches, and his treatises, we find him withholding judgment on some issues, and on others espousing positions that range from the idiosyncratically Ciceronian to the bona fide Stoic, Platonic, or Antiochean. All of this is exactly what we would expect from a "soft"—that is, probabilist—Academic Skeptic. Skepticism does not prevent Cicero from holding a view, or from selecting positive aspects of a variety of philosophies; it does, however, prevent him from accepting any doctrine sight unseen or merely because it comes as part and parcel of a particular philo-sophical system.

Cicero, of course, stands out from most other philosophically interested late Republican Romans for not just espousing philosophical teachings for application to the conduct of his own life, but in addition producing a signifi-cant corpus of philosophical works himself. Cicero's declared reasons for writ-ing philosophy are many and range from introducing his fellow Romans to Greek thought and creating a body of Latin philosophy, to providing comfort and distraction to the author in times of personal and public hardship, to con-tinuing Cicero's politics by other means (see 4.3 below). Long considered derivative and mere expositions of Greek ideas, Cicero's *philosophica* have in re-cent years been rehabilitated and started to be taken seriously as philosophy.[73] In keeping with the purpose of this book, I will not in this and other Cicero-centered sections attempt to offer in-depth interpretations of Cicero's individual philo-sophical works (let alone engage with the copious scholarly literature on each); instead, my focus is on the intersections of the author's written oeuvre, his declared philosophical beliefs, and his social and political actions.

This approach, which aims at a holistic view of Cicero's thoughts and deeds, obviously runs the risk of ignoring or downplaying real differences among the

---

72. See esp. *Tusc.* 5.33, where the Ciceronian speaker rejects his interlocutor's attempt to hold him to an opinion expressed in the earlier *De finibus: cum aliis isto modo, qui legibus impositis disputant: nos in diem uiuimus; quodcumque nostros animos probabilitate percussit, id dicimus, itaque soli sumus liberi* ("You can do this with other people, who argue according to fixed laws. I live from day to day: whatever strikes my mind as probable, that I proclaim, and thus I alone am free").

73. See now esp. Woolf 2015, the first comprehensive monograph on Cicero as a philosopher.

various spheres of Cicero's life and speech. What the author says in a philosophical treatise need not agree with what he says in a speech or a letter, let
alone with how he behaved in real life. Ever the master orator, Cicero was
highly adept at fitting his words to his addressees and circumstances, and it
would be a mistake to accept everything he says at face value, let alone assume
that he never changed his mind. While the reader thus always needs to keep
in mind the specificity of each Ciceronian (speech) act, I believe that it is
nevertheless possible to gain a coherent view of Cicero across his many works
and genres, for the very reason that the author himself throughout his life appears to be focused on telling his own story.[74] Since antiquity, Cicero has
been accused of being self-centered and self-promoting, and indeed a fair part
of his oeuvre is concerned with projecting an image of the author. Cicero
clearly did not think of the various aspects of his personality (the orator, the
statesman, the philosopher) as essentially distinct but, in a sustained effort at
self-fashioning, tried to fuse them into a superior type of public figure, whose
triumphs and tribulations he chronicles in his writings. It is thus possible, indeed desirable, to "read Cicero" (in the phrase of Catherine Steel) across his
genres and areas of activity.[75] Of course, what we end up with this way is
Cicero's own version of Cicero (just as there is the larger danger, owing to the
imbalance of our sources, of our entire view of late Republican Rome turning
out to be fundamentally Ciceronian). We can attempt to modify this image to
some extent by recourse to other information; at the end of the day, however,
what primarily interests me as an intellectual historian is precisely what Cicero
himself thought (or said he thought) he was doing. While this section focuses
on general aspects of Cicero's philosophically engaged politics—or politically
engaged philosophy—and on the period through the end of the Civil War,
Cicero's life and work in the changed situation under Caesar's sole rule will
play a central role in chapter 4.

For all his philosophical training, interests, and commitments, Cicero at
many points in his life and work professed a profound ambivalence about the
role of philosophy in his own life and that of his Roman upperclass peers. As
discussed in 2.1, such statements have often been taken as evidence for a general Roman hostility to philosophy and other intellectual pursuits: a politically
active man like Cicero thus felt the need to justify why he was spending time
reading or even writing philosophy. However, it seems to me that the conflict

74. Compare Gildenhard 2011: 20 on Cicero's construction of his own self: "Taken together,
his self-portrayals amount to nothing less than a political autobiography of sorts, which tells the
fetching story of one of the last heroes of the free republic."

75. See Steel 2005; on Ciceronian self-fashioning and self-mythologizing, see further Dugan
2005, Kurczyk 2006, Scheidegger Lämmle 2016: 75–109, and Bishop 2019.

is instead a specifically Ciceronian one. Cicero viewed himself as first and foremost a politically active citizen, an outlook that accorded with his public role but one that was also philosophically informed. Following Peripatetic and Stoic views of man's natural sociability, Cicero throughout his philosophical work stressed that human beings can flourish only in communities and that political engagement represents the perfection of their rational nature.[76]

This political imperative is developed at greatest length in the preface to the first book of *De re publica*, Cicero's great, if unfortunately now fragmentary, exposition of his political philosophy. There, the author argues against philosophers who believe that the wise man should not engage in politics, or do so only in a crisis. His target appears to be, first and foremost, the Epicureans, who counsel a retreat from politics as an activity nonconducive to the pleasurable freedom from disturbance that is their ethical goal. More generally, Cicero's arguments are directed against any philosophical stance that values the contemplative over the active life. Virtue, he maintains, manifests itself only in action, and the highest form of virtuous action is political governance.[77] Even political theory as practiced by philosophers is inferior to the political know-how of lawgivers and statesmen (*Rep.* 1.2–3), and the idea that the wise man could emerge from his ivory tower at a time of political crisis and take over (as the Epicureans envisage) is perfectly ludicrous (1.10–11).

In the *Dream of Scipio*, the eschatological vision that concludes *De re publica*, Cicero reaffirms his belief in politics as man's highest calling, incorporating it into a grand cosmological scheme, whereby virtuous statesmen, such as the father and grandfather of the dialogue's main protagonist Scipio Africanus, are granted a blessed afterlife among the stars, in the Milky Way. As the elder Africanus explains to his grandson (*Rep.* 6.13):

> omnibus qui patriam conseruauerint adiuuerint auxerint certum esse in caelo definitum locum, ubi beati aeuo sempiterno fruantur. nihil est enim illi principi deo, qui omnem mundum regit, quod quidem in terris fiat, acceptius quam concilia coetusque hominum iure sociati, quae ciuitates appellantur; harum rectores et conseruatores hinc profecti huc reuertuntur.

For all men who have preserved, aided, and increased the fatherland there is a certain place reserved in heaven, where, blessed, they enjoy eternal life. For to that ruler god who governs the whole world, there is nothing more

---

76. That citizens ought to engage in politics was, as Brown 2009 shows, the "dominant ideology" of ancient Greece and Rome. Cicero's attitude is thus wholly in keeping with his society's traditional values, but unusually theoretically informed and self-aware.

77. *Rep.* 1.2: *uirtus in usu sui tota posita est; usus autem eius est maximus ciuitatis gubernatio.*

pleasing (at least among things on earth) than the gatherings and communities of men joined in law, which are called commonwealths. Their rulers and preservers return from there to this place.

It is politicians who go to heaven, not philosophers.

Why is Cicero harping like this on the primacy of politics? It is not an inappropriate argument to make in a treatise devoted to government but it is also not a necessary component of such a work.[78] Did Cicero feel the need, in the mid- to late 50s, to exhort his fellow Romans to political engagement?[79] Was he perhaps concerned specifically about the rise of Epicureanism, deeming it a threat to the social fabric?[80] While it is certainly true that the hedonism and political quietism of the Epicureans was a constant philosophical red flag for Cicero, it is hardly the case that the occasional espousal of Epicurean ideas among upperclass Romans led to a thinning of the political ranks. Instead, in *De re publica*, as elsewhere, Cicero seems to be concerned at least to some extent with his own political and philosophical choices.[81] After all, unlike most of his fellow senators, the *homo nouus* from the *municipia* did have to make a conscious decision to enter politics.

As a highly educated equestrian with a passion for philosophy, Cicero could, one assumes, have opted against a political career—something that would have been very difficult for the sons of established senatorial families.[82]

---

78. Cicero himself justifies his lengthy discussion as follows: *haec pluribus a me uerbis dicta sunt ob eam causam, quod his libris erat instituta et suscepta mihi de re publica disputatio; quae ne frustra haberetur, dubitationem ad rem publicam adeundi in primis debui tollere* ("I have talked about this at greater length for the following reason: in these books, I intend to discuss the commonwealth, and in order for this not to be considered pointless, I first needed to remove any hesitation about entering politics," 1.12).

79. For the view of *De re publica* as a protreptic to politics, see Zetzel 1998 and Blößner 2001.

80. See esp. Maslowski 1974, Andreoni 1979, and Englert 2014 (the first two see Cicero as responding in particular to Lucretius's *De rerum natura*, as does—from a more literary perspective—Zetzel 1998, followed by Gatzemeier 2013: 31–41; see also Fontaine 1966 and Lévi 2014: 117–21 specifically on anti-Lucretian polemic in the *Somnium*). On the popularity of Epicureanism in the late Republic and the issue of Epicurean political disengagement, see 3.3 below. Generally on Cicero's attitudes to Epicureanism, see first and foremost Gilbert 2015, as well as Maslowski 1974; Erler 1992; Lévy 2001 (with the response of Ferrary 2001), 2020; Hanchey 2013; and Maso 2015.

81. Generally on the various permutations of Cicero's choice of the active over the contemplative life, see Kretschmar 1938, André 1966: 279–334, Görler 1990, Perelli 1990: 3–15, and Lévy 2012b.

82. As Cicero says himself in *Rep.* 1.7, his excellent education meant that he could have profited more than others from the leisurely pursuit of his studies. He also mentions that the

Of course, there probably were family pressure and expectations for both Cicero brothers to enter the *cursus honorum*, as indeed both Marcus and Quintus did. At the same time, there were models for an alternative way of life: Cicero's own father, suffering from poor health, had lived a life dedicated to his studies in Arpinum, and his best friend Atticus, a highly talented person with similar interests, had consciously chosen not to pursue politics, very likely influenced by his Epicurean beliefs.[83]

Even given his original decision for a political career, by the mid-50s Cicero could very well have opted to retreat from politics and dedicate himself to his studies. He was over fifty years old, had suffered the hardships of exile, and was politically sidelined owing to the First Triumvirate. Nevertheless, by what one assumes was both inclination and conviction, Cicero stuck to his political imperative. As he explains in the preface to the first book of *De oratore*, written in the same period, the very fact that the political situation does not allow him an *otium cum dignitate* ("leisure with dignity," *De or.* 1.1) means that he cannot opt for *otium* at all but must remain politically involved. Similarly, in the preface to *De re publica*, he uses his own tempestuous career as proof—not that the tribulations of politics are better avoided, but that even greater sufferings than those experienced by himself must be risked for the sake of serving the common good (*Rep.* 1.6–8). As the history of the following decade shows, Cicero remained true to this conviction, ultimately paying for it with his life.

Where does this declared primacy of politics leave philosophy? Cicero grappled with this question throughout his life, coming up with different answers at different times. To some extent, philosophy and *studia* in general simply remained a beloved leisure-time activity for those private moments free from politics. Thus, Cicero has the Muse Urania declare to his character in *De consulatu suo*, the celebratory epic about his own consulship, written in 60 BCE:[84]

---

elder Cato, being "an unknown and new man" (*homini ignoto et nouo*), could easily have chosen to enjoy a life of leisure rather than being so "crazy" (*demens*) as to enter politics (1.1). On the choice of some equestrians not to seek entry into the senate (and a very few cases of men from senatorial families who decided to "drop down" into the equestrian order), see Nicolet 1966–74: 699–722.

83. See 2.1 with n. 32. On Atticus's Epicureanism and rejection of a political career, see 3.3 below. In a number of letters, Cicero discusses the choice between the active and the contemplative life with Atticus, often with reference to the Peripatetic Dicaearchus, who argued in favor of the former: *Att.* 1.17.5; 2.16.3; 7.3.1; 14.20.5. Compare McConnell 2014: 115–60.

84. Fr. 2.77–78 Soubiran. In line 77, I read Davies's *patria* and Madvig's *uacat, id* for the manuscripts' *patriae uocatis.* See further Volk 2013: 105 n. 45. For the same sentiment, see *Off.* 2.4.

tu tamen anxiferas curas requiete relaxans,
quod patria uacat, id studiis nobisque sacrasti.

Soothing your anxious cares in leisure, you have dedicated to your studies
and to us [sc. the Muses] that which is not taken up by the fatherland.

Once Cicero's leisure turned from the desired private time interspersed in
public duty to the enforced *otium* under Caesar, however, philosophy and
other studies were transformed from pastimes into major occupations, providing not only distraction but a refuge and comfort in trying times. As Cicero
himself makes clear, it was the change in political situation and his own status
that enabled and inspired the composition of his philosophical corpus of
46–44.[85] Nevertheless, despite such occasional representations (and, one
assumes, experiences) of philosophy as either a relaxation or a refuge from
politics, Cicero—as we have seen in the quotations at the beginning of this
section—ultimately always sought to combine the two. If philosophy is the art
of life, and if Cicero's life was by definition a political one, then philosophy had
to be made applicable to politics and politics informed by philosophy, both in
theory and in practice. Effecting this kind of mutual reinforcement was one of
Cicero's lifelong projects.

This chapter cannot attempt to analyze Cicero's political philosophy and
philosophical politics in detail, but will instead focus on a few central aspects.[86]
One major concern, in evidence in particular in Cicero's two great works of
the 50s, *De oratore* (55) and *De re publica* (51), is the question of how Greek
learning can be made applicable in a Roman context.[87] As we have seen in 2.1
above, philosophy and other fields of study were represented by Greek teachers, learned individuals of whose expertise Roman aristocrats might avail
themselves, but whose professionalism and theoretical approach they had no
desire to emulate. In his dialogues about the perfect orator and the perfect
statesman (and, of course, these two are ultimately the same person), Cicero
sketches out his new ideal of a man who is steeped in Greek learning while
remaining profoundly Roman in his proudly traditional, practical, public-
spirited outlook. Leaving behind the Greek schoolroom, where she was the

85. For Cicero's attitudes to and uses of philosophy in the 40s, see 4.3.

86. Generally on Cicero's political philosophy, see Wood 1988, Perelli 1990, E. M. Atkins
2000, J. W. Atkins 2013, Zetzel 2013, Woolf 2015: 93–124, and Straumann 2016; for his philosophical politics, see the literature cited in n. 67 above.

87. See Zetzel forthcoming. The date of *De legibus*, apparently never finished or published,
is unclear. Conceived as a sequel to *De re publica*, it is often placed in the late 50s but could have
been written (partly?) in the 40s as well.

butt of mild ridicule, philosophy steps onto the Roman public stage, where she is bound to be taken seriously.

Cicero does not bluntly put forward his project of Romanizing Greek theory and Hellenizing Roman practice, but subtly refracts it through his dialogues' settings and interlocutors. *De oratore, De re publica,* and *De legibus* are self-consciously Platonic, with the participants fully aware that they are enacting Roman versions of the *Phaedrus, Gorgias, Republic,* and *Laws.* The simultaneous closeness to and distance from the Greek models are playfully foregrounded, and the questions of Greek versus Roman and theory versus practice are discussed in multiple transformations by the interlocutors themselves, many of whom have ambivalent attitudes or appear to change their minds. The historical settings of *De re publica* (129 BCE) and *De oratore* (91) allow Cicero to present his protagonists as potential precursors of his own cultural ideal while freeing him from having to maintain that those men of the hallowed past really had the same kind of sophistication Cicero is demanding of himself and his contemporaries.[88] Crassus and his fellow grand old orators, and Scipio and his circle of friends, are important *exempla* of the blending of Greek learning and Roman talent and morals, but they are "not quite there yet"—for which they cannot be faulted, having lived when they did. The implication is that the perfect orator and statesman is still to come, and it is fairly clear that Cicero views himself as the last link in the intellectual genealogies he has created. Of course, Cicero cannot very well say so directly, either in his own voice or in that of his long-dead historical interlocutors. This does not stop him from having contemporary characters, in other dialogues, hint—in the most urbane manner—that there might just be a person among those present who fits the description of, say, "the man who is the leader both in learned studies and in the ruling of the state."[89]

The boldest assimilation of Greek thought to Roman reality occurs in *De re publica,* where spirited Roman aristocrats play out a Platonic dialogue (as well as, in book 3, a Carneadean debate), adapting it to their own purposes while freely criticizing the shortcomings of the original.[90] In the course of the

88. For the construction of settings and interlocutors in Ciceronian dialogue, see Becker 1938; Zetzel 1995: 3–13 (on *Rep.*), forthcoming (on *De or.* and *Rep.*); Gildenhard 2013; Steel 2013; and Hanchey 2014–15.

89. *Leg.* 3.14: *et doctrinae studiis et regenda ciuitate princeps.* It is Atticus who says he believes that such a man exists and that he is one of the three present (*aliquem de tribus nobis*), i.e., Atticus, Quintus, and Cicero himself. Cicero constructs a similar teleology in the *Brutus* (46 BCE), his history of Roman oratory, which—it is implied—culminates in none other than himself. For further discussion of the *Brutus,* see 2.3, 4.2, and 5.3.

90. Criticism of Plato's *Republic*: *Rep.* 2.21–22, 51; 4.4–5 Ziegler.

work it is demonstrated that what political theory has determined to be the best kind of res publica is exactly the mixed constitution that obtains in the Roman Republic (book 1); that it was not one solitary thinker and lawgiver but instead the practical trial and error of numerous politically active individuals through history that perfected the Roman commonwealth (book 2; see further 5.2 below); and that a well-ordered res publica like Rome is fully in accordance with natural law (book 3). The individual polity of Rome is part of the cosmopolis; service to the fatherland is divinely ordained; and great statesmen find their eternal reward in a starry afterlife (book 6).

Books 5 and 6 of De re publica, which are unfortunately nearly entirely lost, treated a topic that was especially important to Cicero: the qualities of the perfect statesman. The meager fragments that survive have occasioned much controversy, with some scholars believing that the figure Cicero refers to as rector, conservator, moderator, gubernator, tutor, or procurator of the res publica or ciuitas is meant to be a person who takes on an extraordinary leadership role that transcends the mixed constitution of the Republic, perhaps even prefiguring the Augustan princeps. It is now largely agreed, however, that Cicero simply lays out his view of the ideal politician, a man who with his superior knowledge and experience serves the commonwealth and, in a time of crisis, has the wherewithal, not to concentrate unwonted power in his own hand, but to restore the political system to order.[91] This is the role envisaged for Scipio when his grandfather tells him in his dream that he will be appointed to the extraordinary office of dictator in order to "restore the Republic" imperiled by the doings of the Gracchi[92]—something that never happened, owing to Scipio's death. It is no doubt also the role that Cicero thought he himself had played in 63, saving the Republic from the clutches of Catiline.

What the rector has at heart throughout is the welfare of the citizens;[93] his opposite is the tyrant (2.51). Fully in keeping with Cicero's cultural program, the perfect statesman is profoundly learned, including in Greek literature and the civil law, yet does not pursue knowledge for its own sake but in order to enable him to administer the commonwealth.[94] Apparently, Cicero saw his rector as additionally playing an educational role, instilling in the populace a sense of shame that would lead to moral behavior (Rep. 5.6 Ziegler). However, our fragments are too scanty to give us a good sense of how the statesman was supposed to go about this.

91. Thus already the classic article of Heinze 1924, arguing against R. Reitzenstein and E. Meyer. For a brief historia quaestionis, with further references, see Zarecki 2014: 9–11.

92. Rep. 6.12: dictator rem publicam constituas oportet.

93. Rep. 5.5, 8 Ziegler.

94. Rep. 5.2, 5 Ziegler.

Being in the unique position of combining political expertise (including as the holder of the highest office available in the Republican system) and philosophical knowledge,[95] Cicero thus formulated in *De re publica* a political philosophy that was itself predicated exactly on the hybridization of Roman practice with Greek theory, a combination of which he himself, he believed, was the best example. But how did this political ideal play out in real life? Did Cicero consciously apply his philosophy to his politics? And how did he fare—in terms of both external behavior and internal experience—in doing so? Since we cannot look into Cicero's head, we can answer these questions only partially. However, we do have a unique source for this particular Roman's decision-making processes and mental states in his extensive corpus of letters, a set of texts that is increasingly being mined as a source for Cicero's theoretical and practical philosophy.

Cicero's letters, especially those to Atticus and a number of other friends, are saturated with philosophy.[96] Philosophical badinage—to use Miriam Griffin's term[97]—is part of a shared language of men joined in *societas studiorum*, who delight in in-jokes, clever allusions, and gentle ribbing of one another's philosophical convictions. Occasionally such urbane displays develop into more serious philosophical arguments, sometimes carried on over an extended correspondence.[98] Atticus in particular also serves as a sounding board for the development of Cicero's own politico-philosophical attitudes: we can often follow the letter writer's process of decision-making (and, not infrequently, unmaking) through his missives to his best friend. No doubt the very act of corresponding with an equally learned and sophisticated addressee was itself an important part of Cicero's philosophical formation.

In the period under discussion here, Cicero had to make some difficult, if not impossible, choices. In the 50s, he needed to chart his own course in relation to both the members of the First Triumvirate and the optimate opposition, as well as to cope with the disaster of his exile and its aftermath. After the outbreak of the Civil War, it quickly came down to choosing sides, once

95. As Wood 1988: 176 points out, "Cicero is the only important political thinker who devoted a life to politics and attained the highest governmental office." Cf. Cic. *Rep.* 1.13.

96. On philosophy in Cicero's correspondence, including many of the letters discussed below, see Boyancé 1936: 302–4; Michel 1977; Brunt 1986; Boes 1990; Griffin 1995, 1997a; Leonhardt 1995; Guillaumont 2002; Gildenhard 2006; Baraz 2012: 44–95; Aubert-Baillot 2014, 2018; McConnell 2014; Gilbert 2015; and Cappello 2019: 11–81.

97. See the pioneering article of Griffin 1995.

98. See, e.g., *Fam.* 15.16–19, a sequence of letters to and from Cassius; cf. the discussion in Gilbert 2015: 163–283 and 3.3 below.

attempts to negotiate peace between Pompey and Caesar had proved elusive. In the letters where we see Cicero striving to make up his mind, he is often employing one of two philosophical techniques: on some occasions, we find him debating different options in the best New Academic manner,[99] while on others, he is attempting to adjust his own actions to what he has determined to be the virtuous course. In those latter cases, Cicero not infrequently measures himself against the ideal statesman as defined in his own *De re publica*.

An early example of Academic self-debate occurs in *Att.* 2.3, written in late 60 BCE. Cicero faced the dilemma of how to react to the agrarian law that the incoming consul Caesar was about to propose. The tone in which he lays out his quandary to Atticus is witty and urbane, but the matter, as he points out, is serious (*Att.* 2.3.3):

> uenio nunc ad mensem Ianuarium et ad ὑπόστασιν nostram ac πολιτείαν, in qua Σωκρατικῶς εἰς ἑκάτερον, sed tamen ad extremum, ut illi solebant, τὴν ἀρέσκουσαν. est res sane magni consili.

> I now come to the month of January and to my political position, concerning which I shall debate in both directions, in the Socratic manner, but to the very end, as they used to do, that is, [to the determination of] my preference. For it is a matter of great importance.

As it turns out, there are not just two, but three options (ibid.):

> nam aut fortiter resistendum est legi agrariae, in quo est quaedam dimicatio sed plena laudis, aut quiescendum, quod est non dissimile atque ire in Solonium aut Antium, aut etiam adiuuandum, quod a me aiunt Caesarem sic exspectare ut non dubitet. nam fuit apud me Cornelius, hunc dico Balbum, Caesaris familiarem. is adfirmabat illum omnibus in rebus meo et Pompei consilio usurum daturumque operam ut cum Pompeio Crassum coniungeret.

> For I must (i) vehemently resist the agrarian law, which means a struggle but a glorious one, or (ii) keep quiet, which basically means retiring to Solonium or Antium, or (iii) support it, which they say Caesar expects from me without even entertaining a doubt. For Cornelius, I mean Caesar's friend Balbus, came to me and assured me that Caesar would make use of my and Pompey's advice in all matters and would try to bring Pompey and Crassus together.

99. On this technique, see Aubert-Baillot 2014, 2018.

Tacitly discarding the second possibility (doing nothing), Cicero quickly boils down the two remaining courses (either supporting or opposing the law) to a choice between the advantageous and the morally right (4):

> hic sunt haec: coniunctio mihi summa cum Pompeio, si placet, etiam cum Caesare, reditus in gratiam cum inimicis, pax cum multitudine, senectutis otium. sed me κατακλεὶς mea illa commovet quae est in libro tertio:
>
>> interea cursus, quos prima a parte iuuentae
>> quosque adeo consul uirtute animoque petisti,
>> hos retine atque auge famam laudesque bonorum.
>
> haec mihi cum in eo libro in quo multa sunt scripta ἀριστοκρατικῶς Calliope ipsa praescripserit, non opinor esse dubitandum quin semper nobis uideatur εἷς οἰωνὸς ἄριστος ἀμύνεσθαι περὶ πάτρης. sed haec ambulationibus compitaliciis reseruemus.

This would mean: intimate association with Pompey, and even with Caesar, if I want; restored relations with my enemies; peace with the people; and an old age in leisure. But that conclusion of the third book [of *De consulatu suo*] gives me pause: "Meanwhile, stick to the course which you have sought with virtuous mind since your early youth and even now as consul, and increase the fame and praise of the good men." Since Calliope herself gave me this advice in a book in which there are many aristocratic sentiments, I don't think I can hesitate to remain true to the maxim "one omen is best: to defend the fatherland." But let's come back to this topic during our strolls on the Compitalia.

Supporting Caesar's legislation would guarantee Cicero an advantageous position vis-à-vis the nascent First Triumvirate.[100] On the other hand, it would be morally wrong, and not in agreement with Cicero's previous political stance and actions.

In keeping with the playful tone of the letter,[101] Cicero voices his moral concerns indirectly, through quotations from two epic poems, Cicero's own *De consulatu suo* (fr. 8 Soubiran) and Homer's *Iliad* (12.243)—a juxtaposition

---

100. As Shackleton Bailey 1965–70 ad loc. points out, the reference to Caesar's attempts to bring Pompey and Crassus together shows that the "Triumvirate" as such did not yet exist.

101. Just before the mention of the agrarian law, Cicero engages in a mock-scientific debate with Atticus over the size of the windows in one of Cicero's villas, which includes a reference to Xenophon's *Education of Cyrus*, a geometrical formula, and a joke about the Epicurean theory of perception (*Att.* 2.3.2). The tone is one of delight in the writer's and addressee's shared cleverness.

that itself can be read as either ridiculous self-aggrandizement or tongue-in-cheek self-deprecation. At the end of Cicero's (recently completed) poem on his consulship, the Muse Calliope exhorts him to stay his political course, a course that is described in optimate terms both in the poem itself (cf. the reference to the *boni*) and in the letter's summary (cf. ἀριστοκρατικῶς), but that is also sanctioned as morally right (cf. *uirtute* in the second verse). It is striking that Cicero presents himself as bound not only by his previous politics, but by his own literary representation of these politics. Calliope speaks to Cicero the epic protagonist—but it is Cicero, the Roman politician, who feels himself to be obliged by her (that is, his own) words.

As for the Homeric quotation, this phrase, uttered by Hector to Polydamas, encapsulates Cicero's imperative: service to the fatherland is the final good of all political action. It is striking how in thinking through his dilemma, Cicero has availed himself of a multitude of techniques and authorities: the Academic debate *in utramque partem*, which comes down to a conflict between perceived *utile* and *honestum*; the appeal to Cicero's own political course, poetically codified and divinely sanctioned; and the quotation from the greatest poetic authority, Homer himself. Even so, Cicero's conclusion is—in the best Academic fashion—both tentative (note the highly qualified *non opinor esse dubitandum quin semper nobis uideatur*, 4) and temporary. The discussion will continue in Atticus's presence and with his input; in an ideal *societas studiorum*, it takes two to philosophize.[102]

Ultimately, Cicero indeed decided not to support the agrarian law, suffering the adverse consequences of setting himself against the First Triumvirate. As the letter shows, he made his choice with open eyes, fully aware of what it meant and what potential advantages he was giving up. In its use of Academic debate and the framing of a policy decision in moral terms, the letter is a prime example of Cicero's application of his philosophy to his politics, and of the literate and urbane terms in which such a decision might be presented to an intellectual and social peer.[103]

---

102. We will return to *Att.* 2.3 in 6.4 below.

103. There is one instance where Atticus himself uses New Academic *disputatio in utramque partem*—without, however, settling on a *probabile* and instead withholding judgment in the "hard" Skeptic manner: when Cicero departed from his province Cilicia in the summer of 50, he needed to leave somebody in charge since no new governor had been appointed. The choice was between Quintus or Cicero's quaestor Coelius, neither of whom was ideal (Cicero in the end went with Coelius). *Att.* 6.6.3 and 6.9.3 refer to Atticus's having written that he was suspending judgment (ἐπέχειν), which may very well have been an urbane way of staying out of this fraught decision—even though Cicero shrewdly remarks that Atticus's failure to come out in favor of his brother-in-law Quintus itself speaks volumes (6.9.3).

We find more debates *in utramque partem* in 49 BCE, when Cicero faced the more harrowing choice of taking either Pompey's or Caesar's side in the Civil War. In *Att.* 9.4, of 12 March, he describes how he is formally debating with himself a list of θέσεις πολιτικαί (1), questions of political principle that are applicable to the current circumstances. He proceeds to provide a long list of such topics of debate (e.g., "Is it politically advisable to live quietly in retirement while one's country is under a tyrant, or should one risk everything for the sake of freedom?"[104]), all in Greek, the language of formal philosophical discussion. As he tells Atticus, he is arguing these issues in each direction, alternating between Greek and Latin (3). Five days later, in *Att.* 9.9.1, he reports that he is still "playing the sophist" (σοφιστεύω) and keeping up practice on his topics of debate, while on 3 April, he is concerned especially with the question of "whether one ought to enter into council with a tyrant if he is about to deliberate about some good,"[105] in light of the possibility of new peace negotiations with Caesar. In adapting set Greek debating topics for his own purpose, Cicero casts Caesar as the stock figure of the tyrant, enabling a set of cultural and philosophical association that would color Cicero's views and actions in the coming years.[106]

Rationally weighing the pros and cons of an action was one way in which Cicero attempted to chart a philosophically informed political course for himself. Another was to measure himself, and others, against a previously determined moral ideal, either such abstract concepts as "duty" or "the good," or otherwise that paragon of statesmanship, the *rector* of Cicero's own *De re publica*.[107] Especially Cicero's letters from Cilicia (51–50)—a place where he actually had some governing to do, at a time when *De re publica* was fresh in his mind—abound in references to Cicero's attempts to measure up to his ideal. While decidedly unenthusiastic about being sent abroad,[108] Cicero was

104. *Att.* 9.4.2: εἰ πολιτικὸν τὸ ἡσυχάζειν ἀναχωρήσαντά ποι τῆς πατρίδος τυραννουμένης ἢ διὰ παντὸς ἰτέον τῆς ἐλευθερίας πέρι.

105. *Att.* 9.1.3: *ueniendumne sit in consilium tyranni si is aliqua de re bona deliberaturus sit.*

106. See Gildenhard 2006 and compare Gildenhard 2011: 85–92, as well as 4.4 below.

107. For "duty" (*officium*), see esp. *Att.* 8.12.5, 8.15.2, as well as Brunt 1986. The criterion of the morally good (*honestum*), often contrasted with the advantageous (*utile*), is a leitmotif of Cicero's ethical considerations in his correspondence (cf. McConnell 2014: 225–26). The Greek technical term τὸ καλόν is used twice to denote the moral excellence from which the Civil War actions of both Caesar and Pompey are far removed: *Att.* 7.11.1; 8.8.2. On Cicero's employing the *rector* from *De re publica* as an ideal against which to measure himself and others, see Zarecki 2014; on the primacy of virtue in Cicero more generally, see 6.4 below.

108. Cicero, who much preferred keeping close to the political scene in Rome, had happily renounced his claim to a provincial posting following his consulship, but was drafted as the

determined to be a just administrator and avoid the corruption and exploitation that typically came as part and parcel of such provincial postings. As he tells Atticus upon setting out, he has six "guarantors" to ensure that he will do his duty, namely, the six books of *De re publica* (*Att.* 6.1.8), and the theme runs as a leitmotif through his correspondence from the province: if Cicero were to fail in his duties as a just ruler, "would I ever dare to read or even touch those books which you praise so much?"[109] Throughout, the conceit is that Cicero has to prove to Atticus—portrayed as an ardent fan of *De re publica*—that he is really living up to his stated principles.

Once Cicero returned to Italy and found the political situation teetering on the brink of civil war, holding reality up to his political ideals became an increasingly depressing exercise. While he reported to Atticus in December 50 that he thought he himself might pass muster in resembling closely enough "that man who is fleshed out in the sixth book,"[110] he had to conclude that both Pompey and Caesar, the two current potential leaders of Rome, were far removed from his ideal. He wrote to Atticus on 27 February 49 (*Att.* 8.11.1–2, citing *Rep.* 5.8 Ziegler):

> consumo igitur omne tempus considerans quanta uis sit illius uiri quem nostris libris satis diligenter, ut tibi quidem uidemur, expressimus. tenesne igitur moderatorem illum rei publicae quo referre uelimus omnia? nam sic quinto, ut opinor, in libro loquitur Scipio: "ut enim gubernatori cursus secundus, medico salus, imperatori uictoria, sic huic moderatori rei publicae beata ciuium uita proposita est, ut opibus firma, copiis locuples, gloria ampla, uirtute honesta sit; huius enim operis maximi inter homines atque optimi illum esse perfectorem uolo." hoc Gnaeus noster cum antea numquam tum in hac causa minime cogitauit. dominatio quaesita ab utroque est, non id actum beata et honesta ciuitas ut esset.

> I spend all my time thinking about the greatness of that man whom I have described in my books, well enough, in your opinion at least. Do you remember the principle according to which I wanted that leader of the commonwealth to act in all things? For Scipio says, I believe, in book 5: "Just as a fair voyage is the goal of the helmsman, health that of the doctor, and victory that of the general, thus to this leader of the commonwealth it is the well-being of the citizens: strong through protection, wealthy in provisions,

---

result of a new law, which obliged earlier officeholders to share in the burden of administering an increased number of provinces.

109. *Att.* 6.2.9. Cf. also *Att.* 6.3.3, 6.6.2; 7.2.4.

110. *Att.* 7.3.2: *illum uirum qui in sexto libro informatus est.*

renowned in glory, and virtuous in morality. This is the task, the best and greatest among mankind, that I want that man to accomplish." That sort of thing never crossed our Pompey's mind, not earlier and certainly not now. Both want power, not to make the citizenship virtuous and happy.

Pompey and Caesar are driven only by their own desire for dominance, without any consideration for the commonwealth. Their actions are not only politically disastrous for Rome; they are also morally wrong, according to the philosophical principles that Cicero has laid down in *De re publica* and by which he himself has tried to live. Comparing his own deeds and fortunes with those of the two warlords, he writes to Atticus on 14 April 49 (*Att.* 10.4.4):

> horum ego summorum imperatorum non modo res gestas non antepono meis sed ne fortunam quidem ipsam; qua illi florentissima, nos duriore conflictati uidemur. quis enim potest aut deserta per se patria aut oppressa beatus esse? et si, ut nos a te admonemur, recte in illis libris diximus nihil esse bonum nisi honestum, nihil male nisi quod turpe sit, certe uterque istorum est miserrimus, quorum utrique semper patriae salus et dignitas posterior sua dominatione et domesticis commodis fuit.

> Not only do I not rank the deeds of those great generals above mine, but not even their fortune—though they appear to have flourished while I was battered about. For who can be happy either having deserted the fatherland or ruling it as a tyrant? And if I have, as you remind me, said correctly in those books that nothing is good except virtue and nothing bad except vice, then surely both of them are miserable in the extreme, seeing that each has always put the well-being and dignity of the fatherland below his own power and private advantage.

For Cicero, the question of the Civil War is a profoundly ethical one, and the criterion for morally good action is the political imperative formulated by him. Both Pompey and Caesar have failed in the supreme duty that is service to the fatherland and are thus doomed to misery, notwithstanding their past and potential future victories and positions of power. Cicero, despite his failure and lack of power, is still morally superior. Even without any influence or ability to take charge of the *res publica*, he remains more of a true *rector* than the most powerful men at Rome.

Given the failures of both Caesar and Pompey, there was no obvious path for Cicero to follow, only a choice of the lesser evil. After much agonized hesitation and months of lying low in the Italian countryside, Cicero finally joined Pompey in Greece in the summer of 49, motivated by both a sense of personal obligation and a conviction that the would-be tyrant Caesar was out to destroy the *res publica*, while Pompey was nominally defending it, however poorly.[111] Cicero did not care for the state of affairs he found in the Pompeian camp and was especially alarmed by the bloodthirsty rhetoric of some of Pompey's followers;[112] he made himself unpopular with his sarcasms;[113] and he missed the final defeat at Pharsalus while stationed at Dyrrhachium with Cato, Varro, and others. As we have seen, Cicero had no taste for carrying on the war in the company of the uncompromising Cato, and instead embarked back to Italy at the earliest occasion, hoping for Caesar's *clementia*. As it happened, he had to spend an uncomfortable year marooned in Brundisium before finally being allowed to return to Rome. This is where we will pick up the story again in chapter 4.

3. Epicurean (Dis)Engagement

As we have seen above, Cicero polemicized against Epicurean attitudes to political engagement in the preface to *De re publica*, and he continued to argue against the school throughout his published work as well as in his letters.[114] By his own admission, Cicero was troubled by the popularity of Epicureanism: in the preface to *Tusculans* 4, he hyperbolically states that the teachings of Epicurus "have taken over all of Italy," and he begins his comparative discussion of ethical systems in *De finibus* with Epicureanism for the very reason that this is a creed that "is very well known to most people."[115] Cicero's concern was not unfounded: Epicureanism indeed appears to have been the philosophical doctrine most widely espoused by late Republican Romans, and we have evidence for the Epicurean leanings of far more upperclass individuals than for any of the other schools.[116]

Philosophical affiliation is not always easy to gauge, however, especially for less well-documented figures, and scholars have differed on which late

---

111. Even if he did not think that Pompey was motivated by considerations of *honestum* (see above), Cicero was still electing what was *honestum* for himself by following Pompey; cf. *Fam.* 4.2.2; 5.19.2.

112. See *Att.* 11.6.2, 6.

113. See further 4.2, n. 65.

114. For Cicero's philosophical exchanges with his Epicurean correspondents, see Gilbert 2015. My discussion in this section owes much to Gilbert's work, not only his 2015 dissertation but also unpublished material that the author has kindly made available to me.

115. *Tusc.* 4.7: *Italiam totam occupauerunt* (the subject is the supposedly numerous writers of Latin Epicurean treatises); *Fin.* 1.13: *Epicuri ratio, quae plerisque notissima est.*

116. On Epicureanism in the late Republic, see Momigliano 1941: 150–57, Castner 1988, Benferhat 2005, Sedley 2009, Gilbert 2015, and Valachova 2018; Castner, Benferhat, and Gilbert provide prosopographical surveys of individual Epicureans.

Republican Romans really qualify as Epicureans. According to a conservative estimate, by Nathan Gilbert, the following mid-first-century senators were definitely adherents of the Garden: L. Calpurnius Piso Caesoninus, C. Cassius Longinus, M. Fadius Gallus, L. Manlius Torquatus, C. Memmius, and C. Vibius Pansa Caetronianus. In addition, we have the Epicurean *equites* L. Papirius Paetus, T. Pomponius Atticus, L. Saufeius,[117] and C. Trebatius Testa. There are a number of other possible candidates, and since we lack information about the vast majority of members of the senatorial and equestrian orders, not to mention the larger populace, this list presumably represents but the tip of the Epicurean iceberg.

Epicureanism has the further distinction of being the first Greek philosophical system to find an expression in Latin writing. We know of three writers of Latin Epicurean prose works, C. Amafinius (late 2nd/early 1st c.), Rabirius (1st half 1st c.), and Catius Insuber (d. 46), and we still possess *De rerum natura*, the monumental didactic poem on Epicurean physics by T. Lucretius Carus (mid-50s). Of course, there were also Greek Epicureans, not only such visitors from the Athenian school as Cicero's and Atticus's teacher Phaedrus,[118] but also men who settled in Italy, gathering around them groups of Roman followers. Two prominent scholars of this type were based in the Bay of Naples, which is why one sometimes speaks of "Campanian" Epicureanism: the prolific prose author and epigrammatist Philodemus lived in Herculaneum, close to the villa of his patron Piso, and Vergil's teacher Siro set up shop in Naples.[119]

Why was Epicureanism so appealing to the Romans? Cicero has a scornful answer (*Tusc.* 4.6):

> cuius libris editis commota multitudo contulit se ad eam potissimum disciplinam, siue quod erat cognitu perfacilis, siue quod inuitabantur illecebris blandis uoluptatis, siue etiam, quia nihil erat prolatum melius, illud quod erat tenebant.

> After his [sc. Amafinius's] books were published, the crowd betook itself to this doctrine above all others (i) because it was very easy to understand, or (ii) because they were lured in by the seductive blandishments of pleasure, or, in addition, (iii) because nothing better was on offer, so they took what was there.

---

117. On Saufeius, see now Haake 2017 and Gilbert 2019.

118. On Phaedrus and his Roman students, see Raubitschek 1949.

119. On Campanian Epicureanism, see, e.g., D'Arms 1970: 56–60 and Sider 1997: 3–24. Many of our ideas about Epicurean activity in the Bay of Naples are based on the assumption that the Villa dei Papiri belonged to Piso, and that Philodemus and other Epicureans congregated there; however, Porter 2007: 98–99 rightly cautions that the evidence linking the villa to Piso is slender.

Cicero's dismissal here is motivated not only by his distaste for Epicureanism as such, but also by the wish to stress the superiority of his own philosophical writing in Latin over that of his Epicurean predecessors.[120] Once we take the author's obvious bias into consideration, however, we can still find some truth in his assessment.

As for reason (i), Epicureans indeed prided themselves on the accessibility of their doctrine, which could be reduced to a number of handy maxims, Epicurus's Κύριαι δόξαι ("Principal Sayings"), which the Epicurean accolyte was encouraged to learn by heart. As for (ii), Epicureanism's promise of a life of easily attainable pleasure and freedom from anxiety may well have seemed attractive to many people, especially in a period of political strife and uncertainty. In the words of Lucretius, "nothing is sweeter than to inhabit the well-fortified, serene temples of the wise, erected by knowledge" and to look down on the rest of humankind as they fret and toil.[121] In mid-first-century Rome, this may have been a particularly appealing scenario.

Cicero's third reason (iii), that people espoused Epicureanism because it was the only game in town, seems ridiculous and is clearly designed to highlight the author's important role in finally creating a decent Latin philosophical literature that transcends the sorry products of an Amafinius. Still, the very existence of these Epicurean treatises in Latin may point to a further reason for the school's relative popularity. Unlike other philosophies, Epicureanism stressed and created a sense of community beyond the original Garden in Athens. Motivated by the high value their creed placed on friendship, Epicureans flocked together, dining in each other's company and no doubt discussing philosophy.[122] We have an epigram of Philodemus that invites Piso to a celebration of Epicurus's birthday (27 Sider), offering evidence that the ritual aspects of Epicurean life, including its worship of the school's founder, had taken root in Italy. Roman Epicureans surrounded themselves with images of the god-like *primus inuentor* of their gospel: as Atticus is made to explain in *De finibus* 5.3, Epicurus's likeness was found on paintings, drinking cups, and rings, so as always to remind his followers of his teachings.[123]

---

120. Cicero disparages the style of Amafinius, Rabirius, and/or Catius at *Acad. post.* 5; *Tusc.* 4.6; *Fam.* 15.19.2.

121. Lucr. 2.7–8: *nil dulcius est bene quam munita tenere / edita doctrina sapientum templa serena.*

122. In a letter to his friend the Epicurean *eques* L. Papirius Paetus, Cicero refers jocularly to Paetus's "Epicurean fellow boozers" (*combibonibus Epicuriis, Fam.* 9.25.2). Allusions to feasting and drinking are frequent in anti-Epicurean polemic but may also reflect the social reality of Epicurean conviviality.

123. For different takes on Epicurean communal life (primarily in the school in Athens), see Frischer 1982, Clay 1983, Nussbaum 1994: 102–39, and Asmis 2004: 134–43.

Epicureanism thus presented not only, like all philosophies, an art of life, but a veritable way of life, and the social and communal aspects of the creed very likely contributed to its popularity. Roman Epicureans had, as it were, their own *societas studiorum*, a subculture within the larger network of learned practices, which followed its own rules and held out to its members the promise not only of sociability and intellectual engagement, but also of a good and happy life. There is reason to believe (and this brings us back to Cicero's concern) that at least some Epicureans actively proselytized. According to the preface of *Tusculans* 4, quoted above, Amafinius's books had the effect of filling Italy with Epicureans, and it is not too much of a stretch to assume that converting readers to Epicureanism may indeed have been the author's purpose. As a matter of fact, we have evidence for the conversion of at least two individuals to the Epicurean school, both in the upperclass milieu that is the subject of this book. In 53 BCE, the *eques* and jurist C. Trebatius Testa, who at this point was part of Caesar's staff in Gaul, became an Epicurean, apparently under the influence of C. Vibius Pansa, a senator and follower of Caesar well known for his Epicureanism.[124] And as an exchange of letters between Cicero and Cassius of 46/45 BCE shows, the latter had converted to the Garden comparatively recently and already proved himself well versed and firm in Epicurean doctrine.[125] Finally, Lucretius's *De rerum natura*, taking the form of a didactic speech of the poet addressed to the senator C. Memmius, presents, as it were, the poetic staging of such a one-on-one Epicurean conversion: as the poem progresses, Memmius and, by extension, the reader turn into fully informed Epicureans ready to confront reality.[126]

The popularity of Epicureanism among late Republican upperclass Romans is remarkable and, from the perspective of this chapter, appears to pose a problem.[127] As we saw in Cicero's discussion at the beginning of *De re publica*,

124. Cic. *Fam.* 7.12.1 (Cicero to Trebatius): *indicauit mihi Pansa meus Epicureum te esse factum* ("my friend Pansa tells me you have become an Epicurean").

125. *Fam.* 15.16–19. On this correspondence, see the discussion of Gilbert 2015: 163–283 and further below (the thesis of Dettenhofer 1990, that these letters are written in political code, and that "Epicureanism" is a cipher for "Caesarianism," has not found adherents). The exact date of Cassius's conversion as well as his former philosophical allegiance have been much debated but are of no importance here; see also 4.4.

126. On the teacher-student constellation of *De rerum natura*, as well as its sense of a developing didactic plot, see Volk 2002: 69–118; on the poem as a conversion narrative, see Asmis 2016. Unfortunately, nothing is known of Lucretius's life and social status beyond the fact of the dedication to Memmius, whose "sweet friendship" (*suauis amicitiae*, 1.141) the poet invokes. For Memmius, see 2.1 with n. 20.

127. It has sometimes been assumed—based on Cicero's scornful assessment of Amafinius's success—that Roman Epicureanism was a popular movement, appealing to an audience outside

Epicurus counseled his followers against political engagement: μὴ πολιτεύεσθαι ("Do not engage in politics," fr. 8 Usener) and λάθε βιώσας ("Live hidden," fr. 551 Usener) were two Epicurean maxims expressive of the belief that public life produces anxieties and emotional disturbances, and that the wise man will stay far from the madding crowd. Thus Lucretius includes political ambition among various factors that make human life miserable, compares the man running for public office to Sisyphus pushing his rock, and states in general terms that "it is so much better to live quietly as a subject than to want to rule the state by power and be a king."[128] This makes perfect sense from an Epicurean standpoint. Still, how were Roman senators who espoused Epicureanism able to reconcile this doctrine with their political careers?[129]

To some extent, this problem is a red herring. As Geert Roskam has shown in his monograph on the λάθε βιώσας provision, Epicurus's interdiction against public life is not an absolute prescription but must be understood in the context of his larger ethics.[130] In the effort to maximize pleasure and minimize pain, Epicureans will employ what has been called the hedonistic calculus, weighing the pros and cons of each action, while taking account of their individual circumstances. For most people in most situations, political activity will not be conducive to a pleasurable life and should thus be eschewed. However, in special circumstances, political engagement might be indicated even for an Epicurean, either because of an emergency or because the person in question is so naturally suited for a life in the public eye that he would experience pain forgoing it.[131] Thus Plutarch reports (De tranq. anim. 465F–466A = Epicurus fr. 555 Usener):

---

of Rome or to members of the lower classes. There is no evidence for such a scenario, which seems intrinsically unlikely (see Gilbert 2015: 40–52).

128. Lucr. 5.1127–28: *ut satius multo iam sit parere quietum / quam regere imperio res uelle et regna tenere.* Lists of anxieties: 2.9–61; 3.41–93; Sisyphus: 3.995–1002. Lucretius's scornful descriptions of political life clearly allude to the political realities of his time, which he refers to as "this bad condition of the fatherland" (*hoc patriai tempore iniquo*, 1.41). Scholars have ascribed various political stances to the poet, from Republican to Caesarian, but I would agree with Roskam 2007: 83–101 that his attitude seems simply Epicurean.

129. Compare my discussion in Volk forthcoming a.

130. See Roskam 2007. It has also been argued that Epicurean doctrine shifted over time and that such 1st-c. Epicureans as Philodemus had a view of political engagement and other matters more in keeping with the values of their Roman patrons; see Erler 1992, Armstrong 2011, Fish 2011, and Valachova 2018.

131. See Roskam 2007: 49–56. Roskam plays down the political emergency scenario, but Cic. *Rep.* 1.10 (discussed in 3.2 above) seems to me a clear indication that this "exception" (*exceptio*) was part of Epicurean doctrine: *negant sapientem suscepturum ullam rei publicae partem, extra*

οὐδ' Ἐπίκουρος οἴεται δεῖν ἡσυχάζειν, ἀλλὰ τῇ φύσει χρῆσθαι πολιτευομένους καὶ πράσσοντας τὰ κοινὰ τοὺς φιλοτίμους καὶ φιλοδόξους, ὡς μᾶλλον ὑπ' ἀπραγμοσύνης ταράττεσθαι καὶ κακοῦσθαι πεφυκότας, ἂν ὧν ὀρέγονται μὴ τυγχάνωσιν.

Not even Epicurus thinks that ambitious men eager for glory should live quietly. Instead they should embrace their disposition and engage in politics and public life, since by nature they will be disturbed and harmed by inactivity if they do not achieve what they desire.

Even so, however, such cases are only exceptions to the rule. It is unlikely that all politically active Roman Epicureans thought they were just stepping up to an emergency or otherwise gratifying a natural disposition to hunt for glory. It seems far more likely that many such men did not consider their political careers a philosophical issue, either because they had never thought the matter through or because they had adopted certain aspects of Epicureanism but not others. While there has been much debate in scholarship about the seriousness and commitment of philosophically inclined Romans in general and Roman Epicureans in particular,[132] it is surely unrealistic to expect each and every person to live up to the stringent postulates of their particular school. In addition, by considering only diehard, card-carrying Epicureans or Stoics, we miss out on the complexity of the intellectual landscape at a particular historical moment. Finally, one suspects that this scrutiny of commitment is, whether consciously or not, still motivated by the old prejudice according to which the Romans must have been intellectual lightweights. We never wonder whether, say, Plato was himself a good Platonist.

For the purposes of this chapter, what interests me, of course, are exactly those cases (if they exist) where Epicureanism did make a difference in a man's political conduct or in the way he thought about it. Did any Roman Epicurean take seriously the injunction to "live hidden," or did Epicurean convictions influence political action in any other way? As usual, our evidence for individual motivation is scanty, but the following brief case studies will demonstrate the range of Epicurean political (dis)engagement in mid-first-century Rome.

On one end of the spectrum, we find Roman politicians acting publicly in, as it were, a traditionally Roman way—while justifying their actions with the Epicurean hedonistic calculus. We are extraordinarily lucky in possessing the

---

quam si eum tempus et necessitas coegerit ("they say the wise man will in no way engage in politics, except when circumstance and necessity force him").

132. Thus, e.g., Castner 1988 throughout dismisses the Roman Epicureans she studies as superficial and frivolous, while Gilbert 2015 is at pains to prove those same men's intellectual seriousness.

firsthand philosophical reflections of a Roman senator (who is not Cicero!) in a letter by Cassius of January 45 (*Fam.* 15.19), which explains how virtuous behavior and the pursuit of pleasure can go hand in hand. C. Cassius Longinus (before 85–42 BCE), an experienced military man whose political career had proceeded as far as the tribunate, had fought on Pompey's side in the Civil War but, like Cicero, had sought Caesar's pardon and been appointed legate. At the time of the correspondence, he was biding his time in Brundisium, anxiously awaiting news of Caesar's Spanish campaign against Pompey's son, whose victory might have spelled repercussions against turncoats like Cicero and himself.

In his letter, Cassius is responding to three previous missives from Cicero (*Fam.* 15.16–18), especially one where Cicero had pointed out the popularity of their mutual friend, the Caesarian and Epicurean Pansa, and argued that Pansa's kindness and support for the exiled Pompeians was such as "to make anyone understand that which you have recently begun to doubt, viz. that 'the good is to be chosen for its own sake.'"[133] Alluding to Cassius's recent conversion to Epicureanism, Cicero challenges his correspondent to explain Pansa's virtuous conduct in a way that avoids what Cicero views as the obvious motivation, namely, the conviction that virtue is choiceworthy as such: betraying his own Epicurean principles, Pansa does the right thing because doing the right thing is a good in itself.

Cicero is here using a time-honored strategy of philosophical polemic, which Gilbert has called the "living refutation argument":[134] Pansa's actions contradict his Epicureanism, therefore the Epicurean position must be wrong. Cicero deploys living refutation arguments throughout his writing, from letters to speeches to philosophical works, not only against Epicureans but against Stoics as well.[135] His use of the technique is connected to what Raphael Woolf has identified as Cicero's general concern with the "transparency" of any philosophic position:[136] can one live one's philosophy openly, or would one have to dissimulate one's true beliefs as being too much at odds with the values of society? The apparently public-minded, virtuous actions of the Epicurean Pansa mean either that he is insincere, caving in to societal strictures because he does not dare actually to behave in an Epicurean fashion, or—on Cicero's charitable reading—that he is in fact a virtuous man, whose sincere

---

133. Cic. *Fam.* 15.17.3: *ut quiuis intelligere posset id quod tu nuper dubitare coepisti*, τὸ καλὸν δι' αὐτὸ αἱρετὸν *esse*. On Cicero's argument, see Griffin 1995: 343–44 and Gilbert 2015: 222–30.

134. See Gilbert 2015: 131–34 and passim.

135. Other anti-Epicurean living refutation arguments are found in *Fam.* 7.12 (against Trebatius) and *De finibus* 1 and 2 (against Torquatus; see below in the text and n. 139). Comparable anti-Stoic arguments are employed in *Mur.* 62–66 and *Fin.* 4.21–22 (both against Cato).

136. See Woolf 2015: 147–50, 160–61, 195–97.

espousal of the good refutes his purported hedonism. Epicureanism has thus been shown to be either discreditable or weak.

In his response, Cassius rises to the challenge put down by Cicero, unabashedly professing his own Epicureanism and mounting a sophisticated proof of the hedonistic motivation of Pansa's virtuous behavior:[137]

difficile est enim persuadere hominibus τὸ καλὸν δι' αὐτὸ αἱρετὸν esse; ἡδονὴν uero et ἀταραξίαν uirtute, iustitia, τῷ καλῷ parari et uerum et probabile est; ipse enim Epicurus . . . dicit: οὐκ ἔστιν ἡδέως ἄνευ τοῦ καλῶς καὶ δικαίως ζῆν. itaque et Pansa, qui ἡδονὴν sequitur, uirtutem retinet et ii, qui a uobis φιλήδονοι vocantur, sunt φιλόκαλοι et φιλοδίκαιοι omnisque uirtutes et colunt et retinent.

It is difficult to convince people that the good is to be chosen for its own sake. But that pleasure and freedom from disturbance are brought about by virtue, justice, and the good, that's both true and easily argued. For Epicurus himself says: "A pleasurable life is impossible without a good and just life." Thus Pansa, pursuing pleasure, retains virtue, and those who by you are called pleasure-lovers, are lovers of the good and just, and retain and exercise all virtues.

Directly contradicting Cicero, Cassius makes the bold claim that by acting virtuously in the political arena, an Epicurean like Pansa is in fact pursuing pleasure, all appearances to the contrary. According to Epicurus himself (Cassius is here partly quoting *KD* 5), true pleasure entails virtue, and the good Epicurean simply cannot help being a good person as well, even if this is not his prime objective.

Cassius's argument raises a number of questions. First, one would like to know how he imagines the details of Pansa's putative hedonistic calculus. What pleasure exactly is Pansa pursuing with his altruistic behavior? Moral satisfaction? Popular applause? Or, ultimately, the creation of a stable political situation conducive to individual tranquility? And second, there is the general question of what "virtue" even means within the Epicurean system, given that it cannot be a good in its own right. Is it simply the moral standard of a given society, whose violation would cause the Epicurean more disturbance than it would be worth? Or is it some intrinsic quality that just happens to be conducive to—or the byproduct of—pleasure?[138]

---

137. *Fam.* 15.19.2–3. On this passage, see Griffin 1995: 344–46, Sedley 1997: 46–47, Gilbert 2015: 230–34, and Roskam 2019: 728–33.

138. Cf. Gilbert 2015: 242: "It is certainly an astonishing coincidence that developing virtuous dispositions has turned out to be the royal road to pleasure in our cosmos."

These issues notwithstanding, Cassius's argument shows how late Republican Epicureans could justify their political activity with orthodox Epicurean arguments and engage in public life without feeling at odds with their philosophical convictions. Of course, Cassius may be imputing to Pansa considerations that never crossed the latter's mind. The letter still remains important evidence for Cassius's own beliefs, and I furthermore consider it plausible that fellow Epicureans discussed such matters among themselves and that Pansa in particular—previously involved in the conversion of Trebatius (see above)—was the kind of man who had given thought to such matters. A few months after the correspondence, Cicero employed living refutation arguments throughout the first two books of De finibus against his Epicurean interlocutor L. Manlius Torquatus, a noble who in 50 BCE, the date of the dialogue, had been elected to the praetorship, but was to die in battle on the Pompeian side in 48.[139] Torquatus, however, is made to reply that even his ancestor T. Manlius Imperiosus Torquatus (4th c. BCE)—(in)famous for both defeating a Gaul in single combat and putting his own son to death for an infringement of military discipline—was in no way motivated by a consideration of virtue as such[140] but simply employed it as a means to the greater hedonistic end. Of course, his Ciceronian opponent is not convinced, and the very choice of Torquatus as an interlocutor constitutes a living refutation argument in its own right: the man's exemplary political career and heroic death for the good cause are meant to disprove his own Epicurean tenets. Even so, the fact that Cicero saw fit to include a Cassius-style Epicurean justification for hedonistically motivated public action in his dialogue may well be an indication that such modes of thought were common among his Epicurean contemporaries.

If Roman upperclass Epicureans could justify their engagement philosophically, is there any way in which their specific political actions might have been informed by their Epicurean convictions? In his letter to Cicero, Cassius expresses the hope that Pansa's behavior—no doubt his conciliatory stance toward the former Pompeians—might show people "how much everybody hates cruelty and loves righteousness and mercy."[141] It is sometimes claimed that there was a specifically Epicurean way of doing Roman politics, one that

139. The argument structures much of the discussion in the two books; see esp. *Fin.* 1.23–25, 34–36; 2.60–1. Gilbert 2015: 243–83 makes the attractive suggestion that Cicero's strategy in the dialogue may have been inspired by his correspondence with Cassius; see also Roskam 2019 specifically on *Fin.* 1.25.

140. *Fin.* 1.35: *uirtutem . . . per se ipsam causam non fuisse.*

141. Cic. *Fam.* 15.19.2: *spero enim homines intellecturos quanto sit omnibus odio crudelitas et quanto amori probitas et clementia.*

was moderate, nonconfrontational, and—in a period of violent civic and military clashes—committed to peaceful solutions.[142]

The prime exhibit for this thesis is L. Calpurnius Piso Caesoninus, the consul of 58 and father-in-law of Caesar.[143] That he was an Epicurean is clear from his close association with Philodemus and from the scathing attacks of Cicero's *In Pisonem*, the speech from 55 BCE in which the orator lashed out against the man who as consul had aided and abetted Cicero's exile.[144] Despite Cicero's depiction of Piso as a monster, this Roman noble comes across in our other sources as a mild-mannered moderate, who before the Civil War attempted to make peace between Pompey and Caesar and after the Ides of March favored negotiations between the senate and Antony. Still, while it is certainly possible that these and other pacifist aspects of Piso's public conduct were influenced by his Epicureanism, there is nothing specifically Epicurean about an aversion to confrontation and the wish to bring about peaceful solutions. Other men behaved similarly in those same situations, and Cassius's "righteousness and mercy" can hardly be considered an exclusively Epicurean slogan.[145]

What is more suggestive is Piso's apparent indifference to personal honors. Cicero makes much of the fact that his enemy—though proclaimed *imperator* by his troops for military achievements during his proconsulship in Macedonia (57–55 BCE)—made no effort whatsoever to secure a triumph, dismissing his lictors before entering the city of Rome upon his return.[146] In Cicero's interpretation, this is a sign of Piso's moral depravity; interestingly, however, Piso himself had openly declared his lack of interest in a triumph. Cicero's report is dripping with sarcasm and burning with outrage:[147]

142. The main proponent of this view is Benferhat 2005, who states that "[i]l y a bien une manière de faire la politique qui est propre aux épicuriens" (232).

143. On Piso's Epicurean politics, see esp. Griffin 2001 and Benferhat 2005: 173–232, who provide detailed documentation of his actions and self-presentation.

144. In the speech, Cicero attacks Piso not so much as an Epicurean but rather as a *bad* Epicurean, one who mistakes the Garden's ethics for an invitation to debauchery: "a product of the pigsty, not the school" (*ex hara producte, non ex schola, Pis.* 37). On Cicero's anti-Epicurean arguments in *Pis.*, see further De Lacy 1941 and Gordon 2012: 162–71.

145. Of course, "mercy" (*clementia*) was, at the time of Cassius's letter, a specifically *Caesarian* slogan, and both Pansa and Cassius were Caesarians (as was Piso). For the often-mooted idea of a connection between Epicureanism and support for Caesar, see further below.

146. See *Pis.* 38–39, 44, 53–63, 74, 97. On Cicero's rhetorical strategy here, see Volk and Zetzel 2015: 208–11.

147. Cic. *Pis.* 56; see also 62–63. Cicero is responding to an actual speech by Piso, and I take it that references to what Piso has said and the senators have heard have a certain truth value,

at audistis, patres conscripti, philosophi uocem. negauit se triumphi cupidum umquam fuisse. o scelus, o pestis, o labes!

But, conscript fathers, you have heard the words of the philosopher. He said he never had any desire for a triumph. You criminal, you plague, you stain!

Cicero explicitly connects Piso's lack of ambition with his philosophy, and hilariously imagines his foe giving an Epicurean lecture to his son-in-law Caesar, who at this point is covering himself in military glory in Gaul: what is the point of public thanksgivings if the gods have no care for human affairs (59), and why should one aim for the trappings of a triumph, which do not in any way contribute to bodily pleasure (60)?

Cicero's invective is highly tendentious, of course, but it is still perfectly plausible that Piso had phrased his disavowal of triumphal ambitions in Epicurean terms, even if he had not explicitly referred to his philosophical convictions. After all, *supplicationes* and triumphs are, from an Epicurean standpoint, indeed empty honors, whose pursuit may provoke far more anxiety than they are worth. That Piso, while progressing through a model political career (he attained all magistracies on the first try, Cic. *Pis.* 2), may have tried to avoid troublesome distinctions is suggested also by his reluctance to assume the censorship of 50 BCE: Cassius Dio reports that he was made censor against his wish (40.63.2) and, unlike his activist colleague Appius Claudius Pulcher, showed no interest in exercising his powers by excluding men from the senatorial or equestrian orders. Miriam Griffin has pointed out that Dio's description of Piso as "generally wishing not to have trouble" is highly reminiscent of Epicurus's own description of the divine as not "having trouble itself or causing trouble to another."[148] If the historian is faithfully reflecting Piso's own motivation or even utterances, the senator apparently felt that the work-intensive censorship with its potential to alienate people was hardly conducive to an untroubled Epicurean life on the model of the gods.

As the examples of Piso, Pansa, and Cassius show, Roman Epicureans engaged in politics and were able to justify their actions with reasoned philosophical arguments. Of course, these three men were born into senatorial families, and going through the *cursus honorum* was simply their default career, whose rejection would have been met with social censure (something that

---

however much Cicero may be distorting his foe's utterances. I thus disagree with the assertion of De Lacy 1941 that Cicero is using boilerplate anti-Epicurean invective that has little to do with Piso himself.

148. Cass. Dio 40.63.4 on Piso: οὔτ' ἄλλως πράγματ' ἔχειν ἐθέλων; Epicurus, KD 1 on the divine: οὔτε αὐτὸ πράγματα ἔχει οὔτε ἄλλῳ παρέχει. See Griffin 2001: 89.

would, perhaps, itself have been counterproductive to ensuring ἀταραξία).[149] What, however, of members of the equestrian order, men like Cicero, who had to make a conscious effort to enter politics as *homines noui*? Were there any Roman *equites* who decided to forgo a political career in favor of the Epicurean hidden life?

As usual, we have next to no information about most individuals' motivations, but among our known Roman Epicureans of equestrian rank, there is one unusually well-documented man whose actions have often been viewed as inspired by his philosophy. T. Pomponius Atticus, Cicero's friend and correspondent, undoubtedly claimed allegiance to the Epicurean school.[150] In his letters to his friend, Cicero repeatedly makes joking references to Atticus's affiliation and involves him in philosophical debates; in the dialogues where he appears, his Epicureanism is referred to in passing, even though he never appears as a spokesman for his creed and is even playfully told to set his convictions aside for the purposes of the discussion.[151] We possess precious first-hand information about Atticus from Cicero's over four hundred letters; in addition, we have the biography written by the historian Cornelius Nepos, who like Cicero was a personal friend. Neither source is unproblematic: the letters tell only the story of Atticus's involvement with Cicero; the *Life* paints a highly idealized picture that glosses over potentially disagreeable details.[152] Taken in conjunction with each other, and with whatever other evidence there is, however, these two contemporary sources can still give us a good sense of what kind of person Atticus was.

Wealthy, well-educated, well-spoken, and well-connected, Atticus would have been well positioned to have a stab at a political career, just as his friend Cicero did. That he did not do so is not surprising in itself: there was no expectation for most *equites* to move up into the higher order, which might at any rate have impeded their business interests and way of living. What is striking, in the case of Atticus, is the extent to which he clearly viewed and represented his choice of life as a concious, well-reasoned decision. Cicero writes to his friend (*Att.* 1.17.5):

> neque ego inter me atque te quicquam interesse umquam duxi praeter uoluntatem institutae uitae, quod me ambitio quaedam ad honorum studium, te autem alia minime reprehendenda ratio ad honestum otium duxit.

149. Compare Fish 2011: 96.

150. Atticus's Epicureanism has been often, and controversially, discussed. See Leslie 1950, Labate and Narducci 1981: 141–56, Castner 1988: 57–61, Perlwitz 1992: 90–97, Benferhat 2005: 98–169, and Gilbert forthcoming.

151. See *Fin.* 5.3–4, 96; *Leg.* 1.21–22.

152. On Nepos's *Atticus*, see Labate and Narducci 1981; Millar 1988; Holzberg 1995; Lindsay 1998; Leppin 2002; Stem 2005, 2019; J. Sauer 2011; Schubert 2015; and Nelsestuen 2019.

I never thought that there was any difference between me and you, except for our voluntary life choices: my ambition led me to the pursuit of honors, but your different, by no means reprehensible, reasoning led you to honorable leisure.

It is established between the two men that both have knowingly chosen a type of life; while Cicero self-deprecatingly speaks of his own motivation as ambition, he ascribes his friend's choice to reason, and generously concedes that both paths are honorable. As for Nepos, Atticus's firm decision never to take an active part in politics runs as a leitmotif through the entire *Life*: *honores non petiit* ("he did not seek offices," 6.2). Not only does Atticus not enter the *cursus honorum* but he also rejects all other public positions that are offered to him in the course of his life; even though he consorts with and indeed privately supports numerous politically active contemporaries, he himself maintains a position of strict neutrality.[153]

Neither Nepos nor Cicero ascribes Atticus's choice explicitly to Epicureanism. As a matter of fact, Nepos never mentions that Atticus was an Epicurean, perhaps out of personal dislike for the school or because he did not think that it fit into his air-brushed portrait (other aspects of Atticus's life, e.g., his moneylending, are likewise elided). The reasons for Atticus's eschewal of public engagement that Nepos adduces, however, are very much in keeping with Epicurean thought: given the current political climate, Atticus had no desire to be tossed "on the waves of civil strife" (*ciuilibus fluctibus*, 6.1) and instead wished to preserve his *tranquillitas* (6.5). Similarly, Cicero's reference, in the letter quoted above, to Atticus's *minime reprehenda ratio* seems to be an allusion specifically to Epicureanism. *Ratio* itself not only means "reason" but can also refer to a philosophical system or school, and as Carlos Lévy has shown (2001), Cicero frequently uses qualifiers of the "really not so bad" kind when speaking of Epicurean doctrine, either out of ostensible fairness or in order to damn with faint praise.

It thus seems fairly certain that Atticus's Epicureanism was a factor in his decision not to pursue a political career. But there may be more. What Cicero calls his friend's *honestum otium* (*Att.* 1.17.5) was not an existence of leisurely retreat but an active life engaged in business and indeed politics.[154] Born into

---

153. The only known exception—not mentioned by Nepos—is Atticus's public appearance as the leader of a group of *equites* to demonstrate support for the consul Cicero during the Catilinarian crisis in 63 BCE (Cic. *Att.* 2.1.7).

154. On Atticus's financial and political activities, see Perlwitz 1992 and Welch 1996, as well as N. K. Rauh 1986: 7–12 specifically on his acting as Cicero's "ancient equivalent of the modern Swiss banker" (12). For Atticus as a historian, see 5.1 below.

a wealthy family, he inherited an additional fortune from his uncle Caecilius in 58 and increased his holdings through a number of business activities, first and foremost money-lending.[155] Profoundly knowledgeable of the political scene—Cicero calls him πολιτικός at *Att.* 2.12.4; 4.6.1—and with personal connections to a large number of senators,[156] Atticus was in a position not only to dispense political advice (as he did for Cicero throughout his career) but also to influence events, not infrequently by means of financial support. Shrewd and discrete, he managed throughout a period of violence and conflict never to get on anybody's bad side, survived civil wars and proscriptions, and died at the ripe old age of seventy-seven in 32 BCE, still hedging his bets by keeping up friendly relations with both Octavian and Antony.

Scholars who discuss Atticus's politics and business practices tend to dismiss his Epicureanism,[157] but a case can be made for viewing the canny *eques* as implementing the hedonistic calculus throughout his life. Nepos stresses Atticus's *prudentia*—meaning both "practical intelligence" and "foresight" (< *pro-uidentia*)[158]—which allowed him to take actions that ensured both his present and future well-being. Security (ἀσφαλεία) is the external state Epicureans endeavor to achieve in order to enable them to maintain their internal freedom from disturbances (ἀταραξία), and Atticus was singularly successful at doing so, arriving, to quote Nepos, "at safety through so many and such dangerous political tempests."[159]

One factor that instrumentally contributed to Atticus's maintenance of his secure state was his undeniable talent for friendship. His intimate relationship with Cicero is well documented and immortalized in Cicero's dedication to his friend of his treatise on the very topic of friendship, *De amicitia*; Nepos too was close to the subject of his biography, being well acquainted with Atticus's private affairs (13.7) and dedicating to his friend his *Lives of Foreign*

155. As Asmis 2004 has shown, Epicureanism (esp. in the late Republican version of Philodemus's treatises *On Wealth* and *On Household Economics*) has a relaxed attitude toward financial resources and their procurement: as long as mental disturbances and excesses are avoided, wealth is preferable to poverty and especially conducive to pleasure when shared with friends. Being a businessman like Atticus is thus in no way incompatible with being an Epicurean.

156. Perlwitz 1992: 100–105 provides a list of forty-six senators associated with Atticus in our sources.

157. Perlwitz 1992: 90–97 comes to the conclusion that Atticus's Epicureanism was largely irrelevant for his actions, while Welch 1996: 451 glosses over the issue in two noncommittal sentences; differently Benferhat 2005: 98–169.

158. The terms *prudens* and *prudentia* are applied to Atticus at 3.3, 9.1, 10.6.

159. Nep. *Att.* 10.6: *ex tot tamque grauibus procellis ciuilibus ad incolumitatem peruenit.*

Generals.[160] Atticus must have been extraordinarily amiable and charming, something that still comes across in the tone of Cicero's letters and that no doubt stood him in good stead as he built up friendly relationships with some of the most prominent late Republican figures on all sides of the various political equations: Sulla, Cicero, the optimate leaders of the 60s and 50s (including Cato and Atticus's special friend Q. Hortensius Hortalus), Caesar and his intimates of the early 40s, Brutus, Antony, and Octavian.

Friendship was prized by all philosophical schools but especially celebrated by the Epicureans, who viewed it as the ideal social relationship and particularly conducive to pleasure. Just like virtue, however, friendship was considered not an end in itself but a means to a secure and happy life.[161] Friends provide many benefits for one another, both emotional and material; crucially, the very knowledge of having a friend allays one's anxieties about the future, since one can rely on the friend for support in any misfortune. Atticus's modus operandi provides an excellent illustration of how this system could work in practice: people liked the sophisticated *eques* and enjoyed his company; at the same time, they profited from his financial assistance, political advice, and social connections. Conversely, Atticus shored up friendly support for himself in all quarters, ensuring his own ἀσφάλεια even in the diciest situations. Most (in)famous is his behavior in 44–43 BCE (see Nep. *Att.* 8–10): as a close friend of Brutus, he supported the liberators and privately offered them financial support while refusing—in keeping with his low-profile policy—to join an official fund the *equites* were trying to organize; shortly thereafter, however, he rendered important services to Antony's wife Fulvia and friend P. Volumnius, taking charge of their affairs in Rome when Antony, declared a public enemy and forced to retreat to Transalpine Gaul after the Battle of Mutina, already appeared to be defeated. This conduct—though criticized at the time and no doubt horrifying to Cicero—paid off when, shortly thereafter, Antony entered into the Second Triumvirate with Octavian and Lepidus. As an associate of Cicero and Brutus, Atticus was immediately proscribed; however, in recognition of his support for Fulvia and Volumnius, Antony struck from the list not only Atticus but Atticus's long-time friend Q. Gellius Canus, who had taken refuge with him. Antony remained Atticus's friend until the latter's death, reportedly corresponding with him even from Egypt, at a time when Atticus was

160. On Atticus's friendship with Cicero, see Shackleton Bailey 1965–70: 1.3–59; on his relationship with Nepos, see Stem 2012: 55–61. On friendship as the leitmotif of Nepos's biography, see Stem 2005, 2019 and Nelsestuen 2019.

161. The strict utilitarianism of Epicurean friendship has been questioned since antiquity (Do Epicurean friends really love each other not for their own sakes but only for the benefits they provide?; see, e.g., Cic. *Fin.* 2.78–85); see Mitsis 2020 for a helpful discussion.

himself on the most amiable terms with Octavian and his followers, having married his daughter to none other than Agrippa.[162]

Of course, it cannot be proved that Atticus's self-interested policy of strict outward neutrality coupled with intensive networking was informed by his Epicureanism, but in light of his attested commitment to the creed and his philosophically inspired rejection of a political career, the scenario remains attractive. If his peculiar brand of "honorable leisure" was colored by the precepts of the Garden, then it lies at one end of the wide spectrum of Roman Epicurean (dis)engagement that we have been examining. A professed Epicurean could wholeheartedly pursue the political career expected from him and justify his public-minded actions with the hedonistic calculus, like Cassius and the Torquatus of *De finibus*; he could deviate from the normative behavior of his fellow senators through Epicurean-inspired political actions, such as Piso's rejection of unnecessary and anxiety-inducing honors; or he could, like Atticus, eschew a political career altogether while following Epicurus's teachings on friendship in building up a social network conducive to his own interests. Of course, some *equites* with Epicurean commitments may have chosen to live an entirely "hidden" life; the reason why we do not know about them is exactly because they were successful at escaping notice.

While there were thus different Epicurean approaches to politics, these do not map onto the support for specific individuals or groups. It has been claimed both that Epicureans were Caesarians or even protomonarchists looking for a sole ruler to enable their quietist life[163] and that they were good Republicans opposed to Caesar.[164] It is true that there seems to be, at certain times, a kind of social clustering of Epicureans around Caesar: Trebatius converted to Epicureanism while in Caesar's entourage and in the company of the likes of Pansa, and something similar may have happened to Cassius; Piso, of

162. Nepos, who provides all these examples of Atticus's friendship, is at pains to stress that there was nothing whatsoever self-serving or opportunistic about them (esp. 9.6, 11.3–4). His suppression of his subject's Epicureanism may be part of the same strategy: Nepos's Atticus had to be above the suspicion of cultivating his friends out of a mere hedonistic calculus.

163. See Grimal 1966, 1978. The contention that Roman Epicureans were looking for a benign monarch in Caesar is often supported by a political reading of Philodemus's treatise *On the Good King according to Homer*, which the philosopher dedicated to Piso. This work, whose date is unknown, is a kind of mirror of princes, explaining kingly virtues with examples from the Homeric poems. It has been variously interpreted but a connection to contemporary politics is not readily apparent; cf. Benferhat 2005: 219–29 (Benferhat throughout her book seeks to demolish the putative link between late Republican Epicureanism and monarchism). For Epicurean ideas of kingship, see McConnell 2010.

164. See Momigliano 1941: 151–57.

course, was Caesar's father-in-law.[165] In addition, there are tantalizing but in-
conclusive hints that Caesar himself had Epicurean leanings.[166] While no contemporary or later author associates him with the school, some of his reported
utterances have a suggestively Epicurean flavor, most notably his observation
(in his speech against the death penalty of the convicted Catilinarians in 63)
that death is not an evil but the end of all evils, and his remark (in the senate
in 46) that he had "lived enough for both nature and glory."[167]

In the absence of further evidence, the question of Caesar's own Epicurean
affiliation must remain open. As for the Epicureans among his followers, there
is no reason to believe that their Caesarianism was philosophically motivated.
Epicureans fought on both sides of the Civil War, with many of them—just
like their non-Epicurean peers—adjusting or switching their allegiances in
keeping with the developments of this turbulent time. Cassius supported
Pompey, then became Caesar's protégé, and finally led the plot against the
dictator's life;[168] the moderate Piso unsuccessfully attempted to negotiate between the parties both before the Civil War and after Caesar's death; and the
ever-careful Atticus maintained his outward neutrality while hedging his bets
and supporting opposing camps behind the scenes. Epicureanism offered no
advice on ideological grounds on whether to choose Pompey or Caesar, Antony or Octavian, even if general Epicurean principles might help the individual
actor make his political decision at a given moment.

The political significance of late Republican Epicureanism is thus similar to
that of the other schools we have been examining. Philosophy did not provide
political ideologies or prescriptions for specific behavior. Instead, it furnished
its adherents with ethical guidelines and techniques for determining their own
actions. Stoicism informed Cato's determined fight for a lost cause; Academic
Skepticism helped Cicero reason out his political attitudes and decisions; and
Epicureanism supplied Cassius, Piso, Atticus, and others with a way of calcu-
lating the long-term hedonistic benefits of their public actions. These men
were Roman senators, and their behavior was circumscribed by the norms and

165. See Fussl 1980, Benferhat 2005: 233–84, and Valachova 2018. How strong this Epicurean-
Caesarian link is depends on which Epicureans one considers Caesarians and which Caesarians
one considers Epicureans. In addition to the names mentioned above, the following have been
suggested by some scholars as belonging to both camps: L. Cornelius Balbus, A. Hirtius, C.
Oppius, and C. Matius.

166. See Volk forthcoming a with ample bibliography, as well as 4.2 below.

167. Death: Sall. *Cat.* 51.20, 52.13; Cic. *Cat.* 4.7. Nature and glory: Cic. *Marcell.* 25. On the
latter incident, see the discussion in 4.2 below.

168. On the philosophical background of the Ides of March, including Cassius's role, see
Sedley 1997 and 4.4 below.

customs of their order. At the same time, they were Stoics, Academics, and Epicureans, and their philosophical beliefs were part of their intellectual and emotional makeup and thus, to a greater or lesser extent, influenced or at least colored what they were doing. In the late Republic, philosophy thus crucially informed, not Roman politics as such, but Roman politicians.

4

Philosophy after Pharsalus

BY THE mid-first century BCE, as we have seen in the preceding chapter, philosophy had become domesticated at Rome and served at least some members of the elite not only as a learned pastime but also as an intellectual and moral tool in shaping and interpreting their actions. The claim of the philosophical schools to providing an art of life capable of enabling human beings to master adversities and achieve happiness was put to the test in a political climate that offered ever more threats not only to mental equilibrium but also to life and limb: as the comparatively quiet 60s gave way to the turbulent 50s, Roman public life became characterized by the machinations of the First Triumvirate, an increasing weakening of political institutions, and the violent gang warfare of Clodius and Milo. The decade ended with the complete breakdown of Republican order when Caesar crossed the Rubicon and the Roman world was plunged into a bloody civil war.

We have already caught some glimpses of how philosophically inclined senators used philosophy in attempting to cope with the crisis: Cato opted for stubborn Stoic resistance against Caesar and ultimately for Socratic suicide; Cicero employed Academic reasoning to determine his political duty; and such Epicureans as Atticus and Pansa made their individual (and widely divergent) Epicurean calculations for maximizing pleasure and minimizing pain. In this chapter, I focus on the role philosophy played in the period following Caesar's defeat of Pompey at Pharsalus on 9 August 48. While the Civil War continued in various theaters throughout the Mediterranean, many Pompeians had given up the fight, and Caesar's position as Rome's de facto sole ruler became ever more institutionalized. How did Roman senators react to a changed political landscape that bore little resemblance to the structure of Republican goverment to which they had been accustomed before? And in which way did philosophy—still, or again, or perhaps more than ever—color and inform their experiences and decisions?

My dicussion in what follows will by necessity be one-sided: for the years 49–43, our evidence for Roman intellectual life largely concerns the anti-Caesarians, the men who had fought or continued to fight for the Pompeian side and those who ultimately joined the conspiracy against the dictator (with a fair amount of overlap between the two groups).[1] The reason is, once again, the Ciceronian bias of our sources: while we know about the military events of the Civil War from Caesar's own *Commentarii*, the social and intellectual world and mood of those years come to life in Cicero's letters, whose cast of characters is strongly Republican. In addition, we have Cicero's extensive rhetorical and philosophical writings from this period, works that raise many questions about their author's intentions, attitudes, and states of mind. As a result, even though we know of philosophically inclined Caesarians (we have already encountered Pansa and will later meet Caesar's friend Matius), this chapter is largely concerned with the uses of philosophy made by those who in the Civil War had sided with Pompey—and perhaps a case could be made that these men, defeated and dissatisfied, had more of a need for the comforts and guidance that philosophy could offer. Thus, I first discuss the consolatory role of philosophy evoked in the correspondence of numerous Pompeians post-Pharsalus (4.1), before turning to their experience of the new political situation, in particular the limits of free speech under Caesar's rule (4.2). This second section will momentarily take us away from philosophy proper and has a strong Ciceronian flavor; in the subsequent section, I remain with Cicero but return to philosophy, in particular the famous philosophical corpus the author rapidly composed in 46–44 (4.3). The final part of the chapter considers the role played by philosophy in the conception, execution, and aftermath of the assassination of Caesar on the Ides of March 44 (4.4).

1. Pompeian Group Therapy

When Julius Caesar defeated Pompey at Pharsalus, dozens of Roman senators found themselves in a tricky situation. They had joined forces with Pompey out of political conviction or personal loyalty, or simply because it had seemed to be the lesser of two evils, and they now had to make up their minds what to do next.[2] Should they follow Pompey and other diehard Republicans and carry on the war in a different locale, or should they count their losses, throw

1. Here and elsewhere, I loosely refer to such men as "Republicans," a term that has little to do with republicanism as defined by modern political science and absolutely nothing with contemporary party affiliations. For variety's sake, I occasionally refer to Caesar as "the dictator," whether he held the dictatorship at a particular moment or not, in light of the fact that he did so for most of the period 49–44.

2. For lists of senators in the Pompeian and Caesarian camps during the Civil War, see Shackleton Bailey 1960 and Bruhns 1978: 31–63.

themselves on Caesar's much-advertised *clementia*, and hope for the best? While a number of senators, most famously the younger Cato, openly continued the anti-Caesarian resistance, many others withdrew from the conflict and endeavored to come to terms with Caesar, hoping to return to Italy and ultimately reenter political life.

Among these recanting Pompeians, some men did better than others.[3] A number were pardoned right away and flourished under Caesar's protection (Brutus and Cassius come to mind); others languished in limbo (witness Cicero's eleven-month stay in Brundisium) before finally being allowed to return; and a third group was still in exile when Caesar breathed his last in March 44—if they had not died in the meantime, as, for example, the polymath and astrologer Nigidius Figulus, who passed away in 45, still waiting for Caesar's pardon. Whatever their individual fates, however, these men shared a number of experiences and concerns. They had seen their own party defeated, an event that involved not only a fair amount of bloodshed but also the apparent end of the political world as they knew it. Many had suffered personal losses, including the death or alienation of family members, destruction or diminution of property, and separation from their homes and loved ones. They were worried about how they would be treated by Caesar and his followers, or otherwise by the remaining committed defenders of the Republican cause. While the Civil War raged on, there was uncertainty about who the victor would be and what he would do; once Caesar had conquered his foes, the depressing realization set in that the perpetual dictator was there to stay. Even apart from any immediate fears, hopes, and anxieties, many of the Pompeian survivors agonized over whether they had made the right decisions, both politically and ethically, and what their present and future actions should be. In sum, these elite Roman men were, to use a modern term, traumatized, and in their attempts to cope with their grief, anger, doubt, and fear, they turned to two sources of support: their social network of like-minded *amici*—and philosophy.

This section explores what I somewhat flippantly refer to as Pompeian group therapy: the various ways in which defeated Pompeians post-Pharsalus used philosophy to cope, and help each other cope, with their difficult situation. The turn to philosophy of one of the most prominent ex-Pompeians, Cicero, is well documented, and the manifold interconnections of his philosophical corpus of the mid-40s with the political situation at the time have elicited much scholarly interest and will be the subject of my discussion in 4.3.

---

3. Pina Polo 2019 traces the fates of individual Pompeians; for Caesar's policy vis-à-vis his defeated foes, see Jehne 1987.

For the moment, however, my focus is on the wider phenomenon of elite Roman uses of philosophy as a coping mechanism or consolation (hence the "therapy" of my heading) as well as on the communality and sociability of such practices (hence "group"). I use as my main evidence Cicero's letters of the period, which document not only the author's interactions with a wide variety of people, but also the ways in which his correspondents relate both to Cicero and to one another. Since especially the collection *Ad familiares* contains not only letters by Cicero himself but also ones addressed to him by his friends and since, in addition, the actions and attitudes of Cicero's addressees can often be inferred from Cicero's own letters, we are able to use the epistolary corpus as a source for not only the life and personality of one prominent individual, but also the practices of a whole network of men in a similar situation.[4]

My time frame extends from Cicero's return to Rome in the fall of 47 to the death of his daughter Tullia in mid-February 45. The latter event was traumatic for Cicero, and concerns in his correspondence shift accordingly, as new grief calls for new forms of therapy. My chosen period is longer than one might think: the year 46 saw the implementation of Caesar's calendar reform, which involved the intercalation of an extra month after February and two additional ones between November and December. It is also a very eventful time, in terms both of larger historical developments and of Cicero's own life. The Civil War continued as Caesar battled the remaining Pompeians first in Africa and then Spain; subsequent to the Battle of Thapsus in April 46, the younger Cato committed suicide, turning himself into a Republican martyr. In Rome, Cicero got divorced from Terentia and married Publilia; he delivered speeches in support of the exiled Pompeians Marcellus and Ligarius; and he embarked on a writing spree, penning his *Brutus, Paradoxa Stoicorum, De optimo genere oratorum, Cato, Orator,* and *Hortensius.* Throughout, he kept up an active correspondence—not so much with Atticus, since the two friends were mostly in Rome together—but with numerous *familiares,* prominently a large number of former Pompeians, including M. Terentius Varro, L. Mescinius Rufus, L. Domitius Ahenobarbus, M. Claudius Marcellus, P. Nigidius Figulus, Ser. Sulpicius Rufus, Q. Ligarius, T. Ampius Balbus, L. Lucceius, A. Manlius Torquatus, C. Cassius Longinus, Cn. Plancius, and C. Toranius.[5]

---

4. Compare my discussion in this section with the treatment of the same corpus of letters in Steel 2005: 96–103 and Gildenhard 2018, who both stress Cicero's attempts at political community-building. I am in general agreement with their reading but more interested in the communality and reciprocity of such efforts, as well as in their philosophical aspects.

5. The fact that so many of these letters survive reflects the choice of the ancient editor(s) of the collection *Ad familiares,* who must have considered Cicero's interactions with other

First, however, let us consider another letter, written *to* Cicero, which has not survived but which we are told about in the *Brutus*. In late 47, Brutus wrote to Cicero a letter that according to its recipient had a remarkable effect: "for you should know that from a long crisis, which affected my entire health, I have been recalled to the light of day, as it were, by this letter."[6] Cicero—either still at Brundisium or just returned to Rome—was suffering from acute depression, and Brutus's epistle was the first thing to cheer him up and, so to speak, bring him back to life and to his previous intellectual pursuits (*ad pristina studia, Brut.* 11). As we saw in 2.3, what Brutus sent was not any old letter, but his philosophical treatise *De uirtute*.[7] This is a pivotal moment in the history of Roman philosophy: the work is one of the very first Latin philosophical prose treatises (preceded, as far as we know, only by Cicero's *De re publica* and perhaps *De legibus*, as well as Amafinius's and Rabirius's Epicurean writings); in it, Brutus, an adherent of Antiochus's "Old Academy," presented an argument to the effect that virtue is sufficient for happiness.[8] *De uirtute* plays an important role in Cicero's thought and work: it kicks off his period of greatest creativity (as discussed in 2.3, the *Brutus* is the author's return gift to his friend, the first of a whole series of works dedicated to Brutus), and its central thesis is one that Cicero was going to grapple with throughout the months to come, not only in the philosophical discussions of *De finibus* and *Tusculans* but also, as we shall see, in the letters.

De uirtute is also a prime example of the phenomenon I am investigating: one ex-Pompeian uses philosophy to cheer up—or, in Cicero words, "advise and console" (*monere . . . et consolari, Brut.* 11)—another, and while we can only guess at the exact arguments Brutus used, we know that the political situation

---

ex-Pompeians of special interest (compare Steel 2005: 96 and Martelli 2017); two books (4 and 6) are dedicated in their entirety to the correspondence with such individuals, and additional letters are found in other books. On the themes and structure specifically of *Fam.* 4, see Gibson forthcoming; on *Fam.* 6, see Grillo 2016; generally on the editorial selection behind the exant corpus of Ciceronian letters, see Beard 2002, esp. 120–30; P. White 2010: 31–61; and Bishop 2019: 219–57. Note that while the vast majority of the passages cited in this chapter come from Cicero's correspondence with members of the senatorial class, I have included a few letters to nonsenators that exhibit similar features and lines of argument.

6. *Brut.* 12: *nam me istis scito litteris ex diuturna perturbatione totius ualetudinis tamquam ad aspiciendam lucem esse reuocatum* (cf. also 11).

7. See Hendrickson 1939 and further 2.3, n. 100.

8. See Hendrickson 1939 for what we know about the content of *De uirtute*; testimonia and fragments are now found in Garbarino 2003. On Brutus's Antiocheanism, see esp. Sedley 1997 and Lévy 2012a: 300–303. Cicero's reponse to *De uirtute* in the *Brutus* is discussed by Dugan 2005: 236–48.

was by no means elided in the treatise. As an *exemplum* of the self-sufficiency of virtue, Brutus cited the Pompeian M. Claudius Marcellus, happy despite his exile on the island of Lesbos. Marcellus was one of Cicero's correspondents during this period and was pardoned by Caesar in the fall of 46 (witness Cicero's speech *Pro Marcello*, discussed in 4.2); in *De uirtute*, Brutus apparently presented Marcellus as a kind of Pompeian philosophical sage, a man who, secure in his *uirtus*, is able to weather all adversity. Interestingly, this is a strategy similar to the one Brutus was going to pursue a few months later with his uncle Cato: as we will see in 4.2, in the pamphlet war following Cato's suicide, Brutus did his best, through both his own publications and those commissioned from others, to cement the image of Cato as a Stoic, anti-Caesarian saint.

Turning now to Cicero's extant correspondence with his fellow ex-Pompeians, we see the same motifs and concerns coming up again and again in letters to and from different people. Cicero and his friends express a strong sense of mutual obligation: not only is Cicero, situated in Rome, actively engaged in the relief effort for those followers of Pompey still abroad, working to bring about Caesar's pardon, but in addition to such more tangible help, there is also an understanding that friends are obliged to provide emotional support to one another. As Cicero writes to Ligarius, "in your present circumstances, I owe it to our friendship to write to you something to comfort you or cheer you up."[9] Occasionally, the letter writer mentions explicitly that he has heard that the addressee is upset,[10] alluding to a network of friends beyond himself and the immediate correspondent: people keep him informed of the addressee's situation and state of mind,[11] and the correspondent is encouraged to turn to mutual friends for additional intellectual and emotional support.[12]

The main work all such letters are supposed to do is that of comforting, *consolari*, the addressee. As the remark to Ligarius just quoted makes clear, Cicero and his correspondents are explicit about this task, and there are numerous places in the letters where the writer reflects on the various ways of providing comfort and their efficacy.[13] Throughout, Cicero and his friends are making valiant and cheerful efforts to alleviate one another's distress; just occasionally, there is an acknowledgment that the present circumstances may be too dire to allow for any *consolatio*. Thus Cicero admits to Marcellus: "if the

9. *Fam.* 6.13.1: *tali tuo tempore me aut consolandi aut iuuandi tui causa scribere ad te aliquid pro nostra amicitia oportebat.*

10. See *Fam.* 4.1.1; 6.1.1, 6 (both letters are discussed in greater detail below).

11. See the examples cited in the previous n., as well as *Fam.* 6.6.2.

12. See *Fam.* 6.1.6 (discussed below in the text), 6.4.5.

13. See *Fam.* 4.3.2–3, 4.8.1, 4.13; 6.1.3–7, 6.3.3–4, 6.4, 6.5.2, 6.13.1, 6.21.1.

great disaster of the commonwealth is distressing you, I am not so ingenious as to be able to comfort you, seeing that I cannot comfort myself."[14]

Of course, the *consolatio* was an established philosophical genre, with which Cicero and his correspondents were well acquainted.[15] In their letters, they adapt it to their unique circumstances, retooling old techniques and employing new ones, and combining common-sensical reasoning with highly philosophical arguments. The basic thesis the consoler is trying to prove to the consoled is that the apparent present evil is not in fact an evil at all, a line of approach based on the typical intellectualism of most ancient philosophy, according to which rational understanding will automatically lead to emotional adjustment.

Some of the arguments employed to prove that things are not as bad as they appear are fairly ad hoc: thus Cicero can maintain to people stuck far from Rome that, contrary to what they may think, being away from the center of all misery is actually a blessing;[16] conversely, when trying to persuade Marcellus to return to the city, Cicero claims that even under the present circumstances, Rome is still the place to be.[17] Another popular misperception that Cicero is trying to clear up is the belief that Caesar is a monster and/or dead set against the correspondent: the man is actually not as bad as all that, and Cicero has it on good authority that he is increasingly favorably inclined to his former enemies.

A special subcategory of the "*x* is not an evil" argument is the claim that the ultimate disaster, death, is not in fact a *malum* at all.[18] This is of course a philosophical commonplace, developed at great length just a few months later in *Tusculans* 1. The reason that Cicero feels the need to assert this repeatedly is not simply that it makes such a good a fortiori argument (If death is not an evil, what can be?), but that in those early months after Pharsalus, with the Civil War still in the balance, proscriptions or a massacre were very much felt to be in the cards, especially if the remaining diehard Pompeians were to prevail over Caesar and take their revenge against Cicero and his turncoat friends.

What is striking is how in the letters, the ad hoc "*x* is really not so bad" line of reasoning frequently morphs into a far more strictly philosophical argument, according to which the reason "*x* is not an evil" is that the only evil is vice:

---

14. *Fam.* 4.8.1: *sin te tanta mala rei publicae frangunt, non ita abundo ingenio ut te consoler, cum ipse me non possim.*

15. On the genre of the *consolatio*, see Kassel 1958 and Scourfield 2013. For *consolatio* in Cicero's letters, see Guttilla 1968–69, Zehnacker 1985, Hutchinson 1998: 49–77, Wilcox 2005, and Schwitter 2017.

16. See *Fam.* 4.3.2, 4.4.2, 5; 6.1.1, 6.4.3.

17. See *Fam.* 4.7–10. Cf. Zehnacker 1985: 77 and Gildenhard 2018: 232.

18. See *Fam.* 5.21.4; 6.3.3, 6.4.4.

since the conduct of Cicero and his friends during and after the Civil War has been blameless, it follows that no evil has befallen them.[19] This is, of course, a classic Stoic argument, one that during this time becomes a central feature of Cicero's intellectual landscape.[20] He returns to it repeatedly in the letters, as well as in his philosophical works, and it is clear that it is a way of thinking that he frequently uses to evaluate his own past and present actions and states of mind.

This thought is developed at some length in the following passage from a letter to A. Manlius Torquatus, which contains a number of the key words and concepts of the communal philosophical therapy shared by Cicero and his friends (*Fam.* 6.4.2):

> hoc loco si uideo augere dolorem tuum quem <u>consolando</u> leuare debebam, fateor me communium malorum <u>consolationem</u> nullam inuenire praeter illam, quae tamen, si eam possis suscipere, maxima est quaque ego cottidie magis utor, <u>conscientiam</u> rectae <u>uoluntatis</u> maximam <u>consolationem</u> esse rerum incommodarum nec esse ullum magnum malum praeter <u>culpam</u>. a qua quoniam tantum absumus ut etiam optime senserimus <u>euentus</u>que magis nostri <u>consili</u> quam <u>consilium</u> reprehendatur et quoniam praestiti-mus quod debuimus, moderate quod <u>euenit</u> feremus.

> If at this point I seem to increase your pain rather than relieving it, as I ought to, by <u>consolation</u>, I must admit that I cannot find any <u>consolation</u> for our common calamities—except one, which (if you are capable of mak-ing use of it) is the most efficacious and which I myself employ more often every day: the greatest <u>consolation</u> in adversity is <u>awareness</u> that one has had the right <u>intentions</u> and that there is no great evil except for <u>guilt</u>. Of the latter, we are entirely free; indeed, our attitude was so correct that only the <u>outcome</u> of our <u>intentions</u> can be faulted, not our <u>intentions</u> them-selves. Since we did what we ought to have done, we will bear the <u>outcome</u> in a self-possessed manner.

The goal remains *consolatio*, which in the depressing political circumstances can be supplied only by the individual's *conscientia*, awareness, that he has done the right thing. No *culpa*, fault or guilt, attaches to Cicero and his fellow

---

19. See *Fam.* 5.21.5; 6.1.4 (discussed below in the text), 6.2.3, 6.3.4, 6.4.2 (discussed below in the text), 6.20.3; 7.3.4; 9.5.2, 9.16.5. Cicero reprises the argument after the death of Caesar in a letter to Cornificius (*Fam.* 12.23.4).

20. See Bringmann 1971: 64–65 and Griffin 1995: 335–36. Cicero's *Paradoxa Stoicorum*, writ-ten in spring 46, sets out to defend this putatively counterintuitive Stoic doctrine by means of effective rhetoric and shows many points of philosophical and political contact with the letters of the same period; see Kumaniecki 1957 and Wassmann 1996: 96–138.

ex-Pompeians: in acting, they had the right intention, *uoluntas* or *consilium*, and if the outcome, *euentus*, was not what they were hoping to achieve, this does not detract from the intrinsic virtue of their actions.[21] This last argument resembles another Stoic tenet: preferred indifferents are to be pursued, but an agent's virtue and hence happiness do not depend on the outcome of this pursuit.

Note, however, that Cicero is not treating the *euentus* he and his friends were hoping for as an indifferent: though he stresses again and again in the letters that there is no *malum* other than *culpa*, he nowhere explicitly makes the converse claim that, as the Stoics maintain, nothing but virtue is a good.[22] While maintaining the self-sufficiency of virtue, Cicero implicitly at least leaves open the possibility that there may be other, lesser goods, as argued, notably, by Antiochus, who held that virtue enables us to live a happy life, but that the *happiest* life additionally requires the presence of external goods; this, as we know, was the position that the Antiochean Brutus took in *De uirtute* as well.[23]

The very fact, of course, that Cicero keeps harping on the point that only *culpa* is an evil shows how far he and his correspondents are from being actual wise men: the sage presumably has no need for *consolatio*, whereas these Roman senators fully acknowledge their wish to comfort and be comforted in turn. This explains the further twist Cicero gives to the "I know I did the right thing" argument. Having *conscientia* (this word shows up frequently in the letters[24]) of the virtuousness of one's own actions is not only helpful for

---

21. Note, though, the tentative way in which Cicero phrases his assertion: awareness of the blamelessness of one's actions is the greatest comfort—if one can accept it (*si eam possis suscipere*). Likewise, he does not claim that there is absolutely no *malum* other than *culpa*—only that there is not "any great" (*ullum magnum*) one. Similarly, in *Fam.* 6.1.3 (discussed below in the text), he does not deny outright that anyone who can sustain himself with *optimorum consiliorum conscientia* is *miser*; rather, he "fears" (*uereor*) that calling such a person miserable would be "blasphemous" (*nefas*). Cicero's disinclination to make stronger claims may have to do with the style and rhetoric of his letters (hitting his addressees over the head with hardcore philosophical tenets would not be in keeping with the polite urbanity of upperclass correspondence), but may also be a sign of his skepticism: it may be probable that there is no evil but vice, but that does not mean that it is an unassailable truth.

22. Pace Griffin 1995: 335–36. Of course, the two points logically entail one another, but it is perfectly conceivable that a person not committed to the Stoic "either/or" approach might take a minimalist view of evil (= only vice) while expecting somewhat more from the highest good (= virtue plus). The question whether virtue is not only necessary and sufficient for happiness but also its only and exclusive source is one that Cicero struggled with throughout his life; cf. esp. the discussions in *Fin.* 3–5 and *Tusc.* 5.

23. Cicero himself ascribes the Antiochean view to Brutus at *Tusc.* 5.12, 21, 30, 34.

24. *Fam.* 4.3.1; 5.13.4 (discussed below in the text), 5.21.2; 6.1.3 (discussed below in the text), 6.4.2 (discussed above in the text), 6.6.12, 6.10.4, 6.13.5; 9.16.6; see also *conscius* in *Fam.* 6.21.1.

reminding oneself that one's virtue guarantees one's ability to live a happy life. It is also pleasant, and hence comforting, in and of itself to recall one's good deeds, either alone or with a like-minded individual. Thus Cicero thanks his friend Lucceius for having given him, in a consolatory letter "pleasant recollections of my good conscience," a phrase that sounds positively Epicurean.[25] The Epicureans, of course, maintained that present distress can be alleviated by the memories of past pleasures, a technique that Cicero scoffs at in *Tusculans*, but one that he may have found not unhelpful in his own situation.[26]

While Cicero's choice of philosophical arguments is eclectic (a practice in keeping with his Academic Skepticism), he is explicit about the role philosophy plays in his efforts to comfort himself and others. Without referring to specific schools, he makes clear that many of his consolatory arguments are philosophical in nature, positing a final goal of *bene* or *beate uiuere*.[27] He also frequently recommends the practice of philosophy as a form of self-therapy, often citing himself as an example for its efficacy.[28] How "philosophical" any given letter is depends on the situation and on the addressee, but considering this body of correspondence as a whole, it is striking to what extent philosophical discourse is part and parcel of Cicero's interactions with his fellow Pompeian Civil War survivors.

It would be interesting—but beyond the scope of this discussion—to trace the continuities between these correspondences and Cicero's philosophical oeuvre of the following years. I just note that in the *Tusculans*, written in the summer of 45 BCE, Cicero provides, as it were, a primer of *consolatio*,

---

Cf. Grillo 2016: 408–9. The term may also have been used in Brutus's *De uirtute*, referring to Marcellus: in *Brut.* 250, Cicero has the character Brutus describe Marcellus on Lesbos as comforting himself (*consoletur*) with his *conscientia optimae mentis*; Hendrickson 1939: 408–9 plausibly suggests that Cicero is here drawing on Brutus's treatise. Further on Cicero's ideas about *conscientia*, see Gildenhard 2011: 104–24, 2018: 229–30.

25. *Fam.* 5.13.4: *das enim mihi iucundas recordationes conscientiae nostrae rerumque earum quas te in primis auctore gessimus. praestitimus enim patriae non minus certe quam debuimus* ("You offer me pleasant recollections of my good conscience and of those things I have done, with you in particular encouraging me. For I certainly served the country no less than was my duty"); see also *Fam.* 6.21.2.

26. See *Tusc.* 3.28–51, with Graver 2002: 96–106. Of course, at first glance, the past pleasures recalled by Epicureans would appear to be a far cry from the past virtues fondly remembered by Lucceius and Cicero. Note however, on the one hand, the Epicurean claim that pleasure always entails virtue (see 3.3 above on Cassius and Pansa) and, on the other, that Cicero himself alludes to the pleasure at least of the recollection itself (*iucundas recordationes*, *Fam.* 5.13.4).

27. See *Fam.* 4.3.3 (discussed below in the text); 5.13.1; 6.1.3 (dicussed below in the text).

28. See *Fam.* 4.3.3–4 (discussed below in the text), 4.4.4–5; 6.4.3, 6.22.2; 15.18.

summarizing the various approaches a consoler can take and linking them up with the philosophical schools that recommend them:[29]

> haec igitur officia sunt consolantium, tollere aegritudinem funditus aut se-dare aut detrahere quam plurumum aut supprimere nec pati manare lon-gius aut ad alia traducere. sunt qui unum officium consolantis putent malum illud omnino non esse, ut Cleanthi placet; sunt qui non magnum malum, ut Peripatetici; sunt qui abducant a malis ad bona, ut Epicurus; sunt qui satis putent ostendere nihil inopinati accidisse <, ut Cyrenaici>. Chrysippus autem caput esse censet in consolando detrahere illam opinionem maerenti, qua se officio fungi putet iusto atque debito. sunt etiam qui haec omnia genera consolandi colligant—alius enim alio modo mouetur—ut fere nos in Consolatione omnia in consolationem unam coniecimus.

> These, then, are the tasks of the consoler: to completely eradicate the dis-tress, or to calm it, or to remove it as much as possible, or to suppress it and prevent it from developing further, or to redirect it to something else. There are those who think the sole job of the consoler is [to show] that there is no evil present at all, as Cleanthes thinks; or that it isn't a great evil, as the Peripatetics. There are those who distract [the mind] from evils to goods, as Epicurus; and those who think it is enough to prove that nothing unex-pected has happened <, as the Cyrenaics>. But Chrysippus believes that the most important thing in consolation is to free the mourner from the belief that he is doing a just and necessary duty. Finally, there are also those who combine all consolatory approaches—for different people are affected in different ways—just as I myself in the *Consolatio* put them all together into one consolation.

Here we learn that the Stoics argue that the perceived evil is not a *malum* at all, the Peripatetics that it is not a great *malum*, the Epicureans swear by the recollection of past *bona*, and so forth. Of course, by this point, Tullia has died, and Cicero has studied every piece of consolatory literature he could get his hands on.[30] As he reports in the passage just quoted, he has found it useful, in the *Consolatio* written to himself, to use a combination of various consola-tory approaches. This same eclectic procedure is in evidence already in the

---

29. *Tusc.* 3.75–76. See also the following paragraphs, *Tusc.* 3.77–84. On Cicero's engagement with the consolatory tradition in *Tusc.* 3, see S. A. White 1995 and Graver 2002.

30. *Att.* 12.14.3: *nihil enim de maerore minuendo scriptum ab ullo est quod ego non domi tuae legerim* ("for nothing has been written by anyone about the lessening of grief that I have not read at your house").

earlier letters to and from his fellow Pompeians, when the *malum* in question was a shared rather than private one.[31]

To illustrate my general observations on the epistolary strategies of the communal Pompeian therapy project, I conclude this section with a closer look at two Ciceronian letters. The first, to Ser. Sulpicius Rufus, was written perhaps in September of 46 (*Fam.* 4.3). The famous lawyer and consul of 51 was an old friend; he had been pardoned soon after Pharsalus, and at the time of the letter was governor of the province Achaea at Caesar's behest.[32] However, just like Cicero, he was anything but happy with the state of affairs. The very opening of the letter demonstrates the group dynamics of Roman *amicitia*, where members of the same social network watch out for each other (*Fam.* 4.3.1):

> uehementer te esse sollicitum et in communibus miseriis praecipuo quo-dam dolore angi multi ad nos quotidie deferunt.

> Many people tell me every day that you are very upset and during our shared suffering are pained by some particular distress.

Cicero expresses his solidarity, saying that he himself is suffering great distress from the upheaval of the *res publica*. However, Sulpicius needs to use his *sapientia* to comfort himself, just as Cicero has derived comfort from the awareness of the moral faultlessness of his own past decisions.[33]

Cicero proceeds to remind his addressee that Sulpicius, too, has absolutely done the right thing (in fact, if people had listened to him during his consulship, the Civil War would not have happened, 4.3.1) and comforts his friend by reminding him of Caesar's favor (4.3.2). Reflecting self-consciously on his consolatory strategy, he states that he is engaging in *consolatio* in order that Sulpicius might learn from his good friend that there are indeed things that can alleviate his distress.[34] However, Cicero emphasizes, the greatest comfort lies in Sulpicius himself: he is a man who from his early youth has dedicated himself to the study of philosophy and to "what the wisest men have had to say about the good life."[35]

31. Compare Zehnacker 1985.

32. We have little direct evidence for Sulpicius's actions during the Civil War, but I agree with Shackleton Bailey 1960: 253–54 n. 7 against Münzer 1931: 854–55 that Cicero's later statements (esp. *Fam.* 6.6.10) strongly suggest that he joined Pompey rather than remaining neutral.

33. *Fam.* 4.3.1: *tamen multa iam consolantur maximeque conscientia consiliorum meorum.*

34. *Fam.* 4.3.3.: *quoad certior ab homine amicissimo fieres iis de rebus quibus leuari possent molestiae tuae.*

35. *Fam.* 4.3.3: *te autem ab initio aetatis memoria teneo summe omnium doctrinarum studiosum fuisse omniaque quae a sapientissimis uiris ad bene uiuendum tradita essent summo studio curaque didicisse.*

Given that at the moment, there is little call for oratory (Cicero's special talent) or law (Sulpicius's expertise), Cicero has transferred all his efforts to philosophy and is confident that Sulpicius is doing the same thing. Philosophy is a real help and comfort in these dark times—but even if it were less useful, it would still provide a welcome distraction.[36]

This is just one of the seven letters that make up Cicero's correspondence with Sulpicius, two of which are by Sulpicius himself.[37] Already before the Civil War, we see the two men agonizing over how to act, a question that is put into quite philosophical terms by Cicero in *Ad familiares* 4.1 and 2.[38] After the defeat at Pharsalus, the friends engage in the kind of mutual therapy that is the topic of this section: in the letter we just looked at and in the one that follows (*Fam.* 4.4), it is Cicero who is comforting Sulpicius; after the death of Tullia, however, Sulpicius takes on the task of *consolatio*, attempting to reach Cicero in his period of deepest grief (*Fam.* 4.5). It is also Sulpicius who in May 45 gives his correspondent the shocking news of the murder of their fellow Pompeian Marcellus, Brutus's philosophical paragon, who, though pardoned by Caesar, never made it back to Rome (*Fam.* 4.12).

Cicero's addressee in the final letter I wish to discuss is far less well known, and there are some questions concerning his exact identity. Most likely, A. Manlius Torquatus was a praetorian of the same age as Cicero, who at the time of the correspondence was living in self-imposed exile in Athens.[39] We have four letters to him, from one of which I have already quoted; they are striking for being among the most technically philosophical of all the letters written to former Pompeians at this period, with the exception perhaps of the—rather different—correspondence with Cassius discussed in 3.3. I here focus on the first extant letter to Torquatus (*Fam.* 6.1), where we find evidence of the same kind of social network we saw in the letter to Sulpicius. Not only has Cicero learned about Torquatus's emotional distress from a common acquaintance,

---

36. *Fam.* 4.3.4: *quae etiam si minus prodessent, animum tamen a sollicitudine abducerent.*

37. *Fam.* 4.1–5, 12. This does not include thirteen letters of recommendation written to Sulpicius in the same period of time (*Fam.* 13.17–28a).

38. See esp. *Fam.* 4.2.2: *si quid rectissimum sit quaerimus, perspicuum est; si quid maxime expediat, obscurum. sin ii sumus qui profecto esse debemus, ut nihil arbitremur expedire nisi quod rectum honestumque sit, non potest esse dubium quid faciendum nobis sit* ("If we are asking what is the right thing [to do], it is obvious; if what is most expedient, it is unclear. But if we are the kind of men we ought to be, ones who do not consider anything expedient except what is right and honorable, then there is no doubt what we ought to do"); cf. 3.2 above on Cicero's philosophical decision-making before and during the Civil War.

39. See Shackleton Bailey 1977: 2.408–9, as well as, for greater detail, Münzer 1928 and J. F. Mitchell 1966.

a certain Philargyrus (probably a freedman), but since Torquatus currently resides in Athens, he can take advantage of the presence of none other than Sulpicius Rufus, a friend who will be able to comfort him "with benevolence and wisdom."[40] Thus, Cicero consoles Torquatus and Sulpicius; Sulpicius consoles Cicero and Torquatus; and many common friends, including Philargyrus, make sure that these men know when one of their group is in need of emotional support.[41]

Once again, Cicero reflects explicitly on his own task as a consoler, mustering a number of arguments, including that Torquatus is missing nothing by being away from Rome; that Caesar may come around; and that any personal afflictions of Torquatus's are just part of the disaster that is affecting everyone (*Fam.* 6.1.1–2). But, Cicero asks himself rhetorically, is not the very existence of such a *commune periculum rei publicae* the very thing that Torquatus finds the most upsetting (6.1.3)? Indeed, and the only true *consolatio* for this kind of distress relies on a person's own strength of mind (ibid.):

> si enim bene sentire recteque facere satis est ad bene beateque uiuendum, uereor ne eum, qui se optimorum consiliorum conscientia sustentare possit, miserum esse nefas sit dicere.

> For if good thought and right action are enough for a good and happy life, I believe it would be blasphemy to call a man miserable who is able to support himself with the awareness of having made the right decisions.

Torquatus and Cicero entered the Civil War not for selfish motivations, but out of a sense of duty toward the *res publica*; since they knew full well that they might end up on the losing side, the actual negative outcome holds no surprise for them (6.1.3–4). Following *ratio* and *ueritas*, they need to take the attitude that the only thing they are answerable for is moral fault (*culpa*)—but that is something of which they are free (6.1.4). As Cicero sums up his argument, "the point of this speech is that even when everything else is lost, virtue nevertheless seems to be able to sustain itself."[42] In other words, virtue is sufficient for happiness, just as Brutus had written in *De uirtute*; the defeated Pompeians thus

---

40. *Fam.* 6.1.6: *beneuolentia et sapientia.* Unfortunately, a couple of letters later Sulpicius has left Athens: *Fam.* 6.4.5.

41. Torquatus himself has consoled Cicero in the past: *Fam.* 6.1.5.

42. *Fam.* 6.1.4: *atque haec eo pertinet oratio, ut perditis rebus omnibus tamen ipsa uirtus se sustentare posse uideatur.* Note the clausula $-\cup\cup\cup--$, which lends the sentence special weight (see Hutchinson 1998: 9–12 on prose rhythm in Cicero's letters), even though *uideatur* ("seems" rather than "is") rings the kind of skeptical, tentative note we have seen elsewhere (compare n. 21 above). In another letter to Torquatus, probably written shortly after *Fam.* 6.1, Cicero

emerge not only as the moral victors of the Civil War, but as true philosophers who know how to effectively console themselves and one another.

2. The Limits of *libertas*

The consolatory strategies found in the Ciceronian correspondence of the early Caesarian period present something of an inward turn: the defeated Pompeians employ philosophy to make themselves and one another feel better, stressing the self-sufficiency of virtue as a guarantee of their own moral recitude and ability to live happily despite the adversities that have befallen them. At the same time, they recommend the study of philosophy as both a means of coping with the situation and a welcome distraction. What, however, of these senators' public lives? On the assumption that their political sympathies were still the same, were they doomed to either serving Caesar without conviction or otherwise retreating into private life? Was there still scope for the kind of "engaged philosophy" that, say, Cato and Cicero had practiced before and throughout the Civil War? Or were any *studia* now confined to, as it were, an *otium sine dignitate*, divorced from all public endeavors? Would members of the Roman upper class still be able to integrate their intellectual and their political activities under the new regime, as they had done before?

Unsurprisingly, we find Cicero, that intensely political animal, grappling with these questions in his post–Civil War letters and published works. As he dispenses philosophical *consolatio* to his friends and to himself throughout the long year 46 and into 45, he is also attempting to define his own role under Caesar's rule and determine—through trial and error, in conversation, letters, and a body of diverse writings—to what extent he still has a public voice and how far he can go in expressing his opinions. As so often, Cicero is the person for whose thoughts and doings in this period we have by far the most evidence, and given his personality and interests, he does present a special case. However, as we will see, others were dealing with the same problems and trying to find their own solutions.[43]

Cicero's conflicting thoughts on how to reinvent himself post-Pharsalus are reflected particularly well in his correspondence with Varro of the first half of 46.[44] Cicero had not previously been overly fond of this most scholarly

---

admonishes his addressee to sustain *himself* by means of his *uirtus*: *tu uelim te, ut debes et soles, tua uirtute sustentes* (*Fam.* 6.4.5).

43. For this section, compare the valuable discussion of J. Hall 2009b.

44. *Fam.* 9.1–7. On these letters, compare Baraz 2012: 78–86, Gunderson 2016, and Cappello 2019: 45–56.

inclined of his fellow senators,[45] but either the shared Civil War experience had brought the two men closer together, or it was Cicero's unilateral initiative after his return to Rome to seek a more intimate bond with a peer of similar interests in the same situation. The letters (all from Cicero; the Varronian side of the correspondence does not survive) attest to the men's anxiety about their precarious situation as defeated Pompeians and worries about how to behave toward the victorious Caesarians and—upon his expected return from Africa—toward Caesar himself. In addition, however, Cicero raises larger questions about what the two senators are now supposed to be doing with their lives.

In his very first extant letter to Varro (perhaps still from late 47), Cicero shares his mental anguish with his friend, but also reports on a new turn his life has taken now that he is back in Rome (*Fam.* 9.1.2):

> scito enim me, postea quam in urbem uenerim, redisse cum ueteribus ami-cis, id est cum libris nostris, in gratiam.

> You should know that after my return to the city, I made up with my old friends, that is, my books.

Using the language of *amicitia*, Cicero expresses his strong emotional bond to his books, that is, his *studia*, but also hints that they have been better "friends" to him than his human associates. In joining the Civil War, Cicero continues, he abandoned his books and their precepts, a decision he has come to regret. However, the old friendship has been rekindled (2):

> ignoscunt mihi, reuocant in consuetudinem pristinam teque, quod in ea permanseris, sapientiorem me dicunt fuisse.

> They forgive me and call me back into our former relationship and say that you, who always remained there, were wiser than I.

The message seems clear: Cicero renounces his party politics and returns to his *studia*, asserting the superior wisdom of Varro, who he claims never abandoned his true vocation.[46]

---

45. On the relationship of Cicero and Varro, see the literature cited in 2.3, n. 90.

46. One wonders what exactly Cicero saw as the difference between himself and Varro: after all, both men joined the war, but only in Cicero's case is this presented as a betrayal of his books and their (no doubt philosophical) precepts: *uidebar enim mihi ... praeceptis illorum* [sc. *libro-rum*] *non satis paruisse* (*Fam.* 9.1.2). Apparently, he viewed Varro as inherently more suited and dedicated to scholarship and able to retreat fully into his *studia* in a way that Cicero himself found difficult (the fact that Cicero was a consular, and proud of it, may also have played a role: perhaps he thought that a mere praetorian like Varro could cede from the political stage more

In the following letter (*Fam.* 9.3), Cicero stresses the benefit he and Varro are at this time deriving from their *artes*, which serve as medicine for their current ills, and in the one after that (*Fam.* 9.2), he exhorts his friend to share in his intellectual pursuits (*una uiuere in studiis nostris*, 5), since these provide not only pleasure (*delectationem*) but—crucial in these dark times—salvation (*salutem*). All this sounds like a retreat from politics into a purely intellectual realm, a safe space where sidelined politicians can find comfort in conversing with their like-minded friends, as well as with their even truer friends, their books.[47]

However, this is not how Cicero thinks about it. After stressing the consolation found in *studia*, he continues letter 9.2 by declaring himself (and Varro) ready to step up immediately should the *res publica* again require their services. If this does not happen, their course of action will be the following (*Fam.* 9.2.5):

> si nemo utetur opera, tamen et scribere et legere πολιτείας et, si minus in curia atque in foro, at in litteris et libris, ut doctissimi veteres fecerunt, gnuare rem publicam et de moribus ac legibus quaerere.

> If no one calls on our help, let us nevertheless both read and write "Republics" and—if not in the senate house and the forum, then in writing and books—serve the Republic as did the learned men of old, and inquire about customs and laws.

For Cicero, *studia* are not an alternative to politics but a different way of *doing* politics. If senate and forum are no longer open to him, writing and books will provide a new venue of public service, in which the speech acts of *scribere et legere* create a new πολιτεία or *res publica*.[48] It is only at the moment when traditional avenues of political activity are closed at Rome that *studia* come to take on—or Cicero wills them to take on—a political role in their own right. As his words to Varro show, Cicero was, already early in 46, actively contemplating a continuation of his political career through his writings. What exact

---

easily). In *Fam.* 9.6.4–5, he expresses his envy of Varro's current scholarly existence at Tusculum and his wish to join his friend in this mode of life.

47. At *Fam.* 9.6.5, Cicero, once again exhorting Varro to a life of *studia*, most uncharacteristically even cites the authority of "many learned men" (*multi docti homines*; cf. *magnorum hominum sententia*)—presumably both Peripatetics and Epicureans—who have exalted the contemplative over the active life: "perhaps not correctly, but with strength in numbers" (*fortasse non recte sed tamen multi*).

48. This is what Baraz 2012 refers to as Cicero's "written republic." Cf. my discussion in 2.3 above. Whether Cicero had at this point any specific (political or legal) work in mind, or whether he was referring in loose terms to any intellectual production with a political significance, is unclear.

shape this new form of public service was going to take is something he discovered through a series of experiments.

Cicero's first work after the Civil War—in fact, his first published work since *De re publica* of 51—was the *Brutus*, a history of Roman oratory. As we have already seen (in 2.3 and 4.1 above), this dialogue, in which Cicero converses with his friends Atticus and Brutus, conjures up an idealized *societas studiorum* and is also explicitly billed as Cicero's return to intellectual activity after the trauma of Pharsalus and its aftermath (11–12, 19). A chronology of orators from the foundation of the Republic to the present, which none too subtly culminates in Cicero himself, the work contains assessments of dozens of historical figures as well as a polemic against contemporary Atticists, who in the eyes of Cicero fail not only to be effective speakers but even to understand what Attic style really consists of. However, while presenting a treasure trove of material, the *Brutus* is anything but a disinterested piece of historiography, and oratory itself is far from being a neutral topic. More than any other Ciceronian rhetorical or philosophical treatise, the dialogue is intrinsically bound up in, and an outspoken comment on, the contemporary political situation.[49]

Despite the amicable banter of the three interlocutors, the tone of the *Brutus* is depressed. The oppressive atmosphere of life in Rome under Caesar is taking its toll: Cicero himself has barely emerged from a period of deep despondency (12), and Atticus vetoes the topic of politics as being too painful (11, 157); as Brutus bluntly puts it, any news at this point would be bad news (10).[50] However, it is not just the dialogue's setting that is gloomy. The very topic of conversation is inherently political and, under the current circumstances, profoundly upsetting.

The subject matter of the *Brutus* is not rhetoric, theoretically considered, but the socially and historically situated practice of oratory in a particular society, Republican Rome. Eloquence is born and dies with well-regulated communities in which free speech obtains and matters are decided by debate, not fiat. Cicero writes, apropos of the flourishing of oratory in democratic Athens (45):

---

49. For various takes on the politics of the *Brutus*, see Gelzer 1963 [1938]; Bringmann 1971: 13–20; Bellincioni 1985; Rathofer 1986; Strasburger 1990: 29–31; Narducci 1995: 7–12 (with a *historia quaestionis*); Wassmann 1996: 160–72; Gowing 2000; Steel 2002–3; Dugan 2005: 172–250, 2012; Jacotot 2014; Martin 2014; Kaster 2020: 5–17; and van den Berg forthcoming.

50. The dramatic date of the *Brutus* appears to be spring 46, before news of Caesar's victory at Thapsus and of Cato's death had reached Rome; a number of anachronisms show that Cicero wrote the work when he already knew the outcome of the African campaign, or perhaps that he worked on the text over a period of time, while events were unfolding (see the brief discussion of Douglas 1966: ix–x; differently Gowing 2000: 62–64).

nec enim in constituentibus rem publicam nec in bella gerentibus nec in impeditis ac regum dominatione deuinctis nasci cupiditas dicendi solet. pacis est comes otique socia et iam bene constitutae ciuitatis quasi alumna quaedam eloquentia.

The desire for oratory does not usually arise among men who are only just constituting a state, or are waging war, or are bound and shackled by the rule of kings. Eloquence is the attendant and companion of peace and quiet, and as it were the fosterchild of an already well-established commonwealth.

Accordingly, the Roman history of oratory begins with Brutus's ancestor L. Brutus, instrumentally involved in expelling the Tarquins and establishing the Republic (53), and has ended, alas, at this very moment. With the collapse of the free *res publica*, the forum has grown silent (6), and the *Brutus*, which starts and ends with a eulogy of the recently deceased orator Q. Hortensius Hortalus (1–9, 317–30), thus functions as a *laudatio funebris* not only of that one great man, but of Roman oratory as a whole.[51] As for Cicero himself, he is deeply distressed that now that real arms hold sway, his own "weapons of counsel, intellect, and authority" are no longer needed; if the voice of Hortensius was silenced by his death, that of Cicero was muzzled by that of the Republic.[52] What is even more distressing is that the rising star Brutus, who should by rights at this point be enjoying a brilliant public career, has been deprived of the opportunity of employing both his rhetorical and his political skills. Night has fallen on the Republic.[53]

The *Brutus* is remarkably outspoken in its expression of distress at the present political situation. While Caesar is not blamed or criticized directly, and even receives lavish, if not unequivocal, praise for his own rhetorical style,[54] one does not need to read between the lines to understand whom Cicero holds responsible for the demise of oratory and the Republic both. As John Dugan puts it, "Rhetoric is not dead of natural causes; Caesar has killed it" (2005: 177). There are even some fairly explicit digs at the victor(s) of the Civil War as Cicero caustically remarks that "those who had learned to use weapons

---

51. The similarity of the *Brutus* to a Roman funeral oration was first pointed out by Haenni 1905: 52 and has been much discussed in subsequent scholarship.

52. *Brut.* 7: *angor animo non consili, non ingeni, non auctoritatis armis egere rem publicam*; 328: *sic Q. Hortensi uox exstincta fato suo est, nostra publico.*

53. *Brut.* 330: *hanc rei publicam noctem.*

54. *Brut.* 252–62. This passage and its significance for contemporary debates about language and style will be discussed in 5.3.

in the pursuit of glory could not figure out how to use them for the public welfare" and "I have never seen a man become eloquent by victory in war."[55]

While some scholars have viewed the *Brutus* as an example of veiled political allusion or "doublespeak," it seems to me that the work makes Cicero's opinion unambiguously clear.[56] What is harder to tell is what purpose its author was pursuing in publishing the dialogue. Are we to read the *Brutus* as a manifesto or "politische Kundgebung"?[57] If so, is it directed specifically at Brutus, whose Republican spirit Cicero is attempting to rouse with references to his antityrannical ancestors L. Brutus and C. Servilius Ahala?[58] Or is Cicero addressing himself primarily to Caesar, pressuring him to restore Rome's political structures and thus enable again the free practice of oratory?[59]

I believe that there is some truth to both views, though it also seems to me that the political message of the dialogue remains fairly general and by no means amounts to a call to any particular act of anti-Caesarian resistance. While Cicero in many ways casts himself as a model and teacher for the dialogue's namesake and tries to shape Brutus as a thinker, speaker, and politician, he is not as of yet attempting to mold him into the conspirator and assassin he was to become—even though in hindsight, the *Brutus* can appear as one of many small steps leading up to the Ides of March. The intervention of the *Brutus* consists not in advocating a course of action but in expressing an opinion—at the very moment when other venues for doing so have been barred, for example, when Cicero is no longer able to give his *sententia* freely in the senate.[60] Oratory has been silenced, but Cicero has not.[61]

55. *Brut.* 8: *arma . . . quibus illi ipsi, qui didicerant eis uti gloriose, quem ad modum salutariter uterentur, non reperiebant*; 24: *eloquentem neminem uideo factum esse uictoria.* Cf. also *Brut.* 255–58.

56. Wassmann 1996: 160–72 and Dugan 2005: 172–250, 2012 are proponents of a more subversive reading that finds "hidden" meaning in the *Brutus*; by contrast, J. Hall 2009b: 108–9 maintains that "Cicero was not in the habit of thinking in terms of doublespeak or of composing subtly subversive literature."

57. The phrase is that of Gelzer 1963 [1938].

58. Thus Balsdon 1958: 91, 94; Rathofer 1986; Strasburger 1990: 29–31; Dugan 2005: 172–250, 2012; and Martin 2014.

59. Thus Gelzer 1963 [1938] and Bellincioni 1985. A scholarly minority view holds that rather than wanting to influence either Brutus or Caesar, Cicero in the *Brutus* is addressing diehard Republicans and attempting to justify his own stance of compromise and conciliation; see Bringmann 1971: 17 and cf. Rathofer 1986: 26.

60. Cicero himself had made the decision not to speak in the senate and stuck to it until October 46, when he delivered the speech *Pro Marcello*, on which see further below.

61. My interpretation of the *Brutus* is thus closest to that of Gowing 2000, who observes how Cicero creates, as it were, a new venue for oratory in his writing: "For while it may be true that the forum may no longer be a place for the free and open exchange of ideas, there exists another

The main political significance of the *Brutus* is thus the speech act that is the *Brutus* itself. Cicero still has a voice and he has carved out for himself a space in which to use it: if not *in curia atque in foro*, then at least *in litteris et libris*. The work's dialogue form reinforces its theme of free expression: in sophisticated conversation among equals, members of the Roman nobility are still able to speak their minds. "I'm not afraid of your contradicting me, for here we are at liberty to say what we think," says Cicero to Atticus and Brutus[62]—pointedly in the very context of an (implied) comparison of himself and Caesar, in the course of which Cicero, as so often, stresses the superiority of civic achievements over military ones. As the traditional political arena has shrunk for men like Cicero, politics has found a new home in the realm of *studia*, which—rather than, as previously, informing politics, have become the locus of politics itself.

How did Caesar react to the *Brutus*? We have no evidence, and since Cicero himself mentions the work only once, very briefly, in the preface to the second book of *De diuinatione* of 44 BCE (4), we do not know anything about the history of its writing or the reaction of any of its early readers, including Brutus and Atticus. It is clear, however, that Cicero did not get into any kind of trouble.[63] Apparently, the measured expression of political opinion in a work of scholarship was considered perfectly acceptable and in keeping with the conventions of learned sociability and exchange that still obtained, even among men who had found themselves on opposite sides of the Civil War. For all its implied criticism of Caesar, the *Brutus* is in part also a learned reply to Caesar's own *De analogia*, whose contents and dedication to Cicero are discussed at some length (252–62). Jon Hall points to the "sense of gentlemanly decorum that had developed between Cicero and Caesar over the previous decades" (2009b: 108) and was still in place. If two gentlemen could agree to disagree over the role of analogy in proper word choice, they could do the same with their divergent views of the state of the Republic.

This is not to say that men like Cicero felt they could freely express their opinions the way they used to. Any critical utterance might be reported to Caesar or his followers and could have repercussions—and even if it did not, the very fear of offending might act as an effective means of self-censorship.[64]

---

venue for expression, specifically, writing. The *Brutus* is in fact a brilliant demonstration of the power of oratory and the written oration, the 'scripta verbis oratio' (328)" (58).

62. *Brut.* 256: *non metuo ne mihi acclametis; est autem quod sentias liber dicendi locus.*

63. Neither did Brutus with *De uirtute*, despite his praise of Marcellus, who had been a particularly fierce enemy of Caesar.

64. It is not entirely clear what repercussions there could have been. As J. Hall writes, "We should certainly not imagine storm-troopers bursting into Cicero's house in the early hours of

This becomes clear in a letter (*Fam.* 9.16) that Cicero wrote in July 46 to his friend Papirius Paetus, an equestrian with Epicurean leanings, who lived on the Bay of Naples and with whom Cicero conducted an especially witty and jocular correspondence. Apparently Paetus had written to Cicero to alert him to the possibility that some of Cicero's sayings had been reported to Caesar and might cause offense, a possibility about which Paetus was clearly worried.[65] Cicero's letter is meant to put his friend at ease, and in the process reveals much about the writer's cautious modus operandi under the new regime.[66]

One of Cicero's strategies, the author explains, has been to cultivate friendships with Caesar's followers—as we know from many other letters, these included especially Balbus, Oppius, Hirtius, and Dolabella—and he believes himself to be well liked by them (*Fam.* 9.16.2). As far as his own behavior is concerned, it is Cicero's policy "not to say or do anything stupidly or rashly against those in power."[67] Times have changed (3):

> ut enim olim arbitrabar esse meum libere loqui, cuius opera esset in ciuitate libertas, sic ea nunc amissa nihil loqui quod offendat aut illius aut eorum qui ab illo diliguntur uoluntatem.

> Once I thought it was my job to speak freely, seeing that thanks to me there was freedom in the commonwealth. Now that freedom has been lost, I think it is my job to say nothing that offends either his wish or that of those whom he loves.

The loss of both political *libertas* and *libertas loquendi* puts Cicero in a difficult situation, one in which he has to walk a fine line—which he is doing, he reassures Paetus, successfully—between offending the Caesarians and losing his

---

the morning to drag him off for torture and interrogation" (2009b: 92; cf. also Strasburger 1990: 64–65). Confiscation of property was a concern, but as Jehne 1987: 329–35 shows, the property appropriated was largely that of Pompeians who had fallen in battle. Characterized by the policy of *clementia*, the Caesarian period was free of the proscriptions of Sulla and the Second Triumvirate or the institutionalized repression of the Empire; this does not mean that people with dissenting views necessarily felt safe or at ease.

65. Cicero was (in)famous for his caustic bon mots (see Beard 2014: 100–105). Plutarch reports some of the bitter jokes he made in Pompey's camp (*Cic.* 38.2–6; cf. Cic. *Phil.* 2.39), probably drawing on a collection of Ciceronian witticisms like the one assembled by Trebonius, for which Cicero thanks the author in *Fam.* 15.21 (perhaps late 46). See Corbeill 1996: 183–89 on the Civil War jokes (with 7 n. 13 and 186 n. 20 on Ciceronian joke collections) and 209–15 on joking and free speech under Caesar.

66. Cf. McConnell 2014: 161–94 on Cic. *Fam.* 9.22, a letter likewise written to Paetus, which discusses the topic of *libertas loquendi* in a highly oblique and playful manner.

67. *Fam.* 9.16.5: *ne quid stulte, ne quid temere dicam aut faciam contra potentis.*

own *dignitas*.[68] Even so, Cicero admits, sometimes his wit runs away with him, and he says something biting and amusing (*acute aut facete*, 3); he couldn't get rid of his reputation for cleverness (*fama ingeni*) even if he tried. Luckily, however, Caesar is an excellent philologist (4) and able to judge the authenticity of any bon mot that is repeated to him: if it is not by Cicero, he will declare it spurious.[69]

Cicero can joke about his predicament, but the letter shows clearly how careful men previously used to aristocratic freedom of speech had to be under the current circumstances. How far could they take their *libertas*? What could they, and what could they not, say? We possess an extraordinary document of the agonizing decision-making process many Romans wishing to enter public discourse must have gone through in a letter from A. Caecina to Cicero of late 46 or early 45.[70] The equestrian Caecina had fought against Caesar in the Civil War, not only by force of arms but also through the publication of an aggressive pamphlet.[71] As a result, Caesar was disinclined to pardon his attacker, despite the fact that Caecina was now trying to churn out Caesar-friendly material.[72] The letter shows Caecina in a state of high anxiety: he has sent the manuscript of his new book to Cicero but begs his correspondent not to let it go into circulation but instead make any revisions he might see fit (1, 6). His previous experience has made him paranoid: "I am still being punished for my pen."[73]

Caecina bitterly points out how unfairly he has been treated (1–2). Of course, all men fighting against Caesar prayed and hoped for their foe to be defeated but only Caecina conveyed his *male dicta* in the medium of a book— as a result, everybody else has been pardoned, while he is still stuck in Sicily. Once bitten, the author is more than twice shy, continuously second-guessing his new work, deleting passages that might cause offense (3), and imagining, as it were, that Caesar is reading over his shoulder (4):

> hoc probabit, hoc uerbum suspiciosum est. quid si hoc muto? at uereor ne peius sit.

> He'll like this, but that word might raise suspicions. Why don't I change it? But then I'm afraid that I'll make it worse.

---

68. *Fam.* 9.16.6: *ego me non putem tueri meum statum sic posse ut neque offendam animum cuiusquam nec frangam dignitatem meam?*

69. *Fam.* 9.16.4: *sic audio Caesarem ... si quid adferatur ad eum pro meo quod meum non sit, reicere solere.*

70. *Fam.* 6.7; compare the brief discussion in Dugan 2013: 221–22.

71. Suetonius refers to it as a *criminosissimo libro* (*Iul.* 75.5); cf. Rosillo-López 2009. For more on Caecina, see 6.2 below.

72. *Fam.* 6.6.8 mentions a book of *Querelae*, which apparently praised Caesar's *clementia*; the text whose difficult genesis is discussed in letter 6.7 seems to be yet another work.

73. *Fam.* 6.7.1: *adhuc stili poenas dem.*

Caecina's nerves are seriously frayed by "the self-criticism that arises from fear and the torment of pointless suspicion, when everything must be written according to another person's conjectured state of mind, not one's own judgment."[74] He ends the letter by imploring Cicero to help him, both by pleading his case with Caesar and by acting as an editor for Caecina's work (6). Sadly, despite Cicero's professed optimism in his own letters to Caecina (*Fam.* 6.5, 6.6, 6.8) and somewhat contrary to Suetonius's assertion that Caesar put up with Caecina's original screed *civili animo* (*Iul.* 75.5), the efforts to have Caecina pardoned came to nothing, and he remained in exile.

In his letter to Cicero, Caecina politely suggests that his correspondent may never have had to exercise self-censorship and try to gauge the reactions of a potentially hostile readership, "since your outstanding and superior genius has armed you for everything."[75] However, only a few months earlier, Cicero himself had been agonizing over what he called "a problem for an Archimedes":[76] his eulogy for Cato. After the news of Cato's suicide had reached Rome in the late spring of 46, Brutus apparently asked Cicero to write a work in praise of his uncle, a task that his friend, by his own admission, undertook only reluctantly.[77] The times, Cicero fears, are "hostile to virtue,"[78] and how, he complains to Atticus, can he possibly avoid giving offense? (Cic. *Att.* 12.4.2):

> non adsequor ut scribam quod tui conuiuae non modo libenter sed etiam aequo animo legere possint; quin etiam si a sententiis eius dictis, si ab omni uoluntate consiliisque quae de re publica habuit recedam ψιλῶςque uelim grauitatem constantiamque eius laudare, hóc ipsum tamen istis odiosum ἄκουσμα sit. sed uere laudari ille uir non potest nisi haec ornata sint, quod ille ea quae nunc sunt et futura uiderit et ne fierent contenderit et facta ne uideret uitam reliquerit.

I won't manage to write something that your drinking buddies will be able to read with equanimity, let alone with pleasure. Even if I were to stay away from his stated views and his every intention and plan concerning the commonwealth and simply wished to praise his seriousness and consistency,

---

74. *Fam.* 6.7.4: *calumnia timoris et caecae suspicionis tormento, cum plurima ad alieni sensus coniecturam, non ad suum iudicium scribantur.*

75. *Fam.* 6.7.4: *quod te ad omnia summum atque excellens ingenium armauit.*

76. *Att.* 12.4.2: πρόβλημα Ἀρχιμήδειον. The reference is presumably to the squaring of the circle.

77. See Cic. *Orat.* 35. Caecina, in the letter just discussed, is quick to spot Cicero's strategy of putting the blame on Brutus; he finds it alarming that even Cicero apparently feels the need for an *ad excusationem socium* (*Fam.* 6.7.4).

78. Cic. *Orat.* 35: *tempora timens inimica uirtuti.*

that alone would be a performance unwelcome to them. But in truth, the man cannot be praised without elaborating on the fact that he saw that what is now going on would happen, and strove that it wouldn't, and left life in order not to see it done.

Even a mere praise of Cato's virtues cannot help being political and thus unpalatable to Atticus's (and Cicero's) Caesarian *conuiuae*.

Despite his misgivings, Cicero completed the *Cato* in the late summer of 46, though strategically did not publish it until Caesar had left Rome for his Spanish campaign in November.[79] Only three fragments of the work survive but, as far as we can tell, Cicero did what he had declared to be impracticable, that is, enumerate Cato's *uirtutes*, an approach that allowed him to avoid the explicit discussion of politics.[80] Even so, however, Caesar and his followers were none too pleased with the glorification of an enemy whose dangerous potential for exemplarity they must have understood all too well. They were quick to reply in what turned into a rapid-fire exchange of publications on the merits and faults of the suicide of Utica—the "Cato Wars," as it were.[81]

Republican Rome did not have public media or venues for political comment, and the need for manual copying and recopying made the distribution of written material sluggish by modern standards.[82] Books circulated among small groups of learned readers and took their time to get around; public oratory and private conversation were more effective means to make one's views known and attempt to garner support. Nevertheless, we do find publications that in modern scholarship are often referred to as pamphlets, a moniker that I here use to include a wide range of texts circulated to influence public opinion.[83] These might include "public" letters meant to be passed on beyond the original addressee; real or fictitious speeches; invective poems; or any other type of writing. The genre is by necessity ill-defined—in some sense, of course, any publication aims at influencing its readership—but it is still a useful category

79. On the chronology, see Tschiedel 1981: 6–12.

80. On Cicero's *Cato*, see Jones 1970, Kumaniecki 1970, and Kierdorf 1978. The content and structure of the work can to some extent be inferred from what we know about Caesar's *Anticato* (see immediately below in the text), which reportedly answered Cicero's praise point by point (cf. Cic. *Top.* 94; Quint. *Inst.* 3.7.28; Mart. Cap. 5.468).

81. Cf. Bardon 1952: 281: "querelle Caton."

82. On political literature in ancient Rome, see Eich 2000 and Rosillo-López 2017: 98–154.

83. On pamphlets in the late Republic, see Bardon 1952: 276–90 and Rosillo-López 2009, 2017: 132–41. On the Cato Wars, see (in addition to the literature specifically on Cicero's and Caesar's interventions) Pecchiura 1965: 25–44, Zecchini 1980, Fehrle 1983: 279–316, Wassmann 1996: 139–59, J. Hall 2009b: 94–100, Gäth 2011: 3–44, and S. H. Rauh 2018.

to describe especially works of a highly political nature that are produced at a time of crisis, in particular, when they spark a process of published attack and counterattack. Caecina's *liber criminosissimus* against Caesar was a pamplet under this definition, as presumably were his subsequent palinodes. As in that case, examples of the genre are often ephemeral and do not survive; owing to the prominence of the combatants, the debate over Cato is unusually well documented.

Cicero's *Cato* must have reached the Caesarian army in Spain in the winter of 46/45. The first to react was Caesar's faithful general A. Hirtius, on whose *Anticato* Cicero reports to Atticus on 9 May 45. Hirtius responded to Cicero's *laudatio* with his own *uituperatio*, presenting a catalogue of Cato's faults (*Att.* 12.40.1). By this point Cicero knew that Caesar himself was working on a response, of which Hirtius's pamphlet was, as it were, a preview;[84] Caesar's own *Anticato*—a substantial work in two books—was available in Rome by August.[85] Meanwhile, however, Brutus was apparently not satisfied with Cicero's production and wrote his own *Cato*, annoying Cicero by misrepresenting Cato's role in the debate over the convicted Catilinarians of 5 December 63: Cicero complains to Atticus about Brutus's historical ignorance and his only lukewarm praise of Cicero's own achievements.[86] We know about yet another *Cato*, from the pen of Cicero's Epicurean friend M. Fadius Gallus and published the following year, and it is attractive to think that the biography of Cato written by Munatius Rufus is part of the same flurry of publications.[87] The controversy is still echoed in Sallust's *Bellum Catilinae*, written at the end of the decade, where Cato is famously compared to his detractor Caesar: now that the latter has come to a violent death as well, and the downward spiral of the Republic continues, these two men have emerged as the outstanding personalities of their generation.[88]

84. Cf. Cic. *Att.* 12.40.1, 12.41.4.

85. Cf. Cic. *Att.* 13.50.1, 13.51.1.

86. See *Att.* 12.21.1. The letter is from 17 March 45 and refers to Brutus's text as a work in progress. It was published at the latest in August (cf. *Att.* 13.46.2).

87. For Fadius, see Cic. *Fam.* 7.24.2, 7.25.1; for Munatius Rufus, see 3.1 above.

88. See Sall. *Cat.* 53–54. With his observation that Cato "wanted to be, rather than seem, a good man" (*esse quam uideri bonus malebat*, 54.6), Sallust may be alluding (in addition to Aesch. *Sept.* 592) to Cicero's claim in his *Cato* (reported by Macrob. *Sat.* 6.2.33), that "there happened in Cato's case the contrary to what happens to most people, namely that everything seemed greater in reality than in reputation; it does not come along very often that experience surpasses expectation and autopsy hearsay" (*contingebat in eo quod plerisque contra solet, ut maiora omnia re quam fama uiderentur; id quod non saepe euenit, ut expectatio cognitione, aures ab oculis uincerentur*). See Jones 1970: 190 and Kumaniecki 1970: 173; differently Kierdorf 1978: 176 n. 36.

Of all the publications of the Cato Wars, Caesar's *Anticato*—explicitly billed as a response to Cicero—is the one about which we know the most.[89] Like Hirtius's precursor, the work was a catalogue of Cato's vices, among them alcoholism, abuses during his administration of Cyprus, and such infractions of familial *pietas* as passing on his wife to Hortensius, committing incest with his half-sister, and sifting the ashes of his brother's pyre in search of the melted-down remains of precious funerary offerings. What is striking about the fragments that we possess is that Caesar's blame—and thus presumably also Cicero's praise—seems to steer clear of the political and fasten onto the personal, which in the case of the eccentric Cato provided ample fodder for both hagiography and gossip. While Caesar appears to have delighted in tabloid-style mudslinging, we have no evidence that he attacked Cato for his political and military opposition to himself. As a matter of fact, the most political moment in all the *Catos* and *Anticatos* we hear of is Brutus's discussion of the debate about the Catilinarians, an episode that, after all, for the first time pitted Cato directly against Caesar. Of course, our information is more than scanty, but if it is true that Caesar largely avoided politics or the Civil War in his *Anticato*, his pamphlet took a different approach from his triumph of September 46, where gruesome images of the death of Cato and other Pompeians were paraded through the streets of Rome (App. *B Civ.* 2.101.420).

Triumphal imagery is aimed at a wide and diverse audience of spectators from all social classes. By contrast, the pamphlets of Cicero, Caesar, and others reached only a small, educated readership of peers. What is striking about the Cato Wars is the polite and collegial manner in which the debate was conducted—despite the inflammatory subject matter, the at least in part aggressive tone of the publications, and the anxiety-inducing power differential among the participants. As we can tell from Cicero's correspondence, the charge and countercharge between Cicero, on the one side, and Hirtius and Caesar, on the other, were managed with the utmost cordiality, no doubt facilitated by Atticus and mutual Caesarian friends. Thus Hirtius prefaced his *Anticato* with "the greatest praise" of Cicero,[90] and rather than being upset by this vituperative response to his own eulogy, Cicero actually took pains to circulate Hirtius's screed.[91] His purpose, as declared to Atticus, was to further Cato's reputation (the implication being that Hirtius's attack was on the clumsy side), though perhaps Cicero also did not mind the kind words about himself reaching a wider audience. Whatever the case may be, though, Hirtius

---

89. See the commented edition of Tschiedel 1981.

90. *Att.* 12.40.1: *cum maximis laudibus meis.*

91. Cf. *Att.* 12.40.1, 12.44.1, 12.45.2, 12.48.1.

must have viewed the broadcasting of his production as a compliment rather than an insult.

As for Caesar's *Anticato*, this work apparently began with a flattering dedication to Cicero, in which Caesar self-deprecatingly asked to be forgiven for his simple style, not to be compared to the superior eloquence of his addressee.[92] When Cicero had read Caesar's book, he let his Caesarian go-betweens Balbus, Oppius, and Dolabella know how much he liked it (*uehementer probasse, Att.* 13.50.1), and also had them vet a complimentary letter to Caesar himself. In reporting on this letter, Cicero assures Atticus that it was by no means a piece of abject flattery (*Att.* 13.51.1):

> nec mehercule scripsi aliter ac si πρὸς ἴσον ὅμοιονque scriberem. bene enim existimo de illis libris, ut tibi coram. itaque scripsi et ἀκολακεύτως et tamen sic ut nihil eum existimem lecturum libentius.

> Really, I wrote no differently than if I were writing to a peer. For indeed, I have a good opinion of the book, as I told you when we spoke. Therefore I wrote without flattery but still in such a way that I think he will read nothing with greater pleasure.

If Cicero knew how to rub Caesar the right way, the opposite was true as well. Just a few days earlier, Balbus had shown Cicero a letter in which Caesar said "many things about my *Cato*," comparing it favorably to Brutus's pamphlet: "he says that reading [my piece] again and again increased his power of speech, while after reading Brutus's *Cato*, he felt that he was already eloquent."[93]

The Cato Wars show the limits of *libertas* under Caesar as men like Cicero were experiencing them. No one could prevent them from speaking their minds or circulating their opinions in written form. At the same time, Cicero felt that he was well advised not only to be careful about what he said but also to pass potentially problematic publications by the likes of Oppius and Balbus first. At the same time, Caesar and his men went out of their way not to offend Cicero's sensibilities and to keep up the trappings of a free exchange of opinions. In their *Cato* and *Anticato*, Cicero and Caesar skillfully played the same game, managing to cross swords without actually injuring the other party. By means of their accustomed aristocratic politeness, helped along—I would

---

92. Plut. *Caes.* 3.2 = fr. 2 Tschiedel; cf. Plut. *Cic.* 39.4 = fr. 3 Tschiedel. Caesar's pointed comparison between himself and Cicero is part of a stylistic debate between the two men that extends from *De oratore* via *De analogia* to the *Brutus* (see above) and beyond; for further discussion, see 5.3 below.

93. *Att.* 13.46.2: *multa de meo Catone, quo saepissime legendo se dicit copiosiorem factum, Bruti Catone lecto se sibi uisum disertum.*

conjecture—by a certain amount of genuine liking and respect, the two men
succeeded in saving face, keeping up the facade of senatorial equality while not
upsetting the changed power structures.[94]

If a Cicero could thus, with all the necessary circumspection and care, make
his opinions about recent and current events known in such diverse genres as
a treatise on the history of oratory and a *laudatio* of a dead friend, was there
perhaps also a way to influence politics more directly—which at this point
meant influencing Caesar himself? Since his return to Rome, Cicero had not
spoken in the senate, presumably preferring to keep quiet rather than appear
to collude openly with the Caesarian regime. As he put it in a letter to Sulpicius
Rufus, "I had determined to remain silent forever, not indeed out of laziness
but out of longing for my former dignity."[95] Cicero, as he views it, has already
seen his *dignitas* diminished, but not to such an extent that he is going to involve himself in a political process in which, since the beginning of the Civil
War, "nothing has been done with dignity."[96] Famously, however, the orator
changed his stance on the occasion of a meeting of the senate in October 46,
when Caesar announced his decision to pardon M. Claudius Marcellus: when
asked his *sententia*, Cicero broke his long silence and delivered a speech of
thanks, whose published version is our *Pro Marcello*.

As mentioned above (see 4.1), the consul of 51 had not sought Caesar's
pardon after Pharsalus but instead retreated to Mytilene, in a spirit of philosophically minded independence. Praised by Brutus in his *De uirtute*, this diehard optimate who—to judge from Cicero's correspondence[97]—showed
little inclination to return to Rome was no doubt an irritant to Caesar, who did
not relish having to contend with yet another *exemplum* of Republican virtue,
in addition to the glorified Cato. It is impossible to tell whether Caesar was
pressured into pardoning Marcellus by the insistence of the exile's cousin, who
at the senate meeting in question threw himself at Caesar's feet, upon which
the whole senate started entreating the dictator (see Cicero's report in *Fam.*

---

94. On "saving face" as the goal of both Cicero and Caesar in their works on Cato, see
Tschiedel 1981: 21. On aristocratic politeness, see J. Hall 2009a; specifically on Cicero and Caesar's
availing themselves of the "dynamics inherent in the conventions of aristocratic courtesy" in
the Cato Wars, see J. Hall 2009b: 97–98 (quotation at 97), as well as 107–8. While it is often
believed that Cicero must have hated Caesar, I am assuming that despite their political differences, the two men, whose acquaintance went back a long time, had a certain affinity.

95. *Fam.* 4.4.4: *statueram non mehercule inertia, sed desiderio pristinae dignitatis in perpetuum
tacere.*

96. *Fam.* 4.4.3: *post has miserias, id est postquam armis disceptari coeptum sit de iure publico,
nihil esse actum aliud cum dignitate.*

97. *Fam.* 4.7–11. On these letters, see Fiocchi 1990.

4.4.3)—or whether this scene had been staged by Caesar himself, who was thus able to foist his *clementia* on his less than enthusiastic opponent.[98] Cicero, at any rate, was positively impressed, seeming to himself "to catch a glance, as it were, of a revival of the commonwealth."[99] Whether the speech the consular delivered on that day in the senate was anything like what he wrote up afterwards is irrelevant for my discussion in what follows. What is important is that Cicero decided to publish, in *Pro Marcello*, a text that directly addresses Caesar—thanking him for his clemency, to be sure, but also offering to the dictator cautiously but clearly phrased advice.[100]

Containing extravagant praise of Caesar, the *Pro Marcello* has been the subject of critical controversy since antiquity.[101] Is the speech an expression of abject flattery, prefiguring the worst excesses of the Imperial period? Or is it an *oratio figurata*, a speech of concealment, which under the cover of praising Caesar is actually indicting him or even calling for his assassination?[102] While most scholars steer between these two extremes, viewing the *Pro Marcello* as combining sincere praise for Caesar's *clementia* with advice for a political reconstruction,[103] they still have to come to terms with the profound ambiguity at the heart of the speech, an ambiguity that is not just a feature of the text,

98. It is perhaps most likely that the delicate negotiations between Caesar and Marcellus's supporters had reached a point where it was clear to both parties that the dictator was about to give in, and that the scene in the senate, though not premeditated, enabled all participants to act out, in a reasonably gracious way, the kinds of roles they had already decided they were likely to play.

99. *Fam.* 4.4.3: *speciem aliquam uiderer uidere quasi reuiuiscentis rei publicae.*

100. We know nothing about the publication of *Pro Marcello*, but I am working on the assumption that it was circulated shortly after the speech was given, presumably in October of 46 (by contrast, Dyer 1990 and Gagliardi 1997: 93–178 place the publication only after Marcellus's death in 45, a dating that greatly facilitates their anti-Caesarian reading [see n. 102] but has no other support). At this time, as mentioned above, the *Cato* was already written but had not yet been made public.

101. See Dugan 2013.

102. This interpretation is attested already in the *Scholia Gronoviana*, 295.32–296.2 Stangl, where the scholiast argues against it. It has been resurrected by Dyer 1990 and (in a more extreme fashion) Gagliardi 1997: 93–178.

103. A formulation often found esp. in Italian scholarhip is that the speech is a hybrid between a *gratiarum actio* ("speech of thanksgiving," the *status* of the speech according to *Scholia Gronoviana* 295.24 Stangl) and a *suasoria* ("speech of persuasion"). Versions of such middle-of-the-road readings are found in Rambaud 1984; Dobesch 1985; Rochlitz 1993: 74–115; Tedeschi 1996, 2005; Kerkhecker 2002; Winterbottom 2002; von Albrecht 2003: 163–74; Krostenko 2005; Gildenhard 2011: 225–33, 361–64; Gotoff 2012: 224–35; Tempest 2013a, 2013b; Bianco 2017; and Scatolin forthcoming. I myself discuss *Marcell.* further in Volk forthcoming a and d, with some

but clearly was an important aspect both of its author's experience and of the times in which he lived.[104] On the one hand, how was Cicero to thank and praise Caesar without appearing to buy into a view of Caesar as a monarchic ruler, characterized by the princely virtue of *clementia*?[105] But on the other, how could he advise Caesar to take a different political path without causing offense? *Pro Marcello* begins with Cicero's claim that from this day on, he will again "say what I wish and what I think in my former manner."[106] *Libertas loquendi* has been restored, or so Cicero says. The following speech will show to what extent this is, or is not, the case.

The speech falls into two main parts. In the first (1–20), Cicero praises Caesar's past deeds, among which the pardon of Marcellus is by far the most splendid; in the second (21–32), he looks forward to Caesar's future accomplishments, first and foremost among which must be the restoration of the Republic. The orator cleverly—or even insidiously—links the two parts via a number of motifs, the most important of which is that of Caesar's wisdom. Caesar is called *sapiens* or associated with *sapientia* nine times in the course of the short speech[107]—high praise indeed, especially for a person of such intellectual interests and abilities as Caesar, but one that, as the speech insinuates, comes with a fair number of strings attached.

Sapientia, of course, is a loose term, and Cicero offers no definition, leaving Caesar's *sapientia* to hover somewhere between practical political judgment and theoretical philosophical wisdom. What the virtue of *sapientia* implies no matter what, however, is rationality. Caesar's truly wise actions are those guided by his reason, which means, on the one hand, that they are truly his alone, not subject to external factors, and bound to gain immortal fame.[108] On the other hand, owing to their very rationality, they can be interpreted and understood. Because Caesar is so *sapiens*, Cicero and his fellow senators can,

---

verbatim overlaps with what follows. For a very different take from mine on how the speech responds to the changed political situation under Caesar, see Connolly 2011.

104. This important point is made by Dugan 2013; see also J. Hall 2009b.

105. Since *clementia* is by definition exercised by a superior toward an inferior, the concept was bound to raise a red flag for Republicans. See esp. Dyer 1990: 23–26; differently Konstan 2005. See further n. 250 below.

106. *Marcell.* 1: *initium quae uellem quaeque sentirem meo pristino more dicendi.*

107. *Marcell.* 1, 7, 9, 18, 19 (2x), 25 (3x). On *sapientia* in the speech, see Rochlitz 1993, esp. 111–15, and Volk forthcoming d.

108. The autonomy of virtue and wisdom is a leitmotif of the speech: Caesar's greatest accomplishments are those that arise from his own self, are not shared with anyone, and are not subject to fortune; it is those, and only those, that will gain lasting fame. See esp. *Marcell.* 6–7, 19, 29.

as it were, read the dictator's past judgments and are even able to predict what he, acting wisely and rationally, is going to do next.

Thus Cicero takes it upon himself to explain what Caesar's *iudicium* was in pardoning Marcellus (*Marcell.* 13). In Caesar's opinion, the Civil War was not a question of nefarious hostility to himself but simply one big misunderstanding: "he judged that most men went to war out of ignorance or a false and empty fear rather than out of desire or cruelty."[109] Caesar's moderate *de bello uoluntas* is thus clear: by pardoning those who advocated peace (including Marcellus and Cicero himself), "he indeed declares that he would have preferred not fighting to winning."[110] And not only that: if he but could, Caesar would bring back from death the fallen Pompeians themselves (17).

In his tendentious exegesis of Caesar's one act of *clementia*, Cicero paints an image of the dictator's mindset whose truthfulness, as the orator maintains, simply cannot be doubted.[111] From his wise and rational act of pardoning Marcellus, we can infer that Caesar never wanted the Civil War to happen and holds no grudge against those who opposed him and who he knows were motivated by neither ideological zeal nor personal animosity. This is a remarkable piece of spin, by which Cicero endeavors to hold Caesar to one very specific interpretation of his past actions. However, this is nothing compared to what the orator does with Caesar's deeds that are yet to come.

Seeing that the well-being of the *res publica* now rests in Caesar's hands, the benefactor of Marcellus has his work cut out for him: he "must . . . raise up" what has been "struck down, . . . set up trial courts, renew faith, curb excesses, see to the propagation of offspring, bind together with strict laws what has collapsed and fallen apart . . . heal all the wounds of the war" and generally "labor for this one end: to reestablish the *res publica*."[112] With his unremitting use of the passive periphrastic, Cicero hammers home to Caesar his obligation to restore the Republic, something that he absolutely needs to accomplish if he wants to garner true *gloria*. Caesar is a wise man—and his wisdom implies that he will do the right thing.

---

109. *Marcell.* 13: *iudicauit a plerisque ignoratione potius et falso atque inani metu quam cupiditate aut crudelitate bellum esse susceptum.* On Cicero's depoliticization of the Civil War in *Marcell.*, see Kerkhecker 2002.

110. *Marcell.* 15: *profecto declarat maluisse se non dimicare quam uincere.*

111. *Marcell.* 15: *nemo iam erit tam iniustus rerum existimator qui dubitet;* 17: *dubitare debeat nemo.*

112. *Marcell.* 23: *omnia sunt excitanda tibi, C. Caesar, uni quae iacere sentis belli ipsius impetu, quod necesse fuit, perculsa atque prostrata: constituenda iudicia, reuocanda fides, comprimendae libidines, propaganda suboles, omnia quae dilapsa iam diffluxerunt seueris legibus uincienda sunt;* 24: *tibi nunc omnia belli uolnera sananda sunt;* 27: *in hoc elaborandum est ut rem publicam constituas.*

As scholars have pointed out, Cicero is here employing a line of argument found in a genre that would come into its own only during the Empire and continue to flourish through the early modern period: the mirror of princes.[113] In this type of protreptic literature addressed to a monarchic ruler, a metaphorical mirror is held up to the prince, in which he can see himself as endowed with all princely virtues.[114] It is because he is already virtuous that he must, and obviously will, act in the beneficial manner advocated by the author of the treatise. While Cicero makes use of the same kind of "obliging praise"[115] in trying to steer Caesar onto a Republican course, there remains, however, a crucial difference. In a typical mirror of princes, the absolute rule of the addressee is an established fact, and it is clear what his role and virtues are supposed to be. With Caesar, that is not the case: his present position is unprecedented and controversial, and it is anything but obvious what he will or should do in the future. Rather than speaking as a subject to a ruler, Cicero—for all his well-turned praise—addresses Caesar as an equal, involving him in a debate that is not a little philosophical.

In his own speech in the senate, Caesar had apparently not only declared his intention of pardoning Marcellus but also painted an image of himself as a victim, not only of Marcellus's harsh attacks in the past but also of assassination threats in the present—no doubt in order to highlight his own magnanimity.[116] Expressing a resigned, if not jaded, attitude to the possibility of his own demise, he even declared that he had "lived enough for both nature and glory."[117] In *Pro Marcello*, Cicero picks up this statement and argues against it.[118] Quoting Caesar verbatim, he labels his quip a *sapientissima uox* (25), which here clearly carries a philosophical meaning: contempt for death is the reasoned attitude of learned men and, as such, might be considered *sapiens*—but that kind of

113. See Rochlitz 1993: 79–115, who discusses the pre-Ciceronian history of the genre as well as its topoi, and compare Tempest 2013b on *Marcell.* as a "Hellenistic" speech. Compare also Levene 1997: 68–77, Gildenhard 2011: 361–64, and Cole 2013: 112–26, who examine the ways in which Cicero assimilates Caesar to a god, a topic that will concern us again in 6.3.

114. The image of the mirror in this context is first found in Sen. *Clem.* 1.1.1.

115. Compare Krostenko 2005: 289: "Cicero's praises also bind."

116. Complaints about Marcellus: Cic. *Marcell.* 3; *Fam.* 4.4.3; death threats: *Marcell.* 21–23.

117. *Marcell.* 25: *satis diu uel naturae uixi uel gloriae.*

118. Cicero mentions that Caesar had expressed the same sentiment on other occasions (in a more self-centered version: *satis te tibi uixisse, Marcell.* 25); cf. Suetonius's report of some people's belief that by the time of his assassination, Caesar "did not wish to live any longer" (*neque uoluisse se diutius uiuere, Iul.* 86.1). On Caesar's utterance, see Narducci 1983, who also shows how Cicero in later works adapts the phrase for himself. On the argument in *Marcell.*, see Tedeschi 1996.

"wisdom" is no good for the *res publica*.[119] Cicero is playing with the concept of *sapientia*: Caesar's stance is "wise" in the sense that it is philosophically informed, but it is not wise in the true meaning of the word.

What is the philosophical stance that Cicero detects in Caesar's words? While contempt for death is an attitude shared by all philosophies, the idea of having lived "enough" from the point of view of nature seems to be particularly Epicurean.[120] The Epicureans held that perfect pleasure cannot be increased by the duration of time and that one might as well quit while the going is good and one has had "enough" (cf. Caesar's *satis*) of good things. Thus in her diatribe at the end of Lucretius, *De rerum natura* 3, personified *Natura* tells the man unwilling to die that "there is nothing that I could additionally contrive and invent to please you: everything is always the same," and that he ought to leave while "sated (*satur*) and full of things."[121] Of course, a true Epicurean has no desire for glory, but Cicero himself points out that this part of Caesar's utterance is heterodox and not part of his Epicurean *sapientia*: "You will not deny that *even though* you are wise, you are most desirous of fame."[122]

From Cicero's perspective, of course, Caesar's view is completely wrong: he may have lived long enough for nature and for glory, "but not enough for the fatherland, which is the most important thing."[123] It is fundamentally mistaken to set one's course of life by the criterion of one's own mental contentment rather than that of public welfare.[124] Arguing, as he so often does in his philosophical works, against Epicurean individualism and retreat from politics, Cicero exalts service to the *res publica* as the highest calling of man in general and Caesar in particular. In fact, truly immortal glory can be achieved

119. *Marcell.* 25: *qua re omitte istam, quaeso, doctorum hominum in contemnenda morte prudentiam: noli nostro periculo esse sapiens.* The *Scholia Gronoviana* 297.1–2 Stangl comment on Caesar's *satis diu* . . . with the explanation *quasi uerba sunt sapientis philosophi uitam contemnentis* ("they are, so to speak, the words of a philosopher who has contempt for life").

120. Whether Caesar had Epicurean leanings has been much discussed. I reconsider the question in Volk forthcoming a, tentatively concluding that while Caesar was probably not a declared Epicurean, some of his attested utterances about death may be informed by Epicurean doctrine. What matters for my discussion here is that Cicero decides to take Caesar's *satis uixi* as having been pronounced in an Epicurean spirit, whether this was what Caesar himself had in mind or not.

121. Lucr. 3.944–45: *nam tibi praeterea quod machiner inueniamque, / quod placeat, nil est: eadem sunt omnia semper;* 960: *satur ac plenus . . . discedere rerum.*

122. *Marcell.* 25: *cuius* [sc. *gloriae*] *te esse auidissimum, quamuis sis sapiens, non negabis.* In *Pis.* 59–61, Cicero humorously contrasts Caesar's desire for glory with the Epicurean lack of ambition of his father-in-law Piso (cf. 3.3 above).

123. *Marcell.* 25: *at, quod maximum est, patriae certe parum.*

124. *Marcell.* 25: *hic tu modum uitae tuae non salute rei publicae sed aequitate animi definies?*

only through political engagement: if Caesar quits now, he will lose his chance of leaving behind a lasting legacy.[125] Pleasure, even the memory of past pleasure, by which the Epicureans set so much store, will end with death (27); only true glory lives on.[126] Therefore, there is only one course possible for Caesar, provided that he is truly *sapiens*, not just imbued with Epicurean pseudo-wisdom (27):

> haec igitur tibi reliqua pars est; hic restat actus, in hoc elaborandum est ut rem publicam constituas, eaque tu in primis summa tranquillitate et otio perfruare: tum te, si uoles, cum et patriae quod debes solueris et naturam ipsam expleueris satietate uiuendi, satis diu uixisse dicito.

> This part is left for you, this deed remains, to this alone you must devote your effort: put the Republic in order, and you first and foremost will be able to profit from it in the greatest tranquility and peace. At that point, once you have paid your debt to the fatherland and—sated with life—have satisfied nature, you may say that you have lived long enough.

The entire *Pro Marcello* is, of course, addressed to Caesar, but it is in the rebuttal of his statement about life and death that Cicero most actively engages his addressee, involving him, as it were, in a philosophical give-and-take. Caesar's phrase is quoted, dissected, and proved wrong; staccato rhetorical questions are employed to overwhelm the interlocutor (25–26); and Caesar's imagined objections are immediately rebutted (*non negabis*, 25; *inquies*, 26). Throughout the entire speech, Cicero uses syllogisms and enthymemes to prove to Caesar by means of strict logic that *if* he desires true fame, and *if* true fame is gained only through service to the fatherland, *then* he must restore the Republic in order to achieve his goal.[127] Cicero addresses Caesar in the language of philosophical discourse, speaking as one learned senator to another, despite the obvious power differential. Making Marcellus's pardon a matter of *sapientia*, the orator attempts to resolve some of the ambiguities inherent in his situation (How to praise Caesar without endangering his own *dignitas*?

---

125. *Marcell.* 26. As Scatolin forthcoming shows, Cicero uses similar arguments in addressing Antony and Octavian in the *Philippics*: praise of the powerful individual remains "hypothetical," contingent on his future virtuous conduct.

126. Here, Cicero must hasten to forestall the Epicurean counterargument that the dead man will not be affected by his continuing glory: "*even if* this will not then concern you, *as some people wrongly believe*, now certainly it is a concern for you to be the kind of person whose praise will never be obscured by oblivion" (*id autem etiam si tum ad te, ut quidam falso putant, non pertinebit, nunc certe pertinet esse te talem ut tuas laudes obscuratura nulla umquam sit obliuio*, 30).

127. For the use of logic in *Marcell.*, see Rambaud 1984.

How to advise him without incurring offense?) and to find a way of clearly expressing his own views in a language that his addressee might find appealing. Even if Caesar did not follow Cicero's advice—and, of course, he did not—he could relish the speech for both its laudatory and its intellectual aspects; Cicero's opinion about the state of the *res publica* was, at any rate, hardly unknown or shocking to Caesar, and the very fact that the consular (one of few alive) had broken his silence in the senate may have been the aspect of *Pro Marcello* most gratifying to the dictator.

Cicero himself attempted once more to dispense philosophical advice to Caesar directly. In May 45, while the Cato Wars were unfolding, Cicero at the suggestion of Atticus drafted a letter to Caesar, which he himself labels a συμβουλευτικόν ("work of advice") and which was presumably intended to be circulated to a wider audience.[128] His model were the letters to Alexander the Great ascribed to Aristotle and Theopompus, but he was having a hard time applying their approach to his own situation (*Att.* 12.40.2; cf. 13.28.2–3):

> sed quid simile? illi et quae ipsis honesta essent scribebant et grata Alexandro. ecquid tu eius modi reperis? mihi quidem nihil in mentem uenit.

> What's the similarity? Those men wrote what was both honorable to themselves and pleasing to Alexander. Can you think of anything in this vein? Certainly nothing comes to my mind.

Cicero nevertheless produced a text, one that he caustically described as "containing nothing not befitting a good citizen—that is, 'good' as far as the times allow."[129] Even so, he decided once more to have his work vetted by Caesarian go-betweens (presumably again Balbus and Oppius)—who promptly asked for major changes. Exasperated, if perhaps also relieved, Cicero decided to abandon the project (*Att.* 13.27.1):

> quod enim aliud argumentum epistulae nostrae nisi κολακεία fuit? an si ea quae optima putarem suadere uoluissem, oratio mihi defuisset? totis igitur litteris nihil opus est.

> What other subject matter did my letter have but flattery? Or if I had wanted to persuade him of what I thought best, would I have lacked eloquence? There is no point whatsoever to this letter.

---

128. *Att.* 12.40.2. The genesis of the work can be followed through numerous letters to Atticus: *Att.* 12.40.2, 12.51.2, 12.52.2; 13.1.3, 13.26.2, 13.27.1, 13.28.2–3, 13.31.3, 13.44.1. For discussion, see Brožek 1961, Rosillo-López 2011, and now McConnell 2014: 195–219, who explores philosophical antecedents and attempts to reconstruct the letter's content.

129. *Att.* 12.51.2: *nihil est in ea nisi optimi ciuis, sed ita optimi ut tempora.*

Despite Atticus's attempts to persuade his friend to try again, Cicero has had enough: he is glad that he has avoided offending Caesar and putting himself in danger (*Att.* 13.27.1) but will not disgrace himself by producing a piece of even greater flattery, even if he were able to come up with something to say (*Att.* 13.28.2). Caesar is no Alexander, and even the brilliant student of Aristotle turned into a cruel tyrant once he had ascended to the throne (*Att.* 13.28.3). It is clear that Cicero feels that Caesar has reached the same point.

Times have changed since the *Pro Marcello*. Cicero no longer glimpses signs of the revival of the *res publica* and he no longer considers it worth his while trying to steer between flattery and advice in an attempt to influence Rome's new ruler. Whether or not in (re)writing his speech of thanksgiving as a philosophical disputation in late 46 he had thought he could actually sway Caesar, by mid-45 he had given up on the idea of playing the wise adviser. After all, even Aristotle had failed with Alexander. In addition, Cicero's private situation had taken a turn for the worse: at the beginning of the year, his beloved daughter Tullia had died from complications following childbirth, plunging her father into despair. Grieving for the loss of both his child and the *res publica*, Cicero once again turned to philosophy—for consolation, but also for a continuation of his political career.

3. Politics by Other Means

Through most of the long year 46, Cicero's literary output is characterized by diversity and a spirit of experiment, as the author tries out various topics and genres, attempting to find his voice in a changed political landscape: he composes a history of Roman eloquence (*Brutus*), a set of show speeches on Stoic philosophy (*Paradoxa Stoicorum*), a treatise on the perfect orator (*Orator*), an encomium of Cato (*Cato*), and his speech *Pro Marcello*, all the while keeping up his usual extensive correspondence. At the end of the year, however, his work begins to focus nearly exclusively on philosophy and to take on a more systematic character. Writing at breakneck speed, Cicero between late 46 and late 44 published over ten works on various fields and topics of philosophy, producing a corpus that was to have a profound influence on the history of western thought and is today one of our major sources for the doctrines of the Hellenistic schools.[130]

130. For information on and summaries of the individual works, see Philippson 1939: 1104–73, MacKendrick 1989, and Gawlik and Görler 1994: 1015–83; for philosophical exegesis and appreciation, see Woolf 2015.

Cicero clearly conceived his series of *philosophica* as a coherent whole—not perhaps in the sense that he planned it in all its details beforehand, but in such a way that each new work responds to and continues the ones that precede it.[131] The sequence begins with a protreptic to philosophy, *Hortensius* (now unfortunately surviving only in fragments), and continues with discussions of the three traditional philosophical subfields of epistemology (*Academica*), ethics (*De finibus bonorum et malorum*), and physics (here focused on theology: *De natura deorum*). Those three foundational works are written in a dialogue format that Cicero apparently invented: adherents of individual philosophical schools present their doctrines, which are subsequently challenged by a spokesman for the skeptical New Academy, who in the second version of the *Academica* and in *De finibus* is none other than Cicero himself.[132]

Some of the other treatises are, as it were, sequels of those initial discussions, picking up unresolved issues or focusing on corollary matters. Thus, *Tusculans* extends in a different format the inquiry of *De finibus* whether virtue is the only good, while *De diuinatione* and *De fato* continue *De natura deorum* by investigating the related topics of divination and fate. In the later stages of the project, a number of works written after the assassination of Caesar in March 44 are connected to one another in their exploration of Roman social practices from a philosophical point of view; these include *De gloria* (on the pursuit of fame, now lost), *De amicitia* (on friendship), and *De officiis* (generally on the ethics of social action).[133]

Cicero frequently cross-references his works, referring back to earlier discussions, and generally shapes the corpus in such a way that individual treatises respond to others without overlapping in terms of contents. In the preface to the second book of *De diuinatione* (written just after Caesar's death), Cicero himself presents the works completed up to this point as part of a sustained effort to "provide [his] citizens with the methods of the most noble arts" and "not allow any area of philosophy to remain that is not made lucid and accessible in Latin writing."[134] After enumerating the treatises written

131. On the unity of Cicero's philosophical corpus, see Gigon 1973: 240–50, Steinmetz 1990, and Schofield 2002.

132. On the originality of this dialogue form, which combines doxography and debate, see Schofield 2008 and cf. Süß 1952 and Leonhardt 1999: 13–88. Still fundamental on ancient dialogues, including those of Cicero, is Hirzel 1895.

133. Other philosophical works of the period include the *Consolatio* (lost), *De senectute* (on old age), the *Topica* (on arguments from commonplaces), and the *Timaeus* (on cosmology; surviving only in part and perhaps unfinished).

134. *Div.* 2.1: *optimarum artium uias traderem meis ciuibus*; *Div.* 2.4: *nullum philosophiae locum esse pateremur qui non Latinis litteris illustratus pateret.*

since late 46, he adds *De re publica*, the *Cato*, and his rhetorical works *De oratore*, *Brutus*, and *Orator*, thus presenting more or less his entire output other than the poetry and speeches as part of a *Gesamtkunstwerk* that is at heart philosophical (*Div.* 2.3–4): invoking Plato, Aristotle, and Theophrastus, Cicero vindicates political theory and rhetoric as subfields of philosophy, while the inclusion of his praise of Cato is justified on the grounds that a "man becomes good and brave through philosophy."[135]

As Cicero avows in the same preface, it was the "dire disaster of the commonwealth" that "provided [his] motivation for expounding philosophy,"[136] and the philosophical works of the 40s are clearly products of Cicero's life under Caesar's rule and in the immediate aftermath of his assassination. This, of course, raises the question of their relationship to contemporary politics and their potential political message. Given that, as we saw in 3.2, Cicero viewed his politics and his philosophy as deeply intertwined, it makes sense to investigate to what extent he continued to practice "engaged philosophy" during the crisis following the Civil War, a question that has occasioned a fair amount of scholarly debate.[137] Since Cicero himself discusses his aims and motivations in his extensive prefaces, these have deservedly figured large in all investigations; in addition, scholars have detected covert strategies within the texts for conveying commentary on contemporary events or making political points. My discussion in what follows will review both types of evidence, all the while keeping in mind that Cicero's intentions and motivations—both as represented and as real—are likely to be highly complex and not easily reducible to one simple formula.[138]

Nearly all the works, and many of the individual books of multibook treatises, have prefaces in which Cicero discusses his project of writing philosophy in Latin.[139] There is amusing evidence that the author did not compose these ad hoc, to fit each individual work, but thought of his prefatory writing as, so to speak, its own genre. In July 44, he writes to Atticus (*Att.* 16.6.4):

> nunc neglegentiam meam cognosce. de gloria librum ad te misi, et in eo prohoemium idem est quod est in Academico tertio. id euenit ob eam rem

---

135. *Div.* 2.3: *philosophia uir bonus efficitur et fortis.*

136. *Div.* 2.6: *mihi quidem explicandae philosophiae causam attulit casus grauis ciuitatis.*

137. On the politics of the philosophical works of the 40s, see esp. Bringmann 1971, Strasburger 1990, Wassmann 1996, and Baraz 2012, as well as Gildenhard 2007 specifically on *Tusc.*

138. Note that while this section largely treats works from before and after the Ides of March as parts of a single corpus, there are also important differences; some of the later treatises will be considered in their specific context in 4.4.

139. On the prefaces, see the discussion in 2.1 above, with the literature cited in n. 23.

quod habeo uolumen prohoemiorum. ex eo eligere soleo cum aliquod σύγγραμμα institui. itaque iam in Tusculano, qui non meminissem me abusum isto prohoemio, conieci id in eum librum quem tibi misi. cum autem in naui legerem Academicos, adgnoui erratum meum. itaque statim nouum prohoemium exaraui et tibi misi. tu illud desecabis, hoc adglutinabis.

Can you imagine my carelessness? I sent you the book *De gloria*, and with it the same preface that is in the third book of the *Academica*. This happened because I have a collection of prefaces, from which I choose when I begin some new work. So when I was in Tusculum and didn't remember that I had used this preface before, I stuck it onto the book I sent you. But when on board ship I read the *Academica*, I noticed my mistake and immediately dashed out a new preface and sent it to you. Cut off the old and glue on the new.

Some scholars have been scandalized by Cicero's cavalier attitude displayed here and have hastened to point out that the actual prefaces do not read like "off the rack" but are carefully adjusted to the works they introduce. This does not, however, prevent Cicero from really having sketched various prefaces in a *uolumen prohoemiorum* (one can imagine that he enjoyed doing so), which he subsequently revised and fitted to individual treatises. What the existence of the *uolumen prohoemiorum* shows is that the author considered his philosophical corpus in progress a coherent whole and that he saw himself as engaged in a sustained effort to explain and position his philosophical writing at Rome.

There are two main sets of purposes that Cicero in the prefaces claims to be pursuing with his composition of philosophical work in Latin. The first is to give comfort to himself, the second to provide a public service. As for the first, Cicero repeatedly mentions that writing philosophy offers him a refuge from, and consolation for, his sufferings, and that he engages in this activity as a form of self-therapy.[140] Occasionally, he less ambitiously describes his work as a (pleasant) distraction or even, not without sarcasm, states that he simply does not have anything better to do.[141] These themes are familiar from Cicero's correspondence with his fellow Pompeians discussed in 4.1 above and also show up repeatedly in his letters to Atticus of spring 45, the period of Cicero's intense grief for Tullia.[142] Shutting himself off from the world, Cicero by his own account "spent all [his] days with reading and writing . . . for the purpose

---

140. *Acad. post.* 11; *Tusc.* 5.5, 121; *Nat. D.* 1.9; *Div.* 2.7.
141. *Acad. post.* 11 (cf. *Fam.* 9.8.2, to Varro); *Tusc.* 2.1; *Div.* 1.11; 2.6; *Off.* 3.3–4.
142. *Att.* 12.16, 12.20, 12.21.5, 12.28.2, 12.38.1, 12.38a, 12.44.4.

of relieving and healing [his] mind."[143] He was working first on his *Consolatio* but then proceeded to continue his more systematic philosophical writing— already begun the previous year with the *Hortensius*[144]—with the composition of the *Academica* and the treatises that follow.

The suffering for which philosophy is supposed to provide a remedy is Cicero's shock and grief at the death of both his daughter and the *res publica*. He experiences these two losses as related: Tullia was his one comfort for the trauma of the Civil War and its aftermath; with her demise, "even those wounds that had appeared to have healed have broken open again."[145] Sulpicius Rufus in his famous letter of consolation-cum-admonition attempts to cheer Cicero with the fact that Tullia died together with the free state,[146] that is, she no longer has to live through the debasement of current life at Rome, but also warns his correspondent to curb his display of grief for political reasons (*Fam.* 4.5.6):

> denique, quoniam in eam fortunam deuenimus ut etiam huic rei nobis seruiendum sit, noli committere ut quisquam te putet non filiam quam rei publicae tempora et aliorum uictoriam lugere.

> Finally, since we have to come to such a pass that we have to watch out even for this sort of thing, make sure people don't think you are mourning not your daughter but the state of the commonwealth and the victory of the other party.

Personal and general calamity are inextricably linked, and Cicero, the erstwhile *pater patriae*, cannot help being deeply wounded by the loss of both his actual child and the political system that he has spent his life fostering.[147]

In presenting his philosophical works as a form of *consolatio*, Cicero thus blends the public and the private in a way that is not only very Ciceronian—he cannot help viewing his personal life in relation to the *res publica*—but also

---

143. *Att.* 12.20.1: *totos dies consumo in litteris . . . leniendi et sanandi animi causa.*

144. The composition of the *Hortensius* is not well documented and scholars disagree about the date. I believe—with Philippson 1939: 1125–26; Bringmann 1971: 91–93; Marinone and Malaspina 2004: 190, 211, 213; and Baraz 2012: 88, among others—that the treatise was (largely) composed in the period from October 46 to February 45, i.e., before Tullia's death.

145. *Fam.* 4.6.2 (to Sulpicius Rufus): *etiam illa quae consanuisse uidebantur recrudescunt.*

146. *Fam.* 4.5.5: *cum res publica occideret, uita excessisse.*

147. Thus Lefèvre 2008: 191: "Die *aegritudo* über die politischen und die persönlichen Umstände ist unteilbar." Compare *Fam.* 9.20.3 (to Paetus, August 46), where Cicero says that he has "mourned the fatherland already longer and more deeply than any mother her only son" (*patriam eluxi iam et grauius et diutius quam ulla mater unicum filium*).

appropriate to the topic: in offering an art of life, philosophy is meant to provide solutions to all human vicissitudes. In addition, Cicero blurs the distinction between philosophizing as private practice and as literary pursuit. Philosophy provides consolation to the individuals who study its precepts and apply them to their lives—but in Cicero's case, the consolation arises also from his writing of philosophical texts (*Nat. D.* 1.9):

> ea [sc. leuatione] uero ipsa nulla ratione melius frui potui quam si me non modo ad legendos libros, sed etiam ad totam philosophiam pertractandam dedissem. omnes autem eius partes atque omnia membra tum facillume noscuntur cum totae quaestiones scribendo explicantur.

> I could enjoy this relief in no better way than by dedicating myself not only to the reading of books but also to the treatment of all of philosophy. For all its parts and divisions become clear once its topics in their entirety are explained in writing.

In endeavoring to expound his philosophical subject matter, Cicero is working out solutions for his own *aegritudo animi*.[148] When he flees into the haven of philosophy—as he so memorably puts it in *Tusculans* 5.4—he seeks refuge at the same time in the haven of philosophical writing.

Writing, of course, is always directed at an audience, and in addition to availing himself of the consolations of philosophy, Cicero wants to bring them to others. At the same time, his ideas for the public aspect of his writings are more ambitious: as he declares repeatedly, his aim is to "benefit as large a number of people as possible" or, more specifically, his "fellow citizens."[149] This wish to be useful or provide a service to the Romans runs through the prefaces as the second leitmotif; it is difficult, however, to grasp how Cicero envisages this public benefit. How exactly are his philosophical writings supposed to benefit their readers and the population at large? At different points, Cicero provides different answers to this question.

In one important sense, Cicero views the composition of his philosophical corpus as a cultural project that, qua intellectual achievement, will further the glory of Rome. Philosophical writing has hitherto, with negligible exceptions,[150] been an exclusively Greek pursuit: "up to now, philosophy has

---

148. This aspect is esp. developed in *Tusculans*, the most explicitly (self-)therapeutic of the works; see S. A. White 1995, Graver 2002, Schofield 2002, Koch 2006, and Lefèvre 2008.

149. *Luc.* 6: *ut plurimis prosimus enitimur*; *Tusc.* 1.5: *ciuibus nostris prosimus*; *Div.* 2.1: *prodesse quam plurimis*; 2.7: *prodessemus ciuibus nostris qua re cumque possemus*.

150. The only known predecessors are the Epicureans Amafinius and Rabirius (disparaged by Cicero: *Acad. post.* 5–6; *Tusc.* 2.7–8; 4.6–7; *Fam.* 15.19.2; see 3.3 above), Brutus's *De uirtute*

lain fallow [at Rome] and lacked the light of Latin literature."[151] In a typically Roman spirit of competitive imitation, Cicero undertakes to transfer this field of study from Greece to Rome and give it a home in the Latin language. He discusses at length the cultural exploits of the two civilizations (a comparison in which the Romans always end up coming out on top; *Tusc.* 1.1–6; 4.1–7) and argues passionately for the possibility and desirability of doing philosophy in Latin (esp. *Acad. post.* 3–12; *Fin.* 1.4–10). Such an undertaking, thus Cicero, is in fact a service to the *res publica* (*Nat. D.* 1.7):

> ipsius rei publicae causa philosophiam nostris hominibus explicandam putaui magni existimans interesse ad decus et ad laudem ciuitatis res tam grauis tamque praeclaras Latinis etiam litteris contineri.

> I thought that I ought to expound philosophy to our people for the sake of the commonwealth itself, in the belief that it makes a great difference for the excellence and glory of the citizenry if such important and outstanding matters are treated in Latin writing as well.

Of course, as a master of Latin style with a deep commitment to giving the most effective and pleasing verbal form to any content, Cicero considers himself uniquely suitable for this undertaking, which is in keeping with his lifelong desire to collapse the boundaries between rhetoric and philosophy. Thus he proudly declares in his last work, *De officiis*: "so far I don't see that any Greek has managed to be active in both genres and practice both that forensic style of speaking and this quieter type of disputation."[152] Cicero views himself as a trailblazer whose works ring in a glorious state of affairs where Rome no longer needs Greek writings since Romans now compose their own philosophical works (*Tusc.* 2.6; *Div.* 2.5–6). Indeed, he contends already in *De natura deorum*—that is, only halfway through the corpus—that his writing has "inspired many people not only to study but to write" philosophy.[153]

(praised: *Acad. post.* 12; *Fin.* 1.8; *Tusc.* 5.1), Varro's *Menippean Satires* and other works (considered only marginally philosophical: *Acad. post.* 8), and Lucretius's *De rerum natura* (known to Cicero [cf. *QFr.* 2.10.3] but never mentioned in the philosophical works).

151. *Tusc.* 1.5: *philosophia iacuit usque ad hanc aetatem nec ullum habuit lumen litterarum Latinarum.*

152. *Off.* 1.3: *id quidem nemini uideo Graecorum adhuc contigisse ut idem utroque in genere elaboraret sequereturque et illud forense dicendi et hoc quietum disputandi genus.*

153. *Nat. D.* 1.8: *multorum non modo discendi sed etiam scribendi studia commouerim* (the claim is repeated at *Off.* 2.2). One would like to know to whom this—no doubt hyperbolic—statement refers. One candidate is Varro, whose *De philosophia* did not yet exist when Cicero wrote the *Academica* (see *Acad. post.* 3) but was possibly inspired by this treatise as well as by *De finibus*.

So far, Cicero's double purpose of (self-)therapy and cultural project seems straightforward and comparatively apolitical. While the need for consolation arises in part from the current state of the *res publica* and the domestication of philosophy is meant to benefit the commonwealth at large, neither motivation translates into a direct intervention into the political situation under Caesar's rule. There are, however, a number of places in the prefaces where Cicero presents the public service his philosophical corpus is meant to render in more concretely political terms. These occur primarily in works written after Caesar's death, when Cicero perhaps felt that he could be more explicit—which does not mean, however, that he did not think along similar lines already when writing his earlier treatises.

First, there are a number of places where Cicero presents himself as being on a pedagogical mission. Such an educational purpose is ascribed in the preface of *De diuinatione* 2 to the entire corpus and occasionally alluded to earlier.[154] What exactly is Cicero teaching? Is it simply a question of making his fellow citizens "more learned" or informing them of "the methods of the best arts"[155]? Or is he aiming at ethical instruction of the Roman youth, much needed in these troubled times (*Div.* 2.4):

> quod enim munus rei publicae adferre maius meliusue possumus, quam si docemus atque erudimus iuuentutem, his praesertim moribus atque temporibus quibus ita prolapsa est ut omnium opibus refrenanda ac coercenda sit?

> What greater and better gift could I offer the commonwealth than to teach and educate the youth, especially given that at this time it is so morally deteriorated that it must be restrained and coerced by all means?

Even so, it is anything but clear what exactly Cicero's moral message would be or how his composing philosophical treatises might contribute to putting supposedly wayward Roman youngsters back on the right path.

The second and most significant avowal of a political dimension in the philosophical works likewise occurs in the preface to the second book of *De diuinatione*, which Cicero apparently wrote shortly after Caesar's death and in which he reflects on his philosophical production up to this point. After

---

Brutus too wrote philosophical works in addition to *De uirtute* (we know of *De officiis* and *De patientia*), but nothing is known about their date.

154. *Div.* 2.4; *Acad. post.* 11; *Fin.* 1.10.

155. *Fin.* 1.10: *ut sint opera studio labore meo doctiores ciues mei; Div.* 2.1: *optimarum artium uias traderem meis ciuibus.*

invoking all the motivations we have encountered so far—consolation, cultural achievement, education—he makes a remarkable final claim (*Div.* 2.7):

> in libris enim sententiam dicebamus, contionabamur, philosophiam nobis pro rei publicae procuratione substitutam putabamus.

> In my books I have been giving speeches in the senate and addressing the assembly, considering philosophy my substitute for administering the Republic.

Philosophy, so Cicero claims, has been for him a continuation of politics by other means, the equivalent of his accustomed activities of speaking to the senate and people of Rome. What is this supposed to mean? Is Cicero simply depicting his philosophical writing as the occupational therapy of a frustrated senator? Is he referring once more to his envisaged public service qua cultural innovation and education? Or is he hinting at a political message of the *philosophica* themselves? The expression of a *sententia* in the senate or address to a *contio* always involves the attempt to get a point across and to inspire a course of action. Is something similar true for Cicero's philosophical works?

A number of scholars—first and foremost Hermann Strasburger, followed by Herbert Wassmann—have seen the philosophical corpus of the 40s and specifically the pre–Ides of March works as deeply political, that is, anti-Caesarian.[156] These critics rely not so much on the prefaces (where, as we have seen, the political claims are rather muted) as on the form and content of the works themselves, pointing to features that they consider, in one way or another, critical of Caesar's rule. Most prominent among these is the prosopography of the dialogues, including the dedicatees, interlocutors, and characters mentioned as historical *exempla*. Most of the treatises are dedicated either to other former Pompeians, first and foremost Brutus but also Varro, or otherwise to such family members or close associates as Atticus, Quintus, or Cicero junior.[157] In addition, many of the dialogues' interlocutors are either such old dyed-in-the wool optimates as Hortensius, Lucullus, and Catulus or otherwise victims of the Civil War and its aftermath like L. Manlius Torquatus, C. Triarius, Cato, and Nigidius Figulus.[158]

---

156. See Strasburger 1990 and Wassmann 1996, as well as Gildenhard 2007 (specifically on *Tusc.*) and Peetz 2008.

157. Brutus: *Fin.*, *Tusc.*, *Nat. D.*; Varro: *Acad. post.*; Atticus: *Sen.*, *Amic.*; Quintus: *Div.*; Cicero junior: *Off.* Exceptions to this tendency are *Fat.* and *Top.*, dedicated to the Caesarians Hirtius and Trebatius, respectively—but only after Caesar's death.

158. Hortensius, Lucullus, Catulus: *Hort.*, *Luc.*; Torquatus, Triarius, Cato: *Fin.*; Nigidius: *Tim.*

This distribution is striking, even more so when one considers that, as Strasburger 1990: 40 points out, it would have made perfect sense for Cicero instead to have dedicated one of his works to Caesar. After all, Caesar had already in 54 addressed his *De analogia* to Cicero and—by the rules of reciprocity that governed Roman *amicitia*—might well have expected a dedication in return.[159] Honoring Caesar in this way would have been highly politic in the early 40s, as realized by the ever-pragmatic Varro, who dedicated his *Antiquitates rerum diuinarum* to Caesar in 46.[160] Cicero not only did nothing of the kind, but consistently kept his philosophical works written before the Ides of March in what we might call a "Caesar-free zone": not only is the cast of characters decidedly unsympathetic to Caesar and what he stands for, but the dictator is never even mentioned, either in the prefaces or in the dialogues themselves. After Caesar's demise, Cicero refers to him a number of times, but then typically in the context of deploring his rule or justifying his assassination.[161]

In addition to the dialogues' prosopography, scholars like Strasburger and Wassmann have identified a number of passages where they suggest Cicero is covertly attacking Caesar. Discussions of the evils of tyranny or the disastrous striving for false glory must, they believe, have been understood as referring to the dictator and contributed to making the philosophical works a sustained anti-Caesarian polemic and, ultimately, a call to arms or—thus Strasburger's title—an "Aufruf gegen die Herrschaft Caesars." Cicero's intention is nothing less than to "reeducate" the Romans "to a more correct view of life," to bring about the "rebirth of a political leadership through the spirit of philosophy," or even to "revindicate mankind out of the rule of violence into the freedom of a divinely guided natural and moral world order."[162]

The strong reading of Strasburger and his followers is very suggestive but ultimately not borne out by Cicero's text. The philosophical works are about philosophy, including fairly detailed doxography, and the teachings one might

---

159. As we saw in 4.3, Cicero made a half-hearted attempt to address Caesar with his *symbouleutikon*, but was relieved to give up the project.

160. This date is not assured but seems likely; see Horsfall 1972: 120–22.

161. See esp. *Off.* 3.19. The justifications of Caesar's murder are discussed further in 4.4.

162. Strasburger 1990: 66: "*Umerziehung* zu einem richtigeren Lebensverständnis" (emphasis his); 55: "Wiedergeburt einer politischen Führungsschicht aus dem Geiste der Philosophie"; 54: "Rückeroberung der Menschheit aus der Herrschaft der Gewalt in die Freiheit der gottgelenkten natürlichen und sittlichen Weltordnung." Strasburger's own anti-Caesarianism—in evidence also in his earlier (1968) book on contemporary judgments of Caesar—is clearly influenced by his experience as a Jew in Nazi Germany. A one-time victim of the "making of history" ("wer einmal bei den 'Spänen' war, als 'Männer, die Geschichte machen', 'hobelten,'" 1968: 81), he has no time for the idealization of "great men."

glean from them are, by their very nature, so general that it is hard to view them as carrying a specific political message. Of course, many of the insights conveyed in the treatises—say, that death is not an evil, virtue is the only good, and nothing is beneficial that is not also honorable—could provide comfort or motivation to people unhappy with Caesar's rule. They are not, however, specific to the situation at Rome in the early 40s, and the works could have been read with profit also by those more sanguine about the political situation, and have indeed been appreciated by many people in many different contexts over the centuries. The mere discussion of philosophy and extolling of virtue are not as such anti-Caesarian; if Cicero wished to issue a call of arms against the dictator, his choice of medium was decidedly poor.

There is also the question of Cicero's target audience. Despite his claims of benefiting his fellow citizens or the Roman people at large, it is clear that Cicero is writing for a small readership of social and intellectual peers. These might, of course, include people more favorably disposed toward Caesar and less enthusiastic about philosophy in Latin than Cicero himself. On the whole, though, it seems likely that the works were written for and read by a group of more or less like-minded individuals, a readership similar—at least ideally—to the interlocutors that people the dialogues themselves. Cicero was not trying to persuade the hostile or unsympathetic; he was preaching to the choir.

The political dimension of Cicero's philosophical works thus consists not in an anti-Caesarian appeal but in the creation of an a-Caesarian space, a private realm that is morally and intellectually superior to the public space dominated by the dictator.[163] Caesar and his followers need not apply:[164] the personnel consists of contemporary and deceased Republicans or otherwise the great men of old with whom Cicero claims an intellectual and political affinity (Cato the Elder in *De senectute* and Laelius in *De amicitia*). Unlike in the contemporary real world, Cicero plays a leading role in the community he has created, orchestrating the dialogues and not infrequently acting as the central interlocutor himself. Here he gets to wield the moral authority that he has lost in the deteriorated political sphere; in his works, Cicero is still, as it were, a *princeps senatus* who gets to speak his *sententia*.

That the Caesar-free zone that Cicero has created is dedicated to the philosophical discussion of truth and virtue is itself a political statement. The

---

163. Compare and contrast scholars' various takes on Cicero's "written republic" (Baraz 2012), "literary republic" (Gurd 2012: 49–76), or "paper forum" (Stroup 2010: 161–67).

164. This is in striking contrast to Cicero's actual social life at the time: he was giving rhetorical lessons to such Caesarians as Hirtius and Dolabella and frequented their banquets (see, e.g., *Fam.* 9.18).

pursuit and content of philosophy are, as we have seen, not anti-Caesarian as such, but Cicero's exclusionary tactics carry an anti-Caesarian charge. In the philosophical works, Cicero's *amici* discuss philosophy—which means that philosophy has become the monopoly of non-Caesarians, who get to call the shots about what is morally right and wrong, and what the good life really consists in. Caesar has staked out for himself near-absolute political power; Cicero retaliates by appointing himself a philosopher king. And while Caesar is extending the Roman empire through questionable wars, Cicero keeps benefiting his people by his peaceful cultural achievements, bringing about Roman supremacy with the pen, not the sword.

Cicero's philosophical works thus do have a strong political dimension, not in the sense that they call for political action, but because they are political interventions in their own right. It is the composition of these treatises itself that makes a point, as a speech act that pointedly bypasses the Caesarian discourse. Caesar could have found nothing to criticize in Cicero's philosophical pursuits—but he would have been well aware of the intellectual and political distance they spelled.

In fact, it seems as though Caesar was clever enough to fasten on an inherent weakness of Cicero's position as created and projected by his treatises. Cicero was an acclaimed master of language, an incisive theorist of rhetoric and philosophy, a cultural trailblazer—and Caesar had, since the 50s, politely hinted that this was his friend's true calling, with the clear innuendo that he should leave politics alone, that is, to Caesar himself. This same strategy of a reduction to the cultural sphere—an attempt, as it were, to lock up Cicero in the world he has created in his treatises—may be discerned in Caesar's visit to Cicero's villa in Puteoli in December of 45. This event is recounted in a letter to Atticus (*Att.* 13.52), a fascinating document that mixes irony, anxiety, pride at having been a good host, and relief that it is all over. Caesar had a good time (*delectatus est et libenter fuit*, 2), and even Cicero has to admit that it was really quite pleasant (*fuit enim periucunde*, 1). The two men enjoyed a nice conversation (*sermone bono*, 1), something that may have been possible because of the chosen topics: σπουδαῖον οὐδὲν *in sermone*, φιλόλογα *multa* ("nothing serious in our talk, much about intellectual matters," 2). Politics was clearly not on the agenda.

Cicero and Caesar had known each other for a long time and knew how to treat each other. Caesar was well aware that the older man fundamentally disapproved of his politics and deeply resented his own powerlessness; Cicero realized that Caesar would have liked to have more of his political support but, barring that, was trying to push the consular into a merely cultural role. Despite these tensions and the obvious power differential, the two Roman aristocrats rose to the occasion and, making use of their excellent social skills, fell back onto the one topic that still united them: their *studia*.[165]

As Cicero learned after Caesar's death from their mutual friend Matius, Caesar considered Cicero extremely easy-going (*facilis*) but realized toward the end that even the most easy-going people were losing their patience. When he saw Cicero among a group waiting to be summoned into the dictator's presence, Caesar remarked (Cic. *Att.* 14.1.2; cf. 14.2.3):

> ego dubitem quin summo in odio sim cum M. Cicero sedeat nec suo commodo me conuenire possit? atqui si quisquam est facilis, hic est. tamen non dubito quin me male oderit.

> Can I doubt I am deeply hated when M. Cicero is sitting there and can't see me at his convenience? If anybody is easy-going, it's him. Still I have no doubt that he hates me very much.

Caesar was correct. People did hate him, and they were not going to put up with his rule any longer. While the easy-going Cicero was not among the senators wielding their daggers on the Ides of March 44, he approved of their action and immediately threw himself into politics again. Far from maintaining the role of the remote intellectual in which Caesar cast him, he at once recalibrated his pursuit of philosophy with his regained role in public life (*Div.* 2.7):

> nunc quoniam de re publica consuli coepti sumus, tribuenda est opera rei publicae, uel omnis potius in ea cogitatio et cura ponenda; tantum huic studio relinquendum quantum uacabit a publico officio et munere.

> But now, since I have begun to be consulted about the commonwealth, I must devote my efforts to the commonwealth and dedicate to it all my thought and care. To this pursuit [sc. the writing of philosophy] will be left however much time is free from my public service.

For a short period from late 46 to early 44, philosophy was for Cicero the only game in town, his only way of playing a public role, of making a political statement by deliberately ignoring the Caesarian new normal. Once Caesar was removed, Cicero changed back from being a philosopher king to being a Roman senator, one who pursues his political agenda and his *studia* in tandem, as the two established aspects of an elite man's active and leisurely lives, respectively. He continued writing his philosophical corpus, all the while embroiled in the tumultuous

---

165. Compare Damon 2008.

happenings after the assassination, trying—in vain—to put the *res publica* back on track.

4. Philosophies of Tyrannicide

The anecdote about Caesar's realizing that he had made himself unpopular even with easy-going Cicero provides a rare glimpse into the mind of the man central to Rome's politics in our period. For all his significance, Caesar remains an enigma. Owing to the loss of his letters and lack of other contemporary pro-Caesarian sources, and perhaps also to the man's tendency—in evidence in his laconic *Commentarii*[166]—to play his cards close to his chest, we have very little understanding of Caesar's view of the political situation and his own role in it. After his momentous crossing of the Rubicon in January 49, his actions had been dictated by the dynamics of the Civil War as he fought the Pompeians in theaters around the Mediterranean, spending only a few months here and there at Rome. It was only with the final victory over Pompey's sons Gnaeus and Sextus at Munda in March 45 and Caesar's return to Italy that the question of what the post–Civil War *res publica* would look like became overwhelming. What did Caesar want?

For those who held out the hope that the dictator would "reconstitute the Republic,"[167] that is, initiate a return to traditional senatorial rule and give up his own position of unconstitutional power, Caesar's actions became increasingly alarming. Rather than stepping down—as Sulla, the last person in a comparable situation had done—Caesar had himself declared *dictator perpetuo* in early 44, signaling that he intended to remain in charge. He also accepted, and occasionally pointedly rejected, increasingly extravagant honors, which symbolically approximated him to a king or even a god, a process that culminated in the famous scene at the Lupercalia of 15 February, where Antony crowned him with a royal diadem. Caesar ostentatiously refused the honor, but the scene left a bad taste for many Republicans.

---

166. Cicero famously referred to the *Bellum Gallicum* as "naked, straightforward, and elegant, stripped of all rhetorical elaboration as if of a garment" (*nudi . . . recti et uenusti, omni ornatu orationis tamquam ueste detracta, Brut.* 262; on this passage, see further 5.3). Note that I am working on the assumption, with the majority of scholars (cf. Raaflaub 2009: 180–82 and Grillo 2012: 178–80), that the *Bellum Ciuile* was published only after Caesar's death and thus not known to people beyond his close circle in the period treated in this book.

167. Already in *Pro Marcello*, Cicero had told Caesar, *in hoc elaborandum est ut rem publicam constituas* (27; see 4.2). Compare the official titles of Sulla, *dictator legibus scribundis et rei publicae constituendae*, and of the members of the Second Triumvirate, *iiiuiri rei publicae constituendae*.

Most historians today do not believe that Caesar had a worked-out plan to make himself a monarch, or even that he had much of a plan at all.[168] Having precipitated and won the Civil War, he now found himself in circumstances that called for political action but did not suggest an obvious course or allow for an easy solution that would have satisfied the divers groups (senators of various persuasions, *equites*, urban and rural populations, and the army) looking to him for support of their own interests. The German historian Christian Meier thus famously suggested that the most powerful man at Rome became increasingly powerless, unable to cope with the situation into which he had maneuvered himself and looking to his projected Parthian campaign as a way to escape the intractable political mess at Rome.[169]

Some contemporaries analyzed Caesar's situation similarly. After the Ides of March, Caesar's friend C. Matius in a deeply gloomy mood told Cicero that "if a man of such genius couldn't find a way out, who will find one now?"[170] But was the dictator really looking for a solution to the constitutional crisis that his own actions had brought about? His increasingly aloof and arrogant behavior did not inspire confidence, nor did his observation, eagerly reported by his enemies, that "the *res publica* is nothing, a mere name without body or shape; Sulla, laying down the dictatorship, didn't know his ABC."[171] Perhaps Caesar had really come to the conclusion that "*res publica*" was just an empty slogan and not something that he or anyone else might put back in order the way Sulla had mistakenly imagined he had done. If the "public thing" was not a thing at all, then Caesar was free to create his own reality. Reportedly, he

168. See, e.g., Gardner 2009: 65: "there is nothing to indicate that Caesar had formulated any definite plans either for his own future in the government of Rome, or for changes to the Republican constitution itself."

169. See C. Meier 1980: 17–100, an essay called "Die Ohnmacht des allmächtigen Diktators Caesar." Meier views Caesar's lack of a political program as a symptom of the late Republic's "crisis without alternative": the Republican system of government was no longer viable but the Romans were incapable of imagining other options; cf. C. Meier 1997.

170. Cic. *Att.* 14.1: *si ille tali ingenio exitum non reperiebat, quis nunc reperiet?* Cicero found this kind of talk upsetting but had himself already in September 46 expressed his belief that Caesar, even with the best intentions, "can't do anything" (*quid faciat tamen non habet, Fam.* 9.17.2). Pelling 1997 suggests that Plutarch's *Life of Caesar*, too, presents the dictator as a victim of circumstances.

171. Suet. *Iul.* 77: *nihil esse rem publicam, appellationem modo sine corpore ac specie; Sullam nescisse litteras qui dictaturam deposuerit.* Suetonius's source is the fierce anti-Caesarian Ampius Balbus, who may of course have invented or distorted the quotation for purposes of propaganda. However, L. Morgan 1997 makes a good case for authenticity, offering a detailed interpretation.

followed up his dismissal of the *res publica* with the ominous threat that "people now ought to speak more carefully to him and take his words for law."[172]

Whatever Caesar's actual thoughts and plans may have been, by the spring of 44 a sizable group senators had decided that the dictator had to go, among them not only many Pompeians who had been pardoned by Caesar but also some old-time Caesarians.[173] Under the leadership of Cassius, Brutus, and Brutus's relative D. Iunius Brutus Albinus, they coordinated the famous assassination, stabbing Caesar to death at a meeting of the senate on 15 March.[174] Since antiquity there has been much speculation about the assassins' motives. Were these self-styled liberators largely driven by personal considerations, whether hatred of Caesar or dissatisfaction with the way they had fared, politically and/or economically, under his regime?[175] It is impossible to be sure about the motivation of dozens of men, most of whose names are unknown to us, and individual conspirators may have had their own reasons for participating in this act of violence. Nevertheless, I believe with the majority of scholars that the assassination was indeed driven by alarm at Caesar's de facto monarchy, a state of affairs that ran counter to the *res publica*'s unwritten constitution and prevented the functioning of the traditional aristocratic system of senatorial rule. When Caesar appeared to be making himself a king, the Republic struck back.[176]

This motivation of the assassination on, as it were, constitutional grounds could be reinforced—in both the deed's conception and its later justification—by philosophical arguments.[177] As we have seen, both Brutus and Cassius were men of strong philosophical interests and convictions, as of course was Cicero. The consular was not himself privy to the conspiracy, but was afterwards claimed as its inspiration by both friend and foe.[178] In the months following the Ides of March, he became the assassination's most vocal apologist.

---

172. Suet. *Iul.* 77: *debere homines consideratius iam loqui secum ac pro legibus habere quae dicat.*

173. Historiographical sources speak of over sixty conspirators; we know twenty by name (see Lintott 2009: 77).

174. On the assassination, see the helpful discussion of Lintott 2009.

175. Thus already our oldest source, Nicolaus of Damascus (*Life of Augustus* 60–65 = FGrH 90 fr. 127); modern proponents of the personal-enmity thesis include Epstein 1987 and Storch 1995.

176. Compare the reconstruction of the pre-Ides mood in Botermann 1992b.

177. The claim of Gotter 1996b: 225 that any such reference to "Greek motifs" ("griechische Motive") is mere "stylization" ("Stilisierung") without substance seems to me far off the mark.

178. Directly after the stabbing, Brutus reportedly held up his bloodstained dagger and exclaimed, "Cicero!" (Cic. *Phil.* 2.28, 30). In *Phil.* 2.25–36, Cicero answers Antony's claim that Caesar was killed at his instigation (*Caesarem meo consilio interfectum*, 25), denying the actual charge but stressing his approval of the deed.

The main argument used by the liberators and their supporters to justify the killing was that Caesar had made, or was about to make, himself a king (*rex*) or tyrant (*tyrannus*).[179] This was a powerful charge that appealed to the convictions of Roman senators on many levels. First, the abhorrence of king-ship was, as it were, part of the Roman political DNA. Ever since Tarquin the Proud had been driven out—by none other than Brutus's supposed ancestor L. Iunius Brutus—and the Republic established in 509 BCE, the Romans had been decided "not to let anyone else rule as king at Rome."[180] Accordingly, the suspicion that a Roman politician was "striving for the kingship" (*regnum adfectare*) could severely damage his reputation, and accusations of such royal aspiration were thus popular weapons in the arsenal of political invective.[181] Such opprobrium attached to the *r*-word that Caesar did his utmost to avoid the term—but in vain: "he was unable to cast off the odium of having aspired to the name of king, even though when the people hailed him as *rex*, he answered, 'I am not Rex but Caesar.'"[182]

By contrast, the tyrant was a Greek import, a dark figure who had become familiar to the Romans in a variety of cultural contexts. There were infamous historical tyrants, including Phalaris of Acragas, Pisistratus of Athens, and Dionysius of Syracuse; there were monstrous mythological tyrants, such as Atreus and Tereus, who made their appearance not only in Greek literature but also on the Roman stage; and there was the tyrant of philosophy, representative of the worst possible political constitution and example of supreme unhappiness despite his position of power. As so often, Cicero's writings provide excellent

179. The Roman discourses on kingship and tyranny are not the same but closely inter-twined, and are often treated together. Discussions of various aspects of the topic—both in general and in relation to Caesar and his assassination—include Sirago 1956, Dunkle 1967, Rawson 1975, Yavetz 1983, Erskine 1991, Martin 1994, Gildenhard 2006 (cf. 2011, index s.v. "tyrant/ *tyrannus*/tyranny"), Pina Polo 2006, Luciani 2009, Wiseman 2009: 177–210, M. Meier 2014, Sigmund 2014, and Baraz 2018.

180. These are the words that Livy puts into L. Brutus's mouth: *me ... nec alium quemquam regnare Romae passurum* (1.59). On L. Brutus and his use as a political symbol, see Martin 2010. Interestingly, the Roman dislike of *regnum* did not translate into a negative view of the six kings who had preceded Tarquinius, who were typically depicted positively; see Classen 1965 and 5.2 on Cicero's treatment of the regal period in *Rep.* 2.

181. See Dunkle 1967 as well as Baraz 2018, who underlines the versatility of the kingship charge, which could be applied to men across the political spectrum.

182. Suet. *Iul.* 79.2: *neque ... infamiam adfectati ... regii nominis discutere ualuit, quamquam ... plebei regem se salutanti Caesarem se non regem esse responderit.* Caesar's joke depends on the fact that *Rex* was also a Roman *cognomen*.

evidence for how the discourse of tyranny became applied to Caesar, a pernicious development that furnished his assassins with their best argument.

Already in *De re publica*, Cicero had inveighed against the evils of tyranny
as a form of government and opposed the tyrant to his ideal statesman.[183]
After the outbreak of the Civil War, when the consular was trying to determine
how to act so as to live up to his own *rector* ideal, Cicero began to cast Caesar
in the contrasting role of the tyrant.[184] In a letter to Atticus of January 49, he
quotes a line from Euripides's *Phoenissae* to indicate that Caesar is committing
numerous crimes "in order to possess the greatest of deities: Tyranny."[185] A
man like this, who is animated by thirst for power rather than *honestas*, must
by definition be unhappy (*Att.* 7.11.2):

> hoc ipsum uelle miserius esse duco quam in crucem tolli. una res est ea
> miserior, adipisci quod ita uolueris.

> I believe that having this very desire is more miserable than being crucified.
> Only one thing is more miserable than this: to achieve what you have thus
> desired.

Cicero himself would rather spend a leisurely hour with Atticus than have "any
kingdoms of this kind."[186]

Cicero continued to think of Caesar as a tyrant, comparing him to Pisistratus and Phalaris and conceiving his own course of action as that of a man living
under tyranny.[187] Of course, the situation was only exacerbated after Cicero's
return from the Civil War: in a letter of August 45, he for the first time referred
to the dictator explicitly as *rex*, in a grimly jocular context.[188] Meanwhile, in
his pre–Ides of March philosophical work, the tyrant continued to play the

---

183. On tyranny in *De re publica*, see Sirago 1956: 190–99. The *rector* is contrasted with the
tyrant at *Rep.* 2.51.

184. See Gildenhard 2006 and compare McConnell 2014: 62–114. On Cicero's application
of the *rector* ideal to his own situation, see 3.2.

185. Cic. *Att.* 7.11.1 = Eur. *Phoen.* 506: τὴν θεῶν μεγίστην ὥστ' ἔχειν Τυραννίδα.

186. *Att.* 7.11.1: *unam mehercule tecum apricationem in illo lucratiuo tuo sole malim quam omnia
istius modi regna.* Cicero redeploys the motif of "a short time in the exercise of virtue/intellectual
activity preferable to a long period of vice/tyrannical power" at *Tusc.* 5.5, 54–56; see Strasburger
1990: 53–54, 60–61.

187. Pisistratus/Phalaris: *Att.* 7.12.2, 7.20.2; 8.16.2; confronting tyranny: *Att.* 7.20.2; 8.2.4; 9.4.2
(this is the Greek *disputatio in utramque partem* discussed in 3.2), 9.13.4; 10.13, 10.12a.1. See also
Att. 7.5.4; 10.4.2.

188. Cicero's nephew Quintus had been denigrating his father and uncle, explicitly warning
Caesar against Marcus's hostility. Cicero comments sarcastically: φοβερὸν ἂν ἦν *nisi uiderem
scire regem me nihil animi habere* (*Att.* 13.37.2). The translation of Shackleton Bailey 1999: 4.123

role of the supremely unhappy man. *Tusculans* 5 features an extensive description of the misery of the elder Dionysius (57–63), whose life full of fear is the
"most horrible, wretched, and despicable" Cicero can imagine.[189] Virtue is
sufficient for happiness; conversely, the tyrant qua most vicious is also most
unhappy.[190]

That the image of Caesar as a tyrant was not peculiar to Cicero but part of
more widespread parlance is clear from a fascinating passage in Cicero's speech
for the Galatian king Deiotarus of November 45. Deiotarus, an old friend of
Cicero's, had been accused of plotting against Caesar, and the orator had been
called upon to plead his case, not in a public trial, but in a private setting with
Caesar himself as the only judge. One of the pieces of evidence adduced by
the accusers was a letter sent to Deiotarus by a confidant, who reported to the
king on the public mood at Rome (*Deiot.* 33):

> ad regem . . . scribere solebat te in inuidia esse, tyrannum existimari, statua
> inter reges posita animos hominum uehementer offensos, plaudi tibi non
> solere.

> He used to write to the king that you [Caesar] are disliked and considered
> a tyrant, that the minds of men are gravely offended by the erection of your
> statue among [those of] the kings, that you don't receive applause.

Cicero hastens to discredit such rumors as "malicious city gossip" and proceeds to assure Caesar that "we free men, born in the greatest freedom of the
Roman people, do not view you as a tyrant."[191]

Needless to say, Cicero's dismissal of the tyranny charge can easily be understood as conveying the opposite of its superficial meaning:[192] it is obvious that
there *are* people at Rome who consider Caesar a tyrant, while it is not so obvious
that men used to their freedom—that is, the Romans in general but perhaps the
senatorial class in particular—are really as sanguine about Caesar's rule as Cicero
blithely asserts. In stressing *libertas*, Cicero is employing a third leitmotif (next

---

hits the mark: "It would be alarming if I were not well aware that H.M. knows me for a
coward."

189. *Tusc.* 5.64: *huius uita qua taetrius miserius detestabilius excogitare nihil possum.*

190. Strasburger 1990: 56–61 and Wassmann 1996: 182–208 read the discussions of tyranny
in *Tusc.* as specifically anti-Caesarian polemic.

191. *Deiot.* 33: *ex urbanis maleuolorum sermiunculis*; 34: *nos liberi, in summa populi Romani
libertate nati, . . . non tyrannum . . . ducimus.*

192. On the anti-Caesarian elements of *Deiot.*, see Botermann 1992a and Peer 2008. The
speech can be understood as both a covert warning to Caesar, the addressee of its delivered version, and a signaling of Cicero's views to his Republican *amici*, the readership of the written text.

to kingship and tyranny) of the discontent with, and ultimate resistance to, Caesar: the Romans have a birthright to freedom, but by making himself sole ruler, Caesar has become a *dominus* ("master") who has reduced the rest of the populace to *seruitus* ("slavery").[193] In the opinion of Cicero and others, the situation calls out for an act of liberation.

This, finally, brings us back to the men who after the Ides of March came to be referred to as *liberatores* ("liberators").[194] Of these, the only ones for whom we have sources that touch on their intellectual makeup and motivations are the brothers-in-law Cassius and Brutus, two Roman senators whom David Sedley does not hesitate to number among "that select band of philosophers who have managed to change the world."[195] How, then, did their philosophy inform their politics with its turn to violence—and what did the tumultuous events of the 40s do to the men's philosophy?

Less well documented, the story of Cassius emerges as comparatively straightforward.[196] This outstanding general, whom our sources describe as spirited and aggressive, had always been a staunch Republican and was most likely the driving force behind the conspiracy. Pardoned and promoted by Caesar—like Brutus, he was praetor in 44—he seems at first to have taken a realistic but resigned view of the dictatorship. In his letter to Cicero of January 45, the time of the Spanish campaign, he expresses his preference for Caesar over Gnaeus Pompeius junior by observing that he would rather "have the old and merciful master than try out a new and cruel one."[197] The term

193. On *libertas*, see Wirszubski 1950; Bleicken 1962; Brunt 1988: 281–350; Arena 2007, 2012; and Cogitore 2011.

194. As Cogitore 2011: 191–93 shows, the use of *liberatores* for the conspirators was pioneered by, and is typical for, Cicero (its first occurrence is *Att.* 14.12.2, of 22 April 44); for detailed discussion, see Leber 2018. There is no unequivocal evidence for its use by Brutus et al. themselves (it occurs in Cic. *Ad Brut.* 1.16.2 in the hyperbolical expression "liberators of the world," *liberatoribus orbis terrarum*, but this letter from Brutus to Cicero has been suspected of being a forgery; see nn. 216, 229 below), though *libertatis auctores* is attested (Cic. *Fam.* 11.28.3; see further Leber 2018: 171 n. 81). Note that I am using "liberators," "assassins," and "conspirators" interchangeably for variety's sake, without implying any valuation of these men's actions.

195. Sedley 1997: 41; Sedley's piece is the classic treatment of the philosophy of Brutus and Cassius. For detailed discussion of the sources on both men, and their various biases, see Rawson 1986. In what follows, I sometimes extrapolate from the brothers-in-law to the assassins as a group, but ultimately, little can be known for certain about the thoughts and beliefs of the other men involved.

196. Cassius has been little studied. In addition to Rawson 1986, see Dettenhofer 1992 and, for his Epicureanism, Sedley 1997 and Gilbert 2015: 163–283.

197. Cic. *Fam.* 15.19.4: *malo ueterem et clementem dominum habere quam nouum et crudelem experiri.* The letter is discussed further in 3.3 above.

used is *dominus*, which shows that Cassius has no illusions about the real nature of Caesar's rule, while the quietist sentiment expressed fits well with the writer's Epicureanism. Concerned solely with the pursuit of his own pleasure, the Epicurean will favor a political situation that offers as little disturbance as possible,[198] and if one must have a master, Caesar is vastly preferable to Pompeius.

While we have no information about the development of Cassius's views over the following year, it is easy to imagine how this at-best-lukewarm Caesarian after the dictator's return from Spain quickly came to the conclusion that living under the *dominatio* of such a would-be king was not something conducive to *ataraxia* after all. Cassius's turning conspirator, or even the conspiracy's mastermind, in no way contradicts his Epicureanism or indicates that he adopted this world-view only for the short period of resigned inaction under Caesar's rule.[199] Of course, under most circumstances, participating in a political assassination is the last thing an Epicurean in pursuit of the hidden life will do. As we saw in 3.3, however, Epicureanism allowed for a political "emergency clause" and for the tailoring of hedonism to a person's personality and values. Cassius, who in his letter to Cicero had argued for the coincidence of *uirtus* and *uoluptas* (Cic. *Fam.* 15.19.2–3), did not violate his Epicurean beliefs by organizing and participating in the murder of Caesar. He would have maintained that freeing Rome from a tyrant was the only way to guarantee greater pleasure for the future.

In his *Lives* of Caesar and Brutus, Plutarch claims that Cassius occasionally (or eventually) betrayed his Epicureanism: right before the attack on Caesar, Cassius invoked the statue of Pompey at whose foot the dictator was to breathe his last (an inspired gesture but not one in keeping with Epicurean rationalism), while before the Battle of Philippi, baleful omens caused even Cassius to abandon his philosophy and be swept away by the general hysteria.[200] Neither of these anecdotes carries any weight. Plutarch is notoriously biased against Epicureanism, while also at pains to denigrate Cassius to the benefit of his true hero, Brutus.[201] There is, however, no need to assume that the stories are malicious inventions (though of course they may well be): it is perfectly

---

198. Something that cannot be said for the ongoing Civil War: Cassius confides to Cicero that he is "very agitated" (*peream nisi sollicitus sum*, Cic. *Fam.* 15.19.4).

199. A joke in Cic. *Fam.* 15.16.3 (January 45) appears to imply that Cassius's adoption of Epicureanism lay two to three years back; this passage has been much scrutinized but does not in fact provide any information about the circumstances of Cassius's conversion or his earlier philosophical views (cf. Gilbert 2015: 228 n. 13).

200. Pompey's statue: Plut. *Caes.* 66.2, cf. Plut. *Brut.* 17.2; omens at Philippi: Plut. *Brut.* 39.6.

201. On Plutarch's idealization of Brutus, see Pelling 1989: 222–30, Swain 1990: 201–3, and Moles 2017.

imaginable that an Epicurean might have availed himself of the symbolism of Pompey's statue for his rhetoric, or been unhappy about the lowering of morale brought about by unfavorable omens before an important battle.[202]

It has also been claimed that the tale in Plutarch of how Cassius attempted to calm Brutus over the appearance of the famous phantom ("Thou shalt see me at Philippi") is meant to disparage his philosophical credibility by putting into his mouth an un-Epicurean explanation of Brutus's experience.[203] It is certainly the case that the details of Plutarch's version of Cassius's discourse, especially the claim that sense perception is unreliable, are not in keeping with orthodox Epicurean doctrine. However, the gist of his words is perfectly Epicurean: such apparitions arise from the mind's faulty arrangement and interpretation of sensory impressions and are therefore not to be taken as real. It is possible that Plutarch, rather than showing up Cassius as a bad Epicurean, simply wanted to replicate what an Epicurean might say in such a situation.[204] While the real Cassius—who had once been engaged by Cicero in an epistolary discussion of the Epicurean theory of vision[205]—would no doubt have been more sophisticated, it is certainly plausible that *if* Brutus had indeed had a nightly vision, his brother-in-law might have tried to allay his fears with philosophical argument along similar lines. As Plutarch maintains, the two men were in the habit of debating such issues, with Cassius making his Epicurean opinions quite clear.[206]

For all the historical significance of Cassius, it was "the noble Brutus" who captured the imagination of contemporaries and posterity alike: considered the symbolic figurehead of the conspiracy already in his own time, he has over the centuries been submitted to a variety of interpretations and judgments, and enlisted in the service of a multitude of causes.[207] As has often been pointed out, Brutus seemed positively predestined to kill Caesar, claiming among his ancestors both L. Iunius Brutus and C. Servilius Ahala (killer of

---

202. Of course, it is also perfectly imaginable for an Epicurean to lose, or waver from, his philosophical faith (compare Volk forthcoming a); my point is simply that our evidence is not sufficient to claim that Cassius did.

203. Plut. *Brut.* 37.1–6; see FitzGibbon 2008.

204. Thus the reasonable suggestion of Brenk 1988.

205. Cic. *Fam.* 15.16.1–2, 15.19.1.

206. Plut. *Brut.* 37.2: περὶ τούτων [sc. Ἐπικούρου λόγων] ἔθος ἔχων [sc. ὁ Κάσσιος] διαφέρεσθαι πρὸς τὸν Βροῦτον ("Cassius was in the habit of disagreeing about these things [sc. Epicurean doctrine] with Brutus").

207. On Brutus, see now Tempest 2017, as well as Raubitschek 1957; Bengtson 1970; Clarke 1981; Wistrand 1981; Ortmann 1988; Dettenhofer 1992; Gotter 1996b, 2000; Sedley 1997; and Balbo 2013.

Spurius Maelius, a supposed *adfectator regni* of the mid-fifth century). Brutus himself advertised his ancestry: he charged Atticus with reconstructing his genealogy and prominently displayed his family tree in his house, and as a *tresuir monetalis* in 54 issued coins with the images of L. Brutus and Servilius Ahala, as well as the goddess Libertas.[208] Cicero, too, who throughout his work uses the two men as models for proper Republican behavior, liked to remind his friend of his illustrious *maiores*, a theme that is especially strong in the *Brutus*.[209] The traditional Roman idea that a man ought to follow the *exempla* of his ancestors, coupled with Brutus's pointed embrace of his family's anti-royal tradition, had the potential to raise expectations—expectations that interested parties could rephrase as demands. As our historical sources tell us, in the weeks before the Ides of March, graffiti kept showing up on the base of a statue of L. Brutus, reading "If only you were alive!," while Brutus's own tribunal was covered with such mocking sentiments as "Are you asleep, Brutus?" and "You are not Brutus."[210]

Brutus's Republican bona fides was, however, not restricted to being descended from the Iunii and Servilii. He was also the nephew of Cato, whose half-sister Servilia was Brutus's mother (as well as—a fact that one assumes rather complicated family dynamics—Caesar's one-time lover). Possibly inspired by his uncle, Brutus already in the 50s expressed strong pro-senate views, inveighing especially against Pompey, for whom he held a special grudge as the one responsible for the death of his father in the civil strife of 77 BCE. Quintilian has preserved for us a fragment of a speech against Pompey's receiving the consulship *sine collega* in 52, in which Brutus issued the abstract and rather philosophically phrased statement that "it is better not to rule over anyone than to serve someone; for without the former one can live honorably, with the second one cannot live at all."[211] Later the same year, he praised Milo's murder of Clodius as the elimination of a *malus ciuis*.[212]

208. Genealogy: Nep. *Att.* 18.3; Cic. *Att.* 13.40.1; coins: RRC 433.1, 2.

209. On Brutus in the *Brutus*, see the discussion in 4.2 and the literature cited there. On Cicero's—not always easy—friendship with Brutus, see Santamaria 2013–14.

210. On the graffiti, see Suet. *Iul.* 80.3; Plut. *Brut.* 9.8; *Caes.* 62.4; Cass. Dio 44.12; App. *B Civ.* 2.112.469; and Morstein-Marx 2012: 204–13 and Hillard 2013: 112–14. On the pressure exerted by Brutus's name, see Lentano 2009: 74–81.

211. Quint. *Inst.* 9.3.95 = Brutus fr. 158.16 Malcovati: *praestat enim nemini imperare quam alicui seruire: sine illo enim uiuere honeste licet, cum hoc uiuendi nulla condicio est.* Note the references to both "slavery" (part of the Roman political vocabulary) and the "good life" (a philosophical concept).

212. Quint. *Inst.* 3.6.93 = Brutus fr. 158.18 Malcovati. Both this speech and the one about Pompey may have been published pamphlets rather than delivered orations. On Brutus as an orator, see Balbo 2013.

Despite his dislike of Pompey and Pompeianism, Brutus joined the campaign against Caesar, but immediately after Pharsalus sought and received the dictator's pardon. In the years of Caesar's rule we find him in a strangely ambivalent position. On the one hand, he flourished under Caesar's protection, being placed in charge of Cisalpine Gaul (46–45) and appointed urban praetor for 44; clearly, Caesar was fond of him and actively pursued his friendship. On the other hand, Brutus continued ostentatiously to display his Republicanism. If he allowed himself to be wooed by Caesar, he did the same with Cicero, graciously receiving, as we have seen, the dedications of the majority of the pre-Ides philosophical works. Brutus's own publications, too, were hardly Caesar-friendly: the praise of Marcellus in *De uirtute* and that of Cato in the *Cato* sent an obvious message, one that was not a little philosophical. Two of Caesar's fiercest opponents were praised as examples of the self-sufficiency of virtue; what role this left to Caesar remained unspoken. Brutus's final Republican provocation was his unexpected divorce from his wife Claudia and subsequent marriage to Porcia, the daughter of Cato and widow of Bibulus (Caesar's powerless fellow consul of 59). Much gossiped about, these nuptials, as it were, anointed Brutus as Cato's successor. When the conspiracy formed, there was general agreement that Brutus's participation was a *condicio sine qua non* if the act was to have any legitimacy (Plut. *Brut.* 10.1–2). Cassius suggested the matter to his brother-in-law, and the rest is history.

Brutus is sometimes viewed as a weak and indecisive person who was pressured into the role of assassin by the combined weight of Iunian, Servilian, and Porcian ideology.[213] As so often, we have no way to look into our man's head, but it seems to me unlikely that even the most *maiores*-obsessed Roman aristocrat would have engaged in an act of bloody violence for the sole reason that hundreds of years earlier a semimythical ancestor had reportedly done something similar. By most accounts, Brutus acted out of genuine conviction, and it is once again Caesar who in one of his bon mots appears to have captured best the character of his faithless friend: "It makes a big difference what he wants, but whatever he wants, he wants very much."[214] Not unlike his uncle Cato, Brutus vigorously pursued whatever course of action he had decided on, something that involved some spectacular about-faces (he both joined and left the Pompeian camp abruptly, and defended Caesar to Cicero only a few

213. Thus, e.g., Dettenhofer 1992: 244–47 and Gotter 2000.

214. Cic. *Att.* 14.1.2: *magni refert hic quid uelit, sed quicquid uult ualde uult.* This anecdote, told to Cicero once again by his and Caesar's mutual friend Matius, is taken up by Plut. *Brut.* 6.7–8. For the interpretation of Caesar's quip, compare Tempest 2017: 65–67.

months before he plunged his dagger into him[215]) and a fair amount of arrogance and rudeness in pushing his chosen aims.[216]

The philosophical aspects of Brutus's personality and politics were apparent already to his contemporaries and later ancient sources. The concept most typically associated with him is *uirtus*, a quality that Brutus appears to have claimed for himself and made, as it were, his trademark.[217] Of course, *uirtus* is a traditional Roman ideal, but it seems that for the author of a philosophical tract *De uirtute*, the term referred not simply to some vague manly excellence but to the knowing exercise of the morally good. When Cicero in *Tusculans* 5 turns to discussion of the axiom that virtue is sufficient for happiness, he calls this Brutus's favorite topic;[218] at other places he praises his friend's "admirable virtues" and "unique and unbelievable virtue."[219] In his ode about his experience of the Battle of Philippi, Horace refers to the defeat of Brutus's party with the extreme shorthand *fracta uirtus* ("virtue [was] broken," *Carm.* 2.7.11),[220] while in Plutarch's *Life*, Brutus is characterized throughout by ἀρετή and concern for τὸ καλόν.[221]

Of course, Brutus's insistence on (his) virtue did not impress or convince everyone equally. In explaining the Horatian phrase just cited, the commentator Porphyrio remarks drily that "Cassius and Brutus were making a big deal of their virtue,"[222] and after Brutus's death, the malevolent legend arose that right before committing suicide, he dramatically renounced virtue by quoting the following verses:[223]

---

215. In *Att.* 13.40 (mid-August 45), Cicero in a tone of incredulous sarcasm reports to Atticus that Brutus has told him that Caesar is "joining the good guys" (*illum ad bonos uiros*, 1), adding, "But where is he going to find them—unless perchance he hangs himself?" (*sed ubi eos? nisi forte se suspendit*).

216. See Gelzer 1918: 985: "Dieser herbe Freimut, der gerade heraus sagt, was er für das Rechte erachtet . . . ist für Brutus charakteristisch." The ever-polite Cicero had to suffer under the younger man's self-righteousness from the beginning of their friendship to its end (see, e.g., *Att.* 6.1.7, 6.3.7). If the letters *Ad Brut.* 1.16, 17 (Brutus to Cicero and Atticus, respectively) are genuine (see nn. 194, 229), they present the remarkable picture of a Roman aristocrat dropping all decorum.

217. See Moles 1987: 63–66 and Tempest 2017: 224–28.

218. Cic. *Tusc.* 5.1: *quam* [sc. *rem*] *tu ex omnibus maxime probas*.

219. Cic. *Orat.* 33: *uirtutum admirabilium*; *Att.* 14.15.2: *singularem incredibilemque uirtutem*.

220. On this Horatian passage, see Moles 1987 and Tempest 2017: 225–28.

221. Ἀρετή: 7.3, 7.7, 29.3, 46.3, 50.5, 52.5; τὸ καλόν: 1.3, 29.3.

222. Porph. ad loc.: *uirtute se Cassius et Brutus praecipue iactabant*.

223. Cass. Dio 47.49.2, cf. Flor. 2.17.11; Zonar. 10.20. The lines come from an unidentified tragedy and in the original were spoken by Herakles. On the anecdote and its likely inauthenticity, see Moles 1983: 775–79.

ὦ τλῆμον ἀρετή, λόγος ἄρ᾽ ἦσθ᾽, ἐγὼ δέ σε
ὡς ἔργον ἤσκουν· σὺ ἄρ᾽ ἐδούλευες τύχῃ.

Oh wretched virtue, you were but a word, but I treated you as real. In fact, you were the slave of fortune.

Even in its attempt to denigrate Brutus, the anecdote buys into his legend: a true Brutus is defeated not by death but by the renunciation of his principles.

Brutus was an adherent of Antiochus's Old Academy and—as David Sedley has demonstrated in a brilliant article—in conceiving the conspiracy availed himself of both philosophy in general and Platonic doctrine in particular.[224] As Plutarch reports (*Brut.* 12.3–4), Brutus submitted potential co-conspirators to a covert aptitude test by involving them in a general philosophical discussion about the role of the wise man in a "law-flouting monarchy."[225] Both Favonius (arguing from a Stoic point of view?) and Statilius (an Epicurean?) flunked the test by maintaining, respectively, that civil war was worse than tyranny and that the wise man would not expose himself to danger for the benefit of the stupid multitude. Only Labeo, who disagreed with both, was taken into Brutus's confidence and made a member of the team.

It is remarkable that decisions about a political assassination were taken in the context of a "joint philosophical debate"[226] among Roman senators, and it also appears to be the case that, as Sedley has argued, Brutus was employing specifically Platonic language in implying that Caesar's rule amounted to μοναρχία παρανόμος: according to Plato, it is exactly the presence or absence of laws that distinguish (good) monarchy from (bad) tyranny and make the latter the worst of all constitutions.[227] Brutus—"nourished on the words of Plato"[228]—had maintained already in his speech against Pompey of 52 that political servitude was a fate worse than death, and after the Ides of March continued to present himself as having acted, not out of personal animus against Caesar, but solely to free the Roman people from his tyranny.[229]

---

224. See Sedley 1997, a piece that once and for all puts paid to the belief, found frequently in older literature, that Brutus was instead a Stoic. On his philosophical motivations for the assassination, compare Tempest 2017: 94–97. On his Antiocheanism, see further Lévy 2012a: 300–303.

225. Plut. *Brut.* 12.3: μοναρχία[] παρανόμο[ς].

226. Plut. *Brut.* 12.3: ἐν τῷ διαλέγεσθαι καὶ συμφιλοσοφεῖν.

227. See Pl. *Plt.* 302e10–12 with Sedley 1997: 48–50.

228. Plut. *Dio* 1.2: τοῖς λόγοις ἐντραφεὶς τοῖς Πλάτωνος.

229. See, among much other evidence, the letters of Brutus and Cassius to Antony in the months after the assassination (Cic. *Fam.* 11.2, 3), which stress *libertas* as the conspirators' past and present goal; the claim in both Plutarch (*Brut.* 8.6) and Appian (*B Civ.* 2.114) that Brutus

As the conspirators and their apologists were to find out at their peril, their claim that the assassination had been a morally justified act of liberation and tyrannicide failed to establish itself as the dominant narrative at Rome. First and unsurprisingly, many of the turbulent events from the Ides of March to the establishment of the Second Triumvirate and beyond were motivated by factors that had little to do with academic (or Academic) considerations about the right constitution or the exercise of virtue. This does not mean, however, that there was not also a reasoned alternative view according to which the killing of Caesar was a moral wrong. As Cicero "explains" to Antony (whom he depicts as needing some help with binary logic) in the second *Philippic*, there are exactly two ways of looking at the matter (*Phil.* 2.31):

> nego quicquam esse medium: confiteor eos, nisi liberatores populi Romani conseruatoresque rei publicae sint, plus quam sicarios, plus quam homicidas, plus etiam quam parricidas esse, siquidem est atrocius patriae parentem quam suum occidere.

> I say there is no middle ground: I admit that if they are not the liberators of the Roman people and the preservers of the commonwealth, then they are worse than killers, worse than murderers, worse even than parricides, if indeed it is more horrible to kill the Father of the Fatherland than one's own.

And indeed, certain Romans (followers of Caesar, of course, but perhaps also others) were not convinced that Caesar had been justly killed; thought men like Brutus had violated their former friendship with the deceased; or did not see why they themselves should not be distressed at the demise of the great man.[230]

This divergence of opinions is in evidence in an exchange of letters between Cicero and Matius.[231] We have already on a number of occasions encountered

---

was opposed to tyranny on principle rather than Caesar in particular; and Brutus's rage, in Cic. *Ad Brut.* 1.16, 17, at Cicero's championing of Octavian, who threatens to undo Brutus's deed of liberation. The authenticity of these last two letters has been much debated (Shackleton Bailey 1980: 10–14 and Tempest 2017: 262 n. 24, 286 n. 50, 287 n. 81 reject them; Moles 1997 defends them; Gotter 1996b: 286–98 remains agnostic, as do I; cf. nn. 194, 216). They provide either a remarkable window into the mind of this famous Roman or otherwise a good sense of how he was imagined after his death. *Ad Brut.* 1.16.9 may serve as emblematic: *quibus enim potius haec uita factis aut cogitationibus traducatur quam iis quae pertinuerint ad liberandos ciuis meos?* ("With what deeds or thoughts might this life of mine be spent better than with those concerned with liberating my fellow citizens?").

230. Cf. Zecchini 2009.

231. Cic. *Fam.* 11.27, 28. On these letters, see Heuss 1956, Bellincioni 1970, Bringmann 1971: 270–77, Heldmann 1976: 93–99, Griffin 1997a, and J. Hall 2009a: 60–66.

this *eques* and friend of both Caesar's and Cicero's who after the Ides of March annoyed Cicero with his doom-and-gloom attitude but also regaled him with anecdotes about the dead man (Cic. *Att.* 14.1). By the fall, Matius had made himself even more unpopular with the party of the liberators by reportedly voting in favor of a law brought by Antony and by joining in the supervision of the funeral games for Caesar organized by Octavian. Cicero was not amused, but when he heard from their mutual friend Trebatius that Matius was distressed at this deterioration of their relationship, he took it upon himself to write a letter and assure Matius of his continuing friendly feelings (*Fam.* 11.27). However, he also ever so gently raised the issue of the ethics of both Caesar's killing and Matius's subsequent behavior (8):

> sed te, hominem doctissimum, non fugit, si Caesar rex fuerit (quod mihi quidem uidetur), in utramque partem de tuo officio disputari posse, uel in eam qua ego soleo uti, laudandam esse fidem et humanitatem tuam qui amicum etiam mortuum diligas, uel in eam qua nonnulli utuntur, libertatem patriae uitae amici anteponendam.

> But it won't escape you, learned as you are, that, if Caesar was king (as indeed it seems to me) there are two possible arguments about your duty: the one that I am accustomed to employ, namely, that your loyalty and humanity in loving your friend even after his death ought to be commended, and the one that some people employ, namely, that the freedom of the fatherland must be put above the life of a friend.

In his response, Matius makes it clear which side he is on (*Fam.* 11.28.2):

> nota enim mihi sunt quae in me post Caesaris mortem contulerint. uitio mihi dant quod mortem hominis necessarii grauiter fero atque eum quem dilexi perisse indignor; aiunt enim patriam amicitiae praeponendam esse, proinde ac si iam uicerint obitum eius rei publicae fuisse utilem. sed non agam astute: fateor me ad istum gradum sapientiae non peruenisse.

> I know well what it is that they have been holding against me since Caesar's death. They blame me for grieving for the death of a friend and being upset that the man whom I loved is gone. For they claim that the fatherland must be put above friendship—as though they had already made their case that his death was a good thing for the commonwealth. But I won't try to be clever: I admit that I have not reached that level of wisdom.

Matius does not accept Cicero's premise that Caesar, having made himself king, needed to be eliminated for the good of the commonwealth, and he also implies strongly that for him, friendship is a duty not to be abandoned out of political considerations. He complains bitterly about the intimidations of the

Republicans who will not let a man grieve for his friend (3) and declares defiantly that their threats will not deter him *ab officio aut ab humanitate* (4). In picking up these key terms from Cicero's letter, Matius stresses his divergent understanding of what duty and humane behavior entail; even though he rejects his correspondent's characterization of himself as *doctissimus* by disdainfully renouncing "cleverness" and "wisdom," it is clear that his position is well reasoned[232] and presents a serious challenge to the moral claims of "those self-styled 'granters of freedom.'"[233]

The question of whether the public good trumps personal loyalties was at the heart of the controversy over the Ides of March. Roman aristocrats took seriously the claims of *amicitia*, however vaguely defined and elastic the concept may have been.[234] This is apparent, for example, from the way in which the letters to and from Matius are not only interventions in a debate about the friendship of Matius and Caesar but also speech acts designed to shore up the *amicitia* between Matius and Cicero themselves. A more striking example is the way in which even Cicero and Antony—men between whom there was never much love lost—publicly dramatized their falling out in September 44 as a matter of friendship betrayed. Throughout his first *Philippic*, Cicero stressed his *amicitia* with Antony, all the while attacking him, which led his opponent to complain in turn that the rules of *amicitia* had been violated—something which in his second *Philippic* Cicero denied, while now accusing Antony of no longer behaving like an *amicus*.[235] If even Antony had a valid claim on Cicero's friendship, what could be said about the obligations of Brutus et al. to Caesar? In promoting their new hierarchy of values, the liberators and their followers had serious work to do.

We can see the liberty-vs.-friendship discourse run through private and public utterances of the months following the Ides of March.[236] In addition to the exchange with Matius, there is Cicero's statement, in the second *Philippic*, about the conspirator Trebonius's being worthy of the public's gratitude "for having preferred the liberty of the Roman people to the friendship of a single

---

232. As Griffin 1997a: 101–4 shows, Matius's arguments are consistent with Epicureanism, which famously prized friendship; however, since he makes no specific reference to Epicurean doctrine (and in fact disavows *sapientia*), it is not clear whether he was—like his friend Trebatius—a follower of the school (Castner 1988: 96–99 is skeptical, Benferhat 2005: 281–84 more positive).

233. Cic. *Fam.* 11.28.3: *ut quidem isti dictitant libertatis auctores.*

234. On *amicitia*, see 2.3 above, with Brunt 1965 and Williams 2012. On Caesar's own construction of *amicitia* in *BCiv.*, see Grillo 2012: 143–49.

235. See *Phil.* 1.11, 12, 26, 28; 2.3, 6, 7.

236. Cf. Wistrand 1981: 5–6.

man and having wished to abolish monarchy rather than take part in it."[237] Meanwhile, Brutus and Cassius were telling Antony in no uncertain terms that while they did not wish to start any *inimicitiae* with him, they "nevertheless valued [their] own liberty more than [his] friendship."[238] And once those *inimicitiae* were in full swing in mid 43, Cassius's legate Lentulus Spinther in a letter to Cicero described his taking the part of the liberators against his friend Dolabella and relative Antony with the words "'loving my country more,' I declared war against all my nearest and dearest."[239]

At least for Cicero, however, the problem of what goals and considerations ought to guide public action was not just a matter of handy slogans. In his post-Ides philosophical writing, he tackles these questions from a theoretical perspective. *De amicitia* ("On Friendship") and *De officiis* ("On Duties") are works of practical ethics that—unlike the treatises of the previous months—have a clear application to Roman society and much more overt pedagogical aim.[240] They provide a code of upperclass behavior that radically rewrites the traditional value system, replacing agreed-upon but unreflected Roman concepts such as friendship and honor with philosophically defined universal virtues.

Thus, Laelius in *De amicitia*, all the while stressing that he is speaking not for the wise but for ordinary Romans, nevertheless redefines the Roman social practice of *amicitia* as Peripatetically inflected virtue friendship, which by definition can exist only between good men.[241] As a result, *amicitia* can never be used as a justification for doing anything dishonorable and especially not anything directed against the *res publica*.[242] A dishonorable person cannot be an actual friend, and tyrants, those deplorable characters who are feared not loved, cannot have any friends at all: "life with a tyrant is different from life with a friend."[243] Cicero need not spell it out: any so-called *amicitia* with Caesar was not really friendship and thus cannot be invoked as a criterion to judge the actions of his assassins.

In *De officiis*, Cicero's handbook of virtuous gentlemanly conduct, the recent tyrannicide is one of many examples to illustrate the work's main argument

---

237. *Phil.* 2.27: *ei res publica gratiam debet qui libertatem populi Romani unius amicitiae praeposuit depulsorque dominatus quam particeps esse maluit.* The motif returns in *Phil.* 5.6.

238. Cic. *Fam.* 11.3.4 (a letter of Brutus and Cassius to Antony of 4 August 44): *uocemus te ad nullas inimicitias, sed tamen pluris nostram libertatem quam tuam amicitiam aestimemus.*

239. Cic. *Fam.* 12.14.7: πατρίδα ἐμὴν μᾶλλον φιλῶν *omnibus meis bellum . . . indixi.*

240. See Bringmann 1971: 182–255, Long 1995b, and Baraz 2012: 187–223.

241. On *De amicitia*, see Bringmann 1971: 206–28, Gotter 1996a, and Griffin 1997a.

242. Cic. *Amic.* 40: *turpis enim excusatio est et minime accipienda, cum in ceteris peccatis, tum si quis contra rem publicam se amici causa fecisse fateatur.* The discussion of the limits of friendship covers *Amic.* 35–43.

243. See *Amic.* 89: *aliter enim cum tyranno, aliter cum amico uiuitur;* see also 52–55.

that—contrary to popular perception—the honorable or morally good (*honestum*) always coincides with the expedient (*utile*).[244] Under normal circumstances, a homicide, and especially the killing of a friend, would be a crime. Not so when the victim was a tyrant (3.19):

> quod potest maius esse scelus quam non modo hominem sed etiam familiarem hominem occidere? num igitur se astrinxit scelere si qui tyrannum occidit quamuis familiarem? populo quidem Romano non uidetur qui ex omnibus praeclaris factis illud pulcherrimum existimat. uicit ergo utilitas honestatem? immo uero honestas utilitatem secuta est.

> What greater crime can there be than to kill, not just a man, but a friend? So did he commit a crime who killed a tyrant even though he was a friend? That is not how it seems to the Roman people, who consider this the most beautiful of all outstanding deeds. So did the expedient trump the honorable? Not at all: the honorable coincided with the expedient.

There is no ethical conflict underlying the conspirators' actions: what is expedient for the *res publica* is also morally right.

In *De re publica*, written in the 50s, Cicero had discussed how a well-established commonwealth, such as the Roman Republic, calls for virtuous statesmen. Ten years, a civil war, an unconstitutional monarchic goverment, and a bloody assassination later, he in *De officiis* stressed conversely that unless public figures behave virtuously, the commonwealth and human society in general will fall to pieces. The message is the same but the emphasis has shifted from the community to the moral makeup of the individual, with recent history providing some of the most striking examples, both positive (the conspirators) and negative (Caesar). The late dictator in his blind pursuit of power, honors, and fame subverted the virtue of justice; his policy of confiscation and redistribution of property was but a parody of the virtue of generosity; and his establishing himself as a—by definition asocial—tyrant led to his failure to make himself loved rather than hated, and ultimately to his death.[245]

Caesar's career and fate thus provide a textbook case for illustrating Cicero's main point: that there is nothing on earth for which one may trade off what is *honestum*—and that any such trade-off is based on wrong assumptions to begin with, since what is achieved at such a cost turns out not to be *utile* after all (*Off.* 3.83):

---

244. On the politics of *Off.*, see the seminal article of Long 1995b, as well as Gabba 1979, Dyck 1996: 29–36, Arena 2007, and Woolf 2015: 170–200; specifically on the topic of tyranny, see Samotta 2009: 157–70.

245. Subversion of justice: Cic. *Off.* 1.26; failure to achieve generosity: 1.43; hateful tyranny: 2.23; 3.32.

ecce tibi qui rex populi Romani dominusque omnium gentium esse concu-
piuerit idque perfecerit. hanc cupiditatem si honestam quis esse dicit,
amens est; probat enim legum et libertatis interitum earumque oppres-
sionem taetram et detestabilem gloriosam putat. qui autem fatetur honestum non esse in ea ciuitate quae libera fuerit quaeque esse debeat regnare,
sed ei qui id facere possit esse utile, qua hunc obiurgatione aut quo potius
conuicio a tanto errore coner auellere? potest enim, di immortales, cui-
quam esse utile foedissimum et taeterrimum parricidium patriae, quamuis
is qui se eo obstrinxerit ab oppressis ciuibus parens nominetur?

Take the man who wanted to be king of the Roman people and master over
all nations, and brought it about. If anybody calls this desire honorable, he
is mad; for he approves of the destruction of law and liberty and believes
their foul and despicable oppression to be a cause for glory. But he who
holds that it is not honorable to be king in a commonwealth that was free
and ought to remain so, but that it is nevertheless expedient for the person
who is able to do so, with what reproach or indeed what abuse should I try
to tear him away from his error? For how, immortal gods, can the most
shameful and disgusting murder of the fatherland be expedient to anyone—
even if the man who has stained himself in this way be hailed "father" by
the oppressed citizens?

According to Cicero, Caesar's politics were a moral failing, based on a fundamental misunderstanding of both *honestum* and *utile*. And as any morally bad
person, Caesar was utterly unsuccessful in achieving the *summum bonum*
agreed upon by all philosophies: the happy life. Playing on one of his favorite
themes, that of *conscientia*, Cicero ends up nearly pitying Caesar: "What fester-
ing wounds of conscience do you think he had in his soul?"[246]

De officiis—addressed, fittingly, to Cicero's son and by implication to the
entire younger generation—analyzes the current Roman crisis as a lack of
moral compass occasioned by a lack of conceptual clarity. Men like Caesar
believe that *imperia*, *honores*, and *gloria* are desirable, without understanding
what true leadership, honors, and fame consist in.[247] Others, like Matius and
Antony, hold that *amicitia* enjoins loyalty to a friend regardless of his merits.
And perhaps a majority of people are convinced that what is expedient cannot

246. Cic. *Off.* 3.85: *hunc tu quas conscientiae labes in animo censes habuisse, quae uulnera?*
247. The three terms occur together at *Off.* 1.26 as misunderstood goals whose pursuit per-
verts justice. The question specifically of false vs. true glory must have been the central topic of
Cicero's lost *De gloria*, written in the same period: like *amicitia*, *gloria* is a traditional value that
Cicero attempts to reinterpret philosophically (see Bringmann 1971: 196–205, Long 1995b:
223–33, and Graver forthcoming).

always be come by honorably, and that many honorable things are in turn fairly useless. What Rome needs, badly, are men who, like Brutus and Cassius, know how to act virtuously and those who, like Cicero, can explain to their fellow citizens what virtuous behavior is. In other words, Rome needs philosophy.

After the Ides of March, Cicero was for a while planning to write a philosophical dialogue specifically about Caesar's murder and its moral justification.[248] What he wrote instead was a general vindication of the primacy of the *honestum* in human behavior, an ideal that he saw realized in the liberators' act. Indeed, the conspiracy against and killing of Caesar stand out in the history of the Roman Republic as a rare event that was primarily ideologically motivated. As is often pointed out, while the assassination itself went off without a hitch, its aftermath was a resounding failure. Apparently, Brutus, Cassius, and the others did not have much of a follow-up strategy and proved fairly incompetent at pulling off whatever plans they may have had. This may have been owing to arrogance, naïveté, or the simple logistical impossibility of coordinating a large group of men beyond the actual stabbing; of course, the actions of other parties, largely unforeseeable, were an important factor as well. The very fact, however, that the liberators did not have in place a mechanism for putting themselves in control of the situation, and perhaps indeed blithely assumed that with Caesar gone, the Republic would just magically reconstitute itself, goes to show to what extent they really were inspired by the abstract concept of liberty: they wanted to kill the tyrant but had no intention of themselves entering into a new struggle for power.[249]

What the assassination shows is that Caesar had seriously misread his fellow senators. Having pardoned so many of his enemies and favored so many of his friends, he must have believed that, in the strongly networked upperclass Roman society, *amicitia* would create durable bonds between himself and the men who had been his peers, even if they increasingly turned into his subjects.[250] Conversely, he may have assumed that his view of the *res publica's*

248. This is (presumably) what he and Atticus are referring to with the shorthand Ἡρακλείδειον ("dialogue in the style of Heraclides [of Pontus]," i.e., one with a main speaker who is not the author); see Cic. *Att.* 14.17.6; 15.3.2, 15.4.3, 15.13.3, 15.27.2; 16.2.6, 16.11.3; *Fam.* 12.16.4.

249. Wistrand 1981: 10 rightly stresses that "it is a most remarkable fact, meriting more attention than it usually receives, that the group of men who killed Caesar made no attempt at all to usurp power or secure personal advantages." Another aspect of the abstract nature of esp. Brutus's reasoning was the decision to kill only Caesar and not Antony as well—a choice much deplored by the more realistic Cicero in the months to come.

250. This is not the place to discuss in detail Caesar's policy of *clementia*, let alone the scholarly literature. It seems clear that Caesar had been hoping to bind people to him by kindness and leniency, a policy that, after his death, his outraged supporters declared to have been a

being just an empty name was being shared by an enlightened upper class disillusioned after decades of civil conflict. As it turned out on 15 March 44, however, a sizable group of Roman elite men showed themselves motivated by the abstract concept of the "public matter" while eschewing the tangible benefits of personal relations with a powerful (and by no means disagreeable) man. For a brief moment, philosophically trained Roman senators behaved— to adapt Cicero's phrase about Cato (see 3.1)—as though they were in the *Republic* of Plato rather than among the dregs of Romulus.

In the turmoil and civil war that followed the Ides of March, it was the outcry over friendship betrayed that won out over the high-minded appeal to liberty and the public good. In the text of their proscription, the members of the Second Triumvirate explicitly targeted those men whom Caesar, "after capturing them, had saved out of pity and, making them his friends, had provided all of them with offices, honors, and gifts"[251]—and who had repaid his generosity by murdering their benefactor. Brutus, Cassius, Cicero, and many others had to pay for this treason with their lives. In one important way, however, the lesson of the liberators lived on: unlike his cynical adoptive father, Octavian/Augustus was careful not to disparage the *res publica*, let alone call its existence into question. Taking a page out of his enemies' book, the emperor claimed that it was *he* who had "liberated" the commonwealth from *dominatio* and handed it back into the power of the senate and people of Rome.[252] It is this very "reconstitution" of the *res publica*, in February 27 BCE, that historians have traditionally viewed as the last breath of the Roman Republic.

---

failure (see, e.g., Cic. *Att.* 14.22.1: *clementiam illi malo fuisse, qua si usus non esset, nihil ei tale accidere potuisse*, "[the Caesarians say] that his clemency was his downfall: if he had not made use of it, nothing like this could have happened to him"). Of course, one flaw (perhaps indeed fatal) in Caesar's putative reasoning was that the royal virtue of *clementia* (which by definition involves a power differential) does not easily result in the Republican practice of *amicitia* (which exists among equals); I remain unconvinced by the claim of Konstan 2005 that in Caesar's time, *clementia* was considered a straightforward virtue without any problematic connotations. The fact that Caesar himself apparently did not use *clementia* (the label that esp. Cicero applied to his policy) but favored other terms that conveyed the same concept (see Griffin 2003: 159–63) makes no difference to my argument.

251. App. *B Civ.* 4.8.32: οὓς ἐκεῖνος δορὶ λαβὼν ἔσωσεν ἐλέῳ καὶ φίλους θέμενος ἐπὶ ἀρχὰς καὶ τιμὰς καὶ δωρεὰς προσήγαγεν ἀθρόως.

252. *Res gestae* 1.1: *rem publicam a dominatione factionis oppressam in libertatem uindicaui*; 34.1: *rem publicam ex mea potestate in senatus populique Romani arbitrium transtuli*. Cf. L. Morgan 1997: 33, 40.

5

The Invention of Rome

IN BOOK 3 of *De finibus*, Cicero compliments his interlocutor Cato on his skilled use of Latin, which helps to make philosophy feel at home in Rome: "in this way you appear to me to teach Philosophy Latin and to give her citizenship, as it were. For until now she seemed to be a foreigner (*peregrinari*) at Rome and not to enter into conversation with us."[1] In a dialogue written just a few months earlier, the *Academica*, Cicero had praised another formidable intellect among his acquaintances, the polymath Varro, for making feel at home in Rome another group of strangers—the Romans themselves (*Acad. post.* 9):

> nam nos in nostra urbe peregrinantis errantisque tamquam hospites tui libri quasi domum deduxerunt ut possemus aliquando qui et ubi essemus agnoscere.

> For when we were wandering disoriented in our own city like strangers, your books led us home, as it were, so that we were finally able to understand who and where we were.

As we saw in the last two chapters, learned Romans of the late Republic were engaged in the project of Romanizing philosophy, making this Greek stranger a familiar presence at Rome. At the same time, members of the same class—and often the very same men—dedicated themselves to the study of what they perceived of as fundamentally Roman: their very own history, political and religious institutions, language, literature, and customs. Just as in the case of *peregrinans* philosophy, this involved a process of familiarization, except that now, it was the *peregrinantes* Romans who through a process of understanding their own city were finally gaining full cultural citizenship.

---

1. *Fin.* 3.40: *itaque mihi uideris Latine docere philosophiam et ei quasi ciuitatem dare. quae quidem adhuc peregrinari Romae uidebatur nec offerre sese nostris sermonibus.* Of course, Cicero is ultimately complimenting himself, the author of the dialogue and thus of "Cato"'s words.

Of course, Rome had always been a major topic of Latin literature, as writers obsessed with their perceived secondariness vis-à-vis the Greeks had explored, and constructed, not only their relationship to their literary models, but also the originality and specificity of Roman culture. Naevius and Ennius celebrated Rome's roots and military exploits, subjects treated more soberly in the elder Cato's programmatically titled *Origines*. Historiography in its various formats flourished throughout the middle and late Republic, and the scholarly study of Latin literary history, Roman religion and law, and the Latin language had its beginnings in the second century.

Even so, the sudden spike in the mid-first century of scholarly interest in Roman origins and institutions, as well as in the Latin language, is remarkable. The 50s and 40s BCE saw a proliferation of works on Roman political and religious institutions and cultural and linguistic practices. It was as if a whole generation were engaged in mapping the physical and conceptual city in which they found themselves as both citizens and strangers, clarifying to themselves and to their readers their cultural identity or, as we might say, inventing their own tradition. Of course, *res Romanae* were not the only topic of the learned pursuits of the period (and we will encounter some of the era's explorations of the larger cosmos in the following chapter). Even so, the overwhelming preponderance of Roman themes in the scholarship of the late Republic gives the impression that it was felt that the proper study of a Roman was Rome.[2]

In this chapter, I first provide an overview of the scholarly practices and genres devoted to the construction of Roman identity, and discuss modern critical approaches to the popularity of Roman topics in the late Republic (5.1). I then offer my own interpretation of the phenomenon in two more detailed studies, one of antiquarian discussions of Roman political and religious institutions, with a focus on Varro and Cicero (5.2), the other of debates about language and style, concentrating on Varro, Cicero, and Caesar (5.3).

1. Narratives of Identity

What defines a people's identity?[3] In his praise of Varro, Cicero singles out the following topics of his friend's work (*Acad. post.* 9):

2. Compare Augustine's observation on Varro's *Antiquitates rerum humanarum* that, despite its title, the work treats human matters "not as concerns the whole world, but as concerns only Rome" (*De civ. D.* 6.4 = ARD fr. 5 Cardauns: *non quantum ad orbem terrarum, sed quantum ad solam Romam pertinet*).

3. For the discussion in this chapter, Moatti 1997 is crucial (esp. chs. 1, 3, and 6; see also Moatti 1988, 2003b). See further Rawson 1985: 233–49 and Dench 2005.

tu aetatem patriae tu descriptiones temporum tu sacrorum iura tu sacerdotum tu domesticam tu bellicam disciplinam tu sedum regionum locorum
tu omnium diuinarum humanarumque rerum nomina genera officia causas
aperuisti; plurimum quidem poetis nostris omninoque Latinis et litteris
luminis et uerbis attulisti.

You have laid open the age of our fatherland; the divisions of time-
reckoning; the law of rites and priests; the practices of war and peace; and
the names, types, purposes, and origins of dwellings, regions, and places
and of all divine and human matters. And you have thrown much light on
our poets and on Latin language and literature in general.

Varro is described as a specialist in chronology, sacred law, topography, religious and civic institutions, and language and literature.[4] These are some of
the major topics that mid-first-century upperclass Romans found fascinating
and wrote about; others include the origins of the city, genealogies of individual families, civil law, and the histories and practices of disciplines ranging
from oratory to augury.

While the era also saw its share of traditional political historiography,[5] my
focus in this chapter is on the kind of writing that has been described as antiquarian. I am here following the famous discussion of Arnaldo Momigliano,
who pointed out that Varro with his *Antiquitates* provided both the inspiration

4. With the first sentence, Cicero appears to refer in particular to Varro's *Antiquitates rerum humanarum* (*ARH*) and *Antiquitates rerum diuinarum* (*ARD*). I am working on the assumption, shared by the majority of scholars, that the *ARD*, dedicated to Caesar, had been published only recently, perhaps in 46 BCE (see Horsfall 1972: 122). As we know from Augustine (*De civ. D.* 6.4 = *ARD* fr. 5 Cardauns), the *ARH* was written earlier, most likely in the 50s. The works on literary history Cicero alludes to may be *De poetis* and *De scaenicis originibus*, as well as Varro's publications specifically about Plautus (*De comoediis Plautinis, Quaestiones Plautinae*). If *litteris* is taken as meaning not (only) "literature" but "letters," this might be a reference to Varro's early work on the Roman alphabet (*De antiquitate litterarum*, before the mid-80s BCE). By the time of the *Academica*'s publication (45 BCE), Varro was working on, but had not yet completed, *De lingua Latina*. The fact that he was planning to dedicate this work to Cicero (as he finally did) was what motivated his friend to include Varro as an interlocutor in his revised version of the *Academica* and to dedicate the dialogue to him (see 2.2, n. 81 above). For Varro's works and what we know of their chronology, see Dahlmann 1935b.

5. Late Republican historiography survives only in meager fragments (collected and commented in *FRHist* and Beck and Walter 2001–4) and, at least according to Cicero, was of medio-
cre quality (*Leg.* 1.5–7). Cicero himself repeatedly played with the thought of writing history
and giving that genre what he thought was a much-needed lift, but these projects came to
nothing. On Cicero as a historian (manqué), see Rawson 1972, Fox 2007, and Gildenhard 2013.

and the name to a long-lived western tradition of inquiring into the past that crucially differs from the standard writing of history:[6]

> (1) historians write in a chronological order; antiquaries write in a system-atic order; (2) historians produce those facts which serve to illustrate or ex-plain a certain situation; antiquaries collect all the items that are connnected with a certain subject, whether they help to solve a problem or not.

Despite its focus on "antiquities," antiquarianism is not concerned with recon-structing the past for its own sake but with using comprehensive knowledge of the past for the purpose of understanding the present. Momigliano thus defines "the Varronian idea of 'antiquitates'" as "the idea of a civilization re-covered by systematic collection of all relics of the past," and Varro in the *ARD* describes himself as providing a service to his fellow Romans by refamiliar-izing them with their own divinities and religious practices, which have be-come forgotten over time.[7] Both individuals and communities need knowl-edge of the past in order to comprehend and embrace their own identities. As Cicero famously put it, "to be ignorant of what happened before one was born means remaining a child forever."[8]

This exploration of the diachronic in the service of the synchronic em-ployed a number of genres and methodologies but—unlike much early mod-ern antiquarianism—was largely based on linguistic and textual analysis. While there is some evidence for the study of material culture,[9] knowledge of the past was for the most part derived from textual sources and from the vocabulary of the Latin language itself. Legal and grammatical study arose in tandem as learned Romans attempted to understand the form and content of such archaic documents as the Twelve Tables;[10] reconstructions of dates and

---

6. Momigliano 1966 [1950]: 3; cf. also Bravo 2007. On the afterlife of, and critical reaction to, Momigliano's views on antiquarianism, see Miller (ed.) 2007 and MacRae 2018. On anti-quarianism in the late Republic, see Rawson 1985: 233–49, Fuhrmann 1987, Moatti 1997: 97–155, and Wallace-Hadrill 2008: 213–58. It has been argued that "there was no such thing as Roman antiquarianism" (MacRae 2018: 138) and that use of this early modern term constitutes an anachronism. I cannot argue this in detail here, but I still find the term, and Momigliano's defini-tion, helpful in conceptualizing certain late Republican investigations of the past.

7. Momigliano 1966 [1950]: 5; Varro *ARD* frr. 2a, 3 Cardauns.

8. Cic. *Orat.* 120: *nescire autem quid ante quam natus sis acciderit, id est semper esse puerum.* The observation occurs in the context of a mention of Atticus's *Liber annalis*, on which see further below.

9. E.g., Varro, *Ling.* 6.4 mentions a sundial in Praeneste, which Varro himself had inspected; cf. Rawson 1985: 239 and MacRae 2018: 147–49.

10. See Moatti 1997: 137–39 and Zetzel 2018: 25–27.

chronology rested on the perusal of *annales* or *commentarii antiqui*; and most information about political, religious, or cultural practices had to be derived from textual material, whether literary, inscriptional, or archival.[11]

At the same time, even in the absence of specific sources, the Latin language itself was felt to hold a key to Roman history and culture. For Varro in particular, etymology was not just a subfield of linguistic study, but a means of uncovering hidden truths about the world through the vocabulary that described it.[12] Since according to Varro's Stoicizing theory of language, words represented reality in some naturally "true" way, they could in turn be used to gain a deeper understanding of this reality. Having been established by such founding figures as Latinus and Romulus (*Ling.* 5.9), the Latin language was thus a repository of information about what it meant to be Roman. Roman scholarship never needed to undergo a linguistic turn: it was firmly based on linguistic expression, whether in written sources or the spoken language of the culture it studied.

While there were thus certain shared interests and methodologies among late Republican investigators of Roman identity, their exploration and construction of the many facets of Rome's past and present could take a wide variety of scholarly forms and genres. To provide a rough, ad hoc taxonomy, we might distinguish among aetiologies; chronologies and genealogies; historical narratives; and stock-taking and sitemaps. As for the first, aetiology is not a scholarly genre but a mode of thought pervasive in Greco-Roman culture as whole: Who was the "first inventor" of an art or artifact? What was the origin of a religious cult or practice? Where did personal and place names come from, and why did words mean what they meant? Individual *aetia* ("[tales of] origins") can thus be found in works on many different subjects, and the aetiological branch of linguistics, etymology, was not only treated systematically by Varro in six books of his *De lingua Latina* (2–7, of which only 5–7 are extant today) but also used, by Varro and others, as a key to unlock the origins of many hitherto unclear aspects of Roman culture.

Beyond this general aetiological habit, however, the Romans had a particular interest in establishing their own origins and pinning down when exactly their city and its institutions and practices had come into being. Owing to

---

11. On the antiquarians' sources, see Rawson 1985: 238–40. On archives in the late Republic, see Culham 1989, who points out that owing to the spottiness of public record-keeping, it was especially the private archives of noble families that provided crucial sources for antiquarian research.

12. On Varronian etymology, its status as a master methodology, and its theoretical underpinnings, see Schröter 1963; Romano 2003: 113–17; Hinds 2006; Blank 2008, 2012: 279–89, 2019; and Volk 2019: 186–90.

Rome's late arrival on the Mediterranean scene and the Romans' persistent sense of secondariness, there was a felt need of inscribing Roman beginnings into an already extant historical narrative. In addition to sorting out the divergent stories of origin (Aeneas or Romulus?), late Republican writers strove to put an exact date on the foundation of their city. Notwithstanding the mythological trappings of the founding twins' divine birth and lupine upbringing, Rome was founded in historical times and at a date that the Romans believed could be scientifically determined. Unsurprisingly, there was controversy among earlier and contemporary authors, but it was the date championed by Varro and Atticus that ultimately won out and remains canonical today: Rome was founded in the third year of the sixth Olympiad or 754/753 BCE.[13] Once this was established, Varro commissioned his friend, the astrologer L. Tarutius Firmanus, to cast the city's natal horoscope—which, needless to say, turned out to be extremely promising.[14]

It was not only Rome itself that had taken off on one particular day. The Romans were convinced that Latin literature, too, had a clear *aetion*: it began with the performance of the first Latin play, composed by the Tarentine Greek Livius Andronicus, who would go on to pen other dramas and also wrote a Latin translation of the *Odyssey*. The idea that Latin literary production had started on a specific date, by fiat as it were (the play was commissioned by the authorities), once more attests to the typical Roman self-consciousness and belief that their ancestors had purposely inscribed themselves into history: they decided to have a literature just as they had decided to found a city. When

13. On the traditional assumption that Rome was founded on the festival of the Parilia, the exact date would be 21 April 753 (but see the following n.). In modern literature, the determination of this date is usually ascribed to Varro; however, our earliest reference in fact credits Atticus (Cic. *Brut.* 72; 46 BCE). Censorinus, *DN* 21.6 reports that Varro championed the date, but he appears to rely specifically on *De gente populi Romani*, which was published only in 43 BCE; the only use of the "Varronian" chronology in an extant Varronian work is *Rust.* 1.2.9, from 37 BCE. Contrary to what is often maintained, Cicero's claim that Varro revealed the *aetas patriae* (*Acad. post.* 9; 45 BCE) need not refer to a precise dating, and the earliest clear *terminus ante quem* for Varro's use of the 754/753 date of which I am aware is the mention of Tarutius's horoscope of Rome (see immediately below and the following n.) in Cic. *Div.* 2.98–99 (44 BCE). See Drummond's commentary on *FRHist* 33 F2, as well as R. M. A. Marshall 2017. The latter plausibly suggests that the friends Atticus and Varro, working on chronological matters at the same time, collaborated or at least discussed the topic with each other; he proposes that from now on we speak of the "Attico-Varronian" date.

14. See Plut. *Rom.* 12.3–6 with Brind'Amour 1983: 240–49 and Grafton and Swerdlow 1986. To judge from the horoscope, Tarutius fixed the exact foundation day not on the Parilia of 753, but on 4 October 754.

exactly this happened was once again controversial, and once again Varro and Atticus—followed by Cicero—carried the day, placing the birth of Latin literature in the consulship of C. Claudius and M. Tuditanus, or 240 BCE.[15]

Such dates, of course, could not be determined in isolation but needed to find support in the larger study of Roman or even world chronology.[16] Around the mid-50s, Cornelius Nepos published his *Chronica*, credited by Catullus with being the first Latin work to "unroll all of time in three volumes."[17] Apparently Nepos synchronized Roman and Greek history, providing a framework that allowed readers to determine which events had taken place at the same time and how Roman history fit in with everything that had ever happened in the entirety of the known world.

Other works were more specifically concerned with establishing the chronology of events at Rome. The most famous of these, thanks to the championing of Cicero, is Atticus's *Liber annalis*.[18] Apparently this was a bare-bones reference work that year by year listed officeholders and significant events from the foundation of the city to the present day. Other attested authors of *annales*, which may have taken a similar format, include Varro and his (and Cicero's) friend L. Scribonius Libo.

Chronologies of this kind allowed the Romans to behold their past encapsulated in a well-ordered artifact, to own it just as they were able to own the scrolls on which it was laid out so *breuiter et . . . perdiligenter*.[19] In addition, such works were invaluable to writers of more specialized histories, who needed to make sure when and in which order things had happened. A chronological subgenre highly popular in the late Republic was the family genealogy. Thus Atticus, whose reconstruction in the *Liber annalis* of who held office when had involved a fair amount of what we would call prosopography, also

---

15. Cic. *Brut.* 72–73, with Drummond on *FRHist* 33 F6. Cicero ridicules the alternative date of 197 BCE, championed by the tragedian and scholar L. Accius. As with the foundation of Rome, it is unclear whether it was Atticus or Varro who first put forth 240 BCE.

16. On late Republican chronological studies, see Bäumerich 1964: 30–78 and Feeney 2007: 20–23.

17. Catull. 1.5–6: *ausus es unus Italorum / omne aeuum tribus explicare chartis*. For fragments and commentary, see *FRHist* 45.

18. As discussed in 2.3, Cicero's *Brutus* is in part a thank-you gift for the dedication of his friend's work; throughout the dialogue, Cicero makes frequent use of, and bestows ample praise on, Atticus's chronologies. Fragments and commentary are found in *FRHist* 33 and Beck and Walter 2001–4: 2.358–67. On Atticus's writings, see further Münzer 1905, A. Marshall 1993, and R. M. A. Marshall 2017.

19. Cic. *Brut.* 14: "briefly and extremely carefully" (on Atticus's *Liber annalis*). On this aspect of late Republican chronological writing, see Oksanish 2016: 275–78.

produced family histories for Brutus, Claudius Marcellus, Cornelius Scipio, and Fabius Maximus.[20] M. Valerius Messalla Rufus wrote a *De familiis*, apparently encompassing a number of noble *gentes*, while Varro compiled *De familiis Troianis*, focusing on those who believed they could trace their ancestors back to the arrival of Aeneas.

Of course, Roman upperclass families had always preserved and celebrated their own histories, proudly displaying their ancestor masks and parading them at the public spectacle of the *pompa funebris*. Educated Romans were well aware that this lent itself to embellishment and mythmaking. Thus, Cicero points out that the inflated rhetoric of funerary orations "has made our history more faulty" by inventing honors and achievements and by falsely connecting more humble families to illustrious ancestors of the same name.[21] He caustically remarks that by the same token, he himself might "claim to be descended from M'. Tullius, a patrician who was consul together with Servius Sulpicius ten years after the expulsion of the kings."[22] According to Pliny the Elder, it was Messalla's indignation at seeing a latter-day Scipio falsely displaying the famous Africanus among the ancestor masks in his atrium that inspired him to pen his *De familiis*.[23]

A more scholarly approach to genealogy thus had the potential to set the record straight—but was, conversely, also capable of lending new authority to cherished, and politically useful, myths about revered ancestors. Atticus's work for Brutus apparently confirmed his (inherently unlikely) descent from the celebrated L. Iunius Brutus who had driven out the kings, a connection that Brutus proudly displayed in his revamped atrium.[24] As we saw in 4.4, this putative family history of resistance to tyranny played a significant role in how Brutus's participation in Caesar's assassination was depicted and perceived. But more than one person could play that game. On the other side of the political spectrum, Caesar himself had stressed his descent from Aeneas, and hence Venus, already in his funerary oration for his aunt Iulia of 69/68 BCE, and the story will no doubt have figured prominently in Varro's *De familiis Troianis*. If Caesar's own contemporaries do not seem to have been overly impressed with his divine credentials, the Augustan age happily elevated the Julian *aetion* to a national myth.

20. Nep. *Att.* 18.3–4 = *FRHist* 33 T1.

21. Cic. *Brut.* 62: *his laudationibus historia rerum nostrarum est facta mendosior.*

22. Cic. *Brut.* 62: *ut si ego me a M'. Tullio esse dicerem qui patricius cum Seruio Sulpicio consul anno X post exactos reges fuit.*

23. Plin. *HN* 35.8 = *FRHist* 42 T2. On the episode and the identity of the Scipio in question, see Billows 1982.

24. Nep. *Att.* 18.3; Cic. *Att.* 13.40.1.

In addition, aetiological and chronological studies were able to underpin or complement more specialized histories of various aspects of Roman public and private life. In both independent monographs and sections of larger works, authors of the mid-first century traced the developments of Roman lifestyle and customs (Varro, *De uita populi Romani*), the Roman constitution and political institutions (Cicero, *De re publica*; Varro, *Antiquitates rerum humanarum*), Roman oratory (Cicero, *Brutus*), religion (Varro, *Antiquitates rerum diuinarum*), and literature (various work by Varro), among others. Work of a largely synchronic or theoretical character, too, often featured an introductory narrative or *historia quaestionis*, such as Cicero's attempts to historicize Roman philosophizing in the prefaces of his philosophical works, most notably that of *Tusculans* 1.

As mentioned above, in the antiquarian spirit of the age the investigation of the past typically formed part of an attempt to comprehend the present. The most ambitious works of the period are of the type that I have called site-maps, encyclopedic attempts to encompass a particular aspect of contemporary Romanness by understanding both what it was and how it had come to be that way. Varro's massive studies of Roman civic and religious institutions and of the Latin language are the most prominent examples of this type,[25] but wide-ranging linguistic investigations were also undertaken by P. Nigidius Figulus, whose *Commentarii grammatici* (of which a total of sixty-four fragments survive) comprised at least twenty-nine books;[26] Caesar's *De analogia* was a more specialized treatise.

Attempts to take stock of specific areas of Roman culture involved Herculean efforts at collecting, systematizing, and interpreting data, whether this involved words, texts, artifacts, or practices. Varro in particular is famous (or infamous) for his attempts to impose order on his vast material, employing multiple partitions and numeric schemes, many of which recur across his works on different topics.[27] However, to some extent his entire generation was engaged in a process of "ordering knowledge":[28] sorting and sifting through their culture's diachronic depths and synchronic diversity, late Republican Romans came up with intellectual and verbal structures through which to make sense of the bewildering mass, and thus make themselves, and their readers, masters of their cultural heritage or citizens of their own city.

---

25. Further mid-Republican works of religious scholarship are discussed in 6.1 and 6.2 below.

26. Gell. *NA* 10.5.1 = Nigidius fr. 42 Swoboda quotes from the 29th book. On this work, see Garcea 2019; on Nigidius, see further 6.2 below.

27. On Varronian (dis)order, see Volk 2019.

28. I borrow this fitting term from König and Whitmarsh (eds.) 2017, though their specific concern is with the Imperial period.

Like all intellectual enterprises of the period, such projects of stock-taking and site-mapping were the diverse initiatives of private individuals with their own interests and purposes. Thus, for example, efforts were made to codify the civil law because men active in the law courts felt the desirability of collecting *responsa* and formalizing the system they thought underlay their practices.[29] It was Julius Caesar who—perhaps under the impression of the centralized monarchy he had witnessed at Alexandria—decided that such isolated and "amateurish" projects ought to be augmented or replaced by top-down efforts at creating Roman repositories of knowledge. In the last years of his life, he was planning a massive codification of the *ius ciuile* as well as the establishment of the first public library at Rome, tapping none other than Varro for the latter undertaking (Suet. *Iul.* 44.2). Caesar's death, however, prevented these projects from being realized, and the public institutionalization of knowledge began for real only with Augustus.

Why did mid-first-century upperclass Romans evince such fascination or even obsession with their own identity and past? Here as elsewhere, we should beware of reductive explanations that offer a single key to understanding a complex set of events; the belief that the phenomenon under investigation is new, unique, and easily studied in isolation; and the urge to see intellectual activity as purely functional in some larger social or political context, and hence as being "about" something other than its own content. As is the case with all late Republican *studia*, investigations into things Roman were conducted by numerous individuals for what were no doubt numerous individual reasons; Rome's past and present had been a topic of Latin writing for at least a century and a half; and people may well have engaged in antiquarianism in the first place because they found such research interesting and enjoyable.[30]

Unfortunately, we have next to no direct evidence for what motivated learned late Republican Romans to investigate their past or what aims they

---

29. On late Republican legal scholarship, see Rawson 1985: 201–14 and Harries 2006, as well as MacRae 2017 on sacred law. Cicero wrote a work *De iure ciuili in artem redigendo*, of which two very brief fragments survive (Gell. *NA* 1.22.7; Charisius 175.18–19 Barwick).

30. That intellectual investigation is a good in and of itself is a philosophical commonplace (predicated on the idea that humans qua rational animals are naturally equipped with the desire for knowledge) found, e.g., throughout Cicero's oeuvre. It is important to keep in mind that this way of thinking about *studia* was part and parcel of the late Republican mental tool kit: even if authors often conceived of and expressed all sorts of ulterior motivations for their intellectual efforts, the idea of study for its own and its contents' sake was perfectly "normalized." Interest specifically in the past was often presented as a basic human impulse shared by the learned and unlearned alike (e.g., Cic. *Fin.* 5.51–52).

were pursuing—or wanted to be understood as pursuing—in publishing their studies. Unlike in the case of philosophy, where we find Cicero and Lucretius in their prefaces and proems reflecting at length on the reasons for and goals of their philosophical writing, the works of Roman antiquarianism have come down to us in fragmentary form and with hardly any prefatory material surviving.[31] Any reconstruction of what Varro and his fellow students of *res Romanae* thought they were doing must therefore rest on what *we* think they were doing—an operation that is obviously fraught with peril.

In modern scholarship on the period we find two main complementary explanations of the antiquarian enthusiasm of the mid-first century BCE, narratives that are attractive in many ways, but risk becoming reductive and not capturing the phenomenon in its full diversity. As for the first, the scholarly focus on the Roman past and Roman identity is often seen as a conservative and nostalgic reaction to the perceived political and moral crisis of the late Republic. As for the second, the efforts at collecting and systematizing information about all matters Roman have been viewed as part of a process of rationalization by which Greek intellectual methods were brought to bear on undifferentiated masses of Roman data, resulting in the creation of an ordered system of knowledge that replaced more traditional ways of viewing the world.

To address the first of these approaches, it is certainly tempting to see a connection between late Republican investigations of Roman identity and the political drama unfolding at the same time. At a moment of upheaval, uncertainty, and estrangement, the Romans endeavored to reassure and reorient themselves, trying to establish in what kind of city they lived—and in what kind they wished to live. Viewing their own time as one of crisis, they looked back to the past in an attempt to recover and restore the grandeur that was Rome.

This standard view of Roman antiquarian studies as fueled by despair at the present and resulting nostalgia for the past is neatly summed up in Andrew Drummond's recent judgment on Varro (2013: 416):

> his preoccupation with the threatened or actual loss of Rome's past, traditional values, and identity undoubtedly represents a reaction, by a man of profoundly conservative outlook, to what he saw as a deep contemporary crisis.

---

31. The only Varronian work that retains its proper prefaces is the late *De re rustica*. *De lingua Latina* 5 begins with a very brief dedication to Cicero, but this is not the beginning of the work as a whole (bks. 1–4 are lost) and contains no information on Varro's goals and motivations.

The same idea is found across scholarship on the period and its protagonists: late Republican Romans were "pessimists," preoccupied with moral decline, and at the same time "romantics," imbued with nostalgia for their glorious past.[32] Their investigation of the past arose out of a perceived "crisis of tradition," the need to recover a cultural identity at the moment when it was felt to be in danger of being lost.[33] Antiquarian research was not purely academic: its purpose was to lead the Romans back to their former greatness and to effect a "renewal through the restoration of the old."[34]

How much of this is borne out by our sources? Praise of the past coupled with lament about a depraved present is a topos found throughout Greco-Roman literature and beyond (already the Homeric epics contrast "men as they are now" unfavorably with the heroes of old); specifically at Rome, reference to the hallowed example of the *maiores* was an ingrained element of thought and discourse applicable to all manner of situations. The idea that things were somehow better in the past was thus readily available and could be put to use in a variety of contexts, from the most sophisticated to the most banal.

But was there something about the situation in the middle of the first century specifically that turned learned Romans into *laudatores temporis acti*? In Cicero and later in Sallust, we find a strong sense of a political crisis coupled with moral decline.[35] Thus, Cicero in the preface to the fifth book of *De re publica* (1) bemoans that while of old, the *res publica* rested on "its ancient customs and its men,"[36] by now the customs have declined and true men are nowhere to be found. As a result, the Roman commonwealth is barely recognizable:

> nostra uero aetas, cum rem publicam sicut picturam accepisset egregiam sed iam euanescentem uetustate, non modo eam coloribus eisdem quibus fuerat renouare neglexit, sed ne id quidem curauit ut formam saltem eius et extrema tamquam lineamenta seruaret.

> But our age, after receiving the commonwealth as if it were an excellent painting, but one already fading with age, not only failed to restore it with

---

32. Pessimism: Fuhrmann 1987: 137; romanticism: Norden 1901: 251–60, Bäumerich 1964: 21–27.

33. See Moatti 1997: 30–39 ("crise de la tradition").

34. See Dahlmann 1935b, Peglau 2003, and Leonardis 2019 specifically on Varro. "Erneuerung als Wiederherstellung des Alten" is the programmatic title of Fuhrmann 1987.

35. On the theme of moral decline in Cicero, Sallust, and beyond, see, e.g., Lintott 1972, T. N. Mitchell 1984, Samotta 2009, and Biesinger 2016.

36. Cicero is quoting the famous Ennian line *moribus antiquis res stat Romana uirisque* (*Ann.* 156 Skutsch).

the colors that it had before, but didn't even take care to preserve its shape and basic outline.

As Cicero sums up: "we retain the commonwealth in name, but in actuality have long since lost it."[37]

In the prefaces to his historical works (written in the late 40s and early 30s BCE), Sallust, too, laments the decline of both Roman *mores* and Roman politics, positing that this pernicious development began with the final defeat and destruction of Carthage in 146 BCE: once the Romans no longer had to fear an outside enemy, they lost their moral fiber and fell prey to such vices as ambition and greed.[38] As a result, the political culture degenerated, leading to such dangerous incidents as the Catilinarian conspiracy—and, we might add, the Civil War and dissolution of the Republican system.

While such narratives of decline are to some extent traditional (already in the mid-second century, the elder Cato maintained that Rome was going downhill[39]), and while it is also not always clear to modern observers what the posited moral deterioration is supposed to consist in,[40] it is not difficult to see why Cicero and Sallust felt that in their lifetimes, political circumstances at Rome had reached a particular nadir. What we do not find in those two writers, however, is a nostalgic turn to antiquarian investigation. Sallust (who at any rate does not belong to the period and cast of characters at the center of this book) is a historian whose works concentrate exclusively on late Republican events—the Catilinarian conspiracy, the Jugurthine war, and contemporary history from the year 78 BCE onward—and who evinces no interest in more remote periods or the pursuit of anything but straightforward political and military history or *res gestae*. Cicero's works are likewise primarily concerned not with gathering and systematizing information on Rome's past and present, but instead with larger theoretical questions concerning oratory and philosophy. Where he touches—as he often does—on Roman customs

---

37. *Rep.* 5.1: *rem publicam uerbo retinemus, re ipsa uero iam pridem amisimus.* Cicero is fond of diagnosing the loss of the *res publica*; see, e.g., *Att.* 1.18.6; 9.5.2; *Fam.* 6.21.3; *QFr.* 1.2.15; *Off.* 2.29; *Phil.* 3.35. Compare and contrast Caesar's quip about the *res publica*'s being nothing more than a word without body or shape (Suet. *Iul.* 77; cf. 4.4 above).

38. See esp. *Cat.* 5.9–13.5; *Iug.* 41–42; *Hist.* 1, frr. 11–12.

39. See Hampl 1959 and, specifically on Cato, Biesinger 2016: 59–92.

40. Surveying Roman foreign politics and military conduct over the course of the Republic, Hampl 1959 finds no particular evidence of moral decline. His approach is somewhat literal-minded, but compare the more theoretically sophisticated discussion of Beard, North, and Price 1998: 1.119–25, who point out that the widespread idea of the deterioration of religious life and neglect of cult sites in the late Republic is contradicted by evidence for the period's vigorous temple building; see also Wardman 1982: 22–62.

and institutions, his attitude is, as we will see in what follows, by no means always one of idealizing or privileging the past.

How about authors of more antiquarian interests? In his biography of Atticus, Cornelius Nepos prefaces his brief discussion of his subject's chronological and genealogical studies by describing Atticus as "an eager imitator of the customs of old and a lover of antiquity"[41]—a suggestive formulation that does not, however, reveal a sustained program or ideology behind the *studia* of the wealthy *eques*. This leaves Varro, and it is indeed on this arch-antiquarian that scholarly claims about the nostalgic conservatism of the age typically rest. That Varro was on a mission to recover elements of an idealized Roman past for his own time is a scholarly commonplace expressed most clearly in Hellfried Dahlmann's magisterial *Pauly-Wissowa* article of 1935: his Varro is motivated by "ein gut Stück Romantik, eine Sehnsucht nach einer besseren Vergangenheit, der er die verkommene Gegenwart gegenüberstellte" (1179). As the above-cited quotation from Andrew Drummond shows, this view remains current in twenty-first-century scholarship.[42]

It is a fact that large parts of Varro's oeuvre are dedicated to the investigation of various aspects of the Roman past and thus a fair guess that the great polymath was genuinely fascinated with *antiquitates*. But do we know that he took a dim view of the present and automatically thought that things were better in the past? And even if he did, was he on a mission to restore an earlier stage of Roman greatness as a remedy for the ills of his own time? More detailed examination of Varro's attitudes to the synchrony and diachrony of *res Romanae* will have to wait until the following sections; I here just offer some preliminary remarks.

As mentioned above, statements about authorial attitude and purpose are few and far between in the surviving Varronian corpus. The work that more than all others exhibits nostalgia for the past and fierce criticism of the *mores* of the present is the *Menippean Satires*, normally dated to early in Varro's career. Since the curmudgeonly attitude exhibited in these texts is, however, part and parcel of the genre, and since—as so often in satire—the author's relationship to his own persona is anything but straightforward and frequently called into question in the course of the text itself, we can hardly ascribe the views of "Marcus" to Varro himself.

41. Nep. *Att.* 18.1: *moris ... maiorum summus imitator ... antiquitatisque amator.*

42. Thus, in the introduction to a 2017 volume on Varro, the editors state as a matter of course that "Varro represented his time as one of crisis, lamenting the loss of past traditions" (Arena and Mac Góráin 2017: 3). For a recent sustained presentation of Varro as a conservative, see Leonardis 2019.

Take *Sexagesis*, a prosimetric satire of which twenty-one lines survive (frr. 485–505 Astbury).[43] It recounts the adventures of a man who—in Rip van Winkle fashion—falls asleep at age ten and wakes up fifty years later. On returning to Rome, he barely recognizes the place and is shocked by all the vices that have crept in during his absence. Unsurprisingly, he receives anything but a fond welcome: together with other querulous old men, he is cast off a bridge into the Tiber.[44] This apparent blatant indictment of present-day degeneration receives an extra twist, however, when a voice pipes up to confront the satirist himself: "You are wrong to accuse us, Marcus. You are chewing over your antiquities (*antiquitates*)."[45] Here, the author seems to satirize his own textual *alter ego* as a conservative stick-in-the-mud who can only regurgitate *antiquitates*.[46] The genre's game of mirrors makes it impossible to ascribe an unambiguous attitude to Varro himself.[47]

In his scholarly works, Varro frequently remarks on the fact that *uetustas*, that is, old age or the passage of time, has obliterated past phenomena and states of affairs, whether these are the etymologies of Latin words or the origins of Roman cult. "Few things," he observes, "have not been distorted by the passage of time, many have been removed."[48] As a result, it is the antiquarian's job "to dig up as best I can what has become covered up by *uetustas*."[49] The situation described is similar to Cicero's faded image of the *res publica*: the original can barely be perceived by this point, and it takes a learned investigator to fill in the lost colors.

For Cicero, of course, the loss of the original form of the Roman commonwealth is not simply an unfortunate side effect of the passage of time, but the result of a moral failing on the part of the Romans themselves. Varro, by

43. On the interpretation of this satire, see Leonardis 2014—who, however, sees it as directly expressive of Varro's own opinions and the putative conservatism of his antiquarian works.

44. This violent act apparently rests itself on an "antiquarian" interpretation of the obscure proverb *sexagenarios de ponte* ("sixty-year-olds off the bridge!"), often associated with the archaic ritual of the Argei. Varro gives a more anodyne explanation of the saying in *De uita populi Romani* fr. 70 Pittà.

45. Fr. 505 Astbury: *erras, inquit, Marce, accusare nos; ruminaris antiquitates.*

46. The term *antiquitates* raises the attractive possibility that Varro is ironically alluding to his own *Antiquitates* (cf. Cardauns 2001: 43), which might enable us to date *Sexagesis* to the (mid-)50s BCE (the presumed publication date of the *ARH*). See Cèbe 1972–99: 12.1907–8 and Leonardis 2014: 22–23 n. 9 for references and discussion.

47. Against reading the *Menippeans* as expressive of nostalgia for the putative good old days of earlier Rome, see Scholz 2003.

48. Varro, *Ling.* 5.5: *uetustas pauca non deprauat, multa tollit.*

49. Varro, *Ling.* 6.2: *quae obruta uetustate ut potero eruere conabor.*

contrast, typically presents the disappearance of information about Roman words and institutions in a more value-neutral manner, as an unavoidable and natural process of change. The most prominent exception—the one instance in Varro's antiquarian and linguistic works of an explicit program amounting to some kind of "restoration of the past"—is a statement at the beginning of *Antiquitates rerum diuinarum*, where the author ascribes the loss of knowledge about the Roman gods to his fellow citizens' negligence (fr. 2a Cardauns):

> se timere ne pereant [sc. dei], non incursu hostili, sed ciuium neglegentia, de qua illos uelut ruina liberari a se dicit et in memoria bonorum per eius modi libros recondi atque seruari utiliore cura quam Metellus de incendio sacra Vestae et Aeneas de Troiano excidio penates liberasse praedicatur.

> [Varro] says that he fears that the gods will be lost, not by an enemy attack but because of the negligence of the citizens, from which he is rescuing them as if from a cataclysm, and placing them in the memory of good men through his books of this kind, saving them with a more useful endeavor than how Metellus is said to have rescued the sacred implements of Vesta from fire and Aeneas the Penates from the fall of Troy.

Varro is on a rescue mission to recover the gods from oblivion and firmly implanting them in the memory of at least the better part of the Roman citizenry (*bonorum*) by means of his antiquarian works. In doing so, he is making himself useful (cf. *utiliore cura*) to his fellow citizens or, as he explains in a fragment likely to come from the same context, offering an *ingens beneficium* by teaching the Romans which god to invoke in which situation (fr. 3 Cardauns). The restoration of lost knowledge is presented less as the nostalgic recreation of the good old days than as the provision of a practical service.[50] As in Cicero's praise in the *Academica*, Varro is first and foremost the helpful guide for the ignorant, not the castigator of the degenerate. The arch-conservative and unquestioning *laudator temporis acti* of modern scholarship is not the man we encounter in his own writings.

---

50. Even this service may be proffered somewhat tongue-in-cheek. How ignorant were Varro's contemporaries really about their gods' respective areas of expertise? The antiquarian's promise that his information will ensure that "we will not do what the mime actors do and ask Liber for water and the Lymphae for wine" (*ne faciamus, ut mimi solent, et optemus a Libero aquam, a Lymphis uinum*, ARD fr. 3 Cardauns) rings a jocular tone and, through the banality of the example, rather calls into question the immediate applicability of the author's religious research. For some more practical applications of antiquarian research in mid-first-century political life, see 6.1 with nn. 59, 62 below.

For all the ready availability of narratives of decline and the topos of the superiority of the *maiores*, the Romans were also capable of telling the opposite tale, that of a progress from hoary *uetustas* to a more advanced present age. In the *Orator*, Cicero argues against linguistic archaism, stating that the fact that some expression "is not found in the ancient authors" is not a valid argument against linguistic usage, and reserving for himself the right to "despise what is old."[51] Both the preface of *Tusculans* 1 and the *Brutus* tell stories of cultural progress, tracing the development at Rome of philosophy and oratory, respectively. According to Cicero, all arts need time to reach their greatest potential: "nothing was invented and perfected at the same time."[52] Of course, Cicero is hinting strongly that such perfection has been reached in his own time, with none other than himself.[53] Similarly, though taking a larger perspective encompassing all of humankind, Lucretius maintains that it was only recently (*nuper*, 5.336) that Epicurus uncovered the *rerum natura*—and even more recently that he himself was able to translate his master's doctrine into Latin (336–37). As in Cicero, cultural progress is a gradual development, and *De rerum natura* 5 ends with the following triumphant declaration (5.1454–57):

> sic unum quicquid paulatim protrahit aetas
> in medium ratioque in luminis erigit oras;
> namque alid ex alio clarescere corde uidebant,
> artibus ad summum donec uenere cacumen.

Thus time and reason gradually bring each and every thing into the light of common knowledge. For [humans] saw one thing after another become clear in their minds, until they reached the highest peak of the arts.

It is the present age that is the pinnacle of cultural achievement, especially at Rome.[54]

In light of these divergent attitudes to past and present, we should beware of positing a moralizing tale of decline as the master narrative of mid-first-century

---

51. Cic. *Orat.* 168: *non erat hoc apud antiquos*; 171: *uetera contemnenti* (of Ennius, whose dismissive attitude toward earlier writers Cicero arrogates to himself).

52. Cic. *Brut.* 71: *nihil est enim simul et inuentum et perfectum.*

53. Sadly, in the case of oratory this recently achieved excellence is now being threatened by the *misera fortuna rei publicae* (*Brut.* 331), i.e., civil war and Caesarian rule (328–33). Thus the "ideal past" is that of a few years prior to the dialogue's date.

54. Even Cicero's praise of Varro in *Acad. post.* 9 (quoted above) can be read in this way: it is only *now* that Romans are enabled to understand their own identity; antiquarian research is itself a sign of cultural flourishing.

antiquarian endeavors. Similarly—and this brings us to the second widespread explanatory model for the flourishing of antiquarian research in the late Republic—we should resist regarding the scholarly efforts of the period exclusively as a project of rationalization, or even the triumph of Reason or Rationality with a capital R.[55] Of course, as the Lucretian passage just quoted makes clear, *ratio*, in the sense of "human reason," was typically seen as driving cultural and intellectual endeavors, while *ratio* as "system" or "systematic account" could be invoked as both topic and methodology by the scholarly authors of the period.[56] I have already mentioned the era's numerous attempts at systematization and codification, in which individuals collected vast amounts of material and then produced ordered accounts of the area of cultural knowledge in question. Such efforts often went hand in hand with a process that has been called "differentiation," that is, the isolation of a topic or field of study out of what had previously been perceived as a continuous spectrum of experience and practice.[57] For example, Roman senators participated in numerous religious practices as a matter of course and part of their political activity, but it took scholarly effort to break these down into clearly defined topics worthy of investigation. Thus, Varro could divide up the organic unity of Roman cult under the headings of "men," "places," "times," "sacred practices," and "gods" (*ARD* fr. 4 Cardauns), while Cicero isolated a particular set of the sacred practices and treated it under the separate heading of "divination."[58]

Any form of scholarly investigation, especially if it leads to a written account, implies some kind of mental ordering or, if one wishes to use this term, rationalization. This phenomenon is by no means peculiar to the first century BCE but instead—as historians of knowledge and scholars in related fields have been studying for many a culture and period—an intrinsic aspect of intellectual activity as such. Even so, the enormous interest in and proliferation of works on the Roman past and present might fairly be seen as a great communal push, as it were, to move, in Claudia Moatti's words, "du désarroi à l'érudition" (1997: 97–155) and to present Roman knowledge in a rationally ordered form. Varro, the great systematizer, naturally stood at the forefront of this movement.

This picture is correct as far as it goes: late Republican scholarly investigators and writers were imposing rational order on their material because that is

55. See Moatti 1997 and Rüpke 2012, and compare my discussion in 1.3.

56. Thus, e.g., Lucretius in a famous programmatic passage describes his task as laying out Epicureanism, *rationem . . . nostram* (1.946 = 4.21), in poetry, a medium whose choice he claims is not irrational nor unreasonable: *non ab nulla ratione* (1.935 = 4.10).

57. See Beard, North, and Price 1998: 1.149–56 and 1.3 above.

58. See Volk 2017: 331. Further on late Republican religion and religious scholarship, see ch. 6.

what scholars do. This does not necessarily mean, however, that they were straightforward proponents of *ratio* in all the senses in which the word could be used at the time.[59] *Ratio*, originally just the "art of reckoning, calculation" (*OLD* s.v. 1a), can also describe, as we have seen, both the human "faculty of reason" (7b) and "a manner, method, means" (14b) or even "a descriptive account" (6).[60] In addition, though, and especially under the influence of Greek philosophy, *ratio* came to mean also "the ruling principle (of natural forces, etc.), law (of nature)" (12a). In other words, *ratio* may be not just what humans employ when comprehending and explaining whatever subject they are contemplating, but an intrinsic element of that subject itself. On that scenario, scholars are applying their reason on something that has reason itself—and the question of what that inherent *ratio* of a phenomenon might be becomes an important aspect of the investigation in its own right. Take, for example, any human language: it is not just the sum of its attested words, but in its phonology, morphology, and syntax follows certain rules, whose identification is the grammarian's first and foremost task.

This question of *ratio*—the putative inherent reason and order of things—has been given top billing in modern scholarly discussions of the period. In many ways, it can be seen as the synchronic equivalent to the diachronic nostalgia that has been posited as the antiquarian's predominant mood: Romans believed (or so it is believed) that a perfect state lay at the temporal beginning of a phenomenon, some time in the far past—for example, the earliest form of Latin was the best and purest—or alternatively, that there is a hidden order waiting to be uncovered in its present, outwardly chaotic, manifestation—for example, an orderly system of *langue* underlies the Latin *langage* as it is spoken. For the best effect, the two models can even be superimposed on each other: one might thus claim that it was in the earliest stages of Latin that the language still fully adhered to its rational order, with *uetustas* bringing about the very loss of *ratio*.

Ideas like the ones just sketched out were indeed of great interest to the late Republican investigators of Roman identity under discussion in this chapter. What I hope to show in what follows, however, is that in contrast to the two master narratives described, the learned men of the period in their scholarly work tended to exhibit neither the kneejerk conservatism nor the enthusiastic rationality that modern scholars have come to expect of them. Rather than advocating an ideal past or perfect order, men like Cicero and Varro often

---

59. For the different meanings of *ratio*, see Wick 2012 and *OLD* s.v.

60. Note also the specialized meaning "proportion, relation" (*OLD* s.v. 3), which in its linguistic sense of "regularity, analogy" will play an important role in 5.3 below.

ended up embracing a far less glamorous aspect of what it meant to be Roman: *consuetudo*, or the sheer force of habit.

2. Not Built in One Day

In book 6 of his *Histories*, the second-century BCE Greek historian Polybius interrupts the flow of his narrative of Rome's acquisition of Mediterranean hegemony to provide a structural analysis of the reasons behind the spectacular rise to power of a once insignificant Italian city-state. The secret to Rome's success (thus Polybius) lies first and foremost in its mixed constitution, where monarchic, aristocratic, and democratic features are weighted against one another in a stable system of checks and balances; the consuls represent the monarchic element, the senate the aristocratic, and the people the democratic one. In addition, Polybius mentions the factor of Roman religion: it is the Romans' reverence for the gods that more than anything else holds together their commonwealth, inspiring among the people an unusually close adherence to the laws.[61]

In the mid-first century, two intellectually distinguished Roman senators composed works in which they discussed the very two features that Polybius had identified as crucial to Roman identity and success. In the mid- to late 50s, Cicero considered Rome's mixed constitution in his *De re publica*, while a few years later, Varro mapped out the Roman religious system in his sixteen-book *Antiquitates rerum diuinarum*.[62] Both Roman authors appear to share the Greek writer's positive assessment of the institutions they treat; even so, their expositions reveal that—when viewed not in the abstract but, as it were, from the ground—the Roman state and its religion present a complex and messy picture, resisting grand narratives and easy generalizations.

As for Cicero, the question of the *optimus status ciuitatis* is the topic of discussion in the first two books of *De re publica*, beginning with Laelius's explicit request to Scipio to discourse on the subject (1.33). Laelius recalls that Scipio

---

61. Polyb. 6.56: τοῦτο συνέχειν τὰ Ῥωμαίων πράγματα . . . τὴν δεισιδαιμονίαν. Belief in their exceptional religiosity was shared by the Romans themselves and was something of a topos. Thus, Balbus in Cic. *Nat. D.* 2.8 maintains that this is the one thing in which the Romans surpass all other nations: *religione, id est cultu deorum, multo superiores* ("in religion, i.e., the worship of the gods, [we are] far superior"). See Pease 1958 ad Cic. *Nat. D.* 2.8 for further documentation.

62. A third feature of Roman culture flagged as remarkable by Polybius is the creation of a strong sense of family history and civic obligation among Rome's upper classes through such rituals as the *pompa funebris* (6.53–54). As discussed in 5.1, this aspect too was of great interest to late Republican scholarship, as seen in the research on the genealogies of individual noble families.

used to discuss the matter with the Stoic philosopher Panaetius in the presence of another friend, the historian Polybius himself (34). Lest the reader think that Cicero here signals Scipio's, and thus his own, intellectual dependence on these Greek authors, Laelius makes it clear that in those conversations, it was actually Scipio who was "teaching" (*docere*) the "two Greek men who were in fact the greatest experts in political matters"[63] and sharing with them his own ideas about the best constitution. It has always been Scipio's belief, we are told, that "by far the best type of government is that which our ancestors have passed down to us."[64]

Much of *De re publica* 1 is dedicated to a theoretical discussion of the three simple constitutions (monarchy, aristocracy, and democracy) and their perverted forms (tyranny, oligarchy, and mob rule). Since any government resting on one of the simple forms alone is inherently unstable, frequent regime changes and movements from one constitutional system to the other are inevitable. The solution, therefore, is a mixed constitution, where monarchic, aristocratic, and democratic elements all play a role, creating a stable balance that ensures the longevity of the system.[65] Such, according to Scipio, is the Republican constitution at Rome, and he proposes, at the end of book 1, to move on to a more detailed account of "both what it is like and how it is the best," and thus to "treat our own commonwealth as an example" of what the *optimus status ciuitatis* looks like.[66]

Scipio's, and thus Cicero's, task presents a a tall order, if not an impossibility. It is one thing to discourse theoretically on the best possible constitution, but

---

63. Cic. *Rep.* 1.34: *duobus Graecis uel peritissimis rerum ciuilium.*

64. Cic. *Rep.* 1.34: *optimum longe statum ciuitatis esse eum quem maiores nostri nobis reliquissent;* see also 1.70.

65. As has often been pointed out, Cicero departs from Polybius in his account of both constitutional change and the nature of the mixed constitution itself. The Greek historian views the development of one form of government into the next as a natural cycle (*anakyklōsis*), where each constitution will change into the one that is, as it were, next in line, and not into any other; Cicero, by contrast, envisages a much more chaotic situation where, depending on the circumstances, an existing constitution can be replaced by various options. As for the mixed constitution itself, Polybius regards this as a system of checks and balances that prevents each party from acquiring too much power; Cicero conceives of it as a harmonious balance of constituencies that all have different things to offer. See J. W. Atkins 2013: 80–119, with references to earlier scholarship; Straumann 2016: 150–90 now argues against Atkins that Polybius's views are much closer to Cicero's than typically assumed.

66. *Rep.* 1.70: *quam* [sc. *nostram rem publicam*] ... *simul et qualis sit et optimam esse ostendam; expositaque ad exemplum nostra re publica, accommodabo ad eam, si potuero, omnem illam orationem quae est mihi habenda de optimo ciuitatis statu;* cf. *Rep.* 2.65–66.

it is another to claim that this best constitution actually exists, and in the very commonwealth in which we (both Scipio and his interlocutors, and Cicero and his contemporary readers) find ourselves right now. Both the author in his preface and the participants at the beginning of the dialogue have already voiced misgiving about the current state of the *res publica*,[67] and even apart from such localized concerns, we may well wonder whether an actual state—as opposed to, say, the one theorized by Plato in the *Republic*—can ever be shown to live up to the ideal criteria posited by political philosophers. As Jed Atkins puts the problem, "Rome, unlike Kallipolis, had a history" (2013: 98).

Cicero's approach to this dilemma is not to gloss over it, but rather to put it front and center in the historical account of *De re publica* 2.[68] In what has been dubbed the *Methodenkapitel*, Laelius sums up Scipio's approach as follows (2.21–22):

> nos uero uidemus . . . te quidem ingressum ratione ad disputandum noua, quae nusquam est in Graecorum libris. nam princeps ille, quo nemo in scribendo praestantior fuit, aream sibi sumpsit in qua ciuitatem extrueret arbitratu suo, praeclaram ille quidem fortasse, sed a uita hominum abhorrentem et a moribus. reliqui disseruerunt sine ullo certo exemplari formaque rei publicae de generibus et de rationibus ciuitatum; tu mihi uideris utrumque facturus.

> We see . . . that you have begun to employ a new approach to the discussion, which is not found anywhere in the Greek sources. For that great man, whom no one could rival in writing, chose an empty space on which to build a city according to his own ideas, one that was perhaps excellent but far removed from the life and customs of human beings. Others have treated the types and principles of constitutions without the shape or example of one specific commonwealth. You seem to me about to do both.

The interpretation of this passage is somewhat controversial, but it seems clear that what is special about Scipio's method is the combination of general constitutional principles with the focus on a concrete case[69]—and one that is not

<hr/>

67. Cic. *Rep.* 1.7, 31–32.

68. For recent interpretations of Cic. *Rep.* 2, see Fox 1996: 5–28, 2007: 80–110; J. W. Atkins 2013: 80–119; J. Müller 2017; and Zetzel forthcoming; my own reading owes much to Zetzel 1995: 22–25. A comparison of Cicero and Varro can be found in Binder 2018, whose conclusions are, however, very different from mine.

69. See Lieberg 1994 and Zetzel 1995 ad loc. Of the two Greek approaches to the best constitution, the first is obviously that of Plato (*princeps ille*), while the second (*reliqui*) would

(like Plato's Kallipolis) a mere thought experiment, but the actual historical city of Rome.

What this focus necessitates, and what Scipio embraces, is a diachronic approach. Rome was not built in one day, nor was its mixed constitution the product of one lawgiver's political wisdom. Already Polybius had remarked that unlike in the case of the mixed constitution of Sparta, which was the brainchild of Lycurgus, the Romans arrived at the similar shape of their own commonwealth "not by reason (διὰ λόγου) but through many struggles and difficulties, and making better choices once they had learned from their setbacks."[70] Scipio takes this unprepossessing tale of mindless bumbling through a process of trial and error and turns the Polybian necessity into a Catonian virtue. At the very beginning of book 2, he begins his speech with a reference to his older contemporary, the famous Censor:[71]

> is dicere solebat ob hanc causam praestare nostrae ciuitatis statum ceteris ciuitatibus, quod in illis singuli fuissent fere quorum suam quisque rem publicam constituisset legibus atque institutis suis, . . . nostra autem res publica non unius esset ingenio sed multorum, nec una hominis uita sed aliquot constituta saeculis et aetatibus. nam neque ullum ingenium tantum exstitisse dicebat ut quem res nulla fugeret quisquam aliquando fuisset, neque cuncta ingenia collata in unum tantum posse uno tempore prouidere ut omnia complecterentur sine rerum usu ac uetustate.

> He used to say that the reason why the constitution of our commonwealth was superior to all others was that in those, there had been single men, each of whom set up his own state with his own laws and institutions . . . But our state belonged to the genius not of one person but of many, and had been established not in one human lifetime but over many ages and generations. For he said that there never existed a single person of such intelligence as never to make a mistake, nor could many minds in cooperation at one single moment command such foresight as to take account of everything, without experience over time.

---

appear to be that of Aristotle and the Peripatetics, viewed here as abstract theorizers (rather than as collectors of actual constitutions).

70. Polyb. 6.10: οὐ μὴν διὰ λόγον, διὰ δὲ πολλῶν ἀγώνων καὶ πραγμάτων, ἐξ αὐτῆς ἀεὶ τῆς ἐν ταῖς περιπετείαις ἐπιγνώσεως αἱρούμενοι τὸ βέλτιον. Polybius himself treated Roman prehistory in a section of book 6 conventionally referred to as his "archeology," which survives only in fragments. How closely, or not, Cicero was following this source in Rep. 2 remains unclear.

71. Cic. Rep. 2.2. Though this has been doubted (Zetzel 1995 ad loc., 2001: 84 n. 6), Cicero here most likely paraphrases a passage from Cato's own writings (see FRHist 5 F131), probably the Origines (a title to which Scipio alludes in 2.3).

In adopting Cato's stress on multiple individual actors, Scipio tells the story of Rome's mixed constitution as a long-term work in progress, beginning with Romulus and terminating with the introduction of the Valerio-Horatian laws in 449, when the restoration of plebeian and tribunician rights after the second decemvirate meant that the mixed constitution had reached its final shape.[72] That the *res publica* is created and upheld by individual statesmen is a leitmotif of *De re publica*,[73] from the political imperative formulated in the preface (see 3.2 above) to the dialogue's aristocratic interlocutors, historical narrative, extensive discussion of the role of the *rector*, and final revelation of celestial rewards for the virtuous politician. The vision is a profoundly Republican one, with individual aristocrats serving the common good out of a sense of moral duty.[74] The Ennian quotation from the beginning of book 5 sums up Cicero's view: the *res publica* rests on *uiri* and their *mores*.[75]

Scipio's narrative of the gradual development of the mixed constitution thanks to the initiatives of a series of individuals is, by necessity, an idiosyncratic one.[76] Not bothering with Aeneas or the Alban kings, he begins his history with Romulus, who within a few sentences appears to acquire, nearly in passing, the *populus* that, with its community of law and interest, is what constitutes a commonwealth in the first place.[77] Not only does Roman history thus start with a *res publica* already in place, but it also is already a mixed constitution of sorts, since among Romulus's greatest achievements is the establishment of the senate.[78] Setting out from a reasonably well-developed

72. As it happens, we are missing the conclusion of the Scipio's narrative, which occurred in a lacuna of four leaves between *Rep.* 2.63 and 64.

73. See, e.g., Perelli 1972; Nicgorski 1991; Zetzel 1995, 2013; Powell 2001; Asmis 2005; and J. Müller 2017.

74. Compare and contrast Binder 2018, who finds in Scipio's account a "gentilicial framework that legitimiz[es] [the] nobility's claim to rule" (170).

75. Cic. *Rep.* 5.1, citing Ennius *Ann.* 156 Skutsch; cf. 5.1 above.

76. See Cornell 2001, who stresses the differences between Cicero's version of early Roman history and other accounts.

77. Cf. Scipio's definition of *res publica* as *res populi* in *Rep.* 1.39. The "social contract" envisaged in this definition appears to be effected, in the case of Romulus, when "all those who at that time lived in the fields where Rome now stands obeyed him readily and willingly" (*omnes qui tum agros ubi hodie est urbs incolebant aequo animo illi libenterque parerent, Rep.* 2.4); cf. Binder 2018: 163–64.

78. Cic. *Rep.* 2.14–17. His organization of the people into tribes and *curiae* (14) furthermore appears to indicate the "democratic" institutions of the *comitia tributa* and *curiata*. The curiate assembly is up and running by 2.25.

political system enables Scipio to make his tale a comparatively peaceful one, where most constitutional changes are incremental, and many helpful individuals (esp. the single kings) are given the opportunity to make their own contributions. Of course, occasional more violent disruptions—such as the expulsion of the Tarquins or the secession of the plebs—do occur, but the main impression we get is that of a gradual and organic development.[79]

This does not mean that the *res publica* is perfect at any of these early stages. Scipio is happy to bestow praise on individual achievements, but makes it clear that—as Cato had observed—no single person had the ability to think of everything. Thus, after the highly complimentary treatment of Romulus, for example, the arrival of Numa Pompilius suddenly reveals serious problems with the founder's rule: the new king finds "the Romans, on account of Romulus's system, inflamed with eagerness for war," to the extent that "they are already savage and bestial in their martial spirit."[80] Numa thus has to take initiatives to restore *humanitas* and *mansuetudo* (27) by introducing a "love of peace and quiet"[81] and, famously, instituting religious rites and observances. Romulus and Numa were both good kings, but they were both needed to move Rome along toward the *optimus status ciuitatis*, as were their many successors, royal or otherwise.[82]

Of course, this incremental[83] history of Rome's path toward constitutional perfection is still a construct, a grand narrative devised by Scipio to make his point about the superiority of the ancestral *res publica*. And Cicero wants us to realize that this is so. Twice in book 2 he has Laelius, his down-to-earth foil for Scipio's idealism, comment ironically on what his friend is doing.[84] After Scipio has showered praise on Romulus for his wise choice of the location of

79. Scipio himself compares the development of the Roman commonwealth to the growing up of a human being: *Rep.* 2.3, 21.

80. Cic. *Rep.* 2.26: *hominesque Romanos instituto Romuli bellicis studiis ut uidit incensos*; 27: *studiis bellandi iam immanes ac feros*.

81. Cic. *Rep.* 2.26: *amoremque eis otii et pacis iniecit*.

82. As Classen 1965 shows, Cicero's positive depiction of the kings (with the exception of Tarquinius Superbus) is in keeping with other Republican treatments: despite the Romans' dislike of *reges*, they typically viewed their own early rulers as revered founding figures and the originators of various customs and institutions (see also Rawson 1975: 152–53). Büchner 1984: 42 lists the achievements of the individual kings in Cicero's account; for Varro's treatment of the kings' contributions to Roman religion, see below.

83. On this aspect, see Perelli 1972: 310–11 and Binder 2018: 167–69.

84. On Laelius's interventions as deconstructing Scipio's arguments, see esp. Fox 1996: 23–28, 2007: 98–100.

his city (2.5–10) and his overall *consilium* (21), Laelius responds by first acknowledging Scipio's unique approach to his subject matter (cited above) before remarking, in what is surely a jocular manner (22):

> es enim ita ingressus ut quae ipse reperias tribuere aliis malis quam, ut facit apud Platonem Socrates, ipse fingere, et illa de urbis situ reuoces ad rationem quae a Romulo casu aut necessitate facta sunt.

> For you proceed in such a way that you prefer to attribute your own insights to others—rather than make it up yourself, as Socrates does in Plato—and in the question of the city's location ascribe to reason what Romulus did by chance or out of necessity.

Historical events take place because of *casus* and *necessitas*, and it is only the biased historian who sees *ratio* at work; as Laelius realizes, Scipio is shaping Roman history according to his own ideas. It is thus no wonder that, as Laelius remarks a little later, "in your speech, the *res publica* is not creeping but flying toward its perfect state."[85] Clearly, Cicero has introduced these interventions to signal that Scipio's story needs to be taken with a grain of salt: even a diachronic account of a real commonwealth with a multitude of actors over time can turn out rather too idealized.

On occasion, however, even Scipio has to admit that Roman history veered, at least momentarily, from the rational trajectory he has in mind. The most infamous such episode concerns the introduction of the tribunate in 493 BCE (2.57–59), a passage whose interpretation remains controversial.[86] A few years after the expulsion of the kings, it came to pass "what the nature of things (*natura rerum*) itself compelled, namely, that the people were demanding rather more rights."[87] This desire, coupled with the hardship of a debt crisis, led first to the secession of the plebs and ultimately to the introduction of the tribunate. As the reference to nature shows, Scipio treats the people's new aspiration as a perfectly expected occurrence within the scheme of changing constitutions. His following remark, however, is rather less clear (57):

> in quo defuit fortasse ratio, sed tamen uincit ipsa rerum publicarum natura saepe rationem. id enim tenetote quod initio dixi, nisi aequabilis haec in

85. *Rep.* 2.33: <neque> *enim serpit sed uolat in optimum statum instituto tuo sermone res publica.* Since the sentence is preceded by a lacuna, it is not assured that Laelius is the speaker, but it seems likely.

86. For different interpretations, see Perelli 1972, Girardet 1977, Büchner 1984 ad loc., Ferrary 1984: 94–97, and Zetzel 1995 ad loc.

87. Cic. *Rep.* 2.57: *id quod fieri natura rerum ipsa cogebat, ut plusculum sibi iuris populus asciceret.*

ciuitate compensatio sit et iuris et officii et muneris, ut et potestatis satis in magistratibus et auctoritatis in principum consilio et libertatis in populo sit, non posse hunc incommutabilem rei publicae conseruari statum.

In this perhaps there was a lack of reason, but the very nature of commonwealths often defeats reason. For remember what I said at the beginning: if in a community there isn't an equitable balance of rights, duties, and responsibilities, such that the magistrates have enough power and the council of leading citizens enough authority and the people enough freedom, then the status of the commonwealth cannot be preserved unchanged.

Scipio still seems to be saying that the people's call for greater power was in line with *rerum publicarum natura*[88] and that the preservation of *aequabilitas* in the *res publica* demanded granting them their wish. It is strange and somewhat alarming, however, that this process "perhaps" (*fortasse*) involved a failure or defeat of reason (*ratio*). In recent scholarship, this *ratio* is usually understood as the power of reason of Rome's political leaders at the time, who first failed to respond adequately to the people's perfectly natural demands but in the end had to yield to them.[89] Unlike at other times, the *maiores* did not distinguish themselves by their wisdom and foresight: the tribunate had to happen, and the political leadership should have realized this earlier than it did.

This reading is correct as far as it goes, but it does not entirely capture the tone of these and the following sentences. A defeat of *ratio* sounds like a bad thing, while a defeat of *ratio* by *natura* sounds like a positive adynaton, given that in contemporary thought, and elsewhere in *De re publica*, nature and reason are often viewed as working in tandem.[90] Even if the outcome was "natural," something clearly went wrong in the 490s, and the question is whether it could or should not have gone otherwise. In the sentence immediately following the reference to the *res publica*'s stability (58), Scipio ascribes political concessions to the people in other states to a failure of *disciplina* and the

88. Pace Girardet 1977, *rerum publicarum natura* here must be the equivalent of *rerum natura* in the previous sentence.

89. Thus, Perelli 1972, followed—with modifications—by Girardet 1977 and Zetzel 1995. More generally on the "limits of reason" in Cicero's political philosophy, see J. W. Atkins 2013, who frequently refers to our passage.

90. See, for example, the Stoically inspired discussion of natural law in Laelius's speech in *Rep.* 3, where "true law" is defined as *recta ratio naturae congruens* (33 Ziegler); in the equivalent section in *Leg.* 1, this *recta ratio* is given to human beings by *natura* (33). Zetzel 2019 points out, however, that while references to *natura* are frequent in late Republican theorizing on all sorts of topics, they often contradict one another; he mentions Cic. *Rep.* 2.57 as an example (198).

impossibility of imposing reins (*frenos*). The image insinuates a negative view of the people as unruly animals that refuse to be governed, which in turn casts doubt on an anodyne understanding of nature's defeat of reason as a mere error in judgment on the part of the ruling classes.[91]

Scipio complicates things further when he states next that "perhaps (*fortasse*) there would have been some method (*ratio*) for our ancestors to resolve the debt crisis,"[92] that is, by providing some debt relief. The meaning of *ratio* here is not the same as in the earlier instance ("method" rather than "reason"), but cannot fail to recall it. It now seems as though the leadership's deficiency of reason consisted not in the inability to see the constitutional need for greater popular freedom and the institution of the tribunate, but in the failure to come up with a better solution. This is what pushed the people over the edge (59):

> quo tum consilio praetermisso causa populo nata est, duobus tribunis plebis per seditionem creatis, ut potentia senatus atque auctoritas minueretur.

> Since at that time no such plan [i.e., of debt relief] was put into effect, the people had a cause, and by means of their revolt, the two tribunes of the people were created—with the result that the power and authority of the senate were diminished.

Unlike a few sentences earlier, the tribunate no longer seems to be a natural development in the constitutional scheme of things, but rather the unfortunate effect of lack of *consilium* on the part of one party and *seditio* on that of the other. The senate lost *potentia* and *auctoritas*, a potentially alarming fact in light of Scipio's claim, a few lines earlier (57, cited above), that in the balanced constitution, *potestas* is the prerogative of the magistrates (who are, of course, senators as well) and *auctoritas* that of the senate. Scipio hastens to add that, even so, the authority of the senate remained significant and the aristocratic leadership of the age was of outstanding wisdom and excellence (59). Nevertheless, the episode leaves a strange taste, an ill-defined feeling that something did not work out quite as well as it could have.

I suggest that these few paragraphs, with their meandering argument and frankly illogical use of such weighted terms as *natura* and *ratio*, are the expression, on the parts of both Scipio and Cicero, of a deep-seated ambiguity about the tribunate. Of course, the tribunate was an established feature of the unwritten Roman constitution, enshrining the values of popular *libertas*, and was as such a positive and necessary institution. At the same time, both the author and

---

91. Powell 2006 brackets the sentence in question as alien to the context; on my reading, the conceptual tension is part of Cicero's strategy.

92. Cic. *Rep.* 2.59: *fuerat fortasse aliqua ratio maioribus nostris in illo aere alieno medendi.*

his character had been personally affected by *popularis* uses of the tribunician power: Cicero had just recently returned from the traumatic exile engineered by his archenemy Clodius, and Scipio (at least in Cicero's version: *Rep.* 6.12) was expected to be appointed dictator to deal with the fallout of the tribunate of Tiberius Gracchus—except that (again in Cicero's version) he was murdered by the Gracchans before this was able to take place.

We may compare the discussion of the tribunate in *De legibus* 3.19–26, where Cicero likewise conveys an ambivalent view, this time by orchestrating a disagreement between himself qua speaker and his brother Quintus as interlocutor. Very much in passing, Marcus the legislator introduces *tribunicia potestas*, claiming disingenuously that there is no need to discuss the matter further.[93] The reactionary Quintus immediately rises to the bait (19):

> at mehercule ego, frater, quaero de ista potestate quid sentias. nam mihi quidem pestifera uidetur, quippe quae in seditione et ad seditionem nata sit.

> But by Hercules, brother, I want to know what you think about this power. For I think it's truly pestilent, especially since it was created both out of and for the purpose of revolt.

His more moderate brother calmly proceeds to explain why—despite his own negative experiences with one specific tribune—the office as such is still a good thing and a necessary component of the lawcode to be laid down. Notwithstanding Marcus's arguments, however, neither Quintus nor Atticus is convinced (26), with the result that the three interlocutors have to agree to disagree before moving on to the next item.

Ultimately, then, Cicero comes down in favor of the tribunate, but his treatments in both *De re publica* and *De legibus* stage his misgivings. To return to Scipio's speech, the episode is just one indication—though perhaps the most striking one—that the history of Rome is complex and that the *res publica*, in spite of its embodying the *optimus status ciuitatis*, is not in fact ideal at any moment in time. As we have seen, Scipio himself draws attention to the incremental nature of constitutional development and the contributions of multiple individuals; Laelius further calls Scipio's bluff by exposing his teleological "history" as abstract political theorizing in disguise; and in the case of the introduction of tribunate, even Scipio himself has to wonder whether this development was a necessary step to the final goal or in fact an aberration.

In summing up his account, Scipio claims that he has succeeded in showing by means of the example of Rome "what it is that rational discourse (*ratio oratioque*)

---

93. *Leg.* 3.19: *de qua disseri nihil necesse est.*

describes,"[94] namely, what the *optimus status ciuitatis* looks like. It has become clear, however, that while Scipio's *oratio* has been excellent, the story he has told does not always exhibit the desired *ratio*. As Laelius has pointed out (2.22), *casus* and *necessitas* may have played an equally important role, and, as Scipio himself has cryptically observed, sometimes *natura* itself defeats *ratio* (57). Roman history did not develop according to reason (cf. Polybius's οὐ ... διὰ λόγου, 6.10); it was a messy affair, with many individuals doing many individual things over many years, of which many were conducive to perfecting the *res publica*, but others perhaps less so.

Cicero, Scipio, Laelius, and the other participants in the dialogue all know this. What is striking, however, is that by and large they do not seem to mind it. Scipio's focus on a specific *res publica* rather than on a Platonic construct is praised by Laelius; the lack of a single founder or master plan is viewed as positive; and the trial and error of constitutional formation are accepted as part and parcel of what it takes to reach the *optimus status*. Even more strikingly, in the end the conversation transcends the very issue of the ideal constitution, recognizing it as being not the most important question to ask. Once Scipio has finished, Tubero politely criticizes his speech for failing to address more significant concerns (2.64):

> nec tamen didici ex oratione tua istam ipsam rem publicam quam laudas qua disciplina quibus moribus aut legibus constituere uel conseruare possimus.

> But I didn't learn from your speech by what method, customs, and laws we might be able to establish and preserve that commonwealth that you praise.

Constitutional theory is all well and good, but what really matters is how "we" (Scipio and his friends, Cicero and his readers) should go about administering the *res publica* so as to keep it in good shape. After all, the establishment of the mixed constitution by the middle of the fifth century is rather old news, and the more pressing issue is that despite representing the *optimus status ciuitatis*, Rome right now is experiencing a fair number of problems (and no doubt has had a few between 449 BCE and the present moment).[95] The entire constitutional discussion has been nothing but a preamble, and the real question Cicero considers in *De re publica* is how individual statesmen ought to act virtuously in order to ensure the welfare of the commonwealth. Rome was not built

---

94. *Rep.* 2.66: *quale esset id quod ratio oratioque describeret.*

95. See Powell 2001: 25, who argues that "Cicero's message . . . is that whatever has gone wrong with the Rome of 129 (or 52) BC, it is not the fault of the constitution"; cf. also Powell 2018: 257–58.

in one day, and long after it has reached its ideal constitution, the *res publica* remains very much a work in progress.

Turning now to Varro's *Antiquitates rerum diuinarum*, published about five years after *De re publica*, we encounter an at least partly similar story.[96] While Varro's massive work deals largely with the synchronic makeup of Roman civic religion, historical aetiologies can be found throughout the text, and the introductory book 1 features a history of the establishment of individual cults.[97] There we find an incremental account comparable to that in Cicero (frr. 35–46b): Rome did not start out with its pantheon in place, but the worship of particular gods was introduced by particular individuals, typically in conjunction with the dedication of a temple. As in Cicero's account, and in keeping with general Roman ideas about the regal period, the seven kings are responsible for subsequently adding most of the familiar gods;[98] however, even in Republican times individual statesmen and generals were able to expand the Roman religious landscape by establishing further cults.[99]

This incremental approach to religious history seems appropriate to a polytheistic system, which remains open to divine newcomers and largely operates on a principle of "the more gods, the merrier."[100] As a result, however, Varro's narrative proceeds in a somewhat erratic fashion, with the vibrant dynamism of Roman religious development occasionally leading to outcomes that are unexpected, unwelcome, or at odds with practices already in place. Under the

96. I focus here on the *ARD* because it is the best preserved of Varro's antiquarian works. If we knew more about the *ARH* and *De uita populi Romani*, a more thorough comparison between Varro's and Cicero's approaches to Roman institutional history might be possible.

97. Thanks to Augustine (*De civ. D.* 6.3 = *ARD* fr. 4 Cardauns), we know how the *ARD* was structured: after bk. 1, bks. 2–4 dealt with religious personnel (*de hominibus*), bks. 5–7 with sacred spaces (*de locis*), bks. 8–10 with religious feast days and festivals (*de temporibus*), bks. 11–13 with sacred practices (*de sacris*), and finally bks. 14–16 with the gods themselves (*de dis*). Since the *ARD* survives only in fragments, much of my discussion must remain speculative. In what follows, I am adopting the reconstruction and fragment numbering of Cardauns 1976, who distinguishes typographically between summaries of Varro's views in indirect speech and presumed verbatim quotations; in block quotations, I use italics to indicate the latter. For what follows, compare Volk 2019 more generally on Varro's scholarly method, with discussion of some of the same passages.

98. *ARD* frr. 35–42. On kings as the originators of Roman institutions, see Classen 1965 and Cardauns 1976 ad fr. 35.

99. Frr. 43–44. On Varro's history of Roman cult in the *ARD*, see Rüpke 2014 and Binder 2018. The former stresses the originality of Varro's historizing approach; cf. Cardauns 2001: 54: "Man könnte ihn durchaus den Begründer der römischen Religionsgeschichte nennen."

100. See Ando 2010. Generally on constructions of Roman identity as defined by openness to outsiders and newcomers, see Moatti 1997: 255–98 and Dench 2005.

Tarquins, for example, we find that the erection of the temple that was to house the Capitoline Triad displaced a number of other gods who already inhabited the hill. To prevent sacrilege, they were ritually asked whether they would yield to Jupiter; most of them graciously conceded, but Mars, Terminus, and Iuventas decided to stay on and share the new temple with the new gods (frr. 40–41). The construction of the Capitoline temple and resultant dominant role of Jupiter in Roman religion also led to the demise of the worship of Summanus, an old god of thunder and lightning who—as Varro wistfully reports (fr. 42)—has by his own time become more or less forgotten.

In other cases, already established religious practices and even altars and temples were abolished by the authorities, often against popular sentiment. Varro mentions the *senatus consultum de Bacchanalibus* of 186 BCE (fr. 45) and the more recent suppression of Egyptian cults by the consuls Piso and Gabinius in 58 BCE.[101] Another factor that keeps the divine personnel in flux is the fact that it is possible for men to become gods: according to Varro, "there are some gods who from the beginning were certain and eternal, and others who turned from human brings into immortals."[102] The latter class includes such well-known sons of divinities as Castor, Pollux, Liber, and Hercules, as well as a number of more local heroes; one wonders, however, whether Varro might not also have been thinking of the work's dedicatee, Julius Caesar, who was in the habit of advertising his family's descent from Venus (as Varro, the author of *De familiis Troianis*, could not help being aware[103]).

As it happens, Varro's attitude to divine lineage is pragmatic if not downright cynical: he maintains that "it is useful for communities . . . if outstanding men believe themselves to be descended from the gods, even if it is false."[104] Such a conviction will inspire the individuals in question with self-confidence and propel them to greater achievements. As for the populace, Varro generally holds that "there are many true things which it is not only not useful for the common crowd to know but which, even if they are false, the people ought to consider otherwise."[105] Already Polybius had suggested that the outstanding religiosity of the Romans was the result of elite control of the masses, and the

101. Frr. 46a, b. For interpretation, see Rolle 2017: 177–85.

102. Fr. 32*: *deos alios esse qui ab initio certi et sempiterni sunt, alios qui immortales ex hominibus facti sunt*; cf. also frr. 30–31.

103. The date of *De familiis Troianis* is unknown, but the Caesarian period has been suggested (see Drummond 2013: 421–22). On Caesar's putative divinity, see further 6.3 below.

104. Fr. 20†: *utile esse ciuitatibus . . . ut se uiri fortes, etiamsi falsum sit, diis genitos esse credant.*

105. Fr. 21†: *multa esse uera, quae non modo uulgo scire non sit utile, sed etiam, tametsi falsa sunt, aliter existimare populum expediat.* Cardauns 1976 ad loc. suggests that this fragment comes from the same context as the preceding one.

idea that religious institutions and practices are often necessarily predicated on an element of deception is found also in Cicero.[106] Varro echoes this pragmatism, though the Caesarian context adds perhaps an extra wryness to his remarks.

The development in Roman religious practice that Varro presents in the most ambiguous terms is the introduction of cult images.[107] Fr. 18 reads:

> antiquos Romanos plus annos centum et septuaginta deos sine simulacro coluisse. *quod si adhuc ... mansisset, castius dii obseruarentur ...* qui primi simulacra deorum populis posuerunt, eos ciuitatibus suis et metum dempsisse et errorem addidisse.

> For over 170 years the Romans worshiped their gods without images. *If this* [*custom*] *still existed, the gods would be worshiped in a purer fashion.* Those who first put up images of the gods for their peoples both removed fear from, and introduced error into, their communities.

This seems to be a fairly strong condemnation, in line with philosophical critiques of divine anthropomorphism found in other sources; it would also be an indication—one of few in the *ARD*—that Varro views Roman religious history as a story of decline. Surprisingly, however, the author elsewhere puts a positive spin on the use of divine images (fr. 225):

> antiquos simulacra deorum et insignia ornatusque finxisse, quae cum oculis animaduertissent hi qui adissent doctrinae mysteria, possent animam mundi ac partes eius, id est ueros deos, animo uidere.

> The ancients devised images, attributes, and vestments for the gods in order that those who had access to the mysteries of knowledge might see in their minds the world soul and its parts, that is, the true gods.

Varro is here promoting a Stoicizing view according to which the divine is the world soul infused in the cosmos. Anthropomorphic images convey this truth to the observer: since human bodies contain human souls, the depiction of the gods in bodily form signals their ensouled nature.[108] Rather than spreading error, divine images thus promote an important theological message, and while Varro maintains that this can be accessed only by those initiated in

---

106. Polyb. 6.56. For Cicero, see 6.1 and 6.4 below.

107. On this issue, see Wifstrand Schiebe 2006, Cancik and Cancik-Lindemaier 2001: 43–49, Van Nuffelen 2010: 182–85, and Volk 2019: 194–95, 202.

108. Fr. 225: *quorum qui simulacra specie hominis fecerunt, hoc uideri secutos, quod mortalium animus, qui est in corpore humano, simillimus est immortalis animi ... ita per simulacrum, quod formam haberet humanam, significari animam rationalem.*

doctrinae mysteria, the symbolism he suggests is fairly straightforward and potentially comprehensible to a fair number of viewers.[109]

So was the introduction of cult images at Rome a good or a bad thing? Varro seems to want to have it both ways or, rather, he can see the advantages and disadvantages of both forms of worship. Roman religious history is not a straightforward progress or decline, but a bewildering story in which gods come and go, religious practices evolve or are abruptly changed, and the fabric of *res diuinae* is growing denser and more complex over time. It is perhaps no wonder if people are confused and unsure which god to invoke when; luckily, Varro is here to help.[110]

The historical accounts of *De re publica* and the *ARD* thus turn out to be similar in that they present a contingent and meandering development of institutions—the mixed constitution and civic religion—that are at the heart of Roman identity. An obvious difference, however, is that Varro's narrative is nonteleological: unlike Cicero's Scipio, he has nothing to prove, and his incremental tale is not meant to culminate in a supposed *status optimus*. Varro does not need to fit his facts to some preconceived ideal (indeed, one gets the feeling that for Varro, it is all *about* the facts), and his account thus appears to be free from the tensions found in Scipio's narrative.

This, however, is not the whole story. As Varro himself avows, there are inherent contradictions that any writer about religion has to face. For what are we talking about when we are talking about the gods? According to Varro, there are three ways of approaching religion, theorized in his famous *theologia tripertita*:[111]

> tria genera theologiae . . . esse, id est rationis quae de diis explicatur, eorum unum mythicon appellari, alterum physicon, tertium ciuile . . . *mythicon appellant quo maxime utuntur poetae, physicon quo philosophi, ciuile quo populi.*

> There are three types of theology, that is, of ways of explaining the gods. One is called the mythical, the second the physical, the third the civil. *They call mythical the one used mostly by poets, physical the one used by philosophers, civil the one used by citizens.*

---

109. In the same fragment, Varro compares the working of divine images as theological signifiers to the banal use of a wine jar as a symbol for wine.

110. See frr. 2–3 with 5.1 above.

111. Varro, *ARD* frr. 6–11 (quotation from fr. 7); *Curio de cultu deorum* fr. 5 Cardauns (where the theory is ascribed to Q. Mucius Scaevola Pontifex; see Cardauns 1960 ad loc. and Ferrary, Schiavone, and Stolfi 2019: 412–15). On the *theologia tripertita*, see Pépin 1956; Lieberg 1973, 1982; McAlhany 2003: 89–96; Rüpke 2005, 2009a, 2012: 172–85; Leonardis 2019: 169–209; and Volk 2019: 196–97.

Theology (lit. "god-talk") is a question of discourse, which may consist of (i) mythological stories about anthropomorphic gods, (ii) rational explanations of the divine along the lines of natural philosophy, or (iii) the description of the religious institutions of particular communities.

Varro's own work falls squarely into the third category.[112] He describes his bluntly realistic approach as follows:[113]

> non se illa iudicio suo sequi quae ciuitatem Romanam instituisse . . . si eam ciuitatem nouam constitueret, ex naturae potius formula deos nominaque eorum se fuisse dedicaturum . . . sed iam quoniam in uetere populo esset, acceptam ab antiquis nominum et cognominum historiam tenere, ut tradita est, debere se.

> It is not by his own judgment that he sticks to the institutions that the Roman commonwealth established. . . . If he were founding that community anew, he would instead set up the gods and their names according to the formula of nature. But since he lives in an already old people, his task is to keep to the tradition of names and epithets as it has been handed down by the men of old.

Varro is not designing a perfect religious system according to his own reasoning or a "formula of nature" that philosophers might identify.[114] Instead, he is describing the handed-down institutions of a real, historically grown community;[115] these may be far from ideal, but their documentation is what Varro considers to be his task. Elsewhere, he states clearly that all such institutions are man-made and literally the products of the communities in which they are found:[116]

---

112. MacRae 2016 thus adopts the term "civil theology" to describe scholarly work on Roman religion by Varro and his contemporaries (see already Rüpke 2009a: 78–80 on Varro as "Bürgertheologe"); he points out that by focusing on the official aspects of religion, these writers present a highly selective view of Roman religious practices (13–52).

113. ARD fr. 12 = August. De civ. D. 4.31; Augustine refers to Varro's statement once more at De civ. D. 6.4.

114. Note that natura here falls on the side of reason (rational philosophical explanation according to the true nature of things, as in the genus physicon of theology); on natura as a polysemous catchword of late Republican theorizing, see n. 90 above.

115. On Varro's claim of living in an "old people," which appears to allude to [Pl.] Letter 5.322a8–b4, see Volk 2016a.

116. ARD fr. 5. The context is Varro's explanation of why he wrote first about human antiquities before turning to the divine ones: quod prius extiterint ciuitates, deinde ab eis haec instituta sint ("because first communities existed, then these [religious practices] were instituted by them").

sicut prior est . . . pictor quam tabula picta, prior faber quam aedificium, ita priores sunt ciuitates quam ea quae a ciuitatibus instituta sunt.

Just as the painter comes before the painting and the builder before the building, thus communities come before the institutions of those communities.

Just as (according to Cato, Scipio, and Cicero) the Roman *res publica* was built over many generations by many people, Roman religion was created by the Roman *ciuitas* in a drawn-out process that has been going on for a long time and is anything but finished. The philosophers' "formula of nature" looks very different.

Or does it? For reasons unknown (no explanation on the author's part survives), Varro in select sections of the *ARD* (parts of book 1, as well as book 16) veers into the *genus physicon*, speculating on the nature of god as such and explaining Roman *di praecipui atque selecti* in philosophical terms, mostly employing Stoicizing methods of allegoresis.[117] The passage about divine images and their symbolism quoted above (fr. 225) comes from such a context: here, Varro connects actual cult practice with a philosophical theory about the divine world soul.[118] Similarly, he attempts to elucidate the true nature of the most prominent members of the Roman pantheon by interpreting symbolically their names and pictorial representations, as well as the cult practices associated with them. Thus, for example, Janus may represent either the sky or the entire universe; he is in charge of beginnings; and his double-faced appearance is meant to signal his multidirectionality and universality (frr. 230–34).

By mixing civil and physical theology and thus, as it were, referring the institutions of a *uetus populus* to the "formula of nature," Varro significantly complicates his project. The author himself treads very carefully, stating in book 16 (fr. 228):

quid putem, non quid contendam, ponam. hominis est enim haec opinari, dei scire.

I will put down thoughts, not arguments. For a human being can have opinions about these things, but only god knows.

---

117. By contrast, Varro has little use for the *genus mythicon*, stating, *maior societas debet esse nobis cum philosophis quam cum poetis* ("we must keep closer community with the philosophers than with the poets," *ARD* fr. 11). Augustine reports that Varro felt free to criticize all *theologia fabulosa* extensively (*De civ. D.* 6.5); in Augustine's own opinion (laid out esp. in *De civ. D.* 6), however, Roman civic religion as described by Varro is wholly contaminated by mythological views of the gods, and it is thus impossible to keep the *genus mythicon* and the *genus ciuile* apart.

118. For Varro's idea that god is in fact the world soul, see *ARD* frr. 23, 226–27.

In the opinion of Augustine, to whom we owe most of Varro's forays into the *genus physicon*, this experiment was bound to fail: "weighed down by the authority of the *maiores*," the pagan author was unsurprisingly unable to make his insights into natural theology work for "the empty and insane lies of civil theology."[119] Modern scholars have occasionally been more positive about Varro's approach, even crediting him with a grand plan fully to integrate the two theologies and offer a satisfactory rational explanation for all of Roman religious practice.[120]

Since the text of the *ARD* is extremely fragmentary and no authorial statement concerning the purpose of the more philosophical passages survives, it is impossible to tell what exactly Varro had in mind. It would appear, however, that these high-minded speculations were marginal to the author's larger project: they are clustered in the first and last books,[121] while the bulk of the work is dedicated to the messy reality of Roman religious practices, which Varro simply describes as he found them.[122] The *ARD* is primarily a work of civil theology and largely deals with contingent human institutions. But why should this prevent the learned author from occasionally adding his own speculations (and as he himself avows, they are no more than that)? Varro is not founding a new religion *ex naturae formula*, but this still leaves him free to wonder whether his old religion may not at least in part agree with the *genus physicon* of theology after all.

By adding an element of rational analysis to his antiquarian description (rather than keeping the various theologies entirely apart), Varro makes his work less straightforward, introducing tension and contradictions. In a way, his trajectory is thus the opposite of Cicero's in *De re publica*. Scipio's account

119. *De civ. D.* 7.17: [*Varronem*] *maiorum premebat auctoritas; huius ciuilis theologiae uanitates et insanias mendaces.* Augustine's statement introduces the quotation from Varro just cited in the text (*ARD* fr. 228). Criticism of Varro's three theologies and their application is found throughout *De civ. D.* 6 and 7, esp. at 6.2–9; 7.5, 23, 28, 33. See Hagendahl 1967: 2.613–17, Lieberg 1972, Burns 2001: 57–62, Ando 2010: 75–79, North 2014a, MacRae 2016: 129–40, and Hadas 2017.

120. Scholars who view Varro as seriously committed to fusing civil and natural theology include Lehmann 1997, Van Nuffelen 2010, North 2014a, and Leonardis 2019. As will have become clear, my own approach is in sympathy with those—including McAlhany 2003: 61–108; Rüpke 2005, 2009a, 2012; Ando 2010; and MacRae 2016—who read Varro as first and foremost a civil theologian.

121. Cf. the statement of the character Varro in Cicero's *Academica*: *in his ipsis antiquitatum prooemiis philosophiae <more> scribere uoluimus* ("in the very opening sections of my *Antiquitates*, I wished to write in a philosophical manner," Cic. *Acad. post.* 8).

122. For Varro's "finding" (*inuenire*) Roman religion in its present state, see August. *De civ. D.* 4.1 = *ARD* bk. 10 test.; 6.4.

begins by positing a *status optimus*, which in the course of his historical narrative becomes less and less well defined and, ultimately, turns out to be less significant than originally assumed. Varro catalogues the multiform messy details of historical reality, only to end up asking whether some *status optimus* hides behind them after all. Ciceronian idealism becomes realism; Varronian realism allows for idealism.

In the end, however, the approaches of both authors are remarkably similar: committed to the historically grown institutions of the Roman *res publica*, they subject them to rational inquiry, exploring to which extent this reality does conform to theory. Sometimes it does; very often it does not. As members of an old people, Cicero and Varro do not seem particularly anxious about this. What counts for these learned aristocrats is not how best to theorize Roman politics or religion; what counts is to know how best to practice them.

3. The Power of *consuetudo*

Written a few years after the *ARD*, Varro's *De lingua Latina* explores another major marker of Roman identity: the Latin language.[123] Six books (5–10) survive of what was once a twenty-five-book work, dedicated to Cicero, who had long and impatiently waited for this honor and may have received the finished treatise not long before his death in December 43.[124] Nowhere in the extant text does Varro provide a sustained history of Latin. Since, however, books 5–7 deal with etymology and are thus by definition concerned with the diachronic aspect of language, we are able to infer some of Varro's larger ideas about the origin and development of the *lingua Latina*. Readers of the *Antiquitates* will not have been surprised to discover that in Varro's depiction, the history of the Romans' mother tongue is no less complex and elusive than that of their religion.[125]

In theory, we once again have a system that is rational and in accordance with some larger truth. All extant Latin words go back to about one thousand

---

123. For text and commentary, see de Melo 2019. Scholarly discussions of particular relevance to what follows include Collart 1954; Schröter 1963; Boyancé 1975; Siebenborn 1976; Grebe 2000, 2001; McAlhany 2003; Blank 2005, 2019; MacDonald 2016; Zetzel 2018: 31–58; Leonardis 2019; Spencer 2019; and Volk 2019.

124. As *Ling.* 5.1 and 7.109 show, Varro originally dedicated bks. 2–4 to his former quaestor P. Septumius; apparently he later inscribed the entire treatise to Cicero. On the history of the work's genesis and publication, see Barwick 1957; Rösch-Binde 1998: 394–470, 2001; and de Melo 2019: 1.4–5. For Cicero's anticipation of the dedication, see Cic. *Att.* 13.12.3; *Fam.* 9.8.1.

125. For what follows, compare Volk 2019. Zetzel 2018: 39 n. 23 points to the similarity of Varro's account to Cicero's depiction of Roman constitutional history in *Rep.*: language, too, was "created by many people over a long period" (39).

uerba primigenia. This base vocabulary apparently denotes its referents in a naturally correct way, by which each *uerbum* is the perfect signifier for its underlying *res.* It was originally introduced by wise men of old, specifically— as we have come to expect—by the Roman or, in this case, even pre-Roman kings (Varro mentions both Romulus and Latinus). All additional vocabulary items came into being through subsequent *declinatio,* a term Varro uses for both derivation and inflection; at least the latter process (dubbed *declinatio naturalis*) is natural and thus perfectly predictable.[126]

In reality, however, things are not so simple. First, the original words may be naturally correct signifiers, but it is impossible for us to understand how this comes about: we just don't know why *equus* is the right word for "horse" (7.4). Second, it turns out that there are multiple origins of Latin vocabulary. Varro never tackles the question of why, if *uerba primigenia* signify naturally, there is more than one language (Is ἵππος somehow another correct word for the same animal?); however, he explains numerous Latin words as borrowings, most notably from Greek and from other Italic languages.[127] Remarkably, he is even willing to entertain the notion that a word could simultaneously have two etymologies, for example, being both Latin and Sabine; the image he uses to illustrate this situation is that of a tree with roots in two different properties (5.74).

Finally, just like Roman religious institutions, the Latin language is a work in progress. New words are still being created, borrowed, and derived; old words change their meanings, their spellings, or their morphology, or otherwise become obsolete altogether. Usage is both in constant flux and very often incorrect, a state of affairs that makes the job of the linguistic antiquarian as difficult as that of the religious researcher.

As in the *Antiquitates,* however, Varro takes these difficulties in stride, accepting the chaotic status quo of the Latin language as he did that of Roman institutions. Admitting that he may never unveil the mysteries of the fourth and final stage of etymology—that is, explain where the *uerba primigenia* come from—he is content to settle for being able to explain their manifold derivatives and inflectional forms.[128] It is enough to know that *equitatus* comes from *eques,* and *eques* from *equus,* even if the etymology of *equus* itself must remain

---

126. *Verba primigenia: Ling.* 6.36–39; natural signification: 6.3 (cf. Blank 2019); kings: 5.8–9 (cf. Schröter 1963 and Boyancé 1975); *declinatio naturalis:* 8.5–6, 21–22; 9.34–5; 10.15 (cf. D. J. Taylor 1974).

127. On Varro's complicated views of the relations of Latin and Greek, see Gitner 2015.

128. On the four *explanandi gradus* of etymology, see *Ling.* 5.7–9; the fourth one, out of Varro's reach, is described in the language of initiation as *ubi est adytum et initia regis* ("where there are the innermost sanctuary and the mysteries of the king," 5.8; with de Melo 2019 and

unclear (7.4). As for the less than rational ways in which the Latin language is employed by contemporary speakers, Varro declares that as an individual, he is required to hew to the usage of the *populus*, just as in the *ARD* he had accepted the religious practice of his "old people."[129]

Varro's ready submission to popular *consuetudo* occurs in the triad of books 8–10, which unlike the earlier etymological books are concerned with the synchronic state of Latin and the question of how a Roman ought to speak now. What is at issue is the choice of the morphologically correct word form (e.g., is the genitive of the word for "senate" *senati*, *senatus*, or *senatuis*?[130]), and Varro stages his discussion as a debate between the supporters of irregularity or "anomaly," who get to make their case in book 8, and those of regularity or "analogy," who get to speak in book 9. Varro himself, *in propria persona*, adjudicates the quarrel in book 10, coming down on a moderately analogical position.[131]

In book 8, the antianalogist defines the conflict at hand as one between *analogia/ratio* and *consuetudo*.[132] As Francesca Schironi has shown (2007: 332–35), *ratio* is one of a number of Latin translations of Greek ἀναλογία, but does not have a direct Greek equivalent. Of course, the Latin word's specialized meaning of "proportion, relation" (*OLD* s.v. 3) makes it a fitting term for a concept that relies on proportional relations (e.g., *bonus : boni :: malus : mali*). At the same time, its well-established sense of "reason; rationality" lends the word, and hence the debate, a farther-reaching significance: viewed in this light, the question becomes one of whether reason ought to be imposed, top-down, on what are the usage and custom of the actual speakers of Latin.

---

others, I follow Scioppius in reading *adytum* for the manuscripts' *aditum*). For the convincing suggestion that this level concerns the etymology of the *uerba primigenia*, see Schröter 1963.

129. Popular *consuetudo*: *Ling.* 9.6, 114; 10.74; "old people": *ARD* fr. 12 and 5.2 above. Generally on Roman ideas of linguistic *consuetudo*, see R. Müller 2001: 183–207.

130. The forms of nominal *u*-stems (what we consider the fourth declension) were highly controversial, as seen from Gell. *NA* 4.16 = Varro, *Ling.* fr. 17 de Melo = Caes. *De an.* F24 Garcea: Varro and Nigidius Figulus favored the genitive *senatuis*, Caesar promoted *senatus*, and writers from Cicero to Sallust actually used *senati*. See Lomanto 1993 and Garcea 2012: 223–28.

131. Ax 1995 suggests that this part of the work was originally conceived as an actual dialogue in the tradition of *disputatio in utramque partem*. Within *Ling.*, bks. 8–10 constitute the theoretical discussion of analogy (cf. 8.24), aiming to establish whether there is such a thing as regularity in language; the lost bks. 11–13 discussed actual applications of analogy. Similarly, the lost bks. 2–4 contained a theoretical discussion of etymology (apparently in a similar pro-con format: 5.1; 7.109), while the extant bks. 5–6 treat individual etymologies (the first book contained an introduction to the whole work). Perhaps a similar structure underlay bks. 14–25, on syntax, about which very little is known.

132. *Analogia* is the more common term; for the explicit contrasting of *ratio* and *consuetudo*, see 8.57, 79.

The antianalogist's answer, of course, is no. Having established that regularity is not a pervasive feature of language (working by a strict falsification principle, he draws from isolated instances of irregularity the general conclusion that "analogy does not exist"[133]), he declares that *consuetudo* alone ought to be the criterion for speech. The point of language being to make onself understood, any and all forms in common usage will do (8.26); if such forms should happen to be regular, just following *consuetudo* will automatically lead to the employment of analogy, "without instruction."[134] By contrast, anyone who uses analogical forms that are not part of *consuetudo* "would have to be rebuked as a madman."[135]

After this spirited attack, the analogist of book 9 needs to do some damage control. He clarifies that the existence of minor exceptions does not vitiate the observation that language is generally regular: after all, the vast majority of forms in usage operate analogically. It is also not the case that the analogists are out willfully to override *consuetudo*.[136] It would be desirable if the *populus* were to use *ratio* to correct any irregularities in its speech (9.5–6), but individual speakers need to follow popular *consuetudo*: "for the people is in its own power, but individuals are in that of the people . . . I am not, as it were, the master of the people's usage, but the people is the master of mine."[137] The language users able to operate with greater freedom are the poets, who enjoy the license occasionally to override *consuetudo* and introduce forms not in current usage.[138]

When Varro himself takes over in book 10, he largely follows the analogist position but puts the discussion on a more sophisticated theoretical footing

133. Versions of *non est analogia* occur at 8.38, 47, 48, 49, 58, 59, 63, 65, 82. As Blank 2005 points out, the antianalogist's skeptical argument is ultimately that, since there exists no regularity in language, the study of language cannot claim the status of a systematic art: no analogy means no grammar. Compare Volk 2017: 337–42 on Cic. *Div.*, where the dialogue's central question is likewise whether divination "exists."

134. *Ling.* 8.33: *praeceptis nihil opus est, quod, cum consuetudinem sequemur, ea* [sc. *analogia*] *nos sequetur* ("there is no need for instructions since when we follow usage, analogy will follow us").

135. *Ling.* 8.33: *pro insano sit reprehendendus.*

136. According to *Ling.* 9.2, the antianalogist has greatly exaggerated the opposition between *consuetudo* and *ratio*: *consuetudo et analogia coniunctiores sunt inter se quam iei credunt* ("analogy and usage are more connected to each other than those people believe"). As a matter of fact, the two are as intrinsically intertwined as body and soul (9.3).

137. *Ling.* 9.6: *populus enim in sua potestate, singuli in illius . . . ego populi consuetudinis non sum ut dominus, at ille meae est.* Wiseman 2009: 107–29 and Spencer 2019: 34–40 use this and similar passages to argue that Varro was a *popularis* committed to the rights of the Roman people (see also Todisco 2017); this seems fanciful to me.

138. See 9.5, 17, 115; 10.73–74.

by defining at length what elements of individual word forms need to be similar in order to constitute analogy. In conclusion, he admits that there is a difference between speaking of analogy in purely linguistic terms (*ad naturam uerborum*, 10.74) and applying it to actual speech (*ad usum loquendi*, ibid.):

> nam prior definienda sic: "analogia est uerborum similium declinatio similis." posterior sic: "analogia est verborum similium declinatio similis non repugnante consuetudine communi." ad quam harum duarum <si> ad extremum additum erit hoc "ex quadam parte," poetica analogia erit definita. harum primam sequi debet populus, secundam omnes singuli e populo, tertiam poetae.

> The first is to be defined thus: "Analogy is the similar inflection of similar words." The second thus: "Analogy is the similar inflection of similar words as long as common usage does not oppose it." If to the second one we add "to some extent," we have defined poetic analogy. The people ought to follow the first, all single members of the people the second, and poets the third.

The debate thus ends in a kind of draw. Of course, and notwithstanding the antianalogist's more polemical arguments, analogy is predominant in language. However, at the end of the day, *consuetudo* remains king, and—unless you happen to be a poet—there is no way that by an appeal to *ratio*, you can override the people's way of speaking. If you did so, instead of being regarded as reasonable, you would be derided as insane.[139]

Why is Varro dedicating so much space to the anomaly-analogy controversy? According to the author, this is a hot topic "about which Greeks and Romans have written many books."[140] Varro himself in the course of books 8–10 refers only to Greek authors, most notably Aristarchus (who is presented as an analogist) and Crates of Mallus (whose stance does not become entirely clear).[141] While scholars used to take Varro's discussion as reflecting a genuine Hellenistic controversy (though one that happens not to be attested outside *De lingua Latina* and later works that depend on it), more recent commentators have held that the author either invented the debate or at least greatly

---

139. The reference to madness comes from the antianalogist (8.33), but the analogist, too, is only too aware that analogical forms that run counter to usage can cause offense (*offendere/offensio*: 9.5, 8, 16, 18, 35, 114) and are to be avoided.

140. *Ling.* 8.23: *de eo Graeci Latinique libros fecerunt multos.*

141. For disagreement between Aristarchus and Crates, see esp. *Ling.* 8.68; 9.1. Beginning with Gell. *NA* 2.25, it has traditionally been assumed that Aristarchus represents an Alexandrian school of analogy and Crates a Pergamene camp of anomalists (see esp. Dahlmann 1932); however, this view has recently lost support. See immediately below in the text with n. 143.

exaggerated it for his own purposes.[142] As David Blank has pointed out, the strict anomalist view presented in book 8 is that of a skeptic bent on disproving the value of linguistic study; the argument is purely destructive and not likely to have been held by scholars themselves engaged in grammatical pursuits.[143]

If the controversy's Hellenistic pedigree is thus nebulous at best and nonexistent at worst, we know for certain that the question of linguistic regularity was widely debated in mid-first-century Rome. At a time when the Latin language was not yet standardized in the "classical" form students learn today[144] and the study of grammar had not yet become codified and professionalized in the ways it would be from the first century CE onward,[145] learned Roman amateurs researched the past and present of their mother tongue and opined on the correct ways of employing it. As with so many other intellectual pursuits of the period, this was not a purely academic endeavor: linguistic mastery, especially in the context of forensic and political oratory, was an important key to social standing, and a man's language was deemed to be a reflection of his character. How to use Latin, and what Latin to use, were thus questions of paramount importance to the self-definition of the Roman elite.

At the heart of the debate was the issue of *Latinitas*.[146] A calque on the Greek rhetorical term ἑλληνισμός "Greekness; linguistic correctness," *Latinitas*

142. See Fehling 1956–57 for the most radical version of the idea that Varro made up the controversy, as well as Blank 2005 on the intellectual pedigree of the antianalogical argument in *Ling.* 8 (see the following n.). De Melo in his recent commentary takes the stance that Varro "may have exaggerated their [i.e., the anomalists'] claims, but . . . did not make them up entirely" (2019: 1.127); he does not, however, engage with Blank's argument.

143. See Blank 2005, who compares Sextus Empiricus, *Against the Grammarians* and suggests that Varro's antianalogical argument may have an Epicurean source. As he points out (2005: 220–38), it is inherently unlikely that Crates of Mallus, famed for his grammatical work, would have held the kind of anomalist view voiced in *Ling.* 8 and suggests that the disagreement between him and Aristarchus (cf. n. 141 above) was in fact one between two proponents of analogy.

144. As Clackson 2015 points out, Latin never developed a "standard" form the way languages have done in the age of print and mass media. Even so, the influence of the prose styles of Cicero and Caesar, coupled with the efforts of the Roman grammarians, led to a significant streamlining of the educated written form of the language (see Clackson 2011).

145. On the history of Roman grammar, see Zetzel 2018, with discussion of first-century BCE language study on pp. 31–58; for the latter, see also Rawson 1985: 117–31.

146. On various aspects of *Latinitas* and its study in the 1st c. BCE, see Siebenborn 1976, Rawson 1985: 121–23, R. Müller 2001: 249–58, Dench 2005: 298–321, Schironi 2007, Clackson 2015, and Zetzel 2019: 38–55. In addition to Varro's *Ling.* and Caesar's *De analogia*, Antonius Gnipho's *De Latino sermone* (cf. n. 150 below) and Staberius Eros's *De proportione* appear to have been specifically devoted to the topic. The debate was not restricted to learned treatises:

was considered one of the so-called *uirtutes dicendi* "criteria of good speech": any orator was expected to express himself in correct, mistake-free Latin.[147] The early-first-century *Auctor ad Herennium* therefore defines *Latinitas* negatively; it is simply "pure speech removed from all error."[148] What would thus appear to be a fairly banal *condicio sine qua non* of informed language use did, however, have the potential of becoming highly contested as soon as there was disagreement over the exact shape and form of such flawless Latin—especially given that *Latinitas* could, depending on the context, take on meaning beyond pure linguistic correctness to connote more general ideas of "Latin" or Roman identity.[149] The analogical books of Varro's *De lingua Latina* can be seen as an intervention in this debate (or even an attempt to settle it), a debate that had been conducted with particular fervor by the two men whose own brands of verbal mastery would turn out to be the most influential in shaping the Latin language for millennia to come: Varro's fellow senators and one-time dedicatees, Cicero and Caesar.

The two men shared a long-standing interest in language and literature, and their conversations and correspondence often touched on such topics, both in light-hearted and in serious circumstances.[150] Thus we find Caesar making fun of Cicero for using an archaism (*Fam.* 7.5.3), while Cicero employs learned quotations from Homer and Euripides to justify to Caesar his actions during the Civil War (*Fam.* 13.15). At what may well have been their last private encounter, the two enjoyed a conversation about φιλόλογα *multa* at Cicero's country house in Puetoli on 19 December 45 (*Att.* 13.52.1; see 4.3 above). Politics was a taboo topic at the time, but their *studia* still provided a safe space in which the two senators could meaningfully meet and interact.

---

practicing orators, too, tried to employ and promote verbal forms that they viewed as correct (see below on Sisenna).

147. Despite the Greek origin of the concept of ἑλληνισμός/*Latinitas*, the topic appears to have been debated with much greater urgency at Rome. Siebenborn 1976: 108 observes that it is nearly only Roman writers who take a prescriptive (rather than merely descriptive) approach to the question of linguistic correctness; furthermore, as Clackson 2015: 317 points out, "all of the Greek grammarians who are known to have composed treatises on *Hellenismós* were at some time in their careers resident or teaching in Rome."

148. *Auct. ad Her.* 4.17: *sermonem purum . . . ab omni uitio remotum.*

149. See Bloomer 1997: 38–72, Dench 2005: 316–21, and Spencer 2019 (and earlier publications) for different interpretations of Varro's efforts to define Roman identity via the Latin language.

150. Cicero and Caesar had some of the same teachers, including the grammarian Antonius Gnipho (Suet. *Gram. et rhet.* 7.2), the author of a treatise *De Latino sermone* (see n. 146), which has sometimes been thought to have inspired Caesar's work on the topic.

One fascinating piece of evidence of such philological interaction, unfortunately undatable, is preserved by Suetonius, who quotes four hexameters by Cicero in praise of Terence, followed by a six-line response from the pen of Caesar.[151] Even more striking, in 54 BCE, when Quintus Cicero served as legate with Caesar in Gaul, the two Cicero brothers were each working on a poem about Caesar's British campaign.[152] This was a time when—between the low points of Cicero's exile and the Civil War—the personal relationship between Cicero and Caesar was at perhaps an all-time high: forced by circumstances and disgusted by the lack of optimate support, Cicero had made a grudging peace with the First Triumvirate, with the result that he was now on most cordial terms with the charming Caesar. At the same time, Quintus was hoping for advancement from the conqueror of Gaul, and Marcus was eager to support his brother's career. Even so, Quintus's work does not seem to have advanced very far, and while Marcus appears to have finished his poem, it has not survived.[153]

What becomes clear from the two brothers' correspondence is how anxious Cicero was for Caesar's approval of his writing.[154] He obviously valued his critical acumen, an estimation apparent even from the gallows humor with which Cicero assures Paetus in 46 that Caesar would never ascribe any purported anti-Caesarian jokes falsely to Cicero: the man has such "keen judgment" that he can tell a real Cicero from a fake.[155] It is fascinating to observe how even when the two eminent men trade political barbs, they still take care to comment favorably on each other's style: Cicero is thrilled when he hears that Caesar finds his own *Cato* better written than that of Brutus, while he himself has nice things to say about his opponent's *Anticato*.[156]

The polemical conversation of the two sometime friends, sometime foes specifically about *Latinitas* stretches over a decade and a number of publications.[157] It begins in 55 BCE, when Cicero treats the topic in *De oratore*. In

---

151. Suet. *Life of Terence* 7 = Cic. fr. 2, Caes. fr. 1 Courtney; on these poems, see Scarcia 1993, Casali 2018, and n. 172 below. Marciniak 2008 discusses Cicero's and Caesar's ongoing exchanges in matters poetic.

152. See Cic. *QFr.* 2.16.4; 3.1.11, 3.4.4, 3.6.3, 3.7.6, with Allen 1955, Byrne 1998, and Kruschwitz 2014.

153. Kruschwitz 2014: 299–301 identifies a possible fragment.

154. In *QFr.* 2.16.5, Cicero mentions Caesar's somewhat ambiguous reaction to another Ciceronian work in progress, the autobiographical poem *De temporibus suis*; he urges Quintus to find out more about Caesar's opinion.

155. Cic. *Fam.* 9.16.4: *peracre iudicium*; compare the discussion of this letter in 4.2.

156. Cic. *Att.* 13.46.2, 13.50.1, 13.51.1; see 4.2 above. For further instances of Cicero and Caesar praising each other's style, see below in the text.

157. The credit for first discovering this chapter in Roman intellectual history goes to Hendrickson 1906; for further discussion, see Dobesch 2002, Dugan 2005: 177–89, Garcea 2012: 49–113, Volk and Zetzel 2015: 211–20, and Rühl 2018: 237–43.

book 3, one of the dialogue's main interlocutors, L. Licinius Crassus, reviews the *uirtutes dicendi*, asking rhetorically (*De or.* 3.37):

> quinam igitur dicendi est modus melior . . . quam ut Latine, ut plane, ut ornate, ut ad id, quodcumque agetur, apte congruenterque dicamus?

> For what manner of speaking is better . . . than to speak (i) correctly, (ii) clearly, (iii) ornately, and (iv) in a way that is fitting and appropriate to the matter at hand?

In Crassus's opinion, however, the four criteria are not created equal: employing attractive embellishment and fitting the speech to the circumstances (= iii + iv) are the real hallmarks of an outstanding orator; by contrast, using correct Latin and making oneself understood (= i + ii) are but the most banal preconditions that any casual speaker of the language needs to fulfill (38):

> atque eorum quidem quae duo prima dixi rationem non arbitror exspectari a me, puri dilucidique sermonis. neque enim conamur docere eum dicere qui loqui nesciat; nec sperare qui Latine non possit hunc ornate esse dicturum; neque uero qui non dicat quod intellegamus hunc posse quod admiremur dicere.

> I don't think you expect me to provide an account of the first two criteria I have mentioned, namely, pure and clear speech. For I am not trying to teach him to be an orator who cannot speak, nor is there hope that he who cannot speak correct Latin is going to speak ornately, or that he who doesn't make himself understood is going to give a speech that we can admire.

Latinitas, "pure" speech without mistakes, is thus an absolute necessity but beneath the notice of those who want to know what really makes an outstanding oration: "no one has ever admired an orator because he was speaking correct Latin."[158] "The whole matter is so easy" and "something that kids learn";[159] Crassus and his friends have more important things to talk about.[160]

---

158. *De or.* 3.52: *nemo enim umquam est oratorem quod Latine loqueretur admiratus.*

159. *De or.* 3.49: *tam facilis est tota res;* 38: *traditur litteris doctrinaque puerili.*

160. Even though he belittles *Latinitas,* Crassus digresses for a while on what it means to speak—and, specifically, to pronounce—Latin correctly, veering into what we would call sociolinguistics (*De or.* 3.40–47). The best Latin is that of the *urbs* itself, without either rustic or foreign features; interestingly, this correct pronunciation is often best preserved by women, whose speech is less exposed to corrupting influences. While ostensibly passing over *Latinitas,* Crassus has thus managed to say something worthwhile about Latin linguistic identity after all;

Cicero finished *De oratore* in November 55 (*Att.* 4.13.2) and apparently presented Caesar with a copy. Despite the fact that the recipient was busy waging war in Gaul, he read the dialogue and within months had penned a work of his own that he dedicated to Cicero: his *De analogia*, in two books.[161] Our sources stress Caesar's impressive multitasking: Suetonius tells us that he wrote *De analogia* while crossing the Alps, while Fronto, even more dramatically, maintains that the work was composed "during the most violent war in Gaul . . . among flying missiles."[162] It is certainly remarkable to what extent Caesar kept up his intellectual activities and networking during his military campaigns, and how often these involve Cicero. The period 55/54 BCE finds Caesar reading, and responding to, not only Cicero's *De oratore* and *De temporibus suis*, but also Lucretius's *De rerum natura*, a work that the Cicero brothers read and discussed at the same time.[163] He is aware of, and apparently eagerly awaiting, at least Marcus Cicero's poem-in-progress about the British invasion, and it has even been suggested that he envisaged Cicero as his ideal reader when writing some of the more learned passages of his *De bello Gallico*.[164]

As far as *De analogia* is concerned, however, its relationship to *De oratore* is first and foremost polemical. Caesar was not happy with the way Cicero had given short shrift to *Latinitas*, for reasons that he explicitly states in his preface and that we will consider shortly. At the same time, there appears to have been a more personal reason, one that had to do with Cicero's and Caesar's speaking practice and stylistic ideals. Cicero was famous for his *copia*, his verbal abundance, and he accordingly considered *ornatus* (Crassus's third *uirtus dicendi*) a crucial feature of any successful speech. Caesar's style, by contrast, was characterized by *elegantia*, an elegant minimalism. The *Auctor ad Herennium* defines the term as follows (4.17):

---

his interlocutor Antonius accordingly compliments him on his "original speech about a hackneyed topic" (*de peruulgatis noua quaedam est oratio tua*, 51).

161. For *De analogia*, see the commented edition of Garcea 2012 (discussion of the date on pp. 24–26), as well as Hendrickson 1906, Dahlmann 1935a, Poccetti 1993, Sinclair 1994: 92–96, Dugan 2005: 177–84, L. G. H. Hall 2009, Willi 2010, Gurd 2012: 57–66, and Pezzini 2018.

162. Suet. *Iul.* 56.5 = Caes. *De an.* T2 Garcea; Fronto, *Parth.* 9, 224.12–17 van den Hout = Caes. *De an.* T1 Garcea: *atrocissimo bello Gallico . . . inter tela uolantia*. Cf. 2.2 above.

163. Caesar reading *De temporibus suis*: *QFr.* 2.16.5 and n. 154 above; Caesar reading Lucretius: Dale 1958 and Krebs 2013; Marcus and Quintus Cicero reading Lucretius: Cic. *QFr.* 2.9.3. As Dale 1958: 182 and Krebs 2013: 772–73 point out, it is quite possible that Caesar learned about *De rerum natura* from the Cicero brothers.

164. Caesar aware of Cicero's poem: Cic. *QFr.* 3.6.3; Cicero as an ideal reader of *BGall.*: Krebs 2018b, specifically about *BGall.* 6.13–14.

elegantia est quae facit ut locus unus quisque pure et aperte dici uideatur.
haec tribuitur in Latinitatem et explanationem.

Elegantia is what brings about that each and everything appears to be expressed correctly and clearly. It is divided into *Latinitas* and clarity.

What makes for *elegantia* are exactly the two criteria—*Latinitas* and clarity—
that Cicero's Crassus had dismissed as too banal to warrant discussion. No
wonder that Caesar was not well pleased.[165]

De analogia survives only in fragments, but we get a sense of the work's
thrust and theoretical underpinnings from a response that Cicero—some
years and a civil war later—included in his *Brutus* of 46.[166] This history of
Roman oratory avoids commentary on living speakers but makes an exception
for two men, whose juxtaposition appears pointed: M. Claudius Marcellus,
the consul of 51 exiled on Lesbos and exalted by Brutus in *De uirtute*,[167] and
Caesar. Marcellus is dealt with comparatively briefly, but the discussion of
Caesar continues for a while, with Cicero delegating most comments to his
interlocutors Brutus and Atticus. Not that such reticence makes much sense:
as Atticus observes, "your opinion about his talent is very well known, and his
about yours is not a secret."[168]

As expected, Caesar is praised for his *elegantia* and is indeed judged to
"speak Latin (*Latine*) most elegantly of nearly all Roman orators."[169] While his
speeches still add some "rhetorical embellishments of speech to that elegance

---

165. Scholars sometimes connect the polemic between Cicero and Caesar concerning *Latinitas* with Cicero's attacks on the so-called Atticists (see esp. *Brut.* 283–91; *Orat.* 23–32, 75–90,
234–36; *De optimo genere oratorum*). Atticism was a movement within Roman oratory that favored a spare and elegant style based on the Attic orator Lysias, disparaging the more exuberant
rhetoric of Cicero and others (see, e.g., Wisse 1995, Dugan 2001, and van den Berg forthcoming).
Caesar, his style, and his linguistic views have occasionally been considered Atticist, but the
evidence is limited; see Garcea 2012: 119–24, Pezzini 2018: 187–88, and Bishop 2019: 194–211.
While there are interesting parallels between the debate over Atticism and that over *Latinitas*,
and Cicero was crucially involved in both of them, I will not discuss the topic further.

166. Cic. *Brut.* 252–62 ~ Caes. *De an.* F1A-C Garcea. See van den Berg forthcoming. For
further discussion of the *Brutus*, see 2.3 and 4.2 above.

167. Cic. *Brut.* 248–51. This Marcellus was most likely the dedicatee of Varro's *De sermone
Latino ad Marcellum* (frr. 33–48 Funaioli), a fragmentary work that may well have dealt to a large
part with questions of *Latinitas* (see Dahlmann 1935b: 1215, Fantham 1977, and Garcea 2012: 79).
This would provide a further reason (in addition to a possible political point) for his being
discussed in proximity to Caesar in the *Brutus*. For more on Marcellus, see 4.1 and 4.2 above.

168. *Brut.* 251: *et tuum de illius ingenio notissimum iudicium esset nec illius de tuo obscurum.*

169. *Brut.* 252: *illum omnium fere oratorum Latine loqui elegantissime.*

of his Latin vocabulary,"[170] it is his *Commentarii* on the war in Gaul that show Caesar at his most daringly minimalist. Cicero himself in his own voice provides the following striking description: "naked, straightforward, and elegant, stripped of all rhetorical elaboration as if of a garment."[171]

As Atticus points out, Caesar's *Latinitas* is not simply the inherited characteristic of an upperclass native speaker, but the result of much thought and study (252). In fact, Caesar has even written a book *de ratione Latine loquendi* and dedicated it to none other than Cicero (253). Having thus obliquely introduced *De analogia* and its dedication to himself, Cicero has Atticus quote from Caesar's preface, where Cicero himself is directly addressed (*Brut.* 253 = Caes. *De an.* F1B Garcea):

> ac si ut cogitata praeclare eloqui possent nonnulli studio et usu elaborauerunt— cuius te paene principem copiae atque inuentorem bene de nomine ac dignitate populi Romani meritum esse existumare debemus—hunc facilem et cotidianum nouisse sermonem num pro relicto est habendum?

> And if many have devoted both study and practice to the task of giving brilliant expression to their thoughts—and we must recognize that you, almost the pioneer and inventor of this kind of abundance, have deserved well of the name and prestige of the Roman people—should we therefore think that knowledge of this easy and everyday speech ought to be neglected?

Caesar pays a handsome compliment to Cicero's championing of *copia* in theory and practice, but makes it clear that in his opinion, the question of *Latinitas* must not be neglected. Correct Latin may appear to be a matter of the "easy" (Cicero himself had used *facilis* at *De or.* 3.49) and "everyday," but is really not as simple as all that.[172]

In describing Caesar's approach, Atticus first gives a narrative of a supposed decline in *Latinitas* (258–60). In the past, speaking correctly was simply a

---

170. *Brut.* 261: *ad hanc elegantiam uerborum Latinorum . . . adiungit illa oratoria ornamenta dicendi.*

171. *Brut.* 262: *nudi enim sunt, recti et uenusti, omni ornatu orationis tamquam ueste detracta.*

172. In light of Caesar's championing *elegantia* versus Cicero's *copia*, it is intriguing that the roles seem to be reversed in their above-mentioned poems about Terence (Suet. *Life of Terence* 7 = Cic. fr. 2, Caes. fr. 1 Courtney). While Cicero unequivocally praises Terence for equaling his Greek model Menander in his "choice speech" (*lecto sermone*; cf. *elegantia*, derived from *eligere*, the correct choice of words), Caesar is only partly complimentary. His Terence is indeed a "lover of pure speech" (*puri sermonis amator*), but the poet's lack of force (*uis*) means that he emerges as only "half a Menander" (*dimidiate Menander*).

matter of *bona consuetudo* picked up from one's family, but by now, owing to the influx of nonurban speakers into the city, linguistic usage has deteriorated (258).[173] The situation calls for an intervention (258):

> quo magis expurgandus est sermo et adhibenda tamquam obrussa ratio, quae mutari non potest, nec utendum pravissima consuetudinis regula.

> Thus the more must speech be purified, and reason—which is not subject to change—must be applied like a touchstone, and the crooked rule of deteriorated usage must not be followed.

Here we find again the contrast between *ratio* and *consuetudo*, with the former called in to correct the latter.

Even so, a rational approach to language entirely divorced from common usage is bound to fail. Atticus tells the cautionary tale of L. Cornelius Sisenna, whose neologisms, though built to rational standards, exposed him to public ridicule when he used them in his speeches (259–60). His mistake: "he thought that speaking correctly meant speaking in a noncustomary way."[174] Caesar, by contrast, got it right (261):

> Caesar autem rationem adhibens consuetudinem uitiosam et corruptam pura et incorrupta consuetudine emendat.

> But Caesar, using reason, corrects faulty and corrupted usage with pure and uncorrupted usage.

Consuetudo, it turns out, is at war with itself, and it takes the combined effort of Caesar and *ratio* to help "good" usage defeat its evil twin.

As far as we can tell, *De analogia* discussed word choice, orthography, phonology, and morphology. On the whole, Caesar emerges as a moderate analogist, choosing among the forms in usage the ones that represent good *consuetudo*, that is, those that are in keeping with analogical *ratio*. Avoiding the mistakes of radical innovators like Sisenna, Caesar advised speakers "to steer away from an unheard-of and unusual word as if from a rock."[175] Even so, he himself was not entirely averse to more radical interventions, most notably in

173. It is unclear whether this narrative of decline represents Cicero's own opinion (it is at odds with the treatment in *De oratore*, which fails to find *Latinitas* in crisis), is meant to be a realistic depiction of Atticus's views, or is a paraphrase of something Caesar wrote in *De analogia*. With Henrickson 1906: 116–18, I incline toward the last scenario.

174. Cic. *Brut.* 260: *recte loqui putabat esse inusitate loqui.* On Sisenna as an analogist, see Rawson 1979: 343–45.

175. Gell. *NA* 1.10.4 = Caes. *De an.* F2 Garcea: *tamquam scopulum, sic fugias inauditum atque insolens uerbum.*

his putting forth the nonexistent *ens* as a logical present participle of *esse* along the analogy *posse* : *esse* :: *potens* : *ens*.[176]

Why did Caesar write *De analogia*? The wish to engage Cicero in a debate about the importance of *Latinitas* was clearly a motivating factor, but that did not necessitate two whole books of very technical material, similar in purview to Varro's discussion in *De lingua Latina* ten years later.[177] It has been suggested that Caesar had a political agenda:[178] in keeping with other *popularis* policies, he wanted to open linguistic know-how to a wider swath of the population, making *Latinitas* not a matter of aristocratic *consuetudo* but a rational system that any reader of his treatise could follow. Perhaps he was even thinking of nonnative speakers such as the Gauls, who needed to be prepared linguistically if they were to interact efficiently with the Roman administrators of their province. Just as a few years later Caesar would reform the calendar and consider other massive top-down cultural projects (such as his public library and the codification of civil law), he was hoping to reform the Latin language, systematizing chaotic usage according to his own superior reason.

This scenario of an intended large-scale language reform is anachronistic.[179] Neither in 54 nor during his dictatorship was Caesar in a position to impose on his fellow Romans his ideas about word choice, spelling, and inflection: unlike the calendar, which was set by the authorities, language usage could not be controlled or easily influenced by any individual or institution. The observation of Varro's analogist, *ego populi consuetudinis non sum ut dominus* (*Ling.* 9.6), was true also for Caesar. And even if he had wished to purify the language of the tribe, a learned technical treatise would hardly have been an effective medium. Rather than being handed as a textbook to anxious Gauls about to go to provincial court, *De analogia* was—like all the

---

176. Priscian 3.239.7–9 Keil = Caes. *De an.* F31 Garcea.

177. Intriguingly, the surviving portion of *Ling.* does not mention *De analogia* (though some of Caesar's specific suggestions may have been discussed in the lost bks. 11–14; cf. n. 182 below for a Varronian fragment that reports one of Caesar's views). I wonder, though, whether there isn't a humorous allusion in *Ling.* 8.31, where the antianalogist, of all people, is championing *elegantia*: if we are striving for *elegantia*, irregularity is the way to go, just as we don't want all our clothes and household items to look the same. In what seems to me a rather cheeky manner, *elegantia* is glossed with *uoluptas*; if we knew that Caesar was an Epicurean, as has sometimes be assumed (see Volk forthcoming a and 3.3 and 4.2 above), this would be especially pointed. Note that Epicurean inspiration has been suggested both for Varro's antianalogist (Blank 2005: 237–38) and for Caesar's analogist stance (Willi 2010: 238–41 and Garcea 2012: 114–18).

178. Different political readings are found in Sinclair 1994: 92–96, Dugan 2005: 177–84, L. G. H. Hall 2009, and Garcea 2012: 3–10.

179. See Willi 2010: 234–37 and Pezzini 2018: 192.

works discussed in this book—meant to be read by a small group of social peers with similar intellectual interests. Caesar wrote his book for the Ciceros and Varros of this world, and if his ideas about language had any influence, it was with them.

As it happens, there is little evidence that any of Caesar's proposals gained widespread acceptance. Intriguingly, we are told that the orator and poet C. Licinius Calvus, whose own preferred genitive of *senatus* was *senati*, used *senatus* when writing to Caesar, apparently using his correspondent's favorite form in order to be polite (or provocative?).[180] The only real success story concerns Caesar's championing of *-i-* as the proper pronunciation and spelling of the so-called *sonus medius* in forms like *optimus* vs. *optumus* (F5 Garcea). While later grammarians still list both options, we are told that the spelling with *-i-* "became common usage (*consuetudo*) on account of the authority of such a great man."[181] And indeed, as Pezzini (2018: 192) points out, on Augustus's *Monumentum Ancyranum* the *-i-* has become standardized. Even in this case, however, it is not clear whether Caesar's preference became known through *De analogia*, or whether it was not rather his own usage (in his speeches, other publications, or incriptions) that had an influence on his contemporaries and later language users.[182]

If *De analogia* was thus not intended as a blueprint for top-down language reform, it is nevertheless the case that the work's ethos fits in with the efficiency, rationality, and control in evidence in other Caesarian projects and achievements.[183] Just as Caesar's supreme military skills cut through the dithering and mistakes of his opponents, just as his *Commentarii* presented the application of these skills in a minimalist style that is maximally effective, just as the calendar reform did away in one fell swoop with the errors and abuses of centuries, and just as other envisaged Caesarian projects might have imposed order on various areas of the chaotic Roman status quo, so *De analogia* too can be viewed as at least a thought experiment in setting, once and for all, a clear standard for *Latinitas*. The man who advertised his victory at Zela with

---

180. Marius Victorinus 6.9.2–3 Keil. For the issue, see above with n. 130.

181. Cornutus apud Cassiodorus, *De orthographia* 7.150.12–13 Keil: *propter auctoritatem tanti uiri consuetudinem factam.*

182. The ample sources that report Caesar's view of the *sonus medius* do not mention *De analogia* (see F5 Garcea with Garcea 2012: 149), but instead appear to refer to his actual usage. Most notably, Cornutus apud Cassiodorus, *De orthographia* 7.150.11–12 Keil cites Varro as reporting that "Caesar was accustomed to pronounce and write such words with *-i-*" (*Caesarem per i eiusmodi uerba solitum esse enuntiare et scribere* = Varro fr. 269 Funaioli).

183. This point is made by, e.g., Sinclair 1994: 92–96, Moatti 1997: 167, Feeney 2007: 197, Schiesaro 2010, Garcea 2012: 5–7, and Pezzini 2018: 184.

the quasi-analogical *ueni uidi uici*[184] may well have been perceived by his contemporaries as attempting to conquer the Latin language with similar ruthless efficiency. This was not a project that endeared him to his aristocratic peers.

Cicero, for one, was allergic to being told how to use language, and in the *Orator*, written in 46 shortly after the *Brutus*, he inveighs against unnamed analogists who attempt "to emend time-honored usage after the fact."[185] These people want to "command" (*iubent*, 157) Latin speakers to employ certain forms and not others, but Cicero is not having it: he knows full well that certain formations are "correct" or "true,"[186] but that does not mean that he is obliged to use them if others are part of common usage (*consuetudo*) and simply sound better. Language is supposed to be beautiful and persuasive;[187] if this is what *consuetudo* provides, let *ars* and *doctrina* be damned. Cicero makes the point repeatedly:

consuetudini auribus indulgenti libenter obsequor. (157)

I willingly follow usage when it pleases the ears.

impetratum est a consuetudine ut peccare suauitatis causa liceret. (157)

Usage has granted permission to make mistakes for the sake of sweetness.

quod si indocta consuetudo tam est artifex suauitatis, quid ab ipsa tandem arte et doctrina postulari putamus? (161)

If untaught usage is such an artisan of sweetness, why should we then look to learned art?

The consummate orator is not going to learn his Latin from a textbook.

Speaking of his own oratorical practice, Cicero stresses his flexibility and openness to variation.[188] "Sometimes I say *pro deum*, sometimes *pro*

184. Suet. *Iul.* 37.2; Plut. *Caes.* 50.2; App. *B Civ.* 2.91. Plutarch draws attention to the homoioteleuton and its effectiveness. Cf. Kraus 2005: 106 and, generally on the phrase and its possible antecedents, Deutsch 1925.

185. Cic. *Orat.* 155: *a quibusdam sero iam emendatur antiquitas*. On the discussion, which covers 155–62, see Garcea 2008: 94–99, 2012: 42–46.

186. *Recte*: Cic. *Orat.* 157; *uerum/ueritas*: 156, 157, 159, 160.

187. See esp. *Orat.* 159.

188. Compare Gurd 2012: 49–76 on Cicero's sociable practice of revision on the basis of peer feedback (see 2.2 above). By contrast, Caesar's *Commentarii*, as Cicero's maintains at *Brut.* 262, emerge from their author's pen fully formed, with the result that they cannot be improved upon. "The perfection of his [Caesar's] style, like his politics, effectively kills communal interest in it, and he can only dominate, not involve, his readers" (Gurd 2012: 59).

deorum."[189] He has changed his pronunciation over time. Knowing that words like *pulc(h)er* and *triump(h)us* were not originally aspirated, Cicero used to stick to this correct if archaic pronunciation; in the end, however, the beauty of popular usage won out (160):

> aliquando, idque sero, conuicio aurium cum extorta mihi ueritas esset, usum loquendi populo concessi, scientiam mihi reseruaui.

> When finally, late in the day, the protest of my ears wrested the truth away from me, I gave in to the usage of the people and kept my knowledge to myself.

This is a remarkable avowal. While Varro, as we have seen, simply states neutrally that the individual speaker needs to hew to popular *consuetudo* and that it is incumbent on the *populus* to make its usage more correct, Cicero willingly and knowingly throws *ueritas* and *scientia* to the wind and embraces what is incorrect but simply sounds better. *Consuetudo* has carried the day.

Of course, Cicero's own style is anything but a reproduction of popular usage. His carefully crafted Latin is characterized by the *copia* and *ornatus*, the flexibility and adaptability, that his own rhetorical writings propound. As Quintilian was to put it, "nothing can be added" to the abundance of a piece of Ciceronian eloquence.[190] By contrast, Caesar in his equally carefully crafted Latin practiced the minimalism he preached.[191] While the corruptions and corrections that his manuscript tradition has undergone no longer allow us to form an accurate picture of his morphological and orthographic choices, the sparseness of his vocabulary and economy of his syntax in the *Commentarii* are in keeping with the spirit of *De analogia*. Cicero's designation *nudi . . . recti et uenusti* (*Brut.* 262) hits the mark: with the garment of *ornatus* removed, Caesar's is Latin at its *elegans* perfection.

Cicero and Caesar, the two foremost stylists of their day, put forth in their theory and practice two vastly divergent ideas of Latinity, which were to change the history and perception of this world language up to the present day. Their fellow researcher into *Latinitas*, Varro, by contrast, never won much admiration for his own style, which is indeed both unadorned (i.e., not Ciceronian) and unsystematic (i.e., not Caesarian).[192] As J. N. Adams and Anna

189. *Orat.* 156: *uel pro deum dico uel pro deorum.*

190. Quint. *Inst.* 10.1.106: *hic nihil adici* [sc. *potest*].

191. On Caesar's style in relation to his linguistic theory, see Oldfather and Bloom 1926–27, Eden 1962: 94–106, Poccetti 1993, Kraus 2005, L. G. H. Hall 2009, Willi 2010, Carducci 2018, Krebs 2018a, and Pezzini 2018: 182–83.

192. Eduard Norden famously opined that *Ling.* was written "in dem schlechtesten lateinischen Stil . . . , den irgendein Prosawerk zeigt," or rather, in no style at all (1898: 195).

Chahoud have recently shown, Varro's loose and nonstandardized way of writing is in fact far more representative of the diversity of actual linguistic usage in the late Republic than that of his more famous contemporaries, and this "messy" style may well be the result not of carelessness but of a conscious decision.[193] After all, as Adams points out (2005: 95), "the most learned Roman of his time . . . could, one assumes, have eliminated 'non-standard' morphology and the old-fashioned or colloquial from his work if he had felt the need to do so." Instead, we have to conclude that, as Chahoud puts it (2015: 18), "Varro's prose . . . was guided, as was his linguistic theory, by his all-governing principle— *consuetudo* 'usage.'"

What has emerged from our exploration of late Republican constructions of Roman identity is a variety of competing scenarios. Some of these are streamlined according to strict rationality, but the majority exhibit a chaotic complexity shaped by custom and habit over a long period of time. The diversity and messiness of "Rome" as described by her antiquarian and linguistic investigators in the mid-first century BCE, and the ongoing contestation of everything from the foundation date of the city to the genitive of *senatus*, owe much to the period's sociology of knowledge. A fair number of the men who engaged in such debates were senators occupied with running the very city and empire that were the objects of their investigations; their individualistic approaches to their subject matter were in keeping with the ad hoc and personality-driven nature of traditional senatorial politics.

It has been suggested that Caesar's interventions into such debates as that over linguistic regularity were the harbinger of a new way of doing both scholarship and politics: good-bye Republican *consuetudo*, hello autocratic *ratio*. There is certainly some truth to this scenario, and the developments of the Augustan period and beyond, including increasing attempts at the top-down organization of knowledge, are evidence that the "Roman revolution" to a monarchic system went hand in hand with significant changes in the patterns of Roman knowledge production as well.[194] Even so, I believe that the real challenge issued by Caesar to his fellow learned senators in a work like *De analogia* was not the threat of creating a scholarly monopoly or an attempt to impose on his peers the use of *optimus* rather than *optumus*. Caesar's plan was not to make himself the leading Roman intellectual at the same time as he was in the process of making himself the leading Roman politician. His far more insidious move was surreptitiously to sever the traditional connection between

---

193. See Adams 2005, Chahoud 2016, and compare de Melo 2019: 1.236–53.

194. Cf. Wallace-Hadrill 1997 and 2008, though see 1.3 above for my reservations about some of his arguments.

political and intellectual activities, even if this meant that his own learned efforts had to take second place (compare 4.3 above).

As we have seen, the preface of *De analogia* contained fulsome praise of Cicero: Caesar declared that by being the pioneer and inventor of *copia*, Cicero had "deserved well of the name and dignity of the Roman people" (Cic. *Brut.* 253). In fact, Cicero was "the first to deserve a triumph in a toga and a laurel wreath for his speech (*linguaeque lauream*) . . . [which is] greater than the laurel of all triumphs."[195] Caesar is here alluding to Cicero's poem *De consulatu suo*, the celebratory epic about his own consulship of 63, which contains the much-maligned line *cedant arma togae, concedat laurea linguae*, "let arms yield to the toga, let the laurel yield to the tongue."[196] There, Cicero had stressed his achievements as a civic, not military leader: he had managed to suppress the Catilinarian conspiracy as consul by means of his leadership skills and eloquence, an accomplishment that Cicero considered superior to the military victories that earned triumphs for their generals.[197] By picking up on his dedicatee's verse, Caesar is paying Cicero a compliment that is, at least on the face of it, both urbane and extravagant.

However, on closer reading Caesar's praise turns out to be double-edged. Yes, Cicero has earned his *laurea linguae* and deserved well of the Roman people—though not for his political achievements but for pioneering stylistic *copia*. In Caesar's book, Cicero is one of those people who have "devoted both study and practice to the task of giving brilliant expression to their thoughts."[198] Cicero's triumphs are thus purely intellectual ones, earned by a verbal mastery that, as Caesar describes it, has no connection to political activity. A Cicero still provides a service to the people, but it is the service of a master of words, not of public affairs. It is not hard to guess who Caesar believes should be in charge of the latter.

195. Caes. apud Plin. *HN* 7.117: *primus in toga triumphum linguaeque lauream merite . . . omnium triumphorum laurea maiorem.* This quotation comes from an extended eulogy of Cicero in Pliny's *Natural History*, part of which the author ascribes to Caesar. It is controversial how far the Caesarian quotation in Pliny's text extends and from which of Caesar's works it comes (I am working on the assumption that it comes from *De analogia*; the *Anticato* has also been suggested). My interpretation follows that of Volk and Zetzel 2015: 211–20; compare and contrast Hendrickson 1906, Tschiedel 1981: 69–76, Dobesch 2002, and Garcea 2012: 81–97.

196. *De consulatu suo* fr. 6 Soubiran. The verse is also cited with the variant *laudi*, "praise," instead of *linguae*. For the suggestion that both versions occurred in Cicero's poem, see Volk and Zetzel 2015: 204–8.

197. That civic achievements rival or surpass military ones is a leitmotif of Cicero's thought; see Nicolet 1960 and compare Volk 2013 and Volk and Zetzel 2015. Dugan 2005 fittingly refers to this as Cicero's "togate discourse."

198. Cic. *Brut.* 253: *ut cogitata praeclare eloqui possent nonnulli studio et usu elaborauerunt.*

In the *Brutus*, Cicero takes Caesar's assessment and tries to make the best of it, stating that "if there is such a man in this city, whoever he is, who has not only thrown light on but given birth to the abundance of speech, he has certainly added more prestige to this people than those who have captured Ligurian forts."[199] "A great orator is far superior to minor generals"[200] (let us not mention major ones like you-know-who), and even if generals are more "useful" to the *res publica*, Cicero would rather be Phidias, who created the famous and beautiful cult statue of Athena, than some master roofer, however much the Athenians may have been in need of having roofs over their heads (*Brut.* 257).

Cicero here accepts the role of the mere artist, elevating it tendentiously over the purely utilitarian function of the general. This, however, is exactly where Caesar wants him: Cicero can bask in his triumph of eloquence, as long as Caesar remains in charge of the *res publica*.[201] The same strategy is in evidence in the *Anticato*, written a few months after the *Brutus*. In the work's preface, Caesar (thus Plutarch reports) deprecated his own style, asking that "the diction of a soldier not be compared to the eloquence of a gifted orator with much leisure for this sort of thing."[202] Now the gloves have come off:[203] Caesar no longer just mock-humbly subordinates his own *elegantia* to Cicero's *copia* but clearly demarcates what he sees as the two men's spheres. Caesar is Rome's military and political leader, while Cicero is a man of letters who can dedicate his *otium* to his *studia*. Why the sidelined consular had so much time on his hands in the long year 46 is, of course, only too obvious.

In the first book of his *Antiquitates rerum diuinarum*, Varro suggests an identity and etymology for the obscure Roman deity Vacuna: she is the same as Victoria, the goddess of victory. Why? "Because those who have free time (*uacent*) for wisdom rejoice the most in her."[204] Scholars believe that this fragment comes from the very preface of the work, the dedication to Julius Caesar: the author is obliquely thanking his dedicatee for his victory at Pharsalus, which has enabled men like Varro to dedicate themselves to their work, including the *ARD* itself.[205] If this was Varro's point, it must have been music to

---

199. Cic. *Brut.* 255: *plus enim certe attulit huic populo dignitatis quisquis est ille, si modo est aliquis, qui non illustrauit modo sed etiam genuit in hac urbe dicendi copiam quam illi qui Ligurum castella expugnauerunt.*

200. Cic. *Brut.* 256: *multo magnus orator praestat minutis imperatoribus.*

201. See Arweiler 2003: 301–6 and Volk and Zetzel 2015: 211–20.

202. Plut. *Caes.* 3.2 = Caes. *Anticato* fr. 2 Schiedel: παραιτεῖται μὴ στρατιωτικοῦ λόγον ἀνδρὸς ἀντεξετάζειν πρὸς δεινότητα ῥήτορος εὐφυοῦς καὶ σχολὴν ἐπὶ τοῦτο πολλὴν ἄγοντος.

203. See Dobesch 2002: 55: "Daß das abschätzig, ja bitterböse gesagt ist, ist nicht zu verkennen."

204. *ARD* fr. 1: *quod ea maxime gaudent qui sapientiae uacent.*

205. See Cardauns 1976 ad loc., following Rudolf Merkel.

Caesar's ears. Men of superior intellects such as Varro and Cicero were only too welcome to enjoy the peaceful conditions that Caesar was striving to bring about, as long as they did not interfere with his own plans and policies. Caesar was happy to praise them, avail himself of their services, accept their dedications, make urbane conversation at their dinner tables—and grant them lots of free time for φιλόλογα *multa* (Cic. *Att.* 13.52.2). While he himself continued to combine, in the best Republican aristocratic tradition, the wielding of political power and the pursuit of learned interests, Caesar had effectively reduced his opponents to a role previously unthinkable in their social class: that of mere intellectuals.

6

Coopting the Cosmos

LUCRETIUS'S *DE RERUM NATURA* begins with a hymn to Venus. The goddess is celebrated as the universal source of sexual desire and procreation, a function that aligns her with the Epicurean pleasure principle and makes her a fitting assistant in the poet's own process of creation. The text's very first address to Venus, however, draws attention to a different aspect of her divinity: Lucretius invokes her as *Aeneadum genetrix* "mother of the descendants of Aeneas" (1.1), conjuring up both her mythological maternal connection to Rome's founding father and her concern for their joint descendants. That Venus is expected to care for Rome is made even clearer in the following prayer, where the poet exhorts the goddess to seduce her lover Mars (another divinity with a prominent place in Rome's ancestry) and, while still in his embrace, persuade the love-drunk war god to grant the Romans peace: "pour sweet words from your mouth, renowned one, asking for placid peace for the Romans."[1] This request is particularly pertinent because Lucretius is writing "in a bad condition of the fatherland" (*patriai tempore iniquo*, 1.41), a situation so alarming that it has the potential of distracting both the poet from writing his work and his addressee Memmius from paying proper attention.[2]

The hymn in general and the prayer for intercession in particular have confused readers and fueled scholarly debate for centuries. What is a call for divine help doing in a work that expounds a philosophy one of whose cornerstones is the conviction that the gods do not care about human affairs and never interfere in them? Already in antiquity, a reader drew attention to this contradiction by noting down in the margins of his text six lines from later in the poem, in which Lucretius himself lays out the Epicurean belief that the gods live

---

1. Lucr. 1.39–40: *suauis ex ore loquelas / funde petens placidam Romanis, incluta, pacem.*

2. When exactly is the *tempus iniquum* of Lucretius's composition? Hutchinson 2001 believes that the urgency of the poet's request points to the Civil War of 49–48, but Volk 2010 and Krebs 2013 provide arguments for maintaining the traditional date of the mid-50s. On Lucretius's political stance, see 3.3, esp. n. 128.

separate from our world, wholly self-sufficient and untouched by emotional disturbances (2.646–51). In the course of transmission, these marginal jottings entered our text as lines 1.44–49, contributing further to the confusion.[3] A plausible way out of the dilemma is the assumption that the poet uses the hymn, with its beautiful imagery and trappings of traditional religion, to lure in Roman readers who might at first be resistant to Epicureanism; the invocation would thus function as the poetic honey-rim on the philosophical cup of medicine as described in the celebrated simile that explains Lucretius's didactic method (1.935–50 ~ 4.10–25). Later in the poem, once readers have become more amenable to the poet's teaching, popular ideas of religion in general and Venus in particular are thoroughly debunked.

De rerum natura is perhaps the intellectual product of the late Republic that most radically and explicitly sets out to demolish traditional views of the cosmos, the gods, and the way human beings ought to live their lives. Even Lucretius, however, for a moment appears to buy into a belief that lies at the heart of Roman self-definition and that will be the topic of this chapter: the idea that Rome is embedded in a cosmic order and enjoys divine favor. Venus watches over the *Aeneadae* and has it in her power to end the strife that rips apart their commonwealth at the moment of prayer. And even though Lucretius later in the poem expresses his disdain for Roman political life and stresses the insignificance of Roman history, he, too, initially places himself at the center of this pro-Roman divine care: just as the senator Memmius is a special protégé of Venus and counts on the goddess's help to justify "taking time off from his concern for the common good" (*communi desse saluti*, 1.43), so the poet will not be able to work "with a calm mind" (*aequo animo*, 1.42) unless Venus brings about peace for the Romans.[4] The fact that the poem proceeds would appear to show that the prayer has been successful.[5] Even the heretical *De rerum natura* owes its existence to the favor of the gods.

3. See Butterfield 2020 for the issues and for why the placement of the lines (included in some modern editions) is unlikely to be original.

4. The poet states that Venus wishes for Memmius "always to distinguish himself, endowed with all gifts" (*quem tu, dea, tempore in omni / omnibus ornatum uoluisti excellere rebus*, 1.26–27). The Memmii traced their family back to one of the companions of Aeneas and—as both their coinage (see *RRC* 313, 349) and Lucretius's words indicate—appear to have claimed a special relationship to Venus. This fits in with both the late Republican rage for constructing ambitious genealogies (see 5.1) and the increased competition for personalized divine patronage (see 6.1 and 6.3 below). The Memmii were in good company: Sulla, Pompey, and Julius Caesar all advertised their being favored by Venus (see Beard 1994: 752–54).

5. See Volk 2010: 128–30.

This chapter explores similar late Republican ways of coopting the cosmos, that is, of claiming for oneself, for one's family or political group, or for Rome as a whole a privileged place within the universe and a favorable relationship with the divine. The Romans traditionally believed that their outstanding religious piety set them apart from other nations and had won them the divine favor that had brought about their hegemony.[6] Accordingly, the proper worship of the gods was of paramount importance in ensuring the continued success of the *res publica*, and the practices and institutions of Roman civic religion were thus geared toward securing the so-called *pax deorum*. With the crisis of the first century, however, this system came under increased pressure, as political factions or even individuals began to claim divine support for themselves and deny it to their opponents. At the same time, intellectual developments in the fields of science and theology, as well as the flourishing antiquarian study of Roman religion, introduced new ideas about the natural world and the divine, raising questions about, and providing new inspiration for, the various ways in which late Republican Romans thought of their place within the universe.[7]

In what follows I consider how, in various political contexts, learned Roman senators employed old and new religious and divinatory practices and made use of old and new physical and metaphysical theories. I first provide an overview of Roman civic religion and consider some of its first-century permutations (6.1). I then turn to two members of the senatorial class who made highly innovative attempts at coopting the cosmos, albeit from opposite ends of the political spectrum: Nigidius Figulus (6.2) and Julius Caesar (6.3). The chapter ends with a discussion of Cicero, who throughout his life and work grappled with the question of how human endeavors relate to a larger cosmic order (6.4).

1. *Pax deorum*

When in 57 BCE, Cicero addressed the college of *pontifices* in the matter of his house, which during his exile had been confiscated and partly converted into a temple, he opened with the following observation (*Dom.* 1):

6. See 5.2, n. 61 for references.

7. In the ancient division of intellectual fields, the disciplines that we refer to as science and theology were not separated but closely related, and could both be viewed as belonging to the philosophical subfield of physics: the study of nature includes the study of the divine. Thus, e.g., Cicero in his philosophical encyclopedia of the 40s, after discussing logic (*Acad.*) and ethics (*Fin.*, *Tusc.*), fills the slot of physics with what has been called his religious trilogy, viz. *Nat. D.*, *Div.*, and *Fat.*

cum multa diuinitus, pontifices, a maioribus nostris inuenta atque instituta sunt, tum nihil praeclarius quam quod eosdem et religionibus deorum im- mortalium et summae rei publicae praeesse uoluerunt, ut amplissimi et clarissimi ciues rem publicam bene gerendo religiones, religiones sapienter interpretando rem publicam conseruarent.

Our ancestors, pontiffs, have devised and arranged many matters in a divine fashion, but nothing is more excellent than their decision that the same men be in charge of the worship of the immortal gods and the governance of the commonwealth, in order that the most eminent and outstanding men, by administering the commonwealth well, might preserve religion, and by seeing to religious matters wisely, might preserve the commonwealth.[8]

Cicero's purpose is no doubt to flatter his audience (and we will return to the remainder of his speech later), but the sentence concisely sums up a funda- mental fact about Roman religion: the public worship of the gods was intrinsi- cally bound up with the administration of the *res publica*, and the people in charge of both were members of the same social class and not infrequently the very same men.[9] What scholars call the Roman state or civic religion com- prises all institutions, practices, and personnel devoted to ensuring a positive relationship with the gods, who in exchange for being properly worshiped were expected to maintain and advance the *res publica*.[10]

The so-called *pax deorum* "peace of/with the gods" was secured through public ritual, including sacrifice; through divinatory practices aimed at ascer- taining the will of the gods; and through expiatory measures once a threat to or rupture in the positive relationship between community and gods had been diagnosed.[11] The members of the three priestly colleges—the *pontifices*, the augurs, and the *XVuiri sacris faciundis*—oversaw different aspects of this web

8. The Latin word *religio* is notoriously polysemous: the *OLD* lists ten major meanings, none of which corresponds exactly to English "religion." In this passage as elsewhere, I translate *religio(nes)* pragmatically as seems to fit the context.

9. On Roman religion in general, see Beard, North, and Price 1998; specifically on religion in the late Republic, see Liebeschuetz 1979: 1–54; Wardman 1982: 22–62; Beard 1994; Beard, North, and Price 1998: 1.114–66; and Rüpke 2012.

10. Roman religious practice was by no means restricted to the manifestations of civic reli- gion, even though the latter have garnered most of the scholarly attention, from Varro to the present day (see Bendlin 2000 and MacRae 2016: 13–52). There existed diverse forms of private worship, both in the city of Rome and throughout the empire; in keeping with the senatorial focus of this book, however, I am here largely concerned with the state religion.

11. The *pax deorum* has often been seen as a steady state of divine favor that the Romans enjoyed as a matter of course, except when some crisis threatened to disrupt it. Recent work by

of human-divine interactions and were recruited from the upper classes and thus, more often than not, senators themselves; Cicero, for example, became an augur in 53, while Caesar had been elected *pontifex maximus* as early as 63 (and was, against precedent, additionally made augur in 47). But it was not only in their roles as pontiffs, augurs, or *XVuiri* that politically active men participated in the civic religion. The entire conduct of politics was so closely intertwined with religious practices that it makes little sense to strictly demarcate two spheres that actors themselves may not have experienced as distinct. The senate, for example, always met in a *templum* (inaugurated space); consuls offered sacrifice; the higher magistrates had the right and duty to take the auspices; and it was up to the senate as a whole whether or not to accept a reported anomalous occurrence as a prodigy and initiate measures to expiate it.

The functioning of civic religion was based on orthopraxy: rituals had to be correctly performed, with scrupulous attention to every detail, in order to be deemed effective. The question where this leaves "belief" continues to be hotly debated in the study of Roman religion. While the absence of a stress on personal faith used to be viewed as an indication of the unsatisfying nature of the "cold formalism" of Roman ritual (especially when compared to Christianity), the scholarly *communis opinio* from the last decades of the twentieth century onward has been that Roman civic religion needs to be understood on its own, orthopractic terms without the introduction of anachronistic notions of belief. In recent years, however, there has been somewhat of a backlash, with scholars deploring the rigidity of the orthopractic model and reintroducing the notion of belief into Roman religious studies.[12] Some of these debates suffer from a lack of definition of what "belief" is—Are we talking about an intellectual "opinion" *that* certain propositions concerning the divine are true or about an emotional "faith" *in* (the) god(s)?—and despite the heatedness of many arguments, most scholars do in fact appear to be in agreement over the basic nature of Roman civic religion. My discussion in what follows is based on my sense of this *communis opinio*.[13]

Without a doubt, the entire system of Roman civic religion is predicated on a set of beliefs (in the sense of "propositional belief," i.e., opinions or convictions), most basically the one laid out at the beginning of this chapter,

---

Santangelo 2011a and Satterfield 2014–15 has shown, however, that the *pax* was never something to be taken for granted, but had to be secured again and again.

12. Recent interventions include, e.g., Linke 2000, Bendlin 2000, T. Morgan 2015: 123–75, Mackey 2017, and Driediger-Murphy 2019.

13. For a clear exposition of the issues, see Linder and Scheid 1993.

namely, that the gods exist, concern themselves with human affairs, and are inclined to favor the *res publica*. Specific religious practices are based on subordinate beliefs, for example, that sacrifice is welcome to the gods or that Jupiter sends auspicial signs for humans to interpret. These beliefs remain largely implicit in the religious practices themselves,[14] while the orthodoxy of the participants may perhaps be tacitly assumed but does not in fact play any active role: the felicity of the religious act depends on its correct execution, not on the belief of the executant. As with other feelings and opinions of past actors, it is near-impossible to determine the level of personal commitment to these beliefs on the part of the Romans who participated in the rituals based on them, and such commitment will no doubt have varied widely among individuals or even in the case of the same person over time. What is clear, however, is that the practices themselves were taken seriously and executed scrupulously, and that the idea that such *pietas* was essential to the *res publica* was expressed frequently and as a matter of course.

Since its inception, this system of Roman civic religion had been in flux and subject to political and social pressures as well as intellectual debate. In the late Republic, however, there were a number of interlocking developments that put an unusual amount of strain on the traditional Roman ways of interacting with their gods, inspiring both new applications of old rituals and introducing new discourses and practices. In the past, scholars often used to view such modifications and innovations as evidence of religious "decline"; such language has become distinctly unfashionable, and, as we saw in chapter 5, even the Romans themselves were not as inclined to diagnose or deplore deteriorations in their cult practices as has often been believed.[15] It is certainly the case, however, that Roman civic religion, with its fundamental belief in divine favor for the *res publica*, was in the last decades of the Republic a significant locus of conflict, a conflict in which—as we have come to expect—political and intellectual agendas were closely intertwined. In what follows, I identify four interlocking developments.[16]

---

14. Linder and Scheid 1993: 48 speak of "croyances implicites."

15. On problems with identifying a decline of religion in the late Republic, see Wardman 1982: 22–62 and Beard, North, and Price 1998: 1.119–25. On the difficulties of positing such a narrative for Varro, see 5.1 and 5.2 above.

16. As so often, the tendencies I describe in what follows did not suddenly emerge in the first century but can be traced back to developments in the second century or even earlier. However, they significantly intensified in the period with which I am concerned, as I hope to show.

First, there is the increased (ab)use of established religious practices for political purposes.[17] By definition, the state cult concerned the welfare of the entire Roman people; since, however, toward the end of the Republic the ruling class was fractured and in a state of perpetual conflict, individuals increasingly began to claim divine support for themselves and their own initiatives while maintaining that their opponents lacked the approval of the gods. Since the religious system was so rule-bound, interventions formally in keeping with established practice could create significant obstacles to individuals and their agendas, with the result that in the mid-first century, politically active Romans again and again found themselves having to cope with religious strictures that hampered the pursuit of their policies and interests.

A famous case that I have already mentioned and will discuss at greater length below is the affair of Cicero's house. Once Cicero had departed into exile in 58 BCE, his archenemy, the tribune P. Clodius Pulcher, not only saw to the plundering and tearing down of the consular's house on the Palatine, but also consecrated on part of the plot a shrine to the goddess Libertas (a pointed choice that advertised Clodius's *popularis* credentials[18]). When Cicero returned the following year and had his house officially restored to him, he was not able to claim the area that was now sacred ground—unless he could prove that the consecration was invalid according to pontifical law. The speech *De domo sua* is concerned with persuading the *pontifices* of this very point. Luckily for Cicero, the college was convinced by his arguments; however, had he not been able to show that orthopraxy had not been maintained, other considerations would presumably not have carried any weight.

An area of religious practice particularly suitable to political use was divination. The Romans had a number of methods of ascertaining the will of the gods through the interpretation of different sets of signs.[19] Prodigies, for example, were anomalous occurrences ranging from monstrous births to unusual meteorological events to the unexpected behavior of animals to abnormal phenomena involving divine images and beyond. When, not long after the restitution of Cicero's house, loud crashing noises were reported from the *ager Latiniensis*, the *haruspices* were consulted by the senate about the meaning of this alarming

17. See L. R. Taylor 1949: 76–97; Liebeschuetz 1979: 7–29; Wardman 1982: 42–52; Burckhardt 1988: 178–209; Bergemann 1992; de Libero 1992: 53–68; Beard, North, and Price 1998: 1.126–29, 134–40; Linke 2000; Engels 2007: 778–97; and Driediger-Murphy 2019.

18. See Clark 2007: 209–12.

19. On aspects of Roman divination, see MacBain 1982, Linderski 1986, Scheid 1987–89, North 1990, Rosenberger 1998, Rasmussen 2003, Engels 2007, Santangelo 2013, Volk 2017, and Driediger-Murphy 2019.

event and in their official response listed a number of sacrilegious events that had evoked the gods' anger. Among them was the purported fact that "sacred and religious places were being profaned,"[20] and Clodius pounced on this opportunity to claim that this referred to Cicero's not having honored his shrine of Libertas. Cicero thus had to revisit the issue and in his speech *De haruspicum responsis* in the senate argued that this and other sacrilegious actions mentioned by the *haruspices* were in fact a series of misdeeds committed by none other than Clodius himself.[21]

The form of divination that most immediately involved the conduct of Roman politics was augury: numerous activities crucial to the business of running the *res publica* could not be conducted unless signs favorable to their undertaking were obtained, or had to be canceled if unfavorable signs were reported (such an obstructive announcement was known as *obnuntiatio*[22]). This included the popular voting assemblies that elected magistrates and passed laws and that thus provided the fundamental legitimation of all policy; the report of negative signs had, at least in theory, the power to prevent or dissolve all such gatherings. Having been used on and off in the history of the Republic, *obnuntiatio* became a veritable fashion in the political struggles of the 50s, spearheaded by the innovative actions of M. Calpurnius Bibulus in 59.[23]

This colleague of Caesar's in what wits referred to as the "consulship of Julius and Caesar" (Suet. *Iul.* 20.2; Cass. Dio 38.8.2) attempted throughout the year to use *obnuntiatio* to invalidate his fellow consul's legislation: after having been driven from the forum at the assembly that passed Caesar's agrarian laws in January, Bibulus spent the rest of his magistracy barricaded in his house, letting the public know through edicts that he was watching the sky (*de caelo seruare*). Bibulus's actions were controversial at the time and remain so today. Modern scholars have often regarded the fact that mere "watching the sky" was believed to impose religious strictures as an indication that augury had deteriorated to an empty formality: if self-declared looking out for a sign was the equivalent of receiving it, the Romans cannot have taken this form of divination seriously. In response to such a view of augury as fabrication, however,

20. Cic. *Har. resp.* 9: *loca sacra et religiosa profana haberi.*

21. On the speech, see Beard 2012; Corbeill 2010, 2012; and Gildenhard 2011: 326–43, as well as 6.4 below. For the *haruspices* and other aspects of the *disciplina Etrusca*, see 6.2.

22. On the technicalities of *obnuntiatio*, see Linderski 1970, 1986 and Driediger-Murphy 2019: 127–60.

23. Burckhardt 1988: 189–204 surveys the history of *obnuntiatio* in the late Republic, showing how the vast majority of cases occurred in the period 58–49. On the Bibulus affair, see now Driediger-Murphy 2019: 127–60, with a collection of all ancient sources on pp. 158–60.

Lindsay Driediger-Murphy has now argued convincingly that Bibulus's *de caelo seruare* did not amount to the report of an actual sign but was the exercise of his right as magistrate of *spectio*, the process of watching for signs. Bibulus simply let people know that he was still on the lookout; since this meant that a negative sign might yet be received, public business could not proceed until the consul was done.[24]

Caesar, of course, was not impressed, and neither was the tribune P. Vatinius, who likewise sponsored significant legislation in 59. A possible objection against the validity of Bibulus's actions was that, after his first failed attempt, he did not make his announcements in person, as expected in cases of *obnuntiatio*, but communicated in writing from his house. In his unparalleled initiative, Bibulus had entered uncharted religious territory, and as a result, both the supporters of the Triumvirate and the beleaguered *optimates* could claim that they had the support of the gods. The Julian and Vatinian laws remained in power but could never shake the suspicion that they had been passed illegally.

The second significant religious development of the late Republic is related to the first. While the traditional practices of the civic religion, aimed at obtaining the *pax deorum* for the entire *res publica*, were increasingly used to further the interests of factions and individuals, there was at the same time a proliferation of new religious ideas and practitioners that catered directly to single members of the political class and especially the "great men" of the period. Inspired by Hellenistic ruler cult and by the honors they themselves often received in the Greek east, powerful Roman statesmen began to advertise the divine favor they enjoyed or even their own (near-)divine qualities.[25] Sulla, for one, excelled in this kind of self-aggrandizement, styling himself a special protégé of Venus and proclaiming his supernatural *felicitas* in military matters;[26] however, even a politician as different in temperament as Cicero could celebrate his own achievements as consul in an epic poem that featured its protagonist interacting with the gods on Olympus and receiving their personal guidance.[27] The game was taken to a new level by Caesar, who had the added advantage of being himself descended from a divinity and who came

24. Driediger-Murphy 2019: 130: "the process of sky-watching itself was technically sufficient to prohibit public business."

25. See Clark 2007: 205–54 on the competitive claim to divine qualities, Miano 2018: 132–55 specifically on *fortuna*, and Luke 2014 on the "personal theologies" of leading members of the late Republican political elite.

26. See Ramage 1991 and Thein 2009.

27. See Volk 2013: 99–105 on the role of the divine in Cicero's *De consulatu suo*, and further 6.4 below.

close to being worshiped as a god in his own lifetime. We will return to this topic in 6.3 below.

The unprecedented rise to power of individual politicians went hand in hand with the development and spread of individualized modes of divination. The strongmen of the first century retained personal seers, consulted astrologers, experienced prophetic dreams, and were the subject of omens and predictions that concerned their own future rather than the welfare of the *res publica*.[28] If fulfilled, such prophecies could be employed to advertise the concerned individual's exceptional status; if ignored, they might tell a cautionary tale, as in the famous case of the *haruspex* Spurinna's unheeded warning that Caesar "beware the Ides of March."[29]

The new mode of prediction making that more than any others encapsulates the change from a Republican to a monarchic form of government is astrology.[30] Developed in the Hellenistic east on the basis of millennia-old Mesopotamian methods of astral divination and supported by Stoic ideas of cosmic sympathy and ineluctable fate, the art of casting horoscopes became popular in late Republican Rome and appealed to individuals who believed, or wanted it to be believed, that they were predestined to greatness. A birth chart applies to one person and one person only; as a result, as Tamsyn Barton observes, "[a]strology belonged with the sole ruler, as the state diviners belonged with the Republic" (1994: 38). Not that the promises held out by the stars were always fulfilled: Cicero reports with a certain glee that Pompey, Crassus, and Caesar had all been assured by their astrologers that they would pass away in old age, at home, and in a state of glory (*Div.* 2.99).

The rise of astrology presents a perfect example of the interconnection of intellectual and political developments in the late Republic. The spread of astronomical knowledge, philosophical theories, and an aesthetic fascination with the night sky (as seen, most prominently, in the enthusiastic reception of Aratus's *Phaenomena*[31]) met, and reinforced, a demand for cosmic reassurance and validation in a time of political uncertainty and uproar. Private citizens may have had their horoscopes cast to find out how they would fare in

---

28. On the rise of personalized divination, see Jal 1961: 399–403, Rosenberger 1998: 223–27, and Engels 2007: 786–97.

29. On this prophecy, see Ramsey 2000.

30. On the rise of astrology at Rome, see Cramer 1954: 44–80, Barton 1994: 38–41, Volk 2009b: 127–37, and 6.2 below.

31. On the popularity of the *Phaenomena* in Rome, see Volk 2015: 262–65; on Cicero's pioneering translation of the poem and its influence, see Gee 2001, 2013: 57–109; Bishop 2016, 2019: 41–84; and Simone 2020: 13–65.

the uncertain future of the *res publica*; leading statesmen did so to learn how they might shape it.

To return to my list of four operative trends conducive to the late Republican attempts at coopting the cosmos, the third development is one we have already encountered, namely, the proliferation of antiquarian study. Among the Roman institutions investigated by first-century writers, religious practices, places, and personnel take center stage.[32] Varro's *Antiquitates rerum diuinarum* is the most prominent example, but there were also numerous specialized studies, including on pontifical law, augury, and the *disciplina Etrusca*.[33] What is especially striking about the numerous works on augury is that they were written by men who were not only members of the college themselves but also highly successful politicians, making it as far as the praetorship or even the consulate: C. Claudius Marcellus (pr. 80), Varro (pr. date unknown), L. Iulius Caesar (cos. 64), Cicero (cos. 63), Ap. Claudius Pulcher (cos. 54), and M. Valerius Messalla Rufus (cos. 53).[34] Most of their books presumably laid out in systematic form the legal and procedural technicalities of the trade; the only significant fragments to survive, from the work of Messalla, concern the definition of the pomerium and the rights and responsibilities of various magistrates (Gell. *NA* 13.14–16).

As we know from Cicero, however, there were also more theoretical debates within the augural college. In *De legibus*, Atticus, one of the dialogue's speakers, observes (*Leg.* 2.32):

> sed est in collegio uestro inter Marcellum et Appium optimos augures magna dissensio (nam eorum ego in libros incidi), cum alteri placeat auspicia ista ad utilitatem esse rei publicae composita, alteri disciplina uestra quasi diuinari uideatur posse.

> But there is a great disagreement in your college between two excellent augurs, Marcellus and Appius (for I have read their books). The one believes that those auspicial rites were instituted for the good of the commonwealth, the other that that discipline of yours is, as it were, capable of divination.

To judge from *De legibus* 2.33 and *De diuinatione* 2.75 (cf. 1.105), Marcellus held that Roman augury had never involved actual communication with the divine

---

32. See Momigliano 1984, Rawson 1985: 298–316, Sehlmeyer 2009, and MacRae 2016.

33. Pontifical law: Veranius, *Quaestiones pontificales*; Granius Flaccus, *De indigitamentis* (dedicated to Caesar); augury: see immediately below in the text and note also Nigidius Figulus, *De augurio privato*; *disciplina Etrusca*: see 6.2 below.

34. On these authors and their works, see Rawson 1985: 302–3, Harries 2006: 162–69, and Sehlmeyer 2009: 67–68. In addition to these insiders, Veranius, too, wrote on augury.

and always served as a mere political tool, while Appius believed that it had been developed and continued to function as a bona fide method of divination.[35] Interestingly, in both dialogues the character Marcus Cicero hedges his bets, allowing that at some time in the past augury may have presented a genuine way of ascertaining the will of the gods, but asserting that with the loss of the relevant knowledge, the practice persists solely for the purpose of running the *res publica*.[36]

This brings us to the fourth and final development, the adoption of scientific and philosophical ideas about the cosmos, which were frequently at odds with the implicit beliefs that underlay civic religion.[37] If, as the Epicureans held, the gods did not concern themselves with human affairs, this rendered the concept of the *pax deorum* moot. If god was the Stoic impersonal divinity coextensive with the cosmos, the question arose of how that entity related to the anthropomorphic gods worshiped in Rome's temples. If all events were fated, as the Stoics thought, and/or determined by the movements of the heavenly bodies, as the astrologers proclaimed, then one had to wonder whether there was any point in expiating prodigies in an attempt to avoid dire consequences. And if the rituals of the state cult, or perhaps even the existence of concerned gods, were simply the benign (or not so benign) inventions of men in power for the purpose of keeping the populace in check,[38] then enlightened members of the upper class had to admit to themselves that when engaging in augury, sacrifice, or any other rite, they were just putting on an elaborate charade for political purposes.

These are the questions that we find the period's learned senators debating. Cicero in the mid-40s dedicated three treatises of his philosophical corpus to religious topics. *De natura deorum* considers the makeup of the universe and characteristics of the gods, pitting the Epicurean world of randomly falling atoms and unconcerned divinities against the orderly Stoic cosmos governed by divine providence. In *De diuinatione*, the two Cicero brothers discuss the question of whether divination "exists," that is, whether there really are divine signs that are correlated to situations and outcomes in the human realm.

---

35. Appius, the brother of Cicero's nemesis P. Clodius Pulcher, not only was deeply committed to his own art of augury, but is also reported to have practiced necromancy (Cic. *Tusc.* 1.37; *Div.* 1.132; see further 6.2); according to *Div.* 1.105, his own fellow augurs used to mock him for his superstition. He dedicated (at least the first book of) his work on augury to Cicero (*Fam.* 3.4.1, 3.9.3, 3.11.4). For Cicero's own provisions on augury in the religious lawcode of *Leg.* 2 as an intervention in contemporary debate about the practice, see Arena 2020.

36. Cic. *Div.* 2.75: *rei publicae causa*; cf. *Leg.* 2.33.

37. Compare Brunt 1989.

38. On the history of this idea, found in many ancient thinkers and sources, see Döring 1978.

Finally, the now fragmentary *De fato* subjects to scrutiny the Stoic view of strict determinism, according to which events follow one another in an unbroken chain of cause and effect.

All three dialogues are informed by Academic Skepticism, presenting a debate *in utramque partem* and ending in aporia after the Skeptic speaker has demolished the dogmatic positions.[39] However, the impossibility of determining the truth about the gods and the possibility of their communicating with humans is specifically not considered an obstacle to the maintenance of the state cult and of such divinatory practices as augury. In *De natura deorum*, the Skeptic Cotta explicitly states that, as a *pontifex* himself, he has a duty to fulfill (*Nat. D.* 3.5):

> ... ut opiniones quas a maioribus accepimus de dis immortalibus, sacra caerimonias religionesque defenderem. ego uero eas defendam semper semperque defendi, nec me ex ea opinione quam a maioribus accepi de cultu deorum immortalium ullius umquam oratio aut docti aut indocti mouebit.

> [Being a pontiff means] that I ought to defend the beliefs that we have inherited from our ancestors, the rites, the ceremonies, the religious obligations. I will always defend them and have always done so, and the speech of no one—be he learned or not—will ever dislodge me from the belief about the worship of the immortal gods that I have inherited from our ancestors.

Cotta the pontiff makes it clear that whatever his private (lack of) theological conviction may be, this will not prevent him from the execution of Roman *religio*, which in the best orthopractic manner he defines as practices: sacred rites, augury, and response to prodigies.[40]

In *De diuinatione*, as we will see in greater detail in 6.4, the augur Cicero is considerably more aggressive and openly cynical about divination, including even the art of his own college. As it is practiced these days, augury is an empty

---

39. In *Div.* and *Fat.*, the Skeptic is Marcus Cicero himself; in *Nat. D.*, it is C. Aurelius Cotta. Tantalizingly, *Nat. D.* ends with the avowal by Cicero that he himself (who purportedly attended the conversation, held in 77/76 BCE, but did not participate) found the Stoic speech "more approximating the appearance of truth" (*ad ueritatis similitudinem ... propensior*, 3.95).

40. *Nat. D.* 3.5: *cumque omnis populi Romani religio in sacra et in auspicia diuisa sit, tertium adiunctum sit si quid praedictionis causa ex portentis et monstris Sibyllae interpretes haruspicesue monuerunt, harum ego religionum nullam umquam contemnendam putaui* ("The religion of the Roman people comprises sacred rites, augury, and as a third the prophetic warnings the interpreters of the Sibyl or the *haruspices* have derived from prodigies and portents. I have never considered any of these aspects of religion to be despised").

ritual that has nothing to do with ascertaining the will of the gods (*Div.* 2.70–83). Should it therefore be abandoned? Absolutely not: the practice is kept up "on account of both the opinion of the common crowd and its great use for the commonwealth."[41] This is, of course, the very point of view of Cicero's colleague Marcellus, whom Marcus cites with approval (2.75). He also unabashedly spells out what the political usefulness of augury consists in (2.74; cf. 2.43 on haruspicy):

> . . . fulmen sinistrum, auspicium optimum quod habemus ad omnis res praeterquam ad comitia. quod quidem institutum rei publicae causae est, ut comitiorum uel in iudiciis populi uel in iure legum uel in creandis magistratibus principes ciuitatis essent interpretes.

> . . . lightning on the left, which we consider a favorable sign for all situations except for the *comitia*. This was established for the sake of the commonwealth, so that the leaders of the state would be the arbiters of the *comitia*, whether for the purpose of criminal trials or passing laws or electing magistrates.

Augury provides the ruling classes with the means of controlling the assemblies through the practice of *obnuntiatio*: the announcement of a negative sign has the power to prevent unwelcome electoral outcomes or the passage of undesirable laws. Accordingly, in the second book of *De legibus*, the speaker Marcus Cicero puts forward religious legislation that mirrors the provisions of Roman civic religion almost exactly, including its divinatory practices.[42] Even when given the chance to invent religious institutions from scratch, Cicero chooses the civic rites that he finds at Rome.[43]

The author Cicero makes his characters Cotta and Marcus display the kind of "brain-balkanization" theorized by Varro in the *theologia tripertita*, that is, the practice of keeping apart different manners of thinking about and doing

---

41. *Div.* 2.70: *et ad opinionem uulgi et ad magnas utilitates rei publicae.*

42. Unsurprisingly, *Leg.* 3.27 argues forthrightly for the usefulness of augury in controlling the assemblies; see Arena 2020.

43. In this hewing to *consuetudo*, Cicero is more committed to civic religion than even Varro, who in the *ARD* asserts that "if he were founding that community anew, he would instead set up the gods and their names according to the formula of nature" (*si eam ciuitatem nouam constitueret, ex naturae potius formula deos nominaque eorum se fuisse dedicaturum*, *ARD* fr. 12 Cardauns; 5.2 above); see Goar 1972: 79. Cicero, too, in *De legibus* 1 explains the concept of "natural law," on which all specific statutes need to be based; how his actual legislation in bks. 2 and 3 is supposed to relate to such universal principles remains a crux in the interpretation of the dialogue. See below in the text for an example of Cicero's supplying new philosophical content to his conservative lawcode, as well as further 6.4 below.

religion.[44] Such mental compartmentalizing may well have been a habit among the learned elite: while they executed the civic rituals in the expected scrupulous fashion and displayed traditional *pietas* in their public utterances, Roman senators may have held any variety of private views, ranging from Appius Claudius's fervent belief in the power of divination, to the political pragmatism of a Marcus Cicero intent on controlling the populace even if that involves deception,[45] to the Epicurean conviction that it makes no sense to ask the gods for their favor but that one might as well adhere to one's community's religious observances. In their villas, the leading men of Rome might debate the nature of the gods;[46] in the forum, in the senate, and on the battlefield, they were models of orthopraxy.

Even if the orthopractic and political nature of Roman state religion allowed for or even encouraged such a disconnect between theological theorizing and ritual practice, however, the exposure of the Roman elite to new ways of conceiving of the cosmos and the divine could not in the long run fail to influence, not only their private thoughts, but also their public statements and actions. Varro kept his forays into physical theology to the opening and closing books of his *Antiquitates rerum diuinarum*, while Cicero too used the final paragraphs of a number of his dialogues to hint at a personal belief in a divinely ordered universe along Platonic and Stoic lines, as when at the closing of *De diuinatione*, Marcus declares that "religion is linked to the knowledge of nature" and that "the beauty of the cosmos and order of the celestial realm compel us to confess that there is some outstanding eternal being."[47] Still, such powerful ideas could hardly remain permanently marginalized, and the interconnectedness that we have observed throughout this book of intellectual and political developments was bound to apply as well, or even more so, to the realm where the most was at stake: the

44. For the term "brain-balkanization," see Feeney 1998: 14–21, who adopts the concept from Paul Veyne.

45. Varro, too, in *ARD* fr. 21† Cardauns asserts that it is useful for the *uulgus* not to know everything or even to hold some false beliefs; see 5.2 above.

46. In *Div.* 2.28, after having first asserted that haruspicy ought to be practiced *rei publicae causa*, Marcus Cicero interrupts himself, reminding himself and his brother that they are having a private conversation: "but we are alone: we can investigate the truth without incurring ill will" (*sed soli sumus: licet uerum exquirere sine inuidia*).

47. *Div.* 2.149: *religio . . . quae est iuncta cum cognitione naturae*; 2.148: *esse praestantem aliquam aeternamque naturam . . . pulchritudo mundi ordoque rerum caelestium cogit confiteri*. Compare the concluding paragraph of *Nat. D.*, mentioned in n. 39 above, and the placement of the *Somnium Scipionis* in *Rep.* For more detailed discussion of Cicero's theology, see 6.4. For the marginal role of physical theology in Varro's *ARD*, see 5.2.

relationship of individuals and the *res publica* to the universe as a whole and any divine beings within it.

To conclude this section, let us return to Cicero's speech about his house, a dramatic moment where we see the convergence of a number of the developments just described.[48] For all his moral outrage at the appropriation of his property, Cicero had to contend with the fact that the consecration of the shrine of Libertas was apparently legal, having been provided for in Clodius's legislation about Cicero's banishment.[49] In the best Ciceronian style, the speech touches on numerous tangential topics in an attempt to discredit Clodius before even coming to the main point.[50] Cicero's main argument relies on a law, the *lex Papiria de dedicationibus*, according to which dedications needed to be authorized by legislation (which that of Clodius was), with the dedicator specified by name (which Clodius was not; 127–37). Cicero cites as a precedent the case of one C. Cassius, who as censor in 154 wished to dedicate a statue of Concord in the senate house but was told by the pontiffs that unless personally authorized by the people, he had no right to do so. Taking Cicero's point, the *pontifices* in their judiciously worded response declared that if "he who claims to have made the dedication" had not been legally nominated to consecrate the area, *then* the piece of land could be returned to Cicero without religious offense.[51] Even though Clodius, supported by his brother Appius, tried to persuade the people that this meant that the pontiffs had decided in *his* favor, the senate sided with Cicero, and the sometime shrine of Libertas was restored to its previous owner.

The case demonstrates the close interconnectedness of the Roman political and religious spheres: the senate referred the issue to the *pontifices*, and the *pontifices* reported back to the senate, but of course, most of the *pontifices* were

---

48. On the speech, see esp. Stroh 2004 and Gildenhard 2011: 300–326, as well as Nisbet 1939; Goar 1972: 45–56; Classen 1985: 218–67; Bergemann 1992: 3–85; Tatum 1993a, 1999: 156–66, 187–93; Lennon 2010; North 2014b; MacRae 2016: 64–68; and Scheidegger Lämmle 2017.

49. On some of the legal issues, see Moreau 1987 and Tatum 1993b.

50. One of Cicero's contentions is that Clodius was never legally a tribune since his adoption into plebeian status was put into effect by a curiate assembly while Bibulus was "watching the sky," which meant that the decisions of the assembly had no force (39). Curiously, we learn that Clodius himself, in an apparent falling-out with Caesar, had on another occasion used Bibulus and his ongoing *spectio* to argue against the validity of the triumvir's legislation (a self-defeating strategy, one would think; 40).

51. Cic. *Att.* 4.2.3: *si neque populi iussu neque plebis scitu is qui se dedicasse diceret nominatim ei rei praefectus esset neque populi iussu aut plebis scitu id facere iussus esset, uideri posse sine religione eam partem areae mihi restitui.*

senators themselves.[52] Clodius's and Cicero's battle over the house/shrine is a further blatant example of the increased use of religion for personal political agendas, as we find the two enemies engaged in a veritable "rivalry in piety" (L. R. Taylor 1949: 89). Clodius in his own speech had presented himself as the upholder of religious propriety, pointing to the sanctity of a consecrated space.[53] Cicero, in turn, denounces his opponent's weaponization of *religio*, which he warns will lead to an end of the system of civic religion as he and the *pontifices* know it (2):

> uobis hodierno die constituendum est utrum posthac amentis ac perditos magistratus improborum ac sceleratorum ciuium praesidio nudare, an etiam deorum immortalium religione armare malitis. nam si illa labes ac flamma rei publicae suum illum pestiferum et funestum tribunatum, quem aequitate humana tueri non potest, diuina religione defenderit, aliae caeri-moniae nobis erunt, alii antistites deorum immortalium, alii interpretes religionum requirendi.

> You have to decide today whether from now on you wish to deprive crazed and depraved magistrates of the support of wicked and criminal citizens, or instead to arm them even with the *religio* of the immortal gods. For if that stain and conflagration of the commonwealth can uphold his pestilent and deadly tribunate, which he cannot defend by appealing to human justice, by means of divine *religio*, then we have to find other rituals, other priests of the immortal gods, other guides in religious matters.

The fight over the *res publica* hinges on who gets to control the religious narrative.

In this battle, antiquarian learning comes to play a role as well. Clodius had obviously done his religious homework, getting his consecration legally au-thorized and executing it properly with the assistance of a *pontifex*.[54] Cicero, however, was able to point to a flaw in Clodius's orthopraxy, pulling out of his hat the obscure case of C. Cassius.

---

52. Thanks to Cic. *Har. resp.* 12, we know the names of the thirteen members of the college (twelve of them senators) and six holders of other priesthoods who were present at the speech. For details, see Bergemann 1992: 25–35; on the political role of the *pontifices*, see North 2014b.

53. Cic. *Dom.* 127: "*dedicatio magnam,*" inquit, "*habet religionem.*" Cicero comments sarcastically, "you'd think Numa Pompilius were speaking" (*nonne uobis Numa Pompilius uidetur loqui?,* 127).

54. Cicero delights in pointing out that this pontiff, L. Pinarius Natta, was Clodius's brother-in-law and had only recently joined the college, and in alleging that he was therefore clueless and not up to the job. He imagines the two men fumbling the ceremony, hence rendering it invalid (134–35, 139–41). See further n. 65 below.

How did Cicero know about this century-old incident? He himself informs the *pontifices* that this *responsum* can be found "in your books."[55] Little is known about the written records of the pontifical college, which our sources refer to as *libri* or *commentarii* and which have been much discussed in scholarship.[56] It is likely that the pontiffs maintained a collection of their official *responsa*, but it is unlikely that this would have been accessible to an outsider like Cicero. Wilfried Stroh proposes that "Cicero probably had it [the *responsum* concerning Cassius] leaked to him by one of the pontifices" (2004: 328). By contrast, John North suggests the case may have been cited as a precedent in a *senatus consultum* of 123 BCE, which Cicero presented in court immediately after his discussion of Cassius and which concerned the case of an unauthorized dedication by a Vestal Virgin.[57] Cicero's reference to the priests' *commentarii* would then be simply a rhetorical gesture at autopsy, while in reality the speaker had never inspected the pontifical archives himself.

Alternatively, it has been attractively suggested that Cicero learned about Cassius's failed dedication from a work of religious antiquarianism, perhaps from one of the works about pontifical law mentioned above (n. 33) or from a similar text.[58] Someone else, quite possibly a pontiff himself, had done the research and made available to a wider public within the learned elite some part of the record of pontifical responses. As a result, men intent on positioning themselves in the religio-political landscape of Rome, or on justifying their own religious actions and interpretations, were able to get a much better sense of precedent and hence of their own options.[59]

---

55. *Dom.* 136: *in commentariis uestris.* Throughout the speech, Cicero keeps asserting that he lacks pontifical insider knowledge and would not dream of encroaching on the pontiffs' area of expertise (32–34, 121–22, 128, 138). To some extent, this is an example of the modesty topos (Cicero in reality knows more than he lets on yet politely pretends his ignorance), but it is also a hint on the part of the orator that one needs not have studied pontifical law to figure out the rights and wrongs of this case (see further below in the text).

56. See Linderski 1985, Beard 1991: 56–58, North 1998, Scheid 2006, Santangelo 2011a: 175–78, and MacRae 2017.

57. See North 1998: 47–49. Finding historical decrees of the senate (which were kept in the *aerarium*) was easier than accessing the archives of the priestly colleges, but still necessitated a fair amount of research effort; see Culham 1989.

58. Thus Linderski 1985: 220–22 and MacRae 2016: 64–68.

59. The late Republic saw a number of politically motivated attempts at reviving archaic sacral and legal procedures, knowledge of which was likely promoted by antiquarian literature. These include the trial of C. Rabirius for *perduellio* in 63, whose driving forces were Caesar and his relative L. Caesar, the author of studies on augury (see Fuhrmann 1987: 131–34 on the trial's probable inspiration in historical or antiquarian writing), and various attempts at *consecratio*

Varro in his *Antiquitates rerum diuinarum* declared that he wanted to teach his countrymen which gods they might profitably invoke in which situation (fr. 3 Cardauns), while Cicero praised his friend for making the Romans feel at home in their own city by providing them with the knowledge of, among other things, "the law of rites and priests" and "the practices of war and peace."[60] This homecoming, whose benefits Cicero describes as purely cognitive—the Romans are "finally able to understand who and where [they] are"[61]—may also take on a practical aspect as the writers and readers of antiquarian literature learn about purportedly time-honored ways of doing things in a properly Roman way. Since political and religious practices were, as we have seen, inextricably intertwined; since, furthermore, much antiquarian work was concerned with the minutiae of ritual orthopraxy; and since issues of religious legitimacy and divine support carried particular weight in a time of political crisis, the study of Roman civic religion was not a purely intellectual pursuit on the part of pedantic sticklers for orthopraxy, but had the potential of packing a real political punch. Men like Clodius, Cicero, and Caesar had read their books on pontifical and augural law and tried to put what they had found there into practice. In the political "rivalry in piety," it mattered who had the better sources.[62]

To return to *De domo sua*, it was clearly Cicero's ability to suggest a technical flaw in Clodius's dedication and to produce a pontifical *responsum* as precedent that made it possible for the *pontifices* to decide the case in his favor. Disproving Clodius's ritual correctness, however, was not the only strategy of the speech. For, obviously, Cicero's main objection to the consecration of his house was not that Clodius had committed a minor procedural error. The real

---

bonorum, a tribune's dedication to the gods of a malefactor's possessions (see Cic. *Dom.* 123–25; the very period of the speech saw what Cicero makes sound like a farcical case of tit-for-tat *consecratio*, with Clodius attempting to expropriate Gabinius and L. Ninnius in turn trying to consecrate Clodius's goods).

60. Cic. *Acad. post.* 9: *tu sacrorum iura tu sacerdotum tu domesticam tu bellicam disciplinam . . . aperuisti.* On Varro's concern specifically with sacral law, see MacRae 2017.

61. Cic. *Acad. post.* 9: *ut possemus aliquando qui et ubi essemus agnoscere.*

62. The same was true for other aspects of public business. Thus, Varro wrote a treatise on senatorial procedure for the use of Pompey, when the latter became consul in 70 BCE (on this work, later reissued for Octavian's reform of the senate in the early 20s, see Todisco 2017). We also have an example of Varro in his own political life sticking to what he had determined to be correct practice, even against current usage: since tribunes of the people did not technically have the right of *uocatio*, that is, of summoning other people, Varro himself refused a tribune's attempted summons and, when tribune himself, never summoned anyone (Gell. *NA* 13.12.6 = Varro, *ARH* 21 fr. 2 Mirsch).

outrage was that a wicked man had abused religion to hurt his personal opponent and further his rabble-rousing political agenda, and Clodius's actions were outrageous whether he had adhered to strict orthopraxy or not.[63] Thus, Cicero states:[64]

> equidem sic accepi, pontifices, in religionibus suscipiendis caput esse interpretari quae uoluntas deorum immortalium esse uideatur; nec est ulla erga deos pietas <nisi sit> honesta de numine eorum ac mente opinio, ut expeti nihil ab iis, quod sit iniustum atque inhonestum, <iustum aut honestum> arbitrere.

> Indeed, pontiffs, I have been told that in the execution of religious obligations it is crucial to determine what the wish of the immortal gods appears to be. There is therefore no real piety as long as one does not have an honorable conception of their divine power and will. One must thus not consider it just and honorable to ask of them anything that is unjust and dishonorable.

Cicero disguises his observation as an established truism (*sic accepi*) but in fact presents a "revolutionary theology" (Gildenhard 2011: 319) at odds with the orthopractic underpinnings of the state cult. What matters in religion is the will of the gods; the gods are the upholders of justice and morality; and it is therefore impossible to employ a religious ritual (however correctly executed) in the service of something unjust and immoral. Even if Clodius had availed himself of the most recondite pontifical know-how and had had the best experts preside over his dedication, "nevertheless there would be no religious force in a crime."[65] The gods, so Cicero, had no desire to move into Clodius's so-called shrine (*Dom.* 107, 141); the dedication therefore has no validity.

That the gods are guarantors of justice was a well-established tenet of Roman popular morality,[66] and presumably one of the implicit beliefs that

---

63. For what follows, see the brilliant reading of the speech in Gildenhard 2011: 300–326, esp. 315–23, though note that the basic interpretation is already found in Tatum 1993a.

64. Cic. *Dom.* 107. The transmitted text of this passage is clearly corrupt. I print the supplements adopted in the *OCT* (Peterson 1911).

65. Cic. *Dom.* 139: *tamen in scelere religio non ualeret*. As Gildenhard 2011: 322–23 shows, Cicero combines this call for orthodoxy with the traditional stress on orthopraxy when he claims that it was *because* of his unholy intentions that Clodius—crazed by the gods—made a mess of the consecration ritual itself (*Dom.* 139–41). See also Lennon 2010 on the language of ritual pollution associated with Clodius throughout the speech.

66. See North 2014b: 75–76, offering a caveat to Gildenhard's interpretation. See further Liebeschuetz 1979: 39–54 and T. Morgan 2007: 207–11, index s.v. "gods."

underlay the state religion (of course, the just gods could be expected to further the inherently just actions of the *res publica*). What Cicero does is make the implicit explicit, elevating justice and morality to the sole criterion (*caput*) of *pietas*, and putting civic religion on its head by demonstrating that there can be no orthopraxy without orthodoxy. In doing so, he is exemplifying the fourth late Republican religious development laid out above, showing himself to be inspired by philosophical ideas of the divine as an entity of perfect moral goodness, whose worshipers accordingly need to exhibit a morally correct inner disposition.

The same thought can be found in *De legibus*, where Cicero provides an archaic religious lawcode in archaic style, but imbues it with new, philosophically informed meaning. The first ritual provision is *ad diuos adeunto caste* "let [worshipers] approach the gods in purity" (2.19). Traditionally, this would denote ritual purity, that is, the correct dress, proper execution of any cleansing rituals, and the like. As the speaker Marcus Cicero explains, however, that is not his primary intention:[67]

> caste iubet lex adire ad deos, animo uidelicet in quo sunt omnia. nec tollit castimoniam corporis, sed hoc oportet intellegi, cum multum animus corpori praestet obserueturque ut casto corpore adeatur, multo esse in animis id seruandum magis. nam illud uel aspersione aquae uel dierum numero tollitur, animi labes nec diuturnitate euanescere nec amnibus ullis elui potest.

> The law orders us to approach the gods in purity—of the mind, of course, in which everything resides. It doesn't exclude purity of the body, but it is understood that, given that the mind is far superior to the body and one needs to approach with a pure body, this provision must be observed even more in the case of the mind. For impurity of body can be removed by a splash of water or the passage of a fixed number of days, but the stain of the mind will not fade in eternity or be washed away by any river.

Orthopraxy is fine, but it is the worshiper's mental and moral disposition that really counts. This comes very close to what the Stoic Balbus has to say in *De natura deorum*: "the best worship of the gods . . . is always to venerate them with pure, unblemished, and uncompromised mind and words."[68]

In the matter of Cicero's house, we are not surprised to learn that the person who exhibits this right disposition toward the gods and is accordingly favored

---

67. Cic. *Leg.* 2.24; cf. Dyck 2004a ad loc. and Gildenhard 2011: 347–49.

68. Cic. *Nat. D.* 2.71: *cultus autem deorum est optumus idemque castissimus atque sanctissimus plenissimusque pietatis ut eos semper pura integra incorrupta et mente et uoce ueneremur.*

by them is none other than Cicero himself. The gods themselves have brought about the speaker's recall from exile,[69] and in an emotional prayer that is crafted as a single period and takes up nearly an entire *OCT* page, Cicero reminds them of a solemn vow (*deuotio*) that he had made to them when driven out of Rome:[70]

> uos sum testatus, uobis me ac meos commendaui, meque atque meum caput ea condicione deuoui ut, si et eo ipso tempore et ante in consulatu meo commodis meis omnibus, emolumentis, praemiis praetermissis cura cogitatione uigiliis omnibus nihil nisi de salute meorum ciuium laborassem, tum mihi re publica aliquando restituta liceret frui, sin autem mea consilia patriae non profuissent, ut perpetuum dolorem auulsus a meis sustinerem.

> I called you to witness, entrusted myself and my family to you, and solemnly bound myself and my life on the following condition: *if* at that moment and earlier during my consulate I had neglected my own comfort, advantages, and rewards and with every care, thought, and watchfulness had labored for the safety of my fellow citizens, *then* I should at some point be allowed to enjoy a restored commonwealth; *but if* my counsels had not been beneficial to the fatherland, *then* I should suffer eternal pain torn away from my nearest and dearest.

The grand gesture of the *deuotio* leaves it up to the gods to decide whether the suppliant has fulfilled the conditions that ought to grant his salvation, laying a heavy curse on him in the event that he has not. Cicero is obviously confident that he has acted virtuously for the benefit of the *res publica* and that, by this logic, the gods are on his side. The ball is now in the court of the *pontifices*, whose task it is to execute the will of the gods and to reward Cicero for his virtuous behavior. A case that started out as legal quibbling over ritual correctness has turned into arbitration in a fight between good and evil.

The conflicts of the last years of the Republic were ultimately decided on the battlefield, but they also involved heated contests over divine favor and cosmic legitimation. The various new forms of knowledge that learned senators had acquired during their *studia* served them in staking out their own religious positions and attacking those of their opponents. In what follows, we will consider how three men of exceptional intellectual ability and originality made use of their scientific and theological learning at a time when fast-moving

---

69. Cic. *Dom.* 143: *diuino me numine esse rei publicae redditum.*

70. Cic. *Dom.* 145. Cicero mentions this vow also at *Red. pop.* 1. On the logic of *deuotio*, see Nisbet 1939: 212–14. Dyck 2004b is mistaken in viewing Cicero's vow as an example of *deuotio ducis*, by which a general sacrifices his own life in exchange for the victory of his army.

political events forced members of the Roman upper classes continuously to adjust their beliefs, words, and deeds to an ever-changing reality.

2. *Pythagoricus et magus*

In his *Chronicle*, Jerome informs us that in 45 BCE "Nigidius Figulus dies in exile."[71] As far as we can tell from our meager sources, this Roman senator had always been an aggressive optimate: during the Catilinarian conspiracy, he supported Cicero both in public and in private; in 60, he pushed for the prosecution of the corrupt C. Antonius Hybrida; his energetic handling of his praetorship in 58 earned Cicero's praise; and he entered the Civil War against Caesar at an early date, possibly fighting with Domitius Ahenobarbus in Italy before joining up with Pompey.[72] Accordingly, Nigidius found himself in exile after Pharsalus, and while a cautiously worded letter from Cicero of 46 holds out the hope of an ultimate pardon (*Fam.* 4.13), Jerome's notice makes it clear that by Nigidius's death the following year, no Caesarian clemency had been extended.

As so often in his post–Civil War letters to fellow Pompeians (see 4.1), Cicero reminds Nigidius of the consolations available to him from his *studia*, *artes*, and *ingenium*, which he believes will enable his correspondent to bear his misfortune "with wisdom."[73] Within the world of late Republican learned senators, however, Nigidius is not simply yet another upperclass man with lively intellectual interests or the occasional treatise to his name. In the opinion of Aulus Gellius, the late Republic excelled in "the manifold forms of learning and the various arts by which *humanitas* is fostered." The "pillars" of this kind of study were Varro and Nigidius, two men Gellius considers "the most learned of the Roman race."[74] Servius too informs us that Nigidius ranks immediately below Varro;[75] the sole reason his works are less widely read than those of his contemporary is (again according to Gellius, 19.14.3) their *obscuritas subtilitasque*.

---

71. Jer. *Ab Abr.* 156.25–26 Helm: *Nigidius Figulus in exilio moritur.*

72. On Nigidius, see Kroll 1936 (with full documentation); Della Casa 1962; Rawson 1985: 123–24, 181–83, 291–92, 309–12; Musial 2001; Ducos 2005; and Flinterman 2014: 343–46. My discussion in this section expands on Volk 2016b: 45–49, 2017: 342–47.

73. See Cic. *Fam.* 4.13.4: *studia ... artes quibus a pueritia floruisti*; 7: *ingenio studioque; quae accident, qualiacumque erunt, sapienter feres.*

74. Gell. *NA* 19.14.1: *aetas M. Ciceronis et C. Caesaris ... doctrinarum autem multiformium uariarumque artium, quibus humanitas erudita est, columina habuit M. Varronem et P. Nigidium*; 4.16.1: *M. Varronem et P. Nigidium, uiros Romani generis doctissimos* (cf. 4.9.1). See also 10.11.2; 11.11.1; 13.10.4; 15.3.5; 17.7.4 for praise of Nigidius's learning without reference to Varro.

75. Serv. *ad Aen.* 10.175: *Nigidius autem solus est post Varronem.*

It is indeed the case that, while Nigidius's publications were wide-ranging in topic and prolific in extent, they have fared poorly by comparison even with Varro's ravaged oeuvre: only about 130 fragments survive, many of them very short.[76] The erudite but luckless senator might thus come across as a kind of second-class Varro: not quite as learned, not quite as successful as an author, and—we might add—not quite as adept at navigating the political vicissitudes of his time. There is, however, an aspect of Nigidius's life and work that sets him apart from his fellow polymath and makes him stand out from the contemporary society of learned Roman aristocrats.[77] What renders Nigidius unusual is evoked in the moniker that Jerome affixes to him in his death notice: strikingly, he labels the late Republican senator a "Pythagorean and sorcerer" (*Pythagoricus et magus*).

What does that mean? Nigidius's Pythagoreanism is attested elsewhere. Most notably, Cicero in the set-up of his fragmentary *Timaeus* introduces Nigidius, one of the dialogue's interlocutors, by praising his intellectual abilities and pursuits as follows:[78]

> fuit enim uir ille cum ceteris artibus quae quidem dignae libero essent ornatus omnibus, tum acer inuestigator et diligens earum rerum quae a natura inuolutae uidentur. denique sic iudico post illos nobiles Pythagoreos quorum disciplina exstincta est quodam modo cum aliquot saecula in Italia Siciliaque uiguisset, hunc exstitisse qui illam renouaret.

> For he was not only accomplished in all the other arts that are worthy of a free man, but also a keen and careful investigator of those matters that seem to have been concealed by nature. Finally, I believe that after those noble Pythagoreans, whose teaching somehow fell into disuse after going strong for some centuries in Italy and Sicily, this man came onto the scene to renew it.

Within the *Timaeus*, a major reason Cicero highlights Nigidius's Pythagoreanism is presumably the fact that he is subsequently made to utter the author's partial translation of the speech of Timaeus from Plato's dialogue: the Platonic Timaeus was often thought to have been a Pythagorean, and it therefore makes sense for a Roman adherent of the same sect to proclaim his cosmological views.

76. Nigidius's fragments have been edited by Swoboda 1889 and Liuzzi 1983; all Nigidian fragments in this section are cited from Swoboda's edition.

77. Cf. Kroll 1936: 210: "Umfang und Charakter der Studien des N. geht über das, was damals bei einem römischen Senator üblich war, erheblich hinaus."

78. Cic. *Tim.* 1. Cicero speaks of Nigidius in the perfect, which means that by the time of composition, Nigidius must have been dead. On the *Timaeus* and the problems of its date and interpretation, see Lévy 2003, Sedley 2013, and Hoenig 2018: 38–101.

Beyond this Ciceronian homage, all we learn about Nigidius's Pythagorean leanings is that he allegedly gathered around him a group of like-minded followers (*Schol. Bob. Cic. Vat.* 14):

> fuit autem illis temporibus Nigidius quidam, uir doctrina et eruditione studiorum praestantissimus, ad quem plurimi conueniebant. haec ab obtrectatoribus ueluti factio minus probabilis iactitabatur, quamuis ipsi Pythagorae sectatores existimari uellent.

> There lived at this time a certain Nigidius, a man outstanding in his learning and studies, who was sought out by many. This association was attacked by critics as if it were an objectionable cabal, though they themselves wanted to be considered followers of Pythagoras.

This may be the same circle that in the pseudo-Ciceronian *Invective against Sallust* is referred to tendentiously as the *sodalicium sacrilegi Nigidiani* ("brotherhood of Nigidian sacrilege," 14), a coterie the speaker claims was frequented also by the future historian maligned in the speech.[79] As these texts show, late Republican "Pythagoreanism" and especially purported Pythagorean group activities could be construed as either praise- or blameworthy. Tellingly, in his speech against Vatinius of 56 BCE, Cicero viciously attacked his opponent's Pythagorean allegiance, accusing him of engaging in magic practices and even child sacrifice; when two years later, he was forced to defend Vatinius, he presented his client's philosophical leanings as something in his favor.[80]

The sources cited in the last two paragraphs present more or less our grand total of evidence not only for Nigidius's Pythagoreanism, but for Pythagoreanism in the late Republic in general. This has not prevented scholars from constructing sometimes positively fantastic narratives of a Roman Pythagorean movement, in which Nigidius appears not infrequently as the "grand master" of what is presented as a secret order.[81] In reality, we know very little about

79. See, however, Santangelo 2011b on various problems, both textual and contextual, with seeing a reference to Nigidius's Pythagorean activities in this passage. Since pseudo-Cicero in the sentence immediately following mentions that Sallust was twice prosecuted in court, scholars have posited that this had to do with his membership in the mysterious *sodalicium*, and that Nigidius too was brought to trial for his purported *sacrilegium* (the case is tentatively listed as No. 278 in Alexander 1990). See Musial 2001: 350–58; Rives 2005, 2006: 63–64; and Santangelo 2011b on why such a scenario is highly unlikely.

80. Blame: Cic. *Vat.* 14; praise: *Schol. Bob. Cic. Vat.* 14.

81. See, e.g., Gianola 1905; Carcopino 1927; Legrand 1931; Ferrero 1955; Della Casa 1962; Freyburger-Galland, Freyburger, and Tautil 1986: 207–35 (quotation at 213: "Nigidius Figulus fut un grand maître de l'Ordre"); Ternes (ed.) 1998; and D'Anna 2007: 65–88, 2008.

what such apparently self-declared Pythagoreans as Vatinius and Nigidius believed or practiced, and the nature of Nigidius's supposed *sodalicium*— surely at best a loose group of like-minded individuals rather than a formal organization—must remain unclear.[82] As it happens, none of the fragments of Nigidius appear to be informed by specifically Pythagorean doctrine,[83] quite unlike the Varronian corpus, where we find a fair number of references to Pythagorean concepts and ideas.[84]

Unlike other philosophical schools, which had an institutional structure and a more or less fixed doctrine laid down in the works of their founders and their successors, Pythagoreanism was largely an invented tradition, in which over time a wide variety of theories and practices became attached to a revered and near-mythical founding figure, and in which individuals could fashion themselves, or be fashioned by their contemporaries or later sources, as initiates into a wisdom hidden from ordinary mortals. Nigidius's "Pythagoreanism" may have been a carefully thought-out philosophical doctrine, or it may simply have been a convenient shorthand to describe his manifold interests in "those matters that seem to have been concealed by nature," as Cicero put it.[85]

Something similar is true for Jerome's second designation, that of *magus*. It is typically assumed that Jerome derived his biographical information and descriptors from Suetonius's *De uiris illustribus*,[86] and his language thus reflects the sensibilities of the second century CE, when a *magus* could be understood to be a hands-on practitioner of "magic," in the broad sense of "a manipulative strategy to influence the course of nature by supernatural . . . means."[87] As historians of religion and magic have shown, however, this understanding of

82. For more sober assessments of late Republican Pythagoreanism and Nigidius's role, see Burkert 1961: 236–46; Rawson 1985: 291–95; Musial 2001, Flinterman 2014: 343–46; Volk 2016b, 2017: 342–47; and Thibodeau 2018. Ancient sources are collected by Horky forthcoming.

83. Pythagorean provenance has often been claimed for Nigidius's linguistic thought, as expressed in his extensive *Commentarii grammatici* (see esp. Della Casa 1962: 55–99); as Garcea 2019 shows, however, there is no basis for this assumption, and Stoic influence is far more likely.

84. This does not mean that Varro was a card-carrying Pythagorean and member of Nigidius's "circle," as maintained, e.g., by Ferrero 1955: 319–34 and Lehmann 1998. See Cardauns 2001: 70–71 for a down-to-earth assessment of Pythagorean elements in Varro's work and Horky forthcoming for a collection of sources.

85. This is the minimalist thesis of Thibodeau 2018: 603–4, who argues that throughout Roman scientific history, "Pythagorean" was simply used as a label "to provide a veneer of respectability for innovative research" (604).

86. See esp. Della Casa 1962: 9–36. Jerome's notice accordingly features as Suet. fr. 85* Reifferscheid.

87. Thus the working definition of Versnel 2012: 884.

magic was only beginning to develop in first-century BCE Rome and did not fully establish itself until the Imperial period, when we find the elder Pliny both theorizing magic and inveighing against it.[88] In the late Republic, by contrast, when the noun *magus* is first used by Cicero and Catullus, it still—in keeping with its origin—refers exclusively to a Persian priest or diviner.[89]

As it happens, Nigidius mentions the *magi* a couple of times in his surviving work[90] and, as we will see, may have engaged in forms of divination that were believed to be of Persian origin. James Rives thus attractively suggests that *magus* could have been a nickname his contemporaries attached to Nigidius, just as Appius Claudius Pulcher was called a "Pisidian" or a "Soran" by his fellow augurs, in allusion to two territories notorious for their superstition.[91] Be that as it may, we can conclude that the designations *Pythagoricus* and *magus* tell us less about the specifics of Nigidius's studies and activities than about a certain aura of mystery that surrounded the learned senator both in his own lifetime and in later periods, even if the two terms would have conjured up rather different ideas for, say, a Cicero than for a Suetonius, let alone a Jerome.[92] To use a more recent analogy, Nigidius Figulus comes across as a kind of "Roman Dr. Faustus" (Cramer 1954: 64), a seeker for arcane wisdom ready to apply his theoretical insights to the practical exigencies of his own life and times. It is time to have a closer look at what we can resconstruct of his works and actions.

Nigidius's oeuvre comprised treatises on grammar (*Commentarii grammatici*), biology (*De hominum naturalibus, De animalibus*), theology (*De dis*), astronomy (*Sphaera Graecanica, Sphaera barbarica*), meteorology (*De uento*), and various forms of divination (*De augurio priuato, De extis, De somniis*, and an adaptation of an Etruscan calendar of thunder omens). What is immediately striking is the nonantiquarian nature of the corpus: unlike, say, Varro, Nigidius was apparently interested not so much in reconstructing the manmade world of Roman *consuetudo* as in determining—in the words of Goethe's

---

88. See esp. Plin. *HN* 30.1–18. For the history of the Roman conceptualization of magic, see Garosi 1976, Le Glay 1976, Graf 1997: 36–60, and Beard, North, and Price 1998: 1.153–57.

89. See Graf 1997: 36–37.

90. Frr. 67, 127. Fr. 67 cites the *magi* explicitly, while frr. 126–28 are quoted by Pliny in the context of discussions of the views of the *magi* (see Dickie 1999: 171–72).

91. See Rives 2005, with reference to Cic. *Div.* 1.105. For Appius, see 6.1 with n. 35. A possible problem with the nickname hypothesis is that the designation *Pythagoricus et magus* is used once more by Jerome, of Anaxilaus of Larissa, the author of a collection of magical tricks, who was banished from Rome and Italy by Augustus in 28 BC (Jer. *Ab Abr.* 163.26–164.2 Helm; cf. Dickie 1999, who discusses both Anaxilaus and Nigidius as examples of the type of the "learned magician" in antiquity).

92. Compare Mayer i Olivé 2012.

Faust—"was die Welt im Innersten zusammenhält,"[93] that is, the hidden order of the real world. His *De dis* apparently treated exactly what Varro had relegated to the marginal and tentative books 14–16 of his *Antiquitates rerum diuinarum*: rather than dealing with antiquities, Nigidius concerned himself with the nature of the gods themselves. The author also comes across as far less Romanocentric than Varro, adducing theological theories attributed to "Orpheus" and the *magi* (fr. 67), as well as the *disciplina Etrusca* (fr. 56). Detailed knowledge of Etruscan forms of divination as well as the Etruscan language can be inferred from Nigidius's work on extispicy and the Etruscan thunder calendar, while his *Sphaera* not only relates Near Eastern star myths, but in addition to the Greco-Roman constellations lists "barbarian," that is, Mesopotamian and Egyptian ones.[94]

Nigidius's surviving fragments and the *testimonia* about his life do not allow us to reconstruct a coherent world-view, but a number of leitmotifs emerge. Drawing from a wide range of sources, the learned author was apparently particularly interested in physics and theology, presenting—we may conjecture—a divinely ordered cosmos. This sense of natural order is apparent even from Nigidius's grammatical writings, whose most famous fragment provides an argument from phonetics for why linguistic signification is a matter of nature and not convention: in pronouncing such first-person pronouns as *nos, ego,* and *mihi*, we direct our breath and organs of speech toward ourselves, while the second-person *uos, tu,* and *tibi* involve a movement toward the addressee.[95]

If the universe can thus be seen to be arranged in a comprehensible and meaningful manner, and if the divine is behind or implicit in this system, a logical next step is the assumption that nature can be read as a system of signs and that divination is possible. We do not possess any indication that Nigidius discussed this matter from a theoretical point of view (though he may well have done so), but to judge from the transmitted titles of his works, he treated such diverse methods of prophecy as extispicy and thunder omens (both associated with the *disciplina Etrusca*), the practice of augury for private purposes (Romano-Etruscan), dream interpretation (prevalent throughout the ancient Mediterranean and Near East), and astrology (of Near Eastern origin but newly popular in Rome).[96] Of course, the scholarly discussion of divination need not imply any belief in the veracity of such practices on the

93. J. W. von Goethe, *Faust* 1, vv. 382–83: "what holds the world together in its inner core."

94. Myths: frr. 98–99; constellations: frr. 102–3. On Nigidius's *Sphaera*, see the seminal work of Boll 1903: 349–63.

95. See fr. 41 with the discussion of Garcea 2019.

96. As Boll 1903: 349–63 shows, the constellations in Nigidius's *Sphaera* were discussed as *paranatellonta*, i.e., in the context of their rising and setting together with the signs of the zodiac, and thus for their astrological significance.

part of the author, as, for example, the noncommittal *in utramque partem* debate in Cicero's *De diuinatione* shows. In Nigidius, however, we encounter not just an author of learned treatises on various forms of prediction making: we meet a late Republican elite man who in our sources is credited on more than one occasion with having practiced fairly spectacular forms of divination himself.

The first piece of evidence comes from Apuleius's *Apology*, where the speaker relates an anecdote that he says he has read in Varro (42):[97]

> Fabium, cum quingentos denarium perdidisset, ad Nigidium consultum uenisse; ab eo pueros carmine instinctos indicauisse ubi locorum defossa esset crumina cum parti eorum, ceteri ut forent distributi. unum etiam denarium ex eo numero habere M. Catonem philosophum; quem se a pedisequo in stipe Apollinis accepisse Cato confessus est.

> When Fabius had lost 500 denarii, he went to consult Nigidius. Nigidius hypnotized some boys by means of a spell, who revealed where the purse with a part of the coins was buried and how the others had been distributed. [They said that] M. Cato the philosopher had one of them, and Cato admitted that he had received it from a servant as an offering for Apollo.

Among the striking aspects of this story is its quotidian upperclass setting. Fabius would appear to be a member of the *gens Fabia*, possibly Q. Fabius Maximus (cos. 45);[98] unable to account for the disappearance of his money, he decides to employ the handy skills of his fellow senator. In a hilarious twist, even the stern Cato is involved, finding himself unwittingly in the possession of one of the coins, apparently in his function as *XVuir sacris faciundis*. Perhaps the thief meant to appease Apollo (or otherwise thank him for his support?) by means of a donation.

Nigidius's method of determining the whereabouts of the money is one of the very first attested ancient cases of divination by child medium, a practice by which a child is brought into a trance through the directions of an adult practitioner and is subsequently able to issue predictions or answer questions.[99] Typically, hypnosis is combined with "gazing," as the child is made to

---

97. Apul. *Apol.* 42: *memini me apud Varronem philosophum ... legere.* It is unclear from which Varronian work Apuleius derived his information; the *logisticus Curio de cultu deorum* has been suggested (see the discussion of the work's fr. 4 below), though Cardauns 1960: 45–50 remains skeptical.

98. See Cardauns 1960: 47.

99. On this practice, see Johnston 2001. Maras 2019: 64–65 suggests a connection with the role of children in Etruscan divination. The suggestion of Mevoli 1992 that the *pueri* were simply Fabius's slaves, whom Nigidius interrogated, seems wide of the mark.

look into a bowl that contains a substance such as water or fire, in order to descry either images or otherwise gods, demons, or other prophesying entities. Apuleius does not mention any gazing in connection with Nigidius's boys, but immediately before this story he relates another tale from Varro: when the town of Tralles used a child medium to learn about the outcome of the Mithridatic War, "the boy gazed at an image of Mercury in the water and sang about the future in 160 verses."[100] It is thus likely that the boys who found Fabius's money also received their prophetic information by means of gazing.

A scenario in which, at the behest of one Roman senator, another casts a spell on children and then tries to discern their utterances as, in their trance, they stare into a bowl may strike us as unexpected and not quite in keeping with how we have come to imagine the genteel learned sociability of the late Republican elite. To some extent, Nigidius is an outlier, and we will encounter more examples of his intellectual idiosyncracies presently. There are, however, some indications that divination by child medium and bowl gazing—the technical term for which is "lecanomancy"—were rather more widespread among the Roman upper classes than one might have imagined.

Consider what Augustine tells us about Varro's version of the prophecies Numa Pompilius allegedly received from his lover, the nymph Egeria. In a rationalizing reinterpretation of the traditional story, Varro maintains that the king only pretended to have access to a nymph, while in reality he received his inspiration through hydromancy, that is, gazing into a bowl of water:[101]

Numa ... hydromantian facere compulsus est ut in aqua uideret imagines deorum ... a quibus audiret quid in sacris constituere atque obseruare deberet. quod genus diuinationis idem Varro a Persis dicit allatum, quo et ipsum Numam et postea Pythagoram philosophum usum fuisse commemorat; ubi adhibito sanguine etiam inferos perhibet sciscitari et νεκυομαντείαν Graece dicit uocari.

Numa was forced to practice hydromancy in order to see in the water images of the gods, who told him what he ought to establish and observe in matters of cult. Varro says that this kind of divination was imported from the Persians and that both Numa and later the philosopher Pythagoras made use of it. He reports that if one uses blood in addition, one can also question the dead and that this is called necromancy in Greek.

100. Apul. *Apol.* 42: *Trallibus de euentu Mithridatici belli magica percontatione consultantibus puerum in aqua simulacrum Mercuri contemplantem quae futura erant CLX uersibus cecinisse.*

101. August. *De civ. D.* 7.35 = Varro, *Curio* fr. 4 Cardauns; for discussion, see Cardauns 1960 ad loc.

Varro replaces the old wives' tale of Numa's assignations with Egeria with an (apparently in his eyes) more plausible account involving the state-of-the-art prophetic technique of bowl divination. The practice is associated with both the Persians and Pythagoras, the two intellectual ancestors that we have seen claimed for Nigidius.[102] Engaging in lecanomancy, as Nigidius appears to have done, might easily give a man the reputation of being *Pythagoricus et magus*.

In addition to run-of-the-mill prophecy, however, Varro tells us that bowl gazing can also be used for the purpose of conjuring up the dead. The combined use of a child medium and lecanomancy was indeed an established necromantic method, and when Cicero tells us that Appius Claudius Pulcher engaged in such practices, this is probably what we ought to imagine.[103] Similarly, when Cicero in his speech inveighs against Vatinius's self-declared Pythagoreanism, he accuses him of participating in "unheard-of and wicked rituals," which involve "summoning up the souls of the dead and sacrificing to the gods of the underworld using children's innards."[104] The orator here is victim to—or otherwise makes cynical use of—a typical misconstruction of necromantic practicalities: the use of children as mediums could give rise to hysterical tales of child sacrifice, a time-honored accusation against suspicious religious groups well known from later cases of agitation against Jews, Christians, or Muslims.[105]

It is this passage of Cicero's speech against Vatinius that elicits the scholion quoted above, with its information about like-minded "Pythagoreans" flocking to Nigidius (*Schol. Bob. Cic. Vat.* 14). While the evidence is patchy and partly tendentious, it has still allowed us to determine that there existed among the late Republican elite a practical interest in divination via child medium-cum-lecanomancy, whether for necromantic or more mundane purposes (Nigidius, Vatinius, Appius). Such practices were theorized as both Persian and Pythagorean (Varro), and there also appear to have been certain individuals who identified as Pythagorean (Nigidius, Vatinius). Finally, if we trust the scholiast, also taking into account what Cicero says in the *Timaeus*, Nigidius took on a particularly active role in this "movement." Needless to say, this does not give us license to reconstruct, say, regular séances at the house of Nigidius in the company of the likes of Appius or Vatinius (or even Sallust?), let alone other organized activities. Nevertheless, we have been able to catch a glance

---

102. Hydromancy is associated with Persia and the *magi* also at Strabo 16.2.39 and Plin. *HN* 30.14.

103. See Ogden 2001: 149–51 for necromancy in the late Republic and 191–201 for the combination of bowl gazing and use of child mediums. For Appius, see 6.1 with n. 35 above.

104. Cic. *Vat.* 14: *cum inaudita ac nefaria sacra susceperis, cum inferorum animas elicere, cum puerorum extis deos manis mactare soleas.*

105. See Ogden 2001: 191–201.

of late Republican intellectual life that goes beyond the sedate Ciceronian philosophical-discussion-at-the-villa model to which we are accustomed.

In the case of Fabius's lost denarii, Nigidius deployed an elaborate divinatory apparatus to solve an everyday problem. Other prophecies ascribed to the *Pythagoricus et magus*, however, are directly linked to the political events of the time and developments that the conservative senator could only view with alarm. Rather than as a hypnotizer of children, Nigidius has gone down in history as an astrologer, as seen prominently in the anecdote about how he received his *cognomen*.[106] In order to demonstrate why twins, though born in quick succession, nevertheless have different fates, Nigidius dipped his finger in ink and twice touched a spinning potter's wheel. Once the wheel was stopped, the marks were found far apart—just as, Nigidius explained, the situation in the rotating heavens changes significantly between the birth of one twin and the other. As a result, Nigidius received the nickname *figulus* "potter."[107]

As his *Sphaera* demonstrates, Nigidius was well versed in the astral sciences, and he is associated in our sources with two stunning predictions concerning current events and the future of the *res publica*. Unfortunately, both prophecies raise strong suspicions of being apocryphal, constructed in hindsight and fathered on a man well known for his divinatory interests and activities. Thus it is unlikely that, when casting the horoscope of a child born to his fellow senator Octavius, Nigidius shocked the unsuspecting father by telling him that the "master" (*dominus*) of the world had been born—a prediction borne out later when the boy became famous as Augustus.[108] The story is reported by both Suetonius and Dio as part of a series of omens and prophecies concerning the birth and childhood of Octavian and would originally have been spread in the context of triumviral or Augustan propaganda.

Even if we doubt the specifics of Nigidius's on-the-mark prediction, however, it is still perfectly possible that he did cast the child's horoscope. Both Suetonius and Dio provide a rather endearing setting for the story, which once again places Nigidius's activities in an everyday senatorial milieu: Octavius is late to a senate meeting;[109] when Nigidius asks him why and learns that his

---

106. Cognomen: August. *De civ. D.* 5.3; schol. Luc. 1.639; astrological prowess: Luc. 1.639–41; Cass. Dio 45.1.4.

107. Sadly, Della Casa 1962: 14 is more likely to be correct with her suggestion that the cognomen might go back to an "attività ceramistica" on the part of one of Nigidius's ancestors.

108. Suet. *Aug.* 94.5: *dominum terrarum orbi natum*; Cass. Dio 45.1.5: δεσπότην ἡμῖν ἐγέννησας. On this episode, see Bertrand-Écanvil 1994; Vigourt 2001: 274–75, 351, 400–404; and Engels 2007: 622–23.

109. Suetonius specifies that the meeting in question concerned the Catilinarian conspiracy (*cum de Catilinae coniuratione ageretur*), which would put it in November or December 63 and

interlocutor's wife has just given birth, he inquires after the specifics and proceeds to work out the birth chart. Perhaps, just as a fellow senator might seek
out the uniquely gifted Nigidius to inquire after his lost money, he was his
peers' go-to person for a horoscope? Or perhaps nerdy Nigidius forced his
astrology on the new father, whether Octavius had any interest or not.

Even if Nigidius's prophecy is reported among the early signs of Augustus's
coming greatness, its formulation is in keeping with the sentiments of a conservative senator opposed to any concentration of power in the hands of a single man.
The birth of a *dominus* can hardly be good news to a Republican, and in Dio,
Octavius is so horrified that he wants to kill the infant and is stopped only by
Nigidius himself, who points out the futility of opposing fate. Warnings against
the rise of a strong individual is something we find also in other prophecies ascribed to Nigidius; if not historical in fact, these at least capture the man's spirit.

Well known to students of Latin literature is Nigidius's cameo appearance
at the end of the first book of Lucan's *Bellum ciuile* (1.638–72). After Caesar
crosses the Rubicon, dire portents abound, and the poet describes in detail
the warning prophecies uttered by three individuals: the *haruspex* Arruns, a
crazed Roman *matrona*, and—sandwiched between the two—"Figulus, whose
endeavor it was to know the gods and the secrets of the heavens."[110] Casting
what is known as a katarchic horoscope (an interpretation of the heavens not
at a birth, but at some critical moment in order to determine the likely outcome of a contemplated action), Nigidius predicts imminent disaster not only
for Rome but for the world as a whole (644–45): the fact that the sky is dominated by the planet Mars (663) points to horrifying wars that will subvert all
laws and values and last for many years (666–69). Even such mayhem, however, is preferable to what will come afterwards (669–70):

> et superos quid prodest poscere finem?
> cum domino pax ista uenit.

> And what is the point of asking the gods for an end? That peace comes with
> a master.

Accordingly, the Lucanian Nigidius concludes his speech with a prayer to
Rome, asking her to extend civil war as long as possible, since this is the last
time that she will ever be free (670–72).

---

not fit the birth of Augustus on 23 September. The Catilinarian connection may have been
chosen to affect a meaningful synchrony and/or because Nigidius played an important role at
the meeting of 3 December (and possibly also 5 December), being one of the senators chosen
by Cicero to take notes of the proceedings (Cic. *Sull.* 42 with Berry 1996 ad loc.).

110. Luc. 1.638–39: *Figulus, cui cura deos secretaque caeli / nosse fuit.*

Nigidius's horoscope and its relation, if any, to activities or publications on the part of the historical Nigidius have been controversially discussed.[111] Clearly, Lucan's highly stylized and rhetorical prophecy in verse cannot be used as reliable evidence for any actual pronouncement made by a historical agent over a hundred years earlier—and could, in theory, be the poet's original invention. It is still worth asking both (i) whether the horoscope (which provides a detailed description of the heavens in 651–65) makes any astronomical and astrological sense, and (ii) whether Lucan might be drawing on a tradition about or even text by the actual Nigidius. Depending on how Lucan's words are interpreted and what astronomical information is used, views on (i) have diverged widely, from the contention that the horoscope is a jumble of nonsense that does not correspond to any real celestial situation, to the claim that it reflects a perfectly good chart but not one that accurately describes the sky in early 49 BCE, to the suggestion that it in fact works well for the historical moment it is supposed to represent.[112] Accordingly, opinions on (ii) vary as well: while many scholars remain skeptical or noncommittal, some consider it possible that Lucan was making use of an actual incident involving Nigidius, or even a real horoscope published by him.[113] An unusual element of Lucan's *katarchē* is the appearance of Orion (665): extrazodiacal constellations normally have no place in horoscopes, which concentrate solely on the position of the planets. As we know from the *Sphaera*, however, Nigidius was especially interested in the risings and settings of the constellations themselves, and the inclusion of such a *paranatellon* may have been a particularly Nigidian touch.[114]

Once again it seems to me that it would have been perfectly in character for the astrologically well-versed Nigidius to cast a horoscope upon Caesar's invasion of Italy, especially since we know that he himself entered the war at an early stage and that his sympathies (unlike those of the wavering Cicero) were apparently clear-cut. Once he had found the prognosis sufficiently dire, he may have publicized his prophecy as part of the ongoing propaganda war, and Lucan could have had in hand—if not Nigidius's horoscope itself—a historical

111. See Boll 1903: 362–63; Housman 1926: 325–27; Getty 1941, 1960; Hannah 1996; Lewis 1998; Domenicucci 2003; Roche 2009: 360–75 (with a *historia quaestionis*); and Rosillo-López 2009: 109–10, 2017: 136–38.

112. Nonsense: Housman 1926: 215–17; astrological accuracy but not applicable to 49 BCE: Getty 1941, 1960 (the historical Nigidius himself made up a chart to fit what he wanted to predict), Lewis 1998 (what Lucan provides is a katarchic horoscope for Nero's acension!); bona fide horoscope for early 49 BCE: Hannah 1996.

113. For versions of the latter view, see Boll 1903: 363, Getty 1941: 22, and Domenicucci 2003: 100.

114. See Boll 1903: 362–63.

source such as Livy, which may have mentioned this and other Civil War pamphlets.[115] A striking similarity between the prophecy in Lucan and the purported Nigidian horoscope of Augustus is the mention in both of a coming *dominus* (Luc. 1.670; Suet. *Aug.* 94.5; cf. Cass. Dio 45.1.5). Within the context of the *Bellum ciuile*, the reference must likewise be to Augustus, the bringer of a peace that spells the end of Roman liberty,[116] and it is once again unlikely that the historical Nigidius would have predicted the rise of a man who at the time of his own death was still an obscure eighteen-year-old. What is more likely is that Nigidius—an alarmed optimate with an unusual penchant for prophecy—made a habit of employing his divinatory expertise to warn in broad terms against the concentration of power in the hands of would-be *domini* and to inveigh against the dangers of civil strife, and he may well have circulated his predictions, as both demonstrations of his learned *studia* and attempts to sway public opinion.

While Nigidius's horoscopes of 63 and 49 BCE are, as we have seen, reported only in later and not necessarily reliable sources, we have one text that is ascribed to the author himself and that may provide further evidence for Nigidius's politically inflected prediction making. The sixth-century CE Byzantine writer John the Lydian ("Lydus") in his *De ostentis* transmits a wealth of Etruscan and Roman lore on celestial and meteorological prophetic signs, providing a number of translations from original sources.[117] Chapters 27–38 consist of a day-by-day list of thunder omens, which uses a calendar of twelve lunar months of thirty days each, starting with June.[118] The entry for each day follows the same format: after the protasis ἐὰν βροντήσῃ "if it thunders," the apodosis explains the meaning of the sign. The laconic predictions range from weather patterns to crop failures to illness to political events to war; while thunder on certain days has a positive meaning, the overall tenor is pessimistic, painting an image of human life at constant risk.

Lydus introduces his text by saying that he is translating verbatim from "the Roman Figulus [who is drawing] from the books of Tages."[119] Tages was a legendary Etruscan prophet, a mysterious child with the appearance of an old man, who had once upon a time sprung up out of a furrow when a farmer was ploughing the earth and proceeded to reveal what became the basis of the

115. On political pamphleteering, including by Nigidius, see Rosillo-López 2009, 2017, as well as 4.2 above on the "Cato Wars."

116. See Roche 2009 ad Luc. 1.670.

117. On *De ostentis*, see now Domenici and Maderna 2007, with an Italian translation of the text.

118. The Greek text is reproduced by Swoboda 1889 as fr. 83; for an English translation and detailed discussion, see Turfa 2012.

119. Lydus, *Ost.* 27: κατὰ τὸν Ῥωμαῖον Φίγουλον ἐκ τῶν Τάγητος.

disciplina Etrusca "Etruscan [religious] knowledge"; his words were believed to have been taken down and preserved in the so-called *libri Tagetici*.[120] What Lydus's text therefore allegedly represents is his own Greek translation of a Latin translation of an Etruscan original.

Unsurprisingly, given the curious nature of the text, the brontoscopic calendar has occasioned a fair bit of controversy, with scholars coming to divergent conclusions concerning its nature and origin.[121] Is the work a Byzantine concoction? Is it the invention of Nigidius? Does it reflect a bona fide Etruscan document, and if so, of which period? Or is it actually a repository of Near Eastern divinatory practice, as suggested by the protasis-apodosis format familiar from Mesopotamian texts, as well as by parallels in content? Most, but not all, scholars today would probably agree that the text exhibits a number of strata: Etruscan prophecy was indeed influenced by Near Eastern practices; Nigidius translated an actual Etruscan text but may have tweaked it; and Lydus in translating again inadvertently introduced a few anachronisms.

What has particularly struck readers is the looming threat of political disintegration projected by the calendar. Again and again, thunder portends civil discord or even civil war, as well as the rise and fall of powerful men, some of whom are deemed praiseworthy while others are condemned. Apart from a few more specific indications (such as the occasional mention of a "king"), the society depicted is fairly generic, as befits a divinatory text that is designed (and perhaps on occasion redesigned) to be applicable to diverse and changing situations.[122] Despite this indeterminacy—or, one might argue, because of it—the generally alarmist tone as well as a number of specific predictions may well have felt particularly pertinent in Nigidius's own time. Consider, for example, the following two entries (Lydus, *Ost.* 28, 30):

> [14 July:] If it thunders, it signifies that power over everything will fall into the hands of one, and he will be the most unjust in public affairs.

> [25 Sept.:] If it thunders, a tyrant [τύραννος] will arise from the disagreement of the citizenship, and he himself will die, but the powerful will undergo unbearable suffering.

---

120. On Etruscan prophecy and divination, see Thulin 1906–9; de Grummond 2006a, 2006b, 2013; Haack 2017; and Rollinger 2017.

121. See Kroll 1936: 207–9, Piganiol 1951, Weinstock 1951, Valvo 1988: 94–101, Ampolo 1990–91, Capdeville 1998: 395 n. 44, Guittard 2003, Domenici and Maderna 2007: 29–30, and Turfa 2012.

122. Turfa 2012 argues at length that the calendar is an Etruscan product of circa 700 BCE and specifically reflects the social and political situation in Etruria at the time; most other scholars allow for greater fluidity in the text's creation and points of reference.

While neither prediction matches exactly a particular late Republican person and event, such warnings of the rise of a strongman speak to the concerns of an aristocratic society threatened by the unprecedented concentration of power in the hands of individuals.[123] Publicizing such warnings would have been entirely in keeping with what we know about Nigidius, who, as we have seen, is credited in other sources with prophesying the arrival of a *dominus*. John the Lydian concludes his report of the brontoscopic calendar with the observation that "Nigidius believed that this calendar of thunder omens did not apply generally, but only to Rome";[124] Nigidius's Roman readers had been warned.

The most likely scenario for the genesis of the calendar's Latin version is that Nigidius translated an actual Etruscan document that he believed contained prophecies relevant to the contemporary political situation at Rome, adding the proviso that Lydus reports.[125] It is also possible, but by no means necessary, that for his own purposes he adjusted the text to make it more "Roman." In publishing his translation, Nigidius produced a document of religious scholarship that at the same time functioned as a political pamphlet, an intervention that is in tune with two related contemporary developments: in the waning years of the Republic, an increase in politically inflected Etruscan predictions goes hand in hand with the proliferation of Roman research into the *disciplina Etrusca*.

Nigidius's brontoscopic calendar has often been compared to other Etruscan prophecies from the first century BCE, including translated documents, the official pronouncements of the body of *haruspices* consulted by the Roman senate, and the predictions of Etruscan freelance diviners.[126] The alarmist tone

123. More specific allusions to the late Republic have been detected in another text in Lydus, a calendar of lightning omens ascribed to the 3rd c. CE Neoplatonic writer Cornelius Labeo (*Ost.* 47–52; 51: Catiline?; 52: Pompey's campaign against the pirates?). It has been suggested that Labeo's Etruscan source had been modified in the 1st c. BCE, possibly by Nigidius, whose work on dreams Labeo cites at Lydus, *Ost.* 45. On this issue, see Bezold and Boll 1911: 11–12 n. 2; Weinstock 1950: 48, 1951; Mastrandrea 1979: 74–88; and Domenici and Maderna 2007: 151 n. 114.

124. Lydus, *Ost.* 38: ταύτην τὴν ἐφήμερον βροντοσκοπίαν ὁ Νιγίδιος οὐ καθολικὴν ἀλλὰ μόνης εἶναι τῆς Ῥώμης ἔκρινεν.

125. If Nigidius translated the calendar single-handedly, he must have known Etruscan, a fact that has led some scholars to suggest that—like other writers on the *disciplina Etrusca* (see below)—he was Etruscan himself; see Harris 1971: 321–22 and Rawson 1978: 138, 152. There is, however, little additional evidence.

126. Since the Romans used the term *haruspex* indiscriminately for the "official" *haruspices*, Etruscan diviners in general, religious personnel in charge of extispicy, and "soothsayers" of all kinds, the status of a person designated a *haruspex* is not always clear (and neither is the

of many of these predictions is expressive not only of anxiety over the political instability at Rome but also of concern over the future of an independent Etruscan identity in the wake of the Social War, when the grant of citizenship to all of Italy south of the Po officially sealed the process of Romanization that had been going on for centuries. I have already mentioned the response of the *haruspices* of 56 that gave rise to competing interpretations by Clodius and Cicero; like the brontoscopic calendar, it warned specifically against discord among the nobility:[127]

> monent ne per optimatium discordiam dissensionemque patribus principibusque caedes periculaque creentur.
>
> They warn that from discord and disagreement among the optimates might arise slaughter and peril for senators and leaders.

Already in 65 BCE, the *haruspices* had interpreted lightning damage to some statues on the Capitol as a sign that, unless the gods could be placated, "bloodshed, arson, the end of law and order, foreign and domestic war, and the downfall of the entire city and empire were approaching"—a prophecy that, in the interpretation of Cicero, nearly became dire reality two years later with the Catilinarian conspiracy.[128] On a more personal note, it was the *haruspex* Spurinna who unsuccessfully attempted to have Caesar "beware the Ides of March."

An element of the Etruscan religious system that rose to particular prominence in the first century BCE was the doctrine of *saecula*.[129] The Etruscans believed that their nation was destined to live through a fixed number of ages—depending on the source, either eight or ten—at the completion of

---

organization of the college of *haruspices* in the late Republic). My intention in what follows is not to disentangle these matters or determine the historicity or authenticity of each event or document, but simply to give a brief generalized picture of the landscape of late Republican Etruscan(-inflected) prophecy. See further Sordi 1972, Rawson 1978: 140–46, Firpo 1998: 263–69, Corbeill 2012, and Santangelo 2013: 84–114.

127. Cic. *Har. resp.* 40. Cicero's citation from the response continues beyond the part reproduced here, but the text is very corrupt. To judge from the orator's paraphrase later in the speech, the *haruspices* also raised the specter of "power falling into the hand of one man" (*ne in unius imperium res recidat, Har. resp.* 54).

128. Cic. *Cat.* 3.19: *quo quidem tempore cum haruspices ex tota Etruria conuenissent, caedis atque incendia et legum interitum et bellum ciuile ac domesticum et totius urbis atque imperi occasum appropinquare dixerunt, nisi di immortales omni ratione placati suo numine prope fata ipsa flexissent.* See also Cic. *De consulatu suo* fr. 2.23–65 Soubiran = *Div.* 1.19–20; *Div.* 2.45–47; and 6.4 below.

129. On Etruscan *saecula*, see Sordi 1972, Valvo 1988, Briquel 1990, Dobesch 1998, Firpo 1998, de Grummond 2006a, and Santangelo 2013: 115–27.

which "the Etruscan name would come to an end."[130] Since the length of a *saeculum* was not fixed, the end of one age and the beginning of another announced themselves through portents that it fell to the *haruspices* to recognize, and in the last decades of the Republic, such apocalyptic signs occurred with alarming frequency. Since according to Etruscan doctrine, not only Etruria but all polities had their own sequence of ages, and since the Romans had adopted a modified system of *saecula* for themselves, it is not always clear who exactly was supposed to be affected by a declared change of *saeculum*: the Etruscans, the Romans, or the world as a whole. No doubt this uncertainty contributed to a heightened sense of living through momentous events and being faced with possible doom.

Thus the so-called Prophecy of Vegoia, often dated to 91–90, warns of a disintegration of the social fabric toward the end of the eighth *saeculum*, which will result in various disasters, including *multae dissensiones in populo*.[131] In 88 BCE, the sign of a trumpet blast from the sky signified, according to Etruscan experts, the arrival of a new *saeculum* (Plut. *Sull.* 7.3), and only forty-four years later, the *haruspex* Vulcanius interpreted the appearance of a comet at Caesar's funeral games as signifying "the end of the ninth age and the beginning of the tenth."[132] As if this were not alarming enough, Vulcanius continued that "since he had divulged secret matters against the will of the gods . . . he was going to die immediately, and in mid-speech collapsed at the very gathering."[133]

While Etruscan diviners were spreading such disconcerting prophecies, members of the Roman educated elite—some of Etruscan origin themselves— were conducting research into the *disciplina Etrusca* and, as we have seen with the brontoscopic calendar, translating some of the Etruscan sacred texts into Latin.[134] In addition to Nigidius and Varro (see n. 130), we have evidence of

130. Censorinus, *DN* 17.6: *finem fore nominis Etrusci*. This observation caps Censorinus's exposition of the ten *saecula* system, which he says he derives from Varro.

131. The Prophecy of Vegoia is transmitted in the corpus of Roman land surveyors (350.17– 351.11 Lachmann, quotation at 351.9) and purports to be the translation into Latin of an Etruscan sacred text (Vegoia/Begoe was another foundational Etruscan prophet). The date connected to the Social War goes back to Heurgon 1959 and is adopted by Harris 1971: 31–40 and Valvo 1988. Note, though, that Adams 2003: 179–82 now argues on linguistic and stylistic grounds that the document is not a translation and was composed in the Imperial period.

132. *Serv. Dan.* ad *Ecl.* 9.46: *sed Vulcanius aruspex in contione dixit cometem esse qui significaret exitum noni saeculi et ingressum decimi*. On Caesar's comet, see further 6.3 below.

133. *Serv. Dan.* ad *Ecl.* 9.46: *sed quod inuitis diis secreta rerum pronuntiaret, statim se esse moriturum: et nondum finita oratione in ipsa contione concidit*. App. *B Civ.* 4.4 reports a similar incident for 43 BCE, which is perhaps a conflation with the alleged event of 44.

134. See Rawson 1985: 304–6, Capdeville 1998, and Turfa 2012: 286–92.

Etruscological studies by Tarquitius Priscus, Fonteius Capito, and Clodius Tuscus (works by the last two are likewise included in John the Lydian's *De ostentis*), as well as Cicero's friend Aulus Caecina. We last encountered this native of Volaterrae in 4.2 as a particularly anxious correspondent of Cicero post-Pharsalus, languishing in exile and worrying about Caesar's reactions not only to his Civil War–time aggressive pamphlet but even to his new, pro-Caesarian compositions. However, Caecina was also a member of the Etruscan aristocracy and had been instructed in the *disciplina Etrusca* by his father;[135] his work on lightning omens proved indispensable to Seneca's discussion in book 2 of his *Natural Questions* and was also used by the elder Pliny. In one of his consolatory letters to Caecina, Cicero urbanely contrasts his own alleged prowess in *diuinatio* with that of his correspondent: Caecina may be an expert in Etruscan prophecy, but Cicero has his own way of telling the future, which allows him to read the signs and predict Caecina's impending pardon.[136] Unfortunately, it appears that on this occasion the prophet was mistaken: we have no evidence that Caecina was ever recalled.

Considering the cases of Nigidius and Caecina, as well as some of the haruspicinal predictions with their warnings against dissent among the nobility and the rise of powerful individuals, one wonders whether first-century Etruscan prophecy was generally conservative and specifically anti-Caesarian.[137] The stance of Etruria during the Civil War has been studied in detail, and it has been shown that there was no Etruscan party line: while many communities and individuals supported Caesar, others resisted him.[138] Even so, Elizabeth Rawson has tentatively suggested that "experts in the *disciplina Etrusca* . . . were likely to be sympathetic to the Roman optimates; and that is likely to have meant opposition to Caesar, at least at certain times of his life" (1978: 146). This makes sense in light of the fact that such experts were, as we have seen with Caecina, themselves the political and cultural elite within their own communities and thus presumably for the most part not sympathetic to political developments perceived as endangering the status quo.

Though likely not an Etruscan himself (see n. 125), the learned Nigidius deftly availed himself of elements of the *disciplina Etrusca* just as he made use of his lecanomantic expertise and his astrological learning, bringing the fruits of his study of "those matters that seem to have been concealed by nature" to

135. See Cic. *Fam.* 6.6.3. Etruscan religious expertise ran in elite families, being passed down from generation to generation. On Caecina, see Rawson 1978: 137–38.

136. Cic. *Fam.* 6.6; 46 BCE. On this letter, see Guillaumont 1984: 109–17, 2000; and Cuny-Le Callet 2005.

137. Compare Rosillo-López 2009 on the anti-Caesarianism of Nigidius and Caecina.

138. See Rawson 1978, Zecchini 1998 (cf. Zecchini 2001: 65–76), and Aigner-Foresti 2000.

bear on his own private and public life. Whether assisting his fellow senators with the recovery of lost money and custom-made horoscopes, or employing learned predictions as political propaganda, Nigidius's attempts to "coopt the cosmos" went beyond the interventions of many of his learned peers. We do not have to believe each and every anecdote about this *homo doctissimus* (even if the stories cannot count as reliable evidence for what the man did, they tell us what he was thought to have been able to do), nor do we have to construct fantastic tales about his activities as a purported Pythagorean ringleader. Of all the learned senators of his period, Nigidius took his *studia* the farthest away from the practicalities of the *res publica*—and then brought them right back to the center of the Roman cosmos, that is, Rome itself.

3. *Diuus*

Attempts such as those of Nigidius to appeal to the secret workings of nature in order to warn against impending dangers are inherently tricky. The occurrence of thunderclaps or the appearance of the heavens may disclose a cosmic pattern that predicts, say, the rising of an undesirable *dominus*—but they may also end up lending legitimacy to the very disaster they foretell. If the universe is arranged in such a way that signs are unfailingly coordinated with outcomes or if—on the strongest reading—human affairs are indeed ruled by fate, then all that prophecy reveals is what must by necessity happen anyway. Such defeatism is apparent in the ex post facto versions of Nigidius's horoscopes of the birth of Augustus and of the situation in early 49; as we have seen in 6.2, the astrologer himself avows in both cases that the predicted arrival of the *dominus* is all but inescapable. Nothing then prevents the opposing party from appropriating the prophecy and reinterpreting it for their own purposes: one man's dire warning becomes another's glorious teleology.[139] And even in the absence of an original prediction, whoever comes out "on the right side of history" can be understood with hindsight to have been destined to do so, enjoying divine favor all along.

In the late Republican race to coopt the cosmos, Nigidius's nemesis Julius Caesar thus emerges as considerably more successful. Unlike Nigidius, Caesar had no interest or expertise in the occult sciences and for most of his illustrious career displayed the traditional religious behavior and public attitudes of a Roman aristocrat, including in the execution of his duties as *pontifex maximus*.[140] There is little room for the supernatural in his *Commentarii*, and

---

139. Thus we find Nigidius's horoscope of Augustus transmitted among other omens and prophecies of the future *princeps*'s greatness.

140. On Caesar and religion, see Wardle 2009.

Caesar's occasional public disdain of omens and general rationalist persona have contributed to the idea that he may have been an Epicurean.[141] As so often with this elusive character, we have no way to gauge his personal opinions and feelings, and therefore cannot tell what Caesar was thinking when, toward the end of his life, he found himself at the center of the most remarkable religious innovation of his time: his own apotheosis. We will turn to this controversial development in the second part of this section. First, however, let us focus on Caesar's calendar reform, a bid for cosmic control that is arguably the dictator's greatest and most long-lived achievement.[142]

The old Republican calendar had twelve months and 355 days, being thus considerably shorter than the solar year. To make up for this discrepancy, an additional month had to be intercalated at regular intervals in order to keep the civic year in line with the cycle of the seasons. Intercalation lay in the hands of the *pontifices*, but especially in the waning years of the Republic, its implementation was haphazard and occasionally did not take place at all. As a result, by the time of Caesar's dictatorship, Roman calendar dates ran ahead of the solar year by about two and a half months; thus, for example, the spring festival of the Parilia was celebrated on a day that was officially 21 April but that, astronomically speaking, fell into early February.

Caesar solved this problem by introducing the calendar that is used to this day in the western world and beyond, consisting of 365 days with an extra day intercalated every four years.[143] To bring the calendar in line with the solar year, he intercalated a total of ninety days in 46 BCE, with the new system beginning on 1 January 45. The ten extra days were carefully added at the end of months, in such a way as to disturb as little as possible the traditional dates of major religious festivals as well as to make sure that the days of the solstices and equinoxes were evenly spaced out. There was thus little disruption of ordinary dating practices except for events in the second half of a month: if, for example, you were born on the twenty-second day of the month Sextilis (later called August) and your birthday had thus always fallen on the ninth day

141. On Caesar's purported Epicureanism, see 3.3, 4.2, and Volk forthcoming a.

142. The main ancient sources for the calendar reform are Plin. *HN* 18.211–12; Plut. *Caes.* 59; Cass. Dio 43.26; Macrob. *Sat.* 1.14; Censorinus, *DN* 20.6–11. Modern discussions include Malitz 1987, Feeney 2007, Wolkenhauer 2011: 208–37, and Rüpke 2018: 63–66.

143. Owing to a misunderstanding of Caesar's rules, intercalation originally took place every third year (*quarto quoque anno* by inclusive reckoning), a mistake that was corrected by Augustus from 8 BCE onward. Even so, the Julian year was about eleven minutes longer than the solar year, which over the centuries added up. This problem was solved by the Gregorian reform of 1582, which abolished intercalation in centennial years (e.g., 1900) unless they are divisible by 400 (e.g., 2000).

before the Kalends of September, it was now, after Caesar added two days to the month, technically on the eleventh day.

What motivated Caesar to his reform? We may once again point to the increased interest at Rome in questions of astronomy, as well as to antiquarian studies of Roman time-reckoning and the religious holidays that punctuated the year (thus, e.g., in Cicero's praise of Varro at *Acad. post.* 9, the polymath's work on *descriptiones temporum* is one of his areas of expertise mentioned[144]). That the traditional 355-day calendar did not agree with the solar year would have been obvious to anyone with basic astronomical knowledge, while those involved in public life would have known that intercalation had turned into a matter of political advantage-seeking, as the additional month could mean the extension of terms of office and the addition of days available for assemblies or trials. We thus find Cicero during his unloved governorship of Cilicia worried about the possibility of intercalation in 50 BCE, which would have kept him away from Rome even longer; as his letters show, uncertainty prevailed until very shortly before the possible extra month (in the end, there was no intercalation).[145]

As we also gather from Cicero's correspondence, there was intensive lobbying for and against individual intercalations: he himself asked Atticus to exert his influence in Cicero's absence (*Att.* 5.9.2), while at the same time the tribune and pontiff C. Scribonius Curio was unsuccessfully trying to make the (in fact perfectly regular) intercalation of 50 happen, allegedly in order to get more laws passed.[146] While our sources generally blame the "negligence of the *pontifices*" for the deterioration of intercalary practice, it is not in fact clear how their decision in favor of adding the extra month was reached, or to which extent the person ultimately responsible was the *pontifex maximus*.[147] From 63 BCE onward, that is, in the very period when calendar and solar year increasingly diverged, that office was held by none other than Caesar himself, who for most of the 50s, however, spent large parts of the year away from Rome.[148] While he therefore may not have been particularly at fault himself, his priesthood certainly meant that he was well aware of the problem.

---

144. On Varro's research into the ordering of time and its affinities with Caesar's reform, see Tarver 1995 and Wolkenhauer 2011: 168–74.

145. See Cic. *Att.* 5.9.2, 5.13.3, 5.21.14; 6.1.12, with Wolkenhauer 2011: 180–83.

146. See Cass. Dio 40.62.1–2; cf. Cic. *Fam.* 8.6.5 with Shackleton Bailey 1977 ad loc. and Malitz 1987: 107–8.

147. Cic. *Leg.* 2.29: *pontificum neglegentia*; cf. Plut. *Caes.* 59.2; Suet. *Iul.* 40.1; Macrob. *Sat.* 1.14.1; Censorinus, *DN* 20.7.

148. As Malitz 1987: 107 points out, no ancient source faults exclusively the *pontifex maximus*, let alone Caesar specifically.

If there was thus a perception that the system was erratic and open to abuse, we have no evidence that anyone at Rome thought that the solution lay in a wholesale reform: after all, the old calendar worked just fine as long as those in charge played by the rules.[149] In *De legibus*, Cicero thus simply stipulates that "the rules for intercalation ought to be diligently observed."[150] King Numa, or so the story went, had devised the Roman year, and apart from the recent hiccups, it had served the Romans well. It took a Caesar to think outside the calendrical box.

Our sources generally cite Egyptian inspiration for Caesar's reform, and it is possible that he conceived of the idea during his sojourn in Alexandria in 48–47. Not that the Egyptian calendar was perfect: it consisted of a 365-day year (twelve months of thirty days plus five epagonal days) and was thus obviously too short. An attempt in 238 BCE by Ptolemy III to intercalate a sixth epagonal day every four years had foundered on the conservatism of the Egyptian priests, an incident that rendered intercalation anathema for the next two centuries.[151] Perhaps the Ptolemaic precedent piqued Caesar's interest or perhaps he was inspired by conversation with astronomers he encountered in Egypt. Pliny credits a certain Sosigenes as Caesar's collaborator on the calendar reform, and it is plausible that this scientist met his patron in Alexandria and then accompanied him to Rome.[152] Then again, nothing is known about Sosigenes beyond Pliny's mention, and both his origin and his exact contribution remain unclear. Plutarch simply tells us that Caesar consulted "the best philosophers and mathematicians" and combined extant solutions to the calendar problem into his own, superior one.[153]

In addition to overseeing the actual reform, Caesar published a treatise *De astris*, which may have been part of a kind of PR effort to justify and explain the new calendar.[154] As we can tell from the fragments and reports, this work contained a parapegma, or astrometeorological calendar.[155] Parapegmata are

149. See Malitz 1987: 106–10 and Wolkenhauer 2011: 175–83 on the lack of a sense of crisis.

150. Cic. *Leg.* 2.29: *diligenter habenda ratio intercalandi est.*

151. See Blackburn and Holford Strevens 1999: 708–9. Nigidius Figulus fr. 98 Swoboda reports that at their coronation, the Egyptian kings had to swear not to take any intercalation initiatives (*iure iurando adiguntur neque mensem neque diem intercalandum iurare*).

152. Plin. *HN* 18.211–12. On Sosigenes, see Rehm 1927.

153. Plut. *Caes.* 59.3: τοῖς ἀρίστοις τῶν φιλοσόφων καὶ μαθηματικῶν. Macrob. *Sat.* 1.14.2 mentions the collaboration of a *scriba* named M. Flavius; his identity is anyone's guess.

154. The testimonia and fragments are collected in Klotz 1927: 211–29. On the work, see Domenicucci 1993 ~ 1996: 85–99 and Wolkenhauer 2011: 216–21, who views it as part of a "Publikationsoffensive" (220) to advertise the reform.

155. Wolkenhauser 2011: 216–21 believes that the parapegma and *De astris* are two different publications; this seems unlikely. Generally on ancient parapegmata, see Lehoux 2007.

devices that track cyclical phenomena, most often the risings and settings of
constellations, which can be correlated to weather conditions and other seasonal events. Apparently Caesar's work contained such a Farmer's Almanack–
style list, except that it was now cued to the new Julian calendar. The elder
Pliny in his description of the agricultural year in book 18 of his *Natural History*
refers throughout to what he calls Caesar's *Italiae ratio* "formula for Italy"
(18.214), that is, his system of correct risings and settings for the location of
Italy. To cite just one short passage, here is what Caesar has to say about the
weather in early spring (Plin. *HN* 18.237):

> a fauonio in aequinoctium uernum Caesari significat XIV kal. Mart.
> triduum uarie, et VIII kal. harundinis uisu et postero die arcturi exortu
> uesperino.

> In the period between the blowing of the westwind and the spring equinox,
> according to Caesar, February 16 brings three days of changeable weather,
> as does February 22 with the appearance of the swallow and the following
> day with the evening rising of Arcturus.

Here we find weather forecasts, season-typical animal behavior, and astronomical events all anchored to dates fixed once and for all in the new
calendar.

It is likely that in addition to the parapegma, *De astris* contained a theoretical discussion of the astronomy that underlay the calendar reform and an explanation of the rationale that had led to its adoption. Thus, for example, Macrobius reports that "Caesar wrote learned books about the motion of the stars"
and a scholium on Lucan speaks of a "book about the computation [of the
year]."[156] We might imagine a discursive and theoretical part followed by the
parapegma, perhaps in tabular form; if Macrobius's *libros* is correct, the work
may thus have consisted of two books.

In keeping with prejudices against the Romans' intellectual achievements
in general and their scientific abilities in particular, both the calendar reform
and *De astris* have often been viewed as mere Roman putting-into-practice (or
putting-into-words) of Greek theory. Caesar, it is maintained, had neither the
astronomical knowledge nor the time to devote himself to the nitty-gritty of
stellar movements and simply did, or wrote, what Sosigenes and others told
him.[157] Given the scarcity of our sources, we have no way of telling how the
collaboration between Caesar and his advisers worked in detail, but there is

---

156. Macrob. 1.16.39: *siderum motus, de quibus non indoctos libros reliquit*; schol. Luc.
10.185 = Caes. *De astris* test. 6 Klotz: *liber ... de computatione* [sc. *anni*].

157. See, e.g., Rehm 1927: 1154.

no reason to believe that the dictator would not have played an independent role. Time pressures were obviously real, but the multitasker who had expounded on grammatical analogy *inter tela uolantia* in Gaul would probably not have found it impossible to write another book even while waging civil war. The subject matter was hardly impossibly technical (nonspecialist authors like Pliny discuss similar topics), and while Caesar presumably neither did his own calculations nor collated extant catalogues of risings and settings, there is no reason to think that he was anything but fully in command of his material.[158]

Caesar's calendar reform is perhaps the only good example of the "rationalization" narrative so often found in modern discussions of late Republican intellectual history.[159] Here we really do see the successful imposition of a new rational system on an old chaotic *consuetudo*, coupled with the wresting away of control from the old aristocracy (in this case, the pontiffs)—even though the new repository of knowledge and control is not some rising class of professionals, but the autocratic ruler himself. That the new calendar was perceived in this way, and thus not necessarily appreciated, is made clear by Plutarch's report that "even this gave his critics and those who resented his power occasion for blame."[160] He continues with an anecdote about Cicero: when someone remarked that the constellation Lyre was going to rise the following day, he retorted, "sure, by decree."[161]

This quip has elicited a certain amount of scholarly discussion, since it is not entirely clear what Cicero was making fun of. The most obvious interpretation is that of Plutarch, who adds the explanation, "as if people were forced to put up even with this."[162] Just as the orator, as we have seen, did not like to be told by Caesar which verbal forms to use, he did not appreciate that the constellations were now supposed to rise and set by command.

As it happens, however, the time for the morning rising of the Lyre given in Caesar's *De astris* turns out to be wrong.[163] According to Pliny, Caesar has the

158. See Malitz 1987: 111–17 on Caesar's intellectual independence, including vis-à-vis learned Greeks. According to Plin. *HN* 18.212, Sosigenes independently published his own *commentationes* in three books.

159. See esp. Moatti 1997 (calendar reform: 136, 167) and Wallace-Hadrill 1997 (16–18), 2008 (239–48), with my discussion in 1.3 and 5.1.

160. Plut. *Caes.* 59.3: καὶ τοῦτο τοῖς βασκαίνουσι καὶ βαρυνομένοις τὴν δύναμιν αἰτίας παρεῖχε.

161. Plut. *Caes.* 59.3: ναί . . . ἐκ διατάγματος.

162. Plut. *Caes.* 59.3: ὡς καὶ τοῦτο πρὸς ἀνάγκην τῶν ἀνθρώπων δεχομένων.

163. See Le Bœuffle 1964 and in Le Bonniec 1972 ad Plin. *HN* 18.234, Holleman 1978, and Malitz 1987: 125–26.

constellation rise on 5 January, though the actual date, found in other sources, is
at the beginning of November.[164] Were Cicero and his interlocutor gloating
over the dictator's error? We can imagine a scene on 4 January 45, one of the
very first days of the new calendar, with two learned Romans checking out
Caesar's brand-new *De astris* and, to their delight, discovering a mistake on
one of the very first pages of the parapegma. The joke is still that Caesar is
ordering the constellation to rise—but he is telling it to rise on the wrong day!
It is perfectly realistic that Cicero would have been able to spot such an error.
He himself had, after all, translated Aratus, and we possess the part of his poem
that mentions the rising of the Lyre (fr. 33.459–61 Soubiran):

> inde Sagittipotens superas cum uisere luces
> institit, emergit Nixi caput, et simul effert
> sese clara Fides.

> Once Sagittarius begins to revisit the light of heaven, the head of Engonasin
> emerges, and at the same time, the bright Lyre lifts itself up.

Cicero's Lyre rises on time together with Sagittarius, that is, in November.
Caesar's Lyre is two months late.[165]

Despite the discomfort felt by Cicero and others at Caesar's taking control
of the cosmos, however, the Julian calendar was, and continues to be, a success.
The unprecedented alignment of civic and solar year led, in the words of Jörg
Rüpke, to a "long-term cognitive reorientation" (2018: 64), as the Romans
became accustomed to the idea that calendar dates stood in an immutable relation to the changing of the seasons. Once this trust had been established, there
was no longer any need to consult alternative parapegmata, let alone watch the
heavens oneself: it no longer mattered whether the Lyre really rose, as long as
it was indisputably 5 January. Denis Feeney has traced the impact of the Julian
reform through the works of Varro and Pliny, showing that in *De lingua Latina*,
written during and shortly after the reform, Varro still discusses religious holidays without anchoring them in the seasons; in *De re rustica*, by contrast,

---

164. See Plin. *HN* 18.234, with Le Bœuffle in Le Bonniec 1972 ad loc. The same date is found
in Columella 11.2.97, while Ov. *Fast.* 1.315 may refer to either 4 or 5 January; both authors clearly
depend on Caesar.

165. An ingenious way of solving this problem was suggested by Le Bœuffle 1964: 329–30,
who follows Boll 1903: 266–68 in positing a second constellation called *Lyra* or *Fides*, with an
origin in the *sphaera barbarica* and alleged appearances in, among other authors, Teucer of
Babylon and Manilius: Caesar's January constellation would then be that second Lyre (and
Cicero would not have realized this). Unfortunately, however, more recent scholars have concluded that the additional Lyre is a mirage; see Hübner 2010: 2.180–82.

published in 37, he ties the agricultural year to the calendar, fixing the beginnings of the seasons "to our civic days, as they are now."[166] When Pliny was writing a century later, he had, as we have seen, wholeheartedly adopted Caesar's *Italiae ratio*.

If Caesar had thus exerted his control over the seasonal year, it was left to Augustus to fill up the calendar with a plethora of celebrations honoring the imperial family.[167] Thus, by the time we come to Ovid's *Fasti* (c. 2–8 CE), the calendar has become truly Julian, containing not only seasonal markers, the risings and settings of stars, and the traditional civic and religious festivals, but also numerous holidays to commemorate the achievements of the *princeps* and his nearest and dearest, including his adoptive father. The most lasting legacy of the two men may be the fact that we continue to use, unthinkingly and as a matter of course, the designations of the two months that were renamed in their honor: July and August.[168]

Caesar's calendar reform emerges as a conscious—and highly successful—attempt at inscribing Rome and its leader into the cosmic order. From the perspective of later periods, however, this project was only the prelude to a far more ambitious endeavor. As Ovid whimsically puts in the *Fasti* (3.159–60):

promissumque sibi uoluit praenoscere caelum
nec deus ignotas hospes inire domos.

[Caesar] wanted to get to know the heaven that was promised to him and not come as a stranger to an unknown domicile.

Caesar's astronomical and calendrical studies were just reconnaissance for a rather more more intimate acquaintance with the celestial spheres: not content with scientific investigation of the skies, the dictator ultimately ascended to heaven himself. Ovid here ascribes a fair amount of planning and agency to the heaven-dweller-to-be; in reality, however, we have no idea what Caesar was thinking when he found himself at the center of the most remarkable religious innovation of his time: his own apotheosis.

The deification of Julius Caesar is surrounded by confusion and controversy, with scholars differing on the nature and sequence of events as well as on the motivations behind them.[169] Apart from a few passing remarks by

166. Varro, *Rust.* 1.28.1: *ad dies ciuiles nostros qui nunc sunt*. See Feeney 2007: 193–201.

167. See Feeney 2007: 184–89.

168. The former Quintilis was named for Caesar already in his lifetime, in 44, while Sextilis became Augustus in 8 BCE.

169. For a recent and admirably clear exposition of the issues, see McIntyre 2016: 16–26 (~ 2019: 14–25). Major scholarly discussions include Dobesch 1966, Gesche 1968, Weinstock 1971, Rawson 1975, Fishwick 1987–92: 1.1.56–72, Zecchini 2001: 553–63, Gradel 2002: 54–72, and

Cicero, there is no contemporary literary evidence, while the main source is the *Roman History* of Cassius Dio, written well over two hundred years after the events as well as in Greek, a fact that makes it difficult to reconstruct the exact wording of some of the Latin titles awarded to Caesar.[170] Even so, it is generally (though not universally) agreed that during his lifetime, the dictator was officially decreed divine honors in three stages.

First, after the victory at Thapsus in 46, the senate resolved that a statue of Caesar be placed on the Capitol and inscribed to him as a ἡμίθεος "demigod," a title whose Latin original is not clear and which the dictator himself later had erased.[171] Second, in the following year, after the Battle of Munda, another statue of Caesar was placed in the *cella* of the temple of Quirinus, with the legend θεῷ ἀνικήτῳ "to the unconquered god" (Cass. Dio 43.45.3). The Latin equivalent would appear to be *deo inuicto,* but it is unclear whether the dative implies a dedication to Caesar himself or whether the statue was meant as a cult offering to Quirinus, who would then be the unconquered god referred to. On the same occasion, Caesar was granted the honor of having his statue paraded at the opening procession of the circus together with the images of the gods (Cass. Dio 43.45.2).

Cicero in his letters to Atticus scoffs at "him of the procession, the tentmate of Quirinus" and does not hide his schadenfreude at the tepid applause Caesar's statue received at the games.[172] In characteristic black humor, he expresses his preference for Caesar's sharing a temple with Quirinus to his being housed with *Salus.*[173] The protection of the goddess of health and salvation is apparently not what Cicero wishes for Caesar at this point, while a demise on the model of Quirinus/Romulus (who, in one version of the story, was murdered by the senators) may have seemed an increasingly appealing scenario. The Greek term Cicero uses for Caesar's status as a joint inhabitant of the temple, σύνναος, is a technical term for a god who shares his shrine with another[174]—which would mean that Caesar was believed to have been made a god on the same footing as Quirinus. Then again, it is not clear whether

---

Koortbojian 2013. In what follows, I cannot discuss in detail the many uncertainties and differences of opinion, but focus on what appears to me the most likely interpretation of the evidence.

170. See Cass. Dio 43.14.6, 43.45.2–3; 44.4–8, with Cic. *Phil.* 2.110; Suet. *Iul.* 76.1; App. *B Civ.* 2.106.

171. Statue and inscription: Cass. Dio 43.14.6; later erasure: Cass. Dio 43.21.2.

172. *Att.* 13.28.3: *hunc de pompa Quirini contubernalem; Att.* 13.44.1: *populum vero praeclarum quod propter malum vicinum ne Victoriae quidem ploditur* ("good for the people that there isn't applause even for Victory on account of her bad neighbor"; apparently statues of Victory and Caesar were paraded side by side).

173. Cic. *Att.* 12.45.2: *eum σύνναον Quirino malo quam Saluti.*

174. Cic. *Att.* 12.45.2. On σύνναος, see C. R. Phillips 2001.

Cicero is using the word in the technical sense or more loosely, similar in tone to the jocular *contubernalis* "tentmate" found in one of the other letters (*Att.* 13.28.3).

At the third and final stage, apparently early in 44 BCE, the senate decreed that a temple be built to Caesar and his *clementia*, and that he receive a *flamen* (a personal priest like those appointed for Jupiter, Mars, Quirinus, and other gods); Antony was chosen for the latter position.[175] These measures amounted to making Caesar an official god of the state cult, providing him with a place of worship and religious personnel.[176] Confusingly, Dio also reports that the senate addressed Caesar as "Jupiter Julius," a title that is not otherwise attested—unless the Greek author's Δία . . . Ἰούλιον (44.6.4) is in fact a misunderstanding or muddled version of *diuus Iulius*, the divine moniker by which the deified Caesar became known later on.[177]

As it happened, Caesar was assassinated shortly thereafter, at which point none of these last deification measures had been put into place. Railing against Antony later in the year, Cicero somewhat schizophrenically both expresses his dismay at the idea of Caesar's being worshiped as a god and berates Antony for failing to take up his position as *flamen* (*Phil.* 2.110–11):

> quem is honorem maiorem consecutus erat quam ut haberet puluinar simulacrum fastigium flaminem? est ergo flamen, ut Ioui ut Marti ut Quirino, sic diuo Iulio M. Antonius. quid igitur cessas? cur non inaugurais? . . . quaeris placeatne mihi puluinar esse, fastigium, flaminem. mihi uero nihil istorum placet. sed tu, qui acta Caesaris defendis, quid potes dicere, cur alia defendas, alia non cures?

> What greater honor did [Caesar] achieve than to have a ritual couch, a cult image, a pediment,[178] a *flamen*? So just as there is a *flamen* for Jupiter, Mars, and Quirinus, so M. Antonius is the *flamen* of the divine Julius. Why then are you hesitating? Why don't you let yourself be inaugurated? . . . You ask

175. Cass. Dio 44.6.4. See also Suet. *Iul.* 76.1, who among many other honors for Caesar enumerates *templa, aras, simulacra iuxta deos, pulvinar, flaminem* ("temples, altars, statues next to the gods, a ritual couch, a *flamen*").

176. Most scholars interpret the evidence in this way, though there are minority views. Notably, Gesche 1968 believes that the measures of 44 were meant to apply to Caesar only posthumously, while on the revisionist reading of Koortbojian 2013, official deification was decreed only after Caesar's death.

177. Scholars are divided over whether Dio could have made this mistake. The title *diuus* is first attested in Cic. *Phil.* 2.110 (September 44), cited immediately below.

178. This was an honorific pediment added to Caesar's official residence, which approximated its appearance to a temple; cf. Plut. *Caes.* 63.6; Flor. 2.13.91.

me whether I like the fact that there is a ritual couch, a pediment, a *flamen*. I don't like any of this! But you, who defend the measures of Caesar, what is your excuse: why do you defend some of them and not take account of others?

Antony's lack of enthusiasm for his flaminate was likely owed to the arrival on the political scene of Caesar's great nephew and posthumous adoptee C. Octavius ("Octavian"), whose advertising of his Julian pedigree and his late father's divinity ran counter to Antony's attempts to shore up his own position in the volatile situation after the Ides of March. Caesar's funeral as well as the games held in his memory in July 44 gave Octavian the opportunity to capitalize on Caesar's legacy and promote his superhuman status.

It so happened that, while Caesar's funeral games were in progress, a comet appeared and was, unsurprisingly, immediately considered a sign.[179] Once again, all our sources date from after the event, but they still allow us to gauge the uncertainty and concern that surrounded the unusual celestial phenomenon. Was it an omen predicting doom? An indication that yet another *saeculum* had come to an end? Or was it, conversely, a sign heralding the future greatness of Octavian?[180] The one interpretation that ultimately won out, however (with a little help from Octavian and Augustan writers and artists), was that the comet indicated the apotheosis of Caesar[181]—or even that it was literally "the soul of Caesar having been received into heaven."[182]

The so-called *sidus Iulium* subsequently became something of an Augustan logo, appearing in poetry as well as on coinage and in artwork.[183] Octavian placed a star over the head of statues of Caesar that he erected in the forum and in the temple of Venus Genetrix, and the same iconography was likely

179. For the comet itself, see Ramsey and Licht 1997 (with a collection of sources), as well as Domenicucci 1996: 29–85. For its shifting representations and interpretations, see Bechtold 2011: 161–225 and Pandey 2013, 2018: 35–82.

180. Bad omen: Cass. Dio 45.7.1; end of *saeculum* (cf. 6.2 above): *Serv. Dan.* ad *Ecl.* 9.46; good omen for Octavian: Plin. *HN* 2.93–94; *Serv. Dan.* ad *Ecl.* 9.46.

181. Plin. *HN* 2.94 (citing Augustus's autobiography fr. 6 Malcovati = 60 *F1 FRHist*); *Serv. Dan.* ad *Aen.* 8.681.

182. Suet. *Iul.* 88: *creditumque est animam esse Caesaris in caelum recepti.* The scenario of an actual catasterism is developed in the greatest detail in Ov. *Met.* 15.745–851, on which see Volk forthcoming c.

183. Both literary and artistic representations oscillate between conceptualizing the celestial phenomenon as a star and depicting it as an actual comet (the latter enters numismatic iconography only in the 20s BCE). This may reflect uncertainty about the nature of the heavenly body observed in 44; concern about the traditionally ill-omened significance of comets; the lack of a precedent for catasterism into a comet; and/or the fact that stellar (but not cometary) imagery was already an established element of honorific iconography.

used for the colossal statue of *diuus Iulius* in the new god's temple, construction of which was begun in 42 and which was finally dedicated in 29.[184] A decree of the senate of 1 January 42 effectively sealed Caesar's apotheosis (Cass. Dio 47.18.3–19.3), doing away with the confusion concerning the dead man's status: the deified Julius was now officially a god.

How did it come to this? How did a Roman senator end up being worshiped in a temple, with the result that from then on, the apotheosis of members of the Imperial family came to be perceived, first, as a distinct possiblity; then, as an expected outcome; and, finally, as a matter of course? It is impossible to determine to what extent Caesar had been stage-managing his own deification. Some scholars have viewed the dictator as executing a carefully conceived master plan, which culminated in his duly becoming a god in early 44; others have seen him carried along by developments that were not of his own making and of which he may or may not have approved. Dio (44.7) describes a kind of race to shower Caesar with more and more honors, motivated by a wish not only to please him, but also to test him or even open him to ridicule or criticism: how far would Caesar go, and when would he—or otherwise his peers—decide that enough was enough? We do not have to accept Dio's claim that some of the honors proposed were deliberately absurd (Did someone really bring a motion that Caesar be granted the right to sleep with as many women as he liked, as the historian reports at 44.7.3?) in order to find them lacking, as it were, in rhyme or reason. The senators who voted for these measures had not thought out what it would mean for Rome to have a cult of a living (or even dead) political leader, a scenario that was completely unprecedented and for which there could be no blueprint. They and, I suspect, Caesar himself were just feeling their way and may have ended up with something that no one had foreseen and many did not care for.

Even so, Caesar's apotheosis did not come out of the blue. What were the conditions that paved the way for *diuus Iulius*, making it conceivable at that moment in history for a human being to "become" a god? As Spencer Cole has shown in his monograph *Cicero and the Rise of Deification at Rome*, diverse ideas about how outstanding men and women might achieve immortality or even divine status had been gaining traction in late Republican Rome, with Cicero, as so often, both providing our best source for the zeitgeist and himself

---

184. The number, placement, and chronology of statues of Caesar surmounted by a star are not entirely clear: Plin. *HN* 2.94 cites Augustus's autobiography to the effect that Octavian erected such a statue *in foro*; Cass. Dio 45.7.1 says he placed one in the temple of Venus; and Suet. *Iul.* 88 simply states that *simulacro eius in vertice additur stella* ("a star is added to the top of the head of his statue").

playing an active role in shaping it.[185] The apotheosis of Caesar was the culmination of a number of interlocking developments, which once again demonstrate the intricate interactions among the period's intellectual and political theories and practices.

First, in an age of antiquarianism, early Roman history and prehistory were able to provide attractive models. Both Aeneas and Romulus had become deified after their deaths, helped, no doubt, by the fact that they were themselves descended from the gods. Caesar, of course, had divine ancestry himself and had been advertising this fact from early in his career. In the famous funeral oration for his aunt Iulia (69/68 BCE), he stressed her descent both from kings (her mother's family were the Marcii Reges, who traced themselves back to Ancus Marcius) and from the gods: "the Julians, the *gens* to which our family belongs, are descended from Venus."[186] Genealogy, that favored antiquarian mode of thought, could easily turn into destiny.[187]

In addition, a number of philosophical ideas were becoming widespread that suggested mechanisms by which a human being could live on after death and even experience a status change from man to god. According to the rationalizing theology of Euhemerus (4th/3rd c.)—known at Rome at least since Ennius's eponymous work—the gods had originally been human benefactors, which meant conversely that outstanding humans had a chance of turning into gods. Varro reports as a matter of fact that "there are some gods who from the beginning were certain and eternal, and others who turned from human brings into immortals."[188] Works of religious antiquarianism demonstrated that the Greco-Roman pantheon was full of divinities with apparently human origin, while discussions of philosophical theology, such as Cicero's *De natura deorum*, showed that there were numerous different ways of conceiving of the divine. Even the Epicureans, often suspected of being atheists, accorded divine worship to their founder on account of his salvific teachings. "It must be said

185. See Cole 2013, as well as Gildenhard 2011: 255–98, 373–84.

186. Suet. *Iul.* 6.1 = Caesar fr. 29 Malcovati: *a Venere Iulii, cuius gentis familia est nostra.* On Caesar's ancestry and the use he made of it, see Badian 2009.

187. We have already encountered Varro's pragmatic attitude to such appeals to divine descent (see 5.2 above): "it is useful for communities . . . if outstanding men believe themselves to be descended from the gods, even if it is false" (*utile esse ciuitatibus . . . ut se uiri fortes, etiamsi falsum sit, diis genitos esse credant, ARD* fr. 20† Cardauns).

188. Varro, *ARD* fr. 32* Cardauns: *deos alios esse qui ab initio certi et sempiterni sunt, alios qui immortales ex hominibus facti sunt*; cf. also frr. 30–31. In the religious lawcode of *Leg.* 2.19, Cicero prescribes equal worship for "both the gods who have always been considered heaven-dwellers and those whom their merits have placed into heaven" (*diuos et eos qui caelestes semper habiti sunt . . . et ollos quos endo caelo merita locauerint*).

that he was a god, a god!," exclaims Lucretius—though in line with his natural philosophy, he also has to admit that "even Epicurus passed away when the light of his life had run its course."[189]

The awkward fact that human beings die posed an obvious problem for their joining the ranks of the gods, who were by definition immortal. The mainstream Hellenistic schools held out little hope for an afterlife, god-like or otherwise: in both Stoicism and Epicureanism, the individual soul does not survive. By contrast, Pythagoreanism and Platonism promoted the immortality of the soul, which opened up a number of possible post-mortem scenarios: continued metempsychosis, punishment for wrongdoings, or otherwise a reward that might take the form of a blessed afterlife not unlike the life of the gods. Most famously, the good statesmen of Cicero's *Somnium Scipionis* after their passing enjoy a heightened form of existence in the Milky Way, and Africanus takes it upon himself to explain to his grandson how this is possible by citing a proof for the immortality of the soul directly taken from Plato's *Phaedrus*.[190]

The Roman worthies of the *Somnium* are not gods, but they are not exactly normal (dead) human beings either. In addition to Platonic theories about the survival of individual souls, Cicero's dream narrative taps into another set of ideas that was becoming more and more widespread at the time: the fascination with the starry sky, which was often considered divine, the repository of divine signs, and/or the locus of a celestial afterlife.[191] The idea that human souls have a stellar origin and therefore return to the heavens after a person's death (*Rep.* 6.13, 15) is found in Plato's *Timaeus* (41d4–42d2), and Cicero's decision to house his well-deserving statesmen in the Milky Way was likely inspired by a cosmological work of the fourth-century philosopher Heraclides of Pontus.

We have already seen how in the first century BCE, astrology became popular in Rome (6.1). So did the *Phaenomena* of Aratus, the Hellenistic didactic poem about the constellations that in the Greek world was used as a textbook of astronomy and had become the object of extensive literary, scientific, and philosophical commentary. Cicero translated the work, ushering in an unparalleled series of Latin versions and adaptations by, among others, Vergil, Ovid, Germanicus, and Manilius.[192] While appealing to the Romans at least in part because of its refined Hellenistic aesthetics, the *Phaenomena* also helped

189. Lucr. 5.8: *dicendum est, deus ille fuit, deus*; 3.1042: *ipse Epicurus obit decurso lumine uitae*.

190. See Cic. *Rep.* 6.27–28 ~ Pl. *Phdr.* 245c5–246a2. Cicero discusses Platonic arguments for the immortality of the soul further at *Tusc.* 1, where he reuses his translation at 1.53–54.

191. See Orth 1994 and Bechtold 2011: 13–160.

192. See the literature cited in n. 31 above.

project a Stoicizing vision of the heavens as a divinely ordered sign system that is there for human beings to contemplate and interpret. In keeping with Greek lore, Aratus's individual constellations were humans, animals, and objects that had been transposed to the sky, often as a reward or otherwise a memorial for their actions on earth. Catasterism—immortalization by stellification—was thus an accepted idea, at least within the realm of mythology (or what Varro would have called poetic theology). If it had transformed Perseus and Andromeda, could it also happen to the heroes of the contemporary world?

It was in the 50s BCE that Catullus translated into Latin the episode of the "Lock of Berenice" from Callimachus's *Aetia*.[193] In 245 BCE, a lock of hair that the Egyptian queen Berenice II had dedicated in a temple had unaccountably disappeared, upon which the astrologer Conon declared that it had been transformed into a new constellation, which he happened to have just discovered (and which to this day is known as *Coma Berenices*). Callimachus immortalized the incident in a whimsical poem written in the persona of the lock itself; the original survives only in fragments, but Catullus's translation gives us an excellent sense of what it must have been like. To his contemporary readers, it afforded a glance at a world not far from Rome, where a charismatic figure could (at least in part) be turned into a heavenly body.[194]

The Lock of Berenice provides an excellent example of the confluence of the political, intellectual, and artistic: a scientist's bona fide discovery and a poet's masterpiece combined to celebrate the ruling family and shore up their superhuman status. Comparable scenarios played out throughout the Greco-Roman world, as theoretical ideas about the divine potential of certain human beings were increasingly applied to real-life situations, sparking diverse verbal and visual representations, and continuously pushing the boundaries of what was deemed imaginable, acceptable, and perhaps ultimately inescapable. Thus, in a form of Euhemerism in action, it had long been customary in the Greek

---

193. Catull. 66; Callim. *Aet.* frr. 110–110f Harder. On the historical incident behind the poetry, see Bechtold 2011: 81–100.

194. There is tantalizing evidence that Augustus made an attempt to commemorate Caesar, *Coma Berenices* style, by granting him a more permanent heavenly abode than that afforded by a passing comet: Pliny in passing mentions a constellation "that in the reign of the divine Augustus was named Caesar's Throne" (*quem sub diuo Augusto cognominauere Caesaris thronum*, *HN* 2.178), and it has been suggested that a strange rectangular shape on the globe of the Farnese Atlas represents this new set of stars. See further Domenicucci 1996: 66–70 and Bechtold 2011: 199–201. There are many problems with the evidence, but if there really was such a move to create a Julian constellation, the Throne of Caesar, unlike the Lock of Berenice, never managed to catch on and was subsequently forgotten.

world to award divine honors to outstanding public figures, and many of the Hellenistic kings, first and foremost the Egyptian Ptolemies, enjoyed ruler cult as a matter of course. In the course of their conquest of the eastern Mediterranean, Roman generals and administrators, too, had become accustomed to receiving divine honors and being hailed as benefactors. Even Cicero was offered "altars, shrines, chariots" during his proconsular stint in Cilicia in 51 BCE (he modestly declined),[195] but this was nothing compared to the honors showered on such successful eastern campaigners as Sulla and Pompey.

As we saw in 6.1, once back at Rome, the warlords of the era continued to advertise their divine favor and potential. For the most part, this played out on the level of association or metaphor. If Sulla called himself ἐπαφρόδιτος "beloved by Venus" or stressed his *felicitas*, he signaled that he was favored by a particular goddess and shared in a divine quality, not that he was literally a god. When Cicero in his speech on the Manilian Law ascribed to Pompey *diuinum consilium* (10) and *diuina uirtus* (36), he did not mean to tell his audience that the general was really "divine." As Cole has argued, however, such "assimilation via metaphor served to lessen the conceptual distance between gods and humans at a time when humans (such as Pompey and Caesar) were being brought into closer relationship with divinity" (2013: 33). If you call someone a god often enough, he may end up becoming one.

What we find, then, in the last decades of the Republic, is a wide variety of concepts and practices that made it increasingly conceivable that a living man might already be in some sense divine or that he might turn into a god after his death. Helga Gesche in her monograph on Caesar's apotheosis helpfully distinguishes between *Vergöttlichung* (*divinization*, approximation to the divine) and *Vergottung* (*deification*, officially declaring somebody a god).[196] As (speech) acts of divinization proliferated and intensified in the mid-first century, coming to a fever pitch during Caesar's dictatorship, the process reached a tipping point in early 44 when actual deification was suddenly on the table—and voted in, just as so many other honors had been ratified.

In the conceptual confusion and political uncertainty that reigned at the time, we cannot be sure that Romans felt that a line had been crossed. Cicero's remarks from 45 about Romulus's tentmate are caustic but no more outraged than his other observations about Caesar. After Caesar's death, Cicero inveighs against the sacrilege of religious cult for a dead man—"I can't bring myself to

---

195. Cic. *Att.* 5.21.7: *statuas fana* τέθριππα *prohibeo*.

196. Gesche 1968. Koortbojian 2013: 23 distinguishes three stages: honoring someone *as* a god; decreeing that someone *is* a god; and *making* someone a god, that is, working out the exact cult and iconography.

link a dead person to the worship of the immortal gods"[197]—and, as we have seen, deplores the existence of a *flamen* for *diuus Iulius*. Even so, concern about Caesar's apotheosis does not seem to have been at the center of his pre- or post-Ides concern. Cicero did not live to witness the senatorial decree of 1 January 42 or the construction of Caesar's temple. He did not realize as yet that Roman civic religion had undergone a momentous shift.

One of the reasons Caesar's increasing divinity may have slipped under the radar is that the religious honors voted for him were only a small part of a long and seemingly never-ending series of offices, titles, powers, and privileges. What really worried a Cicero and other Republicans was less the outlandish idea that Caesar was supposed to have a temple and *flamen* than the very real danger that he was going to declare himself king. The real scandal of early 44 was not the senate vote of apotheosis (which apparently no one was rushing to implement) but the infamous scene at the Lupercalia of 15 February, when Antony offered Caesar the royal diadem (Plut. *Caes.* 61; Suet. *Iul.* 79.2; Cass. Dio 44.11). Again we do not know enough to understand what exactly the men were thinking, but it seems most likely that this was in fact a botched coronation attempt: when he perceived a lack of public approval, Caesar got cold feet and ostentatiously refused the honor. For the likes of Brutus and Cassius, however, the incident was a last straw; a month later, Caesar was dead. That he was able to become a god but failed to make himself king tells us much about the late Republican mentality.

But just as Brutus, Cassius, and their associates could not rewind the clock and bring back a senate-controlled republic, the death of Caesar did not undo the changes in the Roman cultural imagination that had been building up over time yet had been catalyzed by the events of the early 40s. What had become thinkable could not be unthought, and what had been shocking under Caesar became normalized under Augustus: of course Rome was best ruled by a charismatic *princeps*; of course an outstanding man could turn into a god or (take your pick) into a star. The gods continued their providential care for Rome, but now with specific focus on the savior figure of Augustus.

When in the 50s Lucretius at the beginning of *De rerum natura* implored Venus to give peace to the Romans, he addressed her—in a manner that was orthodox from a Republican Roman, though not from an Epicurean, point of view—as a goddess to whom all the *Aeneadae* were dear. When thirty years later Vergil brought on the same goddess at the beginning of the *Aeneid*, she was treated to a speech from Jupiter (1.257–96) that revealed an utterly changed

---

197. Cic. *Phil.* 1.13: *adduci tamen non possem ut quemquam mortuum coniungerem cum deorum immortalium religione.*

outlook: while the Romans as a whole were granted *imperium sine fine* (279), the course of history from the fall of Troy to Vergil's own day was revealed to be the teleological unrolling of the fate of one privileged family, culminating in the *pax Augusta*. In the long-running race to coopt the cosmos, Augustus had won out—and from now on, there would be no other competitors.

4. The Auspices of Virtue

But let us go back to the time when the outcome of that struggle was still unknown. For all his mocking of the Lyre's following a dictator's orders and Caesar's bunking with Quirinus, Cicero too was highly adept at claiming divine support for himself and others, and generally at presenting both Roman politics and his own actions as part of a larger cosmic order.[198] As mentioned above, he was at the forefront of exploring the possibilities of an afterlife or even apotheosis for deserving individuals, and in many a speech invoked the gods and involved them in the affairs of the *res publica* and in his own. To focus on just one particularly striking case of Ciceronian political theologizing, let us consider the religious narrative he constructed around his suppression of the Catilinarian conspiracy during his consulship.

In the course of the four Catilinarian speeches, as events progressed from 8 November to 5 December 63 BCE, Cicero ascribed an increasingly significant role to the gods.[199] The first speech began and ended with appeals to Jupiter Stator, in whose temple the senate was meeting on that occasion and whom Cicero credited with the uncovering of the conspiracy and implored to persecute and eliminate Catiline and his wicked followers (*Cat.* 1.11, 33). In the second speech, addressed to the people after Catiline's departure from Rome, Cicero declared that the gods were openly protecting Rome and guiding his own actions (*Cat.* 2.29):

> quae quidem ego neque mea prudentia neque humanis consiliis fretus polliceor vobis, Quirites, sed multis et non dubiis deorum immortalium significationibus, quibus ego ducibus in hanc spem sententiamque sum ingressus. qui iam non procul, ut quondam solebant, ab externo hoste atque

---

198. For different approaches to Cicero and (his use of) religion, see Heibges 1969a, Goar 1972, Troiani 1984, Gildenhard 2011: 246–385, Luke 2014: 88–112, and the papers in Beltrão da Rosa and Santangelo (eds.) 2020; on Cicero and divination, see Linderski 1982; Guillaumont 1984; and Rasmussen 2000, 2003: 183–98; on Cicero and immortality/apotheosis, see Cole 2013.

199. On religious themes in the *Catilinarians*, see Vasaly 1993: 40–87, Gildenhard 2011: 272–92, V. Sauer 2013, and Beltrão da Rosa 2020.

longinquo, sed hic praesentes suo numine atque auxilio sua templa atque urbis tecta defendunt.

This [viz. taking effective measures against the conspirators], citizens, I promise you, trusting not in my own intelligence and human capacities, but in many reliable communications from the gods; under their lead I have come to my present hopeful attitude. At this point, they are not as in the past defending their temples and the houses of the city from far away against an external and foreign enemy, but do so with their divine power right here in our presence.

In the third speech nearly a month later, Cicero was able to bring the people the happy news that the Catilinarians had been convicted in the senate thanks to the evidence of the Allobroges and that the urban wing of the uprising had thus been effectively suppressed. Cicero ascribed this salvation of the *res publica* in the same breath to both "the greatest love of the immortal gods for you" and "my labors, plans, and dangers."[200]

In this speech, Cicero was also more forthcoming about the specific signs that he and the other Romans had received from the gods.[201] Not only were there plenty of obvious portents during his consulship, such as comets, lightning strikes, and earthquakes (3.18), but the current events also spectacularly confirmed the interpretation of a number of signs that had been observed two years earlier, in the consulship of L. Aurelius Cotta and L. Manlius Torquatus (65 BCE). In that year, lightning had struck and partly destroyed a number of metal objects on the Capitoline hill, including statues of gods and men, bronze tablets with legal inscriptions, and even the sculpture of the she-wolf that had nursed Romulus and Remus (3.19). When the *haruspices* were consulted, they issued dire warnings of "bloodshed, arson, the end of law and order, foreign and domestic war, and the downfall of the entire city and empire,"[202] but as usual also suggested placatory measures by which the disaster might be averted. These were duly executed, except that the authorities apparently dragged their feet concerning the stipulated erection of a new and larger statue of Jupiter. Unlike its predecessor, the new Jove—so the *haruspices*—was to face toward the east and the forum, in order better to be able to communicate to the senate and people any secret plots being hatched against the *res publica* (3.20).

---

200. *Cat.* 3.1: *deorum immortalium summo erga uos amore laboribus consiliis periculis meis*; cf. 3.4, 18–29.

201. Cic. *Cat.* 3.18–22. On these portents, see Engels 2007: 607–11.

202. *Cat.* 3.19: *caedis atque incendia et legum interitum et bellum ciuile ac domesticum et totius urbis atque imperi occasum.* Cf. 6.2 above.

What greater sign of divine support than the fact that this statue was finally put up on the very day the Catilinarians' plot was laid open? Obviously, the denouement of the conspiracy was brought about "at the nod of Jupiter Optimus Maximus."[203] As Cicero stated to the senate in the fourth Catilinarian, "this is the finale the immortal gods wanted for my consulship."[204]

Cicero published his consular speeches in 60 BCE, in an attempt to advance his own version of his consulship at a time when his actions three years earlier were increasingly being criticized. At the same time, he cast about for other media in which to broadcast his own version of his achievements.[205] Thus, he published a Greek prose account of his consulship and, after a failed attempt to commission a Greek celebratory work from the poet Archias, took matters in his own hands and wrote a Latin epic poem about the events of 63.

Cicero's *De consulatu suo* today survives only in fragments, but we know that it consisted of three books and can still tell that it was a work of considerable originality, not least in the fact that its poet was also its protagonist.[206] A striking feature of the narrative is the consular hero's close interaction with the gods: Cicero participates in a divine council, where he is charged by Jupiter with the guardianship of Rome; learns the *artes* from Minerva; and is treated to separate speeches by two Muses, Urania and Calliope.[207] The message is clear: Cicero is not only supported by the gods but privy to their plans, acting as their representative on earth and the faithful executor of their designs. Enhanced by epic grandeur and poetic embellishment, *De consulatu suo* thus sends the same message as the *Catilinarians*.

The parallel is especially pronounced in the speech of Urania, which at seventy-five lines is by far our longest fragment and which rehearses once more the portents cited in the third speech.[208] In a didactic mode, the Muse begins with a Stoicizing description of the cosmos, explaining how the universe is pervaded and ruled by the divine mind of Jupiter (fr. 2.1–10 Soubiran). This provides a physico-theological explanation for the signs that are enumerated in great detail in what follows, including both the portents observed by Cicero himself in 63 and the ones interpreted by the *haruspices* two years earlier (11–65), and culminating once more in the timely erection of the new

203. *Cat.* 3.21: *nutu Iouis Optimi Maximi.*

204. *Cat.* 4.2: *hunc exitum consulatus mei di immortales esse uoluerunt.*

205. See Steel 2005: 49–63 and Volk 2013: 94–95.

206. I discuss the poem and its generic inventiveness in Volk 2013; see further Plezia 1983, Kubiak 1994, Setaioli 2005, Kurczyk 2006: 75–120, and Gildenhard 2011: 292–98.

207. Divine council and Minerva: [Sall.] *Cic.* 4.7; Quint. *Inst.* 11.1.24; Urania: Cic. *Div.* 1.17–22 = fr. 2 Soubiran; Calliope: Cic. *Att.* 2.3.4 = fr. 8 Soubiran.

208. Kurczyk 2006: 95–97 provides a comparative table of the signs mentioned in both texts.

statue of Jupiter on the Capitol. In light of the veracity of these divine signs, Urania concludes that the wise men of old in general and the Roman *maiores* in particular were right to offer worship to the gods (66–70) and that the same pious attitude was promoted also by those who studied "in the shady Academy and shiny Lyceum."[209] One of these philosophically minded paragons is none other than Cicero himself (75–76):

> e quibus ereptum primo iam a flore iuuentae
> te patria in media uirtutum mole locauit.

> Already in your early youth, the fatherland snatched you from among them and placed you right in the middle of the contest of virtue.

Philosophically trained, divinely favored, and virtuously dedicated to the common good, the consul of 63 was the right man for Rome's hour of need.

Like many other fragments of Ciceronian poetry, we owe Urania's speech to the author's self-citation. In the Academic *in utramque partem* discussion of *De diuinatione* (whose composition straddles the Ides of March 44), Quintus Cicero, defending divination, makes a point of using his brother's past actions, utterances, and publications to build a case against him.[210] In his effort to assemble a vast trove of empirical data to demonstrate the existence of reliable divine signs, Quintus quotes from Marcus's *Aratea*, *De consulatu suo*, and *Marius*; refers to *De natura deorum*; mentions a prophetic dream of his brother's and a true prediction to which he was privy during the Civil War; and delights in drawing attention to Marcus's membership in the augural college.[211] He is optimistic that this ad hominem strategy is going to work, since Marcus will hardly wish to embarrass himself by contradicting his own previous prodivination stance (*Div.* 1.22):

> tu igitur animum poteris inducere contra ea quae a me disputantur de diuinatione dicere, qui et gesseris ea quae gessisti et ea quae pronuntiaui accuratissime scripseris?

---

209. Fr. 2.73 Soubiran: *inque Academia umbrifera nitidoque Lyceo.*

210. On *De diuinatione*, see my discussion in Volk 2017: 334–42, as well as Goar 1968; Guillaumont 1984: 45–49, 2006; Denyer 1985; Beard 1986; Schofield 1986; Hankinson 1988; Timpanaro 1988, 1994; Leonhardt 1999: 66–73; Krostenko 2000; Wardle 2006; Fox 2007: 209–40; Schultz 2009, 2014; Ciafardone 2012; Santangelo 2013: 10–36; Woolf 2015: 62–86; Vielberg 2019; and Wynne 2019.

211. *Aratea*: *Div.* 1.13–16; *De consulatu suo*: 1.17–22; *Marius*: 1.106; *De natura deorum*: 1.33, 93, 117; dream: 1.58–59; prediction: 1.68–69; augurate: 1.25, 28, 29, 30, 72, 90, 103, 105. On Quintus's strategy and the problems it raises, see Schofield 1986: 56–58, Krostenko 2000: 380–85, Fox 2007: 230–40, Santangelo 2013: 25–27, Volk 2017: 338–42, Bishop 2019: 286–98, and Vielberg 2019: 53–61.

Can you really bring yourself to argue against my points about divination, you who have done what you have done and written (and very well, too) what I just quoted?

But Quintus has not reckoned with his brother's dogged Skepticism. While Marcus sidesteps his opponent's accusation of self-contradiction,[212] he cheerfully proceeds to demolish all of Quintus's examples, including those taken from his own works. The list of portents surrounding the Catilinarian conspiracy comes in for special sarcasm (*Div.* 2.47):

> Nattae uero statua aut aera legum de caelo tacta quid habent obseruatum ac uetustum? "Pinarii Nattae nobiles; a nobilitate igitur periculum." hoc tam callide Iuppiter cogitauit! "Romulus lactens fulmine ictus, urbi igitur periculum ostenditur, ei quam ille condidit." quam scite per notas nos certiores facit Iuppiter! "at eodem tempore signum Iouis conlocabatur quo coniuratio indicabatur." et tu scilicet mavis numine deorum id factum quam casu arbitrari; et redemptor qui columnam illam de Cotta et de Torquato conduxerat faciendam non inertia aut inopia tardior fuit, sed a deis immortalibus ad istam horam reseruatus est!

What case of long-standing observation is there in the case of the statue of Natta and the legal bronze tablets that were hit by lightning?[213] "The Pinarii Nattae are *nobiles*; therefore danger is threatening from the nobility." How cleverly Jupiter thought that one out! "The suckling Romulus was hit by lightning, thus danger is portended to the city he founded." In what a learned manner Jupiter informs us through signs! "But the statue of Jupiter was erected at the same moment as the conspiracy was revealed." Sure, and you want to believe that this happened at the behest of the gods rather than by chance. And the contractor who had received the job of making the column from Cotta and Torquatus wasn't late because of laziness or lack of funds but because he was held back by the immortal gods until that very hour!

So much for the divine communications the consul Cicero received from the gods. The alleged portents were really chance events that were interpreted in a symbolic fashion that is so painfully banal as to be an insult to the gods' intelligence. If analogy is the name of the divinatory game, anybody can read "signs" like that (*Div.* 2.59):

---

212. *Div.* 2.46; on this passage, see Volk 2017: 338–40.

213. Long-term observation had been stipulated by Quintus as the condition for the establishment of prophetic signs over time.

quod Platonis Politian nuper apud me mures corroserunt, de re publica debui pertimescere.

When recently mice gnawed on my copy of Plato's *Republic*, I should have been afraid for the *res publica*.

Throughout book 2 of *De diuinatione*, Marcus delivers a devastating Skeptic attack on the existence of divination, demonstrating (i) that the many examples adduced by Quintus (including those taken from Marcus himself) inspire no trust, and (ii) that what is entirely missing is any kind of causal explanation of the alleged nexus among signifying gods, prophetic sign, and actual outcome. His merciless debunking of cherished Roman tales and satirizing of his contemporaries' gullibility make for a very entertaining read, but the extension of this destructive attitude to his own utterances and experiences raises uncomfortable questions.[214] As has often been pointed out, Cicero goes out of his way to include in the discussion putative instances of divination previously championed by himself, and additionally draws the readers' attention to them by having Quintus gloat over his personalized strategy. He could perfectly well have written a dialogue on divination without reference to his own past or even without himself as an interlocutor. The way he chose to do it helps move the dialogue's question out of the comfort zone of the Tusculan villa into the open field of Roman public life. Are there really gods who care for us and communicate with signs? As Cicero puts it in the preface, the basic question is "how much weight we should give to the auspices, to sacred rites and religion." If we trust them too much, we risk becoming superstitious; if we trust them too little, we may slide into impiety.[215]

The apparent contradiction between Cicero's stance on divination in *De diuinatione* and his attitude in earlier works—not only the *Catilinarians* and *De consulatu suo*, but also other speeches, as well as the religious legislation in *De legibus*—has called forth diverse scholarly attempts at a solution or explanation. In one widespread interpretation of the dialogue, the problem is a mirage. Following two influential articles published in 1986 by Mary Beard and Malcolm Schofield, many critics read *De diuinatione* as a strictly balanced

---

214. In addition to explaining away the portents of the Catilinarian conspiracy, Marcus also provides a purely psychological aetiology of his own "prophetic" dream (*Div.* 2.136–42) and interprets the frenzied "prediction" he heard in Dyrrhachium during the Civil War as a mere expression of prebattle fear and panic (2.114).

215. *Div.* 1.7: *in quo iudicandum est quantum auspiciis rebusque diuinis religionique tribuamus. est enim periculum ne aut neglectis iis impia fraude aut susceptis anili superstitione obligemur.*

debate *in utrumque partem* that ends in aporia.[216] The fact that the role of the Skeptic is played by "Marcus" does not make him into a mouthpiece for Cicero himself, whose own views do not enter into the debate. In the end, both opinions have been given equal airtime, and it is up the reader to decide.

As I have argued elsewhere, however, this strictly balanced reading does not capture the trajectory of the dialogue.[217] Cicero's method in his Skeptic dialogues aims not at presenting all views as ultimately equally valid, but at establishing different levels of plausibility; thus, for example, in *De finibus* and *De natura deorum*, Epicurean views are dismissed early on while Stoic and Antiochean theories remain in the running.[218] At the same time, not all speakers are given equal roles: the Skeptics, including Marcus in *De diuinatione*, do not put forward dogmatic views but simply demolish the arguments of their interlocutors. What Marcus stands for is not the belief that there is no divination, but the observation that no convincing arguments for its existence have been adduced and that the proposition therefore remains implausible. It is this skepticism that wins the day at the end of the dialogue and is the result of his examination of the issue that Cicero wished to project: that it seems *unlikely* that divination exists. Finally, note that even on a strictly balanced reading, the problem of self-contradiction does not entirely go away: even if Marcus does not stand for Cicero's own view, the fact that the author would in a published work have his own persona dismiss his previously constructed political theology might at least raise a few eyebrows.

One possible explanation of the shift in Cicero's attitude is that he simply changed his mind. Some scholars believe that his Academic Skepticism was a development of the 40s, while earlier philosophical works (including *De legibus*, with its appeal to natural law and religious legislation) are characterized by a Platonist or Antiochean dogmatism.[219] This view has not won widespread acceptance, and most scholars today believe that Cicero was an adherent of Academic Skepticism throughout his life.[220] Of course, the beauty of Ciceronian

---

216. See Beard 1986 and Schofield 1986; scholars who interpret the dialogue in this way include Leonhardt 1999: 66–73; Krostenko 2000; Fox 2007: 209–40; Schultz 2009, 2014; Vielberg 2019; and Wynne 2019.

217. See Volk 2017: 335–37; other scholars who disagree with the Beard/Schofield thesis include Timpanaro 1988, 1994; Setaioli 2005; Wardle 2006; Guillaumont 2006; Ciafardone 2012; and Santangelo 2013: 10–36.

218. See Leonhardt 1999: 13–50, though note that Leonhardt himself espouses the balanced view of *Div.*

219. See esp. Glucker 1988 and Steinmetz 1989.

220. See Görler 1995 for a rebuttal of the Glucker/Steinmetz thesis. The most recent treatment of Cicero's philosophy in its entirety, Woolf 2015, considers the author to have been an Academic Skeptic throughout his career. See further 3.2, n. 70.

probabilism is that one is free to change one's opinion whenever one position comes to appear more probable than another;[221] however, if Cicero really underwent a change of opinion about divination on philosophical grounds, he does not make this explicit.

Alternatively, it has been suggested that there were external factors that caused Cicero to rethink his ideas about divination and divine involvement in public affairs. Was he alarmed by Caesar's use of religion to further his goals?[222] Or was he simply disillusioned after the experience of the Civil War, when all sides had claimed the support of the gods and, as he states in *Div.* 2.53, next to none of the prophecies received actually came true?[223] It is not impossible that right after the assassination of a so-called god, Cicero found himself in a particularly cynical mood as far as religion was concerned. But would that alone have led him to extend his withering wit even to the events of his own cherished consulship?

A different way of accounting for the conceptual tensions between Marcus's speech in *De diuinatione* and other Ciceronian utterances is to argue from context. Scholars often invoke Varro's *theologia tripertita* to make the point that while involved in affairs of state or matters of policy, as in the speeches or *De legibus*, Cicero is, as it were, engaging in civil theology and upholding the practices of the Roman state religion. By contrast, the discussion of the veracity of divination in *De diuinatione* belongs to the field of natural, that is, philosophical theology and need by no means impinge on the execution of traditional public cult. As mentioned in 6.1, the augur Marcus in *De diuinatione*—just as the Skeptic pontiff Cotta in *De natura deorum*—thus explicitly states that he believes that all state-sponsored divination should be kept up for political purposes, even though he himself is deliciously sarcastic about the meaningless rituals of augury.[224]

A related argument can be made about genre. Invocations of the gods are a standard feature of oratory and discussed as such in rhetorical treatises,

---

221. Cf. *Luc.* 121; *Tusc.* 5.33, 83; *Off.* 3.20.

222. See Linderski 1982 and Momigliano 1984: 204–10. Krostenko 2000 even suggests that Cicero in *Div.* is publicly disavowing his religiously inflected poetry as a form of self-representation that, after the experience of Caesar's rule, is no longer acceptable to him.

223. Versions of this view are found in Bländsdorf 1991, Guillaumont 2006, and Santangelo 2013: 10–36.

224. Attack on augury: *Div.* 2.70–83; defense of state religion: 2.70–71, 74, 75, 148. In the opinion of Moatti 1997: 181–83 and Timpanaro 1988: lxxvi–lxxxiii, the failure on the part of Cicero to apply his philosophical convictions to a reform of the religio-political system is a sign of the limits of the Roman "enlightenment."

including Cicero's own.[225] It is also the case that Cicero's speeches to the people more frequently allude to divine signs and interference, as seen in the *Catilinarians*, where the religious theme is more pronounced in the speeches to the *contio* (2 and 3) than in those to the senate (1 and 4), no doubt in an effort to appeal to different audiences. Poetry, of course, follows its own laws and makes use of the gods as mythological characters (Varro's third theology) in such a fashion that no one familiar with the genre would expect the supernatural events recounted in, say, an epic poem to have taken place as such in the real world. This point is nicely made in the opening dialogue of the first book of *De legibus*, where Atticus visits the Cicero brothers in their hometown Arpinum and is looking for the "oak of Marius," a tree associated with a portent concerning Cicero's famous fellow townsman, which Cicero himself had immortalized in his poem *Marius* (*Leg.* 1.1–5). Atticus is quickly disabused of his (pretended?) literalist reading: he learns that rather than being a real tree, the oak "was planted in the imagination" and that "one set of rules must be observed in history writing, another in poetry."[226] Similarly, no one reading *De consulatu suo* would have believed that Cicero really went to a divine council or was addressed by the Muses; obviously, these were poetic manners of speaking.[227]

In a previous discussion of *De diuinatione*, I thus concluded that while Cicero in *De diuinatione* rejects the belief in (as it were, uppercase) Divination, namely, the existence of signs from the gods, this in no way precludes him from skillfully engaging in (lowercase) divination, the numerous practices and (speech) acts traditionally associated with the observation and explication of such putative signs.[228] In the rituals of civic religion, what counts is orthopraxy not orthodoxy; in speeches and poetry, use of the traditional *Götterapparat* furthers the author's purposes. I would even maintain that the references to Cicero's own poetry and experiences in *De diuinatione*, despite Marcus's mockery, still paradoxically serve to add, as it were, a halo of significance to the author's political career. Even if readers take the enlightened position that Muses do not converse with people and lightning damage to statues does not have any symbolic significance, the speech of Urania still signals

---

225. See Cic. *Inv. rhet.* 1.101; *Part. or.* 6; *Top.* 77; Quint. *Inst.* 5.11.42 (with reference to the third *Catilinarian*). On religious themes in Cicero's speeches and rhetorical writing, see Heibges 1969a, 1969b and Guillaumont 1984: 19–24.

226. *Leg.* 1.1: *sata est enim ingenio*; 5: *alias in historias leges observandas . . . alias in poemate.*

227. Even so, Cicero's poetic self-representation as being in close contact with the divine came in for ridicule and criticism; see Cic. *Dom.* 92; [Sall.] *Cic.* 2.3, 4.7; Quint. *Inst.* 11.1.24.

228. See Volk 2017: 334–42.

what it had always signaled: that Cicero's consulship was an extraordinary achievement.[229]

The different explanations mustered in the preceding pages go a long way toward lessening the tension between the Skeptic *De diuinatione* and Cicero's attempts elsewhere at coopting the cosmos: different contexts call for different discourses and practices, and the Skeptic is not bound to stick to a formerly expressed opinion. A master of verbal art and rhetorical *decorum*, Cicero was able to adjust his speech to whatever the occasion and his own purposes demanded, whether it was fervent religiosity or jaded irony. Even so, however, it seems to me that the attitude displayed in *De diuinatione* is not adopted simply for the purpose of a particular dialogue or otherwise an aspect of Cicero's intellectual makeup that—in a case of strict brain-balkanization—was kept apart from his public actions and pronouncements. I suggest that beyond its immediate argumentative purpose, it is expressive of a consistent view of the human condition that we can find throughout Cicero's life and work—a life and work that, as we have seen again and again in this book, was characterized by the intrinsic linkage of politics, philosophy, and personality.

This is not the place to enter into a comprehensive examination of Cicero's world-view or philosophical methodology, let alone review the immense scholarly literature on the subject. What interests me here is an idiosyncratic feature of his philosophizing that has been often observed and variously explained: for a professed Skeptic, Cicero seems at points remarkably ready actually to espouse certain philosophical positions. Does this mean that he was really a dogmatist at heart, a crypto-Platonist, Antiochean, or Stoic—or otherwise that he changed his philosophical persuasion one or more times in the course of his life (see above)? There is no need for such assumptions as long as we keep in mind that Cicero's Skepticism was of a remarkably constructive and flexible kind.[230] He believed that rigorous *in utramque partem* debate could lead to the discovery of the *ueri simile* and was not shy about espousing what he had determined not to be true, but to be probable. In the *Lucullus*, the Marcus character even proudly declares that he is a *magnus ... opinator* ("great holder of opinions," 66), which means that he is not a wise man but willing to live his life based on what is "similar to the truth."

The *ueri simile* (or at least what appears *ueri simile* to one person at any one time) can be determined through careful examination of all positions, and it

---

229. See Volk 2017: 338–42. Fox 2007: 233–34 suggests that the quotation from *De consulatu suo* was, among other things, intended to bring that poem, and thus Cicero's consulship, back into public awareness.

230. For secondary literature on Cicero's Skepticism, see 3.2, n. 70 above.

may well turn out that there is a hierarchy of probabilities: for example, plea-sure is unlikely to be the *summum bonum*, but whether virtue alone ensures supreme happiness, or whether external goods play a role as well, must remain unclear (thus, in a nutshell, the argument of *De finibus*). Woldemar Görler has additionally argued that very often in Cicero's Skeptic explorations, the op-tions present themselves on a rising scale of three levels.[231] The lowest level, often the Epicurean view, can be dismissed; the middle level is typically the sober option of the Skeptic; but the highest level—thus Cicero's language makes amply clear—is the one that the author *would like to be correct* but can only momentarily persuade himself to approve. Thus, for example, Cicero as-pires to the opinions that virtue is sufficient for the happiest life, that the soul is immortal, and that the gods care for human beings, but he can only occa-sionally bring himself fully to espouse these ambitious positions.

Is it thus the case that Cicero would like to believe that there exists reliable communication between caring gods and the humans and communities that are dear to them, but cannot find arguments for the validity of divination that satisfy his Skeptical standards? According to Görler, this is not so: Cicero in his philosophical works never hints at an approval of divination.[232] In the same vein, John Wynne now argues that the position extremely tentatively approved in the companion dialogues *De natura deorum* and *De diuinatione* is that the gods care for human beings, while divination is clearly rejected as superstition.[233]

While this may be strictly speaking true as far as the trajectory of these dia-logues is concerned, it leaves a number of important questions open. On purely philosophical grounds, how do the gods take care of human beings without communicating with them—and if they do so silently, how would we know?[234] On a more pragmatic level, the attempts of Cicero and others at coopting the cosmos for political purposes do not clinically distinguish be-tween divine signs and other instances of divine favor. Is it possible that the gods watch over Rome but we have no way of ascertaining their approval? Was

231. See Görler 1974 and Gawlik and Görler 1994: 1099–1118.

232. See Görler 1974: 53, 60, 142–43.

233. Wynne 2019 considers "Do the gods care about us?" the "Central Question" of the diptych *Nat. D.* and *Div.*, a question that is ultimately answered in the affirmative.

234. According to a standard Stoic argument, if there are gods, it follows that there is divina-tion (*Nat. D.* 2.12; *Div.* 2.41). Differing views are possible (e.g., the Epicurean gods who neither care for nor interact with human beings), and the Stoic Panaetius famously had doubts about divination (*Div.* 1.6); however, the combination of a belief in divine providence coupled with a rejection of divination still seems to be a fairly marginal position, and one open to objections.

Jupiter supporting Cicero throughout the Catilinarian conspiracy but not in fact sending any signs?

If, instead, we allow for an extension of Görler's thesis that takes account also of nonphilosophical texts and circumstances, we might end up with a Cicero who would *like* to believe that there are gods who care for the *res publica* and for his own efforts at serving her, and who furthermore communicate their divine will to us. This would be a Cicero who uses all the verbal skills at his command to project such a world-view in his speeches and poetry, but who ultimately has to admit to himself and, in all honesty, to his readers that he does not in fact have any good philosophical reasons for allowing him to espouse such a position as probable.

Of course, we cannot be sure what Cicero really thought, but a scenario along these lines appears to be at least plausible. Even so, however, I do not believe that it is the whole story. For underlying Cicero's Skepticism, his shifting espousal of more or less probable positions, there are certain truths that he unquestionably and unchangingly deems correct. Crucially, Cicero believes that "virtue" (*uirtus*), morally correct behavior, is the cornerstone of human life, the basis of all polities, and the necessary and sufficient condition for personal happiness. This primacy of virtue in Cicero's personal, public, and philosophical utterances has often been remarked. To quote Gildenhard, "[t]he idea that human beings are endowed with an internal faculty that instinctively knows right from wrong . . . occupies a prominent place in Cicero's thinking about humanity."[235]

One could argue, of course, using a version of the philosophical charity principle, that Cicero must have arrived at his belief in virtue using rigorous Skeptic debate. In this context, one might point to his references, in many philosophical works, to natural law or to accounts of *oikeiōsis*, the ideal development of human beings from birth to adulthood that results in their realizing their full potential as rational animals. Perhaps Cicero, after extensive thought on the matter, determined as *probabile* the position that human beings are rational and that the world is ordered in such a way that their highest calling is to perfect their nature, that is, achieve virtue and wisdom.[236] Perhaps . . . but it seems to me that for Cicero, the primacy of virtue is something

---

235. Gildenhard 2011: 113. Cf. Görler 1974: 129: "Der Glaube an den Primat der Sittlichkeit und an ihre Autarkie ist bei allen vorgeblich objektiven Untersuchungen das ersehnte Ziel; in diesem Glauben *will* sich Cicero immer wieder bestärken, von ihm will er nicht lassen" (emphasis his).

236. Thorsrud 2009 attempts to make a case along those lines, arguing that Cicero relies on a "kind of philosophical and ethical expertise" (97) that allows him to reach an informed position on matters of virtue.

prephilosophical, a *petitio principii* that is never argued for and must simply be accepted.

Thus, in a short history of Academic philosophy provided by the character Varro as an introduction to his speech in the *Academica*, much is made of Socrates's claim not to know anything and of his aggressive mode of questioning his interlocutors, which typically ended in *aporia*. Nevertheless, Socrates's "entire speech was aimed at praising virtue and exhorting people to strive for virtue."[237] It appears that the desirability of "virtue" is not one of those things Socrates does not know; it is a given, and in fact the very reason and purpose why Socrates enters into conversation with people in the first place.[238]

In Cicero's philosophical works, too, *uirtus* is often the starting point, not something that needs to be argued for. In the very first paragraph of the surviving text of *De re publica*, Cicero states as a fact that "such great necessity of virtue has been given to the human race by nature."[239] Similarly, in the preface to *De finibus* 3, after the Epicurean view of ethics has been dismissed, Cicero considers it obvious that "nothing is to be considered the *summum bonum* that lacks virtue, than which nothing can be more excellent."[240] There are many things about which we cannot know anything for certain and which we therefore must debate in the Skeptic manner; virtue, however, is not one of them.

To return to the topic of this chapter, the Ciceronian primacy of virtue applies to questions of theology and cosmology as well. What matters is for human beings to do the right thing, something that is up to them and their own judgment. Somewhat to the consternation of commentators, the *pontifex* Cotta in *De natura deorum* thus claims outright that virtue is not the gift of the gods: "Has anybody every thanked the gods that he was a good man? . . . It is

237. *Acad. post.* 16: *omnis eius oratio tamen in uirtute laudanda et in hominibus ad uirtutis studium cohortandis consumebatur*; cf. also *De or.* 1.204. See Glucker 1997: 72–75 and McConnell 2019: 252–55.

238. That Socrates excels at exhorting people to virtue but then fails to explain what virtue is and how to achieve it is the contention of the titular character of the (pseudo?-)Platonic *Clitipho* (see esp. 408a1–e2, 410b3–c6). For a modern reading of the Platonic Socrates's "aiming at"—while not having knowledge of—virtue, see Vasiliou 2008.

239. *Rep.* 1.1: *tantam esse necessitatem virtutis generi hominum a natura* [sc. *datam*]. Cicero links this gift of virtue with a second natural capacity: *tantumque amorem ad communem salutem defendendam* ("such great desire to defend the common good"). Cicero's "political imperative," as discussed in 3.2, is thus rooted in his ideas of the primacy of virtue, with politics being the first and foremost area where virtue is exercised.

240. *Fin.* 3.2: *nec uero ullum probetur summum bonum quod uirtute careat, qua nihil potest esse praestantius.*

the belief of all men that one must ask the divine for good fortune but take wisdom from oneself."[241]

In *De diuinatione*, this attitude becomes clearest in Marcus's reaction to Quintus's story about their friend, the Galatian king Deiotarus, who is a great believer in the kind of augury practiced in Asia Minor.[242] Tragically, his trust in the bird signs that told him to support Pompey during the Civil War led to the king's loss of power and resources. Deiotarus's story could thus be interpreted as a cautionary tale against the belief in divination, but Quintus attempts to give it a positive spin: the king maintained that "he did not regret those auspices" and that "the birds had counseled him well" to "defend the authority of the senate, freedom of the Roman people, and dignity of the empire," even if these efforts were entirely unsuccessful.[243]

Marcus, in turns, dismisses Quintus's *exemplum* as "perfectly ridiculous."[244] He is quite willing to believe that his unfortunate but upright friend is not regretting his actions during the Civil War, despite the hardships they caused; however, this has nothing to do with auspicy (*Div.* 2.78–79):

> nec enim ei cornix canere potuit recte eum facere quod populi Romani libertatem defendere pararet; ipse hoc sentiebat, sicuti sensit. aues euentus significant aut aduersos aut secundos. uirtutis auspiciis uideo esse usum Deiotarum, quae uetat spectare fortunam dum praestetur fides. aues uero si prosperos euentus ostenderunt, certe fefellerunt. . . . si euenta quaerimus quae exquiruntur auibus, nullo modo prospera Deiotaro; sin officia, a uirtute ipsius, non ab auspiciis petita sunt.

> No crow could tell Deiotarus that he was doing the right thing in preparing to defend the liberty of the Roman people. He himself was feeling this way, and indeed he did. Birds predict good or bad outcomes. I see that Deiotarus made use of the auspices of virtue, which forbids us to look to fortune as

241. *Nat. D.* 3.87: *num quis quod bonus uir esset gratias dis egit umquam?*; 88: *iudicium hoc omnium mortalium est, fortunam a deo petendam, a se ipso sumendam esse sapientiam.* Mayor 1880–85 ad Cic. *Nat. D.* 3.86 comments that the claim that no one ever credited the gods for his virtue "is very far from the truth." Most of the comparative passages that he and Pease 1958 ad loc. adduce testify to the opposite sentiment.

242. *Div.* 1.26–27; 2.78–79. Less than half a year before the composition of *De diuinatione*, Cicero had defended Deiotarus on the charge of having plotted against Caesar; see 4.4 above.

243. *Div.* 1.27: *negat se tamen eorum auspiciorum quae sibi ad Pompeium proficiscenti secunda euenerint paenitere; senatus enim auctoritatem et populi Romani libertatem atque imperii dignitatem suis armis esse defensam, sibique eas aues, quibus auctoribus officium et fidem secutus esset, bene consuluisse.*

244. *Div.* 2.78: *admodum ridiculum.*

we do our duty. But if the birds foretold him a happy outcome, they certainly deceived him. . . . If we are looking at the kind of outcomes about which one consults the birds, everything went wrong for Deiotarus; but if we look at duty, about this he consulted his own virtue, not the auspices.

Bird signs are neither reliable nor can they provide what a person needs most: moral guidance. For this, we need to consult what Marcus calls the "auspices of virtue," our own judgment of what is right and wrong.[245]

Divination thus turns out to be dangerous at worst and useless at best. Faulty predictions have the potential to mislead people, but correct predictions can at most confirm us in doing what we have already determined to be the right thing anyway. As a result, *if* the gods care for us *and* send us signs, we should ourselves be able to figure out what those signs mean, simply based on our moral compass and without any divinatory expertise whatsoever. This is the attitude Cicero takes in *De haruspicum responsis*. While he makes a great show of deference to the *haruspices* and their ancient *disciplina*, the orator ultimately asserts his right to interpret the reported portents himself (*Har. resp.* 20):

> mitto haruspices, mitto illam ueterem ab ipsis dis immortalibus, ut hominum fama est, Etruriae traditam disciplinam: nos nonne haruspices esse possumus?

> Enough of the *haruspices*, enough already of that old method granted to Etruria (or so the story goes) by the immortal gods: can't we be our own *haruspices*?

Cicero proceeds to give a blow-by-blow reading of the divine signs received, all of which he claims concern the nefarious doings of Clodius. No training in the *disciplina Etrusca* is necessary: simply by virtue of understanding the political situation and its moral implications, Cicero is able to interpret the signs correctly. Clodius is an evil man and a menace to the *res publica*; bad omens therefore *must* be warning of him, just as his consecration of Cicero's house must by necessity have been invalid (see 6.1 above). Cicero presents his haruspical pronouncements with a certain amount of humor—at one point, he compares the bands of slaves Clodius brought to the games of the Megalesia to a swarm of bees, only to wonder how the *haruspices* would interpret the appearance of an actual swarm of bees (25)—but his message is entirely serious: never mind the *haruspices* and their portents, the thing that matters is that something needs to be done about Clodius.

---

245. Cf. *Div.* 2.10–11, where Marcus points out that questions of ethics do not fall under the purview of diviners but philosophers: *ad sapientes haec, not ad diuinos referri solent* (11).

This privileging of human moral responsbility over any possible guidance from above is apparent also in Cicero's private statements. In 3.2, we examined a letter to Atticus from late 60 BCE (*Att.* 2.3), in which Cicero describes his mental processes as he tries to decide whether or not to support Caesar's agrarian legislation. After *in utramque partem* discussion of his options (support Caesar and gain political advantages, or oppose him and take the consequences), Cicero invokes the concluding speech of Calliope from *De consulatu suo*, which bids him to "stick to the course which you have sought with virtuous mind since your early youth and even now as consul."[246] Reminding himself of this moral exhortation goes a long way toward inclining Cicero against the Caesarian option, but his own poem is not the last authority he consults; instead, he concludes with a quotation from Homer (*Att.* 2.3.4, citing *Il.* 12.243):

> non opinor esse dubitandum quin semper nobis uideatur εἷς οἰωνὸς ἄριστος ἀμύνασθαι περὶ πάτρης.

> I don't think I can hesitate to remain true to the maxim "one omen is best: to defend the fatherland."

The virtuous man has no need of signs from the gods (or even from Muses whose speeches he has written himself): the best "bird sign" (οἰωνός) is the call to do what is right for the *res publica*, and to know what that is, Cicero only needs to follow the auspices of virtue.

The context of the Homeric quotation is pertinent as well (*Il.* 12.195–250). In the *Iliad*, the speaker is Hector, who in the absence of Achilles has routed the Achaeans and driven them to their wall and ships. His plan is to press on and set fire to the Achaean fleet, when a bird sign appears, which his companion Polydamas interprets as unpropitious: if Hector continues the fight, many Trojans will never return to their city. Hector reacts in anger, aggressively dismissing Polydamas together with his augury. He himself does not believe in birds but is convinced that he knows the will of Zeus, which obviously bids him to do his utmost to defend his city.

As any reader of the *Iliad* knows, this does not end well for Hector. Cicero, of course, knew this as well, just as he knew that opposing the agrarian legislation would get him into difficulties. Unlike Hector, therefore, who blindly trusted in the support of a treacherous Zeus, Cicero followed the "best bird sign" with his eyes wide open, relying on nothing but his own sense of duty.

Cicero's privileging of virtue does not imply that he did not hold everyday beliefs or philosophically grounded opinions about the order of the cosmos,

---

246. *Att.* 2.3.4 = *De consulatu suo* fr. 8 Soubiran: *interea cursus quos prima a parte iuuentae / quosque adeo consul uirtute animoque petisti, / hos retine.*

the immortality of the soul, the nature of the gods and their care for both the *res publica* and individuals, and the existence and interpretability of divine signs. As we have seen, he discussed these topics in his publications, expressed views about them in speech and in writing, and made highly effective use of cosmological, theological, and divinatory themes in both his poetry and his prose. It is simply that for Cicero such metaphysical subjects are up for speculation and, if need be, manipulation, while his ethical obligation is beyond a doubt. The moral world order is a given; it is the cosmic order that needs to be inferred from it, not the other way around.

In coopting the cosmos, then, Cicero does not seek divine legitimation but claims divine support based on what is morally right. Sulla or Caesar may have been successful because they were championed by a partisan divinity or enjoyed some supernatural *felicitas* or *fortuna*. Cicero, by contrast, did not defeat the Catilinarians because he was supported by the gods: the gods supported him (or could be claimed to have done so) because he acted virtuously on behalf of the *res publica*. And while he may have enjoyed depicting himself as hobnobbing with divinities and being addressed by Urania and Calliope in *De consulatu suo*, Cicero needed no divine advice or explication of portents: he was ready to follow his own reading of the auspices of virtue—even if, like Hector, the "best bird sign" ultimately led him to his death.

7

Conclusion

OVER THE PAST SIX CHAPTERS, we have seen the Roman Republic of Letters in action. We have noted how in the mid-first century BCE, members of
the Roman upper classes were highly educated, including in fields with exclusively Greek pedigrees, and how their aristocratic lifestyle typically included
various intellectual endeavors or *studia*, in which they engaged during periods
of *otium*, often in their villas in the Italian countryside. Such learned pursuits
had a strong social component, as men shared the results of their reading and
writing with their peers or collaborated on individual projects. The sociability
of *studia* and the bonds that such joint study could foster were highly valued,
and *societas studiorum* "comradeship of studies" was perceived as an important
aspect of the networks of *amicitia* that held together the senatorial and equestrian orders.

Against this general background, we have observed how a number of especially remarkable members of the senatorial class engaged in the specific intellectual pursuits and produced the particular works that mark the late Republic
as a period of extraordinary cultural flourishing. Cicero, Caesar, Varro, and
Nigidius Figulus left behind books that include some of the classics of Latin
literature, while such well-known contemporaries of theirs as Cato, Brutus,
and Cassius have not found fame as authors but likewise stand out as men who
combined political leadership with intellectual endeavors. These were very
learned times indeed.

As the individuals studied in these pages demonstrate, late Republican
senators did not keep their intellectual and political activities neatly separate,
but experienced both their *studia* and their public engagement as intrinsically
connected parts of their lives. Both spheres involved what were largely the
same circles of *amici*, as intellectual and political sociable practices overlapped.
A Cicero and a Brutus, for instance, when visiting each other's houses, might
equally well talk about the *res publica* and about the history of oratory or the
meaning of virtue, or the discussion might easily segue from one topic to the
other. For the contents of these men's studies were not felt to be remote from

their roles as political leaders: both oratory and virtue were of the highest importance to the public conduct of upperclass Romans and to their administration of the *res publica*, and so were many of the other subjects of their reading, writing, and conversation. As we have seen again and again, intellectual activities had a political charge and application, while political actions were informed by intellectual habits and convictions. A man did not check his *studia* at the door when entering the senate, nor did he leave behind his concern for the *res publica* when arriving at his villa.

As we have also observed, the rhythms and modes of senatorial intellectual activity themselves show intriguing similarity to the Republican political process. The aristocrats who ran the *res publica* by and large did not follow party lines or ideologies, but viewed themselves as individual actors in both competition and collaboration with their peers. Alliances shifted as senators took and changed political positions, making ad hoc decisions and finding compromises. There existed a diversity of opinions and approaches, at the same time as everyone agreed on the importance of hewing to tradition and the oft-invoked practices of the *maiores*. The system was messy and laborious (and, of course, in the very period with which we are concerned, more or less stopped working), but it was predicated on the autonomy of the individual senators, whose joint task it was continuously to create and recreate the identity and policy of the ruling class as a whole. As conflicts arose, men fell back on their assumption of the prevalence of *amicitia* among them and on their well-honed practices of aristocratic politeness. With any luck, opponents who had clashed with each other in the senate or the courts might shortly afterwards find themselves in pleasant conversation or the epistolary exchange of warm appreciation. Similarly, disagreements on the nature of the *summum bonum* or the genitive of *senatus* might be brought to the fore in fierce debates, even as the men who attacked each other kept adhering to their accustomed gentlemanly decorum and presented themselves as happy to agree to disagree. Strikingly, as we have seen, the same rules of aristocratic sociability survived into the period of Caesar's dictatorship with its unprecedented imbalance of power: even such a politically charged intellectual exchange as the pamphlet war over the legacy of the younger Cato was conducted with the utmost politeness and concern to avoid an opponent's loss of face.

If the close interconnection of late Republican intellectual and political history is thus beyond a doubt, the question remains to what extent we should view the mid-first century's golden age of scholarly originality and productivity as having been directly caused by the crisis of the *res publica* that unfolded at the same time. Claims to this effect have often been made. Thus, for example, Elizabeth Rawson in the very first paragraph of her authoritative *Intellectual Life in the Late Roman Republic* maintains that "[o]ne of the causes" of the "great intellectual flowering at Rome" in the 50s and 40s BCE "was the political uncertainty of the time" (1985: 3). While I remain wary of simple narratives of cause and effect, and would also caution against the counterfactual assumption that without the political turmoil of the period, Roman philosophy and scholarship would not have reached the heights that they did, I believe that in many of the cases studied in this book, the political crisis did indeed act as a significant catalyst for developments in the intellectual sphere—and that intellectual theory and practice occasionally had a direct influence on political events. Roman senators would have engaged in *studia* no matter what, but the unusual and uncertain times made them apply their learning in unprecedented ways.

Thus, for instance, Cicero would presumably not have had the time nor found the inspiration to pen his philosophical encyclopedia had he not found himself living under Caesar's dictatorship, and something similar may be true for at least some of the major works of Varro. In addition, Cicero, as well as such other philosophically inclined senators as Cato, Brutus, and Cassius, might not have felt the urgent need to measure their own behavior and that of others against their ethical convictions, and might not have decided to engage in the acts of political and military resistance that ultimately cost them their lives. Conversely, without the powers afforded by his quasi-monarchic rule, Caesar would not have been in a position to reform the Roman calendar, nor would the theological developments of his age have led to his being declared a god in his lifetime and worshiped as one after his death. Nigidius Figulus, by contrast, would not have had occasion to use his divinatory know-how for politically charged predictions. And, finally, while late Republican antiquarian and religious study may not have been directly influenced by the period's political turmoil (unless we wish to see them as inspired by a general conservative dissatisfaction with perceived moral and cultural decline), they would not have taken on the same charged significance we have seen in a number of cases, including, among others, the genealogy of Brutus and the legal precedents for Clodius's consecration of Cicero's house.

Understandably, late Republican writers habitually deplore the political crisis in which they find themselves, maintaining that it threatens not only their public and private lives, but also the learned pursuits of their *otium*. Already in *De oratore* (55 BCE), Cicero complains that in addition to being deprived of the ability to engage in "public business without danger" (*negotio sine periculo, De or.* 1.1), he also lacks "leisure with dignity" (*otio cum dignitate*). Writing at about the same time, Lucretius claims that the "bad condition of the fatherland" (*patriai tempore iniquo*, 1.41) distracts not only himself from writing his philosophical poem, but also his senatorial dedicatee Memmius from paying attention to it. *Studia* are the product of *otium*, not just in the sense of designated leisure time, but also in the meaning of peace and political order.

There is a sense, however, in which these and other contemporary authors' own practices and publications belie their theories about the best conditions for cultural production. Christopher van den Berg has drawn attention to the fact that Cicero's claim in the *Brutus* that "eloquence is the attendant and companion of peace and quiet, and as it were the fosterchild of an already well-established commonwealth" is not exactly borne out by the writer's own successful career as an orator, which unfolded during and was fueled by a series of political crises.[1] In fact, one might argue that it is exactly conflict that provides scope for eloquence. Something similar may well be true for other types of *studia*. While Cicero, Lucretius, and their learned friends may justifiably have felt that the *patriai tempus iniquum* impinged on their lives in a highly unwelcome manner, threatening their abilities to pursue what they wished to pursue, it may paradoxically have been exactly the public upheavals of their times that inspired and enabled some of their greatest achievements.

The Augustan age and Imperial period were the intellectual heirs of the late Republic, as the products of our senators' *studia* continued to shape the cultural landscape. Philosophy became wholly domesticated within the Roman upper classes, with Cicero providing the model for philosophical writing in Latin and Cato serving as an inspiration for the many Romans who adopted Stoicism as a default world-view. The antiquarian studies of Varro and others served as a blueprint for the Augustan restoration of a perceived earlier Roman golden age (as seen, for example, in Ovid's *Fasti*), while the period's linguistic studies contributed to the development of the Latin grammatical tradition. As the belief in and practice of astrology and other occult arts became widespread, Nigidius Figulus emerged as both a trusted source (for example, for Manilius) and a figure subject to mythmaking (*Pythagoricus et magus*). Caesar's apotheosis taught generations of Romans how to think about the superhuman status of their emperors, while his calendar, of course, continues to shape the daily lives of millions of people even today.

Even so, a particular way of "doing" intellectual work disappeared with the death of the men we have been following in this book. Roman letters continued, but the specifically Republican mode of engaging in *studia* came to an end with the Republican political system that had been the lifeblood of its learned ruling class. Under the Empire, Roman senators continued to hold political positions but no longer made politics, since all de facto power had passed into the hands of the emperor. They continued to engage in learned pursuits and intellectual sociability, with some of them emerging as significant

---

1. Cic. *Brut.* 45: *pacis est comes otique socia et iam bene constitutae ciuitatis quasi alumna quaedam eloquentia.* See van den Berg forthcoming.

authors and thinkers (Pliny the Elder and Seneca come to mind). The Republican bond between political power and learned pursuits, however, had been severed forever.

At the same time, the Augustan and subsequent periods finally saw the rise of professionals that scholars have identified as one of the aspects of what has been called the Roman cultural revolution (see 1.3 above). Of course, intellectual activity was never a monopoly of the upper classes, and, as we have seen, both Greek and Roman scholars and teachers, as well as skilled slaves and freedmen, contributed significantly to mid-first-century intellectual life. Even so, the social world of knowledge production underwent significant changes in the decades and centuries to follow, with the emergence of what our learned senators never were: real intellectuals, that is, individuals whose activities were dedicated exclusively to one field of learning, for which they were often specifically employed and received payment. The senatorial dilettante lived on, but he was now confronted by cadres of not only Greek but also Roman grammarians, philosophers, librarians, doctors, architects, and sophists.

In addition, the political change from what was primarily an aristocratic form of government to a bona fide monarchy went hand in hand with a top-down reorganization of knowledge. Starting with Augustus, who picked up where Caesar had left off, the emperors assumed large-scale patronage and sponsorship of artistic and scholarly endeavors by supporting poets, commissioning artists, building libraries, establishing public chairs for grammarians and philosophers, and many other similar endeavors. As a result, the contents of intellectual pursuits came under pressure by the establishment of, as it were, an official Imperial discourse, which had the power to shape the direction that research and publication was to take. As students of Latin literature and Roman culture know, such Imperial ideologies were never monolithic nor capable of entirely dominating artistic and intellectual expression. Even so, however, an author writing, say, under Augustus, would have found it difficult if not impossible publicly to contradict the dominant narrative of the divinely favored *princeps* who had reestablished the *res publica* and brought about peace and a new golden age. What could, and what could not be said, had become considerably circumscribed.

The Roman Republic of Letters as conceived in this book was characterized by the unity of political and intellectual leadership, as well as by the Republican diversity and competitiveness among its noble citizens. This unique constellation disappeared with the fall of the constitutional Republic that had enabled and sustained it. Romans continued to study, read, and write, but an extraordinary chapter of intellectual history had come to an end.

BIBLIOGRAPHY

Adams, J. N. (2003). *Bilingualism and the Latin Language*. Cambridge: Cambridge University Press.

———(2005). "The *Bellum Africum*." In Reinhardt, Lapidge, and Adams (eds.), 73–96.

Afzelius, A. (1941). "Die politische Bedeutung des jüngeren Cato." *ClMed* 4: 100–203.

Aigner-Foresti, L. (ed.) (1998). *Die Integration der Etrusker und das Weiterwirken des etruskischen Kulturgutes im republikanischen und kaiserzeitlichen Rom*. Vienna: Verlag der Österreichischen Akademie der Wissenschaften.

———(2000). "Gli Etruschi e la politica di Cesare." In G. Urso (ed.), *L'ultimo Cesare: scritti, riforme, progetti, congiure*. Rome: L'Erma di Bretschneider, 11–33.

Alexander, M. C. (1990). *Trials in the Late Roman Republic, 149 BC to 50 BC*. Toronto: University of Toronto Press.

Allen, W. A. Jr. (1955). "The British Epics of Quintus and Marcus Cicero." *TAPA* 86: 143–59.

Ambaglio, D. (1983). "La dedica delle opere letterarie antiche fino all'età dei Flavi." In (no ed.), *Saggi di letteratura e storiografia antiche*. Como: New Press Edizioni, 7–52.

Ampolo, C. (1990–91). "Lotte sociali in Italia centrale. Un documento controverso: Il calendario brontoscopico attribuito e Nigidio Figulo." *Opus* 9–10: 185–97.

Ando, C. (2010). "The Ontology of Religious Institutions." *HR* 50: 54–79.

———and Rüpke, J. (eds.) (2006). *Religion and Law in Classical and Christian Rome*. Stuttgart: Steiner.

André, J.-M. (1966). *L'otium dans la vie morale et intellectuelle romaine des origines à l'époque augusténne*. Paris: Press Universitaires de France.

Andreoni, E. (1979). "Sul contrasto ideologico fra il *De re publica* di Cicerone e il poema di Lucrezio (La genesi della società civile)." In (no ed.), *Studi di poesia latina in onore di Antonio Traglia*. 2 vols. Rome: Edizioni di Storia e Letteratura, 281–321.

Arcangeli, A. (2012). *Cultural History: A Concise Introduction*. London: Routledge.

Arena, V. (2007). "Invocation to Liberty and Invective of *dominatus* at the End of the Roman Republic." *BICS* 50: 49–73.

———(2012). Libertas *and the Practice of Politics in the Late Roman Republic*. Cambridge: Cambridge University Press.

———(2020). "Cicero, the *Augures*, and the Commonwealth in *De Legibus*." In Beltrão da Rosa and Santangelo (eds.), 23–43.

———and Mac Góráin, F. (eds.) (2017). *Varronian Moments* (= *BICS* 60.2). London: Institute of Classical Studies.

———and Mac Góráin, F. (2017). "Foreword." In Arena and Mac Góráin (eds.), 1–7.

Armstrong, D. (2011). "Epicurean Virtues, Epicurean Friendship: Cicero vs the Herculaneum Papyri." In Fish and Sanders (eds.), 105–28.

Arweiler, A. (2003). *Cicero rhetor: Die* Partitiones oratoriae *und das Konzept des gelehrten Politikers.* Berlin: De Gruyter.

Asmis, E. (2004). "Epicurean Economics." In J. T. Fitzgerald, D. Obbink, and G. S. Holland (eds.), *Philodemus and the New Testament World.* Leiden: Brill, 133–76.

———(2005). "A New Kind of Model: Cicero's Roman Constitution in *De republica.*" *AJP* 126: 377–416.

———(2016). "Lucretius' Reception of Epicurus: *De Rerum Natura* as a Conversion Narrative." *Hermes* 144: 439–61.

Atkins, E. M. (2000). "Cicero." In C. Rowe and M. Schofield (eds.), *The Cambridge History of Greek and Roman Political Thought.* Cambridge: Cambridge University Press, 477–516.

Atkins, J. W. (2013). *Cicero on Politics and the Limits of Reason: The Republic and Laws.* Cambridge: Cambridge University Press.

Aubert-Baillot, S. (2014). "L'Influence de la *disputatio in utramque partem* sur la correspondance de Cicéron." *VL* 189–90: 21–39.

———(2018). "Terminology and Practice of Dialectic in Cicero's Letters." In T. Bénatouïl and K. Ierodiakonou (eds.), *Dialectic after Plato and Aristotle.* Cambridge: Cambridge University Press, 254–82.

———and Guérin, C. (eds.) (2014). *Le Brutus de Cicéron: rhétorique, politique et histoire culturelle.* Leiden: Brill.

Auvray-Assayas, C. and Delattre, D. (eds.) (2001). *Cicéron et Philodème: la polémique en philosophie.* Paris: Éditions Rue d'Ulm.

Ax, W. (1995). "*Disputare in utramque partem*: Zum literarischen Plan und zur dialektischen Methode Varros in *de lingua Latina* 8–10." *RhM* 138: 146–77.

Badian, E. (2009). "From the Iulii to Caesar." In Griffin (ed.), 11–22.

Balbo, A. (2013). "Marcus Junius Brutus the Orator: Between Philosophy and Oratory." In Steel and van der Blom (eds.), 315–28.

Balsdon, J. P. V. D. (1958). "The Ides of March." *Historia* 7: 80–94.

———(1979). *Romans and Aliens.* London: Duckworth.

Baraz, Y. (2012). *A Written Republic: Cicero's Philosophical Politics.* Princeton: Princeton University Press.

———(2018). "Discourse of Kingship in Late Republican Invective." In N. Panou and H. Schadee (eds.), *Evil Lords: Theories and Representations of Tyranny from Antiquity to the Renaissance.* New York: Oxford University Press, 43–60.

Bardon, H. (1952). *La Littérature latine inconnue.* Vol. 1: *L'époque républicaine.* Paris: Klincksieck.

Barnes, J. and Griffin, M. (eds.) (1997). *Philosophia Togata II: Plato and Aristotle at Rome.* Oxford: Clarendon Press.

Barton, T. (1994). *Ancient Astrology.* London: Routledge.

Barwick, K. (1957). "Widmung und Entstehungsgeschichte von Varros De lingua Latina." *Philologus* 101: 298–304.

Bäumerich, H. J. (1964). "Über die Bedeutung der Genealogie in der römischen Literatur." Diss. Cologne.

Bavaj, R. (2010). "Intellectual History." *Docupedia-Zeitgeschichte* 13.9.2010. docupedia.de/zg/ Intellectual_History.

Beard, M. (1986). "Cicero and Divination: The Formation of a Latin Discourse." *JRS* 76: 33–46.

———(1991). "Writing and Religion: *Ancient Literacy* and the Function of the Written Word in Roman Religion." In M. Beard et al. (eds.), *Literacy in the Roman World*. Ann Arbor: Journal of Roman Archaeology, 35–58.

———(1994). "Religion." *CAH*²: 9.729–68.

———(2002). "Ciceronian Correspondences: Making a Book out of Letters." In T. P. Wiseman (ed.), *Classics in Progress: Essays on Ancient Greece and Rome*. Oxford: Oxford University Press, 103–44.

———(2012). "Cicero's 'Response of the *haruspices*' and the Voice of the Gods." *JRS* 102: 20–39.

———(2014). *Laughter in Ancient Rome: On Joking, Tickling, and Cracking Up*. Berkeley: University of California Press.

———, North, J., and Price, S. (1998). *Religions of Rome*. 2 vols. Cambridge: Cambridge University Press.

Bechtold, C. (2011). *Gott und Gestirn als Präsenzformen des toten Kaisers: Apotheose und Katasterismos in der politischen Kommunikation der römischen Kaiserzeit und ihre Anknüpfungspunkte im Hellenismus*. Göttingen: V&R unipress.

Beck, H. and Walter, U. (2001–4). *Die frühen römischen Historiker*. 2 vols. Darmstadt: Wissenschaftliche Buchgesellschaft.

Beck, M. (2014). "The Socratic Paradigm." In id. (ed.), *A Companion to Plutarch*. Malden, MA: Wiley-Blackwell, 463–78.

Becker, E. (1938). "Technik und Szenerie des ciceronischen Dialogs." Diss. Münster.

Bellincioni, M. (1970). *Marco Tullio Cicerone, Ad familiares 11, 27 e 28: Cicerone e Mazio*. Brescia: Paideia.

———(1985). "Ancora sulle intenzioni politiche del *Brutus*." In D. Pesce and A. Alfieri (eds.), *Sapienza antica: studi in onore di Domenico Pesce*. Milan: Angeli, 47–67.

Beltrão da Rosa, C. (2020). "The God and the Consul in Cicero's *Third Catilinarian*." In Beltrão da Rosa and Santangelo (eds.), 45–58.

———and Santangelo, F. (eds.) (2020). *Cicero and Roman Religion: Eight Studies*. Stuttgart: Steiner.

Bendlin, A. (2000). "Looking Beyond the Civic Compromise: Religious Pluralism in Late Republican Rome." In E. Bispham and C. Smith (eds.), *Religion in Archaic and Classical Rome and Italy: Evidence and Experience*. Edinburgh: Edinburgh University Press, 115–35.

———and Rüpke, J. (eds.) (2009). *Römische Religion im historischen Wandel: Diskursentwicklung von Plautus bis Ovid*. Stuttgart: Steiner.

Benferhat, Y. (2005). Ciues Epicurei: *les épicuriens et l'idée de la monarchie à Rome et en Italie de Sylla à Octave*. Brussels: Latomus.

Bengtson, H. (1970). *Zur Geschichte des Brutus* (= *Sitzungsberichte Bayerische Akademie der Wissenschaften, Philosophisch-historische Klasse* 1970.1). Munich: Verlag der Bayerischen Akademie der Wissenschaften.

Bergemann, C. (1992). *Politik und Religion im spätrepublikanischen Rom*. Stuttgart: Steiner.

Bernard, J.-E. (2013). *La Sociabilité épistolaire chez Cicéron*. Paris: Champion.

Berry, D. H. (1996). *Cicero: Pro P. Sulla Oratio.* Cambridge: Cambridge University Press.

Bertrand-Écanvil, E. (1994). "Présages et propaganda idéologique: à propos d'une liste concernant Octavien Auguste." *MEFRA* 106: 487–531.

Beßlich, B. (2008). "Cato als Repräsentant stoisch formierten Republikanertums von der Antike bis zur französischen Revolution." In B. Neymeyr, J. Schmidt, and B. Zimmermann (eds.), *Stoizismus in der europäischen Philosophie. Literatur, Kunst und Politik: Eine Kulturgeschichte von der Antike bis zur Moderne.* 2 vols. Berlin: De Gruyter, 1.365–92.

Bezold, C. and Boll, F. (1911). *Reflexe astrologischer Keilinschriften bei griechischen Schriftstellern* (= *Sitzungsberichte der Heidelberger Akademie der Wissenschaften, Phil.-hist. Kl.* 1911.7). Heidelberg: Winter.

Bianco, M. M. (2017). "Meritare il perdono, meritare la memoria: equilibrio del discorso e verdetto della storia nella *pro Marcello* di Cicerone." Ὅρμος 9: 472–98.

Biesinger, B. (2016). *Römische Dekadenzdiskurse: Untersuchungen zur römischen Geschichtsschreibung und ihren Kontexten (2. Jahrhundert v.Chr. bis 2. Jahrhundert n.Chr.).* Stuttgart: Steiner.

Billows, R. (1982). "The Last of the Scipios." *AJAH* 7: 53–68.

Binder, V. (2018). "Inspired Leaders versus Emerging Nations: Varro's and Cicero's Views on Early Rome." In Sandberg and Smith (eds.), 157–81.

Bishop, C. (2016). "Naming the Roman Stars: Constellation Etymologies in Cicero's *Aratea* and the *De Natura Deorum.*" *CQ* 66: 151–71.

———(2019). *Cicero, Greek Learning, and the Making of a Roman Classic.* Oxford: Oxford University Press.

Blackburn, B. and Holford-Strevens, L. (1999). *The Oxford Companion to the Year.* Oxford: Oxford University Press.

Blank, D. (2005). "Varro's Anti-analogist." In D. Frede and B. Inwood (eds.), *Language and Learning: Philosophy of Language in the Hellenistic Age.* Cambridge: Cambridge University Press, 210–38.

———(2008). "Varro and the Epistemological Status of Etymology." *Histoire Épistémologie Langage* 30: 49–73.

———(2012). "Varro und Antiochus." In Sedley (ed.), 250–89.

———(2019). "What's Hecuba to Him? Varro on the Natural Kinship of Things and of Words." In Pezzini and Taylor (eds.), 121–52.

Blänsdorf, J. (1991). "'Augurenlächeln': Ciceros Kritik an der römischen Mantik." In H. Wißmann (ed.), *Zur Erschließung von Zukunft in den Religionen: Zukunftserwartung und Gegenwartsbewältigung in der Religionsgeschichte.* Würzburg: Königshausen & Neumann, 45–65.

Bleicken, J. (1962). "Der Begriff der Freiheit in der letzten Phase der römischen Republik." *HZ* 195: 1–20.

Bloomer, W. M. (1997). *Latinity and Literary Society at Rome.* Philadelphia: University of Pennsylvania Press.

Blößner, N. (2001). "Cicero gegen die Philosophie: Eine Analyse von *De re publica* 1, 1–3." *Nachrichten der Akademie der Wissenschaften in Göttingen. I. Philologisch-historische Klasse* 2001.3.

Boes, J. (1990). *La Philosophie et l'action dans la correspondance de Cicéron.* Nancy: Presses Universitaires de Nancy.

Boll, F. (1903). *Sphaera: Neue griechische Texte und Untersuchungen zur Geschichte der Sternbilder.* Leipzig: Teubner.

Botermann, H. (1992a). "Die Generalabrechnung mit dem Tyrannen: Ciceros Rede für den König Deiotarus." *Gymnasium* 99: 320–44.

———(1992b). "Rechtsstaat oder Diktatur: Cicero und Caesar 46–44 v.Chr." *Klio* 74: 179–96.

Bots, H. and Waquet, F. (1997). *La République des Lettres*. Paris: Belin.

Boyancé, P. (1936). "Les méthodes de l'histoire littéraire: Cicéron et son œuvre philosophique." *REL* 14: 288–309.

———(1975). "Étymologie et théologie chez Varron." *REL* 53: 99–115.

Bravo, B. (2007). "Antiquarianism and History." In J. Marincola (ed.), *A Companion to Greek and Roman Historiography*. Malden, MA: Wiley-Blackwell, 491–502.

Brenk, F. E. (1988). "Cassius' 'Epicurean' Explanation of Brutus' Vision in Plutarch's *Broutos*." In I. Gallo (ed.), *Aspetti dello stoicismo e dell'epicureismo in Plutarco*. Ferrara: Giornale Filologico Ferrarese, 109–18.

Brett, A. (2002). "What Is Intellectual History Now?" In D. Cannadine (ed.), *What Is History Now?* New York: Palgrave Macmillan, 113–31.

Brind'Amour, P. (1983). *Le Calendrier romain: recherches chronologiques*. Ottawa: Éditions de l'Université d'Ottawa.

Bringmann, K. (1971). *Untersuchungen zum späten Cicero*. Göttingen: Vandenhoeck & Ruprecht.

———(2003). "Die Bedeutung der Philosophie in Rom zur Zeit der späten Republik." In Piepenbrink (ed.), 149–64.

Briquel, D. (1990). "Les Changements de siècles en Etrurie." In P. Citti (ed.), *Fins de siècle*. Bordeaux: Presses Universitaires de Bordeaux, 61–76.

Brittain, C. (2001). *Philo of Larissa: The Last of the Academic Sceptics*. Oxford: Oxford University Press.

———(2006). *Cicero: "On Academic Scepticism."* Indianapolis: Hackett.

Brown, E. (2009). "False Idles: The Politics of the 'Quiet Life.'" In R. K. Balot (ed.), *A Companion to Greek and Roman Political Thought*. Malden, MA: Blackwell, 485–500.

Brožek, M. (1961). "De Ciceronis epistula suasoria ad Caesarem scripta." In (no ed.), *Atti del I congresso internazionale di studi ciceroniani*. Vol. 1. Rome: Centro di Studi Ciceroniani, 177–85.

Bruhns, H. (1978). *Caesar und die römische Oberschicht in den Jahren 49–44 v. Chr: Untersuchungen zur Herrschaftsetablierung im Bürgerkrieg*. Göttingen: Vandenhoeck & Ruprecht.

Brunt, P. A. (1965). "*Amicitia* in the Late Roman Republic." *PCPS* 11: 1–20 (~ 1988: 351–81).

———(1975). "Stoicism and the Principate." *PBSR* 43: 7–35.

———(1986). "Cicero's *officium* in the Civil War." *JRS* 76: 12–32.

———(1988). *The Fall of the Roman Republic and Related Essays*. Oxford: Clarendon Press.

———(1989). "Philosophy and Religion in the Late Republic." In Griffin and Barnes (eds.), 174–98.

Büchner, K. (1984). *M. Tullius Cicero, De re publica*. Heidelberg: Winter.

Burckhardt, L. A. (1988). *Politische Strategien der Optimaten in der späten römischen Republik*. Stuttgart: Steiner.

Burke, P. (2000). *A Social History of Knowledge from Gutenberg to Diderot*. Cambridge: Polity.

———(2008). *What Is Cultural History?* 2nd ed. Cambridge: Polity.

———(2012). *A Social History of Knowledge II: From the* Encyclopédie *to Wikipedia*. Cambridge: Polity.

———(2016). *What Is the History of Knowledge?* Cambridge: Polity.

Burkert, W. (1961). "Hellenistische Pseudopythagorica." *Philologus* 105: 16–43 and 226–46.

Burns, P. C. (2001). "Augustine's Use of Varro's *Antiquitates Rerum Divinarum* in His *De Civitate Dei.*" *Augustinian Studies* 32: 37–64.

Butterfield, D. (ed.) (2015). *Varro Varius: The Polymath of the Roman World.* Cambridge: Cambridge Philological Society.

———(2020). "Critical Approaches to the Most Difficult Textual Problem in Lucretius." In D. O'Rourke (ed.), *Approaches to Lucretius: Traditions and Innovations in Reading the De rerum natura.* Cambridge: Cambridge University Press, 19–39.

Byrne, S. (1998). "Flattery and Inspiration: Cicero's Epic for Caesar." *Studies in Latin Literature and Roman History* 9: 129–37.

Cancik, H. and Cancik-Lindemaier, H. (2001). "The Truth of Images: Cicero and Varro on Image Worship." In J. Assmann and A. I. Baumgarten (eds.), *Representation in Religion: Studies in Honor of Moshe Barasch.* Leiden: Brill, 43–61.

Capdeville, G. (1998). "Die Rezeption der etruskischen Disziplin durch die gelehrten Römer." In Aigner-Foresti (ed.), 385–419.

Cappello, O. (2019). *The School of Doubt: Skepticism, History and Politics in Cicero's Academica.* Leiden: Brill.

Carcopino, J. (1927). *La Basilique pythagoricienne de la Porte Majeure.* Paris: L'Artisan du Livre.

Cardauns, B. (1960). *Varros Logistoricus über die Götterverehrung* (Curio de cultu deorum). Würzburg: Triltsch.

———(1976). *M. Terentius Varro:* Antiquitates Rerum Divinarum. Mainz: Akademie der Wissenschaften und der Literatur.

———(2001). *Marcus Terentius Varro: Einführung in sein Werk.* Heidelberg: Winter.

Carducci, K. L. (2018). "The First Supine in *Bellum gallicum* and *Bellum civile*: A Study of Caesar as Grammarian, Narrator, and *exemplum.*" *CP* 113: 404–22.

Casali, S. (2018). "Caesar's Poetry in Its Context." In Grillo and Krebs (eds.), 206–14.

Castner, C. J. (1988). *Prosopography of Roman Epicureans from the Second Century B.C. to the Second Century A.D.* Frankfurt: Lang.

Cavallo, G. (1999). "Between *Volumen* and Codex: Reading in the Roman World." In Cavallo and Chartier (eds.), 64–89.

———and R. Chartier (eds.) (1999). *A History of Reading in the West.* Trans. by Lydia C. Cochrane. Oxford: Polity (Italian 1995).

Cèbe, J.-P. (1972–99). *Varron, Satires Ménippées.* 13 vols. Rome: École Française de Rome.

Chahoud, A. (2016). "Varro's Latin and Varro on Latin." In R. Ferri and A. Zago (eds.), *The Latin of the Grammarians: Reflections about Language in the Roman World.* Turnhout: Brepols, 15–31.

Christes, J. (1975). *Bildung und Gesellschaft: Die Einschätzung der Bildung und ihrer Vermittler in der griechisch-römischen Antike.* Darmstadt: Wissenschaftliche Buchgesellschaft.

———(1996). "Der Gebildete im republikanischen Rom im Spannungsfeld von *negotium* und *otium* (mit besonderer Berücksichtigung Ciceros)." In Keck, Wiersing, and Wittstadt (eds.), 111–31.

Ciafardone, G. (2012). "Appunti sulla posizione di Cicerone nel *De divinatione.*" *Euphrosyne* 40: 327–34.

Citroni, M. (ed.) (2003). *Memoria e identità: la cultura romana costruisce la sua immagine.* Florence: Università degli Studi di Firenze.

Clackson, J. (2011). "Classical Latin." In id. (ed.), *A Companion to the Latin Language*. Chichester: Wiley-Blackwell, 236–56.

———(2015). "Latinitas, Ἑλληνισμός, and Standard Languages." *Studi e saggi linguistici* 53: 309–30.

Clark, A. J. (2007). *Divine Qualities: Cult and Community in Republican Rome*. Oxford: Oxford University Press.

Clarke, M. L. (1981). *The Noblest Roman: Marcus Brutus and His Reputation*. London: Thames and Hudson.

Classen, C. J. (1965). "Die Königszeit im Spiegel der Literatur der römischen Republik (Ein Beitrag zum Selbstverständnis der Römer)." *Historia* 14: 385–403.

———(1985). *Recht—Rhetorik—Politik: Untersuchungen zu Ciceros politischer Strategie*. Darmstadt: Wissenschaftliche Buchgesellschaft.

Clay, D. (1983). "Individual and Community in the First Generation of the Epicurean School." In (no ed.), ΣΥΖΗΤΗΣΙΣ: *studi sull'epicureismo greco e romano offerti a Marcello Gigante*. Vol. 1. Naples: Macchiaroli, 255–79.

Cogitore, I. (2011). *Le doux Nom de liberté: histoire d'une idée politique dans la Rome antique*. Bordeaux: Ausonius.

Cole, S. (2013). *Cicero and the Rise of Deification at Rome*. Cambridge: Cambridge University Press.

Collart, J. (1954). *Varron: grammairien latin*. Paris: Belles Lettres.

Collini, S. (2006). *Absent Minds: Intellectuals in Britain*. Oxford: Oxford University Press.

Connolly, J. (2011). "Fantastical Realism in Cicero's Postwar Panegyric." In G. Urso (ed.), *Dicere laudes: elogio, comunicazione, creazione del consenso*. Pisa: ETS, 161–78.

Corbeill, A. (1996). *Controlling Laughter: Political Humor in the Late Roman Republic*. Princeton: Princeton University Press.

———(2010). "The Function of a Divinely Inspired Text in Cicero's *De haruspicum responsis*." In D. H. Berry and A. Erskine (eds.), *Form and Function in Roman Oratory*. Cambridge: Cambrige University Press, 139–54.

———(2012). "Cicero and the Etruscan *Haruspices*." *Papers of the Langford Latin Seminar* 15: 243–66.

Cornell, T. J. (2001). "Cicero on the Origins of Rome." In Powell and North (eds.), 41–56.

Cowan, R. (2015). "On Not Being Archilochus Properly: Cato, Catullus and the Idea of *iambos*." *MD* 74: 9–52.

Craig, C. P. (1986). "Cato's Stoicism and the Understanding of Cicero's Speech for Murena." *TAPA* 116: 229–39.

Cramer, F. H. (1954). *Astrology in Roman Law and Politics*. Philadelphia: American Philosophical Society.

Culham, P. (1989). "Archives and Alternatives in Republican Rome." *CP* 84: 100–115.

Cuny-Le Callet, B. (2005). "La Lettre de Cicéron à Cécina: vers une divination rationelle?" In Kany-Turpin (ed.), 223–39.

Dahlmann, H. (1932). *Varro und die hellenistische Sprachtheorie*. Berlin: Weidmann.

———(1935a). "Caesars Schrift über die Analogie." *RhM* 84: 258–75.

———(1935b). "M. Terentius Varro." *RE* Supp. 6: 1172–1277.

Dale, F. R. (1958). "Caesar and Lucretius." *GaR* 5: 181–82.

Daly, L. W. (1950). "Roman Study Abroad." *AJP* 71: 40–58.

Damon, C. (2008). "Enabling Books." *NECJ* 35.3: 175–84.

D'Anna, N. (2007). *Mistero e profezia: la IV ecloga di Virgilio e il rinnovamento del mondo.* Cosenza: Giordano.

———(2008). *Publio Nigidio Figulo: un pitagorico a Roma nel 1° secolo a. C.* Milan: Archè.

D'Arms, J. H. (1970). *Romans on the Bay of Naples: A Social and Cultural Study of the Villas and Their Owners from 150 B.C. to A.D. 400.* Cambridge, MA: Harvard University Press.

De Giorgio, J. P. (2015). *L'Écriture de soi à Rome: autour de la correspondance de Cicéron.* Brussels: Latomus.

de Grummond, N. T. (2006a). *Etruscan Myth, Sacred History, and Legend.* Philadelphia: University of Pennsylvania Museum of Archaeology and Anthropology.

———(2006b). "Prophets and Priests." In N. T. de Grummond and E. Simon (eds.), *The Religion of the Etruscans.* Austin: University of Texas Press, 27–44.

———(2013). "Haruspicy and Augury: Sources and Procedures." In J. M. Turfa (ed.), *The Etruscan World.* London: Routledge, 539–56.

De Lacy, P. H. (1941). "Cicero's Invective against Piso." *TAPA* 72: 49–58.

———(1977). "The Four Stoic *Personae.*" *ICS* 2: 163–72.

de Libero, L. (1992). *Obstruktion: Politische Praktiken im Senat und in der Volksversammlung der ausgehenden römischen Republik (70–49 v.Chr.).* Stuttgart: Steiner.

Della Casa, A. (1962). *Nigidio Figulo.* Rome: Edizioni dell'Ateneo.

de Melo, W. D. C. (2019). *Varro: De lingua Latina.* 2 vols. Oxford: Oxford University Press.

Dench, E. (2005). *Romulus' Asylum: Roman Identities from the Age of Alexander to the Age of Hadrian.* Oxford: Oxford University Press.

Denyer, N. (1985). "The Case against Divination: An Examination of Cicero's *De divinatione.*" *PCPS* 31: 1–10.

Dettenhofer, M. H. (1990). "Cicero und C. Cassius Longinus: Politische Korrespondenz ein Jahr vor Caesars Ermordung (Cic. fam. 15,16–19)." *Historia* 39: 249–56a.

———(1992). *Perdita Iuventus: Zwischen den Generationen von Caesar und Augustus.* Munich: Beck.

Deutsch, M. E. (1925). "VENI, VIDI, VICI." *PQ* 4: 151–56.

Devillers, O. and Meyers, J. (eds.) (2009). *Pouvoir des hommes, pouvoir des mots, des Gracques à Trajan: hommages au Professeur Paul Marius Martin.* Louvain: Peeters.

Dickie, M. W. (1999). "The Learned Magician and the Collection and Transmission of Magical Lore." In D. R. Jordan, H. Montgomery, and E. Thomassen (eds.), *The World of Ancient Magic.* Bergen: Norwegian Institute at Athens, 163–93.

Dix, T. K. (2000). "The Library of Lucullus." *Athenaeum* 88: 441–64.

———(2013). "'Beware of Promising Your Library to Anyone': Assembling a Private Library at Rome." In König, Oikonomopoulou, and Woolf (eds.), 209–34.

Dobesch, G. (1966). *Caesars Apotheose zu Lebzeiten und sein Ringen um den Königstitel: Untersuchungen über Caesars Alleinherrschaft.* Wien: Österreichisches Archäologisches Institut.

———(1985). "Politische Bemerkungen zu Ciceros Rede Pro Marcello." In E. Weber and G. Dobesch (eds.), *Römische Geschichte, Altertumskunde und Epigraphik: Festschrift für Artur Betz zur Vollendung seines 80. Lebensjahres.* Vienna: Österreichische Gesellschaft für Archäologie, 153–231.

———(1998). "Ende und Metamorphose des Etruskertums: Grundsätzliche Gedanken zu einer konkreten Fallstudie." In Aigner-Foresti (ed.), 29–147.

———(2002). "Caesars Urteil über Ciceros Bedeutung: Gedanken zu Cic. *Brut.* 253 and Plin. *n. h.* 7, 117." *Tyche* 17: 39–62.

Domenici, I. and Maderna, E. (2007). *Giovanni Lido: Sui segni celesti.* Milan: Medusa.

Domenicucci, P. (1993). "Osservazioni sul *De astris* attribuito a Giulio Cesare." In Poli (ed.), 1.345–58.

———(1996). *Astra Caesarum: astronomia, astrologia e catasterismo da Cesare a Domiziano.* Pisa: ETS.

———(2003). "La previsione astrologica attribuita a Nigidio Figulo in Luc. 1, 639–70." *Schol(i)a* 5.3: 85–106.

Döring, K. (1978). "Antike Theorien über die staatspolitische Notwendigkeit der Götterfurcht." *AuA* 24: 43–56.

Dortmund, A. (2001). *Römisches Buchwesen um die Zeitenwende: War T. Pomponius Atticus (110–32 v.Chr.) Verleger?* Wiesbaden: Harrassowitz.

Douglas, A. E. (1966). *M. Tulli Ciceronis Brutus.* Oxford: Clarendon Press.

Driediger-Murphy, L. G. (2019). *Roman Republican Augury: Freedom and Control.* Oxford: Oxford University Press.

Drogula, F. K. (2019). *Cato the Younger: Life and Death at the End of the Roman Republic.* New York: Oxford University Press.

Drummond, A. (2013). "M. Terentius Varro." *FRHist* 1: 412–23.

Ducos, M. (2005). "Nigidius Figulus (Publius–)." In R. Goulet (ed.), *Dictionnaire des philosophes antiques.* Vol. 4. Paris: CNRS Éditions, 703–12.

Duff, T. (1999). *Plutarch's Lives: Exploring Virtue and Vice.* Oxford: Clarendon Press.

Dugan, J. (2001). "Preventing Ciceronianism: L. Licinius Calvus' Regimens for Sexual and Oratorical Self-Mastery." *CP* 96: 400–428.

———(2005). *Making a New Man: Ciceronian Self-Fashioning in the Rhetorical Works.* Oxford: Oxford University Press.

———(2012). "*Scriptum* and *voluntas* in Cicero's *Brutus*." In M. Citroni (ed.), *Letteratura e civitas: transizioni dalla Repubblica all'Impero.* Pisa: ETS, 117–28.

———(2013). "Cicero and the Politics of Ambiguity: Interpreting the *Pro Marcello*." In Steel and van der Blom (eds.), 211–25.

Dunkle, J. R. (1967). "The Greek Tyrant and Roman Political Invective of the Late Republic." *TAPA* 98: 151–71.

Dyck, A. R. (1996). *A Commentary on Cicero,* De Officiis. Ann Arbor: University of Michigan Press.

———(2004a). *A Commentary on Cicero,* De Legibus. Ann Arbor: University of Michigan Press.

———(2004b). "Cicero's *deuotio*: The Rôles of *dux* and Scape-Goat in His *post reditum* Rhetoric." *HSCP* 102: 299–314.

Dyer, R. R. (1990). "Rhetoric and Intention in Cicero's *Pro Marcello*." *JRS* 80: 17–30.

Eden, P. T. (1962). "Caesar's Style: Inheritance versus Intelligence." *Glotta* 40: 74–117.

Edwards, C. (2007). *Death in Ancient Rome.* New Haven: Yale University Press.

Eich, A. (2000). *Politische Literatur in der römischen Gesellschaft: Studien zum Verhältnis von politischer und literarischer Öffentlichkeit in der späten Republik und frühen Kaiserzeit.* Köln: Böhlau.

Eickhoff, F. C. (ed.) (2016). *Muße und Rekursivität in der antiken Briefliteratur*. Tübingen: Mohr Siebeck.

Elder, O. and Mullen, A. (2019). *The Language of Roman Letters: Bilingual Epistolography from Cicero to Fronto*. Cambridge: Cambridge University Press.

Engels, D. (2007). *Das römische Vorzeichenwesen (753–27 v.Chr.): Quellen, Terminologie, Kommentar, historische Entwicklung*. Stuttgart: Steiner.

Englert, W. (2014). "Epicurean Philosophy in Cicero's *De Republica*: Serious Threat or Convenient Foil?" *Etica & Politica* 16: 253–66.

Epstein, D. (1987). "Caesar's Personal Enemies on the Ides of March." *Latomus* 46: 566–70.

Erler, M. (1992). "Cicero und 'unorthodoxer' Epikureismus." *Anregung* 38: 307–22.

Erskine, A. (1991). "Hellenistic Monarchy and Roman Political Invective." *CQ* 41: 106–20.

Eshleman, K. (2012). *The Social World of Intellectuals in the Roman Empire: Sophists, Philosophers, and Christians*. Cambridge: Cambridge University Press.

Fantham, R. E. (1977). "Cicero, Varro, and M. Claudius Marcellus." *Phoenix* 31: 208–13.

———(1996). *Roman Literary Culture from Cicero to Apuleius*. Baltimore: Johns Hopkins University Press.

———(2009). "Caesar as an Intellectual." In Griffin (ed.), 141–56.

Feeney, D. (1998). *Literature and Religion at Rome: Cultures, Contexts, and Beliefs*. Cambridge: Cambridge University Press.

———(2007). *Caesar's Calendar: Ancient Time and the Beginnings of History*. Berkeley: University of California Press.

Fehling, D. (1956–57). "Varro und die grammatische Lehre von der Analogie und der Flexion." *Glotta* 35: 214–70 and 36: 48–100.

Fehrle, R. (1983). *Cato Uticensis*. Darmstadt: Wissenschaftliche Buchgesellschaft.

Ferrary, J.-L. (1984). "L'Archéologie du *De re publica* (2, 2, 4–37, 63): Cicéron entre Polybe et Platon." *JRS* 74: 87–98.

———(2001). "Réponse à Carlos Lévy." In Auvray-Assayas and Delattre (eds.), 77–84.

———(2007). "Les Philosophes grecs à Rome (155–86 av. J.-C.)." In A. M. Ioppolo and D. N. Sedley (eds.), *Pyrrhonists, Patricians, Platonizers: Hellenistic Philosophy in the Period 155–86 BC*. Naples: Bibliopolis, 17–46.

———, Schiavone, A., and Stolfi, E. (2019). *Quintus Mucius Scaevola: Opera*. Rome: L'Erma di Bretschneider.

Ferrero, L. (1955). *Storia del pitagorismo nel mondo romano dalle origini alla fine della repubblica*. Turin: Università di Torino, Facoltà di Lettere e Filosofia.

Fiocchi, L. (1990). "Cicerone e la riabilitazione di Marcello." *RivFil* 118: 179–99.

Firpo, G. (1998). "La polemica sugli Etruschi nei poeti dell'età augustea." In Aigner-Foresti (ed.), 251–98.

Fish, J. (2011). "Not All Politicians Are Sisyphus: What Roman Epicureans Were Taught about Politics." In Fish and Sanders (ed.), 72–104.

———and Sanders, K. R. (eds.) (2011). *Epicurus and the Epicurean Tradition*. Cambridge: Cambridge University Press.

Fishwick, D. (1987–92). *The Imperial Cult in the Latin West: Studies in the Ruler Cult of the Western Provinces of the Roman Empire*. 4 vols. Leiden: Brill.

FitzGibbon, P. M. (2008). "Boethus and Cassius: Two Epicureans in Plutarch." In A. G. Niko-laidis (ed.), *The Unity of Plutarch's Work: "Moralia" Themes in the "Lives", Features of the "Lives" in the "Moralia."* Berlin: De Gruyter, 445–60.

Flinterman, J.-J. (2014). "Pythagoreans in Rome and Asia Minor around the Turn of the Common Era." In C. A. Huffman (ed.), *A History of Pythagoreanism.* Cambridge: Cambridge University Press, 341–59.

Fögen, T. (2000). Patrii sermonis egestas: *Einstellungen lateinischer Autoren zu ihrer Muttersprache.* Munich: Saur.

Föllinger, S. and Müller, G. M. (eds.) (2013). *Der Dialog in der Antike: Formen und Funktionen einer literarischen Gattung zwischen Philosophie, Wissensvermittlung und dramatischer Inszenierung.* Berlin: De Gruyter.

Fontaine, J. (1966). "Le *Songe de Scipion* premier anti-Lucrèce?" In R. Chevalier (ed.), *Mélanges d' archeologie et d'histoire offerts a Andre Piganiol.* Vol. 3. Paris: École pratique des hautes études, 1711–29.

Fox, M. (1996). *Roman Historical Myths: The Regal Period in Augustan Literature.* Oxford: Clarendon Press.

———(2007). *Cicero's Philosophy of History.* Oxford: Oxford University Press.

Frampton, S. A. (2016). "What to Do with Books in the *De finibus.*" *TAPA* 146: 117–47.

———(2018). *Empire of Letters: Writing in Roman Literature and Thought from Lucretius to Ovid.* Oxford: Oxford University Press.

Freyburger-Galland, M.-L., Freyburger, G., and Tautil, J.-C. (1986). *Sectes religieuses en Grèce et à Rome dans l'Antiquité païnne.* Paris: Belles Lettres.

Frischer, B. (1982). *The Sculpted Word: Epicureanism and Philosophical Recruitment in Ancient Greece.* Berkeley: University of California Press.

Fuhrmann, M. (1987). "Erneuerung als Wiederherstellung des Alten: Zur Funktion antiquarischer Forschung im Spätrepublikanischen Rom." In R. Herzog and R. Koselleck (eds.), *Epochenschwelle und Epochenbewusstsein.* Munich: Fink, 131–51.

Fumaroli, M. (2015). *La République des Lettres.* Paris: Gallimard.

Fussl, M. (1980). "Epikureismus im Umkreis Caesars." In J. Dalfen et al. (eds.), *Symmicta philologica Salisburgensia Georgio Pfligersdorffer sexagenario oblata.* Rome: Edizioni dell'Ateneo, 61–80.

Gabba, E. (1979). "Per un'interpretazione politica del *de officiis* di Cicerone." *RAL* 34: 117–41.

Gagliardi, P. (1997). *Il dissenso e l'ironia: per una rilettura delle orazioni "cesariane" di Cicerone.* Naples: D'Auria.

Garbarino, G. (1973). *Roma e la filosofia greca dalle origini alla fine del II secolo A. C.* 2 vols. Turin: Paravia.

———(2003). *Philosophorum Romanorum fragmenta usque ad L. Annaei Senecae aetatem.* Bologna: Pàtron.

Garcea, A. (2008). "*Consule ueritatem*: Cicéron, Varron et un chapitre de l'histoire de la vérité à Rome." *Revue de métaphysique et de morale* 57: 93–110.

———(2012). *Caesar's* De Analogia. Oxford: Oxford University Press.

———(2019). "Nigidius Figulus' Naturalism: Between Grammar and Philosophy." In Pezzini and Taylor (eds.), 79–102.

Gardner, J. F. (2009). "The Dictator." In Griffin (ed.), 57–71.

Garosi, R. (1976). "Indagine sulla formazione del concetto di magia nella cultura romana." In P. Xella (ed.), *Magia: studi di storia delle religioni in memoria di Raffaela Garosi*. Rome: Bulzoni, 13–91.

Gäth, S. (2011). *Die literarische Rezeption des Cato Uticensis in Ausschnitten von der Antike bis zur Neuzeit*. Frankfurt: Lang.

Gatzemeier, S. (2013). *Ut ait Lucretius: Die Lukrezrezeption in der lateinischen Prosa bis Laktanz*. Göttingen: Vandenhoeck & Ruprecht.

Gawlik, G. and Görler, W. (1994). "Cicero." In H. Flashar (ed.), *Die Philosophie der Antike, Band 4: Die Hellenistische Philosophie*. Basle: Schwabe, 991–1168.

Gee, E. (2001). "Cicero's Astronomy." *CQ* 51: 520–36.

———(2013). *Aratus and the Astronomical Tradition*. New York: Oxford University Press.

Gehrke, H.-J., and Möller, A. (eds.) (1996). *Vergangenheit und Lebenswelt: Soziale Kommunikation, Traditionsbildung und historisches Bewußtsein*. Tübingen: Narr.

Geiger, J. (1974). "M. Favonius: Three Notes." *RivStorAnt* 4: 161–70.

———(1979). "Munatius Rufus and Thrasea Paetus on Cato the Younger." *Athenaeum* 57: 48–72.

Gelzer, M. (1918). "(Iunius 53) M. Iunius Brutus, der Caesarmörder." *RE* 10.1: 973–1020.

———(1961). "Der Antrag des Cato Uticensis, Caesar den Germanen auszuliefern." In E. Kaufmann (ed.), *Festgabe für Paul Kirn*. Berlin: Erich Schmidt, 46–53.

———(1963 [1934]). "Cato Uticensis." In id. *Kleine Schriften*. Vol. 2. Wiesbaden: Steiner, 257–85 (first in *Die Antike* 10: 59–91).

———(1963 [1938]). "Ciceros Brutus als politische Kundgebung." In id. *Kleine Schriften*. Vol. 2. Wiesbaden: Steiner, 248–50 (first in *Philologus* 93: 128–31).

Gesche, H. (1968). *Die Vergottung Caesars*. Kallmünz: Lassleben.

Getty, R. J. (1941). "The Astrology of P. Nigidius Figulus (Lucan I, 649–65)." *CQ* 35: 17–22.

———(1960). "Neopythagoreanism and Mathematical Symmetry in Lucan, *De bello civili* 1." *TAPA* 91: 310–23.

Gianola, A. (1905). *Publio Nigidio Figulo: astrologo e mago*. Rome: Tipografia Agostiniana.

Gibson, R. (forthcoming). "*Pro Marcello* without Caesar: Grief, Exile and Death in Cicero *Ad Familiares* 4." *Hermethena* 201.

Gigon, O. (1973). "Cicero und die griechische Philosophie." *ANRW* 1.4: 226–61.

Gilbert, N. (2015). "Among Friends: Cicero and the Epicureans." Diss. Toronto.

———(2019). "Lucius Saufeius and His Lost Prehistory of Rome: Intellectual Culture in the Late Republic (Servius ad *Aen.* 1.6)." *CP* 114: 25–46.

———(forthcoming). "Was Atticus an Epicurean?" In Yona and Davis (eds.).

———, Graver, M., and McConnell, S. (eds.) (forthcoming). *Power and Persuasion in Cicero's Philosophy*.

Gildenhard, I. (2006). "Reckoning with Tyranny: Greek Thoughts on Caesar in Cicero's *Letters to Atticus* in Early 49." In S. Lewis (ed.), *Ancient Tyranny*. Edinburgh: Edinburgh University Press, 197–209.

———(2007). *Paideia Romana: Cicero's Tusculan Disputations*. Cambridge: Cambridge Philological Society.

———(2011). *Creative Eloquence: The Construction of Reality in Cicero's Speeches*. Oxford: Oxford University Press.

————(2013). "Cicero's Dialogues: Historiography Manqué and the Evidence of Fiction." In Föllinger and Müller (eds.), 235–74.

————(2018). "A Republic in Letters: Epistolary Communities in Cicero's Correspondence, 49–44 BCE." In P. Ceccarelli et al. (eds.), *Letters and Communities: Studies in the Socio-Political Dimensions of Ancient Epistolography*. Oxford: Oxford University Press, 205–36.

Gill, C. (1988). "Personhood and Personality: The Four-*personae* Theory in Cicero, *De officiis* I." *OSAPh* 6: 169–99.

Girardet, K. M. (1977). "Ciceros Urteil über die Entstehung des Tribunates als Institution der römischen Verfassung (rep. 2,57–59)." In (no ed.), *Bonner Festgabe Johannes Straub*. Bonn: Rheinland-Verlag, 179–200.

Gitner, A. (2015). "Varro *Aeolicus*: Latin's Affiliation with Greek." In Butterfield (ed.), 33–50.

Glucker, J. (1988). "Cicero's Philosophical Affiliations." In J. M. Dillon and A. A. Long (eds.), *The Question of "Eclecticism": Studies in Later Greek Philosophy*. Berkeley: University of California Press, 34–69.

————(1997). "Socrates in the Academic Books and Other Ciceronian Works." In Inwood and Mansfeld (eds.), 58–88.

Goar, R. J. (1968). "The Purpose of *De divinatione*." *TAPA* 99: 241–48.

————(1972). *Cicero and the State Religion*. Amsterdam: Hakkert.

————(1987). *The Legend of Cato Uticensis from the First Century B.C. to the Fifth Century A.D.* Brussels: Latomus.

Gordon, P. (2012). *The Invention and Gendering of Epicurus*. Ann Arbor: University of Michigan Press.

Görler, W. (1974). *Untersuchungen zu Ciceros Philosophie*. Heidelberg: Winter.

————(1990). "Cicero zwischen Politik und Philosophie." *Ciceroniana* 7: 61–73 (= 2004: 158–71).

————(1995). "Silencing the Troublemaker: *De Legibus* I. 39 and the Continuity of Cicero's Scepticism." In Powell (ed.), 85–113 (= 2004: 240–67).

————(1997). "Cicero's Philosophical Stance in the *Lucullus*." In Inwood and Mansfeld (eds.), 36–57 (= 2004: 268–89).

————(2004). *Kleine Schriften zur hellenistisch-römischen Philosophie*. Ed. by C. Catrein. Leiden: Brill.

Gotoff, H. C. (2012). "Cicero's Caesarian Orations." In J. M. May (ed.), *Brill's Companion to Cicero: Oratory and Rhetoric*. Leiden: Brill, 219–71.

Gotter, U. (1996a). "Cicero und die Freundschaft: Die Konstruktion sozialer Normen zwischen römischer Politik und griechischer Philosophie." In Gehrke and Möller (eds.), 339–60.

————(1996b). *Der Diktator ist tot! Politik in Rom zwischen den Iden des März und der Begründung des Zweiten Triumvirats*. Stuttgart: Steiner.

————(2000). "Marcus Iunius Brutus—oder: die Nemesis des Namens." In Hölkeskamp and Stein-Hölkeskamp (eds.), 328–39.

————(2003). "Ontologie versus *exemplum*: Griechische Philosophie als politisches Argument in der späten römischen Republik." In Piepenbrink (ed.), 165–85.

Gowing, A. (2000). "Memory and Silence in Cicero's *Brutus*." *Eranos* 98: 39–64.

Gradel, I. (2002). *Emperor Worship and Roman Religion*. Oxford: Clarendon Press.

Graf, F. (1997). *Magic in the Ancient World*. Trans. by F. Philip. Cambridge, MA: Harvard University Press (French 1994).

Grafton, A. T. (2009). *Worlds Made by Words: Scholarship and Community in the Modern West.* Cambridge, MA: Harvard University Press.

———and Swerdlow, N. M. (1986). "The Horoscope of the Foundation of Rome." *CP* 81: 148–53.

Graver, M. (2002). *Cicero on the Emotions: Tusculan Disputations 3 and 4.* Chicago: University of Chicago Press.

———(forthcoming). "The Psychology of Honor in Cicero's *De re publica*." In Gilbert, Graver, and McConnell (eds.).

Grebe, S. (2000). "Kriterien für die *Latinitas* bei Varro und Quintilian." In A. Haltenhoff and F.-H. Mutschler (eds.), *Hortus litterarum antiquarum: Festschrift für Hans Armin Gärtner zum 70. Geburtstag.* Heidelberg: Winter, 191–210.

———(2001). "Views of Correct Speech in Varro and Quintilian." *Papers on Grammar* 6: 135–64.

Griffin, M. T. (1976). *Seneca: A Philosopher in Politics.* Oxford: Clarendon Press.

———(1986). "Philosophy, Cato, and Roman Suicide." *GaR* 33: 64–77 and 192–202 (= 2018: 402–19).

———(1989). "Philosophy, Politics, and Politicians at Rome." In Griffin and Barnes (eds.), 1–37 (= 2018: 341–62).

———(1994). "The Intellectual Developments of the Ciceronian Age." *CAH*[2]: 9.689–728 (= 2018: 432–60).

———(1995). "Philosophical Badinage in Cicero's Letters to His Friends." In Powell (ed.), 325–46 (= 2018: 461–74).

———(1997a). "From Aristotle to Atticus: Cicero and Matius on Friendship." In Barnes and Griffin (eds.), 86–109 (= 2018: 495–509).

———(1997b). "The Composition of the *Academica*: Motives and Versions." In Inwood and Mansfeld (eds.), 1–35 (= 2018: 510–31).

———(2001). "Piso, Cicero and Their Audience." In Auvray-Assayas and Delattre (eds.), 85–99 (= 2018: 551–61).

———(2003). "*Clementia* after Caesar: From Politics to Philosophy." In F. Cairns and E. Fantham (eds.), *Caesar against Liberty? Perspectives on His Autocracy* (= *Papers of the Langford Latin Seminar* 11). Cambridge: Francis Cairns, 157–82 (= Griffin 2018: 570–86).

———(2018). *Politics and Philosophy at Rome: Collected Papers.* Ed. by C. Balmaceda. Oxford: Oxford University Press.

———(ed.) (2009). *A Companion to Julius Caesar.* Chichester: Wiley-Blackwell.

———and Atkins, E. M. (1991). *Cicero: On Duties.* Cambridge: Cambridge University Press.

———and Barnes, J. (eds.) (1989). *Philosophia Togata: Essays on Philosophy and Roman Society.* Oxford: Clarendon Press.

Grillo, L. (2012). *The Art of Caesar's Bellum Civile: Literature, Ideology, and Community.* Cambridge: Cambridge University Press.

———(2016). "The Artistic Architecture and Closural Devices of Cicero's *ad Familiares* 1 and 6." *Arethusa* 49: 399–413.

———and Krebs, C. B. (eds.) (2018). *The Cambridge Companion to the Writings of Julius Caesar.* Cambridge: Cambridge University Press.

Grimal, P. (1966). "Le 'Bon roi' de Philodème et la royauté de César." *REL* 44: 254–85.

————(1978). "Le Poème de Lucrèce en son temps." In O. Gigon (ed.), *Lucrèce* (= *Entretiens Hardt* 24). Vandœuvres: Fondation Hardt, 233–62.

Groebe, P. (1905). "Die Obstruktion im römischen Senat." *Klio* 5: 229–35.

Gruen, E. S. (1974). *The Last Generation of the Roman Republic*. Berkeley: University of California Press.

Guillaumont, F. (1984). *Philosophe et augure: recherches sur la théorie cicéronienne de la divination.* Brussels: Latomus.

————(2000). "Divination et prévision rationelle dans la correspondance de Cicéron." In L. Nadjo and E. Gavoille (eds.), *Epistulae antiquae*. Vol. 1. Louvain: Peeters, 103–15.

————(2002). "Les philosophes grecs dans la correspondance de Ciceron." In L. Nadjo and E. Gavoille (eds.), *Epistulae antiquae II*. Louvain: Peeters, 61–76.

————(2006). *Le* De diuinatione *de Cicéron et les théories antiques de la divination.* Brussels: Latomus.

Guittard, C. (2003). "Les Calendriers brontoscopiques dans le monde étrusco-romain." In C. Cusset (ed.), *La Météorologie dans l'antiquité: entre science et croyance.* Saint-Étienne: Publications de l'Université de Saint-Étienne, 455–66.

Gunderson, E. T. (2016). "Cicero's Studied Passions: The Letters of 46 B.C.E." *Arethusa* 49: 525–47.

Gurd, S. A. (2012). *Work in Progress: Literary Revision as Social Performance in Ancient Rome.* New York: Oxford University Press.

Guttilla, G. (1968–69). "La *consolatio* politica di Cicerone." *Annali del liceo classico G. Garibaldi di Palermo* 5/6: 294–348.

Haack, M.-L. (2017). "Prophecy and Divination." In Naso (ed.), 1.357–67.

Haake, M. (2017). "Brüder—Ritter—Epikureer: Lucius und Appius Saufeius aus Praeneste in Latium, Rom und Athen." In M. Haake and A.-C. Harders (eds.), *Politische Kultur und soziale Struktur der Römischen Republik: Bilanzen und Perspektiven.* Stuttgart: Steiner, 429–53.

Habinek, T. N. (1994). "Ideology for an Empire in the Prefaces to Cicero's Dialogues." *Ramus* 23: 55–67.

————and Schiesaro, A. (eds.) (1997). *The Roman Cultural Revolution.* Cambridge: Cambridge University Press.

Hadas, D. (2017). "St Augustine and the Disappearance of Varro." In Arena and Mac Góráin (eds.), 76–91.

Haenni, P. R. (1905). "Die literarische Kritik in Ciceros *Brutus*." Diss. Fribourg.

Hagendahl, H. (1967). *Augustine and the Latin Classics.* 2 vols. Göteborg: Göteborg University.

Hall, J. (2009a). *Politeness and Politics in Cicero's Letters.* New York: Oxford University Press.

————(2009b). "Serving the Times: Cicero and Caesar the Dictator." In W. J. Dominik, J. Garthwaite, and P. A. Roche (eds.), *Writing Politics in Imperial Rome.* Leiden: Brill, 89–110.

Hall, L. G. H. (2009). "*Ratio* and *Romanitas* in the *Bellum Gallicum*." In K. Welch and A. Powell (eds.), *Julius Caesar as Artful Reporter: The War Commentaries as Political Instruments.* Swansea: Classical Press of Wales, 11–43.

Haltenhoff, A. (2003). "Lukrez, der Epikureismus und die römische Gesellschaft." In Haltenhoff, Heil, and Mutschler (eds.), 219–44.

Haltenhoff, A., Heil, A. and Mutschler, F. H. (eds.) (2003). *O tempora o mores! Römische Werte und römische Literatur in den letzten Jahrzehnten der Republik.* Munich: Saur.

Hampl, F. (1959). "Römische Republik in republikanischer Zeit und das Problem des 'Sittenverfalls.'" *HZ* 188: 497–525.

Hanchey, D. (2013). "Cicero, Exchange, and the Epicureans." *Phoenix* 67: 119–34.

———(2014–15). "Days of Future Passed: Fiction Forming Fact in Cicero's Dialogues." *CJ* 110: 61–75.

Hankinson, R. J. (1988). "Stoicism, Science and Divination." *Apeiron* 21: 123–60.

Hannah, R. (1996). "Lucan *Bellum civile* 1.649–65: The Astrology of P. Nigidius Figulus Revisited." *Papers of the Leeds International Latin Seminar* 9: 175–90.

Harries, J. (2006). *Cicero and the Jurists: From Citizens' Law to the Lawful State.* London: Duckworth.

Harris, W. V. (1971). *Rome in Etruria and Umbria.* Oxford: Clarendon Press.

Heibges, U. (1969a). "Cicero, a Hypocrite in Religion?" *AJP* 90: 304–12.

———(1969b). "Religion and Rhetoric in Cicero's Speeches." *Latomus* 28: 833–49.

Heil, A. (2003). "Literarische Kommunikation in der späten römischen Republik: Versuch einer Topographie." In Haltenhoff, Heil, and Mutschler (eds.), 5–50.

Heinze, R. (1924). "Cicero 'Staat' als politische Tendenzschrift." *Hermes* 59: 73–94 (=id. [1960]. *Vom Geist des Römertums: Ausgewählte Aufsätze.* Ed. by E. Burck, 3rd ed. Darmstadt: Wissenschaftliche Buchgesellschaft, 141–59).

Heldmann, K. (1976). "Ciceros Laelius und die Grenzen der Freundschaft: Zur Interdependenz von Literatur und Politik 44/43 v.Chr." *Hermes* 104: 72–103.

Hendrickson, G. L. (1906). "The *De analogia* of Julius Caesar; Its Occasion, Nature, and Date, with Additional Fragments." *CP* 1: 97–120.

———(1939). "Brutus *De Virtute.*" *AJP* 60: 401–13.

Heurgon, J. (1959). "The Date of Vegoia's Prophecy." *JRS* 49: 41–45.

Heuss, A. (1956). "Cicero und Matius." *Historia* 5: 53–73.

Hill, T. (2004). Ambitiosa Mors: *Suicide and Self in Roman Thought and Literature.* New York: Routledge.

Hillard, T. (2013). "Graffiti's Engagement: The Political Graffiti of the Late Roman Republic." In G. Sears, P. Keegan, and R. Laurence (eds.), *Written Space in the Latin West, 200 BC to AD 300.* London: Bloomsbury, 105–22.

Hinds, S. (2006). "Venus, Varro and the *uates*: Toward the Limits of Etymologizing Interpretation." *Dictynna* 3.

Hine, H. (2016). "Philosophy and *philosophi*: From Cicero to Apuleius." In Williams and Volk (eds.), 13–29.

Hirzel, R. (1895). *Der Dialog: Ein literarhistorischer Versuch.* Leipzig: S. Hirzel.

Hobsbawm, E. (1983). "Introduction: Inventing Traditions." In E. Hobsbawm and T. Ranger (eds.), *The Invention of Tradition.* Cambridge: Cambridge University Press, 1–14.

Hoenig, C. (2018). *Plato's Timaeus and the Latin Tradition.* Cambridge: Cambridge University Press.

Höffe, O. (ed.) (2017). *Ciceros Staatsphilosophie: Ein kooperativer Kommentar zu* De re publica *und* De legibus. Berlin: De Gruyter.

Hölkeskamp, K.-J. (1996). "*Exempla* und *mos maiorum*: Überlegungen zum kollektiven Gedächtnis der Nobilität." In Gehrke and Möller (eds.), 301–38.

————(ed.) (2009). *Eine politische Kultur (in) der Krise? Die "letzte Generation" der römischen Republik.* Munich: Oldenbourg.

————and Stein-Hölkeskamp, E. (eds.) (2000). *Von Romulus zu Augustus: Große Gestalten der römischen Republik.* Munich: Beck.

Holleman, A. W. J. (1978). "Cicero's Reaction to the Julian Calendar (PLUT., *Caes.* 59): January 4th (45)." *Historia* 27: 496–98.

Holzberg, N. (1995). "Enkomionstruktur und Reflexe spätrepublikanischer Realität in der Atticus-Vita des Cornelius Nepos." In P. Neukam (ed.), *Anschauung und Anschaulichkeit.* Munich: Bayerischer Schulbuchverlag, 29–43.

Hopkins, K. (1978). *Conquerors and Slaves.* Cambridge, MA: Harvard University Press.

Horky, P. S. (forthcoming). *Pythagorean Philosophy, 250 BCE–200 CE.* Cambridge: Cambridge University Press.

Horsfall, N. M. (1972). "Varro and Caesar: Three Chronological Problems." *BICS* 19: 120–28.

Housman, A. E. (1926). *M. Annaei Lucani Belli Civilis libri decem.* Oxford: Blackwell.

Houston, G. W. (2014). *Inside Roman Libraries: Book Collections and Their Management in Antiquity.* Chapel Hill: University of North Carolina Press.

Howley, J. A. (2014). "*Heus tu, rhetorice*: Gellius, Cicero, Plutarch, and Roman Study Abroad." In J. M. Madsen and R. Rees (eds.), *Roman Rule in Greek and Latin Writing: Double Vision.* Leiden: Brill, 163–92.

Hübner, W. (2010). *Manilius, Astronomica, Buch V.* 2 vols. Berlin: De Gruyter.

Hutchinson, G. O. (1998). *Cicero's Correspondence: A Literary Study.* Oxford: Clarendon Press.

————(2001). "The Date of the *De Rerum Natura.*" *CQ* 51: 150–62.

————(2013). *Greek to Latin: Frameworks and Contexts for Intertextuality.* Oxford: Oxford University Press.

————(2016). "Muße ohne Müßiggang: Strukturen, Räume und das Ich bei Cicero." In Eickhoff (ed.), 97–111.

Iddeng, J. (2006). "*Publica aut Peri!* The Releasing and Distribution of Roman Books." *SO* 81: 58–84.

Inwood, B. and Mansfeld, J. (eds.) (1997). *Assent and Argument: Studies in Cicero's Academic Books.* Leiden: Brill.

Jacotot, M. (2014). "*De re publica esset silentium*: pensée politique et histoire d'éloquence dans le *Brutus.*" In Aubert-Baillot and Guérin (eds.), 193–214.

Jal, P. (1961). "La Propagande religieuse à Rome au cours des guerres civiles de la fin de la ré-publique." *AC* 30: 395–414.

Jehne, M. (1987). "Caesars Bemühungen um die Reintegration der Pompeianer." *Chiron* 17: 313–41.

Jocelyn, H. D. (1977). "The Ruling Class of the Roman Republic and Greek Philosophers." *BRL* 9: 323–66.

Johnson, W. A. (2010). *Readers and Reading Culture in the High Roman Empire: A Study of Elite Communities.* New York: Oxford University Press.

————(2012). "Cicero and Tyrannio: *mens addita videtur meis aedibus (Ad Atticum 4.8.2)*." *CW* 105: 471–77.

Johnston, S. I. (2001). "Charming Children: The Use of the Child in Ancient Divination." *Arethusa* 34: 97–117.

Jones, C. P. (1970). "Cicero's *Cato*." *RhM* 113: 188–96.

Kany-Turpin, J. (ed.) (2005). *Signe et prédiction dans l'antiquité*. Saint-Étienne: Publications de l'Université de Saint-Étienne.

Kassel, R. 1958. *Untersuchungen zur griechischen und römischen Konsolationsliteratur*. Munich: Beck.

Kaster, R. A. (2016). *C. Suetoni Tranquilli De uita caesarum libri VIII et De grammaticis et rhetoribus liber*. Oxford: Clarendon Press.

———(2020). *Cicero: Brutus and Orator*. New York: Oxford University Press.

Keck, R. W., Wiersing, E., and Wittstadt, K. (eds.) (1996). *Literaten—Kleriker—Gelehrte: Zur Geschichte des Gebildeten im vormodernen Europa*. Cologne: Böhlau.

———(1996). "Vorwort der Herausgeber." In Keck, Wiersing, and Wittstadt (eds.), 7–13.

Kerkhecker, A. (2002). "*Privato officio, non publico*: Literaturwissenschaftliche Überlegungen zu Ciceros *Pro Marcello*." In J. P. Schwindt (ed.), *Klassische Philologie inter disciplinas: Aktuelle Konzepte zu Gegenstand und Methode eines Grundlagenfaches*. Heidelberg: Winter, 93–149.

Kierdorf, W. (1978). "Ciceros *Cato*: Überlegungen zu einer verlorenen Schrift Ciceros." *RhM* 121: 167–84.

Klotz, A. (1927). *C. Iulius Caesar*, Commentarii. Vol. 3. Leipzig: Teubner.

Koch, B. (2006). *Philosophie als Medizin für die Seele: Untersuchungen zu Ciceros Tusculanae Disputationes*. Stuttgart: Steiner.

Koch Piettre, R. (2017). "Lucrèce entre Memmius père et Memmius fils: une interprétation de Cicéron, *Ad familiares*, XIII, 1." In Vesperini (ed.), 89–109.

König, J. and Whitmarsh, T. (eds.) (2007). *Ordering Knowledge in the Roman Empire*. Cambridge: Cambridge University Press.

———Oikonomopoulou, K., and Woolf, G. (eds.) (2013). *Ancient Libraries*. Cambridge: Cambridge University Press.

———and Woolf, G. (eds.) (2017). *Authority and Expertise in Ancient Scientific Culture*. Cambridge: Cambridge University Press.

Konstan, D. (2005). "Clemency as a Virtue." *CP* 100: 337–46.

Koortbojian, M. (2013). *The Divinization of Caesar and Augustus: Precedents, Consequences, Implications*. New York: Cambridge University Press.

Kraus, C. S. (2005). "Hair, Hegemony, and Historiography: Caesar's Style and Its Earliest Critics." In Reinhardt, Lapidge, and Adams (eds.), 97–115.

Krebs, C. B. (2013). "Caesar, Lucretius and the Dates of *De rerum natura* and the *Commentarii*." *CQ* 63: 772–79.

———(2018a). "A Style of Choice." In Grillo and Krebs (eds.), 110–30.

———(2018b). "'Greetings, Cicero!': Caesar and Plato on Writing and Memory." *CQ* 68: 517–22.

Kretschmar, M. (1938). "Otium, studia litterarum, βίος θεωρητικός im Leben und Denken Ciceros." Diss. Leipzig.

Kroll, W. (1936). "P. Nigidius Figulus." *RE* 17.1: 200–212.

Krostenko, B. A. (2000). "Beyond (Dis)belief: Rhetorical Form and Religious Symbol in Cicero's *de Divinatione*." *TAPA* 130: 353–91.

———(2005). "Style and Ideology in the *Pro Marcello*." In K. Welch and T. W. Hillard (eds.), *Roman Crossings: Theory and Practice in the Roman Republic*. Swansea: Classical Press of Wales, 279–312.

Kruschwitz, P. (2014). "Gallic War Songs (II): Marcus Cicero, Quintus Cicero, and Caesar's Invasion of Britain." *Philologus* 158: 275–305.

———and Schumacher, M. (2005). *Das vorklassische Lehrgedicht der Römer.* Heidelberg: Winter.

Kubiak, D. P. (1994). "Aratean Influence in the *De consulatu suo* of Cicero." *Philologus* 138: 52–66.

Kumaniecki, K. (1957). "Cicero Paradoxa Stoicorum und die römische Wirklichkeit." *Philologus* 101: 113–34.

———(1962). "Cicerone e Varrone: storia di una conoscenza." *Athenaeum* 40: 221–43.

———(1970). "Ciceros *Cato.*" In W. Wimmel (ed.), *Forschungen zur römischen Literatur: Festschrift zum 60. Geburtstag von Karl Büchner.* Wiesbaden: Steiner, 168–88.

Kurczyk, S. (2006). *Cicero und die Inszenierung der eigenen Vergangenheit: Autobiographisches Schreiben in der späten Republik.* Cologne: Böhlau.

Labate, M. and Narducci, E. (1981). "Mobilità dei modelli etici e relativismo dei valori: il 'personaggio' di Attico." In A. Giardina and A. Schiavone (eds.), *Società romana e produzione schiavistica III: modelli etici, diritto e trasformazioni sociali.* Rome: Laterza, 127–82.

Landwehr, A. (2008). *Historische Diskursanalyse.* Frankfurt: Campus Verlag.

Leber, N. (2018). "Cicero's *liberatores*: A Reassessment." *CQ* 68: 160–77.

Le Bœuffle, A. (1964). "Quelques erreurs ou difficultés astronomiques chez Columelle." *REL* 42: 324–33.

Le Bonniec, H. (1972). *Pline l'Ancien Histoire Naturelle livre XVIII.* Paris: Belles Lettres.

Lefèvre, E. (2008). *Philosophie unter der Tyrannis: Ciceros Tusculanae Disputationes.* Heidelberg: Winter.

Le Glay, M. (1976). "Magie et sorcellerie à Rome au dernier siècle de la République." In (no ed.), *L'Italie préromaine et la Rome républicaine: mélanges offerts à Jacques Heurgon.* 2 vols. Rome: École Française de Rome, 1.525–50.

Legrand, L. (1931). *Publius Nigidius Figulus: philosophe néo-pythagoricien orphique.* Paris: Éditions de l'Œuvre d'Auteuil.

Lehmann, Y. (1997). *Varron théologien et philosophe romain.* Brussels: Latomus.

———(1998). "Pythagorisme et encyclopédisme chez Varron." In Ternes (ed.), 2.81–88.

Lehoux, D. (2007). *Astronomy, Weather, and Calendars in the Ancient World:* Parapegmata *and Related Texts in Classical and Near Eastern Societies.* Cambridge: Cambridge University Press.

———(2012). *What Did the Romans Know? An Inquiry into Science and Worldmaking.* Chicago: University of Chicago Press.

Lennon, J. (2010). "Pollution and Ritual Impurity in Cicero's *De domo sua.*" *CQ* 60: 427–45.

Lentano, M. (2009). "Il debito di Bruto: per un'antropologia del nome proprio nella cultura romana." *MD* 63: 59–89.

Leonardis, I. (2014). "*Vestustas, oblivio* e crisi d'identità nelle *Saturae Menippeae*: il risveglio di Varrone in un'altra Roma." *Epekeina* 4: 19–58.

———(2019). *Varrone, unus scilicet antiquorum hominum: senso del passato e pratica antiquaria.* Bari: Edipuglia.

Leonhardt, J. (1995). "Theorie und Praxis der *deliberatio* bei Cicero: Der Briefwechsel mit Atticus aus dem Jahre 49." *ACD* 31: 153–71.

———(1999). *Ciceros Kritik der Philosophenschulen.* Munich: Beck.

Leppin, H. (2002). "Atticus—zum Wertewandel in der späten römischen Republik." In J. Spiel-vogel (ed.), *Res publica reperta: Zur Verfassung und Gesellschaft der späten Republik und des frühen Prinzipats*. Stuttgart: Steiner, 192–202.

Leslie, R. J. (1950). "The Epicureanism of Titus Pomponius Atticus." Diss. Columbia.

Levene, D. S. (1997). "God and Man in the Classical Latin Panegyric." *PCPS* 43: 66–103.

———(2005). "The Late Republican/Triumviral Period: 90–40 BC." In S. Harrison (ed.), *A Companion to Latin Literature*. Malden, MA: Blackwell, 31–43.

Lévi, N. (2014). *La Révélation finale à Rome: Cicéron, Ovide, Apulée*. Paris: Presses de l'Université Paris-Sorbonne.

Lévy, C. (1992). *Cicero Academicus: recherches sur les Académiques et sur la philosophie cicéroni-enne*. Rome: École Française de Rome.

———(2001). "Cicéron et l'épicurisme: la problématique de l'éloge paradoxal." In Auvray-Assayas and Delattre (eds.), 61–75.

———(2003). "Cicero and the *Timaeus*." In G. J. Reydams-Schils (ed.), *Plato's* Timaeus *as Cultural Icon*. Notre Dame, IN: University of Notre Dame Press, 95–110.

———(2006). "Y a-t-il quelqu'un derrière le masque? À propos de la théorie des *personae* chez Cicéron." In P. Galand-Hallyn and C. Lévy (eds.), *Vivre pour soi, vivre dans la cité: de l'antiquité à la renaissance*. Paris: Presses de l'Université Paris-Sorbonne, 45–58.

———(2012a). "Other Followers of Antiochus." In Sedley (ed.), 290–306.

———(2012b). "Philosophical Life versus Political Life: An Impossible Choice for Cicero?" In W. Nicgorski (ed.), *Cicero's Practical Philosophy*. Notre Dame, IN: University of Notre Dame Press, 58–78.

———(2017). "Cicéron était-il an 'Roman Sceptic?'" *Ciceroniana on line* 1: 9–24.

———(2020). "Cicero." In Mitsis (ed.), 476–85.

Lewis, A.-M. (1998). "What Dreadful Purpose Do You Have?: A New Explanation of the As-trological Prophecy of Nigidius Figulus in Lucan's *Pharsalia* I, 658–63." *Studies in Latin Lit-erature and Roman History* 9: 379–400.

Lieberg, G. (1972). "Varro's Theologie im Urteil Augustins." In (no ed.), *Studi classici in onore di Quintino Cataudella*. Vol. 3. Catania: Università di Catania, 185–201.

———(1973). "Die *theologia tripertita* in Forschung und Bezeugung." *ANRW* 1.4: 63–115.

———(1982). "Die Theologia Tripertita als Formprinzip antiken Denkens." *RhM* 125: 25–53.

———(1994). "Das Methodenkapitel in Ciceros Staat (*Rep.* 2, 11, 21–22)." *Mnemosyne* 47: 12–32.

Liebeschuetz, J. H. W. G. (1979). *Continuity and Change in Roman Religion*. Oxford: Clarendon Press.

Linder, M. and Scheid, J. (1993). "Quand croire c'est faire: le problème de la croissance dans la Rome ancienne." *Archives de sciences sociales des religions* 81: 47–61.

Linderski, J. (1970). "Römischer Staat und Götterzeichen: zum Problem der obnuntiatio." *Jahrbuch der Universität Düsseldorf 1969–1970*: 309–22.

———(1982). "Cicero and Roman Divination." *PP* 37: 12–38.

———(1985). "The *libri reconditi*." *HSCP* 89: 207–34.

———(1986). "The Augural Law." *ANRW* 2.16: 2146–2312.

———(1989). "Garden Parlors: Nobles and Birds." In R. I. Curtis (ed.), *Studia Pompeiana & Classica in Honor of Wilhelmina F. Jashemski*. Vol. 2. New Rochelle, NY: Caratzas, 105–27.

Lindsay, H. (1998). "The Biography of Atticus: Cornelius Nepos on the Philosophical and Ethical Background of Pomponius Atticus." *Latomus* 57: 324–36.

Linke, B. (2000). "*Religio* und *res publica*: Religiöser Glaube und gesellschaftliches Handeln im republikanischen Rom." In B. Linke and M. Stemmler (eds.), Mos maiorum: *Untersuchungen zu den Formen der Identitätsstiftung und Stabilisierung in der römischen Republik.* Stuttgart: Steiner, 269–98.

Lintott, A. W. (1972). "Imperial Expansion and Moral Decline in the Roman Republic." *Historia* 21: 626–38.

———(2008). *Cicero as Evidence: A Historian's Companion.* New York: Oxford University Press.

———(2009). "The Assassination." In Griffin (ed.), 72–82.

Liuzzi, D. (1983). *Nigidio Figulo "astrologo e mago": testimonianze e frammenti.* Lecce: Milella.

Lomanto, V. (1993). "Due divergenti interpretazioni dell'analogia: la flessione dei temi in -*u*- secondo Varrone e secondo Cesare." In Poli (ed.), 2.643–76.

Long, A. A. (1995a). "Cicero's Plato and Aristotle." In Powell (ed.), 37–61.

———(1995b). "Cicero's Politics in De officiis." In A. Laks and M. Schofield (eds.), *Justice and Generosity: Studies in Hellenistic Social and Political Philosophy.* Cambridge: Cambridge University Press, 213–40.

Luciani, S. (2009). "Cypsélos, Pisistrate, Phalaris, Denys et les autres: la figure du tyran dans l'œuvre philosophique de Cicéron." In Devillers and Meyers (ed.), 151–65.

Luke, T. S. (2014). *Ushering in a New Republic: Theologies of Arrival at Rome in the First Century BCE.* Ann Arbor: University of Michigan Press.

MacBain, B. (1982). *Prodigy and Expiation: A Study in Religion and Politics in Republican Rome.* Brussels: Latomus.

MacDonald, C. (2016). "Rewriting Rome: Topography, Etymology and History in Varro De Lingua Latina 5 and Propertius Elegies 4." *Ramus* 45: 192–212.

MacKendrick, P. L. (1989). *The Philosophical Books of Cicero.* London: Duckworth.

Mackey, J. L. (2017). "Das Erlöschen des Glaubens: The Fate of Belief in the Study of Roman Religion." *Phasis* 20: 83–150.

MacRae, D. E. (2013). Review of Rüpke 2012. *AJP* 134: 510–14.

———(2016). *Legible Religion: Books, Gods, and Rituals in Roman Culture.* Cambridge, MA: Harvard University Press.

———(2017). "'The Laws of the Rites and the Priests': Varro and Late Republican Roman Sacral Jurisprudence." In Arena and Mac Góráin (eds.), 34–48.

———(2018). "*Diligentissumus investigator antiquitatis*? 'Antiquarianism' and Historical Evidence between Republican Rome and the Early Modern Republic of Latin." In Sandberg and Smith (eds.), 137–56.

Malitz, J. (1987). "Die Kalenderreform Caesars: Ein Beitrag zur Geschichte seiner Spätzeit." *AncSoc* 18: 103–31.

Mannheim, K. (1936). "The Sociology of Knowledge." In id. *Ideology and Utopia: An Introduction to the Sociology of Knowledge.* Trans. by L. Wirth and E. Shils. New York: Harcourt Brace, 237–80 (German 1931).

Manuwald, E. (1923). "Σχολή und σχολαστικός vom Altertum bis zur Gegenwart: Eine wortbiographische Untersuchung." Diss. Freiburg.

Maras, D. F. (2019). "Children of Truth: The Role of Apprentices in Etrusco-Roman Divination." *Henoch* 41: 60–67.

Marchese, R. R. (2011). *Cicerone:* Bruto. Rome: Carocci.

Marciniak, K. (2008). "Cicero und Caesar: Ein Dialog der Dichter." *Philologus* 152: 212–22.

Marinone, N. and Malaspina, E. (2004). *Cronologia ciceroniana.* 2nd rev. ed. Bologna: Pàtron.

Marshall, A. (1993). "Atticus and the Genealogies." *Latomus* 52: 307–17.

Marshall, R. M. A. (2017). "Varro, Atticus, and *Annales.*" In Arena and Mac Góráin (eds.), 61–75.

Martelli, F. (2017). "The Triumph of Letters: Rewriting Cicero in *ad Fam.* 15." *JRS* 107: 90–115.

Martin, P. M. (1994). *L'Idée de royauté à Rome II: haine de la royauté et séductions monarchiques (du IVe siècle av. J.-C. au principat augustéen).* Clermont-Ferrand: Adosa.

———(2010). "D'un Brutus à l'autre: de la construction d'un mythe de liberté à sa confusion." In M. Blandenet, C. Chillet, and C. Courrier (eds.), *Figures de l'identité: naissance et destin des modèles communautaires dans le monde romain.* Lyon: ENS Éditions, 33–49.

———(2014). "Entre Prosopographie et politique: la figure et l'ascendance de Brutus dans le *Brutus.*" In Aubert-Baillot and Guérin (eds.), 215–35.

Maslowski, T. (1974). "The Chronology of Cicero's Anti-Epicureanism." *Eos* 62: 55–78.

Maso, S. (2012). *Filosofia a Roma: dalla riflessione sui principi all'arte della vita.* Rome: Carocci.

———(2015). *Grasp and Dissent: Cicero and Epicurean Philosophy.* Turnhout: Brepols (Italian 2008).

Mastrandrea, P. (1979). *Un neoplatonico latino: Cornelio Labeone.* Leiden: Brill.

Maurach, G. (2006). *Geschichte der römischen Philosophie.* 3rd rev. ed. Darmstadt: Wissenschaftliche Buchgesellschaft.

Mayer i Olivé, M. (2012). "Publius Nigidius Figulus Pythagoricus et magus." In M. Piranomonte and F. M. Simón (eds.), *Contesti magici.* Rome: De Luca, 237–45.

Mayor, J. B. (1880–85). *M. Tulli Ciceronis De natura deorum libri tres.* 3 vols. Cambridge: Cambridge University Press.

McAlhany, J. C. (2003). "Language, Truth, and Illogic in the Writings of Varro." Diss. Columbia.

McCarthy, E. D. (1996). *Knowledge as Culture: The New Sociology of Knowledge.* London: Routledge.

McConnell, S. (2010). "Epicureans on Kingship." *CCJ* 56: 178–98.

———(2014). *Philosophical Life in Cicero's Letters.* Cambridge: Cambridge University Press.

———(2019). "Cicero and Socrates." In C. Moore (ed.), *Brill's Companion to the Reception of Socrates.* Leiden: Brill, 347–66.

McCutcheon, R. W. (2016). "Cicero's Textual Relations: The Gendered Circulation of *De finibus.*" *Helios* 43: 21–53.

McIntyre, G. (2016). *A Family of Gods: The Worship of the Imperial Family in the Latin West.* Ann Arbor: University of Michigan Press.

———(2019). *Imperial Cult.* Leiden: Brill.

Meier, C. (1980). *Die Ohnmacht des allmächtigen Diktators Caesar: Drei biographische Skizzen.* Frankfurt: Suhrkamp.

———(1997). *Res publica amissa: Eine Studie zur Verfassung und Geschichte der späten römischen Republik.* 3rd ed. Frankfurt: Suhrkamp.

Meier, M. (2014). *Caesar und das Problem der Monarchie in Rom.* Heidelberg: Winter.

Mevoli, D. (1992). "Una 'magia' di Nigidio (APUL. *apol.* 42)." *Studi di filologia e letteratura* 2: 115–25.

Miano, D. (2018). *Fortuna: Deity and Concept in Archaic and Republican Rome*. Oxford: Oxford University Press.

Michel, A. (1977). "Cicéron, Pompée et la guerre civile: rhétorique et philosophie dans la 'Correspondance.'" *AntHung* 25: 393–403.

Millar, F. (1988). "Cornelius Nepos, *Atticus* and the Roman Revolution." *GaR* 35: 40–55.

Miller, P. N. (ed.) (2007). *Momigliano and Antiquarianism: Foundations of the Modern Cultural Sciences*. Toronto: University of Toronto Press.

Miltner, F. (1953). "M. Porcius Cato Uticensis." *RE* 22.1: 168–211.

Minyard, J. D. (1985). *Lucretius and the Late Republic: An Essay in Roman Intellectual History*. Leiden: Brill.

Mitchell, J. F. (1966). "The Torquati." *Historia* 15: 23–31.

Mitchell, T. N. (1984). "Cicero on the Moral Crisis of the Late Republic." *Hermathena* 136: 21–41.

Mitsis, P. (2020). "Friendship." In Mitsis (ed.), 250–83.

———(ed.) (2020). *Oxford Handbook of Epicurus and Epicureanism*. New York: Oxford University Press.

Moatti, C. (1988). "Tradition et raison chez Cicéron: l'émergence de la rationalité politique à la fin de la république romaine." *MEFRA* 100: 385–430.

———(1997). *La Raison de Rome: naissance de l'esprit critique à la fin de la République (IIᵉ–Iᵉʳ siècle avant Jésus-Christ)*. Paris: Éditions du Seuil (English version: [2015]. *The Birth of Critical Thinking in Republican Rome*. Trans. by J. Lloyd. Cambridge: Cambridge University Press).

———(2003a). "Experts, mémoire et pouvoir à Rome, à la fin de la République." *RHist* 305: 303–25.

———(2003b). "La Construction du patrimoine culturel à Rome aux 1ᵉʳ siècle avant et 1ᵉʳ siècle après J.-C." In Citroni (ed.), 81–98.

Moles, J. L. (1983). "Some 'Last Words' of M. Iunius Brutus." *Latomus* 42: 763–79.

———(1987). "Politics, Philosophy, and Friendship in Horace *Odes* 2,7." *QUCC* 25: 59–72.

———(1997). "Plutarch, Brutus and Brutus' Greek and Latin Letters." In Mossman (ed.), 141–68.

———(2017). *A Commentary on Plutarch's Brutus*. Newcastle: *Histos* Supplements.

Momigliano, A. D. (1941). Review of B. Farrington, *Science and Politics in the Ancient World. JRS* 31: 149–57.

———(1966 [1950]). "Ancient History and the Antiquarian." In id. *Studies in Historiography*. London: Weidenfeld and Nicolson, 1–39.

———(1984). "The Theological Efforts of the Roman Upper Classes in the First Century B.C." *CP* 79: 199–211.

Mommsen, T. (1868–69). *Römische Geschichte*. 5th ed. 3 vols. Berlin: Weidmann.

Moreau, P. (1987). "La Lex Clodia sur le banissement de Cicéron." *Athenaeum* 65: 465–92.

Morford, M. P. O. (2002). *The Roman Philosophers from the Time of Cato the Censor to the Death of Marcus Aurelius*. London: Routledge.

Morgan, L. (1997). "*Levi quidem de re* . . . : Julius Caesar as Tyrant and Pedant." *JRS* 87: 23–40.

———and Taylor, B. (2017). "Memmius the Epicurean." *CQ* 67: 528–41.

Morgan, T. (2007). *Popular Morality in the Early Roman Empire*. Cambridge: Cambridge University Press.

Morgan, T. (2015). *Roman Faith and Christian Faith:* Pistis *and* Fides *in the Early Roman Empire and Early Churches.* Oxford: Oxford University Press.

Morrell, K. (2015). "Cato, Caesar, and the Germani." *Antichthon* 49: 73–93.

——— (2017). *Pompey, Cato, and the Governance of the Roman Empire.* Oxford: Oxford University Press.

Morstein-Marx, R. (2012.) "Political Graffiti in the Late Roman Republic." In C. Kuhn (ed.), *Politische Kommunikation und öffentliche Meining in der antiken Welt.* Stuttgart: Steiner, 191–217.

Mossman, J. (ed.) (1997). *Plutarch and His Intellectual World: Essays on Plutarch.* London: Duckworth.

Mouritsen, H. (2017). *Politics in the Roman Republic.* New York: Cambridge University Press.

Müller, G. M. (2015). "Transfer und Überbietung im Gespräch: Zur Konstruktion einer römischen Philosophie in den Dialogen Ciceros." *Gymnasium* 122: 275–301.

———and Mariani Zini, F. (eds.) (2018). *Philosophie in Rom—Römische Philosophie? Kultur-, literatur- und philosophiegeschichtliche Perspektiven:* Berlin: De Gruyter.

Müller, J. (2017). "Ciceros Archäologie des römischen Staates in *De re publica* II: Ein Exempel des römischen Philosophierens." In Höffe (ed.), 47–71.

Müller, R. (2001). *Sprachbewußtsein und Sprachvariation im lateinischen Schrifttum der Antike.* Munich: Beck.

Münzer, F. (1905). "Atticus als Geschichtsschreiber." *Hermes* 40: 50–100.

——— (1928). "Manlius 76) A. Manlius Torquatus." *RE* 14.1: 1194–99.

——— (1931). "Sulpicius 95) Ser. Sulpicius Rufus." *RE* 4A.1: 851–57.

Murphy, T. (1998). "Cicero's First Readers: Epistolary Evidence for the Dissemination of His Works." *CQ* 48: 492–505.

Musial, D. (2001). "*Sodalicium Nigidiani*: les Pythagoriciens à Rome à la fin de la République." *RHR* 218: 339–67.

Narducci, E. (1983). "Cicerone e un detto di Cesare (nota a *pro Marcello* 25 sgg. e a *Cato Maior* 69)." *AeR* 28: 155–58.

——— (1995). *Marco Tullio Cicerone:* Bruto. Milan: BUR.

——— (1997). *Cicerone e l'eloquenza romana: retorica e progetto culturale.* Rome: Laterza.

——— (2003). "La memoria della grecità nell'immaginario delle ville ciceroniane." In Citroni (ed.), 119–48.

Naso, A. (ed.) (2017). *Etruscology.* 2 vols. Berlin: De Gruyter.

Nelsestuen, G. A. (2019). "A Matter of *prudentia*: Atticus and His Friends in Nepos and Cicero." *TAPA* 149: 353–93.

Nicgorski, W. (1991). "Cicero's Focus: From the Best Regime to the Model Statesman." *Political Theory* 19: 230–51.

——— (2016). *Cicero's Skepticism and His Recovery of Political Philosophy.* New York: Palgrave Macmillan.

Nicolet, C. (1960). "*Consul togatus*: remarques sur le vocabulaire politique de Cicéron et de Tite-Live." *REL* 38: 236–63.

——— (1966–74). *L'Ordre équestre à l'époque républicaine (312–43 av. J.-C.).* Paris: De Boccard.

Nisbet, R. G. (1939). *M. Tulli Ciceronis De domo sua ad pontifices oratio.* Oxford: Clarendon Press.

Norden, E. (1898). *Die antike Kunstprosa vom VI. Jahrhundert v.Chr. bis in die Zeit der Renaissance.* Vol. 1. Leipzig: Teubner.

———(1901). "Vergils Äneis im Lichte ihrer Zeit." *NJbb* 7: 249–82 and 313–34.

North, J. A. (1990). "Diviners and Divination at Rome." In M. Beard and J. North (eds.), *Pagan Priests: Religion and Power in the Ancient World.* Ithaca: Cornell University Press, 51–71.

———(1998). "The Books of the *pontifices.*" In (no ed.), *La Mémoire perdue: recherches sur l'administration romaine.* Rome: École Française de Rome, 45–63.

———(2014a). "The Limits of the 'Religious' in the Late Roman Republic." *HR* 53: 225–45.

———(2014b). "The *Pontifices* in Politics." In G. Urso (ed.), *Sacerdos: figure del sacro nella società romana.* Pisa: ETS, 63–81.

Nussbaum, M. (1994). *The Therapy of Desire: Theory and Practice in Hellenistic Ethics.* Princeton: Princeton University Press.

Ogden, D. (2001). *Greek and Roman Necromancy.* Princeton: Princeton University Press.

Oksanish, J. (2016). "Vitruvius and the Programmatics of Prose." *Arethusa* 49: 263–80.

Oldfather, W. A. and Bloom, G. (1926–27). "Caesar's Grammatical Theories and His Own Practice." *CJ* 22: 584–602.

Orth, W. (1994). "Verstorbene werden zu Sternen: Geistesgeschichtlicher Hintergrund und politische Implikationen des Katasterismos in der frühen römischen Kaiserzeit." *Laverna* 5: 148–66.

Ortmann, U. (1988). *Cicero, Brutus und Octavian—Republikaner und Caesarianer: Ihr gegenseitiges Verhältnis im Krisenjahr 44/43 v.Chr.* Bonn: Habelt.

O'Sullivan, T. M. (2011). *Walking in Roman Culture.* Cambridge: Cambridge University Press.

Otto, A. (1890). *Die Sprichwörter und sprichwörtlichen Redensarten der Römer.* Leipzig: Teubner.

Pandey, N. B. (2013). "Caesar's Comet, the Julian Star, and the Invention of Augustus." *TAPA* 143: 405–49.

———(2018). *The Poetics of Power in Augustan Rome: Latin Poetic Responses to Early Imperial Iconography.* Cambridge: Cambridge University Press.

Parker, H. N. (2009). "Books and Reading Latin Poetry." In W. A. Johnson and H. N. Parker (eds.), *Ancient Literacies: The Culture of Reading in Greece and Rome.* New York: Oxford University Press, 186–229.

Parker, L. P. E. (2002). "Just and Tenacious of His Purpose. . . ." *MusHelv* 59: 101–6.

Pease, A. S. (1958). *M. Tulli Ciceronis De natura deorum libri III.* 2 vols. Cambridge, MA: Harvard University Press.

Pecchiura, P. (1965). *La figura di Catone Uticense nella letteratura latina.* Turin: Giappichelli.

Peer, A. (2008). "Cicero's Last Caesarian Speech: The *Pro Rege Deiotaro* as a Final Warning before the Ides of March." *Studies in Latin Literature and Roman History* 14: 189–208.

Peetz, S. (2008). "Philosophie als Alternative? Ciceros politische Ethik." In M. Bernett, W. Nippel, and A. Winterling (eds.), *Christian Meier zur Diskussion.* Stuttgart: Steiner, 181–99.

Peglau, M. (2003). "Varro, ein Antiquar zwischen Tradition und Aufklärung." In Haltenhoff, Heil, and Mutschler (eds.), 137–64.

Pelling, C. B. R. (1979). "Plutarch's Method of Work in the Roman Lives." *JHS* 99: 74–96.

———(1989). "Plutarch: Roman Heroes and Greek Culture." In Griffin and Barnes (eds.), 199–232.

Pelling, C. B. R. (1997). "Plutarch on Caesar's Fall." In Mossman (ed.), 215–32.

Pépin, J. (1956). "La 'Théologie tripartite' de Varron: essai de reconstitution et recherche des sources." *REAug* 1956.2 (= *Mémorial Gustave Bardy*): 265–94.

Perelli, L. (1972). "*Natura e ratio* nel II libro del *De re publica* ciceroniano." *RFIC* 100: 295–311.

———(1990). *Il pensiero politico di Cicerone: tra filosofia greca e ideologica aristocratica romana.* Florence: La Nuova Italia.

Perlwitz, O. (1992). *Titus Pomponius Atticus: Unersuchungen zur Person eines einflussreichen Ritters in der ausgehenden römischen Republik.* Stuttgart: Steiner.

Perrin, B. (1914–26). *Plutarch: Lives.* Cambridge, MA: Harvard University Press.

Peterson, W. (1911). *M. Tulli Ciceronis orationes.* Vol. 5. Oxford: Clarendon Press.

Pezzini, G. (2018). "Caesar the Linguist: The Debate about the Latin Language." In Grillo and Krebs (eds.), 173–92.

———and Taylor, B. (eds.). 2019. *Language and Nature in the Classical Roman World.* Cambridge: Cambridge University Press.

Philippson, R. (1939). "M. Tullius Cicero: Die philosophischen Schriften." *RE* 7A.1: 1104–92.

Phillips, C. R. III (2001). "Synnaos Theos." *Neuer Pauly* 11: 1156–57.

Phillips, J. J. (1986). "Atticus and the Publication of Cicero's Works." *CW* 79: 227–37.

Piepenbrink, K. (2003). "Einführung." In Piepenbrink (ed.), 9–21.

———(ed.) (2003). *Philosophie und Lebenswelt in der Antike.* Darmstadt: Wissenschaftliche Buchgesellschaft.

Piganiol, A. (1951). "Sur le Calendrier brontoscopique de Nigidius Figulus." In P. R. Coleman-Norton (ed.), *Studies in Roman Economic and Social History in Honor of Allan Chester Johnson.* Princeton: Princeton University Press, 79–87.

Pina Polo, F. (2006). "The Tyrant Must Die: Preventive Tyrannicide in Roman Political Thought." In F. Marco Simón, F. Pina Polo, and J. Remesal Rodríguez (eds.), *Repúblicas y ciudadanos: modelos de participación cívica en el mundo antiguo.* Barcelona: Universitat de Barcelona, 71–101.

———(2019). "Losers in the Civil War between Caesarians and Pompeians." In K.-J. Hölkeskamp and H. Beck (eds.), *Verlierer und Aussteiger in der "Konkurrenz unter Anwesenden": Agonalität in der politischen Kultur des antiken Rom.* Stuttgart: Steiner, 147–67.

Plezia, M. (1983). "De la Philosophie dans le *De consulatu suo* de Cicéron." In H. Zehnacker and G. Hentz (eds.), *Hommages à Robert Schilling.* Paris: Belles Lettres, 383–92.

Poccetti, P. (1993). "Teorie grammaticali e prassi della *Latinitas* in Cesare." In Poli (ed.), 2.599–640.

Poli, D. (ed.). 1993. *La cultura in Cesare.* 2 vols. Rome: Il Calamo.

Porter, J. I. (2007). "Hearing Voices: The Herculaneum Papyri and Classical Scholarship." In V. C. Gardner Coates and J. L. Seydl (eds.), *Antiquity Recovered: The Legacy of Pompeii and Herculaneum.* Los Angeles: Getty, 95–113.

Powell, J. G. F. (2001). "Were Cicero's *Laws* the Laws of Cicero's *Republic*?' In Powell and North (eds.), 17–39.

———(2006). *M. Tulli Ciceronis De re publica, De legibus, Cato maior de senectute, Laelius de amicitia.* Oxford: Clarendon Press.

———(2018). "Philosophising about Rome: Cicero's *De re publica* and *De legibus*." In Müller and Mariani Zini (eds.), 249–67.

———(ed.) (1995). *Cicero the Philosopher: Twelve Papers.* Oxford: Clarendon Press.

———and North, J. A. (eds.) (2001). *Cicero's Republic.* London: Institute of Classical Studies.

Raaflaub, K. (2009). "*Bellum Gallicum.*" In Griffin (ed.), 175–91.

Ramage, E. S. (1991). "Sulla's Propaganda." *Klio* 73: 93–121.

Rambaud, M. (1984). "Le *Pro Marcello* et l'insinuation politique." In R. Chevallier (ed.), *Présence de Cicéron.* Paris: Belles Lettres, 43–56.

Ramsey, J. T. (2000). "'Beware the Ides of March!': An Astrological Prediction." *CQ* 50: 440–54.

———and Licht, A. L. (1997). *The Comet of 44 B.C. and Caesar's Funeral Games.* Atlanta: Scholars Press.

Rasmussen, S. W. (2000). "Cicero's Stand on Prodigies: A Non-existent Dilemma?" In R. L. Wildfang and J. Isager (eds.), *Divination and Portents in the Roman World.* Odense: Odense University Press, 9–24.

———(2003). *Public Portents in Republican Rome.* Rome: L'Erma di Bretschneider.

Rathofer, C. (1986). *Ciceros* Brutus *als literarisches Paradigma eines Auctoritas-Verhältnisses.* Frankfurt: Hain.

Raubitschek, A. E. (1949). "Phaidros and His Roman Pupils." *Hesperia* 18:9 96–103.

———(1957). "Brutus in Athens." *Phoenix* 11: 1–11.

Rauh, N. K. (1986). "Cicero's Business Friendships: Economics and Politics in the Late Roman Republic." *Aevum* 60: 3–30.

Rauh, S. H. (2018). "Cato at Utica: The Emergence of a Roman Suicide Tradition." *AJP* 139: 59–91.

Rawson, E. (1972). "Cicero the Historian and Cicero the Antiquarian." *JRS* 62: 33–45 (=1991: 58–79).

———(1975). "Caesar's Heritage: Hellenistic Kings and Their Roman Equals." *JRS* 65: 148–59 (=1991: 169–88).

———(1978). "Caesar, Etruria and the *Disciplina Etrusca.*" *JRS* 68: 132–52 (=1991: 289–323).

———(1979). "L. Cornelius Sisenna and the Early First Century B.C." *CQ* 29: 327–46 (=1991: 363–88).

———(1985). *Intellectual Life in the Late Roman Republic.* London: Duckworth.

———(1986). "Cassius and Brutus: The Memory of the Liberators." In I. S. Moxon, J. D. Smart, and A. J. Woodman (eds.), *Past Perspectives: Studies in Greek and Roman Historical Writing.* Cambridge: Cambridge University Press, 101–19 (=1991: 488–507).

———(1991). *Roman Culture and Society: Collected Essays.* Oxford: Clarendon Press.

Rehm, A. (1927). "Sosigenes 6) Caesars Mitarbeiter an der Kalenderreform." *RE* 3A.1: 1153–57.

Reinhardt, T. Lapidge, M., and Adams, J. N. (eds.) (2005). *Aspects of the Language of Latin Prose.* Oxford: Oxford University Press.

Ringer, F. (1990). "The Intellectual Field, Intellectual History, and the Sociology of Knowledge." *Theory and Society* 19: 269–94.

Rives, J. B. (2005). "The Sacrilege of Nigidius Figulus." Unpublished paper presented at the Classical Association of Canada Annual Meeting.

———(2006). "Magic, Religion, and Law: The Case of the *Lex Cornelia de sicariis et veneficiis.*" In Ando and Rüpke (eds.), 47–67.

Roche, P. (2009). *Lucan: De Bello Ciuili Book I.* Oxford: Oxford University Press.

Rochlitz, S. (1993). *Das Bild Caesars in Ciceros* Orationes Caesarianae*: Untersuchungen zur* clementia *and* sapientia Caesaris. Frankfurt: Lang.

Rolle, A. (2017). *Dall'Oriente a Roma: Cibele, Iside e Serapide nell'opera di Varrone*. Pisa: ETS.

Rollinger, R. (2017). "Haruspicy from the Ancient Near East to Etruria." In Naso (ed.), 1.341–55.

Romano, E. (2003). "Il concetto di antico in Varrone." In Citroni (ed.), 99–117.

———(2006). "Filosofia in latino, latino dei filosofi." In F. Gasti (ed.), *Il latino dei filosofi a Roma antica*. Pavia: Collegio Ghislieri, 15–20.

Rorty, R., Schneewind, J. B., and Skinner, Q. (1984). "Introduction." In Rorty, Schneewind, and Skinner (eds.), 1–14.

———(eds.) (1984). *Philosophy in History: Essays on the Historiography of Philosophy*. Cambridge: Cambridge University Press.

Rösch-Binde, C. (1998). *Vom* δεινὸς ἀνήρ *zum* diligentissimus investigator antiquitatis*: Zur komplexen Beziehung zwischen M. Tullius Cicero and M. Terentius Varro*. Munich: Utz.

———(2001). "*Ego expectatione promissi tui moueor ut admoneam te, non ut flagitem*: Zur Frage der zeitlichen Redaktion und Edition von Varros De lingua Latina." *Papers on Grammar* 6: 223–45.

Rosenberger, V. (1998). *Gezähmte Götter: Das Prodigienwesen der römischen Republik*. Stuttgart: Steiner.

Rosillo-López, C. (2009). "La guerra civil de las letras: religión, panfletarios y lucha política (49–44 a.C.)." *Klio* 91: 104–14.

———(2011). "Praising Caesar: Towards the Construction of an Autocratic Ruler's Image between the Roman Republic and the Empire." In C. Smith and R. Covino (eds.), *Praise and Blame in Roman Republican Rhetoric*. Swansea: Classical Press of Wales, 181–98.

———(2017). *Public Opinion and Politics in the Late Roman Republic*. Cambridge: Cambridge University Press.

Roskam, G. (2007). *Live Unnoticed (*Λάθε βιώσας*): On the Vicissitudes of an Epicurean Doctrine*. Leiden: Brill.

———(2019). "Cicero against Cassius on Pleasure and Virtue: A Complicated Passage from *De finibus* (1.25)." *CQ* 69: 725–33.

Rühl, M. (2018). *Ciceros Korrespondenz als Medium literarischen und gesellschaftlichen Handelns*. Leiden: Brill.

Rüpke, J. (2005). "Varro's *tria genera theologiae*: Religious Thinking in the Late Republic." *Ordia prima* 4: 107–29.

———(2009a). "Antiquar und Theologe: Systematisierende Beschreibung römischer Religion bei Varro." In Bendlin and Rüpke (eds.), 73–88.

———(2009b). "Between Rationalism and Ritualism: On the Origins of Religious Discourse in the Late Roman Republic." *ARG* 11: 123–44.

———(2012). *Religion in Republican Rome: Rationalization and Ritual Change*. Philadelphia: University of Pennsylvania Press.

———(2014). "Historicizing Religion: Varro's *Antiquitates* and History of Religion in the Late Roman Republic." *HR* 53: 246–68.

———(2018). "Priesthoods, Gods, and Stars." In Grillo and Krebs (eds.), 58–67.

Samotta, I. (2009). *Das Vorbild der Vergangenheit: Geschichtsbild und Reformvorschläge bei Cicero und Sallust*. Stuttgart: Steiner.

Sánchez Vendramini, D. N. (2010). *Eliten und Kultur: Eine Geschichte der römischen Literaturszene (240 v.Chr.–117 n.Chr.)*. Bonn: Habelt.

Sandberg, K. and Smith, C. (eds.) (2018). *Omnium Annalium Monumenta: Historical Writing and Historical Evidence in Republican Rome*. Leiden: Brill.

Santamaria, G. (2013–14). "Quasi amici: il rapporto fra Bruto e Cicerone prima delle Idi di Marzo." *Invigilata Lucernis* 35–36: 283–308.

Santangelo, F. (2011a). "*Pax deorum* and Pontiffs." In J. H. Richardson and F. Santangelo (eds.), *Priest and State in the Roman World*. Stuttgart: Steiner, 161–86.

———(2011b). "Whose Sacrilege? A Note on *Sal.* 5.14." *CW* 104: 333–38.

———(2013). *Divination, Prediction and the End of the Roman Republic*. Cambridge: Cambridge University Press.

Saramago, J. (2010). *The Elephant's Journey*. Trans. by M. J. Costa. Boston: Houghton Mifflin Harcourt.

Satterfield, S. (2014–15). "Prodigies, the *pax deum* and the *ira deum*." *CJ* 110: 431–45.

Sauer, J. (2011). "Werte und soziale Rollen in der Atticus-Vita des Cornelius Nepos." In A. Haltenhoff, A. Heil, and F.-H. Mutschler (eds.), *Römische Werte und römische Literatur im frühen Prinzipat*. Berlin: De Gruyter, 113–44.

Sauer, V. (2013). *Religiöses in der politischen Argumentation der späten römischen Republik: Ciceros Erste Catilinarische Rede—eine Fallstudie*. Stuttgart: Steiner.

Scarcia, R. (1993). "La bilancia del critico (Cesare e Terenzio)." In Poli (ed.), 2.507–32.

Scardigli, B. (1979). *Die Römerbiographien Plutarchs*. Munich: Beck.

Scatolin, A. (forthcoming). "Cicero's Praise of Caesar in the *Pro Marcello*—a Reassessment of a Rhetorical Strategy." *Papers on Rhetoric* 14.

Scheid, J. (1987–89). "La Parole des dieux: l'originalité du dialogue des romains avec leur dieux." *Opus* 6–8: 125–36.

———(2006). "Oral Tradition and Written Tradition in the Formation of Sacred Law in Rome." In Ando and Rüpke (eds.), 14–33.

Scheidegger Lämmle, C. (2016). *Werkpolitik in der Antike: Studien zu Cicero, Vergil, Horaz und Ovid*.

———(2017). "On Cicero's *De domo*: A Survey of Recent Works." *Ciceroniana on line* 1: 147–56.

Schiesaro, A. (2010). "Cesare, la cultura di un dittatore." In G. Urso (ed.), *Cesare: precursore o visionario?* Pisa: ETS, 241–47.

Schironi, F. (2007). Ἀναλογία, *proportio, ratio*: Loanwords, Calques, and Reinterpretations of a Greek Technical Word." In L. Basset et al. (eds.), *Bilinguisme et terminologie grammaticale gréco-latine*. Louvain: Peeters, 321–38.

Schmidt, P. L. (1978–79). "Cicero's Place in Roman Philosophy: A Study of His Prefaces." *CJ* 74: 115–27.

Schneider, W. C. (1998). *Vom Handeln der Römer: Kommunikation und Interaktion der politischen Führungsschicht vor Ausbruch des Bürgerkriegs im Briefwechsel mit Cicero*. Hildesheim: Olms.

Schofield, M. (1986). "Cicero for and against Divination." *JRS* 76: 47–65.

———(2002). "Academic Therapy: Philo of Larissa and Cicero's Project in *Tusculans*." In G. Clark and T. Rajak (eds.), *Philosophy and Power in the Graeco-Roman World: Essays in Honour of Miriam Griffin*. Oxford: Oxford University Press, 91–109.

Schofield, M. (2008). "Ciceronian Dialogue." In S. Goldhill (ed.), *The End of Dialogue in Antiquity*. Cambridge: Cambridge University Press, 63–84.

Scholz, U. W. (2003). "Varros Menippeische Satiren." In Haltenhoff, Heil, and Mutschler (eds.), 165–85.

Schröter, R. (1963). "Die varronische Etymologie." In (no ed.), *Varron* (= *Entretiens Hardt* 9). Vandoœuvres-Geneva: Fondation Hardt, 79–100 (discussion 101–16).

Schubert, C. (2015). "Nepos als Biograph: Der Tod des Atticus." *RhM* 158: 260–303.

Schultz, C. E. (2009). "Argument and Anecdote in Cicero's *De Divinatione*." In Harvey, P. B. Jr. and Conybeare, C. (eds.), *Maxima debetur magistro reverentia: Essays on Rome and the Roman Tradition in Honor of Russell T. Scott*. Como: New Press Edizioni, 193–206.

————(2014). *A Commentary on Cicero*, De Divinatione *I*. Ann Arbor: University of Michigan Press.

Schwitter, R. (2017). "Der tröstende Freund: Epistolares Rollenbild und kommunikative Verhaltensweise in Ciceros *Epistulae ad familiares*." *Ciceroniana on line* 1: 369–94.

Scourfield, J. H. D. (2013). "Towards a Genre of Consolation." In H. Baltussen (ed.), *Greek and Roman Consolations: Eight Studies of a Tradition and Its Afterlife*. Swansea: Classical Press of Wales, 1–36.

Sedley, D. (1997). "The Ethics of Brutus and Cassius." *JRS* 87: 41–53.

————(2009). "Epicureanism in the Roman Republic." In Warren (ed.), 29–45.

————(2010). "Philosophy." In A. Barchiesi and W. Scheidel (eds.), *The Oxford Handbook of Roman Studies*. New York: Oxford University Press, 701–12.

————(2013). "Cicero and the *Timaeus*." In M. Schofield (ed.), *Aristotle, Plato and Pythagoreanism in the First Century BC: New Directions for Philosophy*. Cambridge: Cambridge University Press, 187–205.

————(ed.) (2012). *The Philosophy of Antiochus*. Cambridge: Cambridge University Press.

Sehlmeyer, M. (2009). "Auseinandersetzungen mit Religion in antiquarischer Literatur von M. Fulvius Nobilior bis L. Iulius Caesar." In Bendlin and Rüpke (eds.), 57–72.

Setaioli, A. (2005). "Le fragment II Soubiran du *De consulatu* de Cicéron, le *De diuinatione* et leur lecture par Virgile." In Kany-Turpin (ed.), 241–63.

Shackleton Bailey, D. R. (1960). "The Roman Nobility in the Second Civil War." *CQ* 10: 253–67.

————(1965–70). *Cicero's Letters to Atticus*. 7 vols. Cambridge: Cambridge University Press.

————(1977). *Cicero*: Epistulae ad familiares. 2 vols. Cambridge: Cambridge University Press.

————(1980). *Cicero*: Epistulae ad Quintum fratrem et M. Brutum. Cambridge: Cambridge University Press.

————(1999). *Cicero: Letters to Atticus*. 4 vols. Cambridge, MA: Harvard University Press.

Sider, D. (1997). *The Epigrams of Philodemos*. New York: Oxford University Press.

Siebenborn, E. (1976). *Die Lehre von der Sprachrichtigkeit und ihren Kriterien: Studien zur antiken normativen Grammatik*. Amsterdam: Grüner.

Sigmund, C. (2014). *"Königtum" in der politischen Kultur des spätrepublikanischen Rom*. Berlin: De Gruyter.

Simone, A. A. (2020). "Cicero among the Stars: Natural Philosophy and Astral Culture at Rome." Diss. Columbia.

Sinclair, P. (1994). "Political Declensions in Latin Grammar and Oratory 55 BCE–CE 39." *Ramus* 23: 92–109.

Sirago, V. (1956). "Tyrannus: teoria e prassi antitirannica in Cicerone e suoi contemporanei." *RAAN* 31: 179–225.

Skinner, Q. (2002 [1969]). "Meaning and Understanding in the History of Ideas." In id. *Visions of Politics*. 3 vols. Cambridge: Cambridge University Press, 1.57–89 (first: *History and Theory* 8: 3–53).

Sommer, R. (1926). "T. Pomponius Atticus und die Verbreitung von Ciceros Werken." *Hermes* 61: 389–422.

Sorabji, R. (2007). "What Is New on the Self in Stoicism after 100 BC?" In R. Sharples and R. Sorabji (eds.), *Greek and Roman Philosophy 100 BC–200 AD*. Vol. 1. London: Institute of Classical Studies, 141–62.

Sordi, M. (1972). "L'idea di crisi e di rinnovamento nella concezione romano-etrusca della storia." *ANRW* 1.2: 781–93.

Spencer, D. (2019). *Language and Authority in* De Lingua Latina: *Varro's Guide to Being Roman*. Madison: University of Wisconsin Press.

Starr, R. S. (1987). "The Circulation of Literary Texts in the Roman World." *CQ* 37: 213–23.

———(1990–91). "Reading Aloud: *lectores* and Roman Reading." *CJ* 86: 337–43.

Steel, C. E. W. (2002–3). "Cicero's *Brutus*: The End of Oratory and the Beginning of History?' *BICS* 46: 195–211.

———(2005). *Reading Cicero*. London: Duckworth.

———(2013). "Structure, Meaning and Authority in Cicero's Dialogues." In Föllinger and Müller (eds.), 221–34.

———and van der Blom, H. (eds.) (2013). *Community and Communication: Oratory and Politics in Republican Rome*. Oxford: Oxford University Press.

Stein-Hölkeskamp, E. (2000). "Marcus Porcius Cato—der stoische Streiter für die verlorene Republik." In Hölkeskamp and Stein-Hölkeskamp (eds.), 292–306.

Steinmetz, P. (1989). "Beobachtungen zu Ciceros philosophischem Standpunkt." In W. M. Fortenbaugh and P. Steinmetz (eds.), *Cicero's Knowledge of the Peripatos*. New Brunswick, NJ: Transaction, 1–22.

———(1990). "Planung und Plananderung der philosophischen Schriften Ciceros. In id. (ed.), *Beiträge zur hellenistischen Literatur und ihrer Rezeption in Rom*. Stuttgart: Steiner, 141–53.

———(1995). "Ciceros philosophische Anfänge." *RhM* 138: 210–22.

Stem, R. (2005). "Nepos' *Atticus* as a Biography of Friendship." *Studies in Latin Literature and Roman History* 12: 115–29.

———(2005–6). "The First Eloquent Stoic: Cicero on Cato the Younger." *CJ* 101: 37–49.

———(2012). *The Political Biographies of Cornelius Nepos*. Ann Arbor: University of Michigan Press.

———(2019). "Idealizing a Life of Friendship: Cicero's *De Amicitia* in Nepos's *Life of Atticus*." *TAPA* 149: 27–45.

Storch, R. H. (1995). "Relative Deprivation and the Ides of March: Motive for Murder." *AHB* 9: 45–52.

Strasburger, H. (1968). *Caesar im Urteil seiner Zeitgenossen*. 2nd rev. ed. Darmstadt: Wissenschaftliche Buchgesellschaft.

———(1990). *Ciceros politisches Spätwerk als Aufruf gegen die Herrschaft Caesars*. Ed. by G. Strasburger. Hildesheim: Olms.

Straumann, B. (2016). *Crisis and Constitutionalism: Roman Political Thought from the Fall of the Republic to the Age of Revolution.* New York: Oxford University Press.

Stroh, W. (2004). "*De Domo Sua*: Legal Problem and Structure." In J. Powell and J. Paterson (eds.), *Cicero the Advocate.* Oxford: Oxford University Press, 313–70.

Stroup, S. C. (2010). *Catullus, Cicero, and a Society of Patrons: The Generation of the Text.* Cambridge: Cambridge University Press.

Süß, W. (1952). "Die dramatische Kunst in den philosophischen Dialogen Ciceros." *Hermes* 80: 419–36.

Swain, S. (1990). "Plutarch's Lives of Cicero, Cato, and Brutus." *Hermes* 118: 192–203.

Swoboda, A. (1889). *P. Nigidii Figuli operum reliquiae.* Vienna: Tempsky.

Syme, R. (1939). *The Roman Revolution.* Oxford: Clarendon Press.

Tandoi, V. (1965). "Morituri verba Catonis." *Maia* 17: 315–39.

———(1966). "Morituri verba Catonis II." *Maia* 18: 20–41.

Tarver, T. (1995). "Varro, Caesar, and the Roman Calendar: A Study in Late Republican Religion." In A. H. Sommerstein (ed.) (1995), *Religion and Superstition in Latin Literature.* Bari: Levante, 39–57.

Tatum, W. J. (1993a). "Ritual and Personal Morality in Roman Religion." *SyllClass* 4: 13–20.

———(1993b). "The *Lex Papiria de dedicationibus.*" *CP* 88: 319–28.

———(1999). *The Patrician Tribune: Publius Clodius Pulcher.* Chapel Hill: University of North Carolina Press.

Taylor, D. J. (1974). *Declinatio: A Study of the Linguistic Theory of Marcus Terentius Varro.* Amsterdam: Betjemans.

Taylor, L. R. (1949). *Party Politics in the Age of Caesar.* Berkeley: University of California Press.

Tedeschi, A. (1996). "La vita del *sapiens*: finalità e limiti. A proposito di una schermaglia retorico-filosofica in Cic. *Marc.* 25–27." *BStudLat* 26: 464–81.

———(2005). *Lezione di buon governo per un dittatore: Cicerone, Pro Marcello.* Bari: Edipuglia.

Tempest, K. (2013a). "An *ethos* of Sincerity: Echoes of the *De republica* in Cicero's *Pro Marcello.*" *GaR* 60: 262–80.

———(2013b). "Hellenistic Oratory at Rome: Cicero's *Pro Marcello.*" In C. Kremmydas and K. Tempest (eds.), *Hellenistic Oratory: Continuity and Change.* Oxford: Oxford University Press, 295–318.

———(2017). *Brutus: The Noble Conspirator.* New Haven: Yale University Press.

Ternes, C. M. (ed.) (1998). *Le pythagorisme en milieu romain.* 2 vols. Luxembourg: Centre Alexandre-Wiltheim.

Thein, A. (2009). "*Felicitas* and the Memoirs of Sulla and Augustus." In C. Smith and A. Powell (eds.), *The Lost Memoirs of Augustus and the Development of Roman Autobiography.* Swansea: Classical Press of Wales, 87–109.

Thibodeau, P. (2018). "Traditionalism and Originality in Roman Science." In P. T. Keyser and J. Scarborough (eds.), *The Oxford Handbook of Science and Medicine in the Classical World.* New York: Oxford University Press, 593–613.

Thorsrud, H. (2009). *Ancient Scepticism.* Berkeley: University of California Press.

Thulin, C. O. (1906–9). *Die etruskische Disziplin.* 3 vols. Göteborg: Zachrissons boktryckkeri.

Timpanaro, S. (1988). *Marco Tullio Cicerone: Della divinazione.* Milan: Garzanti.

———(1994). "Alcuni fraintendimenti del *De divinatione.*" In id. *Nuovi contributi di filologia e storia della lingua latina.* Bologna: Pàtron, 241–64.

Todisco, E. (2017). "Varro's Writings on the Senate: A Reconstructive Hypothesis." In Arena and Mac Góráin (eds.), 49–60.

Toner, J. (2017). "The Intellectual Life of the Roman Non-Elite." In L. Grig (ed.), *Popular Culture in the Ancient World*. Cambridge: Cambridge University Press, 167–88.

Trapp, M. B. (1999). "Socrates, the *Phaedo*, and the *Lives* of Phocion and Cato." In A. Pérez Jiménez, J. García López, and R. M. Aguilar (eds.), *Plutarco, Platón y Aristóteles*. Madrid: Ediciones Clásicas, 487–99.

———(2007). *Philosophy in the Roman Empire: Ethics, Politics and Society*. Aldershot: Ashgate.

———(2017). "Philosophical Authority in the Imperial Period." In König and Woolf (eds.), 27–57.

Treggiari, S. (1977). "Intellectuals, Poets and Their Patrons in the First Century B.C." *EchCl* 21: 24–29.

———(2015). "The Education of the Ciceros." In W. M. Bloomer (ed.), *A Companion to Ancient Education*. Chichester: Wiley-Blackwell, 240–51.

Troiani, L. (1984). "La religione e Cicerone." *RivStorIt* 96: 920–52.

Tschiedel, H. J. (1981). *Caesars* Anticato. Darmstadt: Wissenschaftliche Buchgesellschaft.

Turfa, J. M. (2012). *Divining the Etruscan World: The* Brontoscopic Calendar *and Religious Practice*. Cambridge: Cambridge University Press.

Tutrone, F. (2013). "Libraries and Intellectual Debate in the Late Republic: The Case of the Aristotelian Corpus." In König, Oikonomopoulou, and Woolf (eds.), 152–66.

Valachova, C. (2018). "The Garden and the Forum: Epicurean Adherence and Political Affiliation in the Late Republic." In H. van der Blom, C. Gray, and C. Steel (eds.), *Institutions and Ideology in Republican Rome: Speech, Audience and Decision*. Cambridge: Cambridge University Press, 147–64.

Valvo, A. (1988). *La "Profezia di Vegoia": proprietà fondiaria e aruspicina in Etruria nel I secolo a.c.* Rome: Istituto Italiano per la Storia Antica.

van den Berg, C. S. forthcoming. *The Politics and Poetics of Literary History in Cicero's* Brutus. Cambridge: Cambridge University Press.

van der Blom, H. (2012). "Cato and the People." *BICS* 55: 39–56.

van Groningen, B. (1963). "ΕΚΔΟΣΙΣ." *Mnemosyne* 16: 1–17.

Van Nuffelen, P. (2010). Varro's *Divine Antiquities*: Roman Religion as an Image of Truth." *CP* 105: 162–88.

Vasaly, A. (1993). *Representations: Images of the World in Ciceronian Oratory*. Berkeley: University of California Press.

Vasiliou, I. (2008). *Aiming at Virtue in Plato*. Cambridge: Cambridge University Press.

Versnel, H. S. (2012). "Magic." *OCD*[4]: 884–85.

Vesperini, P. (2012). *La philosophia et ses pratiques d'Ennius à Cicéron*. Rome: École Française de Rome.

———(ed.) (2017). *Philosophari: Usages romains des savoirs grecs sous la République et sous l'Empire*. Paris: Classiques Garnier.

Vielberg, M. (2019). "Philosophie und Religion in Ciceros Schrift De divinatione." *Gymnasium* 126: 47–71.

Vigourt, A. (2001). *Les Présages impériaux d'Auguste à Domitien*. Paris: De Boccard.

Volk, K. (2002). *The Poetics of Latin Didactic: Lucretius, Vergil, Ovid, Manilius*. Oxford: Oxford University Press.

Volk, K. (2009a). "A New Reading of *Aeneid* 6.847–853." In R. Ferri, J. M. Seo, and K. Volk (eds.), *Callida Musa: Papers on Latin Literature in Honor of R. Elaine Fantham* (= *MD* 61). Pisa: Serra, 71–84.

———(2009b). *Manilius and His Intellectual Background.* Oxford: Oxford University Press.

———(2010). "Lucretius' Prayer for Peace and the Date of *De rerum natura*." *CQ* 60: 127–31.

———(2013). "The Genre of Cicero's *De consulatu suo*." In T. D. Papanghelis, S. J. Harrison, and S. Frangoulidis (eds.), *Generic Interfaces in Latin Literature: Encounters, Interactions and Transformations.* Berlin: De Gruyter, 93–112.

———(2015). "The World of the Latin Aratea." In T. Fuhrer and M. Erler (eds.), *Cosmologies et cosmogonies dans la littérature antique* (= *Entretiens Hardt* 61). Vandœuvres: Fondation Hardt, 253–83.

———(2016a). "A Wise Man in an Old Country: Varro, *Antiquitates rerum diuinarum* and [Plato], *Letter* 5." *RhM* 159: 429–33.

———(2016b). "Roman Pythagoras." In Williams and Volk (eds.), 33–49.

———(2017). "Signs, Seers and Senators: Divinatory Expertise in Cicero and Nigidius Figulus." In König and Woolf (eds.), 329–47.

———(2019). "Varro and the Disorder of Things." *HSCP* 110: 183–212.

———(forthcoming a). "Caesar the Epicurean? A Matter of Life and Death." In Yona and Davis (eds.).

———(forthcoming b). "Philosophy." In R. Gibson and C. Whitton (eds.), *The Cambridge Critical Guide to Latin Studies.* Cambridge: Cambridge University Press.

———(forthcoming c). "*Tod und Erklärung*: Ovid on the Death of Julius Caesar (*Met.* 15.745–851." In F. Farrell et al. (eds.), *Ovid, Death and Transfiguration.* Leiden: Brill.

———(forthcoming d). "Towards a Definition of *sapientia*: Philosophy in Cicero's *Pro Marcello*." In N. Gilbert, M. Graver, and S. McConnell (eds.).

———and Zetzel, J. E. G. (2015). "Laurel, Tongue and Glory (Cicero, *De consulatu suo* Fr. 6 Soubiran)." *CQ* 65: 204–23.

von Albrecht, M. (2003). *Cicero's Style: A Synopsis.* Leiden: Brill.

Wallace-Hadrill, A. (1997). "*Mutatio morum*: The Idea of a Cultural Revolution." In Habinek and Schiesaro (eds.), 3–22.

———(2008). *Rome's Cultural Revolution.* Cambridge: Cambridge University Press.

Walter, U. (2009). "Struktur, Zufall, Kontingenz? Überlegungen zum Ende der römischen Republik." In Hölkeskamp (ed.), 27–51.

Wardle, D. (2006). *Cicero: On Divination, Book 1.* Oxford: Clarendon Press.

———(2009). "Caesar and Religion." In Griffin (ed.), 100–111.

Wardman, A. (1982). *Religion and Statecraft among the Romans.* London: Granada.

Warren, J. (ed.) (2009). *The Cambridge Companion to Epicureanism.* Cambridge: Cambridge University Press.

Wassmann, H. (1996). *Ciceros Widerstand gegen Caesars Tyrannis: Untersuchungen zur politischen Bedeutung der philosophischen Spätschriften.* Bonn: Habelt.

Weinstock, S. (1950). "C. Fonteius Capito and the *Libri Tagetici*." *BSR* 18: 44–49.

———(1951). "*Libri fulgurales*." *BSR* 19: 122–53.

———(1971). *Divus Julius.* Oxford: Clarendon Press.

Welch, K. E. (1996). "T. Pomponius Atticus: A Banker in Politics?" *Historia* 45: 450–71.

Whatmore, R. (2016). *What Is Intellectual History?* Cambridge: Polity.

———and Young, B. (eds.) (2016). *A Companion to Intellectual History*. Chichester: Wiley-Blackwell.

White, P. (2010). *Cicero in Letters: Epistolary Relations of the Late Republic*. New York: Oxford University Press.

White, S. A. (1995). "Cicero and the Therapists." In Powell (ed.), 219–46.

Wick, C. (2012). "Ratio." *ThLL* 11: 152–204.

Wiegandt, D. (2016). "*Otium* als Mittel der literarischen Selbstinszenierung römischer Aristokraten in Republik und früher Kaiserzeit." In Eickhoff (ed.), 43–57.

Wifstrand Schiebe, M. (2006). "Sinn und Wahrheitsgehalt der Kultbilder aus der Sicht der antiken Philosophie: Zur antiken Debatte an Hand des Beispiels Marcus Terentius Varro." In S. Eklund (ed.), Συγχάρματα: *Studies in Honour of Jan Fedrik Kindstrand*. Uppsala: Uppsala Universitet, 189–209.

Wilcox, A. (2005). "Sympathetic Rivals: Consolation in Cicero's Letters." *AJP* 126: 237–55.

———(2012). *The Gift of Correspondence in Classical Rome: Friendship in Cicero's* Ad Familiares *and Seneca's Moral Epistles*. Madison: University of Wisconsin Press.

Willi, A. (2010). "Campaigning for *utilitas*: Style, Grammar and Philosophy in C. Iulius Caesar." In E. Dickey and A. Chahoud (eds.), *Colloquial and Literary Latin*. Cambridge: Cambridge University Press, 229–42.

Williams, C. A. (2012). *Reading Roman Friendship*. Cambridge: Cambridge University Press.

Williams, G. D. and Volk, K. (eds.) (2016). *Roman Reflections: Studies in Latin Philosophy*. New York: Oxford University Press.

Winterbottom, M. (2002). "Believing the *Pro Marcello*." In J. F. Miller, C. Damon, and K. S. Myers (eds.), *Vertis in usum: Studies in Honor of Edward Courtney*. Munich: Saur, 24–38.

Wirszubski, C. (1950). *Libertas as a Political Idea at Rome during the Late Republic and Early Principate*. Cambridge: Cambridge University Press.

Wiseman, T. P. (2009). *Remembering the Roman People: Essays on Late-Republican Politics and Literature*. Oxford: Oxford University Press.

Wisse, J. (1995). "Greeks, Romans, and the Rise of Atticism." In J. G. J. Abbenes, S. R. Slings, and I. Sluiter (eds.), *Greek Literary Theory after Aristotle: A Collection of Papers in Honor of D. M. Schenkeveld*. Amsterdam: VU University Press, 65–82.

Wistrand, E. (1981). *The Policy of Brutus the Tyrannicide* (= *Acta Regiae Societatis Scientiarum et Litterarum Gothoburgensis, Humaniora* 18). Goteborg: Kungl. Vetenskaps- och Vitterhets-Samhället.

Wolkenhauer, A. (2011). *Sonne und Mond, Kalender und Uhr: Studien zur Darstellung und poetischen Reflexion der Zeitordnung in der römischen Literatur*. Berlin: De Gruyter.

Wood, N. (1988). *Cicero's Social and Political Thought*. Berkeley: University of California Press.

Woolf, R. (2015). *Cicero: The Philosophy of a Roman Sceptic*. London: Routledge.

Wynne, J. P. F. (2018). "Cicero." In D. E. Machuca and B. Reed (eds.), *Skepticism: From Antiquity to the Present*. London: Bloomsbury, 93–101.

———(2019). *Cicero on the Philosophy of Religion: On the Nature of the Gods and On Divination*. Cambridge: Cambridge University Press.

Yavetz, Z. (1983). *Julius Caesar and His Public Image*. London: Thames and Hudson (German 1979).

Yona, S. and Davis, G. (eds.) (forthcoming). *Epicurus in Republican Rome: Philosophical Perspectives in the Ciceronian Age*. Cambridge: Cambridge University Press.

Zanker, P. (1987). *Augustus und die Macht der Bilder*. Munich: Beck.

Zarecki, J. (2014). *Cicero's Ideal Statesman in Theory and Practice*. London: Bloomsbury.

Zecchini, G. (1980). "La morte di Catone e l'opposizione intelletuale a Cesare e ad Augusto." *Athenaeum* 58: 39–56.

———(1998). "Cesare e gli Etruschi." In Aigner-Foresti (ed.), 237–49.

———(2001). *Cesare e il mos maiorum.* Stuttgart: Steiner.

———(2009). "Cesare: tirannicidio o sacrilegio?" In Devillers and Meyers (eds.), 209–17.

Zehnacker, H. (1985). "*Officium consolantis*: le devoir de la consolation dans la correspondance de Cicéron de la bataille de Pharsale à la mort de Tullia." *REL* 63: 69–86.

Zetzel, J. E. G. (1995). *Cicero,* De re publica. *Selections.* Cambridge: Cambridge University Press.

———(1998). "*De re publica* and *De rerum natura*." In P. Knox and C. Foss (eds.), *Style and Tradition: Studies in Honor of Wendell Clausen.* Stuttgart: Teubner, 230–47.

———(2001). "Citizen and Commonwealth in *De re publica* Book 4." In Powell and North (eds.), 83–97.

———(2003). "Plato with Pillows: Cicero on the Uses of Greek Culture." In D. Braund and C. Gill (eds.), *Myth, History and Culture in Republican Rome: Studies in Honour of T. P. Wiseman.* Exeter: University of Exeter Press, 119–38.

———(2013). "Political Philosophy." In C. Steel (ed.), *The Cambridge Companion to Cicero.* Cambridge: Cambridge University Press, 181–95.

———(2016). "Philosophy Is in the Streets." In Williams and Volk (eds.), 50–62.

———(2018). *Critics, Compilers, and Commentators: An Introduction to Roman Philology, 200 BCE–800 CE.* New York: Oxford University Press.

———(2019). "Natural Law and Natural Language in the First Century BCE." In Pezzini and Taylor (eds.), 191–211.

———(forthcoming). *The Lost Republic: Cicero's* De oratore *and* De re publica.

Zodorojnyi, A. V. (2007). "Cato's Suicide in Plutarch." *CQ* 57: 216–230.

INDEX LOCORUM

1.638–39: 271n110
1.639–41: 270n106
1.644–45: 271
1.651–65: 272
1.663: 271
1.665: 272
1.666–69: 271
1.669–70: 271
1.670: 273
1.670–72: 271
Lucr. 1.1: 239
1.26–27: 240n4
1.39–40: 239n1
1.41: 97n128, 239, 315
1.42: 240
1.43: 240
1.44–49: 240
1.141: 96n126
1.935–50: 240
1.935: 198n56
1.946: 198n56
2.7–8: 95n121
2.9–61: 97n128
2.646–51: 240
3.41–93: 97n128
3.944–45: 144n121
3.960: 144n121
3.995–1002: 97n128
3.1042: 292n189
4.10–25: 240
4.10: 198n56
4.21: 198n56
5.8: 292n189
5.336–37: 197
5.336: 197
5.1127–28: 97n128
5.1454–57: 197

Macrob. *Sat.* 1.14: 280n142
1.14.1: 281n147
1.14.2: 282n153
1.16.39: 283n156
6.2.33: 136n88

Mart. *Pref.* 1: 70n53
Mart. Cap. 5.468: 135n80

Nep. *Att.* 3.3: 106n158
6: 33n32
6.1: 105
6.2: 105
6.5: 105
8–10: 107
9.1: 106n158
9.6: 108n162
10.6: 106n158–59
11.3–4: 108n162
13.3: 43n69
13.7: 106
14.1: 43n69
18.1: 194n41
18.3–4: 188n20
18.3: 169n208, 188n24
Nigidius Figulus fr. 41: 266n95
fr. 42: 189n26
fr. 56: 266
fr. 67: 265n90, 266
fr. 83: 273n118
frr. 98–99: 266n94
fr. 98: 282n151
frr. 102–3: 266n94
frr. 126–28: 265n90
fr. 127: 265n90

Ov. *Fast.* 1.315: 285n164
3.159–60: 286
Met. 15.745–851: 289n182

Petron. *Sat.* 71.12: 28n15
Plin. *HN* 2.93–94: 289n180
2.94: 289n181, 290n184
2.178: 293n194
7.115: 43n70
7.117: 236n195
18.211–12: 280n142, 282n152
18.212: 284n158
18.214: 283

GENERAL INDEX

Roman names of the Republic and early Empire appear as "nomen cognomen, abbreviated praenomen," with adjustments as needed. Historical figures who also appear as interlocutors in Ciceronian dialogues share the same lemma with their fictionalized counterparts.

A NOTE ON THE TYPE

This book has been composed in Arno, an Old-style serif typeface in the
classic Venetian tradition, designed by Robert Slimbach at Adobe.